Pioneering Conservation in ALASKA

Pioneering Conservation in ALASKA

KEN ROSS

UNIVERSITY PRESS *of* COLORADO

Published by the University Press of Colorado
5589 Arapahoe Avenue, Suite 206C
Boulder, Colorado 80303

Printed in Canada

The University Press of Colorado is a proud member of
the Association of American University Presses.

The University Press of Colorado is a cooperative publishing enterprise supported, in part, by Adams State College, Colorado State University, Fort Lewis College, Mesa State College, Metropolitan State College of Denver, University of Colorado, University of Northern Colorado, and Western State College of Colorado.

∞ The paper used in this publication meets the minimum requirements of the American National Standard for Information Sciences—Permanence of Paper for Printed Library Materials. ANSI Z39.48-1992

Library of Congress Cataloging-in-Publication Data

Ross, Ken, 1937–
Pioneering conservation in Alaska / Ken Ross.
p. cm.
Includes bibliographical references (p.   ) and index.
ISBN-13: 978-0-87081-852-3 (hardcover : alk. paper)
ISBN-10: 0-87081-852-X (hardcover : alk. paper) 1. Nature conservation—Alaska—History. I. Title.
QH76.5.A4R67 2006
333.95'1609798—dc22

2006030330

Design by Daniel Pratt

15 14 13 12 11 10 09 08 07 06   10 9 8 7 6 5 4 3 2 1

to
the North Pacific Right Whale

Contents

Photographs / *ix*
Maps / *xiii*
Tables / *xiii*
Prologue / *xv*
Acknowledgments / *xix*
Chronology / *xxi*

Part I: Early Naturalists and Wildlife Exploitation / 1

1. Sea Otters and Scientists / 4
2. Fur Seal's Friend: Henry W. Elliott / 27
3. Wake of the Whalers / 58
4. John Muir and the Land / 91
5. The Boone and Crockett Club: George Bird Grinnell, Madison Grant, William T. Hornaday, Charles H. Townsend, Charles Sheldon / 116
6. Charles Sheldon and Mt. McKinley National Park / 135
7. Robert F. Griggs and Katmai National Monument / 154
8. John Muir, William S. Cooper, and Glacier Bay National Monument / 176
9. Alaska Natives and Conservation / 192

Part II: Wildlife and Wildlife Managers / 209

10. Bureau of Biological Survey Chiefs: C. Hart Merriam, Edward W. Nelson, Ira N. Gabrielson / 212
11. Alaskan Wildlife Managers: Frank Dufresne, Clarence Rhode, Jim Brooks, Jim King / 237
12. Grizzly Bears in Politics / 259
13. Frontier Justice: Predator Control / 282
14. Game and Fur Mammals / 316
15. Journey of the Salmon / 350
16. Gold and Oil on the Kenai / 378
17. Bob Marshall, Olaus and Margaret Murie, and the Arctic Refuge / 400
18. Evolution of Conservation Values / 427

Notes / 441
Works Employed / 480
Index / 514

Photographs, Maps, and Tables

Photographs

1.1 Sea otters, Amchitka Island, 1949. / 9
1.2 Aleut sea otter hunters, Unalaska, 1891 or 1892. / 10
1.3 Sea otter skins drying, Aleutian Islands, ca. 1890s. / 20
1.4 Robert D. "Sea Otter" Jones, Aleutian Islands National Wildlife Refuge, mid-1950s. / 24
2.1 Fur seal herd, Zapadni rookery, St. Paul Island. / 29
2.2 Henry W. Elliott, San Francisco, 1872, prior to leaving for the Pribilofs. / 37
2.3 William H. Dall, Western Union Telegraph Expedition, San Francisco, July 1865. / 38
2.4 Indian hunter and sealing gear on schooner *Favorite*, 1894. / 43
2.5 David Starr Jordan. / 47
2.6 Killing fur seals. / 48
2.7 Aleut workers at fur seal processing plant, St. Paul Island, ca. 1980. / 54

3.1 Captain William Mogg and bowhead whale baleen, ca. 1916. / 64
3.2 Eskimo whaling station, Cape Prince of Wales, 1891 or 1892. / 66
3.3 Harpoon gunner striking finback whale near Akutan. / 72
3.4 Right whale at Port Hobron whaling station, 1926. / 73
3.5 Remains of villagers starved at St. Lawrence Island, early 1880s. / 78
3.6 Polar bear struck by bullet, off Point Barrow, 1920. / 81
3.7 Walrus sport hunter and trophy, Arctic Ocean, 1913. / 82
3.8 Eskimo carver, Nome, ca. 1887. / 84
3.9 Walrus herd at Walrus Islands haulout, Bristol Bay, ca. 1957. / 85
3.10 Sea lion breeding male, Northeast Point, St. Paul Island. / 87
4.1 Placer miners on American Creek. / 99
4.2 Hydraulic mining on Dan Creek in the Wrangells. / 102
4.3 Fairbanks Exploration Co. dredge on Cripple Creek, twelve miles from Fairbanks. / 103
4.4 Wood yard at Tanana River Railway, ca. 1905–1910. / 107
4.5 Matanuska Colony farm, Palmer, 1937. / 110
4.6 John Muir and John Burroughs at St. Matthew Island, 1899. / 114
5.1 George Bird Grinnell at Yale, ca. 1890s. / 122
5.2 Madison Grant at Yale, 1912. / 124
5.3 William T. Hornaday and buffalo calf, Washington, DC, 1890. / 129
5.4 Charles Haskins Townsend, 1918. / 131
6.1 Members of expedition making first ascent of McKinley's South Peak, 1913. / 139
6.2 Charles Sheldon, in winter camp north of Mt. McKinley, 1907. / 141
6.3 Belmore Browne in climbing gear. / 142
6.4 Dall rams in McKinley Park, June 1966. / 144
6.5 Former market hunter's cabin used by park rangers, 1926. / 146
6.6 Tourist party crossing moraine of Muldrow Glacier, 1927. / 149
6.7 Adolph Murie at McKinley Park, November 1939. / 151
6.8 Charlie Ott, Fairbanks, 1984. / 152
7.1 Village of Katmai after eruption, 1913. / 156
7.2 W.A. Hesse filming Katmai volcano, 1913. / 159
7.3 Katmai volcano ash at Kodiak, 1912. / 160
7.4 Valley of Ten Thousand Smokes; Mt. Mageik (left) and Mt. Katmai in background. / 162
7.5 Laura Griggs and husband, Robert, at Baked Mountain, Katmai National Monument, 1919. / 164
7.6 Father Bernard Hubbard and dog at Katmai Crater, 1929. / 167
7.7 Looking north across head of Geographic Harbor, 1940. / 168
7.8 Abandoned cannery, Kukak Bay, Katmai National Monument, 1951. / 170

7.9 Victor Cahalane at Novarupta, August 1954. / 173
7.10 Adlai Stevenson and party at Brooks Falls, August 1954. / 174
8.1 John Muir. / 178
8.2 S.S. *City of Topeka* at Muir Glacier, 1890. / 179
8.3 William S. Cooper, Blackstone Bay, 1935. / 182
8.4 Park ranger and harbor seal carcass, Glacier Bay National Monument, 1964 or 1965. / 189
9.1 Commercial walrus hunters, Nome, early 20th Century. / 193
9.2 Inupiat Eskimo boy netting auklets, Little Diomede Island, 1930s. / 194
9.3 Eskimo hunter and largha seal, Bering Sea, early 1900s. / 195
9.4 Caribou left in woods by Inupiat hunters, Shungnak, 1949. / 206
10.1 English sport hunter Charles R.E. Radclyffe and guides, Kenai Peninsula, 1903. / 216
10.2 U.S. Bureau of Biological Survey officials at Lone Pine, California, June 13, 1891, after Death Valley expedition. / 223
10.3 Edward W. Nelson, Yukon-Kuskokwim Delta, 1877–1881. / 226
10.4 Edward W. Nelson in later years. / 228
10.5 Dr. Ira N. Gabrielson, July 1939. / 235
11.1 Alaska Game Commission officers, Fairbanks, 1939. / 239
11.2 Cache of illegally trapped skins at Mulchatna River, June 1936. / 240
11.3 Sam White, Noel Wien, and White's TP Swallow, Valdez, 1931. / 243
11.4 Frank Dufresne and friends, upper Newhalen River, June 1940. / 247
11.5 Clarence Rhode at controls of Grumman Goose, Nome, 1949. / 251
11.6 Jim Brooks conducting polar bear research, Chukchi Sea, 1971. / 254
11.7 U.S. Fish and Wildlife Service agent Jim King and Nunamiut Eskimos, Anaktuvuk Pass, mid-1950s. / 257
12.1 Brown bear at Karluk Lake, Kodiak National Wildlife Refuge, 1958. / 261
12.2 Cow killed by brown bear, Pagashak, Kodiak Island, August 1952. / 273
12.3 Hunter and brown bear trophy, Kodiak Island, 1957. / 277
13.1 Eskimos displaying reindeer killed by wolves, mid-1950s. / 293
13.2 Seal blubber cubes used in wolf control, ca. 1956. / 295
13.3 Wolves recovered from poison bait stations, ca. 1957. / 296
13.4 Silver salmon damaged by harbor seals, Stikine River, 1946. / 302
13.5 Government seal hunter and harbor seals, mid-1950s. / 303
13.6 Seal faces gathered for bounty, Chukchi Sea, May 1967. / 305
13.7 Blue fox and seabirds it killed, Gareloi Island, Aleutians. / 307
13.8 Red foxes and predated lamb, Unalaska or Umnak Island, ca. 1958. / 309

13.9 Bald eagle shot for bounty, held by Jim Dolan, Valdez, ca. 1940. / 312
14.1 Rev. Sheldon Jackson, ca. 1880. / 323
14.2 Reindeer loaded aboard revenue cutter *Bear*, Siberia, 1891. / 324
14.3 Eskimo mail carrier, ca. 1905–1910. / 325
14.4 Muskoxen, College, early 1930s. / 333
14.5 Mountain goat released at Hidden Basin, Kodiak Island, 1952. / 336
14.6 Unloading first buffalo, College, ca. 1928. / 337
14.7 Trappers and their catch of furs. / 341
14.8 Wolverine in leg-hold trap, Anchorage vicinity, 1949. / 346
15.1 Fish trap, Thlinket Packing Company, Funter Bay, 1907. / 352
15.2 Brailing a salmon trap. / 353
15.3 Naket Packing Company's Waterfall Cannery near Craig, Prince of Wales Island. / 354
15.4 Alaska Packers Association ship *Santa Clara*. / 355
15.5 Dam on salmon stream, Helm Bay, ca. 1898. / 356
15.6 Athabaskan fish wheel, Tanana, 1918. / 360
15.7 Stream watcher's cabin, Red River Lake, Kodiak Island, 1950. / 366
16.1 Construction train of Alaska Central Railroad, north of Seward, June 1905. / 384
16.2 English hunter Col. Claude Cane and trophies, Kenai Peninsula, 1902. / 387
16.3 Moose at Kenai River, 1920s. / 389
16.4 Henry Lucas, Frank Dufresne, and Lawrence J. Palmer, Kenai Peninsula, 1938. / 390
16.5 Moose in browse cut, Kenai National Moose Range, 1955. / 394
16.6 Arco discovery well, Swanson River field, Kenai National Moose Range, late 1950s. / 397
16.7 Kenai National Moose Range supervisor David L. Spencer and trumpeter swan nest, May 1957. / 398
17.1 Nutirwik and Bob Marshall, upper north fork of the Koyukuk, 1939. / 405
17.2 Captain Roald Amundsen and crew of *Gjoa*, Nome, September 1, 1906. / 415
17.3 Bull caribou, Arctic National Wildlife Range, October 1970. / 416
17.4 Wolf at Old Woman Creek, Arctic National Wildlife Range, 1966. / 417
17.5 Mardy and Olaus Murie, Sheenjek River Valley, 1956. / 419
17.6 Ginny Hill Wood and Celia Hunter, Fairbanks, ca. 1985. / 423

Maps

1. Alaska. / *xxvi–xxvii*
2. Pribilof Islands. / 30
3. Mt. McKinley/Denali National Park and Preserve, 1932 and 1980. / 145
4. Katmai National Monument/Park and Preserve, 1931 and 1980. / 166
5. Glacier Bay National Monument/Park and Preserve, 1939 and 1980. / 184
6. Kodiak National Wildlife Refuge, 1958 and 1980. / 275
7. Kenai National Moose Range/Wildlife Refuge, 1941 and 1980. / 379
8. Arctic National Wildlife Range/Refuge, 1960 and 1988. / 424

Tables

1.1 Russian Fur Cargoes From North America, 1743–1823 / 18
2.1 Reported Harvest of Pribilof Fur Seals, 1786–1950 / 40
3.1 American Whalers and Harvests in the Pacific North of 50 Degrees, 1835–1913 / 61–62
3.2 Shore-Based Commercial Whale Catches in Subarctic Alaska, 1910–1939 / 70
3.3 Recorded Pacific Walrus Harvests by the Whaling Industry, 1849–1914 / 76
4.1 Forest Acreage Burned in Alaska, 1940–1970 / 105
4.2 Agricultural Activity in Alaska, 1940–1969 / 109
10.1 Human Population of Alaska, 1740–2000 / 213
10.2 Game Killed by Radclyffe Party, Kenai Peninsula, 1903 / 215
10.3 Game and Trophies Shipped From Alaska, 1910–1916 / 219
10.4 Game Purchased by Six Fairbanks Stores, Fall 1921 / 232
11.1 Alaska Game Commission Enforcement Actions, 1936–1937 and 1958–1959 / 241
11.2 Alaska Game Commission License Sales, 1926–1959 / 245
11.3 Travel by Alaska Game Commission Agents, 1937–1959 / 246
12.1 Estimated Harvests of Brown or Grizzly Bears in Alaska, 1945–1966 / 278
13.1 Furbearers Purposely and Accidentally Killed in Predator Control, 1951–1952 / 297
13.2 Alaska Bounty Expenditures, 1927–1958 / 299
13.3 Species Bountied and Taken in Predator Control Programs, 1927–1958 / 299
14.1 Estimated Harvests of Big Game Species in Alaska, 1945–1963 / 317
14.2 Ownership, Size, and Locations of Reindeer Herds, 1949 / 328

14.3 Reindeer in Alaska, 1892–1977 / 329
14.4 Successful Transplants of Wild Terrestrial Mammals in Alaska, 1916–1970 / 335
14.5 Selected Land Mammal Furs Shipped From Russian America and Alaska, 1745–1890 / 339
14.6 Reported Fur Exports From Alaska, 1912–1964 / 345
14.7 Values of Wildlife and Other Natural Resources in Alaska, 1952 / 348
15.1 Statistical Profile of Alaska Salmon Canning Industry, 1878–1897 / 361
15.2 Commercial Salmon Catches in Alaska, 1878–1982 / 370
18.1 Environmental Values Expressed by Alaskan Issues and Leaders, 1741–1960 / 436

Prologue

For 250 years Alaska lured fortune seekers and escapees from the boredom and social confines of modernizing society. A theater of quest to try the hardiest of souls, it promised fabulous riches for the taking. Isolated, vast, open, endowed, and dramatically beautiful, it called out to the most primitive urges—greed, excitement, lust for power, freedom. Adventure awaited all who came; riches only a few. No matter, though; the illusions outweighed the reality. And pioneers pursued them in a state of near-religious fervor.

A few early visitors chose to settle in Alaska, especially after the gold rushes of the late 19th Century and the first two decades of the 20th Century. They wanted to be where they could control their own lives and their achievements could be clearly seen; where folks knew a person as an individual, tolerated idiosyncracies, clearly defined manhood and womanhood, and valued honor; where all could tell right from wrong; where people trusted and helped one another; where one could recognize sources of danger and everyone took hardship for granted; where boredom would be rare, adventure common, rules and crowds few; where people and things were what they appeared to be—a realm of wholesome earth, pure water, and bracing air. And a place where one could wrest a living from the land.

In the Alaskan experience of Europeans and Euro-Americans, three competing land ethics emerged. Combining desire for freedom and lust for wealth and power, one urged exploitation and conquest in the name of individual benefit and economic progress. Sweeping relentlessly through the territory, it devastated wildlife populations and Native cultures alike. Only physical barriers could contain it throughout most of its temporal and spatial reign. It threatened, and still threatens, to subdue one of the last great wild places on earth.

A competing idea, utilitarian conservation, sought to bring the freebooting ethic to bay. It envisioned moderate, measured use of natural resources for the long-term well-being of humans and the nation, in contrast to the short-term, self-centered quest for profit that had wreaked so much destruction on the West. If properly regulated by government, forests, minerals, and wild species populations and their numerous benefits could be harvested indefinitely. They would provide a foundation for a gradually modernizing, stable society.

A third contending view drew strength from the experiences of pre-statehood Alaska. In its most advanced form it nurtured a vision of Alaska as a realm of unspoiled Nature. In this conception, like that of its rivals, Nature symbolized freedom. But Nature meant more than freedom; it represented beauty, truth. One felt freedom in closeness to Nature and in the knowledge that Nature existed free. Power and personal gain inhered not in conquest and material acquisition but in observation and contemplation. Humankind would be integral to, not owner of or mere actor upon, the pageant of wild life. Conquest seemed unnecessary, self-destructive, immoral. Far less prevalent than the exploitation and utilitarian notions, the preservation ideal nevertheless constituted a compelling force for those who experienced it. For more than a century it strove tenaciously and won gathering success in creating a public constituency. The story of Alaska is in large part an ongoing struggle among the ethics of conquest, utilitarian conservation, and preservation. It continues unabated into the 21st Century.

Alaska enticed adventurers and exploiters from around the world as long ago as the mid-1700s. Conflicts over its resources informed signal events—the abandonment of Russian empire in North America, the sale of Alaska to the United States, the elections of at least three U.S. presidents, and appointments and removals of cabinet members. In the territorial era, as now, commercialization of natural resources ranked first among the motives. Euro-American visitors aggressively exploited resources in hopes of making fortunes that would allow them to return to the States and live in luxury. Most of the relatively few who stayed in Alaska endeavored to replicate the pattern of Western settlement by converting the wealth of natural resources into increasingly comfortable modern communities.

Yet pre-statehood Alaska contributed mightily to the growth of American environmentalism. It nurtured early leaders of the national environmental movement who shared, and acted upon, the public fascination concerning Alaska. Through their endeavors to conserve habitat and wildlife these leaders fostered values that evolved into principles of modern environmentalism. Ethics of natural resource use in Alaska evolved from untrammeled exploitation to utilitarian conservation and elements of species and ecosystem preservation. Wildlife management passed from private entrepreneurs into the hands of government professionals employing emerging biological sciences.

Some of the conservation pioneers, by their knowledge and standing, directly molded opinion in Alaska. Most augmented environmentalism in the States, in turn ultimately forcing a shift in Alaskan behavior. Alaska's pre-statehood environmental record is a story of physical endeavor and political conflict in a vast and wild land. It is also a vital chapter in the evolution of American environmental values. This book, a companion volume to *Environmental Conflict in Alaska* (University Press of Colorado, 2000), traces the evolution of environmental values through the outstanding land and wildlife issues of pre-statehood Alaska and the leaders who shaped their outcomes. While values have advanced and conditions have changed, many of the issues remain in force to this day.

Acknowledgments

THANKS TO THE FOLLOWING FOR INFORMATION AND ASSISTANCE: EDGAR P. BAILEY, Bruce W. Black, John Branson, Jim Brooks, Cathy Curby, Colin Day, Robert DeArmond, Jim Estes, Joe Geldhof, Sally Gilbert, Stephen W. Haycox, John I. Hodges Sr., Jean T. Holland, Wayne Howell, Mina Jacobs, James G. King, Betty Knight, Philip S. Koehl, Gladi Kulp, Donald B. Lawrence, Calvin R. Lensink, Malcolm Lockwood, Donald E. McKnight, Bruce Merrell, Ted Merrell, Donald C. Mitchell, Sid Morgan, Margaret Murie, J. Richard Myren, Richard K. Nelson, Robert E. Price, Jack Roderick, Pat Roppel, Kay Shelton, David L. Spencer, Nancy Tileston, Peg Tileston, Will Troyer, Robert B. Weeden, Kenton Wohl, Jennifer Wolk, Steve Zimmerman. Thanks also to Darrin Pratt and Laura Furney of the University Press of Colorado and Cheryl Carnahan for editing.

Special thanks to Jason Geck for maps and to Cynthia A. Bily and Mary C. Mangusso for full-text reviews.

Able assistance from many other librarians in Alaska and the Lower 48 is appreciated. Thanks to Adrian College for providing a sabbatical leave in support of this project.

Chronology

11000–9000 B.C.	First recorded humans in Alaska
1725	Peter the Great orders expedition to America
1741	Captain Vitus Bering lands in Alaska, stimulating sea otter trade
1778	Captain James Cook reaches Alaska, begins British/American fur trade
1784	Gregorii Shelikov creates first Russian settlement, on Kodiak Island
1786–1787	Gerassim Pribylof finds Pribilof Islands, begins fur seal industry
1808	Russian-American Company moves to New Archangel (Sitka) as part of plan to extend Russian control down West Coast of North America
1835	Commercial whalers discover right whales in Gulf of Alaska, begin century-long period of commercial whaling
1847	Hudson's Bay Company builds trading post at Fort Yukon, weakening Russian control of Alaska
1848	Whalers *Superior* and *Ocmulgee* enter Arctic Ocean
1865	Western Union Telegraph Expedition prepares to connect North America and Europe by way of Siberia

1866	Commercial pelagic fur sealing begins, leading to international conflict over seals
1867	United States purchases Alaska
1869	Pribilof Islands designated first U.S. wildlife reserve to conserve fur seals
1871	U.S. Commission on Fish and Fisheries created to manage offshore and Alaska fisheries
1872	Henry W. Elliott assigned to Pribilofs as Treasury agent
1877	Edward W. Nelson assigned to St. Michael as meteorologist
1878	First salmon canneries opened at Sitka and Klawock
1879	George Bird Grinnell becomes publisher of *Forest and Stream*, a leading voice in the conservation movement
1879	John Muir first visits Alaska
1880	Gold discovered at Juneau sets off first major gold rush
1884	Organic Act ends military rule, installs appointed governors
1885	Forerunner of U.S. Fish and Wildlife Service created in USDA
1886	George Bird Grinnell organizes first national Audubon Society
1887	Boone and Crockett Club, of elite hunter-conservationists, organized
1891	Reindeer introduced by Sheldon Jackson to stabilize Eskimo economy
1891	Forest Reserves Act empowers president to protect public lands
1892	Afognak Forest and Fish Culture Reserve protects salmon and bears
1892	Sierra Club organized to promote hiking and conservation
1896	Gold discovered at Bonanza Creek, Yukon
1897–1898	Last reported muskoxen killed in Alaska
1898	Nome gold rush begins
1899	Harriman Alaska Expedition of scientists and wealthy easterners
1900	Game and Wild Birds Preservation ("Lacey") Act bans interstate sale of game; first major federal wildlife protection law
1902	Gold discovered near Fairbanks, expands interior development
1902	First Alaska game law limits killing of game species
1902	First commercially viable oil discovery at Katalla
1902–1909	Roosevelt creates reserves including Chugach and Tongass national forests to conserve coal, timber, wildlife
1905	National Audubon Society organized for bird and nature protection
1905	U.S. Forest Service, Department of Agriculture, assumes control of forest reserves, emphasizes utilitarian conservation
1906	Roald Amundsen completes first navigation of Northwest Passage
1906	American Antiquities Act permits creation of national monuments

1908	Second Alaska game law further protects game, establishes wardens
1910–1915	Wolves and caribou exterminated on Kenai Peninsula
1911	Cordova Railway completed to Bonanza copper mine
1911	North Pacific Sealing Convention protects fur seals and sea otters
1912	Katmai volcano erupts, leading to national monument status
1912	Alaska a territory; legislature elected, governors appointed
1913	Taft creates reserves including Aleutian Islands
1913	Migratory Bird (McLean-Weeks) Act gives national government jurisdiction over all migratory birds
1915	Wolf bounty instituted by territorial legislature
1916	Migratory Bird Treaty ratified; coordinates U.S.-Canada policy
1916	National Park Service created for land and wildlife preservation
1917	Bald eagle bounty instituted by territorial legislature
1917	Mt. McKinley National Park created for game protection and tourism
1918	Migratory Bird Treaty Act gives enforcement power to Bureau of Biological Survey
1918	Katmai National Monument created
1919	National Parks and Conservation Association founded to support parks
1920	Olaus Murie assigned to Fairbanks to study caribou
1923	Alaska Railroad completed; intended to promote interior development
1924	White Act attempts to conserve salmon fisheries
1924–1929	National Conference on Outdoor Recreation, a successful federal-private effort to promote wildlife and habitat conservation
1925	Glacier Bay National Monument created for scientific study/tourism
1925	Alaska Game Law creates federal-local body to manage wildlife
1929	Migratory Bird Conservation Act authorizes national wildlife refuges
1929	Bob Marshall assigned to Brooks Range
1930	Muskoxen imported from Greenland to reestablish species in Alaska
1934	Migratory Bird Hunting Stamp Act provides funds for refuges
1935	Wilderness Society organized by Bob Marshall for land preservation
1935	*Alaska Sportsman*, voice for outdoor sportsmen, begins publication
1936	National Wildlife Federation organized
1937	Federal Aid in Wildlife Restoration (Pittman-Robertson) Act funds wildland acquisition and research
1939	Last Alaskan whaling station closes at Akutan

1940	Fish and Wildlife Service created within Interior Department; formerly Bureau of Biological Survey, USDA
1941	Kenai National Moose Range and Kodiak National Wildlife Range created
1942	Japanese occupy Attu and Kiska
1943	Alcan (Alaska) Highway opened to military
1946	Bureau of Land Management created; promotes mining and oil
1946	Indian Claims Act permits Natives to sue United States for land claims
1947	Tongass Timber Sales Act authorizes large-scale logging contracts; sidesteps Native land claims
1948	Federal Predator Control Branch established in Alaska, primarily to control wolves and coyotes
1948	Alaska Highway opened to public; escalates tourism
1949	Territorial Department of Fisheries created to supplement and eventually replace federal management
1953	North Pacific Fisheries Convention regulates ocean salmon fishing by Japan, Canada, United States
1954	Ketchikan Pulp Company mill opens
1954	Alaska Sportsmen's Council, most prominent in territory, organized
1957	Alaska Department of Fish and Game created
1957	Oil discovered on Kenai Peninsula; initiates oil era
1958–1959	Alaska Statehood Act; statehood; guarantees state 104 million acres
1959	Alaska Pulp Company mill opens at Sitka
1960	Alaska assumes control of fish and game
1960	Alaska Conservation Society organized; founds environmental movement
1960	Arctic, Izembek, and Kuskokwim national wildlife ranges created
1971	Alaska Native Claims Settlement Act (ANCSA) allots 44 million acres to Native village and regional corporations
1980	Alaska National Interest Lands Conservation Act (ANILCA) creates parks, refuges, national forests, BLM lands, wilderness areas

Pioneering Conservation in ALASKA

S I B E R I A
A R C T I C
B E R I N G S E A
Wrangell I
Chaun Bay
Icy C
C Lisburne
Pt Hope
Kolinchin Bay
Noatak
Kotzebue Sound
East Cape
Bering Strait
C Prince of Wales
SEWARD PENINSULA
Holy Cross B
Anadir B
Gulf of Anadir
SOVIET UNION
UNITED STATES
Nome
Norton Sound
Oliutorski Gulf
St Lawrence I
St Matthew I
Nunivak I
Kuskokwim Bay
Platinum
Pribilof Islands
Attu I
Near Is
ALEUTIAN ISLANDS
Rat Islands
Andreanof Islands
Atka I
Fox Islands
Unimak I
Dutch Harbor
Unalaska I
East from Greenwich 180° West from Greenwich

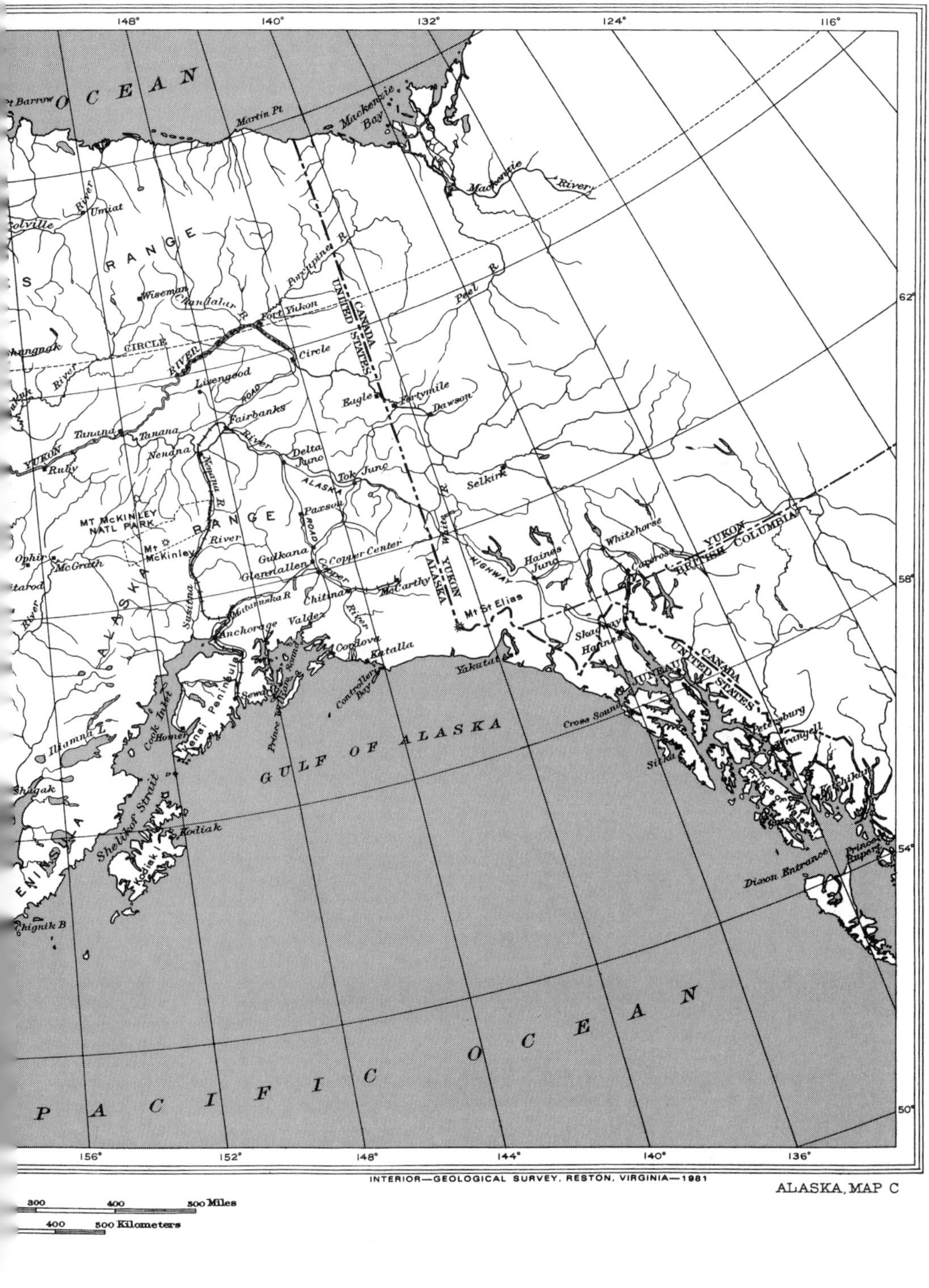

INTERIOR—GEOLOGICAL SURVEY, RESTON, VIRGINIA—1981

ALASKA, MAP C

Part I

Early Naturalists and Wildlife Exploitation

ALASKA'S EARLIEST CONTACTS WITH WESTERN CIVILIZATION AND THE RESULTING environmental crises occurred mainly on the seacoast. There acquisitive nations found valuable fish stocks and the fur, oil, baleen, and ivory of sea mammals. Later, during the gold rushes, the focus of attention shifted inland. Gold seeking introduced unpleasant side effects of forest fires and depletion of fur and game mammals. Physical and psychological separation from centers of civilization made rational resource management difficult and encouraged destructive behavior by Russians and Americans as well as seafarers and explorers from other nations. Disease, liquor, cultural influences, and modern technology weakened Alaska Native societies, and many Natives participated in irresponsible killing of wildlife. Conservation measures ordered by the Russian government, while effecting gains, did not inspire similar behavior by Americans. Repeating the pattern of conquest of the American West, weak and poorly enforced laws governed the disposal of Alaska's natural resources between the purchase of Alaska in 1867 and the 1920s. Such an assault on Nature bore a high potential for ecological damage.

Owing to its wealth of resources and its status as the new American frontier, Alaska attracted numerous government and private scientists, hunters, and adventurers. Some possessed little or no higher education; others held doctorates in science. Their tenures in Alaska ranged from summer trips to decades of residence. Some became prominent government officials, others museum directors or academics. Of those concerned about natural resource policy, most worked out of Washington or New York City. Many wrote for wide audiences, and several founded or led environmental organizations. Some influenced Alaskan environmental issues directly, others indirectly.

Among the pioneer naturalists, private citizens led the way in Alaskan environmental protection. Having come as hunters, adventurers, or young government officials, they fell in love with the scenery and wildlife, especially some of the more visible species of mammals, and did not want to see them disappear. Mainly from privileged backgrounds, they possessed the means to travel, sound education and communication skills, and access to high-level government decision makers. A dozen or more knew and dealt with each other as a social and political elite. In an age when mass public opinion played a relatively minor role, they belonged to a small number of individuals in a position to prod the government into conservation action. Their most influential period extended from about 1890 to 1930. It drew strength from the Progressive movement, a rebellion against the unbridled exploitative behavior of powerful corporations.

Conservationists acted within the context of an upsurge of national interest in Nature, a reaction to rapid urbanization and the loss of natural areas and wildlife. Some, notably John Muir, perceived Nature in spiritual terms and viewed its destruction as a transgression against humankind's proper place in life. They placed a high value on preservation of wildlife habitat and species. Academic scientists and nature enthusiasts worked to set aside unique sites for study of glaciology, vulcanology, or ecology. Others thought it best to manage Nature intelligently for the sustained benefit of humans. Of these utilitarians, outdoor sportsmen tended to focus on maintaining stocks of favorite fish and game species. Government leaders in the conservation movement advocated the controlled use of all natural resources—including water, wood, minerals, soil, and wildlife—to advance human society as a whole. Many activists held elements of both utilitarian and preservationist perspectives, often becoming more preservationist as they advanced in age.

The wholesale slaughter of Western animals, the buffalo in particular, engendered the conservationist conviction that such behavior must not be repeated in Alaska. The presidency of Theodore Roosevelt, a personal acquaintance of several early "Alaskan" conservationists, conferred power and legitimacy on their efforts. Roosevelt espoused a heavily utilitarian variety of conservation that called for scientifically grounded management of natural resources by federal government experts to maximize efficient application of those resources to the needs of the nation. Yet he appreciated birds and other wildlife and responded to preservationist appeals when they did not threaten more frankly utilitarian values. He set aside Alaska lands, and the momentum generated during his presidential terms carried forward for decades, undergirding a broad range of measures to conserve lands and wildlife nationwide.

Through writings and political action supported by sympathetic federal officials, the early private naturalists established legal and administrative foundations for sound management of American, and thus Alaskan, natural resources. They pushed successfully for the first Alaska game laws. They moved the government to set aside special tracts of land for posterity, presaging the world's largest complex of wild parks and refuges, and awakened American elites to the need for conservation of the remaining frontier. Collectively they pioneered modern environmental values of ecosystem sustainability, sustainable utilitarianism, nonconsumptive resource use, science-based management, public participation, and government and corporate accountability. They served as founding environmentalists for Alaska and for the nation.

1 Sea Otters and Scientists

ALASKA'S NATIVES AND WILDLIFE FIRST ENCOUNTERED WESTERN CIVILIZATION BY way of Asia. An aquatic mammal, the sea otter, took center stage in the events that followed. For the better part of three centuries, treatment of the otter marked the tragedies and triumphs of wildlife management and evolving environmental values.

Toward the end of the 1600s Russia's fur trade reached across Siberia to the Bering Sea. An expedition led by explorers F.A. Popov and Semyon Dezhnev rounded the northeastern extremity of Siberia in 1648, followed by others in the late 1600s. They knew, based on reports from Natives, that northwestern North America could not be far to the east. The Russian government sought to enlarge its territorial control and realize economic gain through expanded fur trade and exacting of tribute from Natives. Shortly before his death in 1725, Czar Peter the Great ordered his Kamchatka expedition to send a ship to search for northwest North America. The resultant 1728 sortie under Captain Vitus Bering, a Danish officer serving in the Russian Navy as commander of the expedition, failed to reach the American mainland. Four years later a ship commanded by land surveyor Mikhail S. Gvozdev approached the coast at the present Cape Prince of Wales, following it southward for two days close enough to see Eskimos and their settlements. Unfavorable winds and shallow water prevented a landing, and the crew returned to Kamchatka.[1] They related stories from Siberian Natives of a Russian settlement in "The Big Land" to the east, heard before and to be heard long afterward. Although efforts to confirm the stories never uncovered tangible proof, the consistency and detail of Native accounts suggested that Russians may have settled on the mainland. If so, they probably arrived on some of the four ships lost during the Popov-Dezhnev expedition or from another launched a few years later.[2] Whatever the case, they did not survive to influence subsequent events.

BERING'S ALASKA VOYAGE

The Russian government persisted in its intent to clarify the relative placement of eastern Siberia and northwestern North America. Bering had returned to Russia in 1730 and expressed the belief that he had rounded the tip of Siberia, demonstrating its separation from North America. The government put him in charge of a second major effort to explore the region. Intended to be the greatest geographic expedition ever undertaken, it required years of preparation. As did other such ventures, it called for a wide range of scientific observations. As it turned out, the effort did not succeed in settling the question of physical relationship between the continents. That task lay unfulfilled until the arrival of Captain James Cook who followed the American coast northward to Icy Cape on the Arctic Ocean in 1778. But other adventures and opportunities awaited the Russians when they launched their expedition in June 1741.

Two vessels left Kamchatka, eventually becoming separated. Under Alexei Chirikov, the *St. Paul* crossed the North Pacific and sighted an island near the later-named Prince of Wales Island in Southeast Alaska. Two crews sent ashore disappeared, possibly captured or killed by Native Americans. Chirikov returned westward along the coast without making landfall and arrived at Kamchatka on October 10, seven of the crew having died of scurvy. Captain Bering's *St. Peter*, sailed by Sven Waxell, neared the mainland at Controller Bay and viewed Mt. St. Elias on July 16.[3] Bering fell seriously ill and feared he might not reach Kamchatka before the fall weather; thus he permitted only a brief stop at Kayak Island. On the return trip the *St. Peter* crossed the Gulf of Alaska and followed the Alaska Peninsula and Aleutian Islands westward. In the Shumagin Islands the crew met and traded with Native Americans. In November the ship, its crew sick and dying of scurvy, foundered on the shores of an uninhabited island to be named for the captain. Its crew placed the immobile Bering in an enlarged and unheated fox hole in the bank where a month later he died. Thirty of his shipmates also succumbed that winter. Survivors stayed alive in part by eating the flesh of sea otters, which spent much of their time on land and, at first, trustingly approached the visitors.[4]

Bering's crew included the first person to scientifically examine the sea otter and other Alaskan fauna: Georg Wilhelm Steller (1709–1746). A jay, an eider, a sea eagle, a sea lion, and a sea cow bear the name of this scientist. Also named for Steller are mountains in the Chugach Range and at Katmai National Park and a cove and river on Attu.[5] Of the birds and mammals he studied, the sea cow may have contributed most to Steller's place in history. Unknown to the outside world prior to 1741 and by far the largest of the world's manatees, it attained as much as 42 feet in length and at least 7,000 pounds. It had the misfortune of being born without fear of humans, tasting like beef, and residing directly in the path of fur seekers. A large one could feed a 33-man crew for a month, and its skin could cover a *baidara,* or freighting boat, or be made into boots. Hunters killed them using pikes tipped by long blades, pulled them to shore, and butchered them in shallow water at low tide.[6] Steller biographer Leonhard Stejneger related that

> already in 1743–4 we find Bassoff and his crew wintering on Bering Island, and from that year until 1763 hardly a winter passed without one or more parties spending eight or nine months in hunting fur-animals there, during which time the crews lived almost exclusively on the meat of the sea-cow. But that is not all, for more than half of the expeditions which wintered there did so for the express purpose of laying in stores of sea-cow meat for their farther journey, which usually lasted two to three years or more.[7]

The last reliable sighting of a northern sea cow entered the record in 1768. The spectacled cormorant, also observed at Bering Island by Steller, suffered a similar fate. Flightless and nesting along the fur trade route, it helped fill the stewpots. It disappeared around 1852.[8] Sea cows did not occur in Alaska in modern times, though scientists found their 130,000-year-old bones on Amchitka Island, where they and the spectacled cormorants may have been exterminated by aborigines.[9] Excavations on Bering Island turned up entire sea cow skeletons. By bribing Russian workers, Stejneger obtained a skeleton for the Smithsonian in 1882 or 1883.[10]

Not only did Steller hold the distinction of first natural scientist to visit Alaska, he also became one of the renowned botanists of his era. Son of a church cantor in Windsheim, Germany, he acquired a strong interest in natural phenomena at an early age. A bright and diligent student, he won a public scholarship to study theology at Wittenberg. After a fire destroyed most of his hometown and ended his scholarship he enrolled in medical school at the University of Halle, completing the work in 1734. He qualified as a physician but showed more interest in other natural sciences and had already become an expert in botany.

Peter the Great's awakening of Russia and drive eastward attracted young scientists and adventurers, as would the American West and Alaska in the 19th Century. Hearing of Russian expeditions to Siberia, Steller traveled to Russia bent on joining one. He received a commission in St. Petersburg and crossed Siberia to meet Bering. Illness of the ship's surgeon prompted Bering to sign Steller on as a physician and mineral assayer, a disappointment to Steller who had hoped to research and classify wildlife. Arrogant yet brilliant and competent, Steller alienated the crew and received poor cooperation from them.

Steller experienced extreme frustration when Bering, resentful of Steller's demeanor, nearly prevented him from going ashore at Kayak Island. While on the island he collected a bird that, because of its similarity to the blue jay known to science, he correctly interpreted as proof that the party had reached North America. Bering's anxiety about returning to Siberia restricted the landing party to ten hours ashore over two days, and only Bering's illness and the shipwreck enabled Steller to investigate the sea otter and other life on Bering Island. Steller's discipline and medical expertise proved helpful to the survival of the ship's crew during the winter of 1741–1742 on Bering Island. However, on the return to Kamchatka, space limitations precluded Steller's bringing most of his collection. He left behind the only skin of a sea cow ever to be collected.

Steller's international reputation rested largely on his collections from Kamchatka and the Kurile Islands, where he explored following the return trip from Bering Island. Steller never returned to Alaska or to Europe. Exhaustion and illness overtook him on his way to St. Petersburg and he died in Tyumen, Siberia, at age 37, unaware of the fame that awaited him.[11]

Steller felt sympathy for wild animals, especially sea otters and sea cows. As a descriptive scientist he expressed little of preservationist attitudes or ecological perspectives. Twenty-six years before the final sea cow sighting he speculated, "These animals are found at all seasons everywhere around [Bering] island in the greatest numbers, so that the whole population of the Eastern shore of Kamchatka would always be able to keep itself more than abundantly supplied from them with fat and meat."[12]

What Steller saw happening to the sea otters on Bering Island, on the other hand, turned out to be prophetic for both the otters and Alaska. Crew members gambled constantly, first for money and then for otter skins: "Anyone who had altogether ruined himself tried to recover through the poor sea otters, which were needlessly and thoughtlessly killed merely for their pelts, the meat being thrown away. When this was not enough, some began to steal and stole pelts from the others, whereby hate, quarrels and strife were spread in all the dwellings." "Little work got done," and "on the ship, many necessary materials and objects were ruined, being left in the water—such as compasses and the general journal itself." Otters grew "wary by constant hunting day and night" and began to disappear. At first they could be found within a mile of the Russian camp; by February, within 15 to 20 miles, and by spring hunters had to travel 35 miles or more. Scarcity of food threatened the crew's survival "because we killed them [otters] needlessly only on account of their pelts—yes, frequently letting pelt and meat lie if they were not black enough—it came to such a point that we lost hope of being able to build a ship."[13] Despite Steller's misgivings the crew managed to put together a boat from the remnants of the *St. Peter* and sail it to Kamchatka. They brought back something of great interest to the fur traders: several hundred sea otter pelts and reports of their abundance.

News of the otters sparked efforts to exploit them, for they brought high rewards in the markets of China. Small companies formed by merchants hired crews to build and man vessels to sail from Kamchatka to the Commander (Komandorski) and later the Aleutian Islands, taking enough provisions for three years. As a means of advancing its territorial and economic goals, the Russian government gave the companies permits and loans. It reaped large gains by taxing the furs sold in Russia and to China through the official trading post of Kiakhta, on the Mongolian border south of Lake Baikal, during the mid-18th Century.[14]

SEA OTTER HUNTING UNDER THE RUSSIANS

Promyshlenniki, primarily free peasants and tradesmen who trapped sable in Siberia, and Natives or creoles from Kamchatka and Yakutsk, comprised the bulk of the 30- to 50-man fur-seeking crews in the early voyages. Aleuts later joined the crews. Inexperienced in seamanship, the promyshlenniki had to help build their ships and sail them in forbidding weather through uncharted waters. Lacking nails, in the 1740s they bound the hulls together with whale baleen or willows. Each crew member owned a share in an expedition or worked for someone who did. They owed the company for their provisions if they did not bring back enough furs, a fate that befell many. Government officials expected the crew leaders to conduct exploration, gather information, claim land, collect tribute, and incorporate Natives into the state—tasks they did not relish. A cossack representing the government normally accompanied the crew to collect tributes and record information.[15]

Until the mid-1750s expeditions went to the Commander (Bering and Copper) Islands to acquire sea otter and fur seal pelts for return to Kamchatka or to gather meat and skins and over-winter for the voyage to the Aleutians. On the uninhabited Commanders, promyshlenniki did the meat hunting, fox trapping, and sea otter hunting. In the western and central Aleutians, containing no

Sea otters, Amchitka Island, 1949. By Robert D. Jones. FWS 1092, Alaska Resources Library and Information Services. Sea otters constituted the main attraction for early Russians in Alaska.

indigenous foxes and few fur seals, the men attempted to harvest sea otters by shooting and netting them. They lacked experience in skin boats and frightened off the otters by gunfire; thus they quickly became reliant on the Aleuts. Lacking sufficient trade goods to barter for otter skins, they eventually resorted to coercion to mobilize the Aleut hunters. When the local otter supply gave out, they forced Aleuts to move to new hunting territory.[16]

Natives, primarily Aleuts and Koniag (Alutiiq) Eskimos, carried out sea otter hunts in *baidarkas* (kayaks) carrying one or two persons. About 21 feet long, 18–20 inches wide, and weighing 30 pounds, baidarkas consisted of driftwood frames tied together by baleen and covered tightly by sea lion skin. Hunters sat low in their crafts, feet straight forward, wearing seal-gut raincoats tied around the opening to keep out water. They used stone-tipped spears mounted on throwing handles. Harold McCracken, who knew some of the hunters in their old age, described the chase:

Aleut sea otter hunters, Unalaska, 1891 or 1892. Revenue cutter Bear *coll. 89-193-57, University of Alaska Fairbanks, Alaska and Polar Regions Archives. Employing baidarkas, lances, and guns, Aleuts and Koniag Eskimos conducted most sea otter hunting.*

> A party of anywhere from six to twenty or even a hundred or more skin baidarkas would take to sea together for the hunt. . . . Invariably two men went in each little craft, the one in the front hatch using the spear and the one in the back principally concerned with maneuvering the baidarka with his long, double-bladed paddle. Spread out in a line, they would all move out until a sea otter was seen. The hunter who first sighted the animal would raise his paddle into the air as a signal and his canoe would dart forward as quickly as possible to where the animal went down, remaining on the spot while the other baidarkas quickly formed a wide circle around him. Every eye was now alert to catch the reappearance, which would take place eventually. As soon as this happened, the canoe nearest darted forward in the same manner as the first, while everyone shouted to make the animal dive again, giving it the least possible time to fill its lungs with fresh air. The process was repeated; the sea otter's dives becoming increasingly shorter as the circle gradually closed in. Finally a hunter was sure to be close enough to throw his spear, and these natives were so expert that a sea otter seldom escaped.[17]

Hunters also caught otters by means of sinew nets stretched over kelp beds and across entrances to coastal caves. They paddled up to otters sleeping in seaweed during heavy seas and clubbed them. After catching an otter at sea they skinned it and stowed the pelt inside the boat. Killer whales occasionally took the dead otters and, according to legend, even the hunters.[18]

Tlingit Indians in the Southeast also speared otters and sometimes surprised otters on land and clubbed them. Only partially conquered by the Russians, the Tlingits hunted otters for their own use or for trade to the highest bidders, usually the British or Americans. They resented and frequently opposed Russians and their Aleut and Koniag hunters. In the Southeast, hunting parties organized by Russians used rifles to shoot otters at sea and to protect themselves from the Tlingits. Russians issued rifles only for use south of the fort at Yakutat for fear that their own hunters would turn the guns on the Russians.[19]

Treatment of the Natives

Recurring violence between Russians and Alaska Natives marked Russia's North American adventure. It sprang from many sources: misunderstandings, abuse of women, forced work requirements and tribute payments, resentment of Russian intrusion, rivalries among trading companies, and a history of warfare and slavery among Natives themselves. Either side might initiate an encounter and, within days or weeks, relations might again be peaceful and amiable. Conflict began upon one of the first landings on Attu in 1745. Confusion led to shooting; and, in a separate incident, the abduction of Aleut women by an exploration team culminated in the shooting of about 15 more Aleuts. The surviving guilty parties—a shipwreck on the return trip claimed the cargo and 32 men—received keelhauling as punishment.[20] More extreme Russian behavior followed Native attacks that claimed the lives of numerous Russians and sometimes destroyed their ships. In retaliation Russians killed dozens, probably hundreds, of Aleuts and Koniags. The reprisals pacified the Aleuts and Koniags, ending their internecine wars but facilitating Russian domination.

Some Russians behaved kindly toward the Natives, rescuing and educating orphans and slaves. But orders from Empress Catherine and the Siberian governors to treat Natives fairly tended to be ignored in practice. Tribute payments, banned in 1788, continued until 1794.[21] Promyshlenniki baptized Natives to gain exclusive access to their furs through the status of godfather. Russian clergy, on the other hand, counseled humane treatment of the Natives. First arriving in the mid-1780s, they operated schools, hospitals, and other social services. Both promyshlenniki and clergy tolerated indigenous beliefs and did not actively proselytize. A large percentage of Natives voluntarily converted to Russian Orthodoxy, even before the arrival of the clergy.[22]

As they eliminated otters on the islands nearest Kamchatka, the fur seekers moved progressively eastward through the Aleutians to mainland Alaska. After nearly 40 years of expeditions, a few large corporations, more able to finance bigger ships and crews for greater time spans and distances, replaced the small temporary companies. Merchants Gregorii Shelikov and Ivan Golikov organized the most successful company in 1781.[23] An empire builder, Shelikov wanted to create permanent settlements and strengthen Russian territorial claims in

America as far south as California. Most government leaders approved of land claims but did not encourage large population transfers to what they saw as fur-trading outposts. Nevertheless, Shelikov organized a three-ship expedition to Kodiak Island in 1783 to create a settlement from which trading and expansion inland and along the coast could be facilitated. Upon arrival and in violation of imperial prohibition of violence against Natives, Shelikov's forces attacked and defeated the Koniags. They built a fort and proceeded to establish outposts westward and eastward.

Shelikov pressed Aleuts and Koniags into service while issuing orders to treat them fairly and provide social benefits. He built a school for orphans and sent for more settlers after returning to Siberia in 1786. The deepening enslavement of serfs in Russia made them less available for service in Alaska. A resulting labor shortage caused the company to further impress the Aleuts and Koniags as hunters and fighters while maintaining social services.[24]

On the eastern Aleutians and Kodiak Island during the 1780s and 1790s, exploitation of Natives grew more systematic. Alexander Baranov, aggressive director of the Shelikov-Golikhov Company beginning in 1790, organized them for large-scale fur acquisition. In contrast to small groups of single-hatch kayaks employed earlier, fleets of up to 600 double-hatched kayaks traveled hundreds of miles in search of sea otters. Hunters left home from May until September or later. Upon return they had to trap foxes and land otters or supply meat for the Russians. Women, children, and elderly men remained as hostages, required to gather provisions, make clothing, and perform other chores. Pay for the Natives consisted of small portions of the fruits of their own labor. Women also served as concubines. Given scant opportunity to lay in winter storage for themselves, Natives often starved. Aleut and Koniag hunters endured dangerous seas and attacks by other Natives, particularly Tlingits in the Southeast. Between 1792 and 1805, 751 Koniags died in service to the Russians; 350 Koniags and Aleuts drowned in 1805. Disease, accidents, and other misfortunes reduced the Kodiak Island population from 5,700 in 1792 to 1,500 in 1834.[25] Similarly, an unknown but high percentage of the Aleut population disappeared during the Russian era.[26]

G.I. Dayvidov, a Russian naval officer who visited posts from Kodiak Island to California between 1802 and 1806, recorded the hunting operations of the Russian-American Company. It maintained small posts along the coasts manned by drafted Native hunters directed by one or two Russians. They gathered birds, seals, foxes, and other wildlife for food, clothing, or barter. Kodiak Island had four posts; Afognak two; Ukamok Island, Katmai, and Sutkum one each; Kenai Peninsula two; and Resurrection Bay one. Natives had destroyed the post at Iliamna, as well as the trading post at Yakutat and the main fort at Sitka. Russians had so decimated and intimidated the Aleuts that no such threat remained in the Aleutians.

Russians controlled the Aleuts and Koniag Eskimos and, to some extent, the Chugach Eskimos and Kenaitze Indians, forcing them to do a wide varicty of tasks. In 1803 they sent a party of about 1,000 Aleuts, Koniags, Chugaches, and Kenaitzes southward as far as Yakutat to hunt sea otters and return in August. About 400 more went to Tugidak and Ukamok islands for sea otters and fish. Another 100 or so hunted otters and sea lions in Cook Inlet. A similar party went to Katmai village and Sutkum Island. Aged and weak men, about 80 in all, had to hunt birds for their skins. Not infrequently they died by falling off the nesting cliffs in attempts to fill their quotas of 200 to 300 skins each. In September the company allowed them to return to Kodiak and put them to work carrying supplies or trapping foxes. If a man turned in five black or eight red foxes he received a parka made from the bird skins. Old men were also assigned to catch cod, halibut, and salmon. Whale hunters, if successful, received tobacco and beads.

Koniag women spent the year preparing fish, sewing clothing, digging *sarana* and lily roots, and picking berries for the company. Alaska Peninsula Natives, in addition to hunting sea otters, caught land mammals and gathered roots and berries. The company took the older children to be employed as sailors or workers. Kenaitze Indians similarly gathered food, hunted wildlife, and carried beads and other trade goods into the interior to acquire furs, all to benefit the company. Chugach women and girls gathered roots, berries, and bird eggs. During the winter the company levied a quota of five mountain sheep or three marmots for each Chugach. Natives on the north coast of the Alaska Peninsula had formerly hunted sea otters but had disappeared, abandoning their relatives held hostage by the company.[27]

Competition in the Fur Trade

Effective in 1799, the Russian government granted a fur-trading monopoly to the Russian-American Company, creating a mechanism of imperial power similar to the British East India Company. Unable to project military force to North America, the Russians hoped a powerful trading company would reduce conflict among Russian traders and perpetuate Russian influence.[28] Baranov, manager of the Shelikov-Golikov Company and its successor, the Russian-American Company, from 1799 until 1818, sought to extend Russian control southward along the coast. Progressive depletion of sea otters in the Aleutians and the northern Gulf of Alaska added urgency to the drive. He established forts at Yakutat Bay in 1796 and Novo-Arkangelsk (Sitka) in 1799 but encountered multiple barriers. Native depopulation and resistance worsened the chronic labor shortage. Foreign ships cut deeply into the fur trade. Tlingit Indians in Southeast Alaska not only refused to be dominated but actively made war on the Russians, destroying the Yakutat and Sitka forts. They killed large numbers of Aleut and Koniag hunters who threatened to deplete the sea otters in their waters. Apparently glad to weaken Russian territorial and trading control, British and American traders gave the Tlingits ample supplies of guns and ammunition in exchange for furs. Moreover, the difficulty of importing food from the Russian colonies in eastern Siberia made the Russian-American Company heavily dependent on foreign traders and Native hunters and gatherers.[29]

Baranov and his company superiors resolved to spread their operations southward to California. Sea otters provided the means to this goal and, in 1808, Baranov established a headquarters at Sitka, recaptured from the Tlingits in 1804. From 1803 to 1812 he engaged Yankee captains to carry out the operation—they furnished supplies and transportation, he rounded up Native hunters, and each contracting party received half the otter skins. Beginning in 1809 he sent his own vessels, preferring not to divide the catch. Both ventures reaped profits: tens of thousands of otters. But Spanish authorities in California refused permission for hunting and took measures to stop it, occasionally imprisoning or killing the hunters. After Mexico gained independence, Russians and Mexicans signed otter-hunting contracts between 1823 and 1841. Soon the Russians found themselves junior partners as Mexicans won more control of the industry.[30]

To maintain their presence in California, acquire supplies, and pursue the fur trade, Russians built bases north of Bodega Bay (the Russian Colony, later called Fort Ross) and the Farallon Islands, both in 1812. Disappearance of the sea otters, competition from American hunters, and resistance by Spanish and Mexican officials dried up their fur trade profits. In the Farallons, Russians decimated the otters and exterminated the fur seals before vacating the islands about 1833.[31] At Fort Ross, attempts to produce ships, grain, and livestock failed economically for reasons of climate, cost of supply, and lack of trained personnel. During the 1830s the colony lost an average of 10,000 rubles annually. Mexican hostility and growing British and American influence to the north forced the realization that Fort Ross could not be sustained. The Russians abandoned it in 1842.[32]

Most California sea otter pelts left the hunting grounds in non-Russian vessels. Reports of Alaskan sea otters had reached Boston from Cook's 1776–1780 voyage. British, French, Spanish, and American ships advanced up the Northwest coast in the 1780s to make territorial claims, partly in response to Russian movement into North America. Traders followed them, operating in Alaska after the mid-1780s.[33] British and, increasingly, American seamen plied the waters of Southeast Alaska and Prince William Sound, undercutting Russian trade by bartering goods for sea otter skins and setting sail for China. Baranov estimated that between the end of the 18th Century and the early 19th Century these ships carried away 120,000 sea otter skins. Only two known French expeditions engaged in the trade. Jean Francois La Perouse and his men visited in 1788 and died in a shipwreck in the South Seas. A second expedition by explorer Camille de Roquefeuil contracted with Baranof in 1818. Part of the agreement called for payment of $200 Mexican to the company for each Aleut life lost. A harvest of fewer than 200 otters and the killing of 26 Aleuts by Haida Indians put an end to French interest in the trade.[34]

Sea otters formed an integral part of the newly established China trade of the United States. New England vessels carried goods to the Northwest coast to be traded for furs worth five or six times their cost and exchanged the furs in China for goods to be sold in Boston. Profits for such a three-way trip might reach 500 percent. Between 1788 and 1826 at least 127 ships made the journey. The trade peaked in the two decades after 1790 and fell off sharply as the otters died out.

Sea otters' characteristics abetted their collapse. The hunting season never ended because the animals needed year-round insulation from the cold water, and their pelts remained prime. Mothers refused to abandon their babies, assuring the deaths of both and a disproportionate harvest of females. From 1799 to 1818 about 300,000 sea otter skins went to China ports, not counting those the Russians took to Kiakhta.[35]

Despite a rule against conveying furs to foreign traders, the Russian-American Company traded furs to Americans because they needed foodstuffs and supplies not otherwise available. In 1805 a Yankee shipment of meat, bread, rice, flour, molasses, and sugar warded off starvation at New Archangel. In exchange for food, utensils, guns, blankets, and other supplies, the Americans preferred to take furs. They could sell the sea otter pelts in China more cheaply than the Russians could, in part because the Russians conducted their trade through distant Kiakhta. In return for furs, Russians and Americans got tea, silk fabrics, and porcelain. American ships, predominantly New Englanders, acquired most sea otters directly from Indians in Southeast Alaska. The aggressive sailors ignored Russian attempts to deter them. Indians received guns and ammunition, utensils, metals, nails, hatchets and knives, beads, rum, and molasses. As the sea otters dwindled and Hudson's Bay Company gained control over the land fur trade in the Northwest, Americans withdrew from the Alaska-China fur trade.[36]

Well-provisioned American traders and, later, whalers remained active for several decades, competing effectively against the Russians. Hudson's Bay Company, also able to offer the Natives higher prices and better-quality trade goods for furs than the Russians could, leased most of Southeast Alaska from the Russian-American Company for its trading operations. Hudson's Bay had begun construction of a trading post on the Stikine River, and in 1834 the Russian

Navy fired on a British vessel attempting to provision it. As part of a settlement Hudson's Bay rented the Southeast for 2,000 river otter and lynx skins per year for ten years. The parties renewed the agreement until the United States acquired Alaska in 1867.[37]

In addition to the sea otter trade, Russians bought mink, river otter, and beaver skins from the Tlingits, but they had to pay three to five times what they paid Aleuts and other Natives for furs of similar value. Tanaina Indians of the Kenai Peninsula gathered marten, lynx, bear, river otter, wolverine, beaver, and muskrat skins for the Russians. Koniags, more fully subjugated, trapped on Kodiak Island, and Aleuts in the eastern Aleutians. Russian efforts to set up a fur trade in western Alaska and the lower Yukon valley beginning in 1819 ran into strong competition from Hudson's Bay Company in the upper Yukon Valley.[38]

Low wages, harsh working conditions, and cruel treatment by superiors discouraged young Russian men from going to North America, a cause of the labor shortage. Moreover, most Russians' experience and interests lay in agriculture. Work quality suffered in North America: promyshlenniki, creoles, and most Natives did not produce efficiently and commonly took to alcohol.[39] Russian clergyman Hieromonk Gideon portrayed the acculturation of 150 or so Aleuts who over-wintered at Sitka during the 1820s:

> [T]hey have become accustomed to the Russian way of life, to drinking tea and, more especially, to drinking strong liquor which they like passionately and to which they have become so wantonly addicted, they use every means they can, even illicit means, to satisfy these new needs. Following the example of her husband, who changes his parka of birds' skin, which was so comfortable and so practical, for an overcoat made of dreadnought or cloth or even for a dress coat—an item of clothing already so ridiculous in Europe—the Aleut wife scorns her [skin clothing] and absolutely must have an Indian dress, and a shawl, etc. which she acquires in ways not difficult to guess. The results of these disturbing changes are sickness and a new generation, weak and corrupted from birth.[40]

Baranov's managerial excesses provoked investigations resulting in his replacement and 1819 regulations, again forbidding abduction and other forms of mistreatment of employees and Natives. The 1821 Russian-American Company rules called for a lengthy list of benefits and fair treatment of Russians, creoles, and Natives. They also mandated three-year service by all able-bodied Native men at a minimum of one-fifth the pay of Russians. Notwithstanding the appointment of more enlightened managers, especially Naval officers, the condition of Aleuts and Koniags improved only gradually.[41] Numbering 823 at their high point in 1839,[42] Russians in North America lacked the strength to resist British and American incursions. Their strategic weakness would ultimately bring about the demise of their enterprise in North America.

Indians on the Northwest coast suffered from the fur trade as a whole, partly as a result of their own shortcomings. Traditionally, Indians of Southeast Alaska and coastal Canada actively engaged in a slave trade, typically featuring captives from southern tribes being sold into the interior. Most warfare had the objective of taking slaves. Primarily women and children, the slaves sold for high prices in trade goods; in 1834 Tlingits paid 2 sea otter or 25 beaver skins for each. Wealthy men might own 20 to 40 slaves who performed a variety of tasks including hunting. When trading vessels arrived, the Indians offered their slaves as prostitutes in return for trade items. Some Euro-American traders took up the slave trade to obtain furs, transporting women from as far away as California and Hawaii. Nonslave Indian women also became prostitutes, and venereal diseases spread. Tobacco, alcohol, and violence by guns added to the degradation and death toll. Smallpox killed nearly half of the approximately 800 Tlingits at Sitka in 1835–1836 and similar numbers elsewhere. Measles further reduced and dispirited the Natives, ending their resistance to Euro-American incursions.[43]

Diminishing catches of sea otters had persuaded the Russian government to put conservation measures into effect in 1821, including harvest quotas for districts, bans on hunting in depleted areas, attempts to avoid killing females, and rules for reducing unnecessary disturbance of the otters. The measures lasted until the sale of Alaska in 1867. Conservation worked in the Aleutians and the Pribilofs but not along the mainland where non-Russian traders pursued the otters to near-extermination. Between 1842 and 1862 the Russian total catch averaged 1,347 annually, of which Koniag and Chugach hunters caught about one-fourth in the Kurile Islands north of Japan. Many came from other parts of the Siberian coast and, after the 1840s, virtually none from Southeast Alaska.[44]

A compilation of sales records (Table 1.1) indicated that Russians delivered at least 200,839 sea otters to market in about 129 vessels between 1743 and 1823. Russian, British, American, and French fur seekers took an overall toll of 600,000 to 800,000 sea otters.[45]

SEA OTTER HUNTING UNDER AMERICAN RULE

By the time Russian domination ended, few, if any, full-blooded Aleuts existed and their aboriginal subsistence culture had been altered considerably. To purchase Western clothing and other goods and to construct and maintain their Russian Orthodox churches, they needed cash income. Those not harvesting fur seals in the Pribilofs had to rely on sea otter hunting. Otters survived in substantial numbers in the vicinity of Sanak Island in the eastern Aleutians. Parties of 40 to 50 hunters traveled up to 150 miles from Unalaska Island in two-man baidarkas to pursue them. Hunters camped on Sanak Island and

TABLE 1.1. Russian Fur Cargoes From North America, 1743–1823

Fur seals	2,324,364	Marten	18,121
Sea otters	200,839	Mink	5,349
Blue foxes	108,865	White foxes	5,130
Red foxes	57,638	Bears	2,650
Beavers	58,729	Lynx	1,819
Cross foxes	44,904	Wolverines	1,234
Black & brown foxes	30,158	Walrus ivory	99,700lb
Otters	22,807	Whalebone (baleen)	107,896lb

Source: Berkh, V.N., *A Chronological History of the Discovery of the Aleutian Islands or the Exploits of Russian Merchants* (Kingston: Limestone, 1974), 93.

Note: Figures include otters from Commander Islands but exclude about 17 vessels lacking records of voyage or cargo, in addition to those lost at sea.

paddled out 15 to 20 miles in all directions to look for otters. Lest they alert the animals, the men had to avoid making fires and leaving food scraps on the beaches. An observer noted that "the sufferings to which the Natives subject themselves every winter on the island, going for many weeks without fires, even for cooking, with the thermometer down to zero in a northerly gale of wind, are better imagined than described." Of the sea otter he added that "this animal, of all wild animals, seems to be possessed of the greatest aversion to or dread of the presence, or even the proximity, of man."[46] Otter hunting succeeded best immediately before, during, or after storms, which drove otters near or onto the shore. Young Aleuts using rifles acquired from traders patrolled the shores year-round, firing at any otter near enough to hit. Otters seemed unable to disentangle themselves from the nets western Aleuts threw over seaweed or stretched across cave openings. In the fury of storms, otters landed and pushed their heads under seaweed for shelter. Two Aleut brothers clubbed 78 such otters in 1½ hours. A writer who knew them commented that the money from the otters "would have clothed and fed them for the rest of their natural lives; but, like our own coal-oil Johnny, they quickly squandered their wealth, and are poorer now than ever."[47]

American regulations restricted the taking of otters to Natives and, after 1878, to whites married to Natives. Nevertheless, in territorial waters whites commonly hunted illegally and seldom got caught. In the 1870s and 1880s hunters employed a wasteful practice of shooting otters at sea. Captain Michael Healy of the U.S. Treasury Department's revenue cutter *Corwin* reported that as of 1884, "unprincipled white hunters, tempted by the great value of otter skins, come here and marry the simple girls, force them to accompany them on their hunting trips and do their cooking and work for them, bring two or three children into the world, and then leave their families to get their living as best they can, while they themselves return to enjoy their earnings with other wives in civilization." Healy noted that the hunters illegally used breech-loading rifles and set numerous nets along the shore. He warned of the impending extermination of the otters, adding that "as the Aleuts live almost entirely upon the profits derived from the sale of skins, extreme poverty, if not actual starvation, must follow."[48] In the 1880s, white crews using guns increasingly searched for otters offshore in international waters. Ships carried up to 60 pursuit boats, some driven by steam, permitting longer ranges and periods of hunting.[49]

Compared to a sustainable-yield annual catch of 1,000–2,000 by the Russians between the 1840s and 1867, Americans harvested 12,208 otters in their first four years. The kill rose to nearly 5,000 per year between 1881 and 1890 and by 1909 totaled 107,372.[50] Captain C.L. Hooper, commander of the Revenue Marine Bering Sea Patrol, complained in the 1890s that despite regulations, lack of resources made it impossible for agents to protect the sea otter:

> Being constantly harassed, clubbed and shot on shore, caught in nets by white men, their hauling-grounds made uninhabitable by the camp fires of the hunters and defiled by fisheries and the decaying bodies of their companions, the sea otter of the Aleutian Islands has not only decreased in numbers, but has actually changed its habits. It no longer comes out on the land to feed, rest, or give birth to its young. A floating raft of kelp serves as its only resting-place, and banks of 30 fathoms of water are its feeding-grounds. Even there it is hunted and harassed by hunting schooners from March until August.[51]

Natives willingly engaged in the slaughter. Freed from the oppression of the Russian era, Aleut hunters had a new incentive—cash—to kill as many otters as possible. In 1880 they received $80–$100 per skin from traders. The annual catch peaked in the mid-1880s and sank to 724 in 1896. As otters grew scarce, the price of a pelt rose, reaching $1,200 in London. Of this amount, the few successful hunters got up to $400. Money enabled the Natives to buy guns that hastened the decline of otter populations, despite the fact that the law forbade shooting otters. The relatively vast influx of cash disrupted Native lifestyles and left them more deeply impoverished when the money dried up.[52]

Alcoholic beverages, or the makings thereof, ranked high among the commodities acquired by cash or trade. Through most of its tenure the Russian-American Company prohibited trade in liquor. Moreover, Tlingits in the Southeast refused alcohol lest it weaken them. Late in the 19th Century importation increased despite an 1873 ban by the U.S. government and the initiation of revenue patrols.[53] Based on his inspection tour in the mid-1890s, Assistant Secretary of the Treasury Charles Hamlin commented that

Sea otter skins drying, Aleutian Islands, ca. 1890s. By Samuel Applegate. Core coll. 01-2682, Alaska State Library. For Russians and other fur traders, sea otter skins ranked as the most valuable resource.

> the smuggling of liquor into Alaska and its illegal sale to whites and Indians continues flagrantly and defiantly. . . . Complaint is also made that it is impossible to secure conviction of offenders against the liquor laws by jury trial because of sympathy with the accused. . . . The natives are passionately fond of liquor, and will do anything to secure it. Many murders are directly traceable to liquor obtained in this way; these cases are rarely brought to the attention of the authorities. Much cruelty, such as wife beating and other crimes, is also caused by the use of liquor.

Hamlin recommended strict licensing and control of substances imported for use in making alcoholic beverages.[54]

Samuel Applegate, Aleutian Treasury agent and early recorder of Alaskan wildlife, reflected on the human costs of the fur-seeking era:

> Hundreds, yes thousands of lives lost in the raging sea under lowering northern skies; hundreds of deaths amid swirling snows and chilling blasts; thousands more caused by the hardships and privations inseparable from the hunter's and sailor's life in those high latitudes; hundreds slain in conflicts between native tribes or rival Russians; hundreds more of daring mariners lost in those latter days in reckless pursuit of the precious otter—all these have been sacrificed in addition to money spent and risked, to make up a sum that in these extravagant times does not exceed the wealth of several individuals in the United States.[55]

Applegate might have added reference to the thousands of Natives who lost their freedom and died from forced labor, violence, or introduced diseases.

Treasury agents and other government officials had long protested the unsustainable killing of sea otters. But the international controversy over the fur seal (Chapter 2) overshadowed the sea otter issue and forestalled action. In 1887 and again in 1897 the Japanese, joined in 1897 by the Russians and Americans, urged a treaty to protect both sea otters and fur seals. British interests in freedom of the seas and Canadian interests in pelagic sealing prevented an agreement.[56] Ongoing attempts at resolution of the fur seal dispute lasted from 1887 well past the turn of the century.

SEA OTTER PROTECTION AND RECOVERY

By 1910 sea otters taken in Alaskan waters had fallen to 34. In the 1868–1911 period, Americans harvested a recorded 107,372 otters. Of an estimated original population of 100,000–150,000, only scattered pockets remained. Almost vanished from the earth, sea otters gained firm protection by the 1910 Fur Seal Act and the North Pacific Sealing Convention of 1911. Only Alaska Natives could hunt sea otters, and few did. Further safeguards resulted from the creation of the Aleutian Islands Reserve by William Howard Taft's last-minute executive order on March 3, 1913.[57] In that same year California gave legal protection to the sea otters known to survive there, mostly in the waters near Monterey. Gradually, otters began to recover in the Aleutians, yet they did not go unmolested. A San Francisco trader made annual trips on the mail boat to Attu during at least the period 1916 through 1928, buying poached otter and fur seal skins to be sold in London, Paris, and Berlin. He bought otters for about $300; they sold in Europe for up to $1,500.[58]

American botanist Walter Eyerdam sighted otters off Afognak Island in 1922 and, ten years later, found them fairly common near Atka and Adak islands in the western Aleutians. Aleuts told him that Japanese poaching vessels, normally commanded by Europeans, visited the islands in search of otters. Eyerdam met the English captain of one such vessel in 1930. Eyerdam suggested that otters be reinstated in the Pribilofs or other favorable localities.[59]

Jurisdiction over the sea otters shifted from the Department of Commerce to the Department of Agriculture in 1915. For the next quarter-century a variety of commercial activities took place in the Aleutians: cod fishing extending from mid-19th-Century Russian operations, accelerated fox farming fostered by the Bureau of Biological Survey (BBS), shore-based whaling out of Akutan, sulfur mining at Akun between 1914 and 1922, stocking of reindeer on Unalaska and Unimak islands in 1913, and sheep ranching on Unalaska and Umnak. None of these directly affected the sea otters, but requests by Governor

Walter Clark, interested in economic development, resulted in withdrawal of several large islands from refuge status.

Restoration of sea otter populations remained a high priority for the BBS and its successor, the Fish and Wildlife Service, supervising the renamed Aleutians National Wildlife Refuge in 1940. The BBS undertook several scientific expeditions including one led by Olaus J. Murie and Victor B. Scheffer in 1936–1938 that sighted otters off several islands. Based on reports of otter poaching by Japanese, BBS stationed agents on Amchitka from 1937 to 1940. Amchitka, populated by over 1,000 Aleuts in prehistoric times, had been abandoned in 1849 except for temporary visits by fox trappers. It served as a recovery zone for otters.[60] American poachers took some otters in the 1940s; Alaska Game Commission agents seized three pelts and part of another in 1943–1944.[61]

World War II arrived at the Aleutians in June 1942 when the Japanese seized Attu, Agattu, and Kiska, in part to divert American forces from more strategically vital sectors in the Pacific. Americans launched bombing missions from Dutch Harbor and Umnak but needed more forward positions to reduce the dangers of long flights in bad weather unaided by adequate navigation and communication facilities. They built a field at Adak, landed on Amchitka in January 1943, and laid down a flight strip only 80 miles from Kiska. Army forces recaptured Attu in May at a cost of 549 dead and 1,148 wounded Americans and the deaths of nearly all 2,500 Japanese defenders. Unaware that the Japanese had evacuated Kiska in July, U.S. and Canadian troops invaded in August and suffered 28 dead and 50 wounded by their own firing. Bombers from Amchitka flew about 100 missions to the Kurile Islands, and the U.S. Army prepared runways at Amchitka, Adak, and Shemya for B-29 attacks against Japan, a plan found unnecessary.[62]

The war changed the Aleutians, if not the sea otters. Attu's population of 42 Aleuts went to Japan to be kept as prisoners at Otaru, Hokkaido. Despite rations that starved several to death, 25 survived. Most eventually settled on Atka, and none returned to Attu because the Alaska Indian Service did not want to rebuild the village and maintain services on the remote island 550 miles west of Atka. Officials also declined to pay for the rebuilding of Biorka, Kashega, and Makushin, towns whose combined populations totaled 71. Aleuts from all villages except Attu had been moved to temporary shelters in the Southeast during the war. Loss of their homes and cultural artifacts, and acquisition of new wants and values, dissuaded many Aleuts from returning to their former lifestyles after the war.[63]

GIs on Amchitka dug into all accessible archaeological sites and removed the artifacts, seldom following proper procedures. Some materials found their way into museums; others were dispersed. Accommodation of about 16,000 men on the island necessitated nearly 2,000 Quonset huts and many other buildings, all left behind. The Navy stayed at Adak, but the military abandoned nearly all other sites. Concretized runways and numerous other facilities remained on several islands, and many unexploded bombs lay on Kiska. Vehicles, other equipment, and large piles of junk remained on several islands. Private firms salvaged vehicles in 1951–1952 and nonferrous metals in 1953.[64] Wartime activities apparently had little, if any, significant effect on the sea otters.

Rats brought in on supply ships survived and preyed on bird eggs. The military had no interest in wildlife protection, but Navy pilot Gil Joynt, a biologist, carried out sea otter surveys while on patrol. After the war the War and Navy departments attempted to gain control of some of the main Aleutian Islands. They won expanded use rights, but the islands remained within the refuge.[65]

By the early 1950s Amchitka's otter population had reached its upper limits, and small groups existed elsewhere along the Alaskan coasts. Employing scuba diving for the first time there, refuge manager Bob Jones found the key limiting factor in local otter abundance: when the otters consumed the available supply of rock oysters and sea urchins, their numbers dropped off and the oysters and urchins rebounded as part of a natural cycle.[66] Otters in other locations relied on a wide variety of foods including clams, chitons, crabs, octopi, snails, mussels, and, sometimes, fish. Bald eagles, killer whales, and perhaps sharks are the otters' natural predators.[67]

Apparent overpopulation of Amchitka otters led the Fish and Wildlife Service to try reintroducing them to former habitat, including the Pribilof Islands. But successful movement of otters proved difficult. In March 1951 a team led by Jones captured at least 35 otters on tidal rocks and held them temporarily in shallow mud-bottomed lakes. Within a few days they all died. A second attempt in 1954 compared holding otters in a large wooden tank and on dry grass in a building. All those in the tank died; 3 others survived. In March and April 1955, agents caught 31 and kept them on beds of straw on the way to the Pribilof Islands for release. Of the 19 survivors freed, some died immediately and none appeared subsequently. During 1955 through 1957, experimenters tried to determine the optimal combination of bedding and water access for caged otters, as well as drugs that would reduce stress. Five animals released at Attu in 1956 did not reappear, and an airline flight delay caused the deaths of 6 of the 8 otters taken to the Pribilofs. Experimentation demonstrated the need for clean water and resting places to prevent contaminants from reducing the insulating quality of the fur. Agents applied these lessons in May 1959 and released 7 otters at Polovina Point in the Pribilofs. Three months later fishermen sighted 5 in the vicinity. Funding from the Atomic Energy Commission as part of the 1965–1971 Amchitka nuclear test program enabled much larger translocations.[68]

In 1958 the 10,400-acre Simeonof Island in the Shumagins became a national wildlife refuge for sea otters.[69] Shortly after statehood the Alaska sea otter

Robert D. "Sea Otter" Jones, Aleutian Islands National Wildlife Refuge, mid-1950s. By J. Malcolm Greany. Alaska Game Commission, 18th Annual Report, July 1, 1956 Thru June 30, 1957. Refuge manager Jones advanced knowledge of sea otter ecology by underwater study.

population rebounded from perhaps 2,000 in 1911 to 30,000.[70] The state held management jurisdiction over the otters between 1960 and 1972. Based in part on reports of large-scale starvation of otters caused by overpopulation in the Rat and Andreanof Island groups, the state instituted an experimental, biologically sustainable harvest. Between 1962 and 1971 the program took 2,556 otters from Amchitka, Tanaga, Kanaga, Adak, and Delarof islands. Efforts stemming from nuclear tests at Amchitka Island resulted in the successful transplant between 1965 and 1972 of 708 otters to locations from the Kenai Peninsula to Oregon. Another 341 died in the moving operations, and the 1971 Cannikin hydrogen bomb test killed an estimated 1,000 to 1,350.[71] The 1972 Marine Mammal Protection Act ended state control and prohibited all but Native subsistence use of the otters. Within a quarter-century after statehood, aided by translocation and legal protection, the sea otter recovered most of its original numbers and range in the North Pacific.

Toward the end of the 20th Century four significant problems confronted Alaska sea otters. Pursuant to the Marine Mammal Protection Act, some Alaska Natives hunted the otters. Regulations prohibited sale of whole pelts but permitted parts to be sold as craft items. Natives hoped to develop an industry selling items incorporating otter fur.[72] A second issue, oil spills, found expression in the 1989 *Exxon Valdez* incident that killed an estimated 3,500–5,500 sea otters.[73] Neither of these threats appeared capable of endangering sea otter populations. A third issue, conflict between otters and commercial fishers over food such as clams and crabs, began to manifest itself in Alaska in the 1980s. While far less pronounced than the California dispute over abalone, it might grow in proportion to human demands or otter population increase.[74] The fourth phenomenon eliminated at least 95 percent of otters over a 500-mile stretch of the western Aleutians during the 1980s and 1990s. Marine scientists suspected that a small number of killer whales, possibly as few as four, had eaten the otters. The predation appeared to result from the precipitous decline of sea lions and seals, a normal food supply for the whales. The loss of sea lions and seals, in turn, seemed to be related to one or more of three conditions: predation, overfishing, and climatic warming.

Further investigation indicated that as few as 27–40 killer whales could have caused the decline of sea lions and as few as 5 could prevent recovery. The loss of great whales to commercial hunting could have forced the killer whales to turn to harbor seals, sea lions, and, finally, sea otters.[75] At the onset of the 21st Century Aleutian sea otters may have become, at least temporarily, victims of an ecological collapse.

Sea otter rehabilitation ranks as a noteworthy environmental success for at least two reasons. First, a mammal species inherently attractive and interesting to humans escaped extinction. It became a subject of nonconsumptive use values, including scientific study and direct and indirect viewing. Millions of people have enjoyed watching video presentations of the engaging creature, and many have sought to encounter it through ecotourism. Nearly all, if asked, would consider its extermination unthinkable and would oppose human activities that threatened its well-being.

Second, sea otters in some locations are a keystone species in their ecosystems. They consume large numbers of sea urchins, which in turn feed upon kelp. The kelp beds, essentially undersea forests, provide food and shelter for a vast complex of marine species.[76] Removal of sea otters in the 19th Century might have caused disruption in the coastal North Pacific Ocean. Recovery of the otters may have helped to right natural balances.

The sea otter's hours of peril and salvation in Alaska long pre-dated public awareness of its ecological significance, as well as the existence of video mass media. Far removed from visibility, it lacked the high level of public recognition needed for protective law enforcement. Unmitigated exploitation had reigned until the species nearly disappeared; utilitarian conservation had not been given a chance. Opposition to the otter's overexploitation, expressed by a small number of scientists and government officials, stemmed in part from appreciation of the species. More important, most parties agreed that an economically valuable resource should not be destroyed. Therefore, when the Senate approved the 1910 law and 1911 treaty to conserve the fur seal, it added vital if belated measures for the sea otter. In doing so, it acknowledged the goal of selected species protection and the management objective of sustainable resource use.

Absence of industrial uses for the Aleutians made possible their designation as a wildlife reserve and enhanced the otter's chances for survival. Decades after it had passed the danger point, movies and television magnified public support for the animal and transformed it into a beloved creature. Nonconsumptive use values and public participation entered the equation that would determine the future of the sea otter. Preservation of the species became the main concern. Yet the cumulative pressures of human population growth and alteration of the environment, manifested partly in over-fishing and climate warming, cast doubt on the fate of the sea otter and other marine mammals of the North Pacific.

2

Fur Seal's Friend: Henry W. Elliot

One of the first great international wildlife controversies began immediately after the United States acquired Alaska. In various forms, it lasted more than a century. It gave birth to a prototype environmental campaign and an international treaty centered on a North Pacific sea mammal: the fur seal.

Biologically related to the fur seals of the southern oceans, the northern fur seal gathered on a few subarctic islands each spring and summer for breeding and birth of pups. During the fall and winter the females and young migrated southward in the open ocean while most older males remained in the Bering Sea. On the North American side the herd ranged to the latitude of southern California, swung eastward toward the coast, and followed it northward in the late winter and spring on the way back to the rookeries.

While the sea otter grew harder to find, the fur seal took its place as a mainstay of the Russian fur-trading enterprise in Alaska, furnishing the bulk of profits. Only the superb pelts of the sea otter and black and silver foxes exceeded that of the fur seal in value. Shortly after the mid-18th Century, hunters exhausted the seal rookeries on Bering Island where Steller had encountered them and on nearby Copper Island. Then in 1786 and 1787 navigator Gavriil Pribylov and his crew found the islands that later bore his name. There they discovered by far the largest breeding grounds of the northern fur seal, as well as sea otters and other mammals.[1] Pribilof rookeries hosted about 80 percent of the northern fur seals. Smaller populations bred at the Commander Islands in Siberia, the Kurile Islands and Robben Island controlled by Japan, and San Miguel Island and Castle Rock off California.[2]

FUR SEALING IN THE RUSSIAN ERA

Massive exploitation immediately followed Pribylof's arrival. He returned to Kamchatka in 1788 carrying the hides of 40,000 fur seals, 2,000 sea otters, and 6,000 blue-phase Arctic foxes. For decades thereafter, expeditions tallied similar or greater hauls. The Russians settled Aleuts on the previously uninhabited islands (named St. George and St. Paul) to do the work of sealing, driftwood gathering, and hunting of foxes, birds, and sea lions. They organized an efficient means of harvesting fur seals, as outlined by Russian captain Frederick Litke in the 1820s:

> The hunters form a human chain along the shore and cut off any possible retreat of animals to the sea. They then push them all, without distinction, inland. Then they separate the first and third class males as well as the females and drive them back to the sea. As to the young ones which they intend to kill, they chase them as far as to the settlements—a distance of two or three leagues—but without hurrying them and letting them rest often, for without this precaution the animals could die of exhaustion, especially at a hot and windless time. Once they arrive at the settlement, the hunters kill the animals by blows. On the Island of Saint Paul herds of 3,000 to 4,000 seals can be driven inland this way, and on the Island of Saint George herds of 500 to 2,000.

Occasional signs of empathy for the seals could be seen. Litke observed that "the hunters themselves, hardened as they are to this form of murder, confess that often they can hardly raise their clubs to strike this innocent creature which, lying on its back with its paws in the air and crying plaintively like a baby seems to be imploring mercy."[3]

As soon as feasible, within a few days of the kill, Aleuts removed and cleaned the skins. Women stretched the skins on wooden frames and placed them in drying houses, warmed by heated stones. Workers tied the dry skins in bundles of 50 for shipment. They dried some of the meat for food and stored the remainder of the fat-laden carcasses in a pile to be burned as fuel.[4]

Russians took the fur seal pelts to Kiakhta for trade or sale to the Chinese. British and New England traders, primarily interested in sea otters, also traded

Fur seal herd, Zapadni rookery, St. Paul Island. By Victor B. Scheffer. FWS 1102, Alaska Resources Library and Information Services. Fur seals replaced sea otters as the mainstay of the Alaska fur trade.

or sold fur seal pelts in China. Following the discoveries of the Cook expedition, British merchant ships outnumbered the Yankees from 1785 into the 1790s. New Englanders, who first carried Falkland Island fur seal pelts to China in 1786, quickly surpassed the British in the Northwest fur trade. It formed a vital part of their China trade and helped establish the new nation as a viable economic unit and an important seafaring power.

Many of the fur seals taken to China came from islands off southern South America and, later, off Mexico and California. Sailors went ashore and clubbed them by the tens of thousands, likely exterminating some of the herds. Approximately 150,000 fur seals at the Galapagos, Guadalupe Island, and Baja California, and a similar number on the Farallons off California, fell to the sealers. On Mas Afuera Island alone, sealers killed 3.5 million. The total for Southern waters, Mexico, and California stood at 5 million.[5]

At both Sitka and the Pribilofs the Yankees traded their goods for northern fur seals. Russians needed the rice, tea, sugar, flour, rum, tobacco, and other

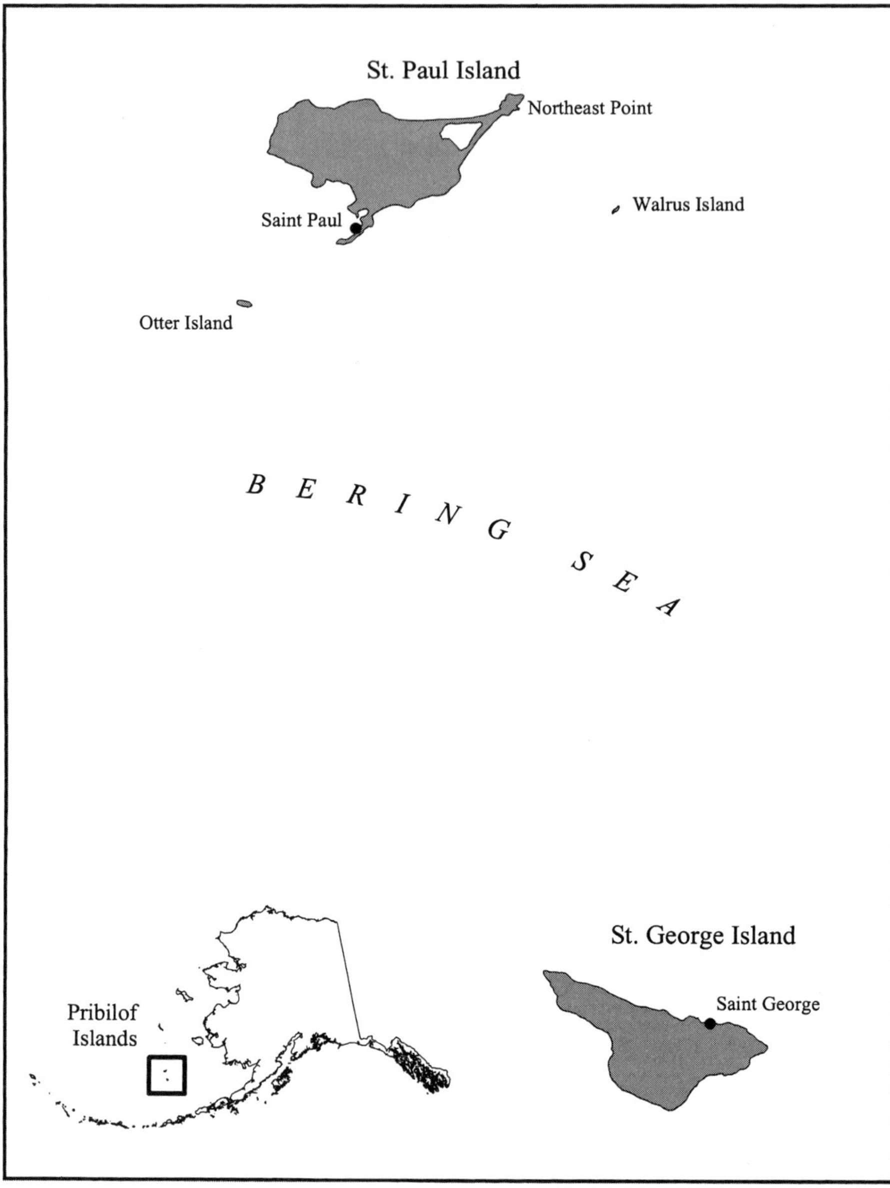

Pribilof Islands. Courtesy Jason Geck

high-quality supplies brought by the Americans but did not want to pay in valuable sea otter pelts. Over a 30-year period beginning in 1799, Americans and other traders acquired at least 700,000 fur seal skins from the Russians.[6]

Until the 1820s no significant market existed for fur seals in Europe or the United States; nearly all skins went to Canton. Limited uses in the United States and Europe included caps, gloves, carriage rugs, trunk covers, and "beaver" hats. Between 1825 and 1870, improved processing, especially in dyeing and guard hair removal, enhanced the quality of pelts. London enterprises handled nearly all fur seal skins by 1870 when fashion began to drive up prices. People now prized seal fur for coats, muffs, and trim. An average pelt sold for less than $5 in the late 1860s and for $40 by 1900. Pribilof seals ranked second-best in quality to those of the South Shetland Islands–Cape Horn. Another, smaller population of southern fur seals bred at the Lobos Islands off Uruguay.[7]

Uncontrolled taking of the Pribilof seals sharply reduced their numbers. In 1802, in an attempt to speed up the drying process, workers spoiled nearly 800,000 skins. Between 1810 and 1813 the Russian-American Company burned at least 100,000 more pelts, apparently to keep the market price high.[8]

Declining seal populations induced conservation measures. Nikolai Rezanof, inspecting for the Russian government in 1805–1806, called an immediate halt to the killing, resulting in transfer of the crews to Unalaska. Sealing resumed on St. George in 1808 and on St. Paul in 1810. Regulations brought additional harvest cessations in 1822–1824 on St. Paul, 1826–1827 on St. George, and 1836–1837 on St. Paul. Notwithstanding a cap of 50,000 per year, the take fell to 7,000 or fewer during the 1830s to early 1850s. Protection of females beginning in 1847–1848 assisted recovery, and the harvest reached 30,000 to 40,000 in the late 1850s and 1860s. By the time of sale to the United States in 1867, the Pribilof herd had rebounded to an approximation of its natural strength of more than two million. During the Russian era, including the Commander Islands, fur seekers had killed about four million fur seals in the North Pacific.[9]

A number of considerations combined to persuade Russian leaders to leave North America, despite the sound financial condition of the Russian-American Company before its lease ended in 1862. British vessels, visiting and mapping the Arctic and subarctic while searching for the lost Franklin Expedition, raised questions about their motives. Russia's military weakness revealed in the Crimean War exposed its inability to deploy defensive forces halfway around the world, and consolidation of the empire in Asia warranted first priority. The British Navy had attacked Russian bases in eastern Siberia and established a base at Esquimault on Vancouver Island. Britain created the crown colony of British Columbia in 1858 and remained an adversary after the war. By contrast, the United States and Russia maintained friendly relations.[10] Discovery of gold in the Stikine River Valley in 1862 set off a gold rush, attracting more Americans. Advances by Britain through the Hudson's Bay Company could not be reversed. Hoping the United States would help balance their geopolitical rival Great Britain, Russians opted to sell Alaska to the Americans.[11]

THE INTERNATIONAL SEALING CONTROVERSY

Americans did not eagerly take possession of Alaska, mainly because they could see little economic benefit. Unlike the contiguous Western territories, settlers could not easily move to Alaska. If they did, they might find no agricultural potential. Hardly any information existed about the mainland. The oceans, by contrast, contained a recognizable store of wealth in the form of sea creatures. Most could be harvested at sea without much reliance on the land. But one valuable exception, the fur seal, came ashore where it could be exploited by whoever owned the land. A fur seal industry might repay the United States in large part for the cost of acquiring Alaska. Eventually it benefited the industry but not the public treasury, and not without 44 years of conflict among nations over who had rights to take the seals.

Management of Pribilof Sealing

In their first year on the Pribilofs, Americans behaved worse than the Russians—introducing liquor and making love to the women while the Aleut men did the work. They showed far less concern for conservation of the seals. For years prior to 1867 the Russians had limited themselves to ensure a sustained yield. American companies, four or more operating in 1868, took an estimated 240,000.[12] Publicity about the high kill rate and pressure from interested investors triggered a congressional investigation, an 1868 ban on commercial sealing, and a March 1869 resolution declaring the Pribilofs a preserve. The Treasury Department announced that only enough seals to feed the Aleut population of 371 would be harvested in 1869, but two commercial companies reaped a total of 85,901 skins. One of the companies, Hutchinson and Kohl of San Francisco, organized the Alaska Commercial Company consortium and won a twenty-year contract for exclusive sealing rights and a monopoly on all fur trading in Alaska between 1871 and 1890. Rules permitted an annual kill of 100,000 fur seals.[13] The company also secured from Russia a monopoly on land sealing at the Commander Islands.[14]

Under the terms of the 1871–1890 lease the Alaska Commercial Company supplied the Pribilof Aleuts with food, firewood, housing, medical care, and schooling for children, and the company discouraged alcohol. It voluntarily paid into a support fund for Aleuts a stipend based on the number of seals harvested, as had the Russians, and it aided widows and orphans. The lease required payment to the U.S. government of a $55,000 annual fee and $2.625 per sealskin. On-site agents of the Treasury Department's Fur Seal Service had responsibility to oversee the operation. In practice the agents exercised substantial power over the lives of the Aleuts, and most adopted a solicitous attitude toward the company.[15]

Ruled by the Russians, the Pribilof Aleuts endured a state of semi-slavery similar to that practiced in Russia. Yet for years before the transition to U.S. rule, they had been paid for their sealing work. Moreover, they retained their traditional chiefs who held considerable influence in village administration. Americans divided administrative duties on the Pribilofs between the Alaska Commercial Company and the U.S. government. At first Treasury agents tried to work through the chiefs chosen by the people. Finding that inconvenient, they resorted to removing and installing chiefs. Rather than paying wages into a community fund to be distributed by the chiefs, as the Russians had, agents took control of the money flow. They tried to stop alcohol consumption and other forms of behavior they considered immoral or unproductive. Offenders paid through fines, imprisonment, forced work assignments, restrictions on their movements, and, sometimes, exile. When an Aleut father refused to send his son to school, "Mr. McIntyre took him from his house, put handcuffs on, and lodged him in the cellar of the company's house, a very cold, damp place, and during all this time the son had been confined in a dark closet in the company's house and kept on bread and water."[16]

Aleuts had readily taken to the schools at first, but they lost interest because they could not study Russian and other aspects of their culture. Treasury Department superiors condoned the actions of their agents, apparently assuming they would improve the Aleuts' behavior and ensure a more productive sealing enterprise.[17] Company managers and Treasury agents got along well. Dr. H.H. McIntyre, the first Treasury agent in the Pribilofs, had helped the Alaska Commercial Company win the 1871–1890 lease and a high annual harvest quota. The company hired him as its superintendent for the Pribilof operation, a post he held for the duration of the lease.[18]

The U.S. ownership of the Pribilofs and their easily accessible breeding colonies permitted the entire harvest to be carried out on land. To help maintain the population, no females could legally be taken. But the harvest plan encountered obstacles in the migration pattern of the seals and in competing claims on them. Native hunters, primarily Indians on Queen Charlotte and Vancouver islands, had long been aware that the seals migrated southward in the fall and north in the spring. They intercepted the mainly female seal herds and speared them for their fur, meat, and oil. Schooner captains from Victoria began trading for the furs in the 1850s. Commercial pelagic sealing began off the British Columbia coast in 1866 and achieved the status of an industry by 1879 as fashion boosted the value of seal pelts. Schooners from the United States and Canada began carrying white and Indian hunters and their canoes to sea to do the hunting. The Alaska Commercial Company's lease kept most vessels away from the Pribilofs, so the schooners hunted along the migration routes. Compared to land-based harvest on the Pribilofs, hunting at sea wasted large numbers of seals: females because they could not be distinguished from males, pelts damaged by bullets and spears, and more lost by sinking or wounding than captured. Commercial sealing vessels numbered a known 34 in 1883 and 115 in 1889.[19]

Sealing vessels sailed out of San Francisco, Victoria, and a few other ports. They started in late winter or early spring, intercepted the migrating seals, and followed them up the coast. Some Indians preferred to hunt offshore in their cedar canoes without schooners. They did well some years but risked being caught offshore in bad weather. In 1875 about 100 perished in a storm off the Washington coast. Most Indians took their chances on schooners, being paid according to the number of seals they killed. Women sometimes accompanied their husbands as cooks or canoe steerers. A few Indians owned schooners; the Makahs sailed ten out of Neah Bay on the Olympic Peninsula in 1893.[20]

As soon as they understood the migration pattern of fur seals in the eastern Pacific, sealers realized they could kill greater numbers near the Pribilof rookeries. And it would be even easier to kill the seals onshore if Alaska Commercial Company personnel could be avoided. In 1874 Martin Kimberley sailed the *Cygnet* from San Francisco to the Pribilofs, carrying Indian hunters. They sealed on or near Otter Island and company officials boarded them. They gave up some skins but took home 135 plus 20 sea otter pelts. The next year Kimberley went to St. George Island and brought back 569 sealskins.[21] In 1876 the *Ocean Spray* raided the Pribilofs, followed by others despite the danger of being fired on by rookery guards. Exploits of pirate sealing captains at the Russian and American rookeries set examples for later American, Canadian, and Japanese raiders and inspired romantic novels by Kipling and London.[22]

Raiding continued on the Pribilofs despite patrols by revenue cutters. In 1884, Lieutenant John E. Lutz of the *Corwin,* detailed to guard St. Paul Island, encountered three poaching vessels. He captured one, engaged the second in a running gun battle, and could not reach the third. The captured *Adele* had German registry, a Scandinavian captain, a Japanese crew, and clearance to hunt in the Kuriles. Lutz left most of the prisoners in the custody of the St. Paul Treasury agent and sailed the *Adele* to Unalaska. Unable to make port, he continued to San Francisco.[23]

Seal poachers operated offshore or on the Pribilof beaches. Usually they came at night or on foggy days to avoid being seen by guards. A journal entry by St. George Island agent A.W. Lavender for June 22, 1885, related: "On the arrival of Mr. Morgan and myself on the ground we found the marauders gone, but their work left on the beach, 120 seal skins and evidence enough to satisfy the Government agent that between 600 and 700 seals had been killed, nearly all females." Lavender frequently made such entries between 1884 and 1889.[24]

During the 1880s critics voiced concern over the extent of seal killing, both onshore and at sea. Treasury agent Charles Goff complained that Aleuts took the initiative to hunt seals at sea: "[M]any thousands are killed by them as they pass through the passes to and from the islands, only for the skins, which are sold and traded for whiskey to poaching vessels." Goff also objected to the regulation permitting the Aleuts to kill 5,000 pups annually at the Pribilofs for food. They did not need them for food or clothing, said Goff; they made the skins into blankets, caps, gloves, and trinkets to be sold to visiting ships.[25]

Pelagic sealers and poachers increasingly contributed to shrinkage of the fur seal herd. An expert on the seals, Henry Wood Elliott, had suggested in his 1881 and 1887 books that no problem existed in the seal population or the actions of the Alaska Commercial Company.[26] Officially the herd in 1886 stood at a robust 4.7 million. But seal counts had been carried out by unscientific methods, if at all. Agent Goff challenged the complacent assumptions in 1889, reporting a sharp drop-off. The Treasury Department sent Elliott and Goff back in 1890 to investigate. What Elliott saw and heard shocked him. His July 1890 report differed dramatically from his earlier assessments; it set the seal count at one million. The Treasury Department decided not to release the document to the public for the time being lest it influence U.S.-British negotiations over rights to pelagic sealing.[27]

Any estimate of seal numbers invited dispute because of its economic and political implications and because no easy method of counting the seals existed. Also, seal totals varied greatly from the post-winter period to the pupping stage. Elliott received vigorous criticism for the 1890 estimate, as he had in the 1870s when he claimed 4.7 million. Yet his had not been the highest 1870s estimate, and other counts in the 1890s confirmed a steep downward trend.[28]

Henry W. Elliott

Widely considered the nation's leading authority on the northern fur seal, Elliott (1846–1930) had been raised in Ohio. He dropped out of high school for a year because of ill health and trained himself in art and science. His father, Franklin, who illustrated his own books on horticulture, encouraged Henry. He took his son to Washington in 1861 and introduced him to Joseph Henry, secretary of the Smithsonian. Impressed by the boy's ability, Henry invited him to work there in an unpaid capacity as a clerk and illustrator. Among other projects, Elliott sketched birds for Spencer F. Baird's volumes on land and water birds of North America.[29]

Meanwhile, interest in Alaska grew rapidly. No telegraph link extended to Russia, diplomatically friendly toward the United States at that time. Western Union devised a plan to route one through Alaska. It arranged for the

Smithsonian to staff an exploratory venture. Elliott signed on as a member and illustrator. The expedition departed in 1865, its scientific section led by Robert Kennicott of Chicago. It visited parts of coastal British Columbia and Southeast Alaska, including Sitka. A transatlantic cable laid in 1866 eliminated the need for an Alaskan route, but the scientific expedition carried on the following summer. Its data and vivid descriptions of Alaskan nature reached Senator Charles Sumner of Massachusetts, chair of the Foreign Relations Committee and prime mover of the effort to purchase Alaska. This and similar information enabled Sumner to counter the "Seward's Folly" and "Walrussia" arguments and reassure the Senate.[30] The treaty approved, Alaska became part of the United States in 1867.

Kennicott (1835–1867), born in New Orleans and raised in Northfield, Illinois, learned to love natural science as he worked in the family horticulture business. His early work in fauna led to study under Baird at the Smithsonian. Poor health prevented his attending university, but the quality of his scientific work put him in charge of a statewide survey of natural science in Illinois at age twenty. He founded the Museum of Natural History at Northwestern University and provided its initial collections. On an 1859–1862 expedition to Canada, funded by the Smithsonian and the Chicago Audubon Society and fully supported by Hudson's Bay Company, he traveled to northern Canada and into Russian territory to Fort Yukon. He ranged widely by boat, dogsled, and on foot, collecting for the museums. After his return in 1862, Hudson's Bay officers continued to send bird and mammal specimens to Chicago and to the Smithsonian.

When the telegraph project got under way in 1865, Kennicott, now curator of the Chicago Academy of Sciences, accepted a position as chief of scientific explorations. In the second year of the expedition he and six assistants left San Francisco in July 1866 and sailed to St. Michael on the Yukon Delta where two parties separated to explore toward Bering Strait and up the Yukon. A third unit, including Elliott, debarked in British Columbia to do preparatory work for the telegraph line along the Fraser River. Kennicott led the Yukon team, and both northern contingents wintered at Unalakleet. Having suffered a heart attack in San Francisco, Kennicott died at Nulato in May 1867. His colleagues ascended the river to Fort Yukon, completing the first exploration of the river by non-Natives.[31]

After Kennicott died on the Yukon, a young Bostonian geographer named William Healey Dall became expedition leader. Dall (1845–1927) pursued a long career in the U.S. Coast Survey and U.S. Geological Survey, completing at least fourteen study trips to Alaska. After retirement he continued to collect material for the Smithsonian and wrote widely into the 20th Century: hundreds of articles and books on mollusks, Alaskan nature, and Native life, the

Henry W. Elliott, San Francisco, 1872, prior to leaving for the Pribilofs. Portrait file 01-3395, Alaska State Library. Devoted to salvation of the fur seals, Elliott conducted a prototype environmental campaign.

best-known being *Alaska and Its Resources* (1870). Dall's porpoise and the Dall bighorn sheep bear his name. Historian Morgan Sherwood titled him "Dean of Alaska's Experts."[32]

William H. Dall, chief of Marine Dept., Scientific Corps, Western Union Telegraph Expedition, San Francisco, July 1865. Smithsonian Archives. Dall, an early American explorer in Alaska, became a leading scientific expert on the territory.

Elliott's experience on the Kennicott expedition opened the door to others. In the summers of 1869–1871 he served as an illustrator on the Hayden Yellowstone expeditions that resulted in the world's first national park. Almost certainly Elliott took note of how photographer William Henry Jackson and artist Thomas Moran, also members of the 1871 expedition, used their work to persuade Congress to pass the park bill.[33]

Fascinated by Alaska, Elliott secured a position in 1872 as assistant to the Treasury agent for the Pribilofs, overseeing the licensed fur sealing operation and researching the seals for the Smithsonian. Baird, in his dual role of Smithsonian administrator and the first U.S. fish commissioner, wanted information on the seals and arranged Elliott's appointment. Soon after Elliott arrived at the Pribilofs he fell in love with the area and married an Aleut woman, Alexandra Melovidova. He studied the seals in depth and created hundreds of drawings and paintings of the seals and other wildlife, scenery, and Aleut life.

In 1874 reports of pelagic sealing caused the Treasury Department to send Elliott back to investigate. He and Lieutenant Washburn Maynard, the latter detailed to check on the Alaska Commercial Company, visited the Aleutian, Pribilof, Nunivak, St. Matthew, St. Lawrence, and Diomede islands and St. Michael on the Yukon Delta. Elliott collected artifacts and did drawings and paintings for the Smithsonian. In 1876 he returned to the Pribilofs on his own and visited the Kuskokwim Delta. Upon returning to Washington he continued his work on the seals and, when the need arose, devoted his talents to their protection. He wrote *The Seal-Islands of Alaska* (1881), the first book on the fur seals. This well-received work and *Our Arctic Province: Alaska and the Seal Islands* (1887) presented a comprehensive profile of the Pribilofs and covered other parts of Alaska. Elliott's articles and illustrations appeared in popular publications; the seals began to acquire a public following.[34]

After leaving his Treasury post in the Pribilofs, Elliott wrote and spoke approvingly of the Alaska Commercial Company, whose operations he had overseen. He wrote articles and testified before Congress to the effect that development funds for Alaska would be a waste of money. Critics believed the company wanted to maximize its control over the fur trade, inland as well as at the Pribilofs. Governor Alfred P. Swineford considered Elliott's negation of Alaskan development part of a strategy to prevent territorial status lest it hinder the company's operations.[35]

Political Tension and Scandal

For the 1891–1910 licensed monopoly on Pribilof sealing the Alaska Commercial Company submitted the lowest bid, as it had in 1871. The highest bidder, another California-based group named the North American Commercial

Table 2.1. Reported Harvest of Pribilof Fur Seals, 1786–1950

Decade	*St. Paul/St. George Is.*	*At Sea*	*Total*
1786–1790	208,879	—	208,879
1791–1800	420,099	—	420,099
1801–1810	422,440	—	422,440
1811–1820	428,460	—	428,460
1821–1830	271,860	—	271,860
1831–1840	104,615	—	104,615
1841–1850	130,814	—	130,814
1851–1860	186,087	—	186,087
1861–1870	624,766	17,483	642,249
1871–1880	1,042,520	71,926	1,114,446
1881–1890	939,103	238,484	1,177,587
1891–1900	165,252	421,300	586,552
1901–1910	163,111	208,611	371,722
1911–1920	197,411	20,834	218,245
1921–1930	268,576	39,401	307,977
1931–1940	555,900	11,698	567,598
1941–1950	664,036	1,106	665,142
Total	6,793,929	1,030,843	7,824,722

Source: Karl W. Kenyon, Victor B. Scheffer, and Douglas G. Chapman, *A Population Study of the Alaskan Fur-Seal Herd,* Special Scientific Report—Wildlife No. 12, USDOI, Fish and Wildlife Service, Washington, DC: June 1954, 47.

Note: Does not include seals killed and lost at sea. Figures before 1910 are least accurate.

Company, won the contract. Two men who had great influence in the Harrison administration, one (Stephen B. Elkins) to be appointed secretary of war, owned most North American Commercial Company stock. The two men opposed land killing limits and pressed for restrictions on pelagic sealing by their competitors. But the first lessee had killed excessively and depleted the seals. It had taken an annual average of 99,081 seals (Table 2.1) and earned $18 million for its fourteen stockholders. North American Commercial Company would kill an annual average of 16,413 but realize nearly $5 million because of higher fur prices. For their part, the Aleuts suffered economically from the harvest reduction, and the government lost $12 million over the first twelve years of the 1891–1910 lease, primarily because of the cost of patrol ships.[36]

Beyond economics and ecology, the fur seal controversy embodied important international dimensions. Beginning in 1886 U.S. Revenue Marine cutters had arrested and confiscated several Canadian and American sealing vessels operating in the Bering Sea outside the traditionally recognized three-mile territorial limit. Noah L. Jeffries, an Alaska Commercial Company lobbyist, wrote articles propounding the theory of U.S. ownership of the Bering Sea. He used his influence to bring about the seizures. When Attorney General A.H. Garland heard about the seizures he ordered the ships released. But the judge in Sitka, persuaded by Jeffries's theory, declined to carry out the order. The legal claim became a part of U.S. policy despite its contradiction of previous American practice, and seizures continued.

Secretary of State John W. Foster later remarked on how "a great government might be betrayed into a line of policy through the machinations of a private corporation, influenced by pecuniary motives, which put in peril its relations with a powerful neighbor and subjected it to the condemnation of an international tribunal for conduct taken unadvisedly and unwisely."[37]

Great Britain and the Canadians demanded compensation for the seizures and asserted their right to hunt seals at sea. Taking the position that the United States owned the seals, in March 1889 Congress passed and President Grover Cleveland signed a law declaring the right to police the Bering Sea and directing the president to send ships to arrest law violators. More seizures took place in the summer of 1889. President Benjamin Harrison ordered revenue cutters again in 1890 to prepare to apprehend pelagic sealers. British foreign secretary Lord Salisbury warned that Britain would be forced to act if more seizures occurred. Five Royal Navy warships at Esquimault, British Columbia, prepared for action, suggesting the possibility of armed conflict.[38] Diplomacy prevented a military clash and the United States arrested no ships, but pelagic sealing proceeded.

Spring 1891 again tested Harrison's administration. The fur seals in the Pribilofs faced the prospect of extinction by hunting—on land by the American licensees and at sea by Canadian sealers. A much greater force of sealing ships prepared for the 1891 season. The disturbing though still-undisclosed study conducted by Elliott for the Treasury Department waited in the wings. It claimed an 80 percent decline in the number of Pribilof seals and recommended a five-year halt on land killing and a permanent cessation of pelagic sealing.

Added to a great power confrontation, administration officials had the 1892 elections to worry about. They dared not be seen as backing down from the British. They needed their powerful friends in the North American Commercial Company but did not wish to be viewed as tools of Big Business. And should Elliott's fur seal report be uncovered, public opinion would demand protection for the seals. The administration chose to leak the study to North American officials, who tried to publicly discredit Elliott. The administration transferred Treasury agent Charles Goff, who at Elliott's urging had recommended prohibition of further killing, away from the Pribilofs. In his place they appointed an inexperienced man. Secretary of State James G. Blaine, having reached a verbal agreement with the British ambassador to stop both pelagic and on-land seal harvest for the 1891 season, nevertheless arranged to give North American a permit for 60,000 kills.

In short order the administration's scheme began to unravel. A woman attending a party in Washington overheard North American's lawyer boasting about the secret deal. She alerted Elliott. Receiving a less than honest response from the official who made the deal, Elliott wrote to the New York *Evening Post* revealing the arrangement and the conclusions of his seal population survey. The *New York Times* picked up the story and called for an investigation of the "sealing scandal."[39] Elliott, a consultant to the State Department, lost his job the day after his letter appeared. Harrison found himself in an embarrassing position and ordered cancellation of the secret agreement between Blaine and North American.

Negotiations resulted in a joint U.S.-British Bering Sea Patrol of revenue cutters and warships to intercept pelagic sealing vessels entering the Bering Sea beginning in 1891. Of the 49-ship fleet leaving Victoria, the patrol fleet stopped 41. Next the two powers signed a treaty, ratified in 1892, instituting a Bering Sea Tribunal to arbitrate the dispute. Harrison lost in the fall election, but the diplomatic process went on. The tribunal convened in Paris in February 1893.[40]

At the tribunal the United States contended that the seals, spending one-third of their lives ashore in the Pribilofs, thereby became American property and needed protection from pelagic sealing. No nation had the moral right, it argued, to destroy the resource at sea. It also claimed jurisdiction over the Bering Sea based on a supposed similar claim by Russia. The U.S. case had been weakened by the reports of Elliott and others documenting wasteful killing by the licensed American company. The tribunal ruled in August 1893 that the United States had no jurisdiction over or ownership of the seals beyond the 3-mile limit. Tribunal guidelines called for both British and American legislation protecting the seals by restricting pelagic hunting in the Bering Sea to licensed, nonmotorized vessels without firearms. No vessel could hunt between May and July or within 60 miles of the Pribilofs. Both parties passed laws by April 1894 incorporating the regulations. The United States paid $423,000 in compensation for seized Canadian vessels.[41]

Height of the Pelagic Sealing Industry

Pelagic sealing continued to exact a high toll despite the regulations. In the 1893 and 1894 seasons, according to London records, pelagic sealers from the northeast Pacific turned in the pelts of nearly 194,000 fur seals.[42] Spears wielded by Natives proved as effective as guns, and the seals breeding at the Pribilofs swam far beyond the 60-mile limit in search of food. Females, pregnant and returning to suckle pups at the rookeries, comprised up to 80 percent of the seals feeding at sea. Killing a female at sea meant the death of a pup as well. One visitor counted 16,000 starving pups at the Pribilof rookeries in 1896. As

Indian hunter and sealing gear on schooner Favorite, *1894. In U.S. Department of the Treasury,* Seal and Salmon Fisheries and General Resources of Alaska, Vol. 4, *Washington, DC: GPO, 1898, p. 473. Skilled coastal Indians and white hunters greatly reduced fur seal herds by hunting at sea. The* Favorite *began a long sealing career out of Victoria in 1873.*

many as one million breeding females may have been killed during the pelagic sealing era (Table 2.1).[43]

Fisheries expert Charles H. Townsend described the machine-like efficiency of a pelagic sealing fleet, all but six of whose vessels employed Indians wielding spears:

> The sealing fleet consisted of 38 schooners, carrying 6 to 20 boats or canoes apiece—the average number being about 12. The boats hunted in all directions, frequently going 10 miles away from the vessels to which they belonged. . . . Pursuing seals in this systematic way, 38 vessels carrying somewhat more than 450 boats, took 31,542 skins in six weeks.[44]

Seals typically slept on their backs, their heads protruding. Indians threw 12- to 14-foot double-pronged spears tipped by detachable spearheads tied by a 30-yard line to the boat. They struck seals at distances of 30 to 35 feet in fairly smooth water. The hunter pulled the seal to the boat and clubbed it. Townsend added that "seals fight vigorously at such times and seldom fail to leave permanent marks of their sharp teeth on boats and canoes, while large bulls are very dangerous to handle."[45]

Indians hunted in two-man canoes and white hunters in threes—one to row, one to steer, and one to shoot. Until banned, a rifle or, more commonly, a shotgun dispatched the seals. Hunters received pay based on the number of seals they took and, to some extent, the condition of the pelts. Bullets usually did more damage than spears, and seals when shot had to be quickly retrieved before they sank. Crew members took their catch aboard the schooner, skinned it, and packed the pelts in salt. In its most successful years a schooner might gather 4,000 skins or more. Between 1887 and 1892, hunter Oscar Scarf chalked up 2,788 seals, including a possible record of 683 in one season. The industry, for a time the most important seafaring pursuit on the Northwest coast, attracted ships from as far away as Newfoundland.[46]

Fur seals, mostly from Robben and the Commander Islands, also migrated down the western Pacific coast to Japan. American hunters decimated the sea otters in the Kurile Islands beginning in 1872 and then discovered small fur seal rookeries on the islands and eradicated them. Following the *C.S. White* in 1890, 82 American and Canadian pelagic sealing vessels arrived off Japan by 1894. The Japanese learned to hunt seals at sea, giving the westerners stiff competition. Seal populations shrank and the price of seal pelts fell in London. An 1897 American law forbade importation of sea otters or fur seals and pelagic hunting under the U.S. flag. Nearly all foreign sealers had left Japanese waters by 1900.[47]

Danger added to the costs of pelagic sealing. In 1894 alone, nearly 10 percent of boats and their crews in northwest Pacific waters went down.[48] A storm off Alaska in 1895 engulfed the Canadian schooner *Walter A. Earle* and its crew of 32. It drove the *C.S. White* onto a snowy shore; 11 drowned or froze and 5 survivors had frozen limbs amputated.[49]

No longer plagued by competition in the northwest Pacific, an active and burgeoning Japanese fleet soon thinned out the seals in nearby waters. Ranging northward, it depleted the seals off the Robben Island rookery, which Japan later gained in 1905 after the Russo-Japanese War. It hunted off the Russian-owned Commander Islands and, to a lesser extent, off the Pribilofs. Not a party to the 1893 tribunal, Japan had no legal obligation to respect the 60-mile limit around the Pribilofs. By 1910, 53 Japanese sealing vessels plied the northern waters.[50]

Subsidized by the Japanese government until 1909, and its boats often captained by North Americans, the fleet adopted aggressive tactics. Two schooners erected facsimiles of funnels to disguise themselves as revenue cutters. A line of schooners would rest three miles off the Pribilofs to intercept females passing by. Boats approached the shore, hunters fired shotguns to frighten the herd off the rookery, and the boats retreated and killed the seals in the water. Some men went ashore to club seals. Five American revenue cutters patrolled the islands and made arrests and confiscations but could not stop the raiders. Thirty or more sealing vessels, bad weather, and sixteen large rookeries on St. Paul and six on St. George made full protection impossible.[51]

Several men died in encounters between poachers and rookery guards. In the most dramatic incident, in 1906 Pribilof rookery guards killed five Japanese poachers, wounded two, and captured twelve. American seizure of Japanese ships and shooting of poachers raised the political stakes of the dispute.[52] Nations could not afford to risk wider conflict over such an issue; it called for international diplomacy.

Resolution of the Conflict

Britain and the United States had agreed in 1891 to send a joint commission of four scientists to the Pribilofs to investigate and make recommendations. C. Hart Merriam and Thomas Mendenhall represented the United States. Unable to agree in the short time allotted, the two teams wrote separate reports. The British-Canadian team downplayed pelagic sealing as a cause of seal decline, and the Americans placed primary blame on pelagic hunting. Unlike Elliott they advocated on-land harvest of young males not necessary for breeding. This position aggravated the split between Elliott and nearly all of the few scientists knowledgeable about fur seals.

Again in 1896 Britain and the United States sent scientists to gather data, and again Elliott did not find himself among those chosen. David Starr Jordan (1851–1931), an ichthyologist who had become president of Stanford University, headed the American team. The rest included Leonhard Stejneger and Frederick Lucas of the Smithsonian and Charles H. Townsend of the U.S. Fish Commission. As had the 1891 team, they condemned pelagic sealing but advocated harvest of surplus males.[53] In a summary document Jordan wrote a critique of Elliott's 1890 report not well engineered to win the heart of its author. While conceding the "general excellence" of the portrayal of the fur seal's life history, Jordan labeled Elliott's 1872–1874 fur seal herd estimates as "gross exaggerations." Citing Elliott's 1870s assertions that government management protected the seal herd, Jordan commented, "This is the only conclusion of his earlier work which he calls into question, and to its undoing his whole 1890 report is dedicated. It is, however, perfectly correct." Whereas Elliott placed little blame on pelagic sealing for the herd reduction, Jordan described it as "the sole cause of the decline." Jordan accused Elliott of "deliberate misrepresentation" of facts: "Whenever any statement made by Mr. Elliott is tried by the records it is found wanting." Jordan's summary judgment on the 1890 report: "We must again express our regret that it was ever printed. It adds absolutely no knowledge to the subject, while it is the source of needless error and confusion. It is wholly lacking in both the methods and spirit of scientific investigation. . . . Its methods and results cannot be too strongly condemned."[54] Jordan and Elliott, the latter of whom considered himself the foremost expert, engaged in a sixteen-year battle over fur seal science and policy. Elliott painted the scientists as tools of a government beholden to sealing interests. They in turn portrayed him as an irrational and unreliable pseudo-scientist.

The United States, Russia, and Japan met in late 1897 and agreed on a temporary pelagic sealing ban pending approval by Canada and Britain. In the 1898 meetings of Canada, Britain, and the United States, Canada attempted to tie the seal issue to settlement of the U.S.-Canada boundary. Canada's proposal would give the Yukon Territory direct access to the sea. The United States refused and the talks failed. But the United States had proposed a new idea: to give Canada a share of the Pribilof harvests in exchange for cessation of pelagic sealing. This proposal would be a crucial element of the ultimate solution.[55]

Studies by Jordan, among others, did not convince the Canadians of the role of pelagic sealing in fur seal decline. Estimates of 20,000 dead pups in 1894 and 16,000 in 1903, allegedly because their mothers had been killed at sea, stimulated the debates. A visit to the Pribilofs by U.S. senators in 1903 determined that the illegal on-land killing of females and yearlings might be as damaging as that done at sea. Congress had entertained, the House passed, and President Theodore Roosevelt suggested a proposal that, absent an agreement, the United States should kill off nearly all the fur seals. However sincerely intended, such a move would put the pelagic sealers out of business and save the cost of revenue cutter patrols.[56]

Disputes among claimants to knowledge of the seals added confusion to the debate and divided conservationists into factions emphasizing preservation and sustainable use. Jordan distrusted Elliott's census figures and his habit of identifying himself as "Prof. Elliott, of the Smithsonian." Elliott possessed neither a professorial appointment nor employment at the Smithsonian, and Secretary Samuel Langley asked him to stop making the claim. Jordan and Elliott campaigned separately for the seals. Jordan published seventeen works on the sealing issue, including a children's book, *Matka and Kotik*, about the life of a seal and her pup. Added to the fictional works of Kipling, London, and Poe, Jordan and Elliott created wide public awareness of Alaska and the North Pacific sealing story.[57]

Elliott had established himself earlier than the others as a writer and an expert on the seals. His illustrations, moreover, may have been more important than the texts. He presented the seals in a highly sympathetic manner, reflecting his own feelings. He drew maps showing the drastic reduction in rookery land area occupied by the seals in 1890 as compared to 1872. When they became available to the press and other interested parties, the maps seemed convincing evidence of excessive killing of the seals. Elliott distributed his pictures and writings to key players in the seal debate, including the British ambassador.

David Starr Jordan. Smithsonian Archives. Jordan, a government-appointed expert and rival of Henry W. Elliott, also worked for protection of fur seals.

And he drew humorous and biting cartoons of his enemies. The artwork added a telling dimension to his campaign.[58]

Jordan held the respect of the scientific community and most government officials, but Elliott appealed to the press, much of the public, and many in Congress. After the breakdown of great-power talks in 1899 and the accession

Killing fur seals. By Henry W. Elliott. RG 22 HE, National Archives at College Park. Elliott's paintings helped generate public support for the seals.

of conservation-oriented Theodore Roosevelt to the presidency in 1901, Elliott tried to reinstate himself as the government's top fur seal expert. He criticized Jordan's thesis, arguing that it exaggerated the impact of pelagic sealing and minimized the effect of land harvest. He proposed a treaty to Secretary of State John Hay that included a ten-year moratorium on harvest at the Pribilofs and a 25 percent share of profits for Canada. He met Roosevelt in the White House in 1904 and offered to go to Canada and negotiate on behalf of the United States. Roosevelt, who admired Elliott's spunk, nevertheless wisely declined the offer. After Hay died in 1905, Roosevelt chose fellow Boone and Crockett Club member Elihu Root to replace him. To Elliott's dismay, Root brought Jordan back as the administration's fur seal adviser. Even though Root offered Canada an agreement similar to Elliott's proposal, Elliott blamed Root when Canada turned it down. He returned to his mode of attack on government fur seal policy.[59]

Elliott found an ally in William T. Hornaday, director of the New York Zoological Park. Like Elliott, Hornaday tended to be egotistical, arrogant, unpredictable, and a preservationist and, therefore, disliked by other prominent conservationists. Also, like Elliott, he displayed extreme tenacity. And he had long since proved his ability to influence the press, public opinion, and Congress. At Elliott's request he set to work on the fur seal issue in 1907. Elliott agreed to remain in the background. Through the Camp Fire Club of America (a group of sportsmen and outdoorsmen he had organized in 1897) and the support of Senator Joseph M. Dixon and President William Howard Taft, Hornaday labored successfully for a 1910 law protecting the fur seals. Henceforth the government would manage the seal herd through the Department of Labor and Commerce in a manner calculated to preserve the herd.[60]

A Fur Seal Advisory Board appointed in 1909 had backed the 1910 legislation, as had Secretary of Commerce and Labor Charles Nagel. Jordan headed the board, and Merriam, Stejneger, and Townsend sat on it. As before, they staunchly opposed pelagic sealing but advocated harvest of males. When Nagel authorized a kill of 12,000 males in the spring of 1910, Hornaday and Elliott went on the offensive. They charged that the kill violated the law and undermined the treaty negotiations. Hornaday argued that no scientific basis existed for killing the males. He questioned the integrity of both Nagel and Jordan. Meanwhile, continuing reports of seal herd decline lent urgency to the negotiations. Various estimates in 1908 and 1909 placed the Pribilof fur seal total at 50,000 to 200,000.[61]

International politics and economics intertwined to bring about the North Pacific Sealing Convention of 1911, the first major international agreement on wildlife. None of the parties wanted armed conflict. Americans wished to avoid extinction of the seals and to maintain the principal share of profits. Russia wanted to safeguard its seal herds, especially from Japanese predation. London had long been a processing point for the furs and stood to lose if extinction occurred. Britain also wanted stable relations with the United States. The Canadians no longer held a significant stake in sealing. Japan still maintained an active sealing fleet as well as its own fur seal herd on Robben Island and stood to gain economically and diplomatically from an accord. The July 1911 agreement, renewed in 1926, compensated the Japanese and Canadians for the loss of their pelagic sealing industries by guaranteeing each of them 15 percent of the skins from Russian and American harvests. Japan in turn agreed to give 10 percent of its pelts to each of the other signatories. The treaty sharply reduced the practice of pelagic sealing. Beyond economics and geopolitics, both the convention and the 1893 tribunal decision set valuable precedents in international cooperation for natural resource protection.[62]

Signing of the treaty did not end the domestic squabble over the seals. Congress held hearings about alleged violations of the law by the North American Commercial Company. Given a more accessible battlefield than treaty negotiations, Elliott and Hornaday carried on the fight to limit seal killing. They and their adversaries, including Jordan and Fisheries commissioner George Bowers, exchanged malicious charges. A congressional committee chairman brought in a trained seal (presumably a California sea lion) during hearings. On the cue "Professor Elliott" it barked and waved its flippers, and at "Commissioner Bowers" it tried to hide beneath a chair.

Both houses of Congress had to approve the treaty because it involved allocation of funds. The House passed the enabling bill in the form desired by the administration. In the Senate, Hornaday and Elliott persuaded Senator Gilbert Hitchcock of Nebraska to attach an amendment to halt all seal killing for ten years. Administration officials could not easily overcome what seemed to be a conservation measure or the argument that the seals ought to know what to do with their young males without human intervention. Congress passed a compromise bill containing a five-year moratorium.[63] The preservationists had prevailed over the utilitarian conservationists.

A *New York Times* article, its rhetoric highly reminiscent of Hornaday's, celebrated the "victory." It left no doubt as to the villainy of

> the people who enjoy killing mothers so that their litter may starve to death, the people who want to wear "furs" without regard as to how their "furs" are got, and the people who see their way clear to make money out of that last desire. These are the three classes that for the last forty years have made organized seal murder under the American flag a profitable industry.
>
> And there are two subsidiary classes. One consists of the so-called experts, headed by Dr. David Starr Jordan, who have supplied the seal murderers with a semblance of argument for their bad cause, and the other consists of the government officials . . . who want to make a commercial record and show they did a big volume of business in this or that fiscal year. These five classes combined to hoodwink that good easy man, Secretary Charles Nagel, and commit the United States Government to the seal slaughtering policy.

At the center of the article stood Elliott in a commanding pose, flanked by an 1872 painting of a rookery full of fur seals and another from 1890 nearly empty.[64]

Even after the treaty ratification, congressional hearings continued on the alleged past mismanagement of the fur seals. A House committee sent Elliott back to the Pribilofs in 1913 for more investigation. He participated in the hearings, carrying on the struggle against his scientific and administrative opponents.[65]

FUR SEALS UNDER FEDERAL MANAGEMENT

Pelagic sealing and the contraction of the fur seal herd worked a hardship on the Aleuts. During the first lease, despite severe restrictions on their freedoms they had prospered economically. Their earnings approximated those of the average American worker. When harvests declined in the 1890s, so did their income. Treasury agents pleaded for subsidies and Congress eventually responded. As Aleut sustenance shifted from seal pelt earnings to donated necessities managed by the agents, the latter increasingly treated the Aleuts as wards rather than employees and took even more control over their everyday lives. A 1909 directive from the Department of Commerce and Labor's Bureau of Fisheries, which had assumed jurisdiction in 1903, specifically authorized agents to (1) draft Aleuts for unpaid labor when needed, (2) remove or install chiefs when necessary, (3) ban sugar to discourage alcohol production, and (4) banish people from the islands when necessary. The orders forbade divulging information on seals or the seal islands. For the next 40 years or more, Pribilof Aleuts lived in a state of dependency and subservience.[66]

The 1910 Fur Seal Act had ended the leasing system, putting the U.S. government directly in control of the Pribilof herd. After the five-year moratorium on commercial sealing at the islands, the Department of Commerce engaged the Fouke Fur Company to conduct a controlled harvest of the herd beginning in 1918. To make use of the meat, fat, and bones, the government built a reduction plant. An observation facility constructed in 1920 accommodated tourists who had been coming to see the seals.[67] During World War I the government tested uses of seal parts for leather, oil, and fertilizer but had difficulty finding economically viable products. Plants operated in 1919–1924, 1928, 1935–1941, and after 1942. They produced oil for tanning leather and meal for feeding foxes, hatchery fish, and poultry. Beginning in 1962 a private firm contracted to supply frozen meat for mink raising.[68]

Indians made relatively modest and declining catches at sea (Table 2.1). The treaty exempted Native Americans from the pelagic sealing ban as long as they hunted without firearms or assistance from motorized vessels.[69] Tlingit Indians had begun commercial sealing in the 1890s, operating from schooners. Between 1897 and the 1920s they used specially designed "Sitka sealers," 25-foot wooden canoes rowed and steered by six-man crews. Unable to legally shoot seals, some kept a gun in a hollowed-out cedar log, plugged at the open end. If approached by a patrol vessel they could toss the log overboard and recover it later. A fur trader confided that nearly all the pelts he bought displayed bullet holes.[70]

U.S.-Japan Tensions

Officially, the Japanese government lived up to the terms of the agreement. But surreptitiously it condoned the continuation of pelagic sealing. Japanese sealers raided the Commander Islands rookeries while the revolution distracted the Russians. They caught seals in Japanese waters for their army to sell in Manchuria. Deteriorating relations between Japan and the United States caused Japan to withdraw from the treaty effective October 1941, terminating it as such, and Japan's pelagic sealing increased.[71] Canada and the United States cooperated through a bilateral agreement from 1941 to 1957.[72]

Wartime tensions bred speculation that Japan might attack the Pribilof herd. Frank Thorne suggested in *Science News Letter* that

> the little men from the East can do immense damage to a major American natural resource. . . . By making even a temporary landing, the enemy could practically wipe out the herd with machine guns and rifles. . . . It can be anticipated that the Japanese will make such a raid—perhaps they already have made it—for they will want all the furs they can steal, in preparation for their anticipated attack on the Soviets in Siberia.[73]

Ben East in *Natural History* repeated the Siberian campaign thesis, adding that the Japanese had held a grudge against the Americans since the killing of their sealers in 1906.[74]

Pribilof sealing had proceeded under Department of Commerce jurisdiction until 1939 when reorganization shifted the responsibility to the Bureau of Biological Survey, renamed the Fish and Wildlife Service in 1940. Its Sealing Division ran the Pribilof operation from Seattle. In 1940 a sealing agent oversaw the work of a population of 294 Aleuts on St. Paul, and a second agent supervised 183 Aleuts on nearby St. George. Most workers and their families lived year-round on the islands as they had since the time of the Russians.

Uncertainty about Japanese intentions, and the desire for military flexibility, led to evacuation of the Pribilof Aleuts as well as those on other islands soon after the Japanese attacks in June 1942. Pribilovians spent the remainder of the war at an abandoned cannery and gold mine site at Funter Bay on north Admiralty Island, and other Aleuts stayed elsewhere in Southeast Alaska. Agency jurisdictional confusion and lack of preparation and funding contributed to disease and many deaths related to inadequate living conditions. In spring 1943 the Fish and Wildlife Service took 116 men back to the Pribilofs to carry out a successful and lucrative sealing operation. The next year a sealing expedition went north to stay, and nearly all of the Pribilof population returned as well.[75]

Postwar Management

Fish and Wildlife Service agents hoped to maintain their control over the sealing in the postwar era. But Aleuts had developed skills and experience as workers during the war, and they pressed harder for change. Frederika Martin, who had lived in the Pribilofs in 1941 and learned their history, wrote a book and articles calling for reform of the treatment of Aleuts. Other reformers in and out of government added their voices, and Congress held hearings in 1949. Laws passed in 1950 and 1962 gave the Aleuts full worker rights. The 1958

Alaska Statehood Act retained federal control of the seals but assigned 70 percent of sealing profits to the state. Aleuts took ownership of most of the Pribilof Islands through the lands settlement acts of 1971 and 1980. They won an $8.5 million judgment from the federal government in 1978 and a $20 million trust fund in 1983 to help them proceed on their own economically.[76]

From an estimated pre-commercial high of about 2.5 million and a low of 215,000 in 1911, the Pribilof fur seal population recovered to about 1.5 million in the 1940s and leveled off. The harvest in the 1940s to early 1950s averaged 66,000 annually. Pelagic sealing, restricted to Natives by the 1911 treaty, tapered off to insignificance by 1950.[77] A renewed Fur Seal Convention in 1957 that included the Soviet Union and Japan retained a profit-sharing arrangement among member nations, including Japan. Japan had lost control of its Robben Island rookery during the war. The new treaty banned pelagic sealing and provided for ongoing research.[78]

In the mid-1950s biologists considered the Pribilof seals to be overpopulated. They believed that by reducing the number of pups born, the rate of pup survival would be greater, thereby boosting the annual sustainable harvest to 65,000–95,000. Accordingly, they reversed an 85-year-old policy and, between 1956 and 1968, included 321,000 females in the kill. The program did not yield the expected result; the sustainable harvest level dropped to 36,000 by 1960. Speculation about the causes of the reduction included hookworm infestation, lessening of food supply by commercial fishing, and entanglement of the seals in discarded nets.[79]

In 1973 the Department of Commerce, now in charge of Pribilof sealing, set aside St. George Island for long-term research. Opposition to seal slaughter by animal rights groups and the advent of synthetic furs contributed to a decline in the industry. Commercial harvest ended in 1984. A rising tourist industry based largely on fur seal viewing helped sustain the Pribilof economy.[80] More important for economic sustenance, the federal government established a trust fund and built port facilities, roads, and other infrastructure, enabling the Pribilofs to operate as a service base for the Bering Sea fisheries.[81]

In the late 20th Century only Pribilof Aleuts purposely harvested fur seals in Alaska. They took about 1,600 annually for subsistence purposes, not affecting the population. However, between 1974 and 1983 the herd shrank from 1.25 million to 877,000, resulting in a 1988 designation of the northern fur seal as depleted under the Marine Mammal Protection Act. One probable cause of the decline, the use of high seas driftnets by Taiwan and Japan, killed an estimated 5,200 seals in 1991. Other fishing gear contributed minimally to seal mortality. International pressure brought high seas driftnetting to an end after 1991. But industrial development on the Pribilofs appeared to be creating disturbances that lowered pup production at some rookeries.[82] A precipitous

Aleut workers at fur seal processing plant, St. Paul Island, ca. 1980. By Jo Keller. FWS 2459, Alaska Resources Library and Information Services. After nearly 200 years, commercial exploitation of northern fur seals ended in 1984.

decline in the fur seal population after 1998 invited speculation and research about killer whale predation, loss of food to commercial fishing, global warming, or a combination of these factors.[83]

ELLIOTT'S LEGACY

One of the first American artists to work in Alaska, Elliott left a valuable record of Aleut life. But he is far better known for his work on the fur seals. Throughout most of the years from 1890 to 1926, he tirelessly lobbied Congress and otherwise publicized the seals' cause. Often neglecting his family, he carried on his single-minded crusade. He objected to the harvest monopoly held by the Fouke Fur Company and lobbied for a 1926 Senate bill to open the market to competitive bidding. After the bill's defeat he moved to Seattle to live with his son John and died three years later at age 80. Some members of Congress remarked that they had never seen such a persistent fighter for a cause.[84]

Elliott had made a last visit to the Pribilofs in 1913, during which he received word that the five-year killing moratorium he had fought for neared approval. Never satisfied, he persisted in his singular quest. Frederika Martin paid tribute in her book *Sea Bears*:

> No posthumous honors have been paid him; the seals he saved, but his reputation, tarnished by the slanders of powerful foes, has still to be rescued. His deeds are permanently recorded in dozens of volumes of Congressional hearings. Few Americans will chance to open even one to chuckle at his barbed rejoinders, his searing caustic epithets, or be impressed by his masterly, insistent repetition of embarrassing facts and statistics. No one following his course through volume after volume of these records will fail to be convinced that had there been no Elliott, the fur seal of the North Pacific might today be an aquatic wraith, companion to its vanished southern relative and the Steller's sea cow.[85]

Elliott, his friends, and some of his adversaries had pioneered Alaskan environmental politics and placed it on the national and world stages.

Elliott's unique background and character helped make possible an environmental victory on a subject greatly removed from the experience of the average person before the age of electronic media. The issue peaked during the Progressive Era when the rapacious behavior of corporations and collusion of government incited strong resentment and suspicion in the body politic. Moreover, curbs on the sealing industry did not threaten the profits of the major natural resource industries of mining, logging, agriculture, or even fishing; nor did sealing benefit the average citizen. And unlike the wolf and buffalo, the fur seal could not disrupt the lives of ordinary people. Thanks primarily to Elliott, the fur seal appeared an innocent, somewhat lovable creature worthy of protection from greedy and brutal exploiters.

To justify suppression of pelagic sealing, technically legal under international law, the United States needed to show evidence of the threat of fur seal extinction and present it as morally offensive. Through its scientists and Elliott and Hornaday, though the men fought among themselves, the effort succeeded. The morality and economics of natural resource use shifted the focus of the dispute from territorial rights to conservation. Also, the gains and losses from the sales of sealskins paled in comparison to the potential costs to the United States of conflict involving the other nations operating in the North Pacific—Russia, Japan, Great Britain, and Canada.

The fur seal controversy promoted the emergence of the national conservation movement. Paralleling the story of the buffalo and the less fortunate passenger pigeon, it helped turn public opinion against market hunting, curbed by the Lacey Act of 1900 and other federal and state laws.[86] Elliott and Hornaday's political campaign, one of the first and most prominent on behalf of wildlife, contained elements to be seen in many to come. Walt Disney, using 20th-Century technology to achieve what Elliott had attempted to do through words and paintings, sent photographers Al and Elma Milotte to the Pribilofs in 1946. The film *Seal Island* appeared in theaters without human actors. To war-weary audiences, an innocent and heartwarming drama of Nature came as a welcome change. The film won an Academy Award in 1948 and its success inspired other nature movies by Disney, laying a foundation of widespread public sentiment for nature preservation.[87]

Far in advance of the modern environmental movement, the fur seal affair modeled several of the movement's key values. Elliott insisted on and ultimately won government and corporate accountability. Management by government experts replaced favoritism toward exploitative commercial interests, and the experts themselves came under closer scrutiny. Through artwork, congressional testimony, and citizen groups, Elliott and Hornaday drew the public into the debate. They and their rivals employed scientific information, though largely in the form of field observation, as a crucial element. Writings and Elliott's paintings of the seals engendered nonconsumptive uses of the seal by a public that would probably never see the creatures in the wild. Not least, international cooperation on seal conservation presaged the common use of treaties to manage natural resources in the post–World War II era.

Under American rule, officials pursued the goal of protecting the fur seal from commercial extinction. Management objectives moved from uncontrolled exploitation to utilitarian sustainability and somewhat beyond. Ecotourism and educational materials testified modestly to the seals' nonconsumptive use value. But nature shows notwithstanding, the seals lacked the sea otters' charismatic image as cuddly, playful, and devoted parents. Managers treated the fur seal herd as a cash crop for the nation until profits fell off in the 1960s; later, the nation subsidized the operation for the benefit of the Aleuts. When commercial harvest stopped in the 1980s, the seals encountered new hazards in the forms of commercial fishing and climatic warming. Their future would depend on the quality of scientific research and the level of political commitment to preserve the ecological integrity of the North Pacific.

3

Wake of the Whalers

During the whaling era, when whales grew scarce in relatively accessible oceans, commercial hunters invaded distant regions. Alaska inevitably drew their attention. Long before the rise of conservation concerns or international agreements on ocean resources, whalers took all they could. Only the limits of commercial value and the vastness of the seas rescued North Pacific whales and pinnipeds from extinction. Public sympathy for ocean species awaited the emergence of nature films and ecological science, probably too late for the North Pacific right whale.

In their relentless quest for comforts and profits, Americans outdid the Russians. Whaling ranked as a prominent commercial venture and a respected social institution. Yankee whalers first visited the North Pacific in the 1830s; they quickly made it their most profitable hunting grounds. Exhausting the concentrations of right and sperm whales in the Gulf of Alaska in the 1840s, they moved north into the Bering Sea in pursuit of bowhead whales. Spearheaded in 1848 by the bark *Superior* under command of Captain Thomas Welcome Roys and the *Ocmulgee* under Captain Fred Manter, they followed the bowheads into the Arctic Ocean, eventually operating east of the Mackenzie River Delta. At their zenith in 1852 an estimated 299 whaleships searched the Bering and Chukchi seas.[1] New England Yankees dominated Alaska whaling until the early 1880s.

Whaling in Alaska originated much earlier. Throwing spears smeared with poison from the monkshood root, the Aleuts took orcas, bowheads, grays, sperms, finbacks, and right whales. Pairs of two-man baidarkas crept up on whales; the hunters struck them and retreated to land for three days in hopes that the whales would die and drift ashore.[2] Koniag Eskimos placed a high priority on whaling and conducted their hunts in a similar manner.[3] Northern Eskimos normally killed whales without the use of poison, using harpoons tipped by stone, bone, ivory, or native copper. They subdued large whales, principally bowheads, by hurling spears attached to sealskin floats designed to tire out the quarry.[4] Eskimos hunted whales at St. Lawrence Island as early as 200 BPE and at Point Hope from about A.D. 800.[5]

In shallower waters, Eskimos pursued *belukhas* (beluga or white whales). Census taker Ivan Petroff described the process he witnessed in 1880:

> Sometimes a hundred or more of the natives proceed to sea on a calm summer day, observing perfect silence and keeping well inshore. As soon as a school of belugas is sighted an old man gives a signal, the kaiaks hurry to seaward of the school, and a tremendous noise begins, with shrill cries and yells, beating of drums and rattles, and splashing of spears and paddles in the water. The hunters gradually approach the shore, driving the belugas before them, until the latter, in the shallow water, fall easy prey to their spears. In former times, when the beluga was more plentiful, from 100 to 200 were secured in a single day in this way.[6]

Koniag Eskimos caught porpoises using spears launched from throwing-boards. Sealskin floats attached to the bone- and stone-headed spears prevented loss of small whales by sinking or escaping. Villagers ate the flesh, blubber, and skin and tanned some hides for boots, kayak coverings, and nets.[7]

Russians, lacking the necessary traditions and skills and preoccupied by the fur business, engaged minimally in whaling. They forced the Aleuts and Kodiak-Afognak Eskimos to hunt whales for food to support fur-seeking operations and sold baleen beginning in the late 1700s. At the Pribilof Islands in 1786–1787, Aleut hunters under Russian control gathered, in addition to fur seal and sea otter pelts, "more whalebone [baleen] than the ship could carry."[8]

Taking note of the lucrative whaling industry conducted by Americans in the 19th Century, Russian-American Company officials explored the possibility of Russian-controlled commercial whaling. In 1841 they complained of American whaleships in the Aleutians boiling down blubber in inshore waters, the smoke driving away sea otters. About 50 New England vessels visited the Bering Sea that year, each capturing ten to fifteen whales. Whalers refused orders to move out of Russian waters. Russian-American Company director Mikhail Tebenkof proposed to respond by going into the whaling business. The czar concurred, but economics and geopolitics plagued the project. A Russian Finland Whaling Company incorporated in December 1850. Its first vessel, the Finnish-built *Suomi*, sailed to the Sea of Okhotsk in 1852–1853 and gathered an impressive 1,500 barrels of oil and 21,400 pounds of baleen. A second ship made a similar catch in Alaskan waters in 1853. War in the Crimea intervened, and an English warship captured and burned the third Russian whaler. A few more whaling voyages produced mediocre results, and the Russians' tenuous position in Alaska induced the Russian government to consider getting rid of its holdings in North America.[9] Among other factors, the presence of hundreds of American whaling ships in Alaskan waters in the 1840s and 1850s helped convince the Russians that the United States would be the region's dominant power, which they preferred to their rival Great Britain.

YANKEE WHALING

Whalers rated the right whale as their top prize for years after they discovered it in large numbers off Kodiak Island. Very similar to the Atlantic right whale so familiar to New Bedford seamen, it moved slowly and contained an average of 125 barrels of oil and 1,250 pounds of baleen. French captain Narcisse Chaudiere sailed the first commercial whaler into Alaskan waters in 1835. His ship *Gange* brought home oil and baleen from seven right whales. Another French whaler arrived in 1836, and at least one American vessel, the *Elbe* out of Poughkeepsie, New York, followed in 1837. As whale stocks in the southern Pacific gave out around 1840 and news of the promising new whaling grounds spread, Yankee whalers moved north. Baleen for corset stays and skirt hoops came into fashion, driving up the price and focusing attention on right whales. Rapidly proliferating numbers of vessels (Table 3.1) quickly exhausted the pods of right whales in the Gulf of Alaska. By the late 1840s whalers moved through the Aleutian passes into Bristol Bay in the Bering Sea.[10]

Inefficient methods of harvesting hastened the decline of the whales. Following a strike by a harpoon, numerous circumstances could result in loss of a whale: the whaleboat being damaged or men injured by flippers or flukes, ropes breaking or being cut by harpoons, men cutting the rope to prevent being pulled down by deep-diving whales or being dragged too far from the ship, harpoons breaking or detaching from the whales, and whales sinking. Men captured well under half the whales they struck, sometimes as few as 20 percent. As whales learned to avoid whaleboats, harpooners had to throw from greater distances, wounding a higher proportion. A large fleet of vessels, each capturing

TABLE 3.1. American Whalers and Harvests in the Pacific North of 50 Degrees, 1835–1913

Year	*Ships*	*Ave. Bbls Oil*	*Total Bbls Oil*	*Bbls Sperm Oil*	*Lbs Baleen*
1835	1	n.d.	n.d.	n.d.	n.d.
1836	1	n.d.	n.d.	n.d.	n.d.
1837	1	n.d.	n.d.	n.d.	n.d.
1838	1	n.d.	n.d.	n.d.	n.d.
1839	2	1,400	2,800	n.d.	n.d.
1840	3	587	1,760	n.d.	n.d.
1841	20	1,412	28,200	n.d.	n.d.
1842	29	1,627	47,200	n.d.	n.d.
1843	108	1,340	146,800	n.d.	n.d.
1844	170	1,528	259,570	n.d.	n.d.
1845	263	953	250,600	n.d.	n.d.
1846	292	869	253,800	n.d.	n.d.
1847	177	1,059	187,443	n.d.	n.d.
1848	159	1,164	185,256	n.d.	n.d.
1849	155	1,334	206,850	n.d.	n.d.
1850	144	1,692	243,648	n.d.	n.d.
1851	138	626	86,360	n.d.	n.d.
1852	278	1,343	373,450	n.d.	n.d.
1853	238	912	217,056	n.d.	n.d.
1854	232	794	184,063	n.d.	n.d.
1855	217	873	189,579	n.d.	n.d.
1856	178	822	146,410	n.d.	n.d.
1857	143	796	113,900	n.d.	n.d.
1858	196	620	121,650	n.d.	n.d.
1859	176	535	94,160	n.d.	n.d.
1860	121	518	62,678	n.d.	n.d.
1861	76	724	55,024	n.d.	n.d.
1862	32	610	19,525	n.d.	n.d.
1863	42	857	36,010	n.d.	n.d.
1864	68	522	35,490	n.d.	n.d.
1865	59	617	36,415	n.d.	n.d.
1866	95	598	56,925	n.d.	n.d.
1867	90	640	57,620	n.d.	n.d.
1868	61	708	43,230	n.d.	627,500
1869	43	890	38,275	n.d.	525,000
1870	46	1,069	49,205	n.d.	659,550
1871	35	n.d.	n.d.	n.d.	15,000
1872	27	730	19,730	n.d.	258,200
1873	30	676	20,295	n.d.	239,300
1874	23	883	20,380	n.d.	222,100
1875	16	1,355	21,680	n.d.	230,460
1876	18	n.d.	5,250	n.d.	35,200
1877	19	1,096	17,530	n.d.	153,800
1878	21	770	13,080	n.d.	114,200
1879	17	n.d.	18,800	n.d.	200,500
1880	19	1,406	26,700	n.d.	409,000
1881	23	1,206	27,740	n.d.	387,000
1882	32	749	22,975	n.d.	360,500

continued on next page

TABLE 3.1—*continued*

Year	*Ships*	*Ave. Bbls Oil*	*Total Bbls Oil*	*Bbls Sperm Oil*	*Lbs Baleen*
1883	38	267	10,155	n.d.	159,400
1884	39	525	20,450	n.d.	318,700
1885	40	533	21,305	635	301,000
1886	53	599	29,950	990	566,301
1887	39	451	17,575	182	367,400
1888	50	273	13,654	280	272,050
1889	46	269	12,395	920	238,100
1890	43	352	15,150	809	314,624
1891	48	352	16,915	1,620	280,400
1892	36	214	7,694	480	317,500
1893	38	204	7,745	3,375	307,940
1894	26	238	6,185	4,605	190,500
1895	14	156	2,185	2,210	111,500
1896	15	182	2,725	1,930	40,580
1897	20	191	3,820	3,610	268,100
1898	13	181	2,350	2,550	34,820
1899	19	231	4,395	4,255	237,365
1900	15	213	3,190	3,630	97,800
1901	15	116	1,735	6,885	21,950
1902	15	109	1,641	3,935	80,500
1903	20	54	1,075	5,800	96,950
1904	16	119	1,905	375	71,200
1905	14	86	1,200	1,400	71,600
1906	5	80	400	140	8,400
1907	10	n.d.	n.d.	n.d.	90,500
1908	10	8	75	1,400	30,500
1909	3	n.d.	n.d.	n.d.	43,000
1910	5	80	400	2,195	10,300
1911	7	143	1,000	2,150	111,000
1912	4	n.d.	n.d.	1,520	n.d.
1913	4	45	180	n.d.	23,500

Sources: 1835–1884 figures from A. Howard Clark, "The Whale Fishery," in George Brown Goode, ed., *The Fisheries and Fishery Industries of the United States, Sect. 5, Vol.2 (Washington, DC: GPO, 1887), 85–86; 1885*–1913 data from Reginald B. Hegarty, *Returns of Whaling Vessels Sailing From American Ports, 1876–1928.* New Bedford: Old Dartmouth Historical Society and Whaling Museum, 1959.

Note: Does not include foreign vessels, about 10–20 percent of total vessels. Harvest data for 1885–1913 listed in year of vessel departure.

whales and leaving many to die of blood loss or infection, soon decimated the North Pacific right whale population.[11]

Whaling Captain Charles Melville Scammon noted that before the whalers laid waste to them, "the right whales are found singly or in pairs; at times, scattered about as far as the eye can see from the masthead. At the last of the season they are sometimes seen in large numbers, crowded together. . . . Having been chased every successive season for years, these animals have become very wild, and difficult to get near, especially in calm weather." Portending the ominous future of the North Pacific right whale, he remarked in 1871, "At the present time, but few right whales are taken."[12] A whaler visited Sitka for repairs in 1891 after grounding in a fog and breaking its rudder while pursuing a wounded whale. It boasted a catch unusual for the time: nine right whales taken in eight days in Prince William Sound. One had dragged a whaleboat underwater and drowned a crew member.[13] Between 1805 and 1914 whalers landed an estimated 14,480 North Pacific right whales, not counting those struck and fatally wounded or otherwise lost.[14]

Whalers sought the sperm whale in the Atlantic and South Pacific and found more in the subarctic waters of the North Pacific. Sperm whales averaged only 45 barrels of oil in their insulating blubber layer. But they carried spermaceti (sperm oil, in the forehead), used to make candles, and the valuable ambergris, an ingredient in perfume. Less favored, the gray whale yielded only 30 barrels of oil and reacted aggressively when attacked. Sulphur bottom (blue), finback, sei, and humpback whales usually swam too fast for the sailing vessels and rowboats.[15]

Commercial whalers most highly valued the bowhead, a close relative of the right whale. It migrated between the Bering Sea and the Arctic Ocean, staying close to the pack ice, hence its other name, "ice whale." When New Bedford whalers first encountered it off the Kamchatka Peninsula in 1843, they realized that it bested the right whale in commercial value. They found bowheads farther north in the Bering Sea.[16] Thomas Welcome Roys examined the reports and determined that there must be a concentration of whales in Arctic waters. As captain of the *Superior* out of Sag Harbor, New York, he signed a crew for the South Atlantic fishery but took them to the North Pacific. There, in the Bering and Chukchi seas, they discovered a treasure trove of large, slow-moving bowheads. Their catch of eleven set off a rush to the Western Arctic, reviving the whaling industry.[17]

A bowhead contained up to 300 barrels of oil (about 100 on average and less as whaling progressed) and a possible 2,500 pounds (1,100 on average) of baleen.[18] Manufacturers used baleen in corsets, women's hats, buttons, upholstery, suitcases and trunks, fishing rods, buggy whips, and springs. Whale oil served in cooking, lamps, soap, candles, paint and varnish, and as a lubricant. Eskimos had relied on the bowhead more than any other great whale and hunted it for over a thousand years, landing a few each year. The meat and oil furnished food and lighting by stone lamps, the bones a variety of tools and weapons. Eskimos used baleen for many implements: ropes, gillnets, crab traps, containers, sleds and sled runners, snares, spring baits, spear and harpoon tips, knife blades, rivets, and toys.[19]

Whalers at first found the bowheads docile, trusting, and easy to kill. After being pursued for a season or two, however, they grew shy and elusive. In 1849, the second year of bowhead whaling in the Chukchi Sea, a ship's log recorded

Captain William Mogg and bowhead whale baleen, ca. 1916. Willoughby coll. 72-116-12n, University of Alaska Fairbanks, Alaska and Polar Regions Archives. Mogg and other Arctic whalers depleted the bowhead whales.

"plenty of whales in sight but all hands too busy [processing whales] to look at them."[20] The catch of North Pacific whales peaked in 1852 during an assault by nearly 300 vessels (Table 3.1), most seeking bowheads.

Whaling ships normally deployed four or five whaleboats propelled by oars and, in the case of bowhead whales, sails to avoid alarming the quarry. Early whalers threw an iron harpoon, let the whale tow the boat by a 600-foot rope until exhausted, and drew alongside and lanced it to death. This method allowed bowheads to escape under the ice. By 1880 inventors devised a darting gun, a harpoon bearing an explosive projectile that, if properly aimed, could kill a whale instantly. The crew towed the dead whale to the mother vessel and fixed it to the side. Then they carved it so its head and blubber could be hoisted aboard, the blubber boiled for oil, and the head stripped of baleen. Cooking an average bowhead lasted about 36 hours. During the return voyage the crew dried the baleen on deck and tied it in bundles of 22 slabs, each weighing about 80 pounds. Crews received pay based on their rank and the value of the catch. Despite risking their lives in difficult work, seamen usually made no financial gain, often owing money to the whaling companies, from which they bought their supplies at inflated prices.[21]

Technological change kept North Pacific whaling alive in the latter half of the 19th Century. Completion of the transcontinental railroad improved the cost-effectiveness of Alaska whaling, as did the invention of the shoulder-fired harpoon gun and a similar device, the bomb lance. Steamships also revised the economics of Arctic whaling, being less subject to entrapment in the ice. The first steam whaler designed for bowheads, the *Mary and Helen* out of Maine, entered the Arctic in 1880. San Francisco became the primary supply, shipbuilding, and whale oil processing center for the Pacific. For fuel, steam whalers tapped coal deposits in northwestern Alaska, although most coal had to be shipped from the States. At a high point in 1887 one vessel tallied 28 whales, and a total of 526,000 pounds of baleen reached San Francisco.[22]

To capture inshore whales, companies set up shore whaling stations, hiring Eskimo or white crews of about twenty men each. Shore stations could operate earlier in the spring, later in the fall, and closer to the ice pack than whaling ships could. Fifteen such stations operated in the Bering and Chukchi seas by the end of the 1880s. Crews killed whales in a traditional manner except for the use of handheld bomb guns. Between 1852 and 1914, company-controlled and independent Eskimo shore whalers captured an estimated 626 bowheads.[23] From 1848 to 1909, pelagic whalers tallied about 29,500 North Pacific bowheads.[24]

Charles Brower—who arrived in 1884, became a shore whaler near Point Barrow, and remained as a trader—dispatched a scout in 1888 to investigate rumors of bowhead whales congregating off the Mackenzie River Delta. The

Eskimo whaling station, Cape Prince of Wales, 1891 or 1892; revenue cutter Bear *offshore. Bear coll. 89-193-116, University of Alaska Fairbanks, Alaska and Polar Regions Archives. Some Natives operated their own shore-based stations, selling the whales or baleen to whaling ships.*

tales turned out to be true, setting off a last surge of Arctic steam whaling. Companies sent north the first ships to over-winter in 1890–1891, and one, the *Mary D. Hume*, stayed two winters. It reaped a plentiful harvest of bowheads on the eastern Mackenzie Delta.[25] As many as fifteen ships remained through the winters, most near Herschel Island, to get an early start on summer whaling.[26] Ship-based whaling continued until 1916 but made few highly profitable catches after 1899. Beginning in 1870 the price of whale oil had sunk as petroleum products became available. But the price of baleen rose, reaching a peak in 1905. Whalers responded by taking baleen only, wasting the remainder of the whale except for those taken at shore stations and given to Eskimos.[27]

Arctic whaling posed dangers for the sailors as well as the whales. Captain Roys related the experience of his bark *Sheffield*, returning in 1850 full of oil and baleen, as a gale drove it toward the cliffs in the Fox Islands passage through the Aleutians:

> With great exertion we got the mainsail upon her. All was done that man could do to save the ship with every man at his post, two men at the helm. Some are weeping, some are praying, some in sullen silence look upon the all exciting scene and calmly await the stroke of death. At this critical moment the gale increases. The tremendous weight of sail is making the ship . . .

> groan throughout her extreme length. The sea is breaking over her, throwing the spray upon her topsails and wetting down the men at her helm, her leerails are under water. No word is spoken, for the proud ship is laboring with destiny and with fearful speed she staggers on, bearing all on board to safety or instant death. Onward she drives, until only one wave is between us and the rocky bottom, here at a distance of about 100 feet [from shore]. Then the memories of years go flying through the brain, the cheek turns pale, the heart beats thick and the boldest hold their breath. In another moment she is free and a shout of joy resounds through the ship. The rocks are passed and orders to reduce sail are obeyed with alacrity and she runs in safety o'er the sea.[28]

Captain Henry Pease of the *Champion* out of Edgartown on Martha's Vineyard recounted an even less enjoyable experience in 1870. After a strenuous whaling effort south of Point Barrow, bad weather forced his vessel southward on October 4. Howling winds and "the heaviest sea I ever saw" drove the ship through Bering Strait, smashing whaleboats, equipment, and barrels of whale oil and leaving the ship covered in ice and oil. It nearly foundered, but the wind slackened just before it would have struck St. Lawrence Island. Pease called the episode "the most anxious and miserable time I've ever experienced in all my sea service."[29]

As might be expected, whaling vessels often came to grief. Normally the unfortunate ones ran into storms and ice, but even war took a toll. During the Civil War, Confederates sank Yankee whalers off the East Coast. In June 1865 their warship *Shenandoah* sailed to the North Pacific and destroyed 38 whaling vessels, unaware that the war had ended.[30]

As dangerous as whaling had been elsewhere, it could hardly outdo the Western Arctic for risk. A combination of ice, storms, and cold conspired to call dozens of vessels and scores of men to untimely ends. Almost every year a few ships went down, and in 1871 most of the Arctic fleet did so. When the bark *Japan* wrecked off East Cape that spring, 8 men died in a long survival march over the ice. As the fleet worked to the northeast between Cape Belcher and Icy Cape, officers chose to ignore warnings by the Eskimos that the wind would drive the ice pack ashore and trap them. The wind changed and the ice came in, crushing some vessels and forcing eighteen into a narrow strip of water not connected to any escape route. At length the captains decided to abandon their ships and transport their 1,219 passengers and crew southward by whaling boats to open water to be rescued by other whaling vessels. They succeeded in saving all hands despite heavy seas that threatened to swamp the rowboats. Thirty-two vessels had been lost, including Captain Henry Pease's *Champion*.[31]

Five years later, in 1876, ice again caught most of the fleet of eighteen American and two foreign whalers. Abandoning their ships to walk to others not icebound, several of the 300 men died of exposure. About 50 elected to remain aboard, of whom only one survived by walking to a village. The fleet lost twelve ships that year and seven more during the next three years. These losses hurt the New Bedford whaling industry, and the Arctic fleet's home port had shifted to San Francisco by 1880.[32]

Arctic whaling revived somewhat as steam whalers entered the trade in the 1880s. But at least seventeen more vessels succumbed between 1888 and 1896 and eleven more between 1899 and 1913.[33] The fleet suffered a telling stroke when ten vessels became icebound off Point Barrow in 1897. About 16 men died trying to reach a rescue vessel. Most of the rest, around 300, remained aboard ship or walked to Charles Brower's whaling station at Cape Smyth. Brower found lodging for the survivors and bade his Eskimo employees hunt caribou to feed them.[34]

Attempts to rescue the stranded whalers led to epic struggles against the elements. Third Mate George Fred Tilton of the *Belvedere* and officer Charles Walker from the *Orca* volunteered to go for help. Walker chose the Mackenzie River route through Canada. Sledging southward accompanied by two Siberian Eskimos on October 1, Tilton reached Point Hope where the Siberians quit the expedition. Tilton enlisted two local Eskimos, Tickey and his wife, Canuanar. The three drove onward through the winter over mountains and treacherous sea ice, so short of food that several times they had to kill dogs to feed the others. Near St. Michael they met Revenue officers planning to drive a herd of reindeer north to relieve the whalers. No one could be certain the reindeer plan would succeed, so Tilton and his companions kept going. They traversed Katmai Pass in early March and spent three days lowering their sleds and dogs down the steep mountain slopes. While crossing a river to get to the small village of Katmai, they lost half their equipment. At Katmai they found an old dory, and Tilton caulked it using his only suit of long underwear. Then, after 1,500 miles by dogsled, the three rowed 37 miles across Shelikof Strait to Kodiak Island. From daybreak to nearly dark, in rare calm water, Tilton rowed while his companions bailed. At St. Paul the Alaska Commercial Company agent demanded an exorbitant fee to take them to Prince William Sound and also charged for their lodging. The three caught a boat to Portland, Oregon, where Tilton wired his company in New Bedford for relief funds. They refused to believe his story, so the three continued to San Francisco, where Tilton found a company willing to send a supply ship. Tilton and his companions arrived in early March and Walker a few weeks later. Vessels not caught in the ice had returned the previous November, prompting a rescue effort by the revenue cutter *Bear*.[35]

While Tilton and Walker strove to alert the outside world to the plight of the whalers, word of the crisis had reached Washington. The revenue cutter *Bear* headed north to aid the rescue but got no farther than Cape Vancouver on

Nelson Island. From there Lt. Ellsworth Bertholf struck out by dogsled carrying provisions to Point Barrow, well over 1,000 miles away. Lt. David H. Jarvis and the ship's surgeon, Dr. Samuel J. Call, separately dog-teamed to St. Michael and on to the Seward Peninsula, where they borrowed two reindeer herds to drive to Point Barrow. Their perilous winter journey in temperatures reaching 60 degrees below zero lasted eleven weeks and ended on March 29, 1898. Lt. Bertholf arrived afterward. Yet their strivings did not turn out to be essential; trader Charles Brower had organized a relief effort and made available all the provisions at his disposal. The contingent of more than 300 whalers suffered negligible loss of life.[36]

20TH-CENTURY WHALING

The invention of spring steel corsets and changes in fashion reduced the value of baleen in 1907, striking a heavy blow against Arctic whaling. High insurance rates and uncertainty of profits took their toll. American commercial whaling nearly ceased in Alaska except for shore stations. A few more vessels ventured north, planning to make the bulk of their profits by bartering trade goods for furs. Arctic shore whaling stations, the first erected at Barrow in 1885, all closed by 1915. A year later two ships carried out the last regular pelagic whaling trip to the Arctic.[37]

Eskimo whaling crews continued to harvest bowheads for subsistence, primarily food, as they had before the era of commercial whaling. Between 1910 and 1969 they landed an average of about twelve per year. Siberian Eskimos killed a smaller number, perhaps four annually, similar to their take in the 19th Century. Canadian Eskimos occasionally took bowheads for food.[38]

Having exhausted the right and bowhead whales and lost most of the baleen market, modern whalers looked for different species found at lower latitudes. Accordingly, southerly shore-based stations lasted longer than those in the Arctic. The first opened in the early 1880s on Killisnoo Island in the Southeast but closed after several years. Tyee Company operated at Murder Cove on Admiralty Island between 1907 and 1913. A wounded whale assisted the station's closing by ramming and sinking one of Tyee's motorized schooners in 1909. The United States Whaling Company at Port Armstrong on Baranof Island caught a record 314 whales in its first year, 1912, but went out of business in 1923. Norwegians opened a station at Akutan in the eastern Aleutians in 1907, joined by the American-owned United States Whaling Company in 1912, the year the station tallied 310 whales. American Pacific Whaling Company took over the Akutan facility in 1917 and ran it until 1939. The company opened a substation at Port Hobron on Sitkalidak Island in 1926.[39] It operated, except for 1931, through 1937.

TABLE 3.2. Shore-Based Commercial Whale Catches in Subarctic Alaska, 1910–1939

Year	*Humpback*	*Finback*	*Blue*	*Sperm*	*Other*	*Total*
1910	—	—	—	—	6 right	146
1911	—	—	—	—	—	(500)
1912	315	235	112	23	—	685
1913	21	29	58	73	3 sei, 1 gray, 1 bottlenose	186
1914	131	259	35	43	14	482
1915	153	239	53	25	—	470
1916	121	161	64	20	21 sei, 1 right, 1 bowhead	389
1917	44	153	138	51	2 bowhead, 26 other	414
1918	58	170	82	92	4 sei	406
1919	132	242	68	95	2 sei	539
1920	75	179	81	90	4 sei	429
1921	75	2	—	1	1 gray	79
1922	95	204	77	69	—	445
1923	155	151	29	16	1 sei, 2 bowhead, 1 right	355
1924	71	148	46	17	1 right	283
1925	208	234	36	33	1 right	512
1926	383	179	15	2	2 right	581
1927	554	122	35	3	3 sei, 1 right	718
1928	220	98	51	24	1 sei, 6 right, 2 gray	402
1929	214	105	53	12	1 right	385
1930	191	50	78	36	—	355
1931	—	—	—	—	(whaling suspended)	—
1932	128	60	78	2	2 right	270
1933	114	61	1	3	1 right, 2 gray	182
1934	166	232	44	21	2 sei	465
1935	141	94	87	70	2 right	394
1936	118	160	41	66	—	385
1937	104	170	45	56	1 sei	376
1938	12	65	33	63	—	173
1939	26	91	5	49	—	171
Total	4,035	3,913	1,455	1,061		11,320

Sources: U.S. Dept. of Commerce, Bureau of Fisheries, Alaska fisheries annual reports, 1910–1939; J.N. Tonnessen and A.O. Johnsen, *The History of Modern Whaling* (Berkeley: University of California Press, 1982), 734.

Note: Does not include figures for Arctic shore whaling stations, for 1908–1909 and 1911, or for 778 belukhas caught between 1917 and 1921. Two of the bowheads listed (in 1917 and 1923) in Bureau of Fisheries data were actually right whales (J.J. Brueggeman, T. Newby, and R.A. Grotefendt, "Catch Records of the Twenty North Pacific Right Whales From Two Alaska Whaling Stations, 1917–39," *Arctic* 39, 1 [March 1986]: 44–45).

Catcher boats from these stations concentrated primarily on the faster-moving sperm, blue (or sulphur bottom), humpback, and finback whales (Table 3.2), although they pursued right whales whenever sighted. A company employee estimated the 1913 value of whale species at: humpback $400, finback $500, blue $600, sperm $1,000, and right whale $2,000. In the same year the United States Whaling Company paid catcher boat gunners $5.50 for each humpback returned, $10.50 per finback, $13 per blue, $30 per sperm, and $50 per right whale. By the mid-1920s, blues surpassed sperm whales in value.

Kills of right whales ceased in the mid-1930s after the adoption of protection measures.[40]

Employing bow-mounted harpoon guns on motor-driven boats, men prowled for whales in the surrounding ocean waters. From a distance of about 120 feet the gunner fired an explosive harpoon into the quarry. Held fast by the rope, the animal would be played like a fish and hauled in by a power winch. Air pumped into the carcass prevented it from sinking. The boat towed the catch to the shore station for processing. Blubber, bones, and meat went into separate cookers for different grades of oil. Oil from the heads of the relatively scarce and valuable sperm whales went into other casks. The United States Whaling Company station at Port Armstrong could handle 500 whales in a season.[41] Whales supplied oil, fertilizer, dog food, hides (in the case of belukhas), and, to some extent, human food.[42] Stations at Cook Inlet and Nome (ca. 1917–1920) and Golovnin Bay (ca. 1920) caught belukhas to sell their skins for white gloves. Settlers sometimes objected to whaling because whales helped fishermen by driving the herring ashore and into their nets.[43]

Between 1910 and 1920, ten shore stations operated from California to the Aleutians. A postwar recession and a glut of oil from Antarctic whaling put most eastern Pacific stations out of business. From the mid-1920s to the mid-1940s only two Canadian stations (Rose Harbor and Naden Harbor in the Queen Charlotte Islands) and two in Alaska (Akutan and Port Hobron) functioned, and not every year. The Great Depression and competition from Antarctic whaling further squeezed the shore stations, closing them for the 1931 season. The 1929 invention of a process to make margarine from whale oil helped keep the industry alive. But aging equipment caused accidents and raised costs. A gun fell backward when fired and killed the gunner. Catcher boats became so frail that the pressure from towed whales nearly stove in their sides. The Akutan station, the only one remaining in Alaska, ceased operation in 1939. Temporarily revived activity at Rose Harbor and Port Ellice, California, ended Northwest whaling in 1942 and 1943 until after the war.[44]

Japan maintained shore-based whaling stations as far north as the Kurile Islands throughout most of the 20th Century. On the eastern side, stations operated from California to Akutan in the Aleutians between 1905 and 1969, run by Americans, Norwegians, Canadians, and Japanese. Whaling at these sites affected Alaska stocks and vice versa because blue, humpback, fin, sei, and gray whales migrated north and south. Blues and seis tended to stay south of the Aleutians, and other species went into the Bering Sea or farther north. Whale migration complicated conservation efforts by adding uncertainty about population levels. It also encouraged the attitude "If we don't get them, someone else will." Periods of high profit, principally during World War I and 1925–1928, inspired greed that sanctioned overkill. Perhaps most important, conservation

Harpoon gunner striking finback whale near Akutan. Core coll. 01-2928, Alaska State Library. Steam- or gasoline-driven ships and harpoon guns enabled whalers to kill the faster blue, finback, sei, and humpback whales.

pleas had to combat the pervasive belief that endless numbers of whales swam the seas.[45]

By the late 1920s the need for whale conservation had begun to alter national policies. Sustainability for the whaling industry rather than demands by conservation groups motivated the change. Norway passed a law in 1929 forbidding its citizens to kill right whales, young or mothers with calves, and immature whales, or to waste body parts. Two years later a League of Nations–sponsored International Whaling Convention adopted protection for right and bowhead whales and the young of most species. Eskimos could take bowheads for subsistence provided they employ nonmotorized craft and primitive weapons.[46] They continued to use explosive weapons but killed only for subsistence.

Worldwide whale harvest shot up by 400 percent during the 1930s and included large-scale killing of immature animals in the Antarctic. Conferences in 1937 and 1938 wrote stricter provisions into whaling regulation. In the North Pacific the agreements protected right, bowhead, and gray whales. They allowed whaling by factory ships only in western waters, a concession to the Japanese whose factory operation had recently been launched. Governments rather than companies would keep statistics on whales caught.[47]

Japan, not a signatory of the 1931 Convention or the 1937–1938 agreements, promised in 1939 to fulfill the agreed-upon provisions but changed its position when war broke out in Europe. Competition among Japan, Germany, Britain, and Norway depleted stocks of blue, finback, and humpback whales in the Antarctic. Whaling continued there until 1941 and revived in 1946, further reducing populations. Meanwhile, a 1946 Washington conference produced

Right whale at Port Hobron whaling station, 1926. Described as "15 feet high, 65 feet long, approximate weight 250 tons." Lagen coll. 7557, University of Washington Archives. Company records list the whale at 62 feet. The weight estimate is almost certainly exaggerated. Commercial whaling nearly destroyed the North Pacific population of right whales.

the International Whaling Commission (IWC) and its related International Agreement for the Regulation of Whaling, which went into effect in 1949. Japan joined in 1951.[48]

Factory ships accompanied by motor-driven catcher boats could gather whales more quickly than shore stations could, although high operating costs limited their use. A California company sailed the first American factory whaler between Mexico and Alaska in 1921, got 158 whales, lost money, and quit. Another repeated the undertaking in 1926–1927 and got 568 whales. It hunted various parts of the North Pacific until 1937. In 1940 Japan sent its first factory ship into the north, capturing 681 whales in waters extending to the Bering Sea icepack. A similar venture reaped 590 whales off the Kamchatka Peninsula in 1941. Even higher kills resulted from revival of the voyages in 1950, ranging as far east as Akutan. The Russians operated a factory ship in the North Pacific continuously from 1934 to 1961 and then added others. They caught large numbers of blue, finback, and sperm whales between Kamchatka and the Gulf of Alaska. By the late 1960s the bulk of the world whale harvest had shifted from Antarctica to the North Pacific, where only Japan and the Soviet Union deployed ships. The IWC made ongoing efforts to persuade the two nations to improve conservation practices.[49]

Japanese whalers captured 69 North Pacific right whales prior to the creation of the International Whaling Commission in 1946. They killed another 13 under "scientific" permits between 1956 and 1968, when the permits for right whales expired. Russians, who also had not signed in 1931 but joined in 1937, caught 10 in 1955 under the permits. Adding a near-fatal blow to an otherwise slowly recovering population, they illegally killed at least 251 in the western Gulf of Alaska and 121 in the southeast Bering Sea between 1963 and 1967.[50]

The IWC banned harvest of gray whales in 1946 and of blues and humpbacks in 1966. These three species, the bowhead, and especially the right whale emerged as the most depleted of the great whales in the North Pacific.[51] The phasing out of the American whaling industry, followed by pressure from a growing environmental movement, placed the U.S. government in the forefront of efforts to preserve the great whales through IWC regulations.

By the 1990s some whale populations had recovered fully, others less so. Eastern Pacific gray whales, migrating between the Arctic and Baja California, had never been intensively hunted. They increased to more than 25,000 and continued at 2.4 percent annually. In 1994 they became the only great whale species to be removed from the endangered species list. Russian Natives annually harvested more than 100, and Makah Indians in Washington occasionally killed them in traditional ceremonial hunts.[52]

Northeast Pacific finback whales ranged from Baja California to the lower Arctic. An estimated 5,000 concentrated for summer feeding in the Bering Sea. Population totals and trends remained unknown. Similarly, no firm estimates existed for sperm whales, ranging widely in offshore waters. Commercial whalers took at least 258,000 of this species in the North Pacific between 1947 and 1987. North Pacific humpback whales included a small population summering along the Aleutians and a larger number summering along the coasts from British Columbia to the northern Bering Sea. Researchers counted 127 near Kodiak Island and 404 in Southeast Alaska. Commercial whalers killed at least 28,000 during the 20th Century and may have reduced the total to as few as 1,000. Biologists believed the population to be increasing in the 1980s and 1990s. Natives did not harvest finback, sperm, or humpback whales.[53]

Western Arctic bowhead whales, originally numbering between 10,000 and 23,000, shrank to an estimated 3,000 as a result of commercial whaling. Tightened protection under the IWC permitted a growth rate of more than 3 percent and an increase from about 5,000 to 8,200 from the late 1970s to the mid-1990s. Eskimos, almost entirely on the American side, harvested a yearly average of 54 in the late 1990s, below the limit of 77 calculated to sustain the population. The far less fortunate North Pacific right whale declined from at least 11,000 to the verge of extinction. Occasional sightings in the Bering Sea in the 1990s included no calves and may have been strays from a small Western Pacific population.

Entanglements in commercial fishing gear and being struck by boats claimed the lives of all great whale species, although not in sufficient numbers to endanger populations other than the right whale. Various disturbances such as airborne pollutants, oil spills, and whale watching posed unquantified but probably minor problems. Researchers could not determine the effects, if any, of climatic warming on North Pacific whales.[54]

COMMERCIAL WALRUS HUNTING

Resource exploiters also found profitable applications for the Pacific walrus. Ivory, one of the commodities sought by Russian fur seekers in Alaska, appeared on returning vessels as early as 1755.[55] In their first year at the Pribilof Islands in 1786–1787, Pribylov's Aleut hunters killed enough walruses to yield 14,400 pounds of ivory.[56] During the 1810s Aleuts collected 7,200 pounds of ivory annually for the Russians, hastening the eventual extermination of walruses at the islands.[57] The last of the Pribilof herd fell in 1891.[58]

Russians forced Aleuts to hunt walruses on the north side of the Alaska Peninsula. Frederick Litke witnessed the process in the 1820s:

> The hunters surround them from the water's edge then rush in upon them, shouting and crying out, and driving them all inwards towards the middle of the sandbank. They then set upon them with pikes, stabbing them where their skin is least thick. One of the most essential precautions is to prevent any of them from getting to the sea because then the whole herd will follow and it becomes difficult to dodge the tusks of these enraged animals and avoid being knocked down by them and dragged into the sea. This dangerous hunt lasts about ten days. When they are preparing to leave for it, the Aleuts always bid farewell to one another.[59]

Between 1799 and 1857 the Russian walrus kill totaled an estimated 500,000.[60]

Whalers turned their attention to the walrus in the late 1850s in the off-season for whaling and as a substitute for whales a few years later (Table 3.3). The bark *Carib* out of San Francisco brought in one of the first large catches: 100 barrels of walrus oil in 1860 or 1861. Whalers found the best hunting on the ice floes of the northern Bering Sea. For several years they harpooned the animals; thereafter they used rifles. Customarily, a boat carrying three men approached a herd from downwind. A rifleman clothed in white stepped onto the ice floe, crept up to the herd, and tried to shoot one dead lest it go into the water followed by the others. If the first one fell in place the rest of the herd would stay, and the rifleman could approach the herd and kill many or all of

TABLE 3.3. Recorded Pacific Walrus Harvests by the Whaling Industry, 1849–1914

Year	*Number*	*Year*	*Number*	*Year*	*Number*	*Year*	*Number*
1849	29	1866	273	1883	3,523	1900	24
1850	180	1867	1,144	1884	665	1901	3
1851	107	1868	2,300	1885	851	1902	4
1852	109	1869	5,998	1886	21	1903	5
1853	68	1870	14,443	1887	144	1904	6
1854	110	1871	6,674	1888	281	1905	32
1855	2	1872	5,775	1989	11	1906	0
1856	0	1873	4,515	1890	10	1907	51
1857	174	1874	9,215	1891	11	1908	0
1858	551	1875	13,080	1892	0	1909	50
1859	946	1876	35,663	1893	0	1910	68
1860	108	1877	13,294	1894	9	1911	0
1861	1,395	1878	13,128	1895	0	1912	30
1862	130	1879	6,699	1896	38	1913	20
1863	58	1880	2,676	1897	77	1914	8
1864	602	1881	0	1898	0		
1865	239	1882	2,624	1899	0		

Source: John R. Bockstoce, "The Harvest of Pacific Walruses by the Pelagic Whaling Industry, 1848 to 1914," *Arctic and Alpine Research* 14, 3 (1982): 187.
Note: Does not include Native subsistence kill or animals killed and lost.

them. Accustomed to the cracking of ice, walruses showed no fear of rifle shots. In this manner one whaling vessel secured 700 walruses in 48 hours and 1,600 in less than three weeks in summer 1877.

After the killing, crew members removed the heads for ivory and the skin and blubber in strips. Occasionally the warm blood caused the ice floe to melt or split, sending the walruses to the bottom and giving the hunters a cold bath. Aboard ship, crews separated the blubber from the skin strips, diced it, and rendered it into oil in the try-pots used for whale blubber. Cooks often fried the liver and heart and made sausages or roasts of the meat.

Ivory went to carvers in New York, London, Japan, and China. Carvers fashioned handles, dice, dog whistles, and other ornaments. American whalers seldom bothered to keep the skins, although Europeans took them for manufacture of harnesses and shoe soles.[61] Weighing 200 pounds or more, skins sold in London for $1–$1.25 per pound for use in metal polishing and other industrial processes.[62] In the peak walrus-hunting years of the 1870s, whalers discarded all but a few of the skins. On average they got 20 gallons of oil from a walrus, graded equal in quality to elephant seal oil and marginally superior to whale oil. A large bull walrus could contain 60 gallons. Between 1869 and 1880 whalers gathered an estimated two million gallons of walrus oil. They wasted many animals; one herd of 1,600 killed on a beach all washed away in a high tide.[63] Catches and herds atrophied.

Effects on Eskimos

Commercial whaling and walrus hunting greatly affected Eskimo culture, mostly in negative ways. It ended the trading system by which Eskimos obtained Russian goods from Siberia and Hudson's Bay goods from Canada. To augment profits or avoid losses, whalers increasingly carried trade goods to the Eskimos. Inland Eskimos moved to coastal towns for access to trade items and to work as whalers or walrus hunters. By the turn of the 20th Century, several shore-based Eskimo crews operated on their own, selling baleen and keeping what they needed for food. The collapse of whale populations reduced food supplies of those still relying on them. Whalers carried diseases, periodically devastating local populations. Influenza and measles killed about 300 people at Barrow between 1900 and 1902. Liquor imported by whalers, traders, or whaler-traders proved irresistible and socially destructive, as it did among other Native Americans. One quart of whiskey could bring $200 worth of furs or other products.[64]

Liquor and disease hurt the Eskimos more than the loss of walruses did. In 1873, primarily because of Indian troubles in the West, the U.S. government banned the sale of liquor and breech-loading rifles to Native Americans. Revenue cutter patrols appeared in the Arctic in 1879, but liquor smuggling persisted and the gun ban made it more difficult for the Eskimos to get food and clothing. Prostitution and venereal disease escalated. In 1890 an estimated half of Barrow's population had syphilis. Large numbers of Eskimos died of introduced diseases, as had other Natives.[65]

In 1877 the whaling brig *William H. Allen* stopped at Cape Prince of Wales and traded liquor for fox furs. That night the Eskimos got drunk. The next day, sixteen men and a woman returned to the ship in an umiak. The men came aboard and demanded liquor. Captain George Gilley, seeing that they had nothing to trade, refused to give them liquor. Becoming more belligerent, the Eskimos began to push the crew around. First Mate Finnegan lost his temper and struck back, whereupon one of the Eskimos stabbed him to death. The Hawaiian crew then attacked the Eskimos, who retreated under the forecastle. They used boat hooks to pull the Eskimos out one by one, clubbed them, and threw them over the rail into the umiak or the sea. Only the woman survived. The incident soured relations between whalers and Eskimos for years and may have induced the murders of several crew members who went ashore.[66]

Hired Eskimos carried out much of the commercial harvest of walruses on which they had traditionally relied for food, boat coverings, dwellings, leather, and ivory to carve into spearheads and other implements. Once at least, their lack of foresight backfired. According to visiting seafarers, in 1878 St. Lawrence Islanders obtained barrels of whiskey from traders. Then came a season of heavy ice, making hunting difficult. Some combination of alcoholism, bad weather,

Remains of villagers starved at St. Lawrence Island, early 1880s. In Michael A. Healy, Report of the Cruise of the Revenue Steamer Corwin in the Arctic Ocean in the Year 1884, *Washington, DC: GPO, 1889, p. 13. A combination of unfavorable weather and depletion of sea mammals visited ruin on island residents.*

absence of whales and walruses, starvation, and disease caused ruin. During the winter of 1878–1879 all the people of three villages on St. Lawrence Island died, and only one of the island's eight villages remained viable. People ate skin houses, boats, and dog harnesses. By 1881 two-thirds of the island's population of 1,500 had died. As news of the disaster spread, some whaling captains brought loads of food to the Eskimos.[67]

Modern analysis led to the conclusion that in 1878–1879 an El Niño event caused warm winds to blow from the south, preventing the normal semi-open ice cover on which walruses and seals hauled out. By contrast, a La Niña event in 1879–1880 blew so cold from the north that it left few openings in the pack ice. In neither year could the St. Lawrence Islanders successfully hunt walruses, already depleted by commercial hunting. Of the fewer than 2,300 people, at least 90 percent died. The population continued to decline for two decades or more despite the immigration of culturally similar Yup'ik from the Chukotka Peninsula. Living patterns changed from dispersed groups to concentration in a few villages. Hunting methods changed from solitary pursuit to groups in umiaks. Ironically, the survivors reaped a valuable harvest of walrus ivory and baleen from the schooner *Lolita*, wrecked on the coast in the fall of 1880.[68]

Ivan Petroff commented in 1880 that

> the trading vessels coming to this [Arctic] region . . . have carried such quantities of alcoholic liquor that the natives have acquired a craving for the same

that no longer can be subdued, and this causes them to look for no other equivalent for their furs, oil, and ivory than the means of intoxication. At the same time they becomc utterly reckless in their pursuit of fur-bearing and other animals, thinking only of satisfying their desire for the present without the slightest thought of the future; and if this state of affairs be continued *the extermination of the people, consequent upon the exhaustion of their means of subsistence, can only be a question of time.*[69]

Captain Michael Healy, commander of the revenue cutter *Corwin*, stated that in 1884 liquor caused the only significant conflicts between whites and Eskimos. He described the Eskimo men as "kindly and hospitable" when sober but "demoniac" when drunk: "The most brutal fights occur when they are in this condition. Their long, sharp hunting-knives make frightful wounds, and their rifles are used without stint and often with deadly effect." Their wives, normally well treated, "are frequently brutally beaten when liquor has frenzied the men." When the *Corwin* crew conducted a liquor seizure, "[T]he women recognized us as their friends and used every exertion to assist us in our search." Healy called for stiffer regulation of liquor and for lifting the ban on repeating rifles and ammunition so Eskimos could more effectively hunt for food.[70] Patrolling by the revenue cutters, however, caused the whaler-traders to take their liquor to the Siberian side. Alaskan Eskimos then traded their furs and ivory for liquor from the Chukotka Natives, who in turn gave the goods to the whaler-traders for more alcohol.[71]

Stories about the walruses surfaced in the mass media. As early as 1869 the *Alaska Herald* of San Francisco lamented, "American whalemen seem to think of [walruses] as of no consequence, being only anxious to secure the tusks, abandoning the carcass." The complaint would become familiar a century and more later, when Eskimos took the place of whalers. An editorial in the *Alaska Appeal* of San Francisco related in 1879:

> Sixteen of the nineteen vessels of the Arctic which have arrived at this port during the past month have brought 27,500 pounds of ivory, consisting entirely of tusks of the walrus, and 4,000 pounds were lost in the *Mercury*. This is an average of 1,853 pounds to the vessel. . . . Let us be moderate in our estimate, and say that 10,000 walruses have been destroyed this season. We have characterized this wholesale destruction as wanton; it were, perhaps, more fitting to term it criminal. . . . [We are told by] intelligent and truthful masters of whaling vessels, that "for every one hundred walruses taken a family is starved." The season's slaughter, then[,] represents the sufferings and death of thirty-five families, and the word *families* implies that at least as many helpless mothers have striven ineffectually to ward off the death pangs of their still more helpless little ones. The total value of the ivory brought to San Francisco this season cannot exceed $3,500, for of late years the market

> has been glutted, and the price at which this article is sold is actually not over ten cents per pound.[72]

People in the villages between Point Hope and Barrow traditionally consumed about 500–600 walruses annually, but by 1890 they seldom got more than 10.[73] One critic of the slaughter, missionary Sheldon Jackson, Alaska's general agent of education, visited northwest Alaska in 1890. He learned of the steep reduction of sea mammals, caribou, and Eskimos over the previous fifteen years. He blamed the commercial whalers directly for the losses of whales and walruses and attributed the disappearance of caribou to breech-loading rifles the Eskimos had recently acquired. At King Island in 1891 he found the inhabitants in a state of starvation, eating seaweed and, in some cases, their dogs. Captain Healy steamed the revenue cutter *Bear* 200 miles to the nearest trading post and bought food to tide the islanders over to the next hunting season. Jackson organized a reindeer industry (Chapter 14) as an alternative economic base for the Eskimos.[74]

Cash wages stimulated wants and needs, many artificial, from industrial society. Visits by whalers, traders, and other Europeans or Euro-Americans reinforced values that weakened Eskimo traditional cultures. The shift toward a cash economy increased dependency on outside technology and income opportunities. Eskimos voluntarily participated in the changes, benefiting in some ways and suffering in others.

20th-Century Walrus Hunting

Predation of walruses did not end when the great whaling fleets no longer journeyed to the Arctic. During the Gold Rush era, passengers on steamships bound to and from the Yukon River shot hundreds of walruses from the rails as they passed by. By 1900 the walrus had virtually disappeared south of Nunivak Island. The entire North Pacific herd had been cut down drastically.[75] The U.S. government halted commercial hunting of the walrus in 1908 after it had become less profitable.[76]

The new law restricted the take of walruses in American waters to Natives for food and clothing, to scientific collectors, and to others in emergencies. But walrus hunters simply moved outside the three-mile limit and resumed operations. Charles Madsen, contracted by the Hibbard Stewart Company in 1909, gathered 100,000 pounds of walrus hides to be used on polishing wheels and for women's handbags. Hunting in Bering Strait and the Chukchi Sea from Nome in the summer, he usually took aboard his schooner *Sea-Wolf* ten Eskimos and their one-man kayaks plus two umiaks. He picked them up at King Island, Cape Prince of Wales, and Little Diomede. They sailed north until they

Polar bear struck by bullet, off Point Barrow, 1920. By J. Hadley. Powell coll. 64-43-201, University of Alaska Fairbanks, Alaska and Polar Regions Archives. Explorers, whalers, sport hunters, and others shot polar bears without concern for the survival of the species.

spotted walruses on ice floes, launched the skin boats, and quietly approached from downwind. First they tried to shoot the lookout animal and, next, as many others as quickly as possible before they slid into the sea. They shot some in the water and speared them with ivory-tipped harpoons tied to sealskin floats to prevent sinking. To be lethal, a bullet had to strike a walrus on the neck vertebrae, in the brain through the eye, or from the side or rear of the head. The Eskimo crew undertook the heavy work of skinning the animals, some weighing 3,000 pounds or more, and feasted on meat, blubber, and clams taken from the stomachs. Successful trips could reap 40 to 50 walruses per day, the skins weighing 300 to 400 pounds each.[77]

Crews salted the hides and stowed them in the hold, to be sold at 7.5 cents per pound and shipped to Seattle for processing. Each member owned an equal share of the ivory, although Madsen received nearly all of it in exchange for trade goods. Much of the meat and blubber went back to the hunters' home villages. The crew also shot many hair seals and polar bears. At least five other walrus-hunting vessels operated at that time: Captain Louis Lane's *Polar Bear*, Olaf Swanson's *Nanook*, C.T. Pederson's *King and Winge*, and the Norwegian *Kit*.[78] The *Kit*, a factory whaler, had arrived in 1912 and returned in 1913 and 1914. Unable to find whales, it took on Eskimo hunters and pursued walruses

Walrus sport hunter and trophy, Chukchi Sea, 1913. In Edward M. Scull, Hunting in the Arctic and Alaska, *Philadelphia: Winston, 1915, p. 124. Sport hunting added, if modestly, to the strain on the walrus population.*

in the Bering Strait and Chukchi Sea. It collected about 2,400 walruses, but the owners lost money on the venture and sold the vessel to Russia.[79]

Like many undertakings in wild corners of the North, walrus hunting offered moments of peril. Chasing a wounded bull in his umiak, Madsen fended off repeated attacks by the enraged beast, which nearly succeeded in sinking the boat. When an Eskimo arrived to assist, the bull tore his kayak to pieces, and the hunter survived by getting behind the bull's head and hanging on to the tusks. A near-drowning followed when the walrus dove, the hunter still clinging to it.[80]

Madsen guided sport hunters for walrus, as did other captains. F.E. Kleinschmidt chartered Captain Larsen's *Abler* out of Nome for a 1913 trip by four wealthy men from the East Coast. They bagged 14 animals but lost at least 24 more killed or wounded. They noted that the *Kit* had taken 900 skins that year, raising protests.[81] Sport hunting, while far more modest in impact than commercial ventures, nevertheless aggravated the scarcity of walruses, to the detriment of Eskimos.

Eskimos, however, on their own killed large numbers of walruses from the American shores. They hunted the animals on the ice, removed the tusks, and left nearly all the bodies. Biologist Joseph Bernard traveled 200 miles along the coast north of Point Hope in the summer of 1923 and counted the walrus bodies that had drifted ashore. He found more than 1,000, two-thirds of which had their tusks cut off. The rest, presumably, had been shot and lost. Walruses no longer dared to come ashore where they could more easily be harvested for food. Bernard recommended that a 25-mile stretch of shoreline formerly used as a walrus haulout be declared a walrus preserve, as had been done by the Chukchis on the Siberian side. The preserve did not materialize, but in 1925 the village council of Gambell on St. Matthew Island imposed restrictions on hunting walruses for ivory only.[82]

During the Great Depression the Bureau of Indian Affairs assisted Eskimos in organizing cooperative stores and a handicraft industry, including ivory carving, as substitutes for the failing reindeer and trapping economies.[83] The 1941 "Walrus Act" limited hunting on the American side to Native Americans. It set no numerical limits on kills or on the export of ivory but prohibited killing solely for ivory. Carving expanded into an industry in the 1940s and, by the early 1950s, the economies of King Island, Gambell, Savoonga, and Little Diomede depended primarily on it. University of Alaska student Jim Brooks, one of the first to do research on the walrus, estimated the kill on Little Diomede at six to ten times what would be needed for food and skins. Regarding hunting methods, he observed that

> harvest techniques now employed unquestionably destroy, without recovery, more walrus than are secured. The Eskimo hunters, at least the older ones, are not ignorant of efficient killing methods, but fail to practice them when game appears abundant. . . . In so far as the writer could discern, the people of the Bering Strait feel absolutely no remorse over the wholesale loss of animals during the hunt; at the onset they stoically expect to lose more than they recover.

Wasteful practices included uncoordinated shooting, failure to use harpoons, and killing to prevent possible attack by immature walruses.[84]

Compared with an original population of possibly 200,000, the walrus herd in the North Pacific dropped to a conservatively estimated 40,000 by the mid-1920s. Russian seal hunters and Eskimos continued to kill them at a high rate between 1931 and 1957 but phased out the killing by 1962.[85]

After mid-century, walruses recovered but ivory hunting increased. In 1956 Congress amended the law to allow sport hunting, again outlawed by the Marine Mammal Protection Act of 1972. Walrus numbers rose gradually during the late territorial period, and surveys done in 1960–1961 placed the total at about 85,000. In 1960 Alaska reserved the Walrus Islands State Game Sanctuary in Bristol Bay. At that time Round Island in the Walrus Islands functioned as the only remaining regularly used haulout site on the American side.[86]

The State of Alaska maintained jurisdiction over walruses between 1960 and 1972, regained it briefly from 1976 to 1979, and then relinquished it. The

Eskimo carver, Nome, ca. 1887. Powell coll. 64-43-213, University of Alaska Fairbanks, Alaska and Polar Regions Archives. A traditional cultural and commercial activity, ivory carving helped sustain the Eskimo economy after World War II.

state encouraged sport hunting before 1972 and stiffened restrictions to discourage ivory hunting. Recorded walrus kills in the postwar and early statehood years averaged fewer than 2,000 annually. Subsistence kills totaled nearly 3,000 in the 1970s. The walrus population swelled to an estimated 140,000–200,000. But so did killing for ivory, even in the more conservation-oriented villages of Gambell and Savoonga. Eskimos killed for ivory to help pay for new boats, television sets, and other modern goods. As snowmobiles replaced dogsleds and aluminum skiffs succeeded umiaks, the need for walrus skins declined. Hunters concentrated on ivory and justified it by citing their right to subsistence. To them, the discarding of walrus bodies could not be considered criminal while such a high and perhaps excess population of the animals existed.[87] Yet the Marine Mammal Protection Act prohibited wasteful killing. In a modern form, conflict persisted among the ideals of mammal protection, communal subsistence living, and modernizing lifestyles.

At the end of the 20th Century, biologists believed North Pacific walruses numbered between 200,000 and 250,000. Eskimos on the American and Russian sides accounted for nearly all known kills; an insignificant number died

Walrus herd at Walrus Islands haulout, Bristol Bay, ca. 1957. By William H. Sholes. Alaska Game Commission, 19th Annual Report, July 1, 1957 Thru June 30, 1958. *The islands became one of the first state wildlife sanctuaries in Alaska.*

in fishery-related entanglements. In the 1990s the annual toll, including a 42 percent loss rate of those struck by bullets, averaged about 5,000. Neither hunting nor other known causes of mortality posed a measurable threat to the walrus herd.[88] But future commercial exploitation of underwater clams could be a problem, and the effects of climatic warming remained to be determined.

SEA LIONS AND HAIR SEALS

Commercial uses for other pinnipeds cut into their numbers during the Russian and American periods. Alaska Natives, especially Aleuts, had traditionally pursued Steller sea lions and hair seals for food, oil, and hides to make clothing and construct baidarkas for sea mammal hunting. A population of about 15,000 sea lions found at the Pribilofs underwent continuous assault during the fur-seeking era. Organized hunts at Northeast Point on St. Paul Island in the early 1870s proceeded as follows: Aleut hunters selected a moonlit night to approach the rookery. They crept onto the beach, frightened the animals inland, spent up to three weeks assembling them into a group of several hundred, and drove them to the village ten to twelve miles away. To avoid stressing the animals to the point to death, the final trip lasted a minimum of three days. After the slaughter, some of the skins went to the Aleutians for sale at 60 cents each.[89] Pribilof Islanders kept some for making boats. Aleuts used dried intestines for waterproof jackets, flipper skins for shoe soles, whiskers for hat decoration, and fat for oil lamps and fire fuel.[90]

By the 1870s white commercial sealers looked for the Steller and California sea lions when other, more profitable seal hunting waned. Some obtained oil or skins to be turned into glue, but they made the easiest money in the "trimmings" trade. Chinese bought the whiskers for toothpicks and opium pipe cleaners, the male genitalia as aphrodisiacs, and the gall bladders for medicinal purposes. Hunters approached a haulout site by land, shot a few males before the herd plunged into the water, cut off what they wanted, and left the carcasses. The Steller population fell precipitously in California and did not recover.[91]

At the high point of exploitation, sea lions grew so scarce in the Aleutians that skins had to be imported from Baja California.[92] Hunters allegedly killed sea lions to reduce the supply available to their competitors.[93] Unregulated taking of the creatures continued into the 20th Century. In 1913 a lack of fur seals induced the Aleuts to kill sea lions on St. George Island, mainly to feed foxes being raised for fur. The rookery ceased functioning in 1916. At Northeast Point, a breeding colony that numbered 10,000 in 1872 dwindled to 120 adults in 1914. To preserve the Pribilof population the island manager banned harvest of pups and females.[94] Tolerance of human activity around rookeries varied widely; in some cases the herds survived repeated incursions by hunters. Relying on such precedents, Fish and Wildlife Service officials permitted Aleuts to take sea lion pups from a revived Northeast Point herd beginning in 1949. A decade later the site, the only Steller sea lion rookery in the world accessible to observers on foot, lay abandoned.[95]

Of the four or five known sea lion rookeries in the Pribilofs active in 1867, none showed breeding activity in 1960, although sea lions visited all of them as haulout sites. Walrus Island, formerly the breeding site of the walrus herd, then operated as the only sea lion rookery in the Pribilofs for its partially restored population of about 6,000. Researchers could not determine whether harassment by hunters and tourists might have driven the animals from Northeast Point to Walrus Island or why the population had not made greater recovery in several decades of restricted hunting.[96]

No longer needed for baidarkas to hunt sea otters and less relied upon for food and clothing by Natives, Steller sea lions recovered in the 20th Century. They became best noted for raiding salmon nets. Fishermen shot many of them, and predator control agents (Chapter 13) killed some in the vicinity of fishing

Sea lion breeding male, Northeast Point, St. Paul Island. By Victor B. Scheffer. FWS 428, Alaska Resources Library and Information Services. Heavily hunted for meat and skins, sea lions abandoned Northeast Point as a breeding colony site.

operations. Fisheries officials investigated possible uses of the animals to take pressure off fish stocks. They found that leather manufacturers did not want the skins because of numerous cuts and scars. The meat, though palatable, would serve only a specialty market. Fox farmers rated it highly as feed, but the fox business evaporated in the 1950s. Pet and fish food would require removal of most of the fat. Processing, preservation, and transportation from distant sites might impose prohibitive costs.[97] A revived fur market prompted the killing of 65,000 pups at rookeries between 1959 and 1972. Then the Marine Mammal Protection Act restricted sea lion killing to Native Americans for subsistence purposes and to fishing operations on a limited permit basis. Management passed from state to federal control.[98]

In the 1970s, populations of sea lions, hair seals, and fur seals started a downhill slide. By the mid-1980s they had shrunk by about half, and the trend continued. An ongoing debate and research program suggested that reduced food supply, possibly caused by commercial fishing or changes in ocean temperature, accounted for most of the losses. In 1990 the National Marine Fisheries Service declared the Steller sea lion a threatened species under the Endangered Species Act.[99] By the end of the century the western population (Aleutians to central Gulf of Alaska) numbered a minimum of 39,000, compared with 140,000 in the late 1950s. Now listed as endangered, it continued to decline at more than 4 percent annually despite measures to restrict fisheries in its feeding zones. The Southeast Alaska population, by contrast, rose by an annual 6 percent through the 1980s to a total of more than 15,000.[100]

Hunters commercially exploited the smaller but widespread harbor seals beginning in 1889 and took large numbers for bounty payments between 1927 and 1967.[101] Alaska Natives traditionally hunted them for subsistence purposes, employing a variety of capture methods. Hunters might sit on the rocks at haulout sites and attract seals by calls and sealskin decoys. When the seals approached, the hunters clubbed or speared them or frightened them into a net stretched offshore. Hunters paddled up to seals sleeping in seaweed, attached hooks tied to sealskin floats, and killed the seals when they tired. Chugach Eskimos stood in the water near haulout sites on stormy nights and speared seals by means of harpoons on long poles. In winter they loaded stones into a skin boat to lower it to the water line and positioned a large piece of ice on the bow. Approaching the quarry, a hunter speared it through a hole cut in the ice. Pulling the dead seal aboard, the hunters threw out an equivalent weight of stones. They repeated the process until they acquired a maximum load of ten or twelve seals.[102]

Tlingits approached swimming seals by canoe or lay waiting in their boats among the ice floes until seals surfaced nearby. They shot or speared the animals and, if the spear had no float attached, they hurried to recover the quarry before it sank. At rookeries they killed pups by clubbing them. Women in camp removed the skin, separated the blubber, and heated it in a pot to render it into seal oil. They dried the skin and soft parts, the latter to be eaten. They sewed skins into footwear, some to be sold as tourist items. Seal oil would be consumed as food or sold for local consumption. A two dollar bounty in 1931, increased to three dollars in 1939, induced some hunters to kill seals for the bounties and discard the bodies. Tlingits used an undetermined percentage of the seals for meat, oil, and handicrafts.

Between 1931 and 1945, hunters, about 85 percent Alaska Natives, collected bounties on approximately 890 seals per year. From 1963 to 1965 a shift in the European fashion industry drove up the price of sealskins, resulting in large-scale killing. A downturn in the fur market and termination of the bounty in 1967 took the pressure off the harbor seals.[103]

A predator control program (Chapter 13) to protect commercial fisheries accounted for about 38,000 harbor seals in the 1950s. From 1927 to 1957 the territory and state paid bounties on more than 358,000 hair seals of all species.[104] The decrease of hair seals may at times have inconvenienced coastal Natives, although no species approached extinction. The 1972 Marine Mammal Protection Act ended all commercial killing but, soon thereafter, harbor seals accompanied the sea lions and fur seals in a steep downward trend.[105] In the late 1990s Alaska harbor seal estimates stood at (1) Bering Sea and Aleutians: a minimum of 13,000, possibly stabilized and increasing; (2) Prince William Sound to Unimak Pass: 29,000 and possibly increasing; and (3) Southeast Alaska: 35,000 and increasing. In general the trend appeared to slow or reverse the declines of the 1970s and 1980s. Direct contact with fisheries accounted for little of the mortality, but possible effects of food supply removal by fisheries remained unknown. Subsistence harvest by Natives approximated 2,700 seals annually, about two-thirds in Southeast Alaska.[106] As for sea lions, fur seals, and sea otters, the central causes of population loss likely included killer whale predation, commercial fishing, and climatic change.[107]

PROSPECTS FOR WHALES AND PINNIPEDS

North Pacific whales, walruses, sea lions, and some hair seals experienced their most intensive exploitation in the near-absence of public commitment to conservation values. Utilitarian regulatory steps to sustain species generally waited until short-term economic advantage no longer existed, especially under American rule. Even the apparent danger to Eskimo populations proved insufficient to curb the commercial slaughter. Government and corporate accountability extended only to the point of avoiding species extinction—even if, as for the right whale, the efforts might well be too feeble and too late. Almost no public participation evidenced itself, and the scant scientific data available had minimal impact on policy.

Apathy toward most sea mammals in the century before Alaskan statehood stood in sharp contrast to the attitudes of the last three decades of the 20th Century. The lack of concern stemmed from a series of particular conditions. Killing took place thousands of miles away, often in international waters, out of sight of video cameras. Insufficient scientific knowledge of far-ranging oceans made them an alien and mysterious world in the eyes of the public. Virtually no one perceived the ocean as a functioning ecosystem. Almost no one could know the whale as a gentle, intelligent creature. Whale products, primarily oil, eased the lives of vast numbers of people, and the whaling industry enjoyed a venerable reputation. The walrus, to the extent that people held any image of it, seemed ugly and perhaps fearsome. Large numbers of sea lions died to supply boats for industrial-scale sea otter hunting, to which few objected. Euro-Americans placed a high value on salmon fishing and readily endorsed the slaughter of seals and sea lions as nuisances. Technology of the period lacked the capacity to accurately count sea mammal populations and permit timely warning of their endangerment. The wide variety of whales and pinnipeds deterred focus on a single species such as the fur seal or sea otter. And no dominant figure like Henry W. Elliott pled the animals' cause. Salvation for the sea creatures awaited changes in economics and communications technology.

All Alaskan sea mammal species survived to statehood, albeit some by a small margin. Beyond statehood they encountered a different set of conditions: waning of markets for their body parts (walrus ivory a glaring exception), rising public interest and concern for their preservation, and degradation of their physical environment by commercial fishing, various disturbances, and pollution. Inexorably they moved into the realm of environmental politics.

As the food demands of an ever-multiplying human population exhausted fishing grounds elsewhere, attention turned to the North Pacific. Directly and indirectly, whales and pinnipeds now had to compete against modern fishing machinery for their space and sustenance. Global climate change introduced worrisome uncertainties. Ecosystem sustainability for either consumptive or nonconsumptive purposes called for advanced ecological understanding and international cooperation in research and management. Survival of the sea mammals would tax the knowledge and wisdom of humans into the foreseeable future.

4

John Muir and the Land

"In God's wildness lies the hope of the world—the great fresh unblighted, unredeemed wilderness. The galling harness of civilization drops off, and the wounds heal ere we are aware."[1] So wrote John Muir, paraphrasing his intellectual forebear Thoreau, in his journal during a climbing trip around the glacier later to bear his name. Muir (1838–1914), a founder of the wilderness preservation movement, may have had the most important indirect influence on Alaska of all its conservation activists. His ideas ultimately bore fruit in protective land designations in Alaska and elsewhere. Yet like many others of his time and afterward, he perceived the territory as so large and isolated that its wilderness character could not be threatened.

Muir learned a love of Nature as a small boy in Scotland where his grandfather took him for walks. He and his brother David liked to roam the countryside and see how many bird nests they could find. They thrilled when the family emigrated to the United States in 1849 and settled in the "glorious Wisconsin wilderness." Muir pursued his interest in Nature in the rare intervals between the chores of a harsh pioneer life on the frontier. As an older child he had to do a man's share of the farmwork, and he once hand-dug a well 90 feet down through sandstone using hammer and chisel, working for months from dawn to dark. On one occasion he barely escaped death by carbonic acid gas poisoning at the bottom of the shaft.

Muir attended the University of Wisconsin between 1861 and 1863, taking courses that interested him, but he had no desire to complete a degree. A pacifist, he went to Canada to avoid the likelihood of being drafted. He traveled, studied plants, and worked in a sawmill until the Civil War ended. His mechanical genius landed him a job as a mechanic in Indianapolis. A shop accident temporarily blinded him in his late twenties, redoubled his appreciation of Nature, and caused him to rethink his priorities. Setting off on a "Thousand Mile Walk" in 1867, he visited Florida and then took a boat from New York to California, arriving in 1868. There he explored and observed the Sierra Nevadas intensely and guided people on wilderness trips. An extraordinarily eloquent and insightful man, Muir deeply impressed others with his discourses about Nature. Friends urged him to publish his views, and he did so beginning in 1871. He wrote of the beauty of Nature and the need for conserving it through better management and the creation of parks. In 1876 he began a long career in public speaking on Nature and conservation.[2]

Travels through time and space took Muir on a parallel philosophical journey. Observations of Nature during his youth caused him to reject his father's fundamentalist view of Nature as an alien, if not evil, force to be conquered. Reading Emerson and other transcendentalist thinkers while at the University of Wisconsin, he moved toward the conception of Nature as God's work created for the benefit of humans. Further reflection, deepened by his experiences in the Canadian woods, the Thousand Mile Walk, and trips into the Sierras, convinced him of the divinity and interrelatedness of all existence. He now saw God as the substance and process of Nature, and humans as an integral part not possessing the right to dominate or destroy the other parts. Humans had the responsibility and the privilege of living in the universe as citizens, respecting and appreciating other living and nonliving elements. Muir held this biocentric, essentially ecological understanding of life decades before its time as a contending view, although he did not attempt to explicitly develop it in his writings. In the words of environmental historian Max Oelschlaeger,

> Muir recognized that whatever humankind might be, one's essential human beingness could be known only in relation to the nonhuman other. Thus Muir's mature idea of wilderness eradicated the boundaries between wilderness and civilization. The flowing whole of nature was the ultimate reality, the process in which life and death (and all other human conceptualizations) were merely part of everything else.[3]

MUIR IN ALASKA

As a lover of mountains and glaciers Muir took an interest in Alaska, making seven trips between 1879 and 1899.[4] They started when Alaska missionary Sheldon Jackson met Muir at a Presbyterian Church convention at Yosemite in the summer of 1879 and alerted him to the departure of a mail steamer in ten days. Muir boarded the ship and went to Alaska.[5] In unbounded enthusiasm he set out, usually alone, on mountain- and glacier-climbing trips. Carrying little food or equipment, he often hiked and camped overnight in rain or snowstorms. He and his 1879–1880 traveling companion, Reverend S. Hall Young, a Presbyterian missionary at Wrangell, became the first non-Natives to fully explore and map Glacier Bay, featuring the great glacier later named for Muir. Twice they journeyed 700 miles from Wrangell to the bay and back by dugout canoe, guided by Tlingit Indians. In a daring rescue following a near-fatal mountain-climbing accident, Muir used his necktie, which he always wore in the wild, to bind Young and pull him from the edge of an abyss.[6] Young's dog Stickeen accompanied Muir on an exploring trip that climaxed in a death-defying crossing of a narrow 70-foot ice bridge on Brady Glacier. The plucky little mutt so impressed Muir that he won abiding fame as the hero of *Stickeen*, the best selling of Muir's several books on Alaska. A tourist stole Stickeen in 1883 and bore him away on a steamer.[7]

Muir's purpose in visiting Alaska involved more nature appreciation than science, although he promulgated theories of glacial movement and carefully recorded a wide variety of natural phenomena. Science, he thought, achieved its highest value by aiding spiritual understanding of Nature. Compared to California, Alaska offered a more perfect place to experience the harmony of Nature because of its unspoiled wild character. Glaciers in particular, in their advances and retreats, displayed what Muir interpreted as Nature's harmonic cycles.[8]

Belief in the spiritual healing power of Nature, and the desire to protect Nature, moved Muir to write. He made vigorous efforts to impress his reading public, believing that, once directly acquainted with natural beauty, people would be motivated to respect and preserve it. Following his 1879 trip through the Inside Passage he wrote, "Never before this had I been embosomed in scenery so hopelessly beyond description. . . . [T]he whole is so tender, so fine, so ethereal, any penwork seems coarse and unavailing."[9] By 1897 he had risen to the challenge: "To the lover of wilderness Alaska offers a glorious field for either work or rest: landscape beauty in a thousand forms, things great and small, novel and familiar, as wild and pure as paradise." This he followed by a 192-word sentence extolling the scenic grandeur of Southeast Alaska.[10]

Sheldon Jackson and John Muir produced the first literature designed to publicize and attract people to Alaska—Muir highlighting natural beauty and Jackson the educational and spiritual needs of the Natives. In an 1880 letter to the San Francisco *Daily Evening Bulletin* Muir asserted, "Alaska is full of food for man and beast, body and soul, though few are seeking it as yet. Were one-tenth of the attractions this country has to offer known to the world, thousands would come every year, and not a few of them would stay and make homes."[11] His descriptions of Glacier Bay persuaded the Pacific Coast Steamship Company to offer large-scale tourist visits to the Southeast, carrying 5,000 passengers annually by 1890. Publicity also attracted hunters and mountain climbers to Southeast Alaska, helped to counter impressions of the territory as a land of ice and cold, and tied it more closely to the rest of the nation.[12] Historian Frank Buske said of Muir, "His magazine articles confirmed his reputation as an Alaskan expert, and conservation efforts with regard to Alaska at the turn of the century had his support. Alaska's reputation as a treasure house of natural beauty and resources began with his reports."[13]

John Muir's Alaska writing may also be seen as part of the process of extending the American frontier. In this context, after Americans conquered and acquired land from the Atlantic to the Pacific, some looked northward to continue the pursuit of their perceived Manifest Destiny. Muir's "discovery" and descriptions of natural wonders and Native culture constituted a form of appropriation that helped fulfill the desire for American expansion.[14] He showed little recognition of this aspect of his work and criticized various impacts of Western civilization on Alaska Natives.

Muir's aesthetic appreciation of the northern land did not necessarily extend to its urban vistas, exponents of the destructive intrusion of civilization. Of Wrangell he wrote,

> It was a lawless draggle of wooden huts and houses, built in crooked lines, wrangling about the boggy shore of the island for a mile or so without the slightest subordination to the points of the compass or to building laws of any kind. . . . The ground in general was an oozy, messy bog on a foundation of jagged rocks, full of concealed potholes. . . . The domestic animals were represented by chickens, a lonely cow, a few sheep, and hogs of a breed well calculated to deepen and complicate the mud of the streets.[15]

Muir strongly disapproved of sport hunting and any other unnecessary form of killing. While visiting prospectors during the 1879 canoe trip Young complained of the lack of meat. Asked by a prospector why they had failed to bag lots of ducks, chief Toyatte replied, "Because the duck's friend won't let us . . . when we want to shoot, Mr. Muir always shakes the canoe."[16] In 1881 Muir traveled through the Bering Sea and into the Arctic Ocean on the revenue cutter *Corwin,* sent to search for the survivors of the cutter *Jeanette*, lost in the Arctic ice. He did not like all that he saw. Having watched the *Corwin* crew shoot three swimming polar bears from the deck as the ship chased them, he expressed disgust:

> They had no chance whatever for their lives, and the whole affair was as safe and easy a butchery as shooting cows from the roof of a barn. . . . The Eskimos hunt and kill them for food, going out to meet them on the ice with spears and dogs. This is merely one savage living on another. But how civilized people, seeking for heavens and angels and millenniums [*sic*], and the reign of universal love, can enjoy this red, brutal amusement, is not so easily accounted for. Such soft, fuzzy, sentimental aspirations, and the frame of mind that can reap giggling, jolly pleasure from the blood and agony and death of these fine animals, with their humanlike groans, are too devilish for anything but hell. Of all the animals man is at once the worst and the best.[17]

Although he occasionally ate meat, Muir opined that, ideally, "people should learn to put their fellow mortals in their hearts instead of . . . their dinners." He valued all creatures including snakes, lizards, spiders, and even flies. He rejected popular notions, overwhelmingly accepted in his time, that animals could be classified as good or bad, moral or immoral.[18]

Muir believed that wild animals, unlike tame ones, could teach humans valuable lessons about life. While trying to avoid anthropomorphizing the creatures and losing the respect of scientists, he saw in wild animals qualities of beauty, grace, and self-reliance from which humans could benefit if they were to appreciate and understand Nature. He contrasted the intelligent, clean, and vigorous mountain sheep to the stupid, dirty, defenseless beast of domestic flocks. He chose not to dwell on the violence inherent in predator-prey relationships and possessed a limited understanding of the connection between population and food supply. In essence he held an animistic philosophy, even though he used the term *God* to describe a causal force behind the evolutionary process.[19]

He rejected the mechanistic Darwinian focus on survival as the most significant aspect of Nature but accepted the concept of evolutionary change and viewed Nature as flowing like a river. He abhorred the notion of Nature as a bank of resources to be conquered, improved upon, and consumed for human benefit. To him the process of manipulating Nature degraded it and humans as well. Wilderness held a store of superior knowledge and wisdom developed through evolution, and its destruction removed the possibility of higher development in humans. As Muir scholar Michael P. Cohen summarized it, "Muir wanted civilized Man to improve his spiritual condition by immersing himself in the flow, not transcending it."[20]

While climbing Muir Glacier the philosopher mused:

> The wilderness, I believe, is dear to every man though some are afraid of it. People load themselves with unnecessary fears, as if there were nothing in the world but snakes and bears who, like the Devil, are going restlessly about seeking whom they may devour. The few creatures there are really mind their

> own business, and rather shun humans as their greatest enemies. But men are like children afraid of their mother. Like the man who, going out on a misty morning, saw a monster who proved to be his own brother.

A reflection later that day: "There is love of wild nature in everybody, an ancient mother-love ever showing itself whether recognized or no, and however covered by cares and duties."[21]

Like nearly all Americans of his time, Muir did not ponder whether Natives, as distinct from the United States, might rightfully own Alaska. Yet as he did for trees and wild animals, Muir felt sympathy toward and spiritual unity with Alaska Natives. He questioned the taking of totem poles for museums. The degrading effects of Euro-American culture on wildlife and the Natives reinforced his view of civilization as an aggressive and pernicious force. He witnessed liquor dismantling the culture and vitality of Native life.[22] In 1879 Muir attended a Tlingit dance depicting deer, porpoise, and bear. He admired the performance but noted the speech given by a dancer: "Dear Brothers and Sisters, this is the way we used to dance. We liked it long ago when we were blind, we always danced this way, but now we are not blind. The Good Lord has taken pity on us and sent his son, Jesus Christ, to tell us what to do. We have danced today only to show you how blind we were to dance in this foolish way. We will not dance any more."[23]

Principled missionaries ("common-sense Christian teachers") merited Muir's favor, and he felt such a relationship with the Tlingits. He found the Tlingits more virtuous than Christians in atonement for their sins and admired the depth of their spiritual thinking. His friend Kadachan exemplified what Muir believed to be their ecological perspective. According to scholar Richard Fleck, the Tlingits "taught Muir that happiness in one's original environment is a true key to wisdom. To be happy in a place is to be at one with it." Muir admired the simplicity and joie de vivre of the Eskimos, whom he regarded as brave and capable. He saw the coming of the white man as a disruption of the Natives' harmonious adjustment to Nature.[24]

Muir made little effort to publicize the lessons Native life might have to offer Euro-American culture, reserving that honor for nonhuman creatures or for Nature as a whole. In his posthumously published *Travels in Alaska* Muir stated of the Tlingits: "[I]n all my travels I never saw a child, old or young, receive a blow or even a harsh word," and "the young are fondly indulged without being spoiled." Crying is rarely heard."[25] But his writings showed no awareness of the legacy of Native warfare and slavery or the brutality and degradation women commonly experienced in traditional cultures of Alaska.

The repeating rifle, Muir judged, encouraged the Natives to waste game. Hall Young told of seeing Muir "furiously angry for the first and last time in my acquaintance with him." Noticing mountain goats on the hills above yet-to-be-named Muir Glacier, Young asked their Tlingit companion to "go up and get us a kid." At length the young man returned carrying a goat, explaining, "I picked the fattest and most tender of those that I killed." Astonished, Hall queried, "What! You killed more than one?" The Indian raised fingers to count to eleven. At that, "Muir's face flushed red, and with an exclamation that was as near to an oath as he ever came, he started for Joe. Luckily for that Indian he saw Muir and fled like a deer up the rocks, and would not come down until he was assured that he would not be hurt."[26]

While Muir lamented the corrupting influences of Euro-American culture on the Natives, he lacked a full understanding of the latter in their relationship to Nature. He interpreted Tlingit fears and superstitions as evidence of separation, whereas the Tlingits viewed themselves as integrally related to Nature. Muir's preservationist conception did not include Native subsistence living as part of an ecosystem. National Park Service philosophy tended to incorporate Muir's concept, encountering little difficulty in the states where, in nearly all cases, Native Americans had been removed from lands that became parks.[27] But in Alaska, notably in Glacier Bay, the continuing use of wildlands by Natives generated conflict that went on through the 20th Century. It centered on questions of "subsistence" rights: Who should be permitted to use natural resources, for what purposes, and by what means of harvest? Should hunting for sport or commercial profit, or by modern technology, be classified as subsistence? At what point should modernization of lifestyle render a person or a group ineligible for subsistence privileges? Should any lands be closed to harvest? These and related issues bore implications for the management of public wildlands and for the philosophies of those supporting environmental protection.

THE GOLD RUSH ERA

John Muir played a minor part in the Gold Rush. Crossing into Canada through the Stikine River Valley in 1879, he made the acquaintance of miners. In a January 1880 letter in the San Francisco *Daily Evening Bulletin* he wrote from Sitka, he speculated that most of Alaska contained gold, that the mountains geologically resembled California. Although he expressed doubt that Alaska goldfields would be as rich as those in the States, his mention of seeing nuggets up to 40 ounces may well have fired the imaginations of would-be prospectors.[28]

Muir chanced to be traveling in Alaska in the summer of 1897 and encountered the driven hordes bound for the Klondike. A newspaper asked him to accompany the gold seekers as commentator. "Do they think I'm daft?" he exclaimed. "When I go into that wild it will not be in a crowd like this or on such a sordid mission." During a brief stay at Skagway and Dyea he wrote articles describing the Chilkoot, White, Chilkat, Taku, and Stikine passes over which the gold seekers traveled into Canada on their way to the Bonanza Creek region. Of the quest for Klondike gold he commented, "The way to Heaven is less anxiously looked for." He adopted a tolerant stand toward gold seeking, considering it preferable to "the mildewed inaction of crowds of purposeless people in big towns." Few would become wealthy, he thought, but each would gain "knowledge better than gold" and attract to Alaska others who would increase their appreciation of Nature. Minimal injury could be done to the land because the cold climate would discourage development. He predicted that abundance of wildlife would allow the Klondikers to exist for years "living off the country as free as a bird."[29] As for himself, Muir asserted, "I never wasted a minute hunting goldmines, knowing that gold dust in one's eyes prevents one from seeing all else. Gold digging is only a dull chore, and no sane man will allow it to blind him and draw him away from the real blessings of existence."[30]

The Alaska-Yukon Gold Rush of the late 1890s and early 1900s highly stimulated public interest in Alaska. World attention focused on the Klondike in Canada's Yukon, although much of the Klondike activity and several other gold strikes took place in Alaska. To the public the Gold Rush signified adventure, trial, freedom, and the vision of instant wealth. Written accounts and tales told by participants, and the fiction of such writers as Jack London, Robert Service, and Rex Beach, elevated the Gold Rush to permanent mythical status. Nature prepared a harsh setting where wits and physical and moral capacities could be tested, fortunes made and lost, legends born. It invited both reader and adventurer to extend the vanishing frontier.[31]

A less noble reality greeted the vast majority of gold seekers. By the time they reached the goldfields nearly all the desirable sites had been claimed. Most men found it necessary to work for claim owners, an arrangement similar to the industrial system they hoped to escape. As historian Kathryn Morse observed, "[W]hatever gold mining was supposed to be, it quickly turned into a familiar round of hirings and firings and bosses, and always too many men for too few jobs." She assessed gold mining as "one of the most unproductive, unpredictable, and generally unpleasant occupations anyone could have chosen."[32]

Misery and danger supplemented drudgery in the pursuit of gold. Miners picked their way through the bodies of scores of horses and mules on White Pass, and more than 50 miners died in an 1898 avalanche on Chilcoot. Survivors again risked their lives in the river rapids descending to the Klondike. Many died of starvation and disease attempting to reach the goldfields through the Copper River Valley. Others braved the North Pacific in aged boats to ascend the Yukon. All but a few arrived too late to realize significant gains.[33]

Miners indeed rarely suffered from "mildewed inaction." In the early days they traveled primarily on foot in the summer and by snowshoe in winter,

Placer miners on American Creek. Core coll. PCA 01-4508, Alaska State Library. Left to right: Charlie Gay, Libby, Allen, Civil War veteran "Dod" Gardner, Jack Coulter. Pole of telegraph line visible at left ran from Eagle (twelve miles away) to Valdez. The Gold Rush era brought a flood of adventurers, and even small-scale mining operations could create long-term environmental impacts.

carrying their supplies by backpack. Sourdough and later U.S. marshal Lynn Smith told of an 1899 incident wherein his boat became frozen in the Yukon ice below Woodchopper Creek. Hearing of a gold strike fifteen miles inland, he set out carrying two days' food but forgot to take extra matches. After walking all day he met his own snowshoe tracks and realized he had lost his way. Encountering a moose, he shot it and used his last match to start a fire. He cooked and ate some of the moose but could not keep the fire going because he had misplaced his hatchet. As a last resort he cleaned out the moose and crawled inside it to sleep. He awoke the next day to find the moose frozen and himself entombed. After two more days he heard a pack of wolves. They approached and tore at the moose. As Smith lay still he could see a black wolf chewing a hole six inches away from him. Eventually the wolves opened up the moose enough for Lynn to force his way out. Perhaps fearing attack, he killed the black wolf and wounded at least four others. The weather had cleared up, and Smith made his way back to the Yukon River.[34]

Muir, who disdained pretentiousness, would probably have approved of the 1896–1897 social arrangements at Circle City detailed by Arthur Walden, who freighted supplies between mining towns by dogsled: "Here was a town made up of men from all parts of the world, intelligent men all. I knew an Oxford man, a younger son, married to a squaw who had blondined her hair: he could quote Greek poetry by the hour when he was liquored up. Another man, raised in the wilds of the Rocky Mountains, never drank and didn't have a squaw, and taught himself to read and write." In Circle City, Walden recalled, "if you look for a fool you find only *one*."[35] The town of 300–400

> had no taxes, courthouse or jail; no post-office, church, schools, hotel or dog pound; no rules, regulations or written law; no sheriff, dentist, doctor, lawyer or priest. Here there was no murder, stealing or dishonesty, and right was right and wrong was wrong as each individual understood it. . . . No firearms were carried for protection; no prayers were said for the dead; but money was raised for the widow. The Indians were treated fairly and squarely and were honest, as no liquor was sold to them. A man could be as wet or dry as he liked, and there were as many dries as in any community. Every man had a right to his own opinions, and was not taunted for them if he did not try to force them on others. There were no hypocrites in Circle City, and there was no need for them. . . . No man was a hero, no matter what he did, and no man was a saint, no matter how good he was.[36]

Stores took payments in gold dust, and one customarily turned one's back while the clerk weighed the poke. Before 1898, Miners' Meetings dispensed justice, operating by consensus. Then, "after the gold rush of '98 conditions here and elsewhere on the Yukon changed. Civilization, with religion, laws, disorder, stealing, education, murder, social life, commercial vice, comforts, and broken pledges, crept in; justice cost money and disease raged."[37]

U.S. Geological Survey officer Josiah Edward Spurr recounted a Circle City dance held in the late 1890s: "The couples gyrated in eccentric curves around in obedience to the cries; the candles flickered in the draft from the open door; and a row of miners too bashful to dance, or who could find no partners, sat on boxes next to the wall, hunched up their legs and spit tobacco juice until the middle of the floor was a sort of island. In short it was the most brilliant affair Circle City ever witnessed."[38] The town emptied almost overnight when it heard news of the Klondike gold strike. Local traders sold the mining supplies upriver for higher profits, so Circle City miners resorted to hijacking steamboats and seizing supplies, although making full payment.[39]

Indians, who sold moose, caribou, and salmon to the gold seekers, paid a fearful price. Introduced diseases including measles, smallpox, diphtheria, influenza, and typhoid fever cut deeply into their numbers. Disease often weakened them to the point where they could not carry out food gathering, causing starvation. Traders sometimes shifted their business to higher-paying miners, leaving Indians without supplies of blankets and ammunition. Market hunting undermined traditional communal patterns of gathering and contributed to shortages of moose and caribou on which the Indians depended for food.[40]

Gold seekers exerted a greater impact on the land than Muir anticipated. In the early years, prospectors dug up streambed gravel in the summer and channeled water into rockers or sluices to settle out the placer gold. By the mid-1890s they worked through the winter, burning piles of wood to thaw holes down to bedrock and then digging laterally, a process called drift mining. When individual gold seekers exhausted the readily accessible placer deposits in the first decades of the 20th Century, companies brought in heavy machinery to dig deeper. They burned wood to heat boilers and piped the steam into the ground to melt the permafrost, enabling them to continue deep subsurface work all summer. As mining advanced in scale and industrial organization, some mining operations applied hydraulic hoses and dredges.[41] When the government raised the price of an ounce of gold from $20.67 to $35 in 1933, Alaskan gold production rose from 469,286 ounces in 1933 to 749,933 ounces in 1940, escalating the environmental impact.[42]

Hydraulic miners wielded high-pressure hoses to remove soil covering gold-bearing deposits. The hoses washed away the organic material, silt, and fine gravel, called the overburden, and flushed it into nearby streams and rivers. Material below the water table could be forced out through an inclined pipe and elevated aggregations torn down. Some gold deposits existed in benches well above the valley floor. At Cripple Creek in the Fairbanks region in 1939, strippers removed hills as high as 140 feet and muck as deep as 140 feet below ground level. Following the hydraulic hoses, a giant dragline dug out nearly 12,000 cubic yards of gravel daily. Stripping commonly prepared the way for dredging operations. Dredging worked best in relatively level areas such as the Yukon and Tanana valleys and the Nome beaches, where gold had settled in large-scale gravel sediments.[43]

After hydraulic hoses tore down the riverbanks and hillsides, gold dredges sifted through the material and converted the valleys into piles of discarded gravel. At Chatanika north of Fairbanks in the mid-1930s the Fairbanks Exploration Company, biggest of its kind in the region, ran a hydraulic gold mining operation. Pipes forced water into the frozen ground to thaw it, and giant hoses blasted away the top layers of soil. Then

> the big dredges follow up and dig out the gold-bearing gravel clear down to bed rock, which is anywhere from twenty to seventy-five feet below the washed surface. . . . They follow the sluicing operation around the valley—up one side and down the other, digging up the whole valley floor in the process. . . . [T]hey are made like barges and float on a pond dug by themselves as they go. . . . A big endless chain of digging buckets projects from the front. By cables fastened to each side of the pond and running over

Hydraulic mining operation on Dan Creek, a tributary of Nizina and Chitina rivers in the Wrangells. Alaska files 8268, University of Washington Archives. Hydraulic mining escalated the impact on the land.

winches in the dredge, it is constantly kept swinging from side to side along a two-hundred-foot front. . . . This digging outfit is a regular four-story factory with engine room and control room, operated on electricity from the

Fairbanks Exploration Co. dredge on Cripple Creek, twelve miles from Fairbanks. Alaska files 8272, University of Washington Archives. Such large-scale operations could permanently alter an entire valley.

> $5,000,000 power station in Fairbanks. . . . The dredge was never stopped, night or day, except for repairs.[44]

Historian Clark Spence characterized the gold dredge as "a marvelous invention, able to do the work of an army of men and to make a profit where none existed before," yet "the seemingly insatiable leviathans wreaked havoc with the environment as few other types of mining have done, leaving behind a wake of desolation and ruin." The Fairbanks Exploration Company furthered natural science in at least one way, donating to the University of Alaska the remains of mammoths and other prehistoric creatures found in the muck.[45]

Extensive removal of trees and topsoil disrupted the ecology of stream valleys, normally among the most biologically productive interior zones. Studies eventually showed that soil loss changed vegetation and that silt from mining could diminish populations of grayling and other fish. Loss of root structures and topsoil, and destruction of mossy wetlands—the latter done in part to discourage mosquitoes—contributed to flooding and loss of evened water flow needed for mining operations.[46] By damaging the environment, miners hurt their own immediate interests as well as those of the Indians and wildlife.

Hard-rock mining for gold seemed even less romantic than hydraulic mining. A visitor to Juneau in the 1890s wrote, "Within two miles of Juneau are the famous Treadwell Mines, the largest in the world. Columns of dense smoke could be seen arising from these great works, surrounding which are mountains, grown white with the timber bleached under the poisonous smoke that comes from the burning of that ore, which cannot be separated from the gold by batteries." Another writer's impression of Douglas during operation of the gold ore crushers: "Nearly two thousand tons of quartz rock are crushed daily at these mills, and the roar made by the eight hundred or more stamps . . . in pulverizing this rock, dwarfs all other rackets I ever heard."[47]

By the end of the 20th Century, regulation had reduced the impact of gold mining in Alaskan lands and waters, but the permissive 1872 mining law, allowing easy access to most federal lands, remained in force.

INTERIOR FORESTS

Alaska's forests felt the impact of gold mining. In contrast to the rainy coastal region familiar to Muir, the interior featured warm and dry summers. Largely because of the Gold Rush, forest fires burned continually. Miners used fire to clear woods and thaw permafrost for prospecting, and wood fueled steamships on the Yukon and other rivers.[48] Miners deliberately set forest fires to scorch and dry out trees to make them more useful as fuel. In the course of a winter a pair of miners might consume 30 to 60 cords of wood. Average-sized steamboats needed 30 cords daily, large ones 50 cords. Between St. Michael on the lower Yukon and Dawson across the Canadian border, a paddle wheeler used 150 to 1,000 cords. At the height of activity after the turn of the century, about 250 steamers plied the Yukon.[49]

In addition to mining operations, white settlers employed fire for camping, signaling, protection from insects, and killing green trees to provide firewood and clear land for agriculture. An 1899 view of the Yukon River above Circle City: "Smoke on all sides fills the air, as camp-fires are built and not extinguished, and the flames slowly climb the mountainside, destroying the much-needed wood, and spoiling the picture otherwise so beautiful."[50] Whites copied some practices from Alaska Natives, who used fire for many purposes, from signaling and driving game to entertainment. Both Natives and whites exercised little care to maintain control of their fires. Escaping or deliberately freed fires had rendered interior Alaska in part an unnatural environment prior to Euro-American contact.[51]

Lightning caused fires in the interior and, before the end of the 19th Century, Indians probably set most of the fires. The Gold Rush accelerated burning. Geologist Alfred H. Brooks observed in 1911 that

TABLE 4.1. Forest Acreage Burned in Alaska, 1940–1970

Year	*Acres Burned*	*Year*	*Acres Burned*	*Year*	*Acres Burned*
1940	4,500,000	1951	221,669	1962	38,975
1941	3,654,744	1952	74,690	1963	16,290
1942	452,510	1953	472,549	1964	3,430
1943	666,773	1954	1,430,645	1965	7,093
1944	110,604	1955	23,582	1966	672,765
1945	117,313	1956	476,593	1967	109,005
1946	1,438,963	1957	5,049,661	1968	1,013,301
1947	1,431,665	1958	317,215	1969	4,231,820
1948	35,190	1959	596,574	1970	113,486
1949	18,147	1960	87,180		
1950	2,063,983	1961	5,100		

Source: (1940–1954): Harold J. Lutz, Ecological Effects of Forest Fires in the Interior of Alaska. USDA Tech. Bull. No. 1133. Washington, DC: March 1956, 14; (1955–1970): U.S. Dept. of the Interior, Bureau of Land Management, Alaska Fire Service, 1992 Fire Statistics. Fairbanks: 1993, 21.

Note: Nearly all acreage is in interior Alaska. Low and high figures reflect reduced activity in war years and climate variations.

> hundreds of square miles of timber have been burned off the Yukon Basin during the last decade. This burning of timber is in part done purposely by both whites and natives in order to get rid of insect pests or to improve the growth of grass near their habitations, and is in part due to carelessness. . . . [T]he amount of timber destroyed by the natives is small compared with that for which the whites are responsible. Many a white man has deliberately started a forest fire which has swept over miles of country solely that he might obtain a few acres of dry wood for winter use. If this willful waste does not stop, the time is not too far distant when there will be a scarcity of timber even for local use.

Settlers commonly believed that fire improved the country by increasing grass and moose browse, killing insects, and easing prospecting. They could see scant use for spruce forests except as fuel and construction material.[52]

An unknown but vast acreage burned between 1898 and 1939, when the Alaska Fire Control Service originated. A fire that started along the Valdez-Eagle trail at Mosquito Fork Flat in 1922 burned a swath 48 miles long by 30 miles wide. Construction workers started fires that consumed more than 100,000 acres at Chatanika River in 1926 and 128,000 acres at Copper River in 1927. A trapper, probably by accident, is believed to have set the Sheenjek River fire that blackened 312,320 acres in 1937. After the Fire Control Service became effective in 1942, aided by reduced activity in the forests, burned acreage dropped precipitously except in dry years (Table 4.1).[53]

Wood consumption rose in the interior as population grew and mining operations became more mechanized. Sawmills cut spruce in the river valleys for lumber and to support World War II construction. Mining operations, especially dredges, continued to consume great quantities of firewood. One gold dredge used up 1,500 cords annually between 1913 and 1947.[54] Steamboats, homes, placer mines, railroads, and other businesses required large volumes. Until mid-century, Fairbanks heated itself primarily by burning wood, directly or in a steam-producing plant.[55] Settled in 1901, the town had to send woodcutters 33 miles to the Salcha River for its supply in 1909. By 1916 the town needed 100,000 cords annually, enough to create a pile 4 feet high and deep, 152 miles long. Mining consumed more than 70 percent of the wood, and heating and power generation about 12 percent each.[56] For great distances around populated or industrial sites, hills stood shorn of trees. When introduction of coal and fuel oil reduced woodcutting, the forests recovered some of their natural character by statehood, nearly a half-century after Muir's death.[57]

In the Southeast, Russians operated sawmills to build ships and other facilities, primarily near their capital, Sitka. Canneries, fish traps, housing, and railroad construction required larger amounts of wood in the American period, as did heating. World Wars I and II called for wood from the Southeast to be used in aircraft and military facilities. Attempts to launch a pulp industry failed between 1913 and the mid-1920s[58] but succeeded in 1954 at Ketchikan and 1959 at Sitka.[59] International demand for pulp and, to a lesser extent, lumber from the Southeast rapidly increased at the time of statehood. Massive clearcutting wrought such violence on old-growth forests and wildlife that environmentalists (including, prominently, John Muir's Sierra Club) and wildlife managers organized to oppose it, setting in motion a struggle that lasted out the century.[60]

Interior forests, while frequently ravaged by fire, did not lend themselves to large-scale cutting for lumber and pulpwood after statehood. Relatively small in diameter and found along scattered river valleys seldom reached by roads, they cost too much to harvest. Only a small market for the wood existed locally, and that need could be met by lumber from Canada or the Pacific Northwest, delivered by the Alaska Railroad.[61] Although fires continued to burn considerable acreage after statehood, the interior suffered only slight habitat degradation and fragmentation from logging roads.

Loss of trees degraded stream valleys, and broader environmental changes followed forest fires. White spruce, the dominant upland tree, burned readily. Aspen and paper birch usually replaced it, and a full return to the white spruce climax stage required about 160 years. Fire tended to kill small furbearers, especially martens, weasels, foxes, and lynx. In that respect it worked a disproportionate hardship on Indians, who relied on trapping for income. Birch and aspen growth favored moose, at least until the trees grew taller. Loss of white spruce and the lichens growing on them and on the forest floor had a direct detrimental effect on caribou. Recovery of lichens took 40 years or more. The Gold

Wood yard at Tanana River Railway, ca. 1905–1910. Cole coll. 76-38-20, University of Alaska Fairbanks, Alaska and Polar Regions Archives. The railroad burned wood in its locomotives, used it for railroad ties, and delivered it to mining sites. Added to forest fires, the use of wood for mining, steamboats, railroads, heating, and power generation stripped many hills and valleys of trees.

Rush, perhaps supplemented by climatic warming, almost certainly reduced caribou populations in subarctic Alaska. Burning added nutrients to the soil but depleted the supply of timber needed for economic development.[62]

Neither Muir nor others of his time could foresee the effects of global warming to be manifested in the 21st Century. Alaska's average temperature rose about 4 degrees F from 1960 to 2000 and promised to continue. A warmer climate favored the spread of bark beetles and fire, reducing the white spruce forests of the interior and associated populations of caribou and marten. Melting permafrost would cause large-scale land erosion, siltation of watercourses, and further loss of spruce forests. Tundra would be progressively converted to steppe. Release of carbon by fire and permafrost melting would increase atmospheric carbon dioxide, accelerating the changes. Rising sea levels would destroy coastal habitat for great numbers of waterfowl and other creatures. Higher ocean temperatures would diminish populations of salmon and affect sea mammals. In the Arctic, sea ice melting would jeopardize the survival of seals and polar bears. Many or most of the glaciers so loved by Muir could disappear.[63] The ecological impact of global warming might well exceed all the depredations of pre-statehood eras.

COAL, COPPER, AND AGRICULTURE

Twentieth-Century development stimulated the use of coal, resulting in both positive and negative effects on the environment. Found in small deposits of varying quality in widely scattered locations around Alaska, coal served the Natives, Russians, prospectors, and settlers. Most frequently burned for residential and mining purposes, it also helped fuel steamships offshore and on the Yukon River. Discovery of large deposits in the Matanuska Valley and south of Nenana appeared to justify building an Alaska Railroad from Seward to Fairbanks, completed in 1923. The railroad, intended to support mining in the interior for economic development, could burn the coal as well as deliver it. Locomotives utilized coal until the late 1940s when they converted to diesel fuel. Coal heated some buildings throughout the territorial period and generated electricity for civilian and military use. Only the Usibelli coal mine at Healy operated after 1971.[64] Coal had taken the pressure off interior forests, and, to a large degree, oil and natural gas replaced coal. Marginal deposits and moderate exploitation of coal permitted Alaska to avoid the pervasive land scarring and water poisoning typical of coal mining regions in the Lower 48.

Next to gold, copper accounted for the most mining activity in Alaska. Natives had used it for centuries, and white prospectors began to look for it in the late 1890s. They found the most productive and accessible lodes in south-central Alaska near Prince William Sound. Among 200 sites along the sound, 8 produced substantial volumes of ore. In 1900, prospectors Clarence Warner and Jack Smith discovered what became the Kennecott Company's Bonanza mine 50 miles up the Copper River from Cordova. The Guggenheim group and others tried to build a railroad to it from Valdez and Katalla, but mountainous territory foiled the attempts. A railway from Cordova, constructed between 1906 and 1911, succeeded. Mining rapidly exhausted the most valuable deposits. Bonanza, the last large mine, closed in 1938. Between 1900 and 1930, Alaska had produced $212 million of copper compared to $400 million of gold.

Copper mining had minimally affected the Alaskan environment, considering that most of the ore went to Washington for smelting. Boosters had hoped the Copper River and Northwestern Railway would be extended into the interior and open it up to settlement and economic development. But the railway folded in 1938 when the mine closed. Copper had not set off a rush as gold did, and the small towns it created either withered away or turned to enterprises such as fishing.[65]

TABLE 4.2. Agricultural Activity in Alaska, 1940–1969

Year	*Farms (full- and part-time)*	*Acres*	*Products Sold ($ million)*
1940	623	11,000	n.d.
1959	367	14,500	3.2
1964	382	16,500	3.8
1969	332	13,000	3.6

Source: Orlando W. Miller, *The Frontier in Alaska and the Matanuska Colony.* New Haven: Yale University Press, 1975, 223–224.

Agriculture, the primary source of environmental degradation in the States, bore far less economic potential in Alaska. Aided by federal funds during the Depression, settlers established commercial farms in the relatively small Matanuska Valley north of Anchorage. Similarly, the Tanana River Valley near Fairbanks produced some commercial crops. Suitable land existed along the west coast of the Kenai Peninsula. Kodiak Island and parts of the Alaska Peninsula and Aleutian Islands could support cattle or sheep grazing to a degree. A few types of vegetables for personal use could be grown in many areas, including the lower Arctic. But commercially viable farming faced numerous obstacles: cool air and ground temperatures; short growing seasons; unfavorable soils; high operating costs including land preparation, processing, transportation, and winter maintenance of livestock; and price competition from food shipped from the States.[66]

Notwithstanding the limits imposed by location, Alaska boosters insisted that the territory possessed the agricultural potential to support large numbers of people, millions by some calculations. If only the federal government would subsidize farm settlement, they believed, agriculture would open up the territory to development. The American pioneer spirit would conquer the wilderness in the name of progress. Besides underwriting the Matanuska Colony, government policy resulted in scattered settlement elsewhere. But agriculture attained only a weak and uncertain position in Alaska's economy (Table 4.2). As historian Orlando Miller described the workings of the frontier myth,

> Local pride, a belief that growth and size mean progress, and an awareness of the gains to be made from rising property values and increased retail trade explain the boosting activities, but in addition promoters, journalists, and politicians swayed to their own incantations. . . . [T]hey eagerly awaited the urban and industrial development that Americans outside sometimes nostalgically regretted and hoped to escape in Alaska. . . . In the postwar period continued frontierism was a means of blinking away complex economic and social problems that could not be escaped in the wilderness. For all but an eccentric or unusual few, pioneer settlement meant not opportunity but poverty.[67]

Matanuska Colony farm, Palmer, 1937. Drawbaugh coll. 89-128-151, University of Alaska Fairbanks, Alaska and Polar Regions Archives. Agriculture made limited inroads into wildlife habitat because of cold, unsuitable soils, and transportation costs.

By the time of statehood only 367 farms, most worked by part-time farmers, produced 14,500 acres of crops, much of it grasses for livestock. A handful of families from the Matanuska Colony still farmed full-time. The Matanuska Valley and its environs produced 70 percent of Alaskan agricultural value. Few, if any, of the conditions inhibiting agriculture improved after statehood.[68]

John Muir committed an oft-to-be-repeated error in assuming that the Gold Rush and related settlement could not hurt Alaska's environment. One dramatic example suggested otherwise: in 1898, prospectors endured weeks or months of the most exhausting and dangerous trials of their lives to reach the remote goldfields of the Klondike. By mid-1900, thanks to the White Pass and Yukon Railway and steamboats in Canada, one could ride in comfort from Seattle to Dawson in less than a week.[69] Other stimuli as powerful as gold—such as war or oil—might similarly break down the barriers to Alaskan wilderness.

Followers of John Muir and other advocates of wilderness preservation have often perceived wilderness as a state of Nature unaltered by humans. The fact that many wildlands have been lastingly influenced by set fires or other human activities has suggested the need for a more flexible concept of wilderness. But what degree of temporary or permanent disruption should make a wild area unworthy of protection? Does the constant change in Nature, with or without human intervention, render the notion of "preservation" meaningless? Should consumptive uses, such as those claimed as subsistence rights, be considered natural or be allowed in protected ecosystems? These questions became part of the debates over disposal of natural resources in Alaska.

MUIR AS POLITICAL ACTIVIST

Years after their Alaskan adventures, Hall Young visited Muir's successful California fruit farm where he found his friend chafing in his harness. "I am losing the precious days," lamented Muir; "I am degenerating into a machine for making money. I am learning nothing in this trivial world of men. I must get out into the mountains and learn the news." Muir's obsessive attention to farmwork also wore down his health. Alaska trips revived him both physically and spiritually, renewing his enthusiasm for Nature. Farm profits enabled him to return his attention to experiencing and writing about Nature.[70]

Muir's writings attracted the attention of Robert Wood Johnson, editor of the prestigious New York magazine *Century*, who acted as a powerful ally in the wilderness preservation movement. Johnson journeyed to California in 1889 and asked Muir to continue writing nature preservation articles for *Century*. They visited Toloumne Meadows in the Yosemite Valley and witnessed the damage being done by logging, mining, and grazing. They decided to launch a campaign to preserve Yosemite and its surroundings. Muir would write supportive articles and Johnson would contact members of Congress and the Harrison administration. In October 1890 their plan succeeded.[71] The resultant Yosemite National Forest Preserve, later named Yosemite National Park, surrounded Yosemite Valley, which had been ceded to California as a park in 1864. Five days before the Yosemite vote and almost certainly influenced by the efforts of Johnson and Muir, Congress created the reserve that evolved into Sequoia National Park. Publicity generated by the Yosemite effort spurred the implementation of the 1891 Forest Reserves Act that enabled President Benjamin Harrison to set aside 13 million acres, including the Afognak reserve in Alaska. Muir and Johnson, among others, co-founded the Sierra Club (1892), dedicated to the enjoyment and preservation of the Sierras. Muir served as president until his death.[72]

Muir increasingly assumed the character of public figure and political activist. Alarmed at the razing of forests by private interests, he assisted the efforts of utilitarian conservationists to create reserves for the public benefit. Like the Progressives coming to prominence, he fought against the social Darwinist idea that natural competition required conquest of Nature and that government should facilitate the process by minimizing regulation. Muir argued that citizens should be educated to appreciate Nature and government should protect it. Uncontrolled exploitation of Nature, such writers as George Perkins Marsh warned, would be disastrous for humans as well. When in 1896 a federal Forestry Commission of scientists chosen to evaluate forest policy invited Muir to participate as an ex-officio member, he accepted. No comprehensive policy had been written for federal wildlands, and Muir and Johnson recognized the opportunity to set a precedent by establishing protection as a goal. Muir acted as unofficial publicist for the commission's activities, expressing spiritual values but cautiously avoiding a preservationist stance. The commission recommended corrective measures, including a ban on grazing, and President Grover Cleveland reserved 21 million acres before he left office in 1897. But the new McKinley administration withheld the report from the public, and Congress passed and McKinley signed a bill removing protective restrictions from the reserves and encouraging commercial development.[73]

Preservationists called on Muir to defend Cleveland's forest reservation decree, under heavy attack from Western senators beholden to logging, grazing, and mining interests. In a pair of *Atlantic Monthly* articles he fought back:

> Any fool can destroy trees. They cannot run away, and if they could they would still be destroyed—chased and hunted down as long as fun or a dollar could be got out of their black hides, branching horns or magnificent bole backbones. . . . Through all the wonderful, eventful centuries since Christ's time—and long before that—God has cared for these trees . . . but he cannot save them from fools. Only Uncle Sam can do that.

Public opposition swelled and a bill to abolish the reserves, having passed the Senate, died in the House.[74]

Muir had befriended and supported Gifford Pinchot, a member of the Forestry Commission and the leading exponent of utilitarian values who later served as Theodore Roosevelt's first chief of the Forest Service. Eventually it dawned on Muir that utilitarianism meant loss of the forests' wilderness character. Hearing of Pinchot's advocacy of sheep grazing in the reserves, Muir personally confronted him in 1897. Their friendship entered a downward course from which it never recovered. From what he had seen in the mountains, Muir regarded sheep as "hoofed locusts," and "[a]s sheep advance, flowers, vegetation, grass, soil, plenty, and poetry vanish."[75] Muir's break from Pinchot, the prime mover of the federal utilitarian conservation effort, constituted both symbol and substance of the division between conservationists and preservationists lasting through the 20th Century.

Only preservation made sense to a thinker so convinced of the spiritual and ecological values of Nature. Yet preservation on public lands could not easily be achieved even on a minor scale. Any restriction on exploitation by Euro-Americans would have to overcome trenchant resistance from corporate interests or settlers. It would have to mobilize significant elements of a public either apathetic or sympathetic toward exploitative behavior. And it would require a variety of compromises. Accordingly, Muir somewhat reluctantly accepted a public role of heroic nature philosopher as a means of generating public influence. He hosted numerous tourists in Sierra parks in hopes that they would gain a love for Nature and support future parks. To these ends, Muir and the Sierra Club even advocated the construction of numerous trails and roads in wild areas.[76]

Although he did not win all his battles, Muir grew increasingly prominent. Both Roosevelt and Taft, while serving as president, visited him during trips to California. Roosevelt described his time alone with Muir, when they camped out in Yosemite during a snowy night in 1903, as "the grandest day of my life." He made a greater concession when Muir asked him, "When are you going to get beyond the boyishness of killing things . . . are you not getting far enough along to leave that off?" Replied the world's best-known hunter, "Muir, I guess you are right." Muir's efforts helped make possible Roosevelt's designation of 148 million acres of forest reserves, including the Grand Canyon, between 1902 and 1909.[77]

Muir participated in the Harriman Expedition, a grand finale for the naturalists' 19th-Century Alaska trips. Paid for and headed by railroad magnate Edward H. Harriman, the expedition combined an exotic vacation and an elite scientific undertaking. A handpicked coterie of 23 top natural scientists—in addition to artists, photographers, and others—boarded a comfortably outfitted ship, the *George W. Elder,* and sailed Alaskan waters from the Southeast to the Arctic and Siberian coasts during the summer of 1899. The plan succeeded in providing a unique experience for all and reinforcing a network of influentials.[78] Harriman's other purposes for the trip achieved mixed success. Like some other wealthy adventurers of the period, he shot a brown bear. He gained temporary status in New York society, but his hope of linking the hemispheres by a railroad tunnel under the Bering Strait fell by the wayside.[79] The expedition's ensuing books and articles expanded awareness of Alaska and its resources, although not especially toward resource conservation.

Muir's ties to Harriman, president of the politically influential Southern Pacific Railroad, paid dividends in the campaign to add Yosemite Valley to the surrounding national preserve.[80] California governor James Pardee had accompanied Muir and Roosevelt on the 1903 Yosemite outing. He promised Sierra Club member William Colby, also in the group, that he would sign a bill to return Yosemite Valley to national control if it could pass the legislature. Muir and Colby made nine lobbying trips to Sacramento, and the Sierra Club–led effort paid off. Another lobbying campaign, supported by the Union Pacific

John Muir (right) and John Burroughs at St. Matthew Island, 1899. By Edward Curtis. Harriman coll. RBD 0201-118, University of Alaska Fairbanks, Alaska and Polar Regions Archives. Through his writings and political work, Muir made lasting contributions to environmental protection in Alaska.

Railroad over which Harriman also presided, culminated in a congressional vote to accept the property in 1906.[81]

As much as he loved Alaska, Muir never returned after the 1899 trip. Embroiled in the fight to save Yosemite, he devoted his time to politics and the education of public opinion. The Yosemite success preceded a long and acrimonious conflict over Hetch Hetchy Valley to the north. In late 1913 Congress approved the dam that would drown the valley. Muir had lost the contest and exhausted himself in the process. He died in December 1914. In addition to the glacier, Muir is remembered by Muir Inlet and Muir Point in Glacier Bay National Park and Mt. Muir in the Chugach Range.[82]

John Muir exercised a powerful, if mainly indirect, impact on Alaska, in the first instance by drawing attention to its natural beauty. His writings stimulated ecotourism and ultimately bore fruit in the establishment of Glacier Bay National Park (Chapter 8). Had he lived longer, he would certainly have approved of this and other Alaskan parkland designations. It is difficult to determine, but doubtful, that by attracting people to Alaska for aesthetic purposes he enhanced the environmental values of settlers.

Muir perceived no significant environmental threat to Alaska, not projecting impacts to a time when visitors and technology would be multiplied. He did not address the question of whether subsistence uses of the land by Natives or others could be considered natural and compatible with wildland preservation. Beyond making his preservation sentiments known, as in the case of polar bear killing, he did not directly participate in Alaskan resource disputes.

In the long run, as an icon of nature preservation, Muir substantially advanced environmental awareness and values in Alaska and elsewhere. The territory held six of the reserves created by Roosevelt, persuaded in some degree by Muir. The Sierra Club evolved into a significant participant in Alaskan environmental issues after statehood. It played a central role in the Alaska lands settlement legislation of 1971 and 1980, two of the most important environmental events in 20th-Century North America. It took the lead in protecting the Tongass National Forest from logging that bid fair to destroy it and participated in nearly all the environmental disputes that marked the statehood period. One of its members, Stephen T. Mather, became the first director and builder of the National Park Service, promoting the establishment of national monuments and parks in Alaska and elsewhere.

Like George Bird Grinnell and Henry W. Elliott, Muir pioneered national publicity and lobbying campaigns for natural resource preservation. In doing so, he won a reputation as the nation's leading spokesperson for wilderness. Perhaps most important, he gave force to an idea that reappeared in the thinking of environmentalists and their public following: that wilderness and its creatures possess beauty, dignity, and merit as elements of the community of life; that humans must learn to see themselves not as owners or conquerors but as fellow citizens of that community.

As a precursor or founder of the modern environmental community, Muir modeled and articulated many of its key values: ecosystem sustainability, nonconsumptive uses of Nature, corporate and government accountability, and public participation in resource disputes. Far ahead of his time, he believed in a holistic relationship of humans to nonhumans, including animal and species rights. He relied more on poetic appeals than on scientific data, although he excelled as a self-trained scientist and, when the need arose, as a political advocate. At the same time, his utopian concept of spiritual fulfillment through immersion in Nature would prove eternally difficult to translate into environmental policy. Nevertheless, he shifted the nation's environmental agenda closer to nature preservation.

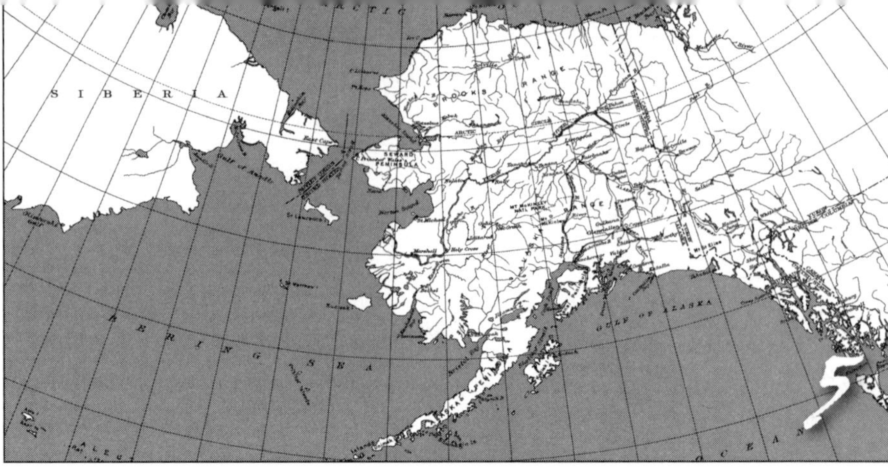

5

The Boone and Crockett Club

George Bird Grinnell, Madison Grant, William T. Hornaday,
Charles H. Townsend, Charles Sheldon

OF ALL THE INDIVIDUALS AND GROUPS RESPONSIBLE FOR THE PRESERVATION OF ALASKAN lands and wildlife, none deserves more credit than the Boone and Crockett Club. This small but highly effective organization fused the power of government and the perspectives of an outdoor-oriented elite to draft a blueprint for national land and wildlife protection. It led wildlife groups during the first decades of the conservation movement and adopted a disproportionate interest in Alaska.

Despite the immensity of the American land, its natural integrity soon withered before the driving force of entrepreneurship. In the face of apathy and opposition from the public and governments, a few early voices called for conservation of wildlife and wildlands. George Catlin pleaded in 1832 for a vast Western park to preserve both the land and the way of life of the Indians. In *Walden* (1854) Thoreau extolled the virtues of Nature as an antidote to industrializing civilization. George Perkins Marsh, having witnessed environmental collapse in the Near East and elsewhere, anticipated the ecological era by more than a century in *Man and Nature* (1864), warning that survival of civilization depended on maintenance of the integrity of the land. Frederick Law Olmsted urged the acquisition of public parks. In the 1870s Interior Secretary Carl Schurz and John Wesley Powell, later chief of the U.S. Geological Survey, advocated conservation of forests and watersheds. Such appeals made almost no impression on a Congress responsive to the demands of settlers and to timber, mining, grazing, railroad, and other acquisitive interests.

At the state level, on the other hand, outdoor sportsmen and nature groups began to press legislatures for conservation measures in the post–Civil War era. National publications, among them outdoor sporting magazines, acted as leading critics of the rampant despoiling of forests and wildlife. Bird watchers and other nature enthusiasts added their voices for reform, and humanitarians, opposed to mistreatment of animals, supplemented the push for conservation measures. An increasingly urbanized society grew less inclined to view Nature as a force to be conquered. Rather, Nature took on status as an asset to be conserved, appreciated, and even romanticized. Darwinian concepts of evolution revised the notion that humans possessed a divine right to dominate and exploit Nature. Not least, the Progressive Era of political reform lent force to the notion that natural resources should be conserved and rationally managed for the good of society.

Motives behind the conservation of wildlife and, therefore, what exactly should be conserved varied. Some like John Muir espoused spiritual values. Others worked for concepts of justice or efficiency, and many valued forms of recreation. Outdoor sportsmen wanted a guaranteed supply of fish and game, as did the arms industries that helped fund their organizations. A few elite hunter groups had broader goals in mind, including habitat preservation. One of these, the Boone and Crockett Club, initiated the effort that moved the federal government to action in wildlife protection. Its originator and leading light, George Bird Grinnell, transformed conservation in Alaska and the United States.

GEORGE BIRD GRINNELL

Grinnell (1849–1938) came from a privileged family in New York City. Huguenot immigrants to Rhode Island in 1630, the Grinnells attained prominent positions in business, education, and politics. George's grandfather represented Massachusetts in Congress, and his father ran textile and investment businesses in New York. An interest in birds gained reinforcement when at age seven George moved to Audubon Park where the family had purchased land from Lucy Bakewell Audubon, widow of John James. Mrs. Audubon, George's academic tutor, shaped his character as well as his interest in Nature. Surrounded by Audubon's paintings, artifacts, and accounts of expeditions, young George grew fascinated by the West. His father, his uncle Tom, and Audubon's sons John and Victor, who lived at Audubon Park, all encouraged his interest in birds and his work in taxidermy.

An undisciplined and indifferent student, George nevertheless entered Yale and graduated in 1870. That summer he joined Yale paleontologist Othniel C. Marsh in a fossil-hunting expedition to Nebraska, Wyoming, and Utah. He returned to employment at his father's investment firm and in 1872 accepted an invitation to participate in a traditional Pawnee buffalo hunt in Nebraska. This experience confirmed a lifelong interest in Indians, about whom he wrote extensively, and a concern about the destruction of the buffalo by market hunters.[1]

Traveling in the plains and Rockies, Grinnell personally encountered much of the American frontier. At least twenty books and as many articles flowed from his adventures with wildlife, hunters, Indians, Cavalry soldiers, and fortune seekers. General Custer chose him as a naturalist for the 1874 Black Hills expedition. The next year Grinnell accompanied the Ludlow expedition to the new Yellowstone National Park. When Custer sent word in 1876 inviting him to join the trip that ended in Little Big Horn country, duties prevented Grinnell from leaving his work at the Peabody Museum.[2]

Witnessing the decline of wildlife in the West, Grinnell derived an interest in conservation work. He inherited his father's investment firm but quickly tired of it and sold it. At the museum he completed a Yale doctorate in osteology and paleontology. In 1876 he signed on as natural history editor and, from 1879 to 1911, as editor-in-chief of the journal *Forest and Stream*, one of the earliest conservation-oriented outdoor magazines. He adopted and elaborated upon a code of "sportsmanship" originating in the British upper class, articulated by his editor predecessor Charles Hallock. The true "sportsman" took game in a restrained, clean, and dignified manner, within the context of an understanding of the quarry and its environment. By contrast, unsportsmanlike hunters killed wastefully, crudely, without great skill or knowledge, or, worst of all, for crass commercial gain. Grinnell also promulgated the British notion that sportsmanlike hunting instilled courage and strength of character, without which a nation would be vulnerable to aggressors.[3]

The gentleman-hunter concept, modified to idealize wilderness adventure as differentiated from the English day-in-the-field, evolved as a reaction to increased urbanization and alienation from Nature in everyday American life after the Civil War. It sought to keep alive pioneer virtues of rugged individualism as the frontier disappeared. A related phenomenon, nature appreciation, expressed the romantic ideal of spiritual fulfillment through closeness to Nature. The noble hunter and nature sophisticate conceptions also enabled established Americans of Anglo-Saxon origin to maintain their distance from the lower classes and southern European immigrants. The two images, popularized by such publications as *Forest and Stream*, spread to less privileged groups and added impetus to wildlife conservation action by government.[4]

Grinnell may also be seen as a practitioner and promoter of the myth of the American frontier superman. In this view, as the nation grew more industrialized and citified it began to lose the manly virtues of physical prowess, courage, self-reliance, integrity, freedom, and individualistic pursuit of progress that appeared to characterize leading men on the frontier. The society seemed to be "going soft," as had Europe. To nurture the frontier virtues, writers, scientists, and adventurers romanticized the West. They set about recording, collecting, and preserving its artifacts. Wealthy Eastern men, whose fortunes had often been made through destructive exploitation of the frontier, sought to link themselves to the frontier myth. They visited the West as explorers, hunters, or absentee ranch owners. However consciously, they wanted to define their manhood and legitimize their leadership in a modernizing world. Further, they considered pioneer virtues vital for the moral integrity of the nation and for the nation's standing in the world.

A model of the neo-frontiersman emerged in the form of the noble hunter-naturalist. As a hunter of big game in the wilderness away from the comforts of civilization, he could prove his courage, physical prowess, self-reliance, and ability to take aggressive action when needed. As a naturalist he demonstrated his education, discretion in taking game, and devotion to preserving the wildlife that gave the wilderness its special character. A successful hunter-naturalist could return from the wilds to the admiration of his colleagues and the public, rejuvenated as a leader in business, military, or civic affairs. Theodore Roosevelt best exemplified the model in the minds of the public. But George Bird Grinnell, Roosevelt's friend, may have done more to shape the hunter-naturalist image than any other person. His vision achieved some of its most enduring expressions in the writings of *Forest and Stream* and the workings of the Boone and Crockett Club.[5]

Convinced that organized greed threatened the very existence of wild resources as demonstrated by the fate of the buffalo, Grinnell embarked on a crusade to end market hunting and protect wildlife. Merging a business management concept and an appeal to democratic ideology, he called for management of forests and wildlife on behalf of the people as a whole rather than leaving their fate to a narrow few who destroyed for monetary gain. Protected forests, he contended, would be necessary for healthy game populations and should be managed by government professionals on a scientific basis for sustained yield. The notion of ownership by and for the public provided a basis for the American national park philosophy.[6]

Grinnell exercised an abiding influence on Theodore Roosevelt, whom he first met in New York in the early 1880s. Having read a Grinnell commentary questioning some of his assertions in *Hunting Trips of the Ranchman*, Roosevelt strode into the offender's office for a showdown. The two men took a liking to one another and met frequently thereafter to discuss mutual interests in Nature and the West, setting the stage for Roosevelt's commitment to conservation.[7] Grinnell persuaded Roosevelt to join the decade-long effort to save Yellowstone Park from ruin by hunters and commercial interests. Grinnell conceived the idea of an elite group of hunter-conservationists to model the ideals of true outdoor sportsmanship and to work for the preservation of game species. Roosevelt liked the plan and arranged a dinner meeting in 1887, attended by Grinnell, at which the Boone and Crockett Club originated. The club adopted its name from two famous frontiersmen who symbolized manly virtues. It received its direction from Roosevelt and from Grinnell, who used *Forest and Stream* as its voice. Through the Yellowstone campaign the club strengthened its public following.[8]

Historian John F. Reiger considered the Yellowstone episode, culminating in protective legislation in 1894, the beginning of the American conservation movement, for several reasons. First, the enabling law recognized the need for continual on-site management, a future standard for national lands. Second, the fight focused on saving the park's buffalo herd from poachers. This generated a national expression of support from the public, who lamented the destruction of the great herds on the plains and realized that wildlife would disappear if not protected. Third, the campaign involved top conservation leaders working together for the first time. Fourth, Yellowstone's designation as a national park presented a model for all forest reservations. The campaign and its outcome perfectly reflected Grinnell's philosophy and cemented Roosevelt's dedication to land and wildlife protection.[9]

A conservation measure crucial for American wildlands, the Forest Reserves Act of 1891, sought to curb the destruction of Western forests and their rapid appropriation by large private interests. General John W. Noble, Benjamin Harrison's secretary of the interior, succeeded in having the measure inserted in a bill in conference committee, and it passed without notice by Congress, which would almost certainly have opposed it.[10] The measure formed the legislative basis of the national forest system. Noble, a Boone and Crockett Club member, proved instrumental in convincing Harrison to support the first reserves.

Afognak Island in Alaska, among other candidates for reserve status, received Grinnell's attention. A study of Alaskan salmon fisheries ordered by Secretary Noble originated the effort. The team's report, reflecting concern over excessive commercial fishing, recommended setting aside part of Afognak as a salmon reserve. Officials called it the Afognak Forest and Fish Culture Reserve, but Grinnell saw it as a refuge for wildlife and applied his editorials and personal influence. Harrison signed the order in 1892.[11] Afognak Island, often cited as the first federal wildlife reserve, contributed to the conservation movement as an important early Boone and Crockett success and a step in involving outdoor sporting groups in national efforts to protect wildlife.[12]

Grinnell reinforced his ties to Alaska by joining the 1899 Harriman Expedition and authoring its report on the salmon industry. As an active member, foremost writer, and long-term president of Boone and Crockett, he directly or indirectly influenced every important Alaskan wildlife issue from the game law of 1902 to the Game Law of 1925 and Glacier Bay National Monument in 1925. He played a prominent role in the passing of the Lacey Act of 1900 to curb commercial exploitation of mammals and birds. He participated in Roosevelt's 1902–1909 forest reserve selections, the Migratory Bird Acts of 1913 and 1918, and the establishment of Katmai National Monument in 1918.

Outside Alaska, Grinnell's initiative led directly to the establishment of Glacier National Park in 1910. In addition to the Boone and Crockett Club, he had founded and directed the forerunner of the National Audubon Society in 1886. It failed because he could not handle the paperwork; 50,000 people had joined by 1888. Local chapters continued and the national organization revived in 1905. Grinnell helped found the New York Zoological Society (1895), Society of American Foresters (1900), North American Wildlife Foundation (1935), and Wildlife Management Institute (1935). He held leadership positions in the National Audubon Society, National Park Committee, and National Parks Association. President Calvin Coolidge presented him the Roosevelt Memorial Service Award in 1925.[13] The citation stated in part, "[N]one has done more to preserve vast areas of picturesque wilderness. . . . [Y]ou have done a noteworthy service in bringing to the men and women of a harried and worried age the relaxation and revitalization which comes with nature."[14]

Historian James B. Trefethen described Grinnell as "a forerunner of the preservationist school of conservation" and assessed his character as follows:

> Grinnell was quiet, modest and self-effacing to the point of shyness, but his personal accomplishments and experience rival fiction. His circle of friends ranged from frontier trappers and Indian warriors to generals, millionaires, leaders in Congress, cabinet members and Presidents of the United States. . . . As Aldo Leopold is recognized as the founder of modern wildlife management, Grinnell in many ways was the spiritual father of Leopold.[15]

New York Times editors titled Grinnell the "father of American conservation."[16]

Politically astute and moderate as well as a hunter, Grinnell could appreciate the viewpoints of nonhunters. As the elder statesman of the conservation movement in the 1920s and 1930s, he bridged the gap between the two groups, making possible many achievements in wildlife conservation. Grinnell molded and moved several of the central American conservation principles of the 20th Century.

George Bird Grinnell at Yale, ca. 1890s. Yale University Archives. Few if any Americans did more than Grinnell to advance wildlife conservation.

Boone and Crockett endured for 40 years or more as one of the leading groups in the conservation movement. During the first three decades of the 20th Century the club operated in close coordination with eight other outdoor sporting and nature organizations: American Bison Society, American Game Protective Association, American Ornithologists' Union, American Society of Mammalogists, American Museum of Natural History, Camp Fire Club of America, National Association of Audubon Societies, and New York Zoological Society. Club members had taken the lead in founding most of these groups. About three dozen prominent men who knew one another sat on their governing boards. This "interlocking directorate," essentially controlled by Boone and Crockett, made up the core of the conservation movement.[17] Roosevelt's presidency (1901–1909) enhanced the movement's power and advanced its goals considerably. Club members enjoyed access, often behind the scenes, to a wide range of top government officials, some of them associate members of the club. For over half a century virtually every chief of the Bureau of Biological Survey and its successor, the Fish and Wildlife Service, held a regular or associate membership.

MADISON GRANT

Grinnell's background and interests closely paralleled those of another leading hunter-naturalist in Alaska's environmental future, Madison Grant (1865–1937). A New York patrician, lawyer, and son of a prominent physician and city health commissioner who won a Congressional Medal of Honor for gallantry in the Civil War, Grant knew how to operate in the political realm. His earlier ancestors had settled in New York and New England in the 1620s and 1630s and become religious, political, and military leaders. One, Robert Treat Paine, signed the Declaration of Independence. The Grant family lived in a mansion on Long Island where Madison played in the surrounding countryside and developed a love for wild creatures. In his teens he studied in Germany.

Following degrees at Yale in 1887 and Columbia Law School in 1890, Grant opened a law office in New York City. Not much interested in law, he pursued an active social life in the exclusive clubs where wealthy men spent their time. He founded and led several organizations. Some of these, such as the Society of Colonial Wars, emphasized the historical prominence of the members' families. Outside of New York, Grant engaged in big game hunting—in the West, Canada, and Alaska's Kenai Peninsula. He met George Bird Grinnell, who nominated him for Boone and Crockett Club membership.[18] Close friends, the two worked together on conservation issues for more than 40 years.

Quickly assuming a leadership role within Boone and Crockett, Grant became the driving force behind its conservation activities. He soon won the confidence of Theodore Roosevelt, another man of highly similar background and interests. After Roosevelt moved to Washington in 1894 to serve on the Civil Service Commission, he left the day-to-day activities in the hands of Grinnell and Grant. They shifted the focus of club activities from social get-togethers toward political action. Grant's quiet demeanor and multiple contacts among the Eastern elite suited the club's lobbying agenda. He organized legislative efforts and moved them forward by meeting key people in private settings. Grinnell, a member of some of the same social clubs, advanced the agenda through *Forest and Stream*.[19]

Grant and Grinnell kept in daily contact to develop political strategy. They first attacked market hunting and worked for state and federal laws to stop it. They understood the need for habitat as distinct from species protection and strove for the creation of forest reserves. Grant persuaded Gifford Pinchot, Roosevelt's chief forester and a fellow Boone and Crockett member, to recommend forest reserves in the West and Alaska. Pinchot opposed wildlife sanctuaries in national parks, however.

Moving in a preservationist direction, Grant pushed for national parks and for game reserves in national forests. He believed, and convinced many of his hunting colleagues including Roosevelt, that other creatures had a right to exist. Boone and Crockett set up a committee on refuges in 1901 and became the most prominent force for American wildland preservation. The committee, largely through Grant, achieved its goal through the establishment of Mt. McKinley, Glacier, Olympic, and Everglades national parks.[20]

Well ahead of his time in thinking about predators, Grant saw them as beneficial in that they weeded out the less fit of their prey. He expressed the belief publicly in 1911. Supplementing the efforts of the American Society of Mammalogists and the New York Zoological Society, Boone and Crockett officially opposed predator control in 1929. Grant helped convince the conservation community that wildlife, like other aspects of society, needed to be managed.

Madison Grant at Yale, 1912. Yale University Archives. Grant and Grinnell led Boone and Crockett Club efforts in wildlife conservation.

Boone and Crockett's game preservation committee officially endorsed game management in 1915, citing the overpopulation of elk in Yellowstone after removal of predators.[21]

Observing the multiplying encroachments on game during his travels, Grant worried about their prospects for survival. Of the Alaska situation he wrote, "It should be clearly understood that the game of Alaska, or any other region, does not belong exclusively to the human inhabitants of that particular region. . . . The interest of the entire people of the U.S. and to some extent that of the civilized world, is centered in the continued existence of the forms of animal life which have come down to us from an immense antiquity through the slow process of evolution." As a hunter and established Boone and Crockett member he pinned the blame for Alaska wildlife depletion on commercial hunting:

> The destruction of game is far more often effected by local residents than it is by visiting sportsmen, but the chief evildoer, and the public enemy of all classes, is the professional hunter, either Indian or white, who kills for the market. Worse still, perhaps, is the professional dealer in heads and antlers, who employs such hunters to provide game heads for the decoration of the banquet halls of the growing class of would-be sportsmen, who enjoy the suggestion of hunting prowess conferred by a selected collection of purchased heads.[22]

Grant's answer to the threat to big game species went beyond game protection laws: "[P]reserves should be set aside in Alaska, while land is yet of little value. . . . Certain islands should also be utilized, particularly in southeastern Alaska. Beyond doubt such refuges will ultimately be established, but it is to be hoped that they can be done before the game is decimated and the forests cut down and burned."[23] It took seven more decades to win protection for the brown bears on Admiralty Island, one of the objects of Grant's concern.

Grant's interest in Alaska and love of wildlife naturally focused on the welfare of game species. The rapid expansion of market hunting to supply the gold miners sparked action by Boone and Crockett. Grant organized a 1901 exploring and collecting expedition led by Andrew J. Stone and funded by the New York Zoological Society, Boone and Crockett, and the American Museum of Natural History. Stone's party traveled down the Mackenzie and Yukon rivers and along the coast to Southeast Alaska. Also in 1901 Grant sent J. Alden Loring to the Cook Inlet region. Loring's portrayals of the waste of wildlife moved Grant and his colleagues to action to stop market hunting in Alaska.

Grant and his friend and fellow Boone and Crockett member, Representative John F. Lacey of Iowa, collaborated to draft a bill to stop the market export of game from Alaska. The first protective game law for the territory, it passed in 1902. Market hunters objected, but Grant insisted that the law would benefit the individual Alaskan by conserving game. He returned to Alaska in 1907 as part of an expedition to dig up a mastodon skeleton and toured the interior to assess the game situation. He gained the impression that, while the export of game had been controlled, irresponsible killing had continued. Alaska Natives, he believed, destroyed more than white hunters did. A 1908 law, influenced by Boone and Crockett, introduced more flexibility in regulations and reduced the number of trophies a nonresident could export.[24]

Outside of Alaska, Grant participated decisively in a long list of important government decisions. He and Lacey co-drafted the Lacey Act of 1900 that increased the national government's responsibility for wildlife. Another monumental measure, the Migratory Bird Act of 1913, owed much to Grant.[25] He took leadership positions in efforts to save the pronghorn antelope, European bison, whales, Galapagos tortoises, mountain gorillas, and numerous other endangered species. These measures and the setting aside of reserves lent both strength and legitimacy to government protection of wildlife. They set precedents to be followed by states, other nations, and subsequent actions by the federal government.

An inveterate joiner, Grant held leadership positions in more than 30 organizations. Of those working on conservation on a national level, he co-founded the American Bison Society (1905), the National Parks Association (1919), and, with John C. Merriam of the University of California, the Save-the-Redwoods League (1919). He founded the American Committee for International Wildlife Protection (1930) and presided over Boone and Crockett for the last twelve years of his life. The 1,605-acre Madison Grant Forest and Elk Refuge (1946) preserves a stand of redwoods in memory of Grant's work. He is also honored in the naming of *Rangifer tarandus granti*, or Grant's caribou. Originally denoting the subspecies encountered by Andrew Stone in 1901 on the Alaska Peninsula, the name later applied to all caribou in Alaska and the Yukon.[26]

Grant's concerns about disappearing wildlife and the necessity of management to maintain populations influenced his social theory. A "splitter" mammalogist, he saw numerous racial distinctions among humans. Like wildlife, he thought, some races are superior to others. He noted the disruption caused by alien wildlife species and the dramatic influx of immigrants in New York. He concluded that immigration, particularly from southern and eastern Europe, posed a threat to both wildlife and the social order. In addition to his respected writings on wildlife, Grant promulgated theories of racial distinction and hierarchy that made him an internationally recognized racist. Notwithstanding his numerous accomplishments in wildlife conservation, the loss of support among scientists caused his conservation work to be nearly forgotten.[27]

Boone and Crockett counted as one of its most significant accomplishments the creation of the New York Zoological Society (NYZS) to oversee a zoological park for New York wherein animals could enjoy semi-natural surroundings. Madison Grant, the prime mover, and C. Grant La Farge succeeded in lobbying the bill through the New York Legislature in April 1895. Boone and Crockett exercised an abiding influence over NYZS through Grant and Henry Fairfield Osborn.[28] The NYZS envisioned much more than a park; it planned to advance wildlife preservation. Even before the New York Zoological Park (popularly called the Bronx Zoo) opened in 1899, writings on endangered species appeared in the society's bulletin. Thereafter NYZS, later renamed the Wildlife Conservation Society, took part in several Alaskan and many national and international efforts to preserve wild creatures.

WILLIAM T. HORNADAY

Grant and Osborn selected as the New York Zoological Park's first director William Temple Hornaday, a noted zoologist and taxidermist. Hornaday (1854–1937) grew up on farms in Indiana and Iowa, where he spent plenty of time outdoors. At sixteen he entered Oskaloosa College for a year, and then transferred to Iowa State College at Ames. There he studied natural sciences for two years and decided on a career in taxidermy and museum work. In 1873 he signed on as an apprentice taxidermist in Ward's Natural History Establishment in Rochester, New York, an institution that fielded collecting expeditions and supplied specimens to museums. Hornaday's excellent work won him a six-year assignment as a collector in the Caribbean, South America, India, Ceylon, the Malay Peninsula, and Borneo. He brought back the greatest aggregation of faunal specimens ever gathered by one person—all of which he had personally prepared. In 1880 he co-founded the American Society of Taxidermists, and in 1882 he became chief taxidermist at the Smithsonian. There he developed his ideas for more realistic displays, including family groupings in natural habitat.

An 1886 trip to the West impressed on him the extent of devastation of wild mammals. He resolved to fight for wildlife protection and in 1889 wrote *The Extermination of the American Bison*.

When Congress appropriated funds for a National Zoological Park, the Smithsonian named Hornaday director. But he could not abide the controlling behavior of the Smithsonian's new director, Samuel P. Langley, so he resigned in 1890 and entered the real estate business. When the Boone and Crockett Club succeeded in launching the New York Zoological Park, Hornaday accepted its directorship in 1896.[29]

Boone and Crockett and New York Zoological Society board members Madison Grant and Henry Fairfield Osborn acted decisively in the formulation of the park and its policies, as well as its spin-off organizations and projects. Hornaday directed the New York Zoological Park until his retirement in 1926. At a meeting hosted by the park, NYZS co-founded the American Bison Society. As co-founder, first president, and a strong champion of the society, Hornaday earned much of the credit for rescuing the buffalo from the edge of extinction. In 1911, through NYZS, he organized the Permanent Wild Life Protection Fund, eventually a leader in the creation of parks and wildlife preserves in Africa and other continents. Hornaday's book *Our Vanishing Wild Life* went into print just in time to aid passage of the federal Migratory Bird Act of 1913. Also in 1913 he authored the key provision of a bill backed by conservation groups, banning the importation of exotic birds for use in women's hats.[30] In all, he wrote twenty books and numerous magazine articles and letters to editors.[31]

Maintaining a lively interest in Alaska even though he never visited it, Hornaday helped bring into being the game laws of 1902 and 1908. In a 1902 article in *Recreation Magazine* he raged against the loss of wildlife and pointed out that "there is not one line of game law to protect the game of Alaska or restrict its slaughter in any manner." He urged readers to support a bill before Congress declaring the Kenai Peninsula a wildlife preserve and empowering the president to create others by proclamation. He called for a game preserve to take in a wide coastal strip from Bristol Bay to Yakutat, including Kodiak-Afognak islands and the Alaska and Kenai peninsulas.[32] He directed heavy criticism at the lack of controls on hunting by Natives and prospectors. "Alaska and its resources," he asserted, "do not belong to the very few people from 'the States' who have gone there to make their fortunes and get out again as quickly as possible." He recommended banning the sale of wild game, quadrupling the warden force, halving the bag limits on big game, and instituting a ten-year moratorium on the killing of walruses for their ivory.[33] Most of these suggestions ultimately became law.

Hornaday worked tirelessly for decades to save wildlife species. He aggressively criticized commercial hunting and the arms industry and incurred the wrath of hunter-conservationists with his opposition to sport hunting. A former hunter for museums, he evolved into militant if somewhat selective preservationism: "The wild life of the world is not ours, to dispose of wholly as we please. We hold it *in trust*, for the benefit of ourselves, and equal benefits to those who come after us. As honorable guardians we have no right to waste and squander the heritage of our grandchildren. It is our duty to stay the hand that strives to apply the torch." He did not hesitate to identify "the hand." Terming them an "army of destruction," he declared, "In the United States there are about 5,000,000 gunners, game-hogs and sportsmen. In that entire multitude I venture to say that there are not over 2,000 men or boys who by reason of *their own high principles* could be trusted in country to hunt wild game *wholly unrestrained by the hand of the law*."[34] He believed "the mental attitude of the men who shoot constitutes a deadly factor in the destruction of wild life and the extermination of species. Fully ninety-five percent of the sportsmen, gunners, and other men and boys who kill big game, all over the world and in all nations, regard game birds and mammals only as things to be killed and *eaten*, and not as creatures worth preserving for their beauty or their interest to mankind."[35]

Like most conservationists of his era, Hornaday thought wildlife needed protection from other wildlife as well as from humans. "Unmoral" animals, predators that killed other animals (of use to humans), needed to be "brought to justice." He made an exception for owls because they ate so many rodents. Reflecting the moralistic humanitarianism of the era and projecting it to non-humans, he foresaw a time when animals would no longer act violently toward one another. But as a zoo director, Hornaday fought back against humanitarian charges of the cruelty of caging wild creatures. He saw "no higher use" for an animal than to be in "comfortable captivity" where people could view it.[36]

Through his writings and political action, Hornaday helped shape environmental issues, including fur seal (Chapter 2) and migratory bird protection and the 1925 Alaska Game Law. After retirement he continued his efforts through the Permanent Wild Life Protection Fund. Summing up his career, he explained that "my chief object in life for the past fifty-four years has been to try to bring the wild creatures of the world to the human millions who cannot get to them. . . . But as an ethical estimate, my thirty-five years of fighting to preserve some wild life has ranked far above that academic work."[37] Never satisfied with the progress made by conservationists, he declared at age 80 that the thought of the ongoing destruction of wildlife still put him in a "red rage," inspiring him to continue his work.[38]

Hornaday resented not being accepted as a Boone and Crockett member despite his outstanding deeds as a big game collector. At length he gained associate membership. His tenacity, arrogance, and abrasiveness, backed by a rare

William T. Hornaday and buffalo calf, Washington, DC, 1890. Smithsonian Archives. A prominent museum director and ardent conservationist, Hornaday pushed for wildlife protection laws in Alaska.

talent for skewering his adversaries with well-chosen words, severely strained his connections to other conservationists.[39] His dedication and combative character also called attention to his causes and won support in the media and the public. He could claim among his admirers Theodore and Franklin Roosevelt. From his deathbed he wrote FDR asking him to do all he could to preserve wildlife; FDR replied that he would do so.[40] At FDR's request, Mt. Hornaday in Yellowstone National Park received its name following Hornaday's death.[41]

CHARLES H. TOWNSEND

Research scientist and associate Boone and Crockett member Charles Haskins Townsend (1859–1944) also cared about Alaskan environmental conditions. Townsend, a Pennsylvanian, studied zoology at Ward's Natural History Establishment and the Academy of Natural Sciences in Philadelphia. He then served the U.S. Fish Commission and as a field naturalist for the Smithsonian. He first visited Alaska in 1885 on the USS *Corwin* expedition up the Kowak (Kobuk) River. During nine years in the Pacific aboard the research vessel *Albatross,* he studied birds, walrus, sea lions, fur seals, and fish in the Bering Sea. Annual summer inspection trips to the seal rookeries in the Pribilofs between 1891 and 1897 led to membership on the Bering Sea and fur seal commissions. In 1902 he began a 35-year career as director of the New York Aquarium, a facility controlled by the New York Zoological Society. A leading authority on water life around the world, Townsend headed the effort for preservation of the Galapagos tortoises. Among Alaskan topics, he wrote on birds, sea mammals, fish, mammoths, and reindeer.[42]

While serving in 1911 on the Fur Seal Advisory Board, Townsend endorsed a limited harvest of male fur seals on the Pribilofs, thereby running afoul of his colleagues William T. Hornaday and Henry W. Elliott. An unpleasant encounter wherein his position met with defeat soured Townsend's feelings toward Hornaday.[43] Attempting to head off a congressional vote to postpone the seal harvest for five years, Townsend had written an article in the influential journal *Science*. The proposal, he said, originated from "men who had not been on the islands for twenty years [Elliott] and who cannot appreciate the recent detailed investigations. Severe criticisms have also been made by men [Hornaday] who have not been there at all, and whose opinions on the subject are of little value."[44]

Townsend had represented both the Cleveland and Taft administrations in fur seal negotiations. He possessed considerable knowledge of the animals, whereas Hornaday did not. David Starr Jordan and Bureau of Biological Survey chief C. Hart Merriam, also experienced in fur seal policy, backed Townsend, as did Boone and Crockett's game preservation committee. They adopted a utilitarian position advocating limited harvest, whereas Hornaday adamantly opposed any killing. Madison Grant tried in vain to smooth over relations between his friend Hornaday and the others. The dispute over the fur seals ended in a compromise five-year moratorium on killing at the Pribilofs.[45]

Townsend and Charles Sheldon worked for two decades on the game preservation committee, influencing a variety of Alaskan issues including the

Charles Haskins Townsend, 1918. Smithsonian Archives. A government marine scientist and aquarium director, Townsend began research in Alaska in 1885.

Game Law of 1925. The two men also helped lead the National Conference on Outdoor Recreation, Townsend chairing its fish committee.[46]

CHARLES SHELDON

Boone and Crockett recruited yet another and by no means the least significant of Alaska's early conservation leaders: Vermonter Charles Alexander Sheldon (1867–1928). Like Grinnell, Grant, and Roosevelt, Sheldon personified the ideals of the hunter-naturalist. A privileged first child of a prominent family that owned a prosperous marble business, Sheldon spent much of his youth outdoors. He entered Yale in 1886 and graduated in 1890 as a civil engineer, but the family business had failed, so he took a management trainee position in the Lake Shore and Southern Michigan Railway Company. His honest and friendly character showed in his peaceful settlement of a strike. From 1894 to 1898 he managed an Albany, New York, company that made heaters for railroad cars. His leadership skills came to the attention of investors who held railroad and mining interests in Mexico. On behalf of his investors he acquired a mine that turned out to be Mexico's top producer of silver; his share in the mine made him wealthy.[47]

Sheldon left Mexico in 1902. He had hunted big game there and found mountain sheep and grizzly bears especially appealing. He knew that the Bureau of Biological Survey (BBS) collected fauna from all over North America. In 1903 he went to Washington and met BBS chief C. Hart Merriam and Edward W. Nelson, the latter in charge of the Mexico field operation. They suggested that he combine hunting and collecting for the Smithsonian. In all, he contributed 554 specimens to the museum, 120 of them big game mammals.

Nelson had collected the first white mountain sheep from Alaska (and named the subspecies for William H. Dall) and wanted more information and specimens. BBS arranged a collecting trip to the Yukon, and Sheldon, BBS biologist Wilfred Osgood, and wildlife artist Carl Rungius arrived there in 1904.

Upon Sheldon's return home to New York the Boone and Crockett Club, at Nelson's recommendation, elected him to membership. There he befriended George Bird Grinnell, who trained him in conservation activism, and Theodore Roosevelt, whom he often visited at the White House and Sagamore Hill on Long Island.[48]

Sheldon hunted brown bears on Prince William Sound, Alaska, in May 1905. Next he collected sheep in the Yukon mountains until October. He wrote a popular book, *The Wilderness of the Upper Yukon*, about his experiences. A year later he stalked sheep and grizzly bears around Mt. McKinley from July to October. In summer 1907 he returned and, assisted by Alaskan outdoorsman Harry Karstens, built a cabin and remained over the winter to study Dall sheep. Sheldon had made himself the foremost authority on the subspecies. On their honeymoon trip in 1909, Sheldon and his bride camped and watched brown bears on Admiralty Island.[49]

Sheldon perceived the grizzly bear as the prime symbol of Alaskan wilderness and worked to protect it. Displaying astute political judgment and moderate utilitarian conservationist views, he succeeded in cultivating Alaskan support for the 1925 Game Law, for which he performed double duty as a principal author and a leading lobbyist.[50]

Upon discovering the notes from Sheldon's 1907–1908 Mt. McKinley adventure, his son asked him why they had not been published. "I've said enough about myself," replied Sheldon. Following his death the family published his best-known book, *The Wilderness of Denali*.[51] Sheldon's experiences in the Denali region inspired him to lead the successful drive (Chapter 6) to designate it a national park in 1917.

Sheldon persevered as a political activist. Like Grinnell and Grant, he preferred quiet diplomacy and allowed others to receive the credit for his achievements. Working closely alongside Grinnell and Nelson as chair of the game preservation committee, Sheldon committed himself to nearly full-time effort in wildlife protection. He moved the family to Washington in 1916 so he could more effectively carry out his work. Their home became a gathering spot for conservationists, hunters, and explorers, including Edward Nelson, Amundsen, and Byrd. Sheldon went on a few more collecting trips to the Southwest and worked to save the vanishing pronghorn antelope. After his death, Boone and Crockett raised money for a Charles Sheldon National Antelope Range in Nevada, so designated in 1931 and expanded to 540,000 acres by FDR in 1936.[52] It became the Sheldon National Wildlife Refuge.

Sheldon's philosophy derived from his own experience and that of the club: "Wildlife conservation will best be promoted by the encouragement of legitimate sport; of scientific interest in natural history; and by building up the public opinion to make and enforce wise laws."[53] Like some of his colleagues,

Sheldon believed that people, Americans in particular, derived moral and spiritual strength and physical well-being from closeness to Nature. He advocated a nationwide recreation plan, coordinated by the federal government, to establish parks and wild areas at national, state, and local levels.[54]

Sheldon served as leading organizer and a member of the permanent committee of the National Conference on Outdoor Recreation (1924–1929). The conference brought together government agencies and private groups to make numerous recommendations on wildlife management and the setting aside of natural areas. It succeeded in getting a high proportion of its resolutions translated into government policy, thus materially promoting modern wildlife management. It also helped raise outdoor recreation to national prominence as a valued realm of activity. Historian James B. Trefethen regarded the conference as Boone and Crockett's greatest single contribution.[55]

Of Sheldon's character C. Hart Merriam observed: "Sheldon was a splendid type of vigorous manhood; self reliant, courageous, of pleasing personality, possessed of sober, earnest dignity, unassuming, simple in tastes, kindly, generous and when estimating others always fair, giving due weight to their environment and opportunities."[56] Trefethen ventured that "probably no individual in the history of biological inquiry has possessed the rare combination of scientific curiosity, dedication to a cause, physical stamina, and financial independence that made his research possible." Roosevelt regarded him as a model Boone and Crockett member.[57] A man of such social standing and virtue fit the mold for national leadership in the conservation movement, and Sheldon filled the role.

By all appearances in good health, Sheldon died of a heart attack at age 60 at the family's summer home in Nova Scotia. His achievements and writings helped confirm Alaska's reputation as a wild, forbidding arena of adventure fit to challenge the best that a man could muster. At the same time, he left a priceless legacy to Alaskan wildlife conservation. But the ingredients of success for people like Sheldon, Grinnell, and Grant—a wealthy, influential, urban, Eastern elite who determined the fate of Alaska's resources from power bases in New York and Washington—fostered an image of outside control that embittered Alaskan attitudes toward the federal government for decades to come.

The scientists and hunter-naturalists of Boone and Crockett practiced stout advocacy of an advanced form of utilitarian conservation. In addition to the goal of protecting favored species, they called for refuges embodying many aspects of ecosystem sustainability. To the extent practicable they gathered scientific data and urged that wildlife management be government-controlled and science-based. Their devotion to wildlife, especially large land mammals, reached well beyond guaranteeing a supply for hunters; they believed the animals possessed inherent value. Hornaday and, to some extent, Grant articulated elements of species rights philosophy.

Boone and Crockett activities constituted an early, if elite, form of public activism, but the club formed productive alliances with nature associations and with outdoor sporting groups more narrowly interested in hunting and fishing. The club's inordinate access to decision-making power enabled it to see its ideas through to completion. Initially, its contributions to environmental thinking showed more in the States than in Alaska. Yet broad-scale Alaska land and wildlife protection, and specific accomplishments such as Mt. McKinley National Park and the 1925 Alaska Game Law, owed much to its efforts.

6

Charles Sheldon and Mt. McKinley National Park

CHARLES SHELDON STOOD OUT AMONG BOONE AND CROCKETT CLUB LEADERS IN expressing interest in Alaska. His experiences on the slopes of Mt. McKinley culminated in Alaska's second (after the 1910 Sitka National Historical Park) and most prominent national park. Originally intended to protect game species, the park evolved into a standard for ecosystem preservation in Alaska and the nation.

A fortuitous combination of circumstances made possible the preeminent Alaskan national park. Albeit the territory embraced numerous sites worth saving, any attempt to do so sparked resistance from Alaskan politicians, business interests, and other boosters. They interpreted such restrictions as unfair impediments to their birthright to use the land for immediate profit and rapidly growing prosperity, as had been done in the States. To them, a group of incompetent Washington bureaucracies, unconcerned about the welfare of local citizens, ruled the territory. Boosters wanted the national government to build the infrastructure for them and then get out of the way, letting them exploit the resources. They suspected, to some extent justifiably, that elites from the States fashioned the rules to suit their own narrow interests.

The seating of a legislature in 1913, and verbal commitments from Washington to develop Alaska, increased the difficulty of land withdrawals. Setting aside a large park, especially if near a populated area or a mining zone, would require just the right conditions. The land would have to be extraordinary in some way, Congress would have to feel a sense of urgency, Alaskans would have to see value for themselves, and astute leadership would be needed to orchestrate the process. No Alaskan would likely take the initiative. But a leader from outside would need qualities of manliness, humility, diplomacy, and knowledge of the North country to win the respect of Alaskans. One of the few such men in existence, Charles Sheldon, stepped forth.

MT. McKINLEY

Sheldon's studies of wildlife near Mt. McKinley had convinced him it should be preserved. He may have been unaware that the Denali area would eventually be world-famous as the site of 20,320-foot-high Mt. McKinley, the tallest peak in North America, but he appreciated its extraordinary presence and radiance. As he topped a foothill above Wonder Lake in the Alaska Range on a clear day in July 1906, Sheldon beheld a scene that would thrill millions, even those never to visit Alaska:

> Three miles below lay the Muldrow Branch of McKinley Fork, fringed on both sides by narrow lines of timber, its swift torrents rushing through many channels. Beyond, along the north side of the main Alaska Range, is a belt of bare rolling hills ten or twelve miles wide, forming a vast piedmont plateau dotted with exquisite little lakes. The foothill mountains, 6,000 or 7,000 feet in altitude and now free from snow, extend in a series of five or six ranges parallel to the main snow-covered range on the south. Carved by glaciers, eroded by the elements, furrowed by canyons and ravines, hollowed by cirques, and rich in contrasting colors, they form an appropriate foreground to the main range.
>
> Denali—a majestic dome which from some points of view seems to present an unbroken skyline—rises to an altitude of 20,300 feet, with a mantle of snow and ice reaching down for 14,000 feet. Towering above all others, in its stupendous immensity it dominates the picture. Nearby on the west stands Mt. Foraker, more than 17,000 feet in altitude, flanked on both sides by peaks of 10,000 to 13,000 feet that extend in a ragged snowy line as far as the eye can see.[1]

The centerpiece of the region is Mt. McKinley (or Denali, a Tanana Athabaskan word for "The Big One" or "The High One").[2] In its first recorded reference, Captain George Vancouver saw "distant stupendous mountains" from Cook Inlet. Russian explorer Andrei Glazunov adopted the Native name

Tenada, but the mountain did not appear on the map employed in the transfer to U.S. jurisdiction, and the name Tenada lost its opportunity for permanent recognition.[3] Prospector Frank Densmore wrote of it after an 1889 trip, leading to local usage of the term "Densmore's Mountain." Mt. McKinley acquired its enduring name in 1896 from prospector William A. Dickey, a Princeton graduate. He and his partner, he said, tired of a free silver harangue from a pair of mining colleagues and retaliated by naming the mountain for presidential nominee and gold standard advocate William McKinley. Dickey related his adventures to the New York *Sun* and, despite protests from the U.S. Geological Survey, the name stuck.[4]

The great mountain had been noticed because it could be seen for 200 miles in clear weather. But its distance from the coast and from easily traveled rivers, added to the ruggedness of the terrain, kept traders and prospectors away until the early 20th Century. The Klondike Gold Rush precipitated efforts to find access from the southern coast into the interior, to avoid the difficult routes through Canada and up the Yukon River. In 1898 Congress assigned the U.S. Geological Survey (USGS) the responsibility of mapping routes to the interior. Later that year a USGS expedition led by Josiah Edward Spurr made the first known traversal by explorers of the Alaska Range in the environs of Mt. McKinley. Also that summer another USGS team, George Eldridge and Robert Muldrow, crossed the range to the headwaters of the Tanana River. Muldrow measured the height of Mt. McKinley as more than 20,000 feet.[5]

The U.S. Army continued explorations begun earlier in the territory and sent teams up the Susitna River Valley in 1898 and 1899. Under the command of Captain Edwin F. Glenn, William Yanert and George Vanschoonoven passed through the Alaska Range at Broad Pass in 1898. A year later Lieutenant Joseph Herron and his group crossed the range, but they ran out of food as fall approached. Athabaskans, whose ancestors had hunted in the region since the last Ice Age, rescued the party and outfitted them for travel by dog team. Herron's group became the first Euro-Americans to reach the Yukon River from Cook Inlet. A 1902 expedition led by USGS geologist Alfred Hulse Brooks mapped the northeast end of the Alaska Range, approaching the base of Mt. McKinley. All of the USGS and Army explorations between Cook Inlet and the interior prepared the way for the railroad and auto road that eventually followed.[6]

Publicity about the mountain inspired attempts to climb it. Federal Judge James Wickersham launched the first sortie from the new gold strike boomtown of Fairbanks in 1903. Wickersham's party attained about 11,000 feet. A few weeks later a team directed by noted polar explorer Frederick A. Cook, approaching from Cook Inlet, gained a similar height. Cook's 1906 expedition catapulted Mt. McKinley into an international controversy. Unable to find a route to the top in an exploration of the mountain's south side, the party returned to Cook Inlet and disbanded. Cook and a companion then set out again for the mountain. Returning, he announced that he had reached the mountain and climbed to the summit in a period of twelve days. Original team members Belmore Browne and Dr. Herschel C. Parker disputed the sensational story, but debate among adherents clouded the issue until 1908 when it merged with Cook's claim to have been first at the North Pole. Evidence mounted against Cook; two investigatory expeditions in 1910 rendered judgments that he had not climbed Mt. McKinley. Browne and Parker discovered and photographed the "fake peak" Cook had represented as the summit, a foothill twenty miles from the top. Ed Barrill, Cook's 1906 partner, concurred, adding that Cook had dictated fraudulent journal entries. Shorn of nearly all credibility, Cook held to his contentions until his death in 1940.[7]

Sheldon played two small parts in the Cook affair. Believing at first that Cook had conquered the mountain, he agreed to contribute a chapter on Alaskan Indians to Cook's forthcoming book *To the Top of the Continent.* By the time the truth became clear, the book had already been published. Years later when Amundsen visited his friend Cook in Leavenworth prison, newspapers published the false impression that Amundsen supported Cook's claim to the North Pole. The National Geographic Society withdrew an invitation to Amundsen to address its meeting. Sheldon tried to defend Amundsen, to no avail, and resigned his society membership in protest.[8]

Listening to the claims and counterclaims and convinced that Alaskans could do the job themselves, Fairbanks prospector Tom Lloyd raised funds and handpicked a team of miner acquaintances—Pete Anderson, Billy Taylor, and Charley McGonagall—for an attempt in 1910. A surveyor, the only scientifically trained member, soon left the expedition in the wake of a dispute. At the end of the climb the three prospectors went straight to their mining sites. Lloyd returned to Fairbanks, declaring that all four men had surmounted both the north and south peaks. Without proof, the "Sourdough Expedition" met disbelief.

Parker and Browne made a bid in 1912 by a northeast route first suggested by Charles Sheldon and Harry Karstens in 1906. Karstens had tried unsuccessfully to interest Sheldon in attempting the route, but the sourdoughs had followed it in 1910. Browne, Parker, and Merl LaVoy got to within 300 vertical feet of the top when, despite the gentle final slope, a storm forced them back.

Archdeacon Hudson Stuck's expedition reached the top on June 7, 1913. Walter Harper, son of a trader-prospector-explorer and an Athabaskan woman, led the first climb to the summit. Stuck, Robert Tatum of Tennessee, and Harry Karstens joined Harper at the top. On the north peak, 2 miles distant and 850 feet lower, they could see the flagpole left by the sourdoughs in 1910. Pete Anderson and Billy Taylor, wearing shoepacs and without ropes, had carried

Members of the expedition making first ascent of McKinley's South Peak, 1913. Denali National Park Archives. Left to right: Robert Tatum, Esais, Henry B. "Harry" Karstens, Johnny, Walter Harper. Absent, probably photographer: Archdeacon Hudson Stuck. Mt. McKinley, later the park's centerpiece, played no significant role in its designation. Karstens, a former prospector and dog teamer, became the first park superintendent.

the 14-foot spruce pole from 11,000 feet to the top and returned in eighteen hours—one of the great feats of mountaineering.[9]

ALASKA'S PREMIER NATIONAL PARK

During his 1906 visit, Sheldon had conveyed to Karstens his idea of national park status for the Mt. McKinley environs. His main motivation lay in the desire to save the magnificent populations of large mammals: Dall sheep, the prime focus of his study, as well as caribou, moose, and grizzly bears. Gold mining in the Fairbanks vicinity had proliferated after 1902, and a 1905 boomlet in the Kantishna country attracted thousands of miners to the Alaska Range. Mining activity meant increased consumption of game.[10] Sheldon presented the park idea to his Boone and Crockett game preservation committee colleagues in 1908. But resentment in Alaska over the 1908 game law and lack of urgency in Congress made it an inopportune time to appeal for an Alaskan park. Circumstances changed, however, over the next few years. Alaska became a territory, and the Taft and Wilson administrations initiated efforts to develop it economically. The 1912 territorial act contained a rider calling for a railroad commission to determine routes into the interior. Congress authorized a railroad in 1914, and Wilson chose the Seward-to-Fairbanks route in 1915. As construction began, Boone and Crockett leaders recognized the imminent danger to sheep populations in the Denali region through which the railroad would pass. They feared the railroad would generate mining, market hunting, or other intrusions—all detrimental to wildlife.

Charles Sheldon and Madison Grant took the initiative. In an October 1915 letter to Edward W. Nelson, soon to be promoted to director of the Bureau of Biological Survey, Sheldon laid out his strategy. First he would contact Alaska's congressional delegate and Mt. McKinley climber James Wickersham, whose acquaintance he and the Boone and Crockett Club had made. Without Wickersham's support no park would be possible, and Wickersham could nominally lead the effort by introducing the bill in Congress. Sheldon would contact Secretary of the Interior Franklin K. Lane and a few key members of Congress, then kick off the campaign officially at a club dinner. Sheldon persuaded Stephen T. Mather, newly in charge of national parks, to secure Lane's backing, and he succeeded in less than a month.[11]

Boone and Crockett's election of Mather to club membership at its December 1915 meeting did nothing to discourage his cooperation. Mather asked Thomas Riggs Jr., then in charge of the railroad planning survey, to lay out boundaries similar to Sheldon's proposal. Satisfied that mining could continue unhampered, Wickersham introduced one of several bills. All incorporated Sheldon's boundaries, but none adopted his proposed name of "Denali National Park."[12]

One of the Mt. McKinley climbers, Belmore Browne, had begun in 1912 to work for a park in the Alaska Range through the Camp Fire Club of America. Browne (1880–1954), a hunter-painter-author-naturalist, belonged to a privileged New York family funded by his father's work as a stockbroker. Several years of residence in Europe cultivated young Belmore's appreciation of art and mountains. After a vacation trip to Southeast Alaska in the late 1880s, the family settled in Tacoma, Washington, to engage in the lumber business. Belmore attended private schools in the East and roamed the wilderness of the Cascades during the summers. A financial downturn prevented his attending Harvard, and he chose the New York School of Art.

In 1902, 1903, and 1904–1905 Browne served as a hunter and artist in collecting expeditions of Andrew J. Stone and others on the Alaska and Kenai peninsulas and in the Yukon and Southeast Alaska. Author of several books and articles on hunting, mountain climbing, and other outdoor subjects, Browne painted on similar themes and composed natural history dioramas for museums. He directed the Santa Clara School of Fine Arts for several years. During World War II he operated out of Ladd Field in Alaska as a consultant on Arctic survival training.[13]

Charles Sheldon, in winter camp north of Mt. McKinley, 1907. Portrait file 01-3394, Alaska State Library. A Boone and Crockett activist, Sheldon led the drive to establish Mt. McKinley National Park.

Upon hearing of Sheldon's efforts in late 1915, Browne offered his assistance. Sheldon called a meeting of the Boone and Crockett game preservation committee, attended by representatives of the Camp Fire Club and John B. Burnham's American Game Protective and Propagation Association. Those present selected Burnham to head the congressional lobbying campaign. The three groups controlled the private-sector effort for the park. They employed as their strongest argument the impending threat to the game mammals.[14] In the Camp Fire Club pamphlet Browne warned,

> [W]hile the Mt. McKinley region is the fountainhead from which come the herds of game that supply the huge expanse of south-central Alaska, that fountainhead is menaced. Slowly but surely the white man's civilization is closing in, and already sled loads of dead animals from the McKinley region have reached the Fairbanks market. Unless a refuge is set aside, in which the animals can breed and rear their young unmolested, they will soon "follow the buffalo."[15]

Belmore Browne in climbing gear. Portrait file PCA 01-3441, Alaska State Library. Browne nearly succeeded in being the first person to climb Mt. McKinley and assisted the formation of Mt. McKinley National Park.

Public lands committees of both congressional houses held hearings in the spring of 1916. Burnham, Browne, Grinnell, and Sheldon testified before a sympathetic House Subcommittee on Public Lands in May. Browne and Sheldon extolled the beauty and wildlife of the region and, accepting the inevitability of the railroad, emphasized the park's potential for tourism and economic development in Alaska. They reiterated the necessity of protecting the land from commercial meat and headhunters but insisted that miners be allowed to take game from the park, in part because regulations prohibiting it would be unenforceable. They pointed out the lack of evidence that the proposed park held any significant mineral reserves.[16]

U.S. Geological Survey officer Stephen R. Capps, detailed to investigate the matter of sheep killing in the proposed park, made an inspection trip in the summer of 1916. His report appeared in *National Geographic* in January 1917, shortly before the new Congress voted on the park bill. Capps related that in the early days Fairbanks hunters found sheep in "the mountains just south of Fairbanks and east of the Nenana River." When they had cleaned out that source, hunters went to the Alaska Range: "I talked with several men who take sheep meat to Fairbanks for sale, and one of them estimated that each winter for the last three years from 1,500 to 2,000 sheep have been taken from the basin of Toklat and Teklanika Rivers. Only a part of these reaches Fairbanks, for the sled dogs must be fed during the hunt and on the trail, and some hunters leave behind all but the choicest hind quarters." Growth of the town of Nenana and the projected Alaska Railroad, to pass within fifteen miles of the park boundary, also bode ill for wildlife.[17]

Sheldon spoke before the National Parks Conference in Washington shortly before the final congressional vote on the park bill. Recalling his first view of Mt. McKinley, he declared, "I felt just exactly the same impression that I had when I was alone in the Grand Canyon, that feeling of reverence and awe produced by grandeur." But he placed the most emphasis on the wildlife, the "principal reason" for the park. He wondered why the enthusiastic descriptions of beauty in the parklands so seldom mentioned animals. He invoked the traditional scenery of Europe for comparison:

> In more civilized countries, on mountains and hills that have been more stamped with civilization for centuries, the adornments, the little castle with its spires, the Moorish castles in Spain—they enhance the landscape. . . . Well, it's exactly the same in the wilderness. Does not . . . a wild animal, the product of that environment, so adorn it that we feel that it is complete? That feeling, that completeness of all your feelings that is aroused by such wild scenery will in this region be constantly gratified to the utmost.[18]

No one disputed the danger to game populations, and no powerful opposition to the bill materialized. The measure passed and President Woodrow Wilson signed the McKinley Park bill on February 21, 1917.[19]

MANAGEMENT OF THE PARK

Sheldon, who had personally delivered the bill to President Wilson for signature, continued to lobby for management funds for the park. He had promised to support Harry Karstens for the position of superintendent, and Karstens occupied that position until 1928. Karstens energetically built what facilities he could, given minimal appropriations, and he made an earnest effort to enforce

Dall rams in McKinley Park, June 1966. By Adolph Murie. A. Murie coll. Box 13, University of Alaska Fairbanks, Alaska and Polar Regions Archives. Preservation of wildlife, and the Dall sheep in particular, inspired the initial movers to create the park.

the law protecting game animals. But his aggressive manner in relating to local citizens and subordinates led to his forced resignation.[20]

The enabling bill drew Mt. McKinley Park to extend about 100 miles along the Alaska Range, totaling 2,200 square miles. Miners retained the right to hunt so as to feed themselves. Congress provided no money for protection or construction of facilities until 1920–1921 when the National Park Service acquired jurisdiction. Sheldon organized an effort to extend the park boundary 10 miles eastward to protect it from disruptive influences related to the railroad. As a result, in 1922 Congress added 445 square miles to the park, and Karstens

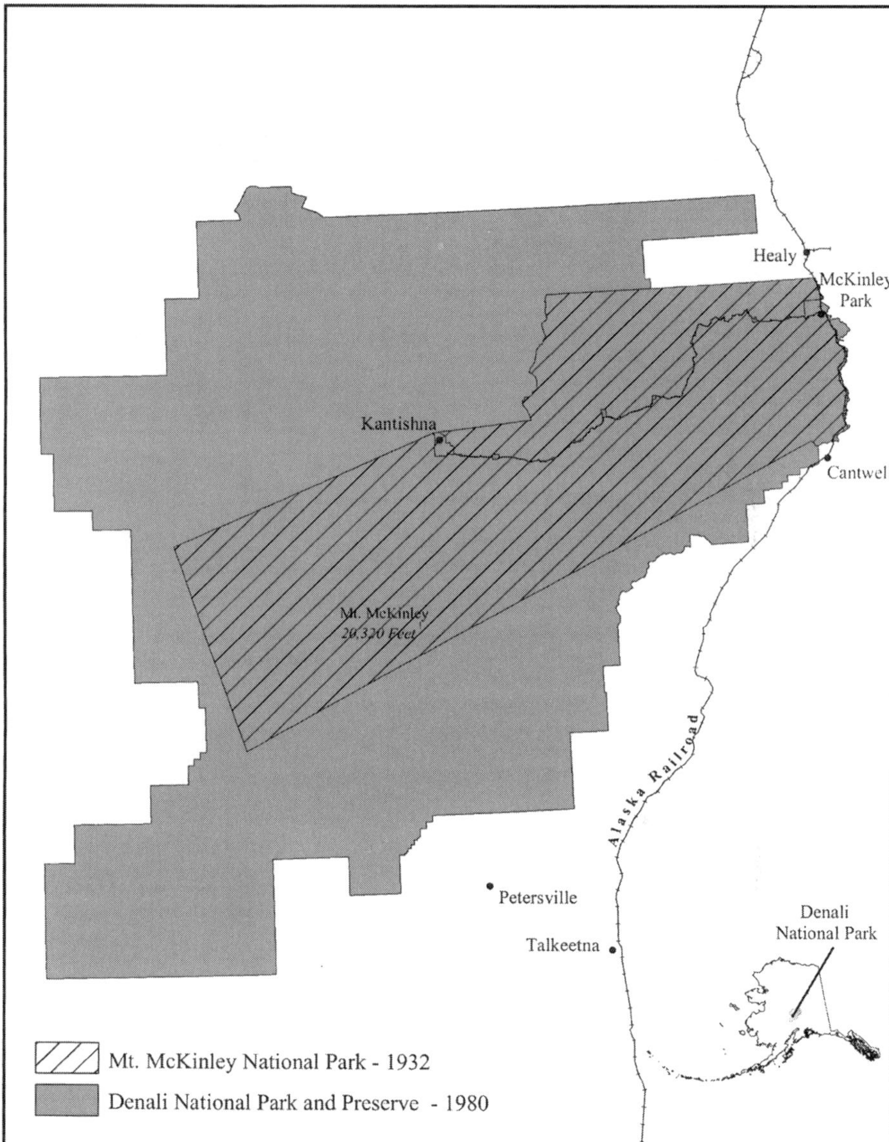

Mount McKinley/Denali National Park and Preserve, 1932 and 1980. Courtesy Jason Geck

moved the headquarters from Nenana to McKinley Park station on the Alaska Railroad east of the park boundary. A quarter-million-acre addition in 1932 took in Wonder Lake and wildlife habitat bordering on the Nenana River, increasing the park's size to nearly two million acres.[21]

Former market hunter's cabin used by park rangers for night shelter, 1926. RG 79G Box 11, National Archives at College Park. Commercial hunting threatened wildlife populations, especially as railroad construction neared the park. Park status prohibited sport hunting, and the Park Service banned all hunting in 1928.

As in the case of other parks and reservations, no one consulted Alaska Natives about the establishment or management of McKinley Park. Tanana Indians had traditionally lived along the region's main rivers and hunted and fished in what eventually became the park. Although relatively isolated, they eventually succumbed to the influences of the Euro-American invasion: disease, alcoholism, and cultural change. Some worked for wages in mining or otherwise served miners and travelers. Some trapped for the fur trade but lost their territories to the more aggressive white men. By the time the park materialized, very few Indians hunted within its boundaries.[22]

Wildlife Protection

Dedicated by law both to the preservation of unspoiled Nature for future generations and to access for tourism and other recreation, the National Park Service faced a dilemma. Virtually none of the parks in the States contained enough acreage to be an intact ecosystem for large mammals, and as tourists multiplied, wilderness declined. Mt. McKinley National Park embodied advantages and disadvantages in relation to the Park Service's mission. In addition to scenic splendor, it featured a community of wildlife unprecedented for a national park and offered a chance of retaining it. Wildlife protection had motivated the conservation clubs to push for park status, but Alaskan politicians and other boosters valued the park more for its economic development potential. They wanted to maximize mining and tourism, and they tolerated game preservation as a benefit to local hunters. In evolving forms, the tension between development and preservation dogged the park throughout its existence.

Wildlife continued to be central to park affairs. Imminent danger from commercial hunting had helped create the park, and instances of excess killing of game prompted a 1928 ban on hunting. The small number of miners involved could acquire game outside park boundaries. Appreciation of the value of protecting game stocks enabled Alaskan support for park boundary extensions, which otherwise would have been opposed. But Alaskan opinion erupted in virulent form over the alleged depletion of Dall sheep by wolves (Chapter 13). This episode, lasting more than two decades, forced the Park Service to partially abandon ecological principles in park management. Research by Adolph "Ade" Murie, added to work by his brother Olaus and biologists George M. Wright and Joseph S. Dixon, helped turn public opinion toward an understanding of the park's ecological function and reinforced the Park Service commitment to maintenance of ecological integrity as a core goal. National Park Service historian William E. Brown described Ade Murie as probably "the single most influential person in shaping the geography and the wilderness-wildlife policies of the modern [Denali] park."[23]

Mining, permitted by the enabling bill, jeopardized the park's scenery, wildlife, and wilderness quality. Kantishna, the most active district, lay just outside the northern boundary, and boosters wanted a road through the park to connect the district to the Alaska Railroad for ore hauling. The road, adopted as a goal by the Park Service, would also ease tourist access to the north side of Mt. McKinley. Miners found modest deposits of gold and copper in the 1920s but not enough to overcome the costs of operation. Fewer than twenty miners remained year-round in the Kantishna vicinity in the early 1930s. Governmental setting of gold at $35 per ounce, and the completion of the park road in 1938, revived gold mining during 1937–1942. An antimony deposit proved valuable for wartime needs. Then the government shut down gold mines as nonessential to the war effort. No significant resurgence of mining took place in the region until the United States abandoned the gold standard in 1971 and the value of gold escalated. But in 1965 the Park Service and Bureau of Land Management arranged a withdrawal of the region surrounding Kantishna to protect wildlife habitat.[24] In 1976 legislation ended new mining claims in the park, and after 1980, no mining could be conducted in the park.

Tourism

As soon as the park came into existence, Stephen Capps declared in *Travel* magazine that "the area on the north flank of the Alaska range is of unrivaled value as a national playground not only because of its abundant big game, but because it contains America's most stupendous mountain scenery."[25] Tourism commenced in 1922, by which time the park could be reached via the Alaska Railroad. Sixty-two tourists appeared in 1924 and 206 in 1925. Cars and buses took them 12 miles into the park to Savage River camp, and they could go farther on horseback. The 90-mile road reached its terminus at Kantishna in 1938. Tourism declined during the early Depression years but peaked at 2,900 in 1939. The park's visibility had been stimulated by the first climb of both peaks of Mt. McKinley in 1932 by superintendent Harry Liek and ranger Grant Pearson, accompanied by Minneapolis lawyer Alfred Lindley and Norwegian skier Erling Strom. Unlike later expeditions that flew to glaciers at high altitudes, the Liek expedition traveled to its base camp by dog team.[26]

In 1942 the U.S. Army requisitioned the park as a recreation area for service men and women, hosting as many as 8,000 per month. The army relinquished the park after the war, but the Alaska Highway opening in 1948 guaranteed a steep upswing in visitors to the park. Plans called for a hotel by Wonder Lake at the far western end of the park road. It would supplement campgrounds along the road and the hotel built in 1939 at McKinley Park near the entrance.[27] A 1951–1952 recreation survey report by the Interior Department exuded unrestrained enthusiasm for tourism potential. It recommended that

> comfortable accommodations and facilities for eating and sleeping should be developed somewhere in the park where there is a good view of Mt. McKinley. The Wonder Lake vicinity has excellent possibilities as a site for a lodge. . . . The accommodations and facilities that will be needed when the park is connected with the Richardson Highway should be constructed as soon as possible. Roads and bridges should be added and improved. In addition to the campgrounds and lodge mentioned above, there will be a need for a store, gas station, automobile repair facilities, restaurants, and more housing. Once the park is readily accessible by automobile, it is reasonable to assume the attendance figures will skyrocket. . . . Facilities should be constructed that would enable a visitor to participate in summertime activities such as tennis, golf, and swimming [and] winter sports activities. . . . Means should be found to improve the park program so that visitors will be encouraged to stay in the park for a few days, rather than to treat it as a target for "quickie" sightseeing trips.

This scenario apparently did not trouble the writers as undermining the values for which visitors came to the park, especially if numbers continued to escalate. Rather, the writers worried that "it will take years to overcome the bad publicity

Tourist party crossing moraine of Muldrow Glacier, 1927. RG 79G Box 11, National Archives at College Park. From a trickle in the 1920s, park visitors multiplied to hundreds of thousands by the end of the century.

that will reach potential tourists in the States if the first group of motorists brings back word that facilities are lacking."[28]

Park officials realized that such infrastructure would severely diminish the park's wild character. A 170-mile road, the Denali Highway, connected the entrance eastward to the Richardson Highway in 1957, giving auto-borne tourists their first direct access to the park. The expected Parks Highway from Fairbanks to Anchorage, completed in 1972, would pass by the entrance and again multiply the number of visitors.

Slow funding during the 1950s and the emergence of wilderness advocacy groups tipped the balance toward keeping the park more natural. Olaus and Adolph Murie, Aldo Leopold, Sigurd F. Olson, and others had lent their voices, and the Fairbanks chapter of the Pioneers endorsed further park expansion to protect wildlife. Park planners, prompted by a survey conducted by Olson, pushed for an expansion that ultimately more than doubled the size of the park to 5.7 million acres in 1980. Renamed Denali National Park and Preserve, it retained the name Mt. McKinley for its famous centerpiece. Planners did not build the recommended hotel at Wonder Lake and arranged for buses rather than private automobiles to take visitors through the park.[29] But the ongoing growth of traffic near and into the park, and the conversion of mining claims at Kantishna to tourist facilities, left the future of Denali's wilderness quality in doubt.

Mt. McKinley (later Denali) National Park won renown as the central focal point of Alaska's wilderness image, one of the nation's flagship parklands, and a unique national treasure. In mounting numbers people came from around the world to take in its dramatic scenery, to climb the mountain, to view its wildlife, to be touched by Nature on a grand scale. In no small part, their interest had been generated by the photography of Charles J. "Charlie" Ott. Raised on a farm in Wisconsin, Ott visited the park in the late 1940s following military service during the war. Superintendent Pearson offered him a job as a maintenance man and mechanic. Ott spent his spare time exploring the wildlands with his friend Ade Murie, eventually becoming one of the park's leading naturalists. Honing his skills as a photographer, Ott produced many of the images that made the park famous. A committed conservationist, he joined numerous environmental groups and donated his photographic slides to them. After retirement in 1974 he studied birds in the Southwest and spent summers at his cabin near McKinley Park. The University of Alaska awarded him an honorary doctorate in 1989.[30]

Park visitors might encounter any of 37 species of mammals—including black and grizzly bears, moose, caribou, Dall sheep, wolves, wolverines, and lynx—and 137 species of birds.[31] Perhaps unknowingly, they would glimpse Mt. Sheldon and Browne Tower near Mt. McKinley, named for the park's two founders.[32] They would not soon forget their adventure in the shining land of the North, and they told the story to anyone who would listen. Almost certainly, the excitement and wonder experienced by American visitors to the park swelled the outpouring of approval for the 1980 Alaska National Interest Lands Conservation Act that expanded Denali and preserved tens of millions more acres in Alaska.

The formation and management of McKinley Park reflected significant changes in environmental values. Before 1917 and, in effect, before the assignment of rangers in 1921, only the weakly enforced game law of 1908 safeguarded wildlife. Mining operations had free rein under the dominant paradigm of free-enterprise exploitation of natural resources as the presumed basis for economic progress. Absence of scientific information and effective regulation cast doubt on the long-term viability of a unique ecological asset. But ownership of the land by the federal government, and the vigilance of conservationists in the States, made possible a reversal of the downward trend. Boone and Crockett and the Bureau of Biological Survey insisted on a minimal goal of selected species protection and, by their advocacy of a large game reserve, moved the goal toward habitat, if not ecosystem, preservation. Based on their mandate to retain

Adolph Murie at McKinley Park, November 1939. Denali National Park Archives. Dr. Murie made notable contributions to the science of predator-prey relationships and to the preservation of wilderness values in the park.

Charlie Ott, Fairbanks, 1984. By Malcolm Lockwood. Ott's wildlife photos enhanced the popularity of Mt. McKinley National Park.

unspoiled Nature, National Park Service officials aspired to ecosystem protection as an explicit goal for the park. Yet all had to accommodate Alaskans and tourism entrepreneurs, who showed little interest in ecosystem protection as such. Park management objectives included elements—the road to Kantishna, hotel-building, and temporary wolf control—that fell short of nonconsumptive human use or even sustainable use of the land and wildlife.

Charles Sheldon had initiated the effort to provide the science necessary to validate ecologically oriented goals and management objectives. Stephen Capps produced timely and telling evidence of the need for legislation to conserve the Dall sheep. Prompted by the wolf control controversy, Adolph Murie and other biologists promoted a more explicit ecological perspective and agenda. Delays caused by the Depression, World War II, and the Korean War kept McKinley Park relatively unspoiled. Then the growing environmental community, increasingly backed by public opinion, lent its weight to ecosystem preservation and nonconsumptive uses of the park.

In terms of decision-making power, the enabling act forced the Park Service to accommodate miners and Alaska Railroad supporters, who stood to benefit from mining and tourism. The 1928 hunting ban and the gradual phasing out of mining left management more firmly in the hands of government experts. But pressure to increase tourist access to the detriment of Denali's ecosystem continued to rise. Not until after statehood would there be Alaskan environmental organizations ready to participate in management deliberations in support of ecological values. They, their stateside environmentalist colleagues, and the Park Service fought against repeated efforts by the state and some federal administrators to increase commercial exploitation of the environs of McKinley/Denali Park.

7

Robert F. Griggs and Katmai National Monument

LATE IN THE SPRING OF 1912 A NATURAL DISASTER CONCEIVED A SUPERLATIVE ALASKAN parkland. A geologic event on the Alaska Peninsula between Kodiak Island and Bristol Bay claimed a place among the greatest volcanic eruptions ever recorded. In doing so it triggered a series of events that produced one of the nation's largest national parks and finest examples of ecosystem preservation.

American Pete, the Aleut chief of Savonoski and among the few recorded eyewitnesses of the event, recalled, "The Katmai Mountain blew up with lots of fire, and fire come down trail from Katmai with lots of smoke. We go fast Savonoski. Everybody get in bidarka. Helluva job. We come Naknek one day, dark, no can see. Hot ash fall."[1] The town of Savonoski had been evacuated because of volcanic rumblings, but American Pete and his companions had returned to a camp on the Katmai trail 18 miles from the explosion to retrieve hunting equipment. They barely escaped by a 75-mile paddle to Naknek on Bristol Bay.[2]

Three days after the explosion a Russian at Kaflia Bay on Shelikof Strait, 30 miles east of and downwind from the eruption site, wrote a letter to his wife, Tania:

> A mountain has burst near here, so that we are covered with ashes, in some places 10 feet and 6 feet deep. All this began on the 6th of June. Night and day we light lamps. We cannot see the daylight. In a word, it is terrible, and we are expecting death at any moment, and we have no water. All the rivers are covered with ashes. Just ashes mixed with water. Here are darkness and hell, thunder and noise. I do not know whether it is day or night. . . . Perhaps we shall see each other again. . . . Pray for us. Your husband, Ivan Orloff.[3]

At the time of the eruption most of the people along Shelikof Strait in the Gulf of Alaska either worked at canneries on Kodiak Island or fled southwestward from their villages to Puale Bay or eastward to Afognak. Some from the villages of Katmai and Kaguyak (Douglas) remained at Kaflia Bay where a salmon saltery operated. Six days after the eruption the Revenue Marine Service evacuated the people at Kaflia Bay to Afognak. Later in the summer the service resettled most of them, 78 in all, at Perryville 200 miles southwest of Katmai village. Katmai, Kaflia Bay, and Kaguyak on the Gulf side and Savonoski and two other small settlements on the Bristol Bay side were never reestablished. By the time the sites became habitable by humans, perhaps ten to twenty years after the eruption, the sites had been incorporated into a national monument.[4]

The Katmai eruption threw up more than 6 cubic miles—29 billion tons—of material. At Seward, 250 miles away, sulfuric acid killed vegetation. A ship's bell at Cape Spencer, 750 miles away, tarnished twenty minutes after being polished. Dust could be seen and booms heard 750 miles away at Juneau, and fumes were detected in British Columbia and Washington State. Ash covered 950 square miles 3 feet deep and 30,000 square miles an inch deep. Europeans noticed a haze, and the Northern Hemisphere experienced an unusually cool summer, averaging 1.6 degrees Fahrenheit below normal.[5]

A colorful legacy preceded the 1912 eruption at Katmai. In 1789 the Russians set up a trading post at the Koniag Alutiiq village of Katmai; Aleuts wiped it out. Alexander Baranov, manager of the Shelikov-Golikov Company, reestablished it in the early 1790s. When the United States purchased Alaska, a series of geographical expeditions immediately set forth to inventory the territory's resources. Several visits to the Katmai coast beginning in 1867 turned up no evidence of important mineral resources in the region.[6] In 1868, Hutchinson, Kohl & Company assumed control of the trading post at Katmai, and its successor Alaska Commercial Company opened a post at nearby Douglas in 1878. Earning substantial amounts of money from sea otter pelts in the 1870s and 1880s, the Aleuts converted to a cash economy. When the otters disappeared by about 1886, the Aleuts lapsed into poverty, relieved in part by employment in salmon canneries.

Katmai Pass, the high point of a trail across the Alaska Peninsula to Bristol Bay, served Alaska Natives for centuries and Russians for decades. Ivan Petroff

Village of Katmai after eruption, 1913. By Mel Horner. KATM 40415, Lake Clark Katmai Center. Natives abandoned Katmai and five other small villages during the eruption and did not reestablish them; the sites became part of Katmai National Monument.

passed through the divide while conducting the 1880 census and felt "compassed on every hand by the grandest visions of Alpine scenery, snows and glaciers."[7] Crossing from Savonoski in the north to Katmai on the south side, Petroff's group hoped to find a ship to take them to Kodiak. Finding none, they paddled in baidarkas. A local weather forecaster's judgment turned out to be wrong, and they underwent a hazardous thirteen-hour voyage in rough seas, partly at night.

Briefly, the U.S. Postal Service carried over the pass. Beginning in 1899 hundreds of prospectors followed the route as a shortcut to the goldfields of Nome, avoiding the hazards of ocean travel through the Aleutian passes.[8] In the howling winds and sudden storms of winter, Katmai Pass could be a death trap. Its fame spread after an 1889 visit by Hugh Cecil Lowther, the Fifth Earl of Lonsdale. Leaving England to escape publicity of his affair with an actress, the earl sought adventure in the American North. He traveled up the Mackenzie River Valley, along the coast of the Arctic Ocean, across the Brooks Range to the Porcupine River, and by dog team down the Yukon and south along the Bering Sea coast. Expected to negotiate the pass in mid-February and thinking the weather prohibitive, his Native companions balked. Lowther, impatient to get home, threatened to shoot anyone who resisted. This persuaded the Natives, who had just seen Lowther repay a dog that had bitten him by shooting it in the head at a distance of 150 yards. After crossing the divide, Lowther wrote, "We began to descend but the storm was terrible, gale very strong we could hardly stand, snowing, drifting & freezing hard. I could not see the man in front of me at all times & he was only 4 or 5 paces ahead." A momentary lift in the weather revealed three large glacial crevasses nearby. Separated from the main party on the way down the south slope, Lowther had to camp in another storm. The starving dogs ate the rawhide from the sleds and snowshoes, and two dogs died before the party made it to Katmai.[9] Before long such adventures as Lowther's would be replaced by scientific expeditions.

VOLCANIC STUDIES

U.S. Geological Survey geologist Josiah Edward Spurr examined the Katmai region in 1898. Like Petroff he traveled from Naknek to Katmai, but he made the trip in mid-October. He described the snow-covered Katmai Pass as

> extremely wild and rugged. . . . For several miles on both sides of the summit there is no trace of vegetation. . . . Many Natives have perished here by being caught in gales, for during storms, even in summer, the wind blows with piercing intensity and coldness. At such times stones of considerable size are picked up by the wind and carried through the narrow defiles where the traveler must walk, and we found many of these stones lying on the snow. Owing to this danger the Natives can not be induced to cross except in perfectly calm and clear weather.

Spurr noted a small earthquake, hot springs, and other evidence of volcanic activity on the south side of the pass.[10]

Native lore made no mention of eruptions; the 1912 event surprised everyone and stimulated great curiosity. Canadian explorer Jack Lee, first to visit the scene, arrived a week after the explosion.[11] Mt. Katmai had lost 800 feet of its 7,500-foot elevation and displayed a new crater lake 3 miles across and 3,500 feet deep that observers assumed to be the locus of the explosion. Actually, Novarupta, 5 miles distant, had erupted, and the loss of material beneath the surface had caused the top of Mt. Katmai to collapse. Semimolten sand then flowed into the valley west of Katmai Pass, burying it an average of 100 feet deep and causing fumaroles of gas and steam to shoot upward.[12] Lee reported that Katmai had not been the source of the explosion, a thesis finally proven correct in the 1950s. A few days after Lee's visit geologist George C. Martin arrived representing the National Geographic Society. A year later curiosity seekers William A. Hesse of Cordova and Mel A. Horner of Seward arrived, climbed into the mountains, and became the first to view the agglomeration of fumaroles in the sand-covered valley soon to be famous as the Valley of Ten Thousand Smokes.[13]

One organization showed strong interest in Katmai: the National Geographic Society, sponsor of seven expeditions beginning in 1912 to study botany and vulcanology at Katmai. Articles in *National Geographic* followed most of the expeditions. Immediately upon hearing of the eruption the society dispatched Martin, who had surveyed the Katmai coast as a member of a U.S. Geological Survey team in 1904. He arrived in the town of Kodiak on Kodiak Island four weeks after the event, having interviewed witnesses in several places along the way. The town had been plunged into darkness for nearly 60 hours and had lost radio transmission capability. The steamer *Dora*, headed for Kodiak, instead had to run out to sea in midday darkness so deep the crew could not see the ocean surface. Captain C.B. McMullen reported that "heavy thunder and lightning commenced early in the afternoon and continued through the night. Birds of all species kept falling on the deck in a helpless condition. The temperature rose owing to the heat of the volcanic ash, the latter permeating into all parts of the ship." The *Dora* proceeded to the Kenai Peninsula and again ran into darkness created by ashfall.[14]

A series of heavy explosions and earthquakes, followed by gigantic clouds of ash, had occurred for the first three days after the eruption, and lesser activity persisted throughout the summer. Martin found ash layers 3.5 inches deep on parts of Afognak Island 113 miles downwind from the presumed volcano, about 12 inches deep at Kodiak 100 miles east and directly downwind of the source, and 55 inches deep at Amalik Bay on the Katmai coast 15.5 miles southeast of the source. Rafts of pumice a foot thick floated in the bay. Nearly all vegetation at the bay had been buried or killed, and only fox tracks testified to the presence of mammals. Three dogs survived at the nearby village of Katmai, whose few residents had left just before the eruption. On Kodiak and Afognak islands, hungry and partially blind brown bears reportedly attacked cattle. As far away as Iliamna Lake the ash blinded rabbits and killed a wide variety of small birds and mammals. Fewer salmon could be found in the streams, and barnacles and mussels died. Two or three people at Kodiak died after breathing the volcanic dust. Martin regarded the inconveniences to humans as temporary and judged that "the soil will probably be improved."[15]

On southern Afognak Island the ash lay 10 inches deep and covered 70 percent of the vegetation. But when the surface dried and cracked after rains, the taller and stronger plants emerged through the cracks. Foxes virtually disappeared from the island, and the following winter trappers complained that the abrasive ash had ruined furbearer pelts by wearing them down and matting them. Spawning salmon and steelheads choked on sediment in the streams, and relatively few sockeye fingerlings returned to the sea the following year. Ash also

W.A. Hesse filming Katmai volcano, 1913. Greely coll. PCA 66-368, Alaska State Library. The Katmai eruption drew scientific and public interest, ultimately producing a national park.

Katmai volcano ash at Kodiak, 100 miles downwind, 1912. Thwaites coll. 0182-1252A, University of Washington Libraries Special Collections. Ashfall from one of history's greatest volcanic explosions temporarily disrupted agriculture and ecosystems.

killed worms and insects needed by fish. In the salt water, sea urchins, clams, and cockles died and the growth of kelp appeared to be retarded. The near-complete destruction of mosses caused postponement of a plan to introduce reindeer for sustenance of the Natives.[16]

Botany professor Robert Fiske Griggs (1881–1962) of Ohio State University first visited the Katmai area in 1913; and in 1915, 1916, 1917, 1919, and 1930 he headed expeditions. A native of Columbus and 1903 graduate of Ohio State, Griggs earned a master's degree at the University of Minnesota and a doctorate at Harvard. His kelp study on the Alaskan coast caught the attention of National Geographic Society officers, who chose him to lead most of the organization's safaris to Katmai.[17]

Volcanic debris rendered the Katmai region difficult to negotiate and potentially dangerous to visitors. A landslide had dammed up Katmai River, forming a large lake in the valley. In early 1915 the dam burst, sending a wall of water down the valley at 70 miles per hour, moving boulders the size of houses.[18] In places the water washed away ash and revived buried vegetation. When Griggs and his partner Lucius G. Folsom arrived that year, they found most trees dead but some regenerating. On the beaches around Katmai Bay they saw tracks of fox and brown bear. Salmon ascended the streams to spawn. A year later they encountered numerous signs of additional predators—wolves and wolverines—and by 1919 abundant evidence of moose and caribou.[19]

Griggs and his colleagues paid the most attention to vegetative recovery, the key to rejuvenation of Katmai's ecosystem. Several elements inhibited regrowth: ashfall, ranging up to 40 feet deep, buried many plants. Some trees, notably willows, survived by protruding above ground level. Horsetail, one of the oldest plants on earth, could push up through three feet of ash. Grasses and other plants could penetrate thinner layers. Streams might rescue plants by exposing roots, but they often changed course in the unstable volcanic material. Katmai's frequent high winds lowered ash levels in many locales but also contributed to surface instability by constantly moving material, and flying particles damaged vegetation. Seeds could germinate in the ash if given water and protection from wind. Yet lack of nitrogen and humus retarded soil stability and plant growth. Brown bears contributed to recovery by leaving deep footprints in which seeds could find increased moisture and protection from the wind.[20]

The 1915 research team set up vegetation observation stations on the Katmai coast and near the village of Kodiak. When he arrived in June, Griggs marveled at the rapidity of change:

> It was not the same Kodiak that I had left two years before. The mountains were everywhere green. . . . Where before had been barren ash was now rich grass as high as one's head. Everyone agrees that the eruption was "the best thing that ever happened to Kodiak." In the words of our hotel keeper, "Never was any such grass before, so high or so early. No one ever believed that the country could grow so many berries, nor so large."[21]

At Kodiak, particles lay in three sizes: a light gray dust on top, medium-sized grains, and angular grains the size of fine sand on the bottom. Wind blew away most of the gray dust and some of the medium-sized material. Wind and water exposed hilly areas, facilitating vegetative growth. Trees still carried coats similar to snowfall, but most survived. Numerous plants arose from roots buried as long as three years. Seedlings could be seen in 1916, and earthworms had begun to mix the soil and create humus. But sphagnum bogs did not recover, and in some spots the ash formed a hard layer that acted like quicksand when water-saturated.[22] Whatever the effect on animals, the eruption disturbed most vegetation only temporarily.

Griggs returned in 1930 to observe the change in vegetation since 1919. He found widespread growth of small plants and willows, largely from roots not killed by volcanic ash. Others such as grasses had taken root from the surface where seeds, plants, and small amounts of organic material had been blown in by the wind. In the Valley of Ten Thousand Smokes, covered by ash essentially devoid of nitrogen, he found extensive and luxurious growth of two species of liverwort. He theorized that the plants had somehow managed to fix nitrogen in a sterile environment and would provide organic material for succeeding

Valley of Ten Thousand Smokes; Mt. Mageik (left) and Mt. Katmai in background. Jasper Sayre coll. KATM 7696, Lake Clark Katmai Studies Center 7696. The fumaroles, a determining factor in Katmai's park designation, proved short-lived.

plant life. The uncontaminated ash bed at Katmai offered a rare opportunity to examine plant colonization and succession.[23]

Griggs and Folsom first sighted the Valley of Ten Thousand Smokes, so named by Griggs, on their 1916 expedition. The once-green valley below Mt. Katmai, about seven miles wide by fifteen miles long, now appeared as a barren plain punctuated by highly active steam vents. For years it represented the most dramatic expression of volcanic activity in North America, attracting the notice of writers and visitors. Even though he knew of Hesse and Horner's 1913 sighting of the valley, Griggs for some time regarded himself as its discoverer and generally received credit for it. Similarly, he erroneously believed his party had been the first to view the crater of Mt. Katmai.[24]

Donovan B. Church, Griggs's photographer on the 1917 expedition, recounted his impressions of the valley:

> It seemed to me, as we stood on the edge of Novarupta, that this was the Devil's own private corner in hell itself. It seemed, as I gazed at the seething steam clouds that rushed from the cooling lava plug, and at the shattered, steam-smothered furnace that filled the vale beyond, that there was some vague, fantastic form, a horrid dream, a hideous, potent "thing" which was

> not for human eyes to see nor human ears to hear. . . . As, homeward bound, we skirted Cerberus, the steamers turned in the dying sunlight to shimmering gold and the snowy crests of distant mountains glinted yellow. I forgot the heavy pack which bowed my shoulders as I glanced backward at the growing beauty which filled the valley. Through its giant gateway the "Valley of the Ten Thousand Smokes" sank from sight as we dropped over the pass, and the sky above reddened to a crimson halo in the fading rays of the sinking sun.[25]

Such descriptions, supplemented by photographs in *National Geographic* and by scientific articles, shifted public attention away from botanical studies and identified the Katmai region as primarily a volcanic phenomenon.

KATMAI BECOMES A PARK

Katmai so impressed Griggs that while in camp during the 1916 expedition he resolved to work for its status as a national park. National Geographic Society president Gilbert Grosvenor liked the idea and arranged expeditions for 1917 and 1918, in part to support the park status effort. Most of the politics took place behind the scenes. Grosvenor contacted society board member Franklin K. Lane, who happened to be secretary of the interior. Lane referred him to acting National Park Service director Horace M. Albright, who approved of the project. Albright advised that the 1917 designation of Mt. McKinley National Park made it unwise to ask Congress for another park so soon, that Katmai should be designated a national monument by presidential proclamation.[26]

National Geographic expeditions and articles generated a favorable public attitude toward Katmai, as did a few other magazine articles. Griggs pulled out the stops in an August 1918 issue of *Nature*: "The Valley of Ten Thousand Smokes . . . is traversed by hundreds of fissures extending along its margin or criss-crossing its floor. These fissures are the seat of several millions of volcanic vents of all sizes, from great volcanoes pouring forth columns of vapor more than a mile high, down to minute jets of gas." For readers more difficult to sway he declared, "As a spectacle of the grandest of all the forces of Nature, the Valley of Ten Thousand Smokes is so far beyond anything else known to us on the globe as to make it quite certain that it will rank as the first wonder of the world." Moreover, the reader might share directly in the glory: "Were the means of transportation provided, it would be quite possible to land from an ocean liner in the morning and cover the whole of the district in a single day by automobile."[27] Having read Griggs's articles, Alaska congressional delegate Charles Sulzer offered to introduce a park bill if needed, adding that "we have the highest mountain in the continent enclosed in a national park in Alaska; why shouldn't we have the biggest volcanic crater in the world similarly enclosed?"[28]

Laura Griggs and husband, Robert, at Baked Mountain, Katmai National Monument, 1919. National Geographic Society Katmai Expedition No. 6491, University of Alaska Anchorage Archives. Griggs led five NGS expeditions to the Katmai region and succeeded in gaining monument status for it.

One question had an important bearing on Katmai's status: whether the 10,000 smokes, a potential tourist attraction, constituted a permanent phenomenon or just temporary releases of trapped water. In 1918 the National Geographic Society declared the phenomenon permanent. This assessment may have made the difference in Lane's favorable recommendation to President Wilson. No organized opposition surfaced, and no public debates or hearings had been conducted. *National Geographic* articles had left an impression of the region as essentially a scientific curiosity of no economic value except for tourism. Preoccupied by the war and sensing no controversy, Wilson signed the order for the 1,700-square-mile monument on September 24, 1918.[29] The proclamation cited the work of the National Geographic Society as the determining element in the monument's creation.[30]

Several groups of sightseers and filmmakers visited the monument in the 1920s and 1930s. But the distance from population centers and travel routes restricted access to a relatively wealthy and adventurous few. No one could afford to invest in comfortable facilities at or near the monument, and this lack of accommodations in turn retarded the flow of tourists.[31]

Father Bernard Hubbard, the adventurous "glacier priest" and geologist who had climbed extensively in the Alps and elsewhere, enhanced Katmai's magic appeal by making seven visits between 1927 and 1934. Accompanied by his friend Red Chisholm and two graduate students in 1929, he climbed Mt. Katmai and traversed the Valley of Ten Thousand Smokes. Atop Katmai, Hubbard peered into the gigantic caldera, three miles across and a half-mile deep: "a vivid mosaic in yellow, violet, orange, green and vermilion, emphasized by bold lines of black and studded with glaciers glinting like jewels in the sun." He descended to the blue lake at the bottom. On the way to the fabled valley the party cowered in their tents, pelted by pumice stones driven by a 36-hour blizzard. Hubbard described the valley as they viewed it on a clear morning: "On either side rose a line of lofty, smoking mountains, ash-yellow slopes hung with snow fields and sparkling blue glaciers. The feet of those volcanoes were gashed with fissures red as blood. The smooth valley floor was yellow, but punctuated by fumaroles ringed with brilliant red, blue, violet and orange." He noticed, however, that the valley "is growing cold. . . . Instead of thousands of smokes, there are now only hundreds." Hubbard also took note of one of the sources of post-eruption recovery. During blizzards the men watched numerous small trees and bunches of grass fly past, uprooted from elevations far below.[32]

Hubbard's crews compiled the most complete motion picture record of the Katmai region available in the 1930s. In 1934 they found access to the interior still difficult. Men and pack dogs sank up to their waists and bellies in the soft sand. They walked through a dead forest left by the explosion:

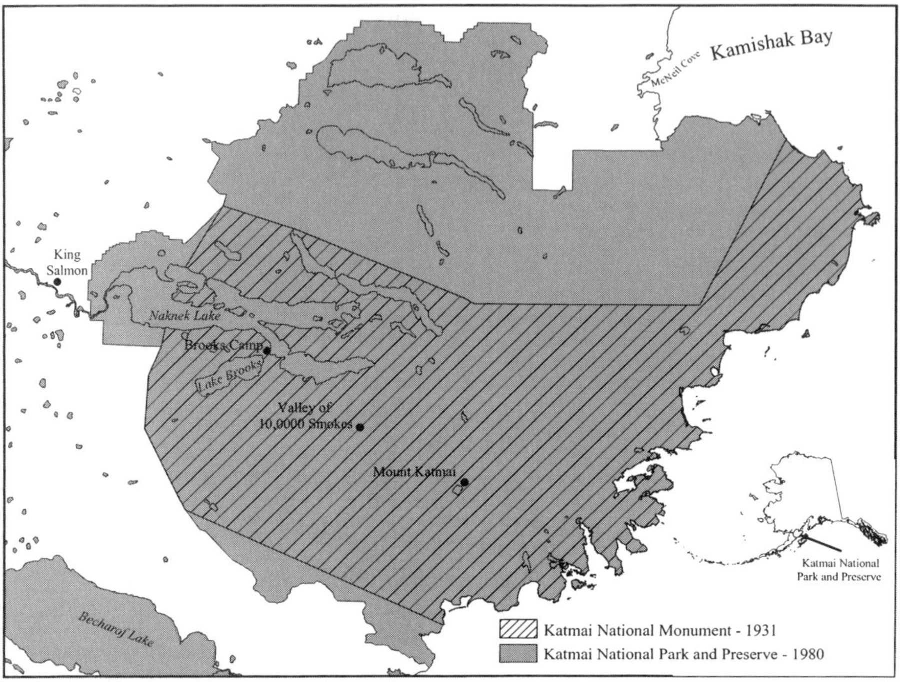

Katmai National Monument/Park and Preserve, 1931 and 1980. Courtesy Jason Geck

> Stark, gaunt trunks of fallen giants sprawled about the ground, their limbs flung out in reckless abandon as though they had grasped for life as life was departing. Dead trees stood upright, without leaf of foliage, without color save the ghastly color of death. . . . This phantom forest stretched for miles, and in all that expanse we and our dogs were the only living things. Curiosity led us to strike some of the dead branches—they snapped like pistol shots; and when we examined them they showed no sign of decay. There was no appreciable weight to the wood, either, and logs of impressive size could be heaved about as though we were giants of prodigious strength playing with twigs.[33]

In the valley Hubbard found "tough grasses a foot or more in height, and large patches of flowering Alaska cotton." As for the smokes, Hubbard judged them "a great disappointment. [The valley] is so inaccessible, so totally different from the enthusiastic descriptions of its first explorers, and finally, so belies the predictions of what might be expected of it, that it should be discontinued as a National Monument, and the trappers who made an honest living in the Valley should be allowed to return there."[34] Hubbard therein touched on a weak point in Katmai's standing; namely, whether restrictive monument status represented a higher use of the land. Other critics had challenged the designation, and more would do so in the coming decades.

Father Bernard Hubbard and dog at Katmai Crater, 1929. Hubbard coll. VTS 29-03, Santa Clara University Archives. Hubbard, the "glacier priest," compiled the first moving picture record of Katmai National Monument.

Looking north across head of Geographic Harbor, 1940. By Victor B. Scheffer. RG 79G Box 9, National Archives at College Park. Snowy Mountain at upper left. Vegetation has risen through the ashfall in many places.

CHALLENGES TO THE PARK

Like other federal attempts to protect land in Alaska, Katmai met opposition from settlers and politicians. The monument designation happened not long after the closure of coalfields in 1906 and oil lands in 1910. Alaska's governor Thomas Riggs remarked pointedly in his 1918 annual report that "practically all of the reservations should be eliminated." In 1920 he declared that Katmai Monument "serves no purpose and should be abolished." But the writings of Griggs and others, promising tourism dollars, helped dampen criticism. In 1923 the U.S. Geological Survey sent two teams into the monument to assess mineral potential. They reported a low likelihood of finding significant mineral deposits. Thereafter, governors' reports focused on tourism potential rather than mining.[35]

Prospects for immediate tourism expansion faded in the 1920s. But another Park Service goal, preservation of wilderness and wildlife, emerged. Charles Sheldon, expressing the interest of the Boone and Crockett Club, had recognized the potential for a brown bear sanctuary and drafted revised monument boundaries for that purpose. As the brown bear controversy (Chapter 12) heated in the late 1920s and the 1930s, Griggs, Stewart Edward White, and others rose to the bears' defense. After Griggs visited Katmai in 1930 he pointed out in a report to the Interior Department that only in the monument did brown bears live unmolested. Boundaries needed to be extended north and west, he contended, to sustain the bears on a long-term basis. Writings in defense of the bears helped prompt President Herbert Hoover's signing of a 1931 order enlarging Katmai National Monument to 4,214 square miles, for "features of historical and scientific interest and protection of the brown bear, moose and other wild animals."[36] Thus the rationale for the park broadened to encompass status as a wildlife sanctuary. This change would prove vital in National Park Service efforts to prevent decommissioning of the monument, by now the largest in the national park system.

In spite of its size, Katmai maintained a tenuous hold on monument status. Remoteness and lack of facilities deterred tourism, and the scarcity of tourists in turn inhibited budget appropriations for facilities. Katmai received virtually no money during its first three decades. Its headquarters were in Mt. McKinley National Park 400 miles away, itself underfunded. Neglect of Katmai encouraged poaching of wildlife and other intrusions and a revival of demands for abolition of the monument.[37]

Alaska Game Commission wardens reported frequent illegal trapping in Katmai in the mid-1930s. Unable to field a ranger, the Park Service relied on the wardens, who had enormous territories to cover. Trapping resumed whenever surveillance slackened. Some violators operated from islands along Shelikof Strait. To prevent such encroachments a 1942 presidential order altered the monument boundary to include all islands within five miles of the shore. The service finally brought trapping under control by deputizing warden Carlos Carlson in 1949. A year later it initiated summer ranger patrols.[38]

During World War II the army built an air base and two recreation camps near Naknek. Soldiers engaged in illegal hunting and fishing in the monument. Private air carriers, having flown in small numbers of visitors since 1929, now brought numerous cannery workers to fish the lakes and streams. These activities put pressure on wildlife, but the Park Service tolerated them—in part for lack of enforcement capacity and in part because it wanted to encourage tourism.[39] Sport fishing held potential to open Katmai to development minimally damaging to wilderness values.

Other interests sought economic exploitation or discontinuance of Katmai. In 1941 Alaska's Territorial Department of Mines pushed for termination of the monument, claiming mineral potential. The Park Service managed to forestall the effort. In 1945–1946 commercial clammers and fishers launched another attempt at abolition, backed by a territorial legislative resolution. The

Abandoned cannery, Kukak Bay, Katmai National Monument, 1951. By Lowell Sumner. Courtesy Lake Clark Katmai Studies Center. Clamming and other commercial activities threatened to revoke Katmai's national monument status.

petitioners received permission from the Park Service to clam below high tide and fish offshore.[40] In 1947 an Anchorage entrepreneur investigated use of the Katmai pumice deposits to manufacture building blocks for construction. He pressed for a law opening the monument to mining. Meanwhile, he illegally entered the monument and set up a pumice extraction operation at Geographic Harbor. When tested the material proved inadequate, and the operation ceased. Yet long afterward the law passed, opening Katmai to pumice mining by permission of the secretary of the interior.[41]

Trappers and commercial salmon fishers tried unsuccessfully to reduce the size of the monument or to gain entry. The Naknek Civic Club, assisted by Alaska congressional delegate E.L. "Bob" Bartlett, made concerted bids in 1950 and 1953 for trapping access. Trappers argued that beaver dams impeded salmon migration upstream, a claim not supported by experience. Fishers accused brown bears of damaging the salmon runs by catching large numbers of fish on their way to spawn. Again the Park Service, aided by the National Parks and Recreation Association, staved off the assaults.[42]

Park Service biologist Lowell Sumner, carrying out a boundary survey in response to calls for reduction of the monument, recommended an overall *increase* in size. He noted that of all the national park units, "only Katmai appears to contain all its native species *in approximately their original numbers.*"[43] Higher-level officials defended the proposed expansion, reinforcing the National Park Service commitment to wildlife preservation values as articulated in its original mandate and in the 1931 Katmai proclamation.

Park status moderately affected area Natives. Once a locus of villages living on seafood, salmon, and land resources, the Katmai coast lost most of its population to disease during the Russian era. Survivors permanently abandoned the nearby small villages when the volcano erupted in 1912. Some Natives made subsistence use of Brooks River salmon until the 1950s when Park Service priorities and sport fishing discouraged their activity. Absence of Natives along the river, a mile-long stream between Brooks and Naknek lakes, changed the ecology of the area. Humans had lived there for about 4,000 years, most of the river's geological time span. After they left, the brown bear presence gradually expanded. Rarely seen on the river in the 1930s and 1940s, bears proliferated in the late 20th Century to a park total of 1,500 to 2,000, and as many as 40 at a time visited the river. The large gathering of bears so appreciated by tourists and regarded as a primeval scene may never before have existed at Brooks River.[44]

The many actual or potential intrusions on the natural integrity of the park included a fishway at Brooks Falls. Fisheries agents had noticed that sockeye salmon had difficulty jumping the 5- to 8-foot waterfall, especially in times of low water. In 1920–1921 they cut a channel through the falls at one end. To complete the project, in 1949–1950 the Fish and Wildlife Service, assuming it had permission from the Park Service, built a concrete fishway in the channel. Park Service officials insisted no such permission had been granted and objected to the visibly intrusive structure that altered migration patterns and ended the spectacle of salmon jumping the falls. Park Service research in 1984–1985 indicated that the fishway did not significantly enhance fish migration and might harm genetically distinct populations of sockeye salmon spawning below and above the falls. Accordingly, the service proposed to the Alaska Department of Fish and Game (ADF&G), the agency holding jurisdiction since statehood, that the fishway be removed. ADF&G denied approval, arguing that the fishway did allow more fish upstream and that removal of the structure would violate state and borough coastal management programs, which emphasized fish production.[45] The issue remained in contention.

To combat critics of the monument and claims on its resources, the Park Service carried out a research program in 1953–1954. Called the Katmai Project, it combined the efforts of federal agencies and university scientists to study Katmai's geology, biology, and archaeology. In February 1953, a few months before researchers arrived, Mt. Trident erupted. It spewed out lava and ash sporadically for two years and offered an unexpected opportunity to observe a volcano in action. Of the fifteen recently active volcanoes in the monument, about half steamed in 1953–1954. Vulcanologists also observed two rare phenomena: five glaciers buried by the 1912 explosion and the glacier formed inside Mt. Katmai's crater, the only known glacier whose date of origin could be determined.[46]

A study by University of California–Berkeley geologist Garniss H. Curtis and his graduate student Jack Sheehan revised the theory of how the 1912 explosion occurred. They measured the depth of fallen ash at selected sites and found that concentric circles of similar depth surrounded Novarupta, not Mt. Katmai. They found no large stones around Katmai as would be expected from a source. They speculated that an underground connection caused Mt. Katmai to cave in when Novarupta expelled the material.[47] Their interpretation won acceptance.

In the Valley of Ten Thousand Smokes a few fumaroles remained active. The vegetation had changed as well. The liverworts found in abundance by Griggs in 1930 had disappeared, but numerous species of plants—including willows—grew on the hillsides. Botanists set up plots to record future vegetative growth.[48]

To justify the monument to Alaskans, the Park Service needed to accelerate tourism. In a December 1953 letter to Interior Secretary Douglas McKay, congressional delegate Bob Bartlett made the case that, given the disappearance of nearly all the smokes,

> the very purpose for which the Monument was established no longer exists. Notwithstanding, I for one believe that the beauty of the area and its other special features warrant a national monument there. But it should be realistic in respect to size and should not deny to residents of the area land which has no proper place within the Monument. It is interesting though discouraging to note that while in the years gone by the Interior Department has resisted uniformly and successfully any attempt to restore to the public domain any of the area within the boundary, it has never done anything at all—that statement is almost literally true—to open the Monument to public use.[49]

Bartlett's lament articulated the essence of the booster perspective: brown bears had no place, a modest reserve might be tolerated as long as it brought in money, and the Park Service goal of ecosystem preservation for posterity should be sacrificed for the slightest economic advantage of the smallest number of people.

National Park Service officials warded off nearly all competing claims on Katmai, and its recreational value gradually advanced to the fore. Ray Petersen, owner of a flying service named Northern Consolidated Airlines, had made bush flights in the Katmai vicinity since 1935. Acting on Park Service approval, he built Brooks and Grosvenor camps on-site in 1950 to accommodate tourists.

Victor Cahalane at base of Novarupta, August 1954. By George Schaller. RG 79G Box 9, National Archives at College Park. National Park Service chief biologist Cahalane and others surveyed Katmai National Monument in the 1950s and fought successfully to include wilderness preservation in the monument's purpose.

Brooks Camp sat in the middle of prime bear habitat, causing long-standing conflict between ecological values and tourist preferences. The Park Service built a ranger station at Ukak River between 1955 and 1957. Under pressure from

Adlai Stevenson (second from left) and party at Brooks Falls, August 1954. By George Schaller. RG 79G Box 79, National Archives at College Park. Others identified: guide Don Holbrook (left) and John Fell Stevenson (with camera). Controversial fish ladder is out of sight at left. Katmai lost much of its appeal as a scientific curiosity but became famous for fishing and wildlife viewing. Remoteness deterred tourism until the 1950s.

Senator Ernest Gruening it constructed a road in 1962 from Brooks Camp to the Valley of Ten Thousand Smokes. This sparked requests to continue the road to the East Coast, but cost and resistance from Park Service officials doomed the idea. Money spent on the valley road delayed construction of a park headquarters, completed at King Salmon in 1964.[50]

Katmai had achieved recognition as a recreational resource as well as a wildlife sanctuary. In 1969 President Lyndon Johnson increased the size to 4,361 square miles, and in 1980 it became Katmai National Park and Preserve.[51] To a perpetually growing tourist population Katmai offered a variety of scenic and scientific attractions: evergreen forests, lakes and streams, tundra, volcanic features, glaciers, and archaeological sites as much as 4,500 years old.[52] Mt. Griggs, named for the monument's founder, overlooks the now-cooled Valley of Ten Thousand Smokes.[53] Of the four million acres, 85 percent is designated wilderness. Katmai hosts at least 117 species of birds[54] and 27 species of land mammals, including a large and viable population of brown bears, as well as moose, wolves, wolverines, lynx, red foxes, river otters, beavers, porcupines, and Arctic hares. Offshore swim sea otters, seals, sea lions, and several species of whales. Its fresh waters hold northern pike, Dolly Varden, Arctic char, grayling, and sockeye, chum, silver, king, and pink salmon.[55] A rare geological event in a remote region, followed by timely and intelligent efforts of a few dedicated individuals, made possible one of the world's largest and finest national parks.

More than almost any other American national park, Katmai embodied values of ecosystem preservation. The initiation of the monument involved a classic case of collusion between government and a small but influential interest group, the National Geographic Society. But the society planned no detrimental use of the land and did not interfere in government efforts to manage it. Initially, Griggs and the National Geographic Society intended to preserve a scientific wonder analogous to Yellowstone National Park (1872). Action by Sheldon, Griggs, and others on behalf of the brown bears moved the purpose closer to species preservation and ecosystem sustainability. Additions by Presidents Hoover, FDR, Johnson, and Carter reinforced the sustainability value.

Scientific information in the form of field observation precipitated a crucial but erroneous judgment about the park's geology. Later, research demonstrated the lack of potential for significant resource extraction. Had the land potentially benefited the mining or logging industries, it probably would not have become a park. The *National Geographic* articles overcame the inaccessibility and interested the attentive public enough to warrant its designation as a monument. National Park Service biologists, backed by their superiors, clarified and fought for the park's wildlife and wilderness values. When Katmai eventually drew tourists in numbers, it increasingly demonstrated the strength and economic vitality of nonconsumptive use values. As one of the five largest national parks in the United States, Katmai marked a signal victory in ecosystem preservation.

8

John Muir, William S. Cooper, and Glacier Bay National Monument

Compared to Katmai, a much more difficult and lengthy struggle preceded the final form of Glacier Bay National Monument. Unlike Katmai, Glacier Bay had been seen by large numbers of people, sat closer to populated areas, and contained gold and other valuable minerals. Moreover, nearby Tlingits possessed credible claims to ownership or, at least, subsistence uses of the land. Glacier Bay's preservation therefore required more public support and incurred greater resistance. Like Katmai, however, as in the case of nearly all national parks, Glacier Bay possessed far more scenic value than mineral or logging potential. And, like Katmai, Glacier Bay attracted university scientists and inspired one to lead an effort for its permanent protection.

VISITORS TO GLACIER BAY

Glacier Bay, now more than 50 miles long, extends northwest of Chichagof Island into the center of the monument. Its best-known feature, Muir Glacier, crucially influenced the attainment of monument status. The glacier filled the bay when the first westerners, a crew sent out by Captain George Vancouver of the HMS *Discovery*, visited it in 1794. The ice receded and U.S. Navy Lieutenant Charles Erskine Scott Wood, who reached it by canoe from Sitka in 1877, explored the bay in its modern form. Also by canoe came John Muir, S. Hall Young, and their Tlingit guides in 1879 and 1880.[1]

Of all the grandeur he had surveyed, few places moved Muir as did Glacier Bay. There he spent many days climbing, hiking, and studying vegetation and glaciation processes. After witnessing the calving of Muir Glacier he wrote:

> When a large mass sinks from the upper fissured portion of the wall, there is a keen, piercing crash, then a deep deliberate, long-drawn-out, thundering roar, which slowly subsides into a comparatively low, far-reaching, muttering growl; then comes a crowd of grating, clashing sounds from the agitated bergs that dance in the waves about the newcomer as if in welcome; and these, again, are followed by the swash and roar of the berg-waves as they reach the shore and break among the boulders. . . . When the sunshine is pouring and sifting in iris colors through the midst of all this wilderness of angular crystal ice, and through the grand, flame-shaped jets and sheets of radiant spray ever rising from the blows of the falling bergs, the effect is indescribably glorious.[2]

Muir thrilled his reading audience with his portrayal of a morning on the bay. As a spectacular sunrise faded,

> the green waters of the fiord were filled with sun-spangles; with the upswinging breeze the fleet of icebergs set forth on their voyages; and on the innumerable mirrors and prisms of these bergs, and on those of the shattered crystal walls of the glaciers, common white light and rainbow light began to glow, while the mountains, changing to stone, put on their frosty jewelry, and loomed again in the thin azure in serene terrestrial majesty. We turned and sailed away, joining the outgoing bergs, while "Gloria in excelsis" still seemed to be sounding over all the white landscape, and our burning hearts were ready for any fate, feeling that whatever the future might have in store, the treasures we had gained would enrich our lives forever.[3]

Muir had been drawn to Alaska not only by his love for Nature but also by a desire to learn more about glaciers and how they shaped the earth, a continuation of his investigations in the Sierras. His writings for the public highlighted the spectacles of Southeast Alaska, most prominently the glaciers. Thus the 300-foot-high and two- to three-mile-wide Muir Glacier, the largest and most accessible at tidewater, became a "frozen Niagara," a source of pride for Americans who wished to believe they possessed grander treasures than could be found in Europe. The first tourists, eager to see what Muir had described, arrived in 1883 in the *Idaho* under the veteran coastal shipmaster James Carroll. Captain Carroll is said to have given Muir Inlet and Muir Glacier their names.

John Muir. Muir Woods coll. P83-143.050, San Francisco Maritime National Historical Park Archives. Muir's writings, and those of Sheldon Jackson, Eliza Scidmore, and others, focused national attention on Alaska.

S.S. City of Topeka *at Muir Glacier, 1890. Reid coll. 115-24, Alaska State Library. By the 1890s outheast Alaska had become a favorite vacation destination for elites.*

His sojourn in the *Idaho* heralded a steady stream of visitors in other vessels, including the Pacific Coast Steamship Company's *City of Topeka*, *George W. Elder*, and *Queen*.[4] The spreading fame generated by enthusiastic vacationers and by the 1899 Harriman Expedition moved Glacier Bay toward ultimate status as a park.

Lituya Bay on the Pacific coast enriched the history of Glacier Bay National Monument. For years it hosted the largest Tlingit settlement on the Fairweather coast. Tlingits also visited to take advantage of its abundant resources. But Nature made Lituya Bay a dangerous place. Two French vessels under Commander Jean Francois de Galaup de La Perouse, hoping to make territorial claims, paid the first European visit to the bay in June and July 1786. They passed through the narrow entrance at an unusual slack tide and nearly foundered. Once inside, they found their exit barred by rolling waves continuously sweeping the entrance from shore to shore. It turned out to be an agreeable place to be confined, endowed by plentiful fish, berries, herbs, wood, and freshwater. Many mammal species lived on the land and sea otters along the coast. Of the scenery La Perouse remarked, "I doubt whether the profound valleys of the Alps and Pyrenees exhibit a picture equally terrific." He voiced less appreciation for the local Tlingit men, who stole at every opportunity, "always quarreling among themselves, indifferent to their children, absolute tyrants to their women, who are incessantly condemned to the most laborious occupations."[5]

While reconnoitering the exit, a boat commanded by an able officer was pulled into the waves by the powerful current. Attempting a rescue, a second boat followed. Both sank, drowning all 21 men. After more than three weeks' delay the ships gained the ocean, only to be wrecked and ending the lives of the remainder of the 200-man expedition in the Solomon Islands.[6] Evidence of the Alaska stay survived in dispatches La Perouse sent back to France by way of Kamchatka.[7]

Hearing of the French landing and planning to extend their own territorial control down the Northwest coast, the Russians entered Lituya Bay in 1788 and buried a copper plate as a symbolic land claim. Nothing came of the French visit, and the Russians built forts at Yakutat and Sitka. Their hunting crews killed 1,800 sea otters in or near Lituya Bay in 1788 and quickly stripped the region of otters. In retribution the Tlingits attacked and destroyed the forts at Sitka in 1802 and Yakutat in 1805.

Tlingits also suffered from disasters at Lituya Bay. In 1788 a war party of ten canoes overturned in the breakers and 80 men drowned.[8] Legend spoke of an entire village disappearing beneath an enormous wave. The legend came alive in July 1958. As three trolling vessels operated in the bay an earthquake struck, sending down 90 million tons of rock from a mountainside and 1,300 horizontal feet of ice from Lituya Glacier. A gigantic wave climbed the wall of Gilbert Inlet opposite the slide, scouring off vegetation to a height of 1,700 feet. At 100 miles an hour a surge of water raced down the bay toward the ocean, engulfing 2 vessels and claiming 2 lives. The *Edrie* snapped her anchor chain and rode out the wave, passing over a forested spit 80 feet above the trees. When the water calmed, great rafts of logs spread for miles out to sea.[9]

William H. Dall in 1874 conducted one of the first scientific observations of Lituya Bay.[10] The bay attracted gold seekers as early as 1880, and prospectors found placer gold in the beach sands not far from the bay entrance in the late 1880s. Mining peaked in 1896 when upwards of 200 men worked the sands. Lituya Bay Placer Gold Mining Company manager Hans Nelson, his wife, Edith, and three other employees stayed through the winter of 1899–1900. In the fall of 1899 one of the men shot dead a fellow worker, wounded another, and aimed the gun at Edith. Hans knocked him down and subdued him. Unable to take the accused to court or effectively guard him, the miners held a trial and sentenced the man to death. Edith carried out the sentence by hanging him. The company left the area in 1900.[11]

Ownership of the Glacier Bay region lay in dispute during most of the 19th Century. An 1825 Anglo-Russian treaty described the boundary in vague terms. In 1887 Canada advanced a claim interpreting the treaty in its favor, to include the Glacier Bay area. The Gold Rush forced the issue, necessitating clear ownership of mines and ports. Negotiations completed in 1903 resolved the issue in favor of the United States and established Glacier Bay and its surroundings as U.S. territory.[12]

John Muir's articles about Glacier Bay attracted the attention of academic scientists who studied glaciers to understand Ice Ages. Tour vessels enabled them to reach Alaska, and the first scientist, George Frederick Wright of Oberlin College representing the U.S. Geological Survey, arrived in 1886. A second team under Harry Fielding Reid of the Case School of Applied Sciences entered the inlet in 1890, finding John Muir on the site measuring glacial movement. Others continued the investigations in the 1890s, among them the scientists of the Harriman Expedition. Grove Karl Gilbert, a member of the Harriman party representing the U.S. Geological Survey, initiated a focus on plant succession in the wake of the retreating glacier. Then, weeks after the expedition departed, earthquakes apparently caused the face of Muir Glacier to collapse into the bay, leaving it full of ice. This ended visits by tourists for a decade. For many years, tour boat companies took their clients to Taku Glacier near Juneau.[13]

Lack of access to Glacier Bay also suspended glacial research for well over a decade. But the writings of John Muir and the glacial scientists sparked the curiosity of Detroit native William Skinner Cooper (1884–1978), a botany professor at the University of Minnesota. Fascinated by mountains after accompanying his father on outings, Cooper made numerous trips to the Colorado Rockies beginning at age eighteen. Earning a degree in botany and ecology from Alma College in 1906, he completed a PhD at the University of Chicago in 1911. He spent four years in California examining the redwoods, chaparral, other plant communities, and sand dune morphology. In 1914 he studied postglacial vegetation in British Columbia and took a side trip to Alaska looking for a site to assess plant growth in the wake of a rapidly receding glacier. A colleague later suggested Glacier Bay, and Cooper found what he sought when he returned to do research in 1916, 1921, 1929, and 1935.[14]

Cooper had been mentored by Harry Fielding Reid and had taken courses in plant succession from Henry Chandler Cowles, a prominent theorist in plant ecology. When he started work at Glacier Bay in 1916, Cooper and his colleague John V. Hubbard laid out quadrats to be examined in periodic surveys of plant species and growth rates in the soil where the glacier had receded. Rapid plant growth, and known locations of the glacier front at various points in time, made Glacier Bay an ideal site for measurement of successional processes. On nine quadrats, three each on land first exposed in 1879, 1892, and 1899, Cooper compared vegetation growth between 1916 and 1921. He found a high mortality rate in individual plants but a net gain in numbers and surface area

William S. Cooper, Blackstone Bay, 1935. University of Minnesota Archives. Botanist Cooper studied plant succession at Glacier Bay and spearheaded the effort to make it a park.

covered. One pioneer species in the evening primrose family declined while others increased:

> The major part of the advance in the establishment of the vegetation cover was due to the activities of a few individuals which survived and persisted from the many that germinated. The most important of the persisting individuals were the *Dryas* [in the rose family] and the willows, all mat-formers and therefore extremely effective in covering the ground.
>
> The gradual acceleration of the successional process, evident in general observation study, has already begun even at this early stage.

Cooper's work culminated in the presentation of a paper in 1922 at the Ecological Society of America, and the ensuing discussion gave birth to the idea of preserving Glacier Bay. The society appointed Cooper chair of an exploratory committee.[15]

MONUMENT STATUS FOR GLACIER BAY

Cooper's committee launched a survey of the bay area and proposed boundaries to encompass all the desired ecological features. Robert F. Griggs sat on the four-member committee. Reflecting on his Katmai experience and congressional responsiveness to extractive interests, Griggs suggested, "A national monument is created by presidential proclamation, whereas a national park is made by an act of Congress. In the first case it is necessary to convince only one man of the advisability of the action, whereas in the second, six hundred, more or less, must be converted to the idea."[16] This lesson had inspired the design of the Forest Reserves Act of 1891 and of the Antiquities Act of 1906, the legal basis for nearly all Alaskan preserves between 1892 and 1978.

Warren Harding, the first president to see Alaska, visited Glacier Bay in 1923 and expressed a desire to see it protected. More than 80 organizations endorsed the plan of the Ecological Society of America, including the National Research Council, American Geographical Society, National Parks Association, Explorers Club, Associated Mountaineering Clubs of North America, American Forestry Association, Botanical Society of America, and American Society of Geologists.[17] Proponents cited five attractive features of the proposed monument: (1) numerous tidewater glaciers, not found in any other park or monument, (2) accessibility for tourists, (3) a pristine coastal forest, (4) opportunity for study of glaciation, and (5) historical associations from Vancouver to Muir.[18]

In Juneau and Haines, the chambers of commerce registered their objections. Cooper's committee had emphasized the lack of economic potential at Glacier Bay but had thought it best to seek the advice of the U.S. Geological Survey's chief representative in Alaska, Alfred H. Brooks. Mining appeared at that time to be the main land-based means of developing the Alaskan economy. Based on a brief assessment reporting gold, silver, and molybdenum, the Geological Survey prepared to oppose monument status. But the influential Council on National Parks, Forests, and Wild Life endorsed the monument. Secretary of the Interior Hubert Work recommended a presidential executive order withdrawing land in the wide parameters recommended by Cooper's committee, pending a review by the Interior Department. President Calvin Coolidge's signature on the order on April 1, 1924, provoked a negative reaction from the Juneau *Daily Alaska Empire* and settlers in Southeast Alaska.[19]

A *Daily Alaska Empire* editorial, citing concern for loss of mining and homesteading opportunities, ventured,

> The suggestion that a reserve be established to protect a glacier that none could disturb if he wanted and none would disturb if he could or to permit the study of plant and insect life is the quintessence of silliness. And when it is proposed to put millions of acres, taking in established industries and agricultural lands and potential resources that are capable of supporting people and adding to the population of Alaska, it becomes a monstrous crime against development and advancement. It leads one to wonder if Washington has gone crazy through catering to conservation faddists.[20]

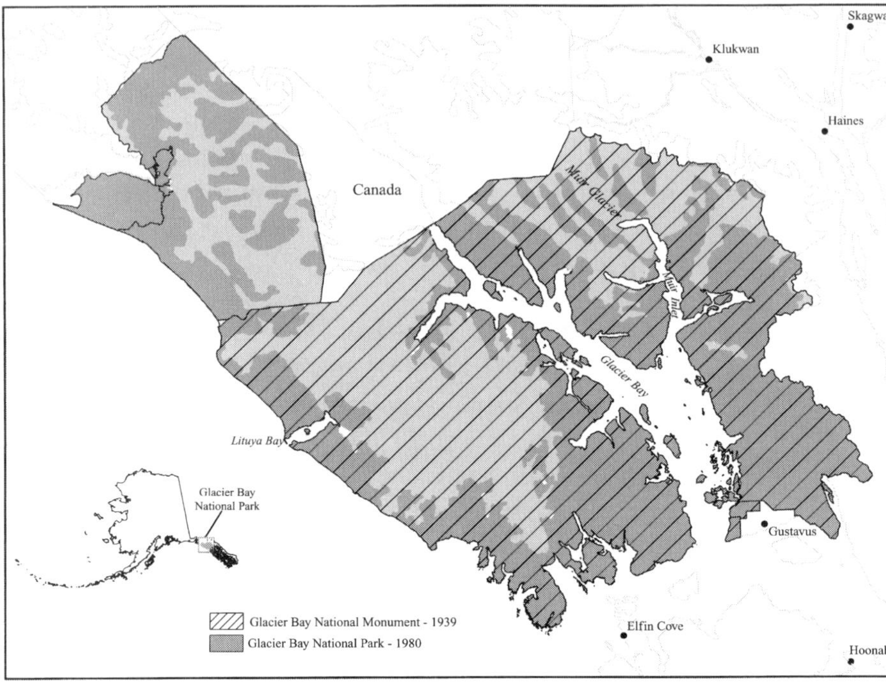

Glacier Bay National Monument/Park and Preserve, 1939 and 1980. Courtesy Jason Geck.

Cooper replied in part that "the time is not too far distant when, due to destruction, and to proper use as well, our forests will have lost their primeval magnificence. We [wish] to reserve a few small areas so that our children may enjoy the bounties of nature untouched by man." He added that Alaska could expect, as in the cases of Yellowstone and Yosemite parks, to reap economic benefits from tourism.[21]

Secretary Work sent General Land Office official and soon-to-be Alaska governor George A. Parks to do the economic assessment of Glacier Bay. Parks, an advocate of Alaskan development, listed in his report every such activity actually or potentially occurring in the proposed monument: fox farming, timbering, mining, homesteading, fish traps and canneries, Native allotments, and agriculture on the 90,000-acre Gustavus forelands. He recommended against monument status for more than a core segment of the withdrawn lands, if any at all. Cooper's committee called forth another massive expression of demand for monument status from citizen groups. In negotiations toward a compromise, the Geological Survey insisted on access for mining, and the Forest and National Park services both sought control of the monument. Cooper fought for inclusion of some forest perimeter. He achieved it in the boundaries eventually accepted, but, for the time being, the monument consisted mostly of a mountainous core. The Park Service won control over a monument closed to mining in the presidential proclamation of February 26, 1925. The edict cited—in addition to the traditional scenic values—scientific study of glaciology and ecology, protection of forests, and historic values based on famous visitors.[22]

MANAGEMENT PROBLEMS

A scattering of small-scale economic activities existed within the monument lands. Salmon salteries and canneries operated at Bartlett Cove from 1888 to 1890, Dundas Bay from 1900 to 1931, Dry Bay from 1910 to the mid-1940s, and Excursion Inlet from 1908 throughout the remainder of the century. A sawmill operated at Excursion Inlet from shortly after 1900 to the late 1930s. Fox farms occupied Lemesurier, Beardslee, Strawberry, and Willow islands between 1920 and the late 1930s when the value of fox fur went down. Nearly all the lands occupied by these ventures passed to monument status.[23] During World War II the army constructed a storage base at Excursion Inlet, cutting down acres of surrounding forest. At Gustavus it built an air base to accommodate B-29s that might strike Japan from the Aleutians. Neither facility proved necessary for the war effort, and the lands reverted to National Park Service control.[24]

Mining in the Monument

Mining presented a problem for the monument. In 1936 a second move to permit mining in the monument brought Cooper back to chair a committee assembled to combat it. He had the sanction of 150 groups including Audubon, Isaac Walton League, National Parks and American Forests associations, American Nature Association, and the new Wilderness Society. Nevertheless, not all public sentiment in the States could be counted on. Popular Hearst writer Rex Beach, author of many Alaskan adventure stories and champion of the small man, envisioned a movement of prospectors exploiting Alaska's mineral wealth as an antidote to the Great Depression. He took up the cause of miners working a claim prior to designation of the monument. Joe Ibach and his wife, Muz, prospected at Reid Inlet in 1924 and found gold in two locations, filing their claims in the late summer after Coolidge's withdrawal. Six months later monument status specifically prohibited mining. Although the Ibachs probably had a legal right to proceed, officials advised them not to develop the claims. Their protests failed until Rex Beach visited in 1935. Beach had known Joe as a guide in 1915 and felt sympathy for him.[25] Beach touted the mining bill and went to see FDR. Roosevelt wanted to avoid alienating the Hearst papers, but he also wanted compromise among the federal agencies and environmental groups involved. In a week's time and without notice to the conservationists, the mining bill rushed through congressional committees and passed both houses, and Roosevelt signed it.[26]

More than sympathy may have motivated Beach's efforts. He returned to join Joe Ibach in prospecting, and in 1936 they staked a group of claims. The venture did not pan out. Never discouraged, the Ibachs engaged another partner, Captain Tom Smith. After two years of effort the three split their total profits of $26. Joe and Muz worked their original claims until 1956.[27]

Contrary to the hopes of economic boosters, prospectors discovered few promising mineral deposits in Glacier Bay National Monument. Miners dug in numerous locations, finding copper and nickel deposits, albeit none of outstanding commercial value. The U.S. Geological Survey, territorial and state politicians, and development interests backed mining in the monument but ultimately lost the contest. In 1976 the Mining in the Parks Act ended new claims and permitted buyouts of old claims.[28]

Boundary Changes

Although the 1936 mining law dismayed conservationists and National Park officials, another issue promised to change the picture. Since the mid-1920s, Forest Service and National Park Service planners had contemplated widening the monument's boundaries to the west and south to encompass Lituya Bay and forest habitat suitable for a brown bear sanctuary. The Forest Service felt pressure from brown bear advocates to designate Admiralty and Chichagof islands as national parks. Large stands of commercially exploitable timber covered both islands; the Forest Service therefore preferred expansion of, and national park status for, Glacier Bay. National Park Service directors concurred, reasoning that Admiralty and Chichagof offered comparatively little except for brown bear populations. Bureau of Biological Survey chiefs, Alaska Game Commission officials, and Governor Parks favored the Glacier Bay National Park option. Interior Secretary Harold Ickes visited Glacier Bay in 1938 and indicated approval of eventual national park status.

After FDR opened Glacier Bay to mining in 1936, advocates of expansion had begun to consider retaining monument status. Some believed mining in a national park would set a bad precedent and that conservationists might oppose such a plan. FDR signed a proclamation in April 1939 adding 905,000 acres of national forest and other lands, including Lituya Bay, to Glacier Bay National Monument.[29] The additions increased the size of the monument from 1,820 to 3,850 square miles.[30]

Soon after the 1939 boundary change, residents in the settlement of Gustavus on Strawberry Point at the edge of the monument complained that potentially valuable agricultural land had been closed to them. Some blamed the decline of cattle herds, down by half from a high of 278, and the decrease of settlers, from 35 to 10, on monument expansion. Alaska congressional delegate Bob Bartlett contacted park officials in the mid-1940s suggesting deletion of much of the lowland near Gustavus. National Park Service officials rated the land as submarginal for cattle or crops, noting that cattle herds had shrunk before the boundary change. They predicted that loss of the flatland, including a small airfield, would result in elimination of wolves and bears in the monument within reach of the private lands. Moreover, in the words of Chief Architect Thomas C. Vint, "Anyone taking up a homestead would certainly be doing so for the future, as a business property in connection with the airport and the National Monument, rather than for future farming." He proposed that to avoid an array of administrative problems, the government should acquire all private plots in the Gustavus area.[31]

Part-time Gustavus resident Charles Parker organized a campaign to remove the disputed land from the monument. In a December 18, 1954, letter to the Juneau *Daily Alaska Empire* he termed it "disheartening to see this virgin 10,000 acres of agricultural and stock-raising land dormant and unused." Pointing to the Cold War buildup he pronounced, "It is time every red-blooded Alaskan and American write his delegate and Congressman and insist that pressure be put on and the release of Gustavus Land from the Glacier Bay National Monument be secured at once. Then we can settle this section with veteran fighting men, and come what may, we will be able to produce thousands of tons of food for our people and military force."[32] The campaign triumphed in 1955 when President Dwight Eisenhower signed an order deleting about 18,000 acres for "an airfield for military purposes" and "limited type of agricultural use."[33]

As in many other Alaskan disputes, national security claims provided more excuse than reason for the deletion. A *Daily Alaska Empire* editorial came closer to the truth: "Although the farming possibilities of the area have long been known, to many the new release order is more important in that a large area has been thrown open to duck hunters for the first time in 16 years. Geese and ducks by the thousands stop to rest on the Gustavus flats and in the many sloughs that criss-cross the grassy coastal plain, but when the 1939 order took in the area, hunting was forbidden." No airfield materialized and, eighteen months after the opening of the "agricultural" area, only one party had filed for a homestead. Within three months they abandoned their farming project.[34]

Native Claims

Tlingit Indians possessed far broader and more long-standing claims to Glacier Bay than did either miners or settlers. At least since the most recent Ice Age glacial retreat, Tlingits had hunted seals and mountain goats, fished for salmon, gathered gull eggs, and picked berries on its lands and in its waters. Implicitly, and notwithstanding the designations of the Tongass National Forest and Glacier Bay National Monument, they could insist on ownership of at least part of the monument. But in the process of designating and adding to the monument in 1925 and 1939, neither conservationists nor the National Park Service paid attention to Tlingit concerns. They focused on a vision of parklands as "natural," or unspoiled by human activity. They viewed mining as the foremost potential threat and also sought to eliminate fish traps, canneries, fox farming, trapping, logging, hunting, and other consumptive activities. Monument status precluded nearly all of these, mining being a glaring exception.[35]

After the 1925 proclamation, Tlingits in the 800-person village of Hoonah 25 miles south of the monument continued to visit it for hunting, fishing, and gathering. They may have been unaware of the new law, and, in any case, no Park Service personnel lived within many miles of the monument. Park Service planners avoided the questions involved in Native land claims, in part because they had no experience accommodating such claims in parks in the States. Also, Native Americans as well as whites commonly accepted the goal of assimilation in the 1920s and 1930s. Hoonah Tlingits had engaged in cannery labor and commercial fishing since well before the turn of the century and actively sought wage work during World War II. Park Service leaders interpreted this as evidence of progressive integration into the cash economy and corresponding abandonment of economic dependence on, and cultural ties to, subsistence use of natural resources. In this light, hunting and fishing in the monument appeared as poaching. If done for cash or commercial sales, the taking seemed unnecessary or even immoral.

Moreover, hunting in the park ran counter to tourists' desire for close-up views of trusting animals. This applied particularly to harbor seals, the most numerous marine mammal species at Glacier Bay. Hoonahs traditionally hunted them for meat, seal oil, and skins for clothing. During the territorial period they killed seals in large part for a two- or three-dollar bounty and, later, for skins to be sold on the European market. Park rangers came upon the remains of 243 seals killed at Bartlett Cove in 1963. Nearly all the meat had been left. Another Tlingit hunter killed 300 seals at Glacier Bay in 1964. Such incidents fed a determination to end hunting in the monument, a goal the Park Service finally accomplished in 1974.[36]

For their part, the Hoonah Tlingits believed they possessed a legitimate right to enter the monument lands for subsistence to fulfill cultural traditions

Park ranger and harbor seal carcass, Glacier Bay National Monument, 1964 or 1965. Fol. 2, 00524, Glacier Bay National Park Archives. Tlingits killed seals to sell the skins and claimed it as a legitimate subsistence activity; Park Service officials regarded the practice as wasteful and illegal.

and that the Park Service had unfairly restricted them. Research indicated that they retained a significant level of dependence on Glacier Bay resources, even during the high-wage years of World War II. They considered seal hunting for bounties and hides essentially the same as subsistence hunting.[37]

The 1968 resolution of *Tlingit and Haida Indians v. United States*, first brought in 1929, acknowledged Tlingit rights to land ownership in the Tongass National Forest and Glacier Bay National Monument. The court ordered compensatory payment of $7.5 million. Passage of the Alaska Native Claims Settlement Act (ANCSA) in 1971 extinguished land claims in exchange for cash and land selections, not to be made in national parks or monuments. While the Hoonah Natives could not own land in the monument, ANCSA and the 1980 Alaska National Interest Lands Conservation Act both supported subsistence use rights on most federal lands. The Marine Mammal Protection Act of 1972 permitted Native Americans to hunt seals and other creatures for traditional purposes if not done in a wasteful manner.[38]

Unlike Katmai, Glacier Bay's formation featured a cultural, philosophical, and political clash over Native rights. Preservation-oriented conservationists and Park Service officials thought their insistence on unspoiled Nature a just goal that outweighed Tlingit prerogatives. Hoonah Tlingits eventually received land claims compensation in the form of cash payments and land selection outside the monument, and the Park Service eventually ended hunting. The experience suggested, but did not illuminate or resolve, some basic questions about natural resource protection: Is it fair to exclude traditional users from a park for the presumed benefit of society? Could or should "nature preservation" include human consumptive activities? If so, where should the lines be drawn between "natural" and disruptive or destructive activities? What motives, needs, traditions, and technologies should determine the limits of use? Who should be eligible for consumptive use rights, and would the arrangement be politically viable and manageable? These questions plagued the Park Service into the 21st Century in the dispute over commercial and subsistence fishing in Glacier Bay.

Park Service officials had for years pointed to the apparently wasteful killing of seals and tried to exclude all subsistence hunting and fishing in the monument. But jurisdiction over the waters beyond low tide had not been legally determined. Exercising interim control, the State of Alaska permitted commercial and, in 1989, subsistence fishing in Glacier Bay. At the onset of the 21st Century, fishing vessels contested whale-watching and sightseeing tourist boats for space in Glacier Bay in the heart of the monument.[39]

Tourism picked up rapidly in the 1970s. Whereas small private boaters had done most of the visiting in the 1940s and Canadian cruise ships in the 1950s, American cruise vessels reappeared in 1969 and escalated their trips over the following decades.[40] The mixture of fishing and tourism operations threatened to injure the park's ecological integrity and degrade the value of visitation. Nevertheless, as tourism multiplied over the years, Glacier Bay rivaled Katmai as proof of the appeal of nonconsumptive use values.

National Park Status

Glacier Bay National Monument, like Katmai, survived for decades despite challenges to its integrity and a near-absence of supervision and funding.

Physical remoteness and relative lack of pressure from extractive commercial enterprises helped protect the units. Concerted action by astute Park Service leaders fended off challenges in Washington. Territorial officials, viewing the units as potential tourist attractions, began to call for their development rather than their abolition. Seasonal rangers appeared in both units in 1950, and year-round supervision began in the mid-1960s. Glacier Bay's government-owned tourist lodge opened in 1966 and Park Service on-site headquarters in the early 1980s.[41]

At the 1966 dedication of the Park Service lodge at Bartlett Cove in the southeast corner of the monument, honored guest William S. Cooper predicted that "Glacier Bay National Monument will become Glacier Bay National Park."[42] Upon passage of the Alaska National Interest Lands Conservation Act two years after Cooper's death, his prophecy came true. Glacier Bay National Park and Preserve soon proved a highly popular scenic and wildlife viewing attraction, one of the best-known parks in Alaska. More than 200 bird species can be seen on its 3.3 million acres (5,322 square miles), encompassing colonies of nesting sea birds. Despite its mountainous character it is home to brown bears, black bears (some in the blue or "glacier bear" phase), wolves, moose, mountain goats, coyotes, wolverines, and smaller land mammals. In its waters swim humpback, minke, and killer whales, harbor and Dall's porpoises, sea lions, harbor seals, sea otters, and four species of salmon.[43] Mt. Cooper, within its boundaries, honors its founder, the botany professor.[44]

First intended as a reserve for tourism and science, Glacier Bay evolved into an outstanding example of ecosystem preservation. Quite similarly to Katmai National Monument, it offered scientific curiosities in the form of glaciers. Publicity by John Muir and others, followed by thousands of sightseers including President Harding, generated stateside interest in its preservation. A dedicated advocate, Cooper effectively mobilized public support. Like Katmai, Glacier Bay held almost no appeal for mining or logging companies or agricultural interests. A thoroughly unscientific claim of agricultural potential cost the park an ecologically valuable waterfowl feeding site, but a political compromise added a brown bear sanctuary. Visitors cherished the birds and mammals, thereby confirming ecosystem preservation as a central purpose of the park. Designation in the 1990s as part of a 27-million-acre U.S.- and Canada-managed Glacier Bay–Kluane-Tatshenshini-Wrangell/St. Elias World Heritage Site broadened the park's role to participation in a holistic plan for international cooperation in ecosystem maintenance.

9

Alaska Natives and Conservation

NOTWITHSTANDING EUROCENTRIC NOTIONS, NATIVE AMERICANS DESERVED THE status of Alaska's "discoverers," first human explorers, and, perhaps, rightful owners. The story of Western exploitation of Alaskan natural resources is in large part a record of destructive impact on the Natives. Russians (Chapters 1 and 2) enslaved the Aleuts and some of the Koniag Eskimos, Kenaitze Indians, and Chugach Eskimos and fought the Tlingit Indians. Whalers (Chapter 3) hired Eskimos to deplete the sea mammals and caribou on which the Eskimos themselves relied for food. Gold seekers (Chapter 4) dried up stocks of game in the interior. Commercial salmon fishers (Chapter 15) often refused to honor Native fishing territories. Federal officials (Chapter 8) ignored Tlingit claims in establishing the Tongass National Forest and Glacier Bay National Monument. Wildlife managers (Chapter 11) paid more attention to the needs of white trappers and hunters than to those of Alaska Natives. The national and territorial governments overrode and deferred Native land claims, although not denying them in principle. Accidentally introduced disease did by far the most damage to Native populations, but reductions of wildlife also took a toll. More

Commercial walrus hunters, Nome, early 20th Century. Newman coll. 97-201-113, University of Alaska Fairbanks, Alaska and Polar Regions Archives. Natives often engaged in industrial killing of wildlife they might need for their own subsistence. Some vessel captains took walrus meat to the villages.

dependent than the transient whites on fish and mammals, Alaska Natives faced poverty and even starvation when wildlife became scarce. But Native hunters (Chapters 3, 5, 10, 16) killed excessive numbers of animals for commercial sale of antlers, horns, hides, ivory, and meat.

Scholars have debated whether European and Euro-American intrusion in Alaska is a case of an environmentally consumptive culture replacing an environmentally responsible and stable system. Were Natives the first environmentalists? Did they see themselves as integrally related to their natural environments? Did they believe in sustainability or practice prudent use of resources? The answers have implications not only for cultural understanding but also for future prospects for sustainable use of natural resources in Alaska.

In addressing questions of aboriginal conservation, observers often cite ecologically oriented statements of Native American leaders and the relatively unaltered state of the natural environment when Europeans arrived. Others point to the extirpation of the mammoths and ancient bison in part by hunting and argue that Natives simply did not possess the technology to do more damage. Anthropologists examining these questions have found it difficult to distinguish Native American culture from the influences of European and Euro-American (or Western, or white) culture that have existed for so long. They also point out

Inupiat Eskimo boy netting auklets, Little Diomede Island, 1930s. Keys coll. 88-174-113, University of Alaska Fairbanks, Alaska and Polar Regions Archives. Low technology and, possibly, a conservation ethic prevented extinction of most wildlife species before the arrival of Europeans.

the difficulty of translating one belief system into terms that can be understood by the other.

EVIDENCE FROM ALASKA

Alaska, having encountered European and Euro-American culture later than most contiguous American colonies and territories, offered a better opportunity to find uncontaminated evidence of aboriginal behavior. Even there the coastal Natives have been affected for more than 200 years. Only fragments of relevant evidence are available for generalized conclusions about conservation practices in pre-contact Alaska.

George Bird Grinnell thought many Native Americans practiced conservation. He cited an incident recorded near Lake Champlain in 1687 in which Indians trapped deer but let the pregnant females go. He believed Algonquins, Athabaskans, and Aleuts had hunting territories carefully managed by families within a framework of overall tribal jurisdiction so as to maintain long-term abundance of wildlife. Grinnell's conclusion: "We sometimes think of the Indian as an improvident savage but in his control of the game supply he showed a wisdom which it has taken his white successors generations to ac-

Eskimo hunter and largha seal he has speared, Bering Sea, early 1900s. Lomen coll. 72-71-3225, University of Alaska Fairbanks, Alaska and Polar Regions Archives. In varying degrees, Eskimos, Aleuts, and Indians continued to rely on wildlife for subsistence throughout the 20th Century.

quire. Had we followed his ways from the beginning, the story of American big game would have been quite different."[1] Grinnell, however, spent little time in Alaska and based his judgment on anecdotal evidence rather than the findings of modern anthropology. Attempts to identify aboriginal conservation practices among Alaska Natives have been made in recent decades, yielding some relevant information.

Aleuts

Based on Russian accounts, researchers have affirmed aboriginal Aleut use of hunting territories, a system broken up during Russian control.[2] Some scholars viewed the Aleuts as ideally integrated into their oceanside environment in a sustainable manner. They argued that Aleuts exercised an ecologically beneficial, stabilizing effect; for example, consuming sea otters that might otherwise overexploit sea urchins and generate high population oscillations. Other information suggested that Aleuts had taken too many otters at Amchitka Island,

and, as a result, sea urchins must have multiplied and eaten up the kelp beds that harbored and fed fish and other creatures.[3] Russian cleric Ivan Veniaminov noted that Aleut hunters sought status by trying to "kill as many . . . wild animals as possible."[4]

Henry W. Elliott described the method used by Aleuts in the 1870s to catch finback and blue whales congregating in herds in the Aleutian Island passes:

> They tip a large number of spear handles with glass heads deeply notched (in primitive days they used slate), and paddling out quietly into a herd unconsciously feeding, they drive these weapons into forty or fifty of the whales, if the day is a favorable one. The glass head works in a day or two into the vitals of the creature, causing first inflammation, then death; and after a certain amount of time the carcass floats, and the currents carry the burden to the beach or else far out to sea, where it is never heard of again. If the natives manage to secure one whale this way, even though they strike hundreds, they feel well repaid for their labor.[5]

Given that the blue and finback whales are the two largest known vertebrate species ever to have lived on Earth, it is difficult to imagine a more ecologically costly means of acquiring food.

Southeastern Indians

Tlingit, Haida, and Tsimshian Indians of the Southeast also divided their hunting, fishing, and gathering areas into clan-controlled territories and, to a degree, exercised care not to overtax the resources. Economist George Rogers summarized their system:

> [T]he Indian had managed to create institutions and organizations which permitted a sound and rational relationship of man to his environment and a balanced utilization of the natural resource base to support something far greater than a bare subsistence existence. . . . [T]he picture is one of a highly rational relationship of population to resource base, a series of striking studies in balanced human ecology. . . . [T]he clans practiced a fairly sophisticated form of sustained-yield resource management in the best "modern" sense.

Other analysts concluded that Southeast Indian land use patterns had been oriented more to ownership than to conservation and that waste of wildlife occurred in the aboriginal culture.[6]

Anthropologist Frederica de Laguna, in a lengthy study of Yakutat Tlingits, found an essentially religious relationship between humans and nonhuman animals. The latter possessed moral standing approximately equal to humans and, according to one myth, had once been humans. They could understand human thoughts and affect the well-being of humans. To take a life of another species, a hunter had to observe correct preparatory behavior. After the kill the hunter explained, often in a song, why he had taken the creature's life. Body parts had to be treated in specific ways; for example, a bear's head would be covered and left facing inland, and salmon bones would be burned. Unnecessary killing and waste of body parts also constituted disrespect for the animal taken. Failure to observe proper etiquette could bring bad luck to the hunter or his relatives, or punishment in the next life. Familial groups maintained hunting territories for their own benefit, not for conservation in the modern sense of conscious sustainable use.[7]

Athabaskan Indians

For reasons not well understood, evidence of conservation practices is much stronger for Athabaskan Indians, living predominantly in the interior, than for other Alaska Native groups. Dena'ina Indian elder Andrew Balluta, a noted bear hunter, told of a traditional form of utilitarian conservation of brown bears in the Lake Clark vicinity. Certain stream valleys where the bears fished for salmon would be set aside. No activity that disturbed the bears would be allowed. The reserve kept the bears well fed, thus available for use and not hungry enough to be a nuisance to villagers.[8]

In his studies of the Koyukon (upper Koyukuk River) Indians, anthropologist Richard K. Nelson discovered a pattern of utilitarian conservation and ecosystem maintenance. Koyukons knew every stream, every patch of woods, every stretch of the river. They knew how many fish, mammals, and plants could be gathered from each and took care not to waste or exhaust the resources. Nelson observed that "Koyukon tradition contains an enormous wealth of empirical knowledge covering the entire spectrum of natural history. This includes a sophisticated understanding of interrelationships among natural phenomena, an ecological perspective essentially identical to that recently evolved in Western scientific thought." At the same time, the Koyukons proffered spiritual explanations for their relationship to Nature and did not appear to perceive any conflict between the two perspectives.[9] Nelson noted that "one of the basic themes in Koyukon ideology is a prohibition against wasting anything from nature. . . . Although avoidance of waste is based on spiritual sanctions, Koyukon people also believe it has practical significance in maintaining populations of resource species. They are always encouraged to harvest only what they can use, and to use anything they harvest."[10]

Beyond the avoidance of waste, "[S]ustained yield considerations are important to the entire spectrum of hunting, trapping, fishing, and gathering activities. This empirically based approach to conservation of resources derives from the Koyukon people's practical understanding of ecological dynamics." Nelson advised, however, that insufficient data existed to prove in scientific terms the effectiveness of Koyukon conservation practices.[11] He also detected a conservation ethic among the Black River Kutchin Indians of northeastern Alaska, although he cautioned that the idea may not have pre-dated Western influence.[12]

Historian Melodie Webb found that, in the upper Yukon Valley in the 1930s, Athabaskan trappers displayed a much more conservative attitude toward game regulations than white trappers did. Relying primarily on trapping for income and apparently desirous of ensuring adequate furbearer stocks, Indians seldom overtrapped their territories. Webb believed the behavior stemmed from cultural ties to the land.[13]

Research on wood bison in the upper Yukon drainage suggests a lack of sustainable behavior on the part of Athabaskans. Oral tradition consistently described the animals as common in the early 1800s. Buffalo Shirt Mountain in the Sheenjek River country is said to have received its name when a large herd passed over its slope, appearing to cover it. Hunters easily killed the beasts using versatile bows and arrows, dogs, and snowshoes in winter. According to one account they drove herds off a cliff. Stories also blamed excessive hunting for eradicating the bison and causing starvation. Wolf and bear predation could have contributed little to the extirpation, nor would climate or vegetation change likely have had such an impact over a relatively short period.[14]

Examining subarctic Indians including Koyukons and Chipewyans, cultural historian Calvin Martin found their relationship to wildlife to be grounded in a fundamentally different conception of reality than that of Western civilization. The latter viewed Nature as matter to be dominated and exploited, whereas for the Indians,

> [a]nimals lived the majority of time as spirits in the bush, the spirit realm, and were every bit as intelligent and sophisticated as man. . . . Hunting these animals was a series of spiritual maneuvers designed to engage the spirit of the game so that it would agree to make a sacrifice of its flesh to the needy hunter. Hunting was a kind of contract between man and animal: animals, as conscious and intelligent beings, were well aware that their flesh was necessary for man's survival and they willingly donned fleshy clothing from time to time and surrendered themselves to the hunter. But they in turn demanded respect. Respect lies at the heart of North American hunting; it forms the core of the man-animal relationship in Amerindian society.

Therefore, Martin concluded, hunting represented "much more than a straightforward pursuit. It is an act that embraces all of life; it is a relationship of reciprocating esteem and courtesy. . . . Animals are members of man's social universe, and man a member of theirs."[15]

Martin perceived three deterrents to overexploitation of wildlife: the small number of Native Americans, the low level of technology, and the lack of economic incentives. Of these, Euro-American influence removed the second and third. Disease and Christianity weakened faith in traditional values and, added to the fur trade, destroyed the spiritual relationship of mutual respect and obligation between the Natives and wildlife. As a result the Natives became aggressively exploitative; in effect, they declared war on wildlife. However, Martin attributed the extinction of ground sloths, mammoths, horses, and other plains mammals more to climate changes than to slaughter by Natives.[16]

Eskimos

Robert F. Spencer cited evidence of conservation practices among Eskimos[17]: "In the aboriginal culture, the foxes were hunted by means of traps between December and April. . . . [O]nly five of each kind of fox could be taken at a time. The theory was the five skins were sufficient for a parka of matched skins and the fox was offended if more that five of his kind were killed."[18] The same rule applied to the wolf and wolverine. Ethnographer Knud Rasmussen noted that the Icy Cape Inupiat trapped no more than five wolves or wolverines in a season lest the hunter lose his catch or be attacked and killed by the animals.[19] As in Indian beliefs, logical sustained-yield principles melded into spiritual explanations. Animals could think and communicate like humans; they sensed human thoughts and actions and could bring bad luck, including reduced hunting success, if mistreated.

In the central Brooks Range, Nunamiut Eskimos reduced Dall sheep populations to low levels between 1885 and 1910. Anthropologist John M. Campbell determined that, following an absence of 600–800 years, the Eskimos moved into the mountains in substantial numbers around 1750. Relying primarily on migrating caribou, they hunted sheep in the summer and at other times when caribou did not appear. They employed bows and arrows and, even more effectively, snares. Periods of starvation came to pass in 1906–1907 and 1910–1911 when few caribou or sheep remained. By 1920, in part because of diseases introduced by whalers, virtually no Eskimos lived in the area. Campbell concluded that sheep had either been gradually hunted out over generations or overutilized during the period of caribou scarcity around the turn of the century. As of the late 1930s, in the near-absence of hunters, sheep herds had recovered.[20]

Moose and muskox populations also reflected hunting pressure by Eskimos on the North Slope. Both had existed in the region during the Pleistocene Era. As moose began to move northwest to recolonize the area in the 1800s, Nunamiut hunters probably killed off most of the few that crossed the Brooks Range into the northern river valleys. Study of climate, vegetation, and wolf predation indicated that none of these would have been a deterrent to moose range extension. After the Nunamiut left the Brooks Range in the early 20th

Century, moose dispersed from populations south of the range and established themselves in the north.[21]

Fragmentary fossil evidence suggested that muskoxen existed in small numbers relative to other grazers. Climatic change turned steppes into forest during the Holocene, restricting muskox populations to northern coastal Alaska and the northern foothills of the Brooks Range where they could find suitable feed. Bernik, Inuit, and Nunamiut hunters stalked the creatures from several thousand years BPE into the 19th Century. They ate the meat, used the skins for warmth, and carved ladles and other implements from the horns. Like mountain sheep, muskoxen served as a reserve meat supply in times of scarcity of caribou or, for the Inuit, whales and other sea mammals. Introduction of an improved dogsled permitted hunters to range more widely and find the small and isolated herds. Dogs could be trained to force the animals into their defensive arcs where they could be killed by bow and arrow. Native hunters, therefore, probably caused the virtual extinction of Alaskan muskoxen before the advent of whaling or firearms.[22]

Anthropologist Ann Fienup-Riordan found that Yup'ik Eskimos on Nelson Island traditionally perceived themselves as integrally and reciprocally related to nonhumans. Both possessed souls, and each could influence the thoughts and behavior of the other. As creatures of equivalent moral standing, humans could not be stewards or owners of others. Humans could justifiably take the lives of nonhumans provided it was done in a proper, respectful manner. In the harvest of herring, individuals earned the right to particular fishing spots through long-term demonstration of appropriate behavior toward the fish by them and their relatives. Failure to fulfill obligations toward wildlife could induce the prey creature to go into hiding or otherwise refuse to make itself available for harvest in the future. If a creature presented itself for harvest, the hunter felt obliged to take it lest it be offended. All creatures eventually returned to life after death; humans could cause local or temporary disappearance of species but not extinction. Therefore, in fulfillment of their obligations, the Yup'ik sometimes engaged in what Euro-Americans would consider unnecessary killing and waste of wildlife, and their belief in reincarnation precluded any concern for species preservation.[23]

Ecosystem Sustainability

Regarding maintenance of ecosystem integrity, few opportunities for assessment of aboriginal practices have appeared. Sustainable harvest of wildlife by Koyukons and others afforded a degree of ecosystem integrity, if only incidentally. But their care for wildlife did not necessarily apply to vegetation, a vital foundation for wildlife populations. Citing fragmentary evidence, historian

Harold Lutz believed Natives sometimes abused the environment through fire. Eskimos and Indians used fire for a variety of purposes, among them campfires, signaling, warding off mosquitoes, repairing birch bark kayaks and canoes, and felling trees. Carelessness prevailed, and fires often went out of control. An observer wrote in 1898 that in the upper Yukon Valley "the Indian also has a way of signaling by burning trees. When in a locality where he expects to find his friends or family, he sets fire to a tall spruce, and then calmly sits down and watches the horizon for an answering column of smoke. The wind will fan these flames into a fierce forest fire in a short time, and the Indians are too utterly indifferent to think about putting them out." White men, judged Lutz, exercised even less care in using fire than Natives did.[24]

Athabaskans in the upper Tanana region, like Algonquins in Canada, employed fire as a tool in a planned strategy to raise the productivity of the taiga. Regularized, prescribed burnings increased furbearers, waterfowl, and big game, especially moose. Fires set in the village periphery suppressed vegetation that might endanger the village in case of wildfire.[25] Uncontrolled fire could wreak widespread havoc in the interior but had virtually no capacity to do large-scale damage to the tundra regions of northern and western Alaska or to the rainforest of the Southeast. Except for destruction of wildlife populations, Natives possessed no means of dismantling these ecosystems. Some spoke of the sacredness of the land and the importance of their ties to it, and some tribes allotted territories for harvest. But the notion or practice of ecosystem preservation as such may not have existed.

INTERPRETING THE EVIDENCE

Whether aboriginal Natives can be considered "environmentalists" or "conservationists" depends in part on definitions. It seems clear that Alaskan aboriginal societies felt close to or part of Nature and respected other creatures. Rituals for taking wild creatures might have had the effect of preventing depletion of species. A society that practiced sustainable use of natural resources, however indirectly, might well be considered conservationist. Utilitarian conservationism in the modern sense would call for institutionalized and conscious restraint in harvest of natural resources based on awareness of their limited availability. To be environmentalist, the society would take steps to protect the ecosystem as well and would order itself so as to perpetuate a sustainable relationship to the ecosystem. Such a holistic system would integrate social beliefs, feelings, behavior, technology, and population levels with the characteristics—including resource limits—of the natural environment.

Perhaps no human society, ancient or modern, has achieved an ideally holistic relationship to its natural environment. Numerous barriers have existed, among them lack of understanding of the environment, changes in the environment, interference by other societies, dissident behavior or beliefs, self-centeredness, and lack of population control. Assessing the evidence for aboriginal environmentalism is not a matter of searching for perfect societies. It is an attempt to find responsible practices by some tribes and individuals that may reflect on their wisdom or, more importantly, may be useful in a modern era of environmental distress.

The apparent infrequency of species extinction and the existence of tribal societies within the land's carrying capacity, said anthropologist Raymond Hames, led people to assume that aborigines practiced conservation. Many myths, taboos, and rituals reinforced the impression. But Hames insisted that "if a people have a conservation ideology but do not act as conservationists, then they are not conservationists. . . . [C]onservation is a matter of performance, not intent." The best proof of conservation behavior would be data on the relationship of hunting practices to wildlife populations. In the case of declining prey species, hunters should reduce their take. Yet tribal societies had caused the extinction of some species on islands. Based on his study of Amazonian tribes, Hames believed that none practiced conservation. For conservation to work in a tribal culture, he posited the need for internal rule enforcement to prevent fellow tribesmen from cheating and external defense to prevent outsiders from taking the resources. The former required strong chiefs and the latter some form of territorial control. Amazonians lacked both, but the Polynesians and Micronesians, who possessed both, enforced effective conservation on their fishing grounds. Hames suggested that coastal Alaska Natives, having strong chiefs and territories, may well have practiced conservation.[26]

Numerous observers have commented on the tendency of Alaska Natives to waste wildlife such as caribou, deer, and sea creatures.[27] To the extent that Eskimos thought about population balances, some of this profligacy may have been related to the large groupings and migratory nature of the animals in question. Unlike the interior Indians less dependent on migratory mammals, coastal Eskimos would have found it difficult to acquire a sense of the ecology of the sea and how their behavior could influence it. A premium might then have been put on killing as many (whales, walrus, seals) as possible, never knowing for certain when they might reappear. Similarly, it would have been difficult to imagine that the massive herds of migratory caribou, for example, could be threatened by wasteful killing at a particular time and place.

The extravagant slaughter and waste of whales by the Aleuts, as related by Elliott, may have involved an assumption that the supply could not be exhausted. Given a small number of consumers in a large ocean, the practice by itself would probably not have endangered a species. Added to commercial whaling, it might have contributed materially to whale declines. Whatever the effect, in comparison to the later use of handheld guns, it represented a rare case of primitive technology being as destructive as modern methods.

Introduction of technologies such as the gun, said Hames, did not necessarily increase the killing of game. It might mean the hunter simply spent less time hunting. But market hunting—for skins, feathers, furs, pets, and other purposes—could quickly exhaust wildlife populations. Contact with modern civilization also encouraged settlement near schools, hospitals, missions, and trading posts, resulting in depletion of natural resources in the vicinity.[28]

Much of the prodigal behavior of Alaska Natives probably stemmed from the adoption of Western values and technology. When John Muir upbraided a Tlingit for needlessly shooting a gull, the Indian replied that he had learned careless killing of wildlife from whites.[29] The impact of just one implement, the gun, exceeded the ability of social norms to evolve fast enough to control the weapon's use. Western culture overpowered the Alaska Natives in several ways. As in nearly all pre-modern societies it has encountered, it weakened the legitimacy of traditional beliefs and practices. It taught Natives to think of wild creatures as commodities to harvest for personal material gain. Knowing that by killing large amounts of wildlife they could earn money to purchase prized luxuries such as guns and alcohol, many Natives did so even though it eroded their life-support base.

Alaska Natives eagerly adopted technologies—the match, rifle, powerboat, modern heating and lighting, medicine—that yielded material comforts and ease of taking game. All of these turned out to be two-edged swords, creating dependency on outside income and resources and undermining traditional culture. Resource exploiters, traders, missionaries, teachers, government officials, and other representatives of Euro-American civilization implicitly or explicitly conveyed a sense of the superiority of white culture. Before the mid-20th Century most educated whites thought assimilation to be in the Natives' best interest. Many or most Natives adopted these judgments and willingly engaged in behavior that damaged their own heritage. Each village and ethnic group contained individuals for and against Westernization, and considerable regional variation existed. Traditional views prevailed more among tribal leaders, the elderly, and the Athabaskans.

Unlike modern technology, adaptation to the core values of Euro-American culture proved extremely trying. Excepting the Southeast coastal Indians and perhaps the Aleuts, traditional Alaska Native culture emphasized group orientation, cooperation, sharing. It differed vastly from Western industrial values of individualism, aggressiveness, and material acquisitiveness. It sought to minimize skills and attitudes necessary for competitive "success." Caught between making the difficult transition and returning to traditional material culture often viewed as a form of poverty, Natives experienced identity crises.

High rates of alcoholism, school dropout, violence, suicide, and mental illness followed.[30]

Some Alaskan aboriginal beliefs and practices demonstrated ecological orientation in a sense of community and mutual obligation with natural surroundings or in awareness of ecological processes. Natives valued animals for a variety of nonconsumptive reasons and regularly granted them a form of rights. Some articulated an appreciation of the land or the ecosystem as a whole. Natives evolved elements of a holistic sense of connectedness to the land that in important respects surpassed the wisdom of the Euro-Americans.

Other Alaska Native practices, especially among Athabaskans, manifested utilitarian conservationist principles, managing and using resources for sustained yield. In some cases this wise use principle may have been a product of the fur trade, an attempt to maximize trapping income by conserving furbearer populations. Groups and, probably, individuals varied in their beliefs and behavior. Practice did not necessarily correspond to belief, as witnessed by many Natives' swift adoption of the wasteful and disrespectful habits of outsiders. Nor did the felt sense of obligation toward wild creatures always protect hunted species from extirpation.

Alaska Natives engaged in constant efforts to survive, as did other organisms, and the value of physical survival implied the need for a value of sustaining the resources on which they depended. Moreover, the hunted species had an implicit need for survival and, arguably, a corresponding right to exist. It seems relevant, therefore, to consider whether Natives engaged in sustainable use of Nature.

Compared to that of Euro-Americans, Alaskan aboriginal treatment of Nature appears to have been relatively benign. As to whether aboriginal Alaskans qualified as conservationists, the evidence suggests that some people, to some degree, in some places practiced elements of conservation, if the criterion is behavior that had the deliberate effect of conserving natural resources. Similarly, some Natives practiced aspects of environmentalism, including a holistic relationship to the land and an acknowledgment of nonhuman rights. By changing technology, attitudes, and land ownership patterns, Euro-American civilization distorted Native environmental practices and social systems as a whole. Whatever the degree of traditional commitment to environmental protection, not much evidenced itself by the time of statehood.

IMPLICATIONS OF THE EVIDENCE

Many scholars and others who attributed ecological wisdom to aboriginal cultures hoped it could be an object lesson to Western civilization, which they viewed as destructive and unsustainable. To the extent that aboriginal Alaskans practiced principles of modern environmentalism, in particular an ecocentric perspective and ecologically sustainable natural resource use, they lacked the power to transfer those values to arriving Europeans and Euro-Americans. Most outsiders thought they had little to learn from the Natives in the realms of philosophy and economics. In the post-1960s era, Alaska Native environmentalism may have marginally affected the thinking of Alaskan environmentalists, who discovered elements of holism by other means.

Calvin Martin described North American Indians' reciprocal relationship to Nature as "inherently conservationist" but added that the idea that Western society might adopt it seemed "preposterous." The gap in perspectives, he argued, is too great. Even the philosophies of Thoreau, Emerson, Muir, and George Perkins Marsh, he thought, had been ethnocentric in that they saw Nature as God's work. And Aldo Leopold's land ethic implied a form of human dominance, if benign in intent, of the land. "Surely," said Martin, "we deluded ourselves when we imagined that the Indian could teach us his particular land ethic; we did not understand that it was not just a land ethic but a comprehensive way of life. Anyway, as far as the Indian is concerned, it isn't he who does the teaching but rather the land."[31]

A second reason for asking whether Natives practiced conservation would be to assess the prospects for sustainable living by present-day tribal societies. In post-statehood Alaska many Natives relied substantially on the land for subsistence and cultural identity. Could these values be maintained, and, if not, what would be the fate of the people? Speaking of tribal societies in general, Hames postulated that social and ecological deterioration did not have to occur: "[S]imultaneous conservation of ethnic and biological diversity is possible. Native peoples can exist in equilibrium with game populations if the technology they use is regulated, if hunting and fishing are aimed solely at meeting nutritional demands, and if settlement patterns remain dispersed, mobile, and at low population densities."[32]

As applied to Alaska, Hames prescribed a difficult set of criteria for social and ecological viability. Resource politics reflected some of the obstacles. Use of wildlife and other natural resources lay at the core of long-standing disputes over Native rights and subsistence rights. Alaska Natives had won a large land settlement through the Alaska Native Claims Settlement Act of 1971, but the state and national governments retained jurisdiction over fish and wildlife. State wildlife managers, like the federal officials they succeeded in 1960, tended to reflect the interests of sport hunters. Management focused on enforcement of licensing, seasons, bag limits, and methods (e.g., snowmobiles and aircraft), backed by biological research aimed at maintaining viable game populations. Natives commonly ignored the regulations and the science, harvesting wildlife according to custom or convenience. Wildlife managers understood little of

Caribou left in woods by Inupiat hunters, Shungnak, 1949. By Ray Woolford. FWS 1214, Alaska Resources Library and Information Services. Alaska Game Commission agent Woolford required the hunters to retrieve the caribou. Numerous instances of wildlife waste by Natives generated an ongoing controversy about causes and management options.

Native culture and judged Native hunting behavior in terms of its adherence to regulations. Finding the Natives frequently in violation of the law, they reacted unsympathetically to appeals for special Native rights to wildlife. Constitutional principles of equality cast doubt on claims of special rights. Also, changes in Native society raised questions of what constituted Native culture and led many non-Natives to conclude that modernizing Natives no longer needed or deserved special resource use rights. A cultural and political gap existed over who should have priority rights to wildlife and what level and type of use met the criterion of fulfillment of a true need.[33]

The gap in perspectives and the remoteness of many Alaska Native hunting grounds resulted in weak enforcement of regulations. Yet some conservation progress occurred. State and federal laws gave Natives a partial priority status in uses of wildlife and included Natives on regulatory panels. Natives found themselves at a disadvantage in competing through the regulatory process, especially in state proceedings. Cooperative management of some federally controlled wildlife, such as bowhead whales and polar bears, incorporated Native participation and succeeded in protecting both wildlife populations and cultural traditions.[34] At the onset of the 21st Century some species had been safeguarded by cooperative management, some had not, and the broader question of subsistence rights had yet to be resolved.

Hames's prescription called for controls on technology in taking wildlife and restriction of the harvest to traditional needs. For some species and locales such as bowhead whales and polar bears along the northern coasts, these goals could be feasibly met. Large animals taken near a small number of villages could be easily monitored. For smaller or more dispersed species such as waterfowl or wolverines, monitoring would be much more difficult. Swift and long-range snowmobiles, powerboats, and aircraft carried the potential for excess killing of wildlife. Enforcement of rules restricting harvest to nutritional needs would be expensive and politically contentious. Acceptance of such rules could grow only gradually among hunters who, by historical experience or traditional beliefs, had not practiced conservation of wildlife. Moreover, Natives could hardly be expected to give up the comforts and pleasures of modern society to which they had become accustomed. Yet these advantages and implements depended on substantial monetary income, not easily achievable for many Natives. To the extent that higher income derived from increased consumptive exploitation of natural resources, such as timber and walrus ivory, sustainability would be put in jeopardy.

On the whole, Alaska Natives have behaved much the same as non-Natives in their treatment of natural resources since statehood. Yup'ik Eskimos depleted goose populations but, after intervention by the Fish and Wildlife Service, cooperated in restoration measures. Hoonah Tlingits opposed clearcut logging in their vicinity but engaged in unsustainable logging elsewhere. Gwitch'in Indians opposed oil drilling in the Arctic Refuge for fear it would undermine their traditional lifestyle and caribou supply, while the Alaska Federation of Natives, and Eskimos who stood to gain from oil revenues, advocated drilling. Some individuals, and some groups such as the Koyukon Indians, emphasized conservation values. Others, especially those active in regional corporations, favored rapid exploitation of resources. In environmental controversies, Alaska Natives and environmentalists have made selective and temporary alliances.[35]

Hames also envisioned dispersed, mobile, and small human populations as necessary for cultural and ecological sustainability. Most Alaska Native villages are widely separated and small, but seasonal migration for subsistence has all but disappeared. The last nomadic group, Nunamiut Eskimos, settled at Anaktuvuk Pass in 1947.[36] Television and other influences attracted the young to outside popular culture, almost certainly eroding their ties to the land. Most villages could not support themselves economically; they relied on the land for part of their sustenance and on cash transfers from outside. Native regional corporations, designed for commercial exploitation of natural resources as a path to modernization, undertook environmentally destructive logging and mining operations. But population growth constituted the most serious problem. Between 1990 and 2000, Alaska Natives increased at three times the rate of white Alaskans (Table 10.1). This trend alone, if continued, would preclude living in harmony with the land and would probably undermine cultural pride as well.

Remnants of aboriginal beliefs supportive of species or ecosystem sustainability could supplement and enrich modern science in resource management. Each could learn something from the other. Management science might become more holistic, developing a broader understanding of human ties to the land. Conversely, ecological science could help Natives understand the dynamics of wildlife populations and the imperatives of balancing human population and resources. Cooperative wildlife management has achieved this in some degree. Broader success would depend in part on whether aboriginal culture has been ecologically responsible and, even more, on whether Natives and non-Natives believe it to be so.

Part II

Wildlife and Wildlife Managers

As Aleutian fur catches shrank in the 1790s, Russians extended the range of their trade to the Alaskan mainland. Americans and the British arrived shortly after Cook's 1778 visit and aggressively sought furs both on land and at sea. The quasi-governmental Russian-American Company could not control or compete against American whalers, who operated at will in Russian waters. Hudson's Bay Company, long arm of Russia's rival the British Empire, established a trading presence in Southeast Alaska by the 1830s. It moved west from the Mackenzie River Valley and in 1847 set up a post at Fort Yukon in Russian-claimed Alaska. Vulnerable to potential hegemonic moves by the British and Americans and realizing modest fur profits, the Russians concluded that they had no viable future in Alaska. Not wanting the British on their eastern border, they resolved to sell the territory to the United States.

The United States assumed jurisdiction over all of Alaska claimed by Russia, even though the Russians had controlled very little of it. It set aside the question of Native claims for future consideration. It placed the land under military rule, but traders, gold seekers, and other exploiters carried on almost unsupervised. After the opening of salmon canneries in 1878 and the Juneau gold strike of 1880 the non-Native population swelled, generating an obvious need for law and order. The 1884 Organic Act made Alaska an administrative district overseen by an appointed governor. It permitted mining claims by whites on lands not occupied or claimed by Natives.

From the beginning, a strained relationship existed between the non-Native elements and the federal government. Settlers demanded more services, autonomy, and control over resources, accusing the government of obstructing progress and favoring salmon canning companies and other outside corporate interests. The salmon industry, for its part, did long-term biological damage to runs of salmon. Federal officials looked upon Alaskans as unprepared for self-government and irresponsible in their treatment of natural resources. They viewed the resources as belonging to the nation, not just to white settlers or Alaska Natives.

While gold rush dramas played themselves out, events in the States had been building for decades toward state and federal wildlife protection. An ornithology office within the Department of Agriculture evolved into the Bureau of Biological Survey and ultimately the Interior Department's Fish and Wildlife Service. It gained power and responsibility through the Lacey Act of 1900, bird and mammal conservation laws, and the assembling of a complex of wildlife refuges. Well before the turn of the century Alaskan wildlife issues caught the attention of federal officials and their allies in private conservation groups. Natural resource abuses in the States, and laws attempting to curb them, echoed in federal policy toward Alaska. Unlike the other territories where the damage had largely occurred prior to federal protective action, Alaska offered the nation a chance to take a preemptive stand against wholesale loss of Nature.

During the gold rushes of 1880–1910 the rising non-Native population intensified the pressure on game mammals. Commercial slaughter for meat, hides, and antlers progressed into a booming industry, depleting several species of mammals in the early years of the 20th Century. At the urging of federal officials, the Boone and Crockett Club, and other conservation groups, Congress enacted laws between 1900 and 1925 in an effort to curb the abuses. A similar series of laws attempted to stop the overexploitation of salmon. Distance from Washington and prevailing attitudes of local citizens and fortune seekers obstructed law enforcement.

When Alaska gained territorial status and a legislature in 1912, the federal government retained jurisdiction over natural resources through the appointed governor and natural resource agencies. But the legislature mirrored local antagonism toward federal wildlife management jurisdiction and policies, especially protection of the grizzly bear and oversight of commercial salmon fishing. And neither the territorial nor the federal government permitted the Natives much say in natural resource policies.

Alaska's naturalist-wildlife managers spent time in Alaska varying from months to years; some worked in the territory and others out of Washington. Three directors of the Bureau of Biological Survey and the Fish and Wildlife Service belonged to their ranks. All loved wild Alaska, or aspects of it, and committed themselves to its defense. They incorporated the values of the Progressive Era conservation movement that guided federal wildlife management. Like the private naturalists, their brands of conservation ranged from utilitarian to moderately preservationist. Most approved of predator control, and some endorsed species translocations or other projects of dubious ecological or economic wisdom. They participated in the writing of wildlife protection laws and worked to gain public support. Traveling by dogsled and boat and later by bush plane, they came to know the country and people, building respect for conservation and guarding fisheries and land mammals. A few, notably Bob Marshall, Olaus and Margaret Murie, and Ira Gabrielson, bestowed lasting gifts in the preservation of large tracts of land as parks and reserves. They assisted and built upon the endeavors of the early private naturalists to complete a vital phase in the development of conservation in Alaska.

Government biologists, through their work on lands and wildlife, reinforced the values of species sustainability for consumptive use (utilitarian conservation). To some extent, as in the Arctic National Wildlife Range, they advocated ecosystem preservation and nonconsumptive use. Ecological science led some to oppose aggressive predator control. Bob Marshall and the Muries forthrightly articulated nonconsumptive use values. All respected and furthered the application of science as a means to sound management. In retirement and sometimes during government service, several mobilized the public through writing or political action. Their efforts sowed seeds of modern environmentalism in both the States and Alaska.

10

Bureau of Biological Survey Chiefs

C. Hart Merriam, Edward W. Nelson, Ira N. Gabrielson

BETWEEN 1902 AND 1924, JURISDICTION OVER ALASKA'S LAND MAMMALS AND MIGRATORY birds came under the purview of the Agriculture Department's Bureau of Biological Survey (BBS). For most of the first half-century of its existence, members or associate members of the Boone and Crockett Club directed the agency. At least three of these well-educated men maintained a strong interest in Alaska and used their contacts in government to implement its first game laws and some of its wildlife preserves. Evidence of decimation and waste of wildlife, largely a product of the Gold Rush and the salmon industry, firmed their resolve to conserve Alaska's game animals.

ABUSE OF LAND MAMMALS

Alaska's land mammals and birds escaped the brunt of the assault by the early fur seekers. This began to change when the Russians moved inland and American and Hudson's Bay traders arrived. In their quest for furbearers, some traders introduced alcohol to the Natives, cheated them, and undermined their

TABLE 10.1. Human Population of Alaska, 1740–2000

Year	*Native American*	*White*	*Other*	*Total*
1740	74,700	—	—	74,700
1840	40,016	700	—	40,716
1880	32,996	430	—	33,426
1890	25,354	4,298	2,298	32,052
1900	29,542	30,450	3,600	63,592
1910	25,331	36,400	2,625	64,356
1920	26,558	27,883	595	55,036
1930	29,983	28,640	655	59,278
1940	32,458	39,170	896	72,524
1950	33,884	92,973	1,976	128,643
1960	43,081	174,546	8,540	226,167
1970	(52,000)	236,767	(12,000)	300,382
1980	64,357	311,968	25,526	401,851
1990	85,698	415,492	48,853	550,043
2000	98,043	434,534	94,355	626,932

Sources: George W. Rogers and Richard A. Cooley, *Alaska's Population and Economy: Regional Growth, Development, and Future Outlook, Vol. 2: Statehood Handbook.* College: University of Alaska, Institute of Business, Economic and Governmental Research, 1963, 28; U.S. Dept. of Commerce, Census Bureau, annual census data, 1970–2000, Washington, DC

Note: 1970 figures for Native American and Other are approximate.

culture in a variety of ways. The Gold Rush era, however, affected land mammals more detrimentally than the land fur traders did. Russians found gold in parts of Alaska but did little or no prospecting. Men attracted by the 1880 Juneau gold strike, as well as salmon canners, put heavy hunting stress on the deer in the Southeast. Then came the great Klondike strike of 1896 and its aftermath. Gold fever drove people from around the world to explore the creeks of the Yukon and of Alaska, whose non-Native population jumped 750 percent between 1890 and 1900 (Table 10.1). Gold seekers killed accessible wildlife to feed themselves or pay their bills. They caught furbearers by any means possible, including poisons and destruction of beaver lodges. Meat hunters, many of them Indians, supplied the miners. Widespread reckless slaughter of game mammals took place. Game and some furbearers dwindled, especially in river drainages where the gold seekers traveled and worked.

Settlers, sport hunters, and commercial trophy hunters added to the toll of wildlife, often wastefully. Treasury agent Joseph Murray described in 1895 what he had witnessed in the Southeast: "[T]he smell from decaying deer carcasses became horribly offensive around the towns and villages. White men go out and kill the animals for fun, just to see who can knock down the most in a given time. The natives kill them, because they can get a drink of whiskey, valued at 25 cents, for each skin secured."[1] An investigative report by J. Alden Loring for the New York Zoological Society in 1901 stated, "It is believed by responsible men that five moose are killed for every one that is used." One Indian reportedly shot 50 moose in a summer, when the meat would not be at its best. Hunters killed many so the largest antlers could be picked out for sale and left the rest of the bodies. They shot thousands of deer for the hindquarters or for the skins alone, which sold for 10 to 20 cents each.[2] Many deer died for even lesser reasons. A Mr. Britten recalled a winter day in 1901 when deep snow had driven deer down to the shore to feed on seaweed in Wrangell Narrows: "Soon a five dory halibut boat came along with, I think, five guns shooting. They simply shot the deer, leaving them lay, not even putting a boat down to pick one up. I counted 28 deer killed below the snow line, with bloody tracks leading into the woods where cripples had escaped, to die later. This took place within a stretch of five or six miles."[3] At Sand Point in 1911, F.E. Kleinschmidt encountered a Native offering 82 caribou tongues at 50 cents each. The remainder of the animals lay in the field on the Alaska Peninsula where they fell.[4] In various localities hunters eradicated herds of mountain sheep.[5] Governors' reports stated that beavers approached extinction and that furbearers in general had become scarce.[6]

Trophy hunting got under way before the turn of the century, mainly in the relatively accessible Southeast and the Alaska and Kenai peninsulas where settlers first appeared about 1898. It took two forms: sport hunting by wealthy individuals who sought adventure, social status, and decorations for their dens and clubrooms; and commercial gathering of animal parts to be sold outside Alaska. Both groups of hunters looked for the largest specimens they could find of moose and caribou antlers, sheep horns, and bear heads and hides.

British military officer Colonel Claude Cane, who visited both peninsulas in 1902, exemplified the gentleman-hunter perspective. Reflecting on his sheep hunt on the Kenai, he reasoned, "Some people, I know, will blame me for shooting four rams in one day and five in another, and call it massacre and not sport; but they must remember I had come thousands of miles to get these specimens, and had already hunted many blank days and put in a great deal of hard work without results."[7] By contrast, his sporting friend Frances Paget

> had just come down from the headwaters of the Indian, and had got six nice rams, though he said they were neither so plentiful as they were the year before, nor did there seem to be as many good heads. This was not to be wondered at, as two brothers had spent the whole winter in this ground, and had brought out twenty-five big heads, besides, as we afterwards found out, leaving a good many smaller ones, which they did not think worth the trouble of packing out, to rot on the ground.
>
> Such slaughter as this is inexcusable, and cannot even be profitable, as the fur dealers will pay only five dollars each for sheep heads, and it is to be hoped that the new Alaskan Game Law will effectively put a stop to it in the immediate future.[8]

TABLE 10.2. Game Killed by Radclyffe Party, Kenai Peninsula, 1903

Species	*Number*	*Species*	*Number*
Brown bear	13	River otter	1
Black bear	2	Wolverine	1
Moose	6	Porcupine	6
Dall sheep	15	Snowshoe hare	31
Caribou	7	Eagle	3
Seal	3	Grouse & ptarmigan	108
Fox	2	Goose, duck, other birds (sp.)	60

Source: C.R.E. Radclyffe, *Big Game Shooting in Alaska* (London: Rowland, Ward, 1904), 73.
Note: Includes some sheep and caribou shot by guides for food.

Regarding moose, Cane pointed to the Berg brothers as having

> killed and shipped out during the last winter to taxidermists in the States twelve moose with heads more than 65 inches in spread, a number which, most sportsmen will agree, is somewhat excessive, even in a country as full of game as the Kenai Peninsula.
>
> It is this demand for trophies by people who go no farther in search of them than the nearest taxidermist's shop which is doing all the harm—at least on the American continent—and closing so many districts which only a few years ago were teeming with game, to legitimate sportsmen.[9]

By implication, many other moose may have been shot to pick out those carrying the largest antlers. Cane himself had killed four moose, nine Dall sheep, and three brown bears on the trip.[10] Apparently an educated and conscientious person, Cane believed sport hunters deserved priority status in taking wildlife and that they would not become so numerous or kill so much as to place a species in jeopardy.

Having heard the accounts of his fellow countryman Cane and others, Charles R.E. Radclyffe and two companions traveled to the United States in 1903. After personal briefings by BBS officials C. Hart Merriam and Theodore Palmer, they set out for the Kenai Peninsula. They took a considerable toll of wildlife (Table 10.2). Radclyffe argued, however, that

> sportsmen . . . have been so few and far between in the country up to the present date, that they have not been to any extent a real menace to any kind of big game. The real danger at present lies in the indiscriminate killing of bears, moose, caribou, and sheep by the natives for the sale of the hides and horns, and also for the sake of the meat of the last three species which is sold by the natives and others to ships, canneries, and miners throughout the country. For the last-named purpose males, females, and young of all kinds of game have hitherto been killed at all seasons of the year.[11]

English sport hunter Charles R.E. Radclyffe (left) and guides pose over record brown bear he shot, Kenai Peninsula, 1903. In C.R.E. Radclyffe, Big Game Shooting in Alaska, *London: Rowland Ward, 1904, frontispiece. As hunting grounds in other parts of the world became exhausted, wealthy sportsmen turned their attention to Alaska in the 1890s. Commercial and sport hunting for heads, hides, or meat led to the Alaska game laws of 1902, 1908, and 1925.*

Sport hunters from faraway nations answered Alaska's call. In 1907 Charles Madsen guided Austrian Baron von Guttman on a hunt lasting several weeks. After bagging eleven walruses and four polar bears north of Bering Strait, the baron killed eight mountain sheep and fourteen brown bears on the Kamchatka Peninsula in Siberia. At Herendeen Bay on the Alaska Peninsula he got seven bull caribou; then he wound up the trip by shooting nine Dall sheep and six bull moose on the Kenai Peninsula, considerably more than the law allowed. In recounting the hunt, Madsen accurately observed that "game was in theory under the protection of the territorial governor . . . but in reality there was little control."[12] F.E. Kleinschmidt organized a similar hunt in 1913. First the group of four American hunters collected fourteen walruses and five polar bears in the north. Then at Pavlov Bay on the Alaska Peninsula they bagged eight caribou and a brown bear. On the Kenai Peninsula they added eighteen Dall sheep, seven moose, and four black bears. One of the polar bears and all four of the black bears were cubs or yearlings.[13]

Whatever the sport of killing nearly defenseless animals with a high-powered rifle, the excursions often entailed danger and hardship. Madsen had a close call when he tried to skin a sleeping brown bear he thought had been shot, and the next day another bear injured him. Kleinschmidt's party lost a rudder, narrowly escaped being frozen into the Arctic icepack, and nearly foundered on the rocks of the Alaska Peninsula. On the Kenai they boated into the interior and backpacked far into the mountains. On the way out they carried their trophy heads and skins and pulled their loaded boats eighteen miles up the fast-moving Kenai River in subfreezing temperatures. One of the guides froze his feet as the thermometer approached zero. Yet as they left the hunting grounds in late October they met English hunters coming in.[14]

Gold miners, often too busy to hunt, relied on commercial meat hunters. In 1903, a year after Felix Pedro discovered gold near Fairbanks, moosemeat sold for 40 cents a pound and caribou for 20 cents. Mountain sheep and fresh salmon fetched even higher prices. Between 1903 and 1908 Tom and Elmer Gibson, among others, supplied mining camps, restaurants, and meat markets in the region. Journeying hundreds of miles in winter by dogsled and carrying large quantities of meat, they engaged in a difficult and dangerous occupation. Construction of the Tanana River Railway in 1905 made transportation much easier. On November 12, 1907, the Gibson brothers shipped 2,430 pounds of meat to Fairbanks; on the 24th, 1,905 pounds; and on the 27th, 1,554 pounds. By that time entrepreneurs had begun to import livestock in quantity from the States via the Gold Rush routes, undercutting the meat-hunting business.[15]

THE 1902 AND 1908 GAME LAWS

Depictions of wildlife abuse alarmed stateside conservation groups. Boone and Crockett, American Ornithologists' Union, New York Zoological Society, and other organizations applied their weight. Aided by the Bureau of Biological Survey, they lobbied through a series of wildlife protection laws, including the Alaska game laws of 1902 and 1908. These laws built upon the Lacey Act of 1900, which prohibited interstate transportation of game taken in violation of state statutes. The 1902 law transferred jurisdiction over most land mammals, plus walruses and sea lions, to the Department of Agriculture, Bureau of Biological Survey. Land mammals classified as furbearers remained under the Department of Commerce, Bureau of Fisheries, until 1920.

The 1902 law sought to curb the trade in deer and bear hides, moose antlers, and sheep horns and to head off plans to increase the market export of meat. It prohibited sale of hides, horns, and heads of game mammals, excluding furbearers, in or from Alaska. It permitted shipment of game parts and live animals from Alaska to the outside as registered trophies and by scientific permit. It outlawed killing of female and yearling ungulates and set bag limits for all land game mammals and birds, including brown bears but excluding black bears. In any one year a hunter could kill two moose, walrus, or sea lions; four caribou, mountain sheep, mountain goats, and adult brown bears; and eight deer. The law instituted hunting seasons and allowed sale of meat until fifteen days beyond closing of the season. It authorized the secretary of agriculture to make rules, such as halting the taking of an endangered species for up to five years. However, it left enforcement to existing federal marshals, burdened by other duties and reluctant to impair their local ties by upholding an unpopular law. Moreover, local citizens complained that well-connected outside sportsmen received favored treatment in being permitted to ship out their trophies.[16]

Criticism of the 1902 law led to a revision in 1908 empowering the governor to appoint wardens and issue licenses for hunting and exporting game. In response to complaints about protection of brown bears, the law compromised by removing the season limit on bears north of 62 degrees, a line running across south-central Alaska. It reduced annual bag limits on large mammals to two moose; one walrus or sea lion; three each of caribou, sheep, and brown bear; and (by regulation), six deer, reduced again to three by 1916. It tightened the rules for shipping hides, trophies, and scientific specimens and retained the other key provisions of the 1902 law. While the governor's wardens enforced the law, the Bureau of Biological Survey wrote the regulations.[17]

Alaska Natives, who did the bulk of commercial hunting, suffered most from the prohibition of hide and horn exports and sale of game meat out of season. Except for work in the salmon industry and selling items to tourists, coastal Natives had few opportunities to earn money. But Boone and Crockett leaders and other supporters of the game laws firmly believed excess killing and waste by Natives jeopardized wildlife populations. They fought off attempts to revise the laws to ease the impact on Natives. In 1916 the Bureau of Biological Survey prohibited the sale of sheep and moose to railroad construction camps, another source of cash for Natives. When the BBS assumed responsibility for furbearer management in 1920, it banned the shooting of muskrats and beavers. In 1923 it temporarily outlawed trapping of beavers statewide, even though the animals had been depleted only in some locations. Indians in the interior, who relied on furs for most of their cash, saw their income lowered.[18]

In legal terms, the Migratory Bird Treaty Act of 1918 also impinged upon the Natives' economic well-being. To protect nesting geese and ducks it banned hunting between December 15 and September 1. Almost all the birds left Alaska by early fall, especially in the interior. Adherence to the law would deprive Natives of vital food supplies and put sport hunters at a disadvantage relative to those in the States where most of the birds wintered. Yup'ik Eskimos on the Yukon Delta, a major nesting area, ignored the law and harvested geese and

TABLE 10.3. Game and Trophies Shipped From Alaska, 1910–1916

Specimen	*1910*	*1911*	*1912*	*1913*	*1914*	*1915*	*1916*
Brown bear skin	10	26	15	7	19	22	35
Glacier bear skin	3						
Sheep head/horns/skin	10	34+	15	31	30	19	28
Moose head/antlers	6	21+	13	18	17	11	9
Caribou head/antlers	—	3	1	1	4	5	11
Goat head/horns/skin	—	2+	—	1	6	6	1

Source: Annual Report of the Governor of Alaska on the Alaska Game Law, 1910–1916.
Note: Does not include an unknown number of trophies shipped in personal baggage or killed but left in Alaska.

ducks in the spring and summer.[19] The conflict went unresolved until long after statehood.

Wardens, being gubernatorial appointees, acquired a reputation as political hacks who exhibited little will to enforce the law. In one case a warden reportedly participated in a "side hunt," a sport calling for a group of hunters to choose up sides for a day and kill every wild creature they could find. Players assigned points to different creatures, and the side tallying the most points won. Although some wardens performed their duties well, many lacked competence and ignored blatant lawbreaking.[20] In any case, the governor needed personnel and funds to police the enormous territory. Seven wardens, occasionally supplemented by Bureau of Forestry officials, carried the responsibility in 1911. In 1918 fish and fur wardens from the Department of Commerce, as well as forest rangers, assisted eight regular game wardens under the Department of the Interior. Until 1924 three departments shared jurisdiction over Alaskan wildlife, creating confusion and duplication of effort.[21] Despite the enforcement weaknesses, the 1902 and 1908 laws appeared to succeed in shutting off the commercial export of wild animal parts. Sport hunting (Table 10.3) took a modest toll of game.

When Alaska achieved territorial status in 1912, its federally appointed governor retained the power to hire game wardens. The new legislature, unlike those in other territories, had no jurisdiction over fish, furbearers, or game. For decades, resolutions called for territorial control of wildlife, for an end to land restrictions by the federal government, and for surveys and other measures to facilitate settler ownership of land. A typical 1913 resolution demanded that the land "be thrown open for the general use of the prospector, miner, and settler." Withdrawals of the Tongass and Chugach national forests in 1903–1907 provoked anger; then parks and monuments at Mt. McKinley, Katmai, and Glacier Bay later appeared, followed by numerous military reservations in the 1940s. Territorial governor and later U.S. senator Ernest Gruening, an inveterate booster, lamented that "the story of land in Alaska is one of contrast between natural and man-made restriction. It is a tale of continuous effort by Americans there to secure a small share of this abundant ground. It is, no less, a necrology of their legitimate aspirations through the thwarting by a distant government. Its full narration would be depressing. It begins in 1867 and it is still 'to be continued.'"[22]

Alaska's population had been calculated at 64,000 in the 1910 census, about 37,000 of it white. By 1939 the total stood at 72,524, including 39,170 non-Natives. The 1912 report of the congressional House Committee on Territories described the enabling act as containing "more than the usual safeguards against unwise or vicious legislation."[23] Federal politicians and administrators did not want to entrust such a huge territory to so few people, and entrepreneurial Alaskans strongly resented the government's barring their full access to the resources. The difference in attitudes informed virtually all natural resource disputes in the territorial period and during statehood as well.

C. HART MERRIAM

Clinton Hart Merriam (1855–1942) can be considered, at least in a jurisdictional sense, one of Alaska's first wildlife managers. Brought up near the Adirondacks in a wealthy family at Locust Grove, New York, Merriam acquired an interest in natural science. His father, a former congressman, introduced him to Smithsonian director Spencer F. Baird. Impressed by the boy's work in taxidermy, Baird arranged a position for him on the Hayden Yellowstone expedition of 1872. This experience confirmed the sixteen-year-old's desire to do taxidermy. Medical degrees at Yale and Columbia, and work as a doctor between 1879 and 1885, diverted him from professional pursuit of his passion. But in his spare time he earned a reputation as a highly competent student of birds and mammals. When an elite group of ornithologists formed the American Ornithologists' Union (AOU, 1883), Merriam assumed leadership as a founding member, secretary, and chair of the migratory bird committee. He organized a volunteer reporting network to track migration routes in North America.[24] Through AOU he made the lifelong friendship of Theodore Roosevelt. Later he befriended John Muir; they spent time in the field together.

Merriam ranks as an ancestor of the U.S. Fish and Wildlife Service. AOU members feared the imminent extermination of the passenger pigeon, Carolina parakeet, and other species and sought government intervention. Through AOU lobbying the Agriculture Department created a position for an ornithologist in 1885 and hired Merriam. The office advanced to Division of Economic Ornithology and Mammalogy in 1886, Bureau of Biological Survey in 1905, and Fish and Wildlife Service in 1940. Merriam directed the agency from 1885 until his retirement in 1910.[25]

Merriam presided during a pivotal era in government and public attitudes toward wildlife protection. Modeled by such writers as John Muir and John Burroughs, nature appreciation grew popular after mid-century. It found organized expression in private groups like AOU and the Audubon societies. Scientists in and out of government began to show active concern in the 1870s. Baird of the Smithsonian Institution applied his connections to help create the U.S. Commission on Fish and Fisheries (1871), perhaps the first federal government unit expressly dedicated to conservation of wildlife species. Similarly, through AOU Baird pushed for the ornithology office within the Agriculture Department. Now able to operate both inside and outside of government, AOU worked for laws protecting birds. George Bird Grinnell tried to complement the group's mainly scientific membership by organizing a national Audubon Society to involve the public more directly.[26]

Public and private naturalists recoiled at the slaughter of the passenger pigeon, fur seal, and other species. They objected to the fashion in women's hats, lasting from about 1890 to 1910 and causing mass killing of egrets and other birds for their feathers. As the naturalists sought legislation to halt commercial hunting, a peculiar event involving Alaska cropped up to assist them. Rumors of a gigantic harvest of wild bird eggs in Alaska and northwest Canada attracted national attention in 1895. Allegedly, the commercial photography and prepared food industries bought and used the eggs. Grinnell of *Forest and Stream* investigated the claims, finding them untrue. Nevertheless, coming at a time of heightened concern about commercial abuses of wildlife, the affair strengthened public sentiment for a protective law passed in 1900.[27]

Outdoor sporting groups had proliferated after the Civil War and held significant potential for wildlife protection. Attempts to organize them to that end produced the League of American Sportsmen (1898), the most active private group supporting the Lacey Act. Its leaders included Merriam, William T. Hornaday, and Ernest Thompson Seton. The league, the Audubon societies, scientists led by AOU's Joel A. Allen and New York Zoological Society's Hornaday and Henry Fairfield Osborn, and the supporting Boone and Crockett Club and Bureau of Biological Survey made up the first broad-based American coalition for wildlife conservation. Their victory in the Lacey Act advanced wildlife protection to prominence within federal policy and in the conservation movement of the 20th Century.[28]

Merriam and his small staff conducted fieldwork over much of the United States, Canada, and Mexico, collecting and classifying thousands of specimens of fauna for the Smithsonian. On a research expedition to Arizona in the late 1880s, Merriam noticed the differences in flora and fauna at different altitudes. He found that each layer, based on temperature, hosted a distinct community of plants, birds, and mammals. Relating altitude to latitude and terming the habitats "life zones," he projected the concept onto the map of North America, identifying seven life zones from the Arctic to the Florida tropics. Approaching the description from the perspective of habitat rather than plant and animal identification, Merriam significantly advanced the emerging science of ecology. Scholars later modified his theory to account for moisture differences in understanding ecological zones and communities.[29]

In 1891 superiors recalled Merriam from a Death Valley expedition to go to the Pribilofs and investigate the fur seal controversy. Ignoring warnings about robbers, he took a shortcut alone across the Tehachapi Mountains. He spotted two armed men following him. When they separated in an apparent pincers movement, he readied his rifle, crouched behind a rock, and picked them both off. As a scientist who had studied the fur seals, in 1909 he received appointment to the Fur Seal Advisory Board. He took a more conservative position than that of Henry W. Elliott, whom he could not abide.[30]

In his capacity as a government scientist and administrator, Merriam raised public awareness of the beneficial nature of most birds, especially those that controlled rodents and insects. He worked for legal protection of birds but harbored no such charitable views of mammals. He testified in a 1908 hearing that the "great bulk of mammals are pests. Except the badgers, weasels, skunks, bats, moles and shrews, very few of our mammals are of service to man." Merriam expressed a highly utilitarian perspective oriented particularly to the interests of Western agriculture, a potent force in government. Congress had forced a more directly economic role on the renamed Bureau of Biological Survey in 1905, including a rodent control program that widened to target a variety of mammalian predators. Merriam preferred a research emphasis but did not object to predator control as such. He considered rodents, coyotes, and wolves bad. Although he revised his stand on predators late in life, the Bureau of Biological Survey acted as the prime mover in efforts at predator control that decimated some species and begot decades of controversy in Alaska and elsewhere.[31]

Founder and first president of the American Society of Mammalogists (1919), Merriam authored more than 500 books and articles on birds, mammals, plants, Indians, and the life of William H. Dall. His mastery of taxonomy won widespread adoption of his methods of classification of animals. He dominated the early evolution of the modern science of mammalogy, even though he possessed only a partially ecological view of the environment.

Merriam participated in, organized, and chose the scientists for the Harriman Alaska Expedition of 1899 and supervised the publication of its voluminous reports. As a result, Mt. Merriam in Glacier Bay National Park is named for him.[32] His positions as chief of the Division of Economic Ornithology and Mammalogy and the successor Bureau of Biological Survey gave him supervi-

U.S. Bureau of Biological Survey officials (left to right): Vernon Bailey, C. Hart Merriam, Theodore S. Palmer, and Albert K. Fisher at Lone Pine, California, June 13, 1891, after Death Valley expedition. Bancroft Library, University of California at Berkeley. The BBS, forerunner of the U.S. Fish and Wildlife Service, initiated federal wildlife management.

sory responsibility for the Alaska game laws, but he had no taste for politics. Except for efforts to save the brown and grizzly bears, in which he adopted a special interest, Merriam shied away from environmental disputes. He devoted most of his time after retirement, funded by a grant from the Harriman Foundation, to research on California Indians.[33]

THEODORE S. PALMER

Merriam chose as his Biological Survey assistant in charge of game Dr. Theodore Sherman Palmer (1868–1955), a Californian and self-taught scientist who had studied birds and other wildlife in Alaska. As had Merriam, Palmer earned an M.D., but he did not practice medicine. Arriving at BBS in 1890, Palmer led the Death Valley expedition in 1891 and collected and wrote descriptions of fauna. Supported by Merriam, he initiated the bureau's emphasis on wildlife protection and maintained connections between the bureau and outdoor sporting and nature preservation groups. In addition to work on the Lacey Act and the Alaska game laws of 1902 and 1908, Palmer wrote the initial draft of the Migratory Bird Treaty of 1916 and the regulations for the Migratory Bird Treaty Act (1918).

A leader in the National Audubon Society for 30 years, Palmer also served as a biographer in the American Ornithologists' Union. He assisted states in drafting game laws and helped create the programs that evolved into the national wildlife refuge system. As a member of Boone and Crockett he remained active in wildlife protection after retirement, serving on the committee on birds at the National Conference on Outdoor Recreation. He wrote on jackrabbits, rodents, and other game and nongame species and their protection. At the Smithsonian between 1928 and 1933 he helped draft the first whale protection treaty.[34]

JOHN B. BURNHAM

Much or most of the credit for the actual drafting of the Migratory Bird Treaty belongs to John B. Burnham (1869–1939), the first president of the American Game Protective and Propagation Association founded in 1911. The arms industry, promoting wildfowl protection laws as essential to its future in a time of rapidly waning flocks, organized the association. George Bird Grinnell, for whom Burnham had worked at *Forest and Stream*, recommended him for the directorship.[35]

Burnham played a leading role in the passage of the Federal Migratory Bird (McLean-Weeks) Act. Critics widely regarded as unconstitutional a law placing all migratory species under federal protection; President William Howard Taft had vowed to veto such a measure. It passed through Congress as a rider to an appropriations bill and reached Taft's desk on March 4, 1913, his last day in office. Turning the clock back to prevent his term from legally expiring, Taft signed the bill, apparently taking no notice of the migratory bird provisions. Courts later affirmed the measure's constitutionality.

During the Gold Rush in 1897–1898, Burnham crossed White Pass to Lake Bennett and returned through Chilcoot Pass. He undertook no scientific study and spent only a short time in Alaska but maintained a strong concern for conservation of its wildlife. For much of his career he served as a New York state game official.[36] His game protection association joined the Camp Fire Club of America and the Boone and Crockett Club to reserve Mt. McKinley National Park (Chapter 6), and he served as the group's chief congressional lobbyist. These groups, and the National Association of Audubon Societies, then assisted passage of the 1925 Alaska Game Law.[37]

EDWARD W. NELSON

In 1916 the directorship of the Bureau of Biological Survey passed to another prominent naturalist, Edward William Nelson (1855–1934). Born in Amoskeag, New Hampshire, Nelson spent the next few years in Manchester. His patriotic father joined the Grand Army of the Republic in 1861, and his mother followed suit by volunteering as a nurse in Baltimore. She sent Edward to live on his grandparents' farm in the northern Adirondacks where he experienced a reintroduction to Nature. His first overnight trip into the woods to pick blueberries sparked a lifelong desire to explore wild places.

Shortly before the war ended, Edward's father died in battle. His enterprising mother moved the family to Chicago and established herself as a successful dressmaker. School and play in the nearby woods furthered Edward's interest in natural science, above all, birds. The high school principal encouraged him, and a friend shared the first bird books, Wilson's and Nuttall's, he had seen. A prominent entomologist interested him in bug collecting, but fate intervened. His home and his mother's shop burned in the 1871 Chicago fire. As the family fled in a stream of refugees, Edward momentarily put down his insect collection box. Within seconds it disappeared. He lost interest in entomology.

While skinning birds, Edward contracted a disease for which a doctor ordered mountain air. Accordingly, in 1872 he traveled west on a biological expedition through the Rockies and to California. A teaching position following normal school did not satisfy him, so he went to see Spencer Baird at the Smithsonian, seeking a field research position. No opening existed, but a year later, in 1877, Baird called him to act as meteorologist at the St. Michael station at Norton Sound, replacing Lucien M. Turner. Nelson exulted in striking off immediately for Alaska, not least because in addition to the mundane task of weather recording he would gather geographical, ethnological, and zoological data. This would accomplish Baird's real object. The Smithsonian lacked funds for studies of Alaska but wanted to develop its collections of data and specimens. Baird served simultaneously at the Smithsonian and as the first U.S. fish commissioner. This enabled him to get his people assigned to such government agencies as the Army Signal Corps and have them collect on the side. Arranging for others to do meter readings, Nelson embarked on collecting and exploring expeditions, covering thousands of miles by kayak and dogsled in all seasons for four years.[38]

Travel called for endurance of harsh conditions. During a 1,200-mile trip through the marshy Yukon and Kuskokwim drainages in 1878, Nelson encountered "violent storms of snow, rain and sleet accompanied by high winds."

> [M]y bedding became saturated with moisture, as did also my clothing, and day after day forced marches were made over a country covered with slush

Edward W. Nelson on the Yukon-Kuskokwim Delta, 1877–1881. National Portrait Gallery. An intrepid explorer and collector, Nelson headed the Bureau of Biological Survey from 1916 to 1927.

> and water. At night a miserable shelter was improvised from our sledges or found in the underground huts of the natives. These were reeking with moisture and decaying filth which the warm weather had thawed out, so that the floor, forming our resting-place, was a soft mass of all descriptions and varying in depth from one inch or two to six inches.

When he reached a half-flooded shelter on the seacoast south of Cape Vancouver just ahead of a storm, "Here my interpreter and myself crouched against the wall in silent misery for two days, while one of the most violent tempests I ever witnessed swept over the desolate tundra."[39] From this he caught pneumonia, which plagued him for the rest of his life. But he grew to be a leading authority on Alaska, manifested in his authorship of over 200 books and articles on birds, mammals, and Eskimo life.

William Fitzhugh of the Smithsonian characterized the St. Michael achievements as "pioneering ethnographic work": 10,000 artifacts collected, extensive ethnographic notes, about 100 photographs, and a continuous sequence of 12,000 meterological observations. "During the course of this work, much of it conducted in the face of great adversity and physical danger, Nelson established a record unparalleled in extensiveness and diversity of subject matter for any individual in the history of North American arctic studies."[40] Nelson Island and Nelson Lagoon bordering the Bering Sea commemorate his achievements in the region.[41]

In 1881 Nelson made the acquaintance of John Muir while assigned as a naturalist on the *Corwin* expedition. Stops along the Arctic coast, including the first landing on Wrangel Island by Euro-Americans, enabled him to secure additional Eskimo artifacts. His study of Nature eventually led to his naming of numerous species and subspecies of mammals (including the Dall sheep), birds, plants, insects, and other life forms. When he returned to the Smithsonian, tuberculosis forced him to reduce his work schedule. He spent most of the 1880s in the Southwest, where he and his brother ran a cattle ranch and he served as county clerk. He joined Merriam's Death Valley expedition in 1890–1891 and from 1892 to 1908 traveled throughout Mexico and Guatemala as a field agent of the Bureau of Biological Survey. Ignoring a damaged lung and heart, he climbed the twelve highest peaks in Mexico. He advanced to chief field naturalist and, in 1916, to director of the bureau.[42]

Nelson continued to pay attention to Alaska after leaving in 1881. His habit of sending talented young men to Alaska produced Alfred M. Bailey, an ornithologist who opened the first Bureau of Biological Survey office in the territory in 1919 and who later became curator of the Denver Museum of Natural History. Nelson also recruited Lawrence J. Palmer, an agricultural expert who studied the ecology of caribou, reindeer, muskoxen, and moose. Not least of Nelson's finds, Olaus J. Murie matured into a national leader in wilderness

Edward W. Nelson in later years. RG22 WB Box 59, National Archives at College Park. Nelson shaped the 1925 Alaska Game Law and numerous other wildlife protection measures.

preservation. On Nelson's second and final trip to Alaska in 1920, Palmer and Murie accompanied him up the Yukon to Fairbanks, whence Murie undertook his survey of the caribou herds that led to his prominent place in conservation history.

Nelson directed the Bureau of Biological Survey until 1927. He helped formulate the 1916 Migratory Bird Treaty, the Migratory Bird Conservation Act

(1929), and the Migratory Bird Hunting Stamp Act (1934), all fundamental to the creation of bird refuges.[43] His philosophy of conservation fit well into the utilitarian mode and paralleled the thinking of wildlife managers and his Boone and Crockett associates:

> The game and wild life of this country . . . is of great value from several points of view but mainly in supplying a highly prized form of food; as affording sport to a multitude of men and employment to others; and as a source of renewed health and vigor to numberless men attracted by it to a period of vigorous life in the open each year. . . . It is a blot on the custodianship of the wild life of the country, however, that commercial slaughter should have been permitted to the extent that the supply was ruthlessly wasted both as regards large and small game and game birds.[44]

THE 1925 ALASKA GAME LAW

Nelson closely followed Alaskan affairs and expressed concern over the plight of its wildlife. But Alaska game laws could be no better than their enforcement. It proved exceedingly difficult to control the behavior of people who saw themselves as fighting for survival in a wilderness and who had seldom encountered enforcement of game laws, commonly regarded as imposed by an outside urban elite. And the 1902 and 1908 game laws permitted the sale of game within Alaska, a practice widely condemned by sport hunters and conservation groups in the States. When the United States entered World War I, Alaska's congressional delegate Charles A. Sulzer introduced a bill intended to meet the needs of Fairbanks residents, who viewed the 1908 law as an obstacle to their food supply. In effect, the bill would seriously weaken the law. Nelson and Charles Sheldon went to see Sulzer and persuaded him to modify his position.[45] The resulting compromise bill would shift the hunting season later into December and eliminate the rule restricting the sale of game to fifteen days after being killed. Abolition of the August season would reduce spoilage of meat, and the indefinite period of sale would enable residents to avoid the high prices charged by the "beef trust" over the winter. The new law would apply only to Alaska north of 62 degrees latitude and stay in force one year beyond the end of the war.[46]

In February 1918 the House Committee on Territories held hearings on the bill. Speaking for the Bureau of Biological Survey and also identifying himself as a member of Boone and Crockett's game preservation committee, Nelson endorsed the bill as a useful temporary measure. He cautioned, however, that "there is no question that the continuous commercialization of game at the present time will bring about its extinction in any part of North America." Sheldon, representing Boone and Crockett, stated that the club had not had time to pass a formal resolution but that the leaders objected only to a clause explicitly endorsing the sale of game. Sheldon insisted that "the spirit of cooperating with [Alaskans], and understanding their point of view, and winning them over—winning each individual over to the idea of protecting game . . . will be the most valuable thing." He added, "If this privilege is not accorded the people will go in and kill the game anyhow."[47]

William T. Hornaday testified on behalf of the New York Zoological Society and the Permanent Wild Life Protection Fund. He adamantly opposed the selling of game and contended that no existing law clearly authorized it. Pointing out that the sale of buffalo parts directly caused destruction of the great herds, he predicted, "If you commercialize the sale in Alaska any further, it is good-bye to the game."[48] Belmore Browne, speaking for the Camp Fire Club, concurred. He pointed to a case wherein meat hunters had killed an entire herd of 47 caribou but delivered very few to Fairbanks because of the distance. He declared:

> When meat is made a business, there is no such thing as sentiment or ethics. . . . I know of many cases where 10 caribou have been shot and left because other caribou were found nearer the sea, nearer the roads, or nearer the main trails. . . . I have seen corporations of different kinds feed their men openly out of season on wild game, including steamship lines, cement companies, mining companies, and construction companies.

Marshall Scull and Henry W. Elliott, both experienced in Alaska, seconded the arguments against game sale.[49] Lack of information about game populations and uncertainty about the probable results of the bill infused the hearings. No bill passed the House, and Nelson lost an opportunity to create goodwill between Alaskans and the Bureau of Biological Survey.

Nelson and Sheldon enjoyed a working relationship with Alaska governor Thomas Riggs, based in part on their cooperative success in establishing Mt. McKinley National Park. They had tried to compromise on the sale of game issue but met defeat by Hornaday and other militant wildlife protectors. For his part, Riggs intensely resented the militants' attitude. He labeled their views "sentimental but ignorant propaganda." Conservationists, he charged, "have done nothing but befog the situation. Alaska has suffered and is still suffering so severely from ill-advised so-called conservation measures that the average Alaskan sees red when the very word 'conservation' is mentioned." Conservation had "ruined so many people" and "retarded territorial growth." The conservationist "thinks he is rendering unselfish aid to the cause of conservation by putting himself on record against what has been put up to him evilly and falsely as wanton slaughter of living animals." Riggs insisted that Alaskans believed in conserving game, "and if the Legislature of Alaska should be given control, there would be sane and stringent laws, better enforced and more cheerfully obeyed than any laws promulgated by self-chosen champions of wild life."[50]

Alfred Bailey's 1921 report graphically illustrated the difficulties of game law enforcement:

> The average person considers a game warden as being a seeker of a "soft" job; he is condemned for such a position, and is considered as doing an injustice to a person if he makes an arrest, and is a damned loafer if he does not. This past season, Mr. Folta, Secretary to the Governor, saw several men kill three goats on the mountain tops near Juneau. He informed the warden, and was severely criticized for so doing. It is almost impossible to get a conviction for deer killing, for a jury trial is necessary, according to Judge Jennings, and the person accused is invariably turned loose, or assessed a minimum fine, say of twenty-five dollars. What could be more discouraging to a warden than to take a prisoner over a hundred miles in his little boat, and then have him turned loose, or assessed such a low fine?
>
> Many deer were killed and the meat canned in the salmon canneries. Others were used for sport shooting: Many nonresidents come to Alaska each summer, cruising about in their own boats, and bringing an arsenal with them. The game suffers severely from these people, and females and young are the usual victims. Aliens to a great extent are responsible for the wanton killing, shooting just to see the animals fall.[51]

Jim Russell told Bailey, "Speaking of wasting deer, six years ago, in Douglas, I saw about one hundred deer scattered about in front of the Indian houses, where they had spoiled because the whites wouldn't buy them. It wasn't because the average white wouldn't buy either, but just because an Indian is too lazy to gut the deer, if they get them near the beach, and of course they sour. The dogs were chewing a few." Bailey noted that the law allowed Alaska Natives to take game virtually without limit, adding, "[t]here should be some line drawn between natives living a civilized life, and those still in a primitive condition, as in the interior. This question would of course be settled in the revision of the game laws which must come soon."[52] His speculation turned out to be wildly optimistic; the question of Native rights bedeviled wildlife management throughout the century. Bailey's other recommendations, however, laid a foundation for a revised game law.

Nelson's Bureau of Biological Survey gained jurisdiction over Alaskan fur-bearing land mammals in 1920. But Nelson's most immediate concerns involved ungulates—moose, caribou, sheep, and Sitka deer, all subject to exploitation to fulfill demands for meat. He wanted a strengthened and comprehensive game law to overcome the weaknesses of the 1902 and 1908 acts. His 1920 visit to the territory allowed him to appraise the situation and make contacts. He directed his agents to gather as much information as possible on game populations and harvests. Warden Olaus Murie reported a strong reliance on purchased game for food in the Fairbanks vicinity in 1921 (Table 10.4). Stores paid their suppliers

TABLE 10.4. Game Purchased by Six Fairbanks Stores, Fall 1921

	Model Café	*Merchants Café*	*U.S. Grill*	*Waechter Bros.*	*Lavery & Bailey*	*Golden's Grocery*
Moose	30	8	2	8	15	(2)
Caribou	100	24	7	20	—	—
Sheep	25	12	1	—	(5)	(8)
Sharptail grouse	500	100	—	—	—	—
Ruffed grouse	200	50	—	—	—	—
Spruce grouse	125	20	—	—	—	—
Willow ptarmigan	200	200	—	—	—	—
Grouse (all species)	—	—	60	—	144	80

Source: Olaus J. Murie, letter to Edward W. Nelson, Chief, Bureau of Biological Survey, January 7, 1922. Alaska State Library, Historical Section, USFWS MS 51 Group 162, Entry 162.

Note: Murie advised that "these figures are very conservative, as some of the dealers showed an inclination to minimize the quantity of game used." Figures in parentheses include parts of animals, e.g., hindquarters.

as follows: moose $0.20-$0.25 per pound, caribou $0.20, sheep $0.30, and grouse $5.00–$7.50 per dozen.[53]

BBS could afford to field only a few agents in the vast territory. Like most in the early days, Murie traveled by boat in summer and dogsled in winter. Game management relied heavily on comments from trappers, miners, and settlers, often reflecting local or temporary conditions or biased by some form of vested interest. By the time a trend became clear, it might be too late to prevent depletion of a wildlife population.

Nelson enlisted the backing of most major national conservation groups, spearheaded by Boone and Crockett. His fur wardens, chosen by the BBS rather than the governor, appealed to the Alaskan game clubs. Nelson demonstrated the economic value to the territory of hosting outside sport hunters. A relatively stable postwar and post–Gold Rush population responded positively to the idea of sustaining wildlife through federal professionals advised by representatives of the Alaskan public.[54] At the March 1924 hearings in Washington, all major players submitted statements in favor of the proposed reform bill: the Interior and Agriculture departments, the Permanent Wild Life Protection Fund (Hornaday), Boone and Crockett (Sheldon), American Game Protection Association (Burnham), Camp Fire Club (W.B. Greeley), and National Association of Audubon Societies (T. Gilbert Pearson). Nelson pointed out the advantage of having one agency manage both game and fur mammals. Hornaday pronounced the bill "perfectly sane and just." Alaska congressional delegate Dan Sutherland, who had introduced the bill in 1921, described it as "agreed upon by virtually all the people of the territory."[55] Absent significant opposition, Congress passed the law effective January 13, 1925.[56] Several months earlier, in June 1924, Congress had placed all enforcement of Alaska land game laws under the Bureau of Biological Survey.[57]

The Alaska Game Law of 1925, strongly oriented to utilitarian conservation, crafted a prudent compromise between federal control and local autonomy. A five-member federally appointed Alaska Game Commission, consisting of residents from each of Alaska's four judicial districts and a chairman-director representing the Bureau of Biological Survey, made fur, game, and sport hunting regulations, subject to approval by the secretary of agriculture. Federal officers chosen for their skill, integrity, knowledge of the country, and ability to convince local Alaskans of the value of wildlife conservation acted as wardens. Big game guides applied to the Game Commission for licenses. Written and oral exams focusing on skills, reputation, and attitudes toward conservation produced a corps of guides known for honesty and competence.[58] During the 35 years of its operation, the 1925 Alaska Game Law and its management earned a widespread reputation for success in wildlife management.

BUREAU OF BIOLOGICAL SURVEY ACTIVITIES

From its inception in the mid-1880s, the BBS carried out much of the fieldwork necessary for knowledge and conservation of North American flora and fauna. In its mature form in the 1930s the BBS engaged in (1) basic research in North America and elsewhere; (2) identification and control of wildlife diseases; (3) control of pests and predators; (4) propagation (e.g., fox farming) and distribution of useful plants (such as duck feed) and animals (such as quail); (5) protection and habitat restoration for game mammals and birds, especially migratory birds; (6) acquisition and maintenance of wildlife refuges; and (7) educational activities including scientific publications and assistance to museums, educational institutions, government agencies, and private groups. The bureau applied its influence to encourage the passage of state wildlife protection laws. In Alaska BBS reintroduced muskoxen and attempted to create a reindeer industry. It managed terrestrial and some oceanic wildlife through the semi-independent Alaska Game Commission.[59]

Plans for a network of national wildlife refuges gathered momentum in the 1920s and 1930s. They drew strength from shortages of ducks and geese caused by market hunting and later by droughts. Outdoor sporting groups and nature preservationists united in support of refuges and migratory bird protection laws. The 1929 Migratory Bird Conservation (Norbeck-Anderson) Act, supplemented by the 1934 Migratory Bird Hunting Stamp Act, generated funds for refuge acquisition. Franklin Roosevelt, a nature enthusiast and former chair of the New York Senate Committee on Forests, Fish and Game, presided over a vast expansion of the wildlife refuge system. As a means of assisting farmers during the Depression, the federal government purchased more than 40 million acres of marginal lands and converted much of it into refuges. Bureau of Biological Survey director Jay N. "Ding" Darling, an ardent conservationist who held office from 1934 to 1935, employed his position to organize the National Wildlife Federation (1936) and headed it after leaving government. The federation, in turn, lobbied successfully for the Pittman-Robertson Act (1937) that funded wildlife research and habitat restoration.[60]

IRA N. GABRIELSON

Another committed promoter of the refuge effort, Ira Noel Gabrielson, directed the Bureau of Biological Survey from 1935 to 1940 and its successor, the Fish and Wildlife Service, until 1946. Gabrielson (1889–1977), an Iowa farm boy, graduated from Morningside College in 1912. He liked science but planned to major in chemistry so he would not have to do biological drawings. When a professor noticed his photographs of birds and his impressive knowledge about them, Gabrielson decided to switch to biology. He left a position as a high school biology teacher to start a career in wildlife management in 1915. He authored books on wildlife conservation, botany, wildlife refuges, and birds of Oregon and coauthored *Birds of Alaska*. His early government work consisted primarily of economic ornithology and rodent control.[61] Beginning in the 1930s he worked to expand the national wildlife refuge complex for migratory birds, moose, and Kodiak bears.

Gabrielson held membership in Boone and Crockett and the Audubon Society and, accordingly, practiced an enlightened form of utilitarianism. A classic example of his thinking appeared in his book on wildlife conservation: "If this country continues depleting the soil, destroying the forests, and wasting the animal and plant life, it will, in time, become a poverty-stricken land inhabited by a constantly decreasing population facing a hopeless future. Such a fate has overtaken other lands with the exhaustion of their resources. It can well happen here."[62] A strong believer in predator control during his first two decades at the Bureau of Biological Survey, he resigned from the American Society of Mammalogists in 1931 to protest its criticism of the bureau's predator policy. His respect for the mounting scientific evidence persuaded him to reverse his position during his tenure as BBS director.[63]

Gabrielson made numerous trips to Alaska and monitored its wildlife issues. In 1941 he effected the designation of the Kodiak and Kenai wildlife refuges. Upon retirement in 1946 he accepted the presidency of the Wildlife Management Institute, until that time closely related to the sporting arms industry. He maintained independence from the industry and earned wide respect within the national environmental community. Presiding over the institute until 1970, he

Dr. Ira N. Gabrielson, July 1939. RG22 WB Box 46, National Archives at College Park. A national leader in wildlife conservation both within and outside government, Gabrielson secured protective status for the Kodiak National Wildlife Refuge and Kenai National Moose Range.

chaired its board until his death in 1977. Like Grinnell in the 1920s and 1930s, Gabrielson played a prominent and active part in the 1950s and 1960s, bridging the gap between hunting and nonhunting groups. He became an increasingly knowledgeable and influential voice in wildlife and habitat conservation.[64] People who met him liked his friendly, down-to-earth manner; he claimed to have climbed "more mountains than any other fat man." Those who knew him regarded him as a highly competent naturalist and a man of integrity.[65] He became the "Grand Old Man of Conservation" of the postwar era.[66]

Before the turn of the century the Bureau of Biological Survey had been primarily a research agency, concentrating on the effects of birds and mammals on agriculture. The passage of wildlife protection laws, from the Lacey Act of 1900 to the Alaska Game Law in 1925, gave the bureau law enforcement jurisdiction over nearly all Alaskan land mammals and birds. Through the bureau and the Fish and Wildlife Service, federal officials managed the wildlife until the state assumed control in 1960. The service retained responsibility for migratory birds and for millions of acres of national wildlife refuges created between 1903 and the passage of the Alaska National Interest Lands Conservation Act in 1980. Merriam, Nelson, and Gabrielson personified the evolution of wildlife protection values among government officials from the 1880s to the 1940s. All worked for conservation of species excepting a few predators. All believed firmly in wildlife management by government experts. Gabrielson in particular labored for a complex of wildlife refuges, thereby achieving a measure of ecosystem preservation. In lobbying for Alaskan game protection the three relied on interest groups, often led by the Boone and Crockett Club to which all belonged as members. They believed in science as a wildlife management tool and a basis for settling disputes. As directors of the leading wildlife management agency, they possessed considerable power to conduct research and formulate environmental policy. But they avoided honest examination of predator-prey relationships because of pressure exerted by the livestock industry on their parent Agriculture Department. They cared most about game mammals and birds and felt closest to outdoor sporting and nature groups. As utilitarians responsible for sustainable production of game and fur, they seldom made reference to aesthetic or spiritual values of wildlife, much less species rights. Yet Nelson and Gabrielson, at least, valued ecological integrity and some species of wildlife on their own terms. All three admired the grizzly bear and worked to protect it. They all employed the science available to wildlife management in their time. Hand in glove, they and their nongovernmental Boone and Crockett colleagues and similar allies contributed directly to the evolution of Alaskan conservation practices and prepared the way for subsequent, more preservationist values in all 50 states.

11

Alaskan Wildlife Managers

Frank Dufresne, Clarence Rhode, Jim Brooks, Jim King

BETWEEN 1925 AND STATEHOOD, THE ALASKA GAME LAW UNDERGIRDED LAND game management. Directors of the new Alaska Game Commission represented the Bureau of Biological Survey, Department of Agriculture, and, after 1939, the Fish and Wildlife Service in the Department of the Interior. They, their agents, and the men who managed the Alaska Department of Fish and Game beginning in 1957 put into practice the evolving philosophies of wildlife management. Leaders among them made lasting contributions to habitat preservation and to public acceptance of wildlife protection and science.

THE ALASKA GAME COMMISSION

In addition to creating the Game Commission and structure for enforcing regulations, the 1925 Alaska Game Law directly set forth some conservation provisions. It prohibited killing cow, yearling, and calf moose and female and young deer or sheep and molesting beaver or muskrat houses. But "any Indian, Eskimo, prospector or traveler [may] take animals and birds during the close season when he is in absolute need of food and other food is not available." Heads and horns could not be marketed, nor could game birds and mammals be sold to commercial boats or canneries. No aircraft or powerboat could be used to directly pursue game nor any poison employed except by predator control agents controlling wolves, coyotes, and wolverines. Of these three species the law classified only the wolverine as a "land fur-bearing mammal."[1]

Under the Game Law, oversight of the land lay in the hands of professional wildlife managers, hardy and practical men whose experience in the bush made law enforcement feasible. Agents possessed a broad, in some cases scholarly, knowledge of Alaskan wildlife. The overwhelming majority of Alaskans prior to World War II engaged in hunting and fishing for subsistence rather than for sport, and wildlife agents viewed their central task as protecting wildlife populations for consumption by humans. Top law enforcement priorities aimed at preventing market hunting, use of poison by trappers, shooting of beavers and cow moose, and excessive trapping of martens. Field agents traveled by road, canoe, or small steamboats in summer; dogsled and snowshoe in winter. They sometimes employed packhorses, the Alaska Railroad, and aircraft on an experimental basis beginning in 1930. During the late 1920s nine men covered Alaska's half-million square miles. They endured arduous working conditions: a lynx severely mauled one agent, and another disappeared on a solo trip up the Chickamin River. Threats from game violators added to the perils, as did accidents, especially in isolated locations, on fast rivers, or in cold temperatures. Arrests, however, yielded a high conviction rate. Agents normally assembled only once annually, and some never met during their careers. Mail from headquarters in Juneau often took several weeks to reach them.[2]

Alaska Natives exercised very little influence on Game Commission deliberations, although the rules affected them considerably. Both the 1902 and 1908 laws gave them the right to hunt game out of season for food or clothing. The 1925 law weakened the provision, allowing hunting out of season when "in absolute need of food and other food is not available." The commission interpreted the clause very strictly, granting the privilege to Natives not "adopting a civilized mode of living" or "exercising the right of franchise." Going beyond the law, the commission required signed application forms stating that the applicant had no work opportunity or alternate food source. It withdrew the form in 1938 after using it for thirteen years.[3]

While the Game Commission and 1925 Game Law represented a substantial upgrading of wildlife management and won the cooperation of many Alaskans, the arrangement did not satisfy the territorial legislature, which perpetually insisted on control of natural resources. In a 1935 joint memorial addressed to the president, it pleaded that

Alaska Game Commission officers (from left) Sam O. White, Jack Benson, Pete McMullen, Frank Dufresne (executive director of Alaska Game Commission), Clarence Rhode, Jack O'Connor, Grenold Collins, and Frank Glaser, Fairbanks, 1939. Courtesy Jim King. Under the 1925 Alaska Game Law, the Game Commission and its officers won a reputation for competence and public service.

> WHEREAS, the actions of the Alaska Game Commission have largely been and are oppressive and repugnant to a large majority of the people of the Territory of Alaska [and the commission] has made unreasonable, oppressive and unenforceable regulations governing the taking and marketing of skins and fur-bearing animals resulting in large financial losses and great inconvenience to trappers and fur dealers. . . . WHEREFORE, your Memorialist respectfully requests, That the repeal of the Alaska Game Laws and the abolishment of the Alaska Game Commission be made at the earliest possible date and that the legislative power of the Legislature of the Territory of Alaska be extended to include the game laws and laws relating to fur-bearing animals.[4]

The resolution shared the fate of numerous other pre-statehood Alaskan requests and demands for jurisdiction over wildlife.

Alaska Game Commission responsibilities included enforcement of the Lacey Act, Migratory Bird Act, Alaska Game Law, Migratory Bird Hunting Stamp Act, and Walrus Act. Between 1944 and 1956 the commission assisted in enforcement of the White Act governing commercial fisheries. Commission

Cache of illegally trapped skins at Mulchatna River, June 1936. By Hosea Sarber. RG22B Box 48, National Archives at College Park. Excessive trapping of beavers and marten occupied a high priority in game protection.

activities consisted of (1) pursuing law violators; (2) issuing licenses and permits for hunting, fishing, trapping, fur raising and dealing; for serving wild game as food in nonprofit facilities; for taking wildlife for scientific, educational, or propagation purposes; and for special hunting of wolves, coyotes, and wolverines; (3) predator control; (4) public relations; (5) research; and (6) miscellaneous.[5]

Most enforcement actions involved illegal taking of wildlife (Table 11.1). In January 1936 warden Hosea Sarber arrested a man for using poison to kill foxes. The man forfeited 25 fox pelts, paid a $300 fine, and spent 140 days in jail. Later that year Sarber carried out several seizures of illegal beaver skins in the Dillingham district, including one cache of 536 pelts. Normally, agents visited trappers before the end of the season to seal the pelts, certifying them as legal.[6]

Agents arrested a particularly unscrupulous pair of outlaws in 1938 in the Stony River country of the Kuskokwim drainage. The wardens found them operating traplines more than 100 miles in length nearly two months after the close of the season. They had killed no fewer than ten moose and cached much of the meat along the trail for dog feed, and it had spoiled. Their packs contained poison, and they had driven the Stony River Indians out of the country at gunpoint. A thirteen-year-old son of one of the men had been told to main-

TABLE 11.1. Alaska Game Commission Enforcement Actions, 1936–1937 and 1958–1959

Violation	*Prosecutions*	*Convictions*	*Fines/ Costs*	*Days in Jail*	*Seizures w/o Court Action*
Aliens w/o license	28	28	2,830	770	61
Aliens buying/selling furs	3	3	900	180	—
Residents	4	4	575	—	1
Nonresidents hunting/ trapping/dealing furs	23	23	454	670	6
Taking/possessing game/ fur/birds	68	67	3,316	2,575	97
Dealing in protected game/birds	10	10	165	210	3
Taking furbearers by illegal methods	3	3	100	3	8
Possession/use of poison	2	2	175	180	—
Assaulting officer	3	3	1,000	540	—
Total (1936–1937)	144	143	$9,515	5,125	185

Seizures: guns 117, furs 47, game animals and birds 2, other 19

Violation	*Prosecutions*	*Convictions*	*Fines/ Costs*	*Days in Jail*	*Seizures w/o Court Action*
1958–1959	363	340	$36,567	1,972	42

Violation	*Number*
Hunting/fishing/trapping in closed area	100
Hunting/fishing/trapping w/o license	81
False statement on license	72
Hunting/fishing/trapping in closed season	62
Taking protected sex/species	46
Hunting/fishing/trapping with illegal devices	30
Migratory bird violations	27
Illegal possession of game/fur/birds/fish	26
Illegal transport of fur/game/trophy	23
Exceeding bag limit	14
Removing evidence of sex/identity of game	10
Wanton destruction of game	7
Illegal purchase/sale of game/fur	7
Walrus act violations	5

Seizures: licenses 160, guns 50, traps & snares 30, moose 55, deer 18, caribou 16, bear 16, sheep 8, mountain goat 5, elk 1, furs 43, birds 73, fish 23

Sources: Alaska Game Commission, *13th Annual Report of Alaska Game Commission to the Secretary of Agriculture, July 1, 1936 to June 30, 1937* (Juneau, 1937) 17–27; Alaska Game Commission, *20th Annual Report, July 1, 1958 Through December 31* (Juneau, 1959), 34–35.

tain the camps until the men served their one-year jail terms. The court ordered arrangements for the boy to attend school.[7]

To collect Alaska bounty payments, men smuggled wolf and coyote skins in from Canada. In 1937–1938 agents apprehended a fur dealer who had imported

42 coyote skins. He paid a fine of $350 and returned $850 in bounty money.[8] The next year, in cooperation with the Royal Canadian Mounted Police, agents Sam White and Clarence Rhode set out on a month-long, 3,500-mile sortie into northeast Alaska during March and early April. Flying a rented four-seat Curtiss Thrush they patrolled the border region between Snag Creek and the Arctic Circle at temperatures of minus 30 to minus 40 degrees. Accompanied by Constable W.W. Sutherland they arrested a dozen men involved in taking furbearers by strychnine poison and smuggling wolf and coyote skins into Alaska. In quick trials seven men received convictions. Stopping at Fairbanks on the return trip, the agents discovered a cracked propeller hub that, if the plane had flown for another hour, would likely have caused a fatal crash. Nevertheless, Rhode concluded that

> this trip has further proved that airplanes are the only possible means of properly patrolling our districts. Likewise, they offer the cheapest method. The inspection that can be given the ground from a low altitude is almost unbelievable. The tracks of nearly every type of game or fur can be readily distinguished and it is easily possible to note where sets have been made along trails. All types of game can be observed from the air that would never be seen from the ground and such things as hidden cabins or caches are easily discovered. With hundreds of miles of remote country in all of our interior districts and the short period when patrol is essential for results, we can never fully police this country until we have our own planes to depend on.

Rhode suggested that lighter planes such as that flown by agent Grenold Collins would enable more flexibility in monitoring the ground and landing for quick action.[9]

The interior, vast and relatively inaccessible by water or land, made law enforcement far more difficult than in the coastal regions. Sam White, stationed at Fairbanks beginning in 1927, pioneered the use of aircraft in law enforcement. Taught to fly by Ralph Wien in 1928, he bought a TP Swallow and flew it on duty from 1930 to 1937. Thereafter he piloted aircraft rented by the Game Commission. A strong advocate of aerial law enforcement, he incurred the wrath of executive director Frank Dufresne in the mid-1930s by criticizing the purchase of expensive but poorly built boats instead of light planes. Frustrated by the slow pace of change, he resigned in 1941.[10] The commission acquired five planes for patrol by 1943 and escalated aerial activity in 1948 under the predator control program (Chapter 13).

Agents rendered assistance in wildlife censuses and in the work of other federal agencies. They helped private parties in emergencies such as plane crashes. Edible meat from law enforcement seizures and railroad and automobile collisions went to Native villages or charitable institutions. In 1955, a typical year

Sam White (left), Noel Wien, and White's TP Swallow, Valdez, 1931. Noel Wien coll. 60-959-35, University of Alaska Fairbanks, Alaska and Polar Regions Archives. White learned to fly in 1928 and pioneered airborne wildlife law enforcement in 1930.

for the 1950s, the Game Commission donated (in pounds): moose, 106,500; caribou, 2,000; deer, 500; and game fish, 258.[11] When not in the field, agents engaged in public education and goodwill by attending fairs, meetings of outdoor sporting groups, school assemblies, and other gatherings. They showed films, gave radio talks, and visited Native villages.

World War II, a time when the military comprised one-third of Alaska's population, inexorably changed the territory. Wildlife law enforcement reflected the new conditions of population increase and demand for access to wildlife. Military personnel wanted outdoor recreation and found hunting and fishing opportunities far superior to what they had seen in the States. When they gained the full right to take fish and game during the war, problems multiplied. Wildlife managers had feared that a quantum increase in the number of hunters would put intolerable stress on big game at the expense of local subsistence hunters. Congress passed a bill, signed into law in July 1943, permitting armed services personnel to buy resident hunting and fishing licenses after living in the territory for a year. Anticipation of the law may have motivated the Interior

Department's 1941 decisions to designate the Kodiak National Wildlife Refuge and the Kenai National Moose Range. Military and related civilian workers provided justification for the wildlife managers' concerns in 1945 and 1946. Seeing their last chance to kill an Alaskan game animal before going home, large numbers engaged in unnecessary, wasteful, and often illegal slaughter. In one locale near a highway they left the bodies of twelve cow moose.[12]

Wartime activities created hundreds of miles of new roads and numerous airports. Proliferating numbers of aircraft, both civilian and military, transported people to far corners of the territory. Trappers flew to their traplines, hunters to big game, and waterfowl shooters to flocks of ducks and geese. Pilots sometimes used their planes to drive the birds to waiting hunters. Wardens needed aircraft to seal beavers, curb violations, and perform other field tasks.[13]

The war, and requests from Alaska's congressional delegate Anthony Dimond, prompted construction of the Alcan (Alaska) Highway. Arguably, the military neither wanted nor needed it to prosecute the war, although it provided valuable support for the air supply route to Russia.[14] Strategic matters aside, a highway link to the States removed some of the isolation felt by Alaskans and embodied in stateside perceptions of Alaska. Tourists quickly seized the opportunity to travel the highway. When it opened to the public in 1948 it carried 18,604 travelers and, in 1951, 49,564 drove it. War construction had left roads, airports, seaports, railroad improvements, housing, and other facilities. It also added people; many former GIs stayed in Alaska. The territory's nonmilitary population nearly doubled, from 75,000 in 1940 to 138,000 in 1950. Cold War events continued the effects of World War II; Alaska's strategic position attracted $250 million annually in combined military and nonmilitary construction from 1949 to 1954. Greatly enlarged cash flows and road access accelerated and dispersed economic development.[15]

After the war, hunting activity rose faster than the population. Resident hunting/fishing licenses (Table 11.2) escalated from 28,316 in 1941–1945 to 124,836 during 1951–1955. Nonresidents bought 1,149 licenses in 1941–1945 and 11,141 in 1951–1955. Trapping fell off, however; resident fur dealer licenses declined from 1,249 to 792 in the same period. More roads, vehicles, and aircraft carried more people into wild areas. Sport hunting by aircraft climbed rapidly, greatly simplifying big game kills. Wildlife managers responded by employing aircraft and radio, increasingly complicated regulations, and research.[16] In 1948 the Game Commission fielded 9 enforcement agents working out of Ketchikan, Petersburg, Juneau, Seward, Fairbanks, and Dillingham. By 1950 permanent posts had been added at Craig, Wrangell, Sitka, Cordova, McGrath, and Kotzebue, and enforcement staff totaled 21. More aircraft, boats, and automobiles, most of them radio- and telephone-equipped, improved the reach and efficiency of field operations.[17] Agents increasingly traveled by aircraft and au-

TABLE 11.2. Alaska Game Commission License Sales, 1926–1959

	1926–30	*1931–35*	*1936–40*	*1941–45*	*1946–50*	*1951–55*	*1956–59*
Res. hunt/fish/trap	12,209	19,225	26,191	17,663	26,521	28,122	23,710
Nonres.hunt/ fish/trap	456	420	517	478	1,868	2,128	3,959
Alien special	467	202	216	106	93	53	114
Res. hunt/fish	—	—	22,627	28,316	59,970	124,836	114,313
Nonres. hunt/fish	86	69	135	1,149	4,897	11,141	6,969
Res. fish	—	—	—	2,793	10,017	28,254	34,355
Nonres. fish	—	—	—	2,021	22,678	61,671	46,695
Alien fish	—	—	—	19	124	447	854
Res. fur dealer	1,843	1,637	1,567	1,249	1,322	792	490
Nonres. fur dealer	17	70	81	51	68	27	16
Alien fur dealer	29	11	2	8	4	—	—
Guide	336	397	396	293	688	832	450

Source: Alaska Game Commission, *20th Annual Report, July 1, 1958 Through December 31, 1959* (Juneau, 1959), 36.

Note: Does not include export permits, fur farm or walrus licenses, or 1,063 special bear licenses in 1959.

tomobile (Table 11.3). As competition for fish and wildlife intensified, predator control, previously a matter of helping trappers and reindeer herders catch raiding wolves and wolverines, changed into a widespread and systematic undertaking conducted by aircraft.

Federal agents retained control over fish and wildlife management until the transfer of most responsibility to the new state on January 1, 1960. At Alaska's Constitutional Convention, wildlife management sparked one of the salient controversies. Outdoor sporting groups lobbied vigorously for a bipartisan commission to manage sport and commercial hunting and fishing. The commission would be established in the constitution rather than created by the legislature and managed by the governor. Proponents argued that it would protect natural resources by taking them out of the realm of politics. Opponents believed the commission would usurp the proper role of the people and their legislature. The proposal lost 35-20, and a Board of Fish and Game, divided in 1975, managed the state's fish and wildlife.[18] The commission would probably have enhanced the power of the outdoor sporting groups in wildlife management, regardless of whether it would have better promoted conservation.

FRANK DUFRESNE

The Alaska Game Commission owed much of its success to strong personalities in leadership positions. Edward W. Nelson had set the stage for professional wildlife management by hiring competent agents such as Olaus Murie, Lawrence Palmer, Seymour Hadwen, and Frank Dufresne. Dufresne (1896–

TABLE 11.3. Travel by Alaska Game Commission Agents, 1937–1959

	FY 1938	*FY 1943*	*FY 1948*	*FY 1953*	*FY 1958*
Commercial steamer	12,313	4,157	—	—	—
AGC patrol boat	31,073	22,580	25,433	23,552	17,563
Outboard motor	9,869	5,571	n.d.	9,046	13,302
Automobile	35,377	37,680	78,352	184,559	254,514
Railroad	2,657	3,824	1,362	897	775
Airplane	25,349	120,031	112,046	315,037	325,754
Dog team	1,161	675	n.d.	3	—
On foot	4,879	4,299	3,551	7,255	5,202
Horseback	—	—	—	762	—

Sources: Alaska Game Commission, *14th Annual Report of the Executive Officer to the Alaska Game Commission, July 1, 1937 to June 30, 1938* (Juneau), 2; Alaska Game Commission, *4th, 9th, 14th,* and *17th Annual Reports, 1943,* 3; *1948,* 23; *1953,* 29; *1958,* 45 (all Juneau).

1966) became one of the best known of the warden-naturalists. Like Nelson he came from New England. As a boy in the White Mountains of New Hampshire he learned to love Nature. Following a stint in the trenches in France, he struck out for Nome on an adventure trip. He hoped to find an uncle who had left for the Gold Rush and never returned. His uncle turned out to be the mayor of Nome and still had gold fever. Attempts to get young Frank interested missed the mark. In Dufresne's words, "The more I thought about it, the more convinced I became that the real gold of Alaska had wings and fins and hair on it." He had planned a short visit but, when offered a job as a deputy U.S. marshal, he stayed. His investigations of the outdoors produced an article that caught the attention of Nelson, who wrote to offer him a position as wildlife survey agent. Dufresne accepted enthusiastically. His reports to Nelson aided the writing of Alaska's 1925 Game Law.

Dufresne's extraordinary zeal for exploring Alaska's wild almost cut short his career on his first winter dogsled journey. Nelson had instructed that he travel with a companion. Inspired by Roald Amundsen, in Nome training for a solo dogsled and plane trip to the North Pole, Dufresne thought, "If Captain Amundsen can do it, so can I." He departed full of confidence until traveling down a remote stretch of the Aghiapuk River, where he and the team went through overflow ice into armpit-deep water. Soaked, he and the dogs managed to get to shore, and immediately his feet, hands, and face began to freeze. Struggling to the top of the bank, he beheld a trapper's cabin and entered. Dunc McBain, an old trapper and the only person living on the river, had not seen anyone for months. He continued to cook flapjacks as he absorbed the situation. Then he rushed out, retrieved and fed the dogs, and insisted that the young man stay to thoroughly dry his clothes and gear. Their friendship lasted many years.[19]

Frank Dufresne (left), Corey Ford, Alistair MacBain, and Field & Stream *editor Dan Holland examining rainbow trout, upper Newhalen River, Bristol Bay drainage, June 1940. By Dan Holland. Courtesy Jean T. Holland and National Park Service/Lake Clark. Dufresne and others in the Alaska Game Commission maintained close ties to the outdoor sporting community.*

As an administrator Dufresne hoped to be away from the desk and in the field as much as possible. As a lover of wild creatures he preferred research to law enforcement. He believed persuasion rather than arrest and conviction would be the most effective means of instilling obedience to the law. In the early years around Nome he became known for meetings in Eskimo villages in which he explained game regulations, warned of the consequences of violation, and gave elders the responsibility for monitoring compliance.[20]

Dufresne worked for sixteen years in the northwest, north central, and Southeast as a warden and surveyor of wildlife species. In 1936 he received appointment as executive director of the Alaska Game Commission and in 1946 as director of information for the Fish and Wildlife Service in Washington.[21] Upon retirement he signed on as West Coast editor for *Field and Stream* and wrote several popular books on his experiences in Alaska.

As did most other game managers, Dufresne articulated a predominantly utilitarian environmental philosophy. He passionately loved wild creatures but advocated predator control, particularly against wolves. He voiced deeply felt concern for the grizzly bear's future in the face of aircraft hunting, logging, and other threats.[22] Yet he saw hunting as not only permissible but as actually beneficial. He protested the 1964 Wilderness Act and "raids" on national forest lands to create national parks, where hunting would be prohibited.[23] Of Admiralty Island and other brown bear country in the Southeast, he wrote, "Because Alaska's abounding fish and game resources are a resource needing to be cropped to hold them in bounds, National Park status is seldom recommended. Instead it is recommended that the region be managed with an eye to its recreational features in the years that lie beyond our own scope of life."[24] In a more private moment he told friend and writer Corey Ford, in reference to wild animals, "They were on earth long before we were, they have the prior right, and now that we're on top after millions of years they deserve our respect and help."[25]

Dufresne made two notable contributions to the Alaskan environment. He popularized wildlife, issuing somewhat ambiguous pleas for its protection. He nurtured the growth of and respect for game laws and their enforcement. His broad personal experience and connection to people in the bush fostered a cooperative relationship between citizens and game officials. On the other hand, Dufresne's person-to-person approach to law enforcement did not comfortably fit the coming age of air and radio. Preferring the riverboat and dogsled, Dufresne resisted the development of an air wing, thereby losing the services of such talented officers as Sam White. Nevertheless, the Game Commission began to purchase aircraft for law enforcement before the end of Dufresne's term in 1946.

CLARENCE RHODE

Wildlife management took a new direction under one of Dufresne's successors, Clarence Joseph Rhode (1913–1958). Rhode hailed from Colville, Washington, the son of a state fish hatchery operator. A deputy warden at age fifteen, he attended business college but never completed a degree. Deciding to devote his life to wildlife management, he left for Alaska in 1934 and became a warden and Dufresne's assistant in 1936. He picked up the idea of flying patrol from Sam White. Eventually, Rhode would encourage all wardens to do flying, and most did so. In 1948 he advanced to regional director for the Fish and Wildlife Service and executive director of the Alaska Game Commission.[26]

Rhode viewed the airplane as the key to effective law enforcement in the bush. On one occasion while flying his west-central district, he spotted five bull moose resting in the snow. They had been killed illegally and propped up so a flying warden would think they were sleeping. Rhode banked, passed over again, landed, and arrested Smoky Nikita, the violator. Rhode had noticed magpies perched on the antlers, something a live moose would not permit.[27]

Flying agent Jim King described the day-to-day work of airborne wardens:

> The pilot agents learned to monitor the activities of people by reading their tracks in the snow. This required the ability to identify suspicious activity from the air and then to pick safe landing spots in the wilderness so apprehensions could be made. Agents had to be prepared to land at any location used by airborne hunters, including high lakes, ridge tops, sand bars, glacial rivers, beaches, and so on. Agents had to be prepared to snowshoe long distances, camp overnight, and heat up their airships after letting them stand in subzero temperatures. A successful flying warden had to master landings on skis, floats and tires.[28]

While crossing his territory during closed season on martens, agent Grenold Collins spied marten tracks and indications of an active trapline. Passing the trapper, he flew ahead to the cabin, entered, and prepared supper. When the trapper arrived Collins advised him that the situation had been radioed to base. The two sat down and ate, swapped stories, spent the night, and went out the next day to snap the traps shut. Then they loaded the illegal skins and flew back to the base where the trapper would face trial. In cold weather, pilots had to drain the oil soon after landing and heat it up in a pot and pour it back into the engine to restart it. Sam White witnessed a flyer who, having lost his oil through a leak, boiled down moose and bear fat. He poured it into the engine and returned to base.[29]

"No other pilot traveled so widely or monitored activities on the ground so closely," King wrote of the wardens. In addition to investigation of fishing activities and smuggling of wolf skins over the Canadian border, "USFWS [U.S. Fish and Wildlife Service] pilots delivered letters and messages, provided supplies to those in need, took the sick to medical help, reported medical emergencies, and saved lives. By the time of statehood, the 'flying game wardens' were regarded not as an outside and unwelcome force inflicted on the country but rather as an element of local society that provided a local service."[30] Citizens responded by assisting the agents, such as when they experienced mechanical troubles.

Aircraft changed the nature of hunting as well as law enforcement in Alaska. Transportation from other parts of the world and to hunting sites grew far easier after the war. Reflecting on the changes, Russell Annabel wrote that, in prewar years, "you used to see the same men year after year in the northern game ranges. . . . The Alaska game lands, because of the outrageous cost of getting into them, were virtually the private preserve of this group." Traveling to and from hunting sites typically required three weeks to a month by a pack train of horses that had to be purchased and shipped to Alaska. "Now, however, the war-hastened development of aviation here has made the entire length and breadth of the north . . . wide open to you." The first postwar polar bear hunter's Kotzebue guide had spotted bears in the vicinity and "radioed his customer to come north at once. It was a pleasant trip. Luxury liner from Detroit to Seattle, from Seattle to Nome; Alaska Airlines feeder-line plane from Nome to Kotzebue. Comfort all the way. Meals served aloft. No delays." Within three days of leaving home the sportsman had been flown out over the ice and landed near a bear. Assisted by a hired Eskimo, he had taken possession of his long-dreamed-of trophy. Annabel welcomed the changes in hunting and fishing convenience "because so many more gunners and anglers can take part in it."[31]

Aircraft-facilitated hunting drew a different response from a National Research Council committee chaired by Olaus Murie and including Aldo Leopold and Robert F. Griggs. They considered the airplane "an intrusion on the wilderness" that could destroy "the incomparable sense of remoteness which comes to those who, upon entering the wilderness, place themselves beyond the 'sights and sounds' of civilization." Ease of entry by motorized vehicles would cause a loss of "self-reliance and a series of skills and woodsmanship which have social values as antidotes for mechanization."[32]

Moreover, Murie's panel believed aircraft could be a threat to fish and wildlife. They cited an outdoor sporting magazine advertisement guaranteeing a polar bear for $1,500 and promising "transportation to bear by airplane." Entrepreneurs planned a 44-room luxury resort at Kotzebue Sound for hunting polar bears, whales, walrus, seals, waterfowl, and ptarmigan. "Similar reports have come from the field," noted the panel, "pointing clearly to: New problems in law enforcement; the danger to wildlife species, especially such as walrus and polar bear, which obviously cannot survive the new refinement in hunting; and a new factor in the character of field sports, tending to reduce further the element of woodsmanship and sportsmanship already otherwise deteriorated." The committee recommended that aircraft and other motorized transportation be banned in wilderness or wild sections of federal lands, that private inholdings in wildlands be purchased, and that no hunting or shooting by aircraft be permitted.[33] Hunting of polar bears and killing of wildlife from moving planes ended in 1972. The luxury resort at Kotzebue did not materialize.

Regardless of whether aircraft diminished the "sport" of hunting, they could immediately jeopardize populations of some species. Over a two-day period in the spring of 1955 one of Rhode's flying agents followed the tracks of twelve brown bears in the Anchorage vicinity. Each trail ended at a skinned bear carcass. Airborne hunters had simply followed the highly visible tracks of bears emerging from their winter dens into the spring snow, landed, and dispatched the animals. A February 1957 regulation by the Game Commission closed brown bear hunting in April and May to end the practice.[34] Controversy over the use of aircraft and snowmobiles in hunting carried on into the 21st Century.

Clarence Rhode at controls of Grumman Goose, Nome, 1949. FWS 1115, Alaska Resources Library and Information Services. Game Commission director Rhode built an effective air wing for law enforcement.

Rhode's views typified those of the game warden–conservationists of the era. He felt a strong commitment to the protection of game through vigorous law enforcement against all violators, the worst being commercial killers and those who wasted wildlife. Predators—wolves and coyotes at least—did not qualify as "game" and needed to be controlled. Politics, in his estimation, subverted the agent's work by failing to appropriate adequate enforcement funds and by interfering in professional game management.[35]

Rhode's Euro-American perspective and law enforcement orientation inevitably grated against hunting practices by Alaska Natives. Having seen and heard of wildlife waste by Natives, he determined to apply the law. Little or no enforcement had been done previously in the Arctic. At Shungnak in 1949 agent Ray Woolford and his partner apprehended some Eskimos for leaving piles of caribou in the woods after killing them. They required the Eskimos to bring in the caribou. The Eskimos argued that the caribou had been left for one day pending pickup and that, meanwhile, federal agents had found the carcasses and spread poison on them to kill wolves. The incident, and attempts to enforce the law at Anaktuvuk Pass and elsewhere, created enmity between Natives and the wildlife management community. It lent impetus to the movement for Alaska Native land and subsistence rights in the 1960s and 1970s.[36]

Rhode professionalized Alaskan wildlife management to a high degree. For a time he accepted only 2 percent of applicants as agents. He hired university-trained wildlife biologists and helped institute a department of wildlife management at the University of Alaska.[37] An intense, competitive, and highly capable organizer and manager, Rhode induced strong loyalties and resentments. His administrative interests lay much closer to law enforcement than to wildlife biology. Territorial fisheries biologists disliked him; they felt he short-changed fisheries research to build his air-based program. The belief that the federal government had mismanaged the salmon fisheries, and weak cooperation between the Fish and Wildlife Service and the Territorial Department of Fisheries, generated negative feelings between federal and territorial officials. Rhode did care about wildlife habitat, however, and firmly endorsed the proposed Arctic National Wildlife Range (ANWR) and Izembek and Yukon-Kuskokwim Delta wildlife refuges.[38]

In August 1958 Rhode took off in a Grumman Goose accompanied by his son Jack and Fish and Wildlife officer Stanley Fredericksen, preparing for a visit by Wildlife Management Institute leaders Ira Gabrielson and Clint "Pink" Gutermuth in furtherance of the effort to establish ANWR. On their return trip south they planned to cross over the headwaters of the Ivishak River, one of the highest mountain passes in the eastern Brooks Range. Twenty-one years later hikers found the wreckage of their aircraft on a rocky slope below the pass.[39] Agency officials memorialized Rhode in the Clarence Rhode National Wildlife Range along the Bering Sea, absorbed in 1980 by the Yukon Delta National Wildlife Refuge.

JIM BROOKS

Boone and Crockett member James Washington "Jim" Brooks (1922–) careered as an official of both federal and state wildlife agencies in Alaska. Raised in Detroit, Brooks gained an interest in Nature through outdoor forays and the books of Ernest Thompson Seton. He left home at age seventeen without benefit of a high school diploma and headed west for adventure, riding freight trains and staying in hobo jungles. Arriving in Alaska in 1940, he worked at a Civilian Conservation Corps camp, an airport, a gold ore processing mill, and on the Alaska Railroad; washed dishes, cut wood, did farmwork, and fished commercially for salmon. In 1941 he took over a trapline in Kantishna country.[40]

Later that winter, Brooks heard about Pearl Harbor from Indians. He continued trapping until three of his four dogs ganged up on the other, his favorite, and killed it. Returning to Nenana, he met the U.S. marshal, who accused him of draft dodging. When Brooks proved his age of nineteen, the marshal apologized and insisted he stay for dinner. But the invitation suffered from unfortunate timing. In an overheated house, Brooks wore thick long underwear and he had not bathed for some time. He could not enjoy the food as he sat there roasting and growing riper by the minute. Nor did it help matters that the marshal's attractive daughter sat close by. Never had he been so happy to hit the trail again.[41]

In Fairbanks, Brooks worked at the airport where he met many of the early aviators. He drove trucks and heavy equipment for the construction of the Alaska Highway. In September 1942 he joined the U.S. Army Air Corps and applied successfully for flight training. In January 1945 he began piloting 15th Air Force B-24s out of southern Italy on seventeen missions through the flak clouds of Austria and northern Italy. After the war he did bush flying for a year around Bristol Bay and then entered the University of Alaska, intending to study pre-dentistry. A weather service position at Wales rekindled his interest in sea mammals. While at Wales, in 1949 he made a hazardous January flight in a snowstorm to rescue an Eskimo whose two companions had perished on the Bering Sea ice. After accompanying him two years later on a trip, during which he gave all the leftover food and fuel to an old trapper, outdoor writer Jim Rearden remarked, "I learned what it is to be an Alaskan from Jim Brooks."[42]

Returning to the University of Alaska in 1949 Brooks majored in wildlife management, writing a master's thesis on walrus in 1954 that became a standard work on the subject. He then entered the Territorial Department of Fisheries, where he conducted research on sea lions and belukhas to determine their impact on salmon. Put in charge of predator control of harbor seals, a program he did not favor, he helped phase it out. In 1957 he transferred to the new Alaska Department of Fish and Game. An appointment as director of the newly organized game division, a post he held from 1959 to 1967, cut short his doctoral study in wildlife management at the University of British Columbia. In addition to the game program, his duties included establishing the state complex of game refuges. From 1967 to 1972 he served in the U.S. Fish and Wildlife Service, where he designed the polar bear research program and engaged in planning for the Alaska Native Claims Settlement Act and the trans-Alaska oil pipeline. He held office from 1972 to 1977 as commissioner of fish and game and, until retirement, as director of enforcement in the Alaska office of the National Marine Fisheries Service, managing ocean fisheries involving Canada and other nations.[43]

In his travels throughout much of Alaska and innumerable contacts with people of every station, Brooks absorbed what he termed a "generalized sourness" toward the federal government. He had witnessed unfair treatment of the Inupiat at Wales, heard of favoritism toward the outside-owned salmon canning companies, and regarded the reindeer industry as an example of federal mismanagement. Unlike most wildlife managers in the territory he looked forward to statehood and state control of fish and wildlife.

Jim Brooks conducting polar bear research, Chukchi Sea northwest of Cape Lisburne, 1971. Courtesy Jim Brooks. Trained in a modern ecological perspective, Brooks headed the game division of the new Alaska Department of Fish and Game.

Empathetic toward both wild creatures and people, Brooks steered a course midway between the conservationists and the advocates of vigorous exploitation of wildlife. He recoiled at the extravagant waste of walruses by his Little Diomede hunting companions, who killed large numbers only for the ivory. He proposed a bill that passed in 1956 permitting sport hunting of walruses, hoping that guiding would help the local economy. It did, but ivory hunting continued to increase. This and other experiences made Brooks skeptical toward claims of subsistence hunting rights. He regarded much of the predator control by both territory and federal governments as excessive and used his influence to limit it.[44]

Brooks represented the ecologically trained wildlife managers, increasingly from the University of Alaska, who replaced the traditional law enforcement–oriented agents. Professors John Buckley (a student of Aldo Leopold), Neil Hosley, Brina Kessel, and Jim Rearden initiated the university's program. Their students, who set the direction of Alaskan wildlife management from the late 1950s through the 1960s, included Brooks, John Hakala, David R. Klein, Calvin J. Lensink, Jack Lentfer, A. Robert Rausch, and Ronald O. Skoog.

Brooks disliked the bounty system and the wolf control effort. He stopped the program of predator poisoning in 1960 and worked to get rid of bounties. He hired other ecologically oriented agents, encouraged research, and established a habitat division, giving the Alaska Department of Fish and Game a nationwide reputation for progressive research and management. Though not a strong supporter of parks and game refuges, Brooks personally moved the selection and designation in 1960 of the Walrus Islands State Game Sanctuary and furthered the establishment of the McNeil River State Game Sanctuary as a fishing site for Alaskan brown bears.[45] In 1989 he received an honorary doctorate from the University of Alaska. During the wolf controversy in the 1990s he facilitated ballot initiatives in which the public opposed the use of aircraft to pursue wolves, land, and shoot them.[46]

JIM KING

One federal wildlife manager, James Gore "Jim" King (1927–), carried on his environmental activities into the 21st Century. Born in Portland, Maine, where his father wrote for newspaper editor and future Alaska politician Ernest Gruening, King grew up in Massachusetts and Connecticut. Following Marine Corps service he attended Harvard and eventually completed a degree in wildlife management at the University of Alaska–Juneau in 1958. His first wildlife management position consisted of summer employment in 1950 as a park ranger at Mt. McKinley National Park, and in 1951 he began a Fish and Wildlife Service career. As an Alaska Game Commission agent out of Fairbanks he performed wildlife studies, waterfowl banding, and law enforcement. During 1962–1964 he managed the first Fish and Wildlife Service station at Bethel, overseeing the Clarence Rhode refuge on the Yukon Delta and adjacent Bering Sea islands. Between 1964 and 1983 he supervised Alaska bald eagle and waterfowl surveys, compiling 33 years of accident-free flying. As a retiree he did aerial surveys on a part-time and contract basis for the Fish and Wildlife Service and published numerous articles on eagles, ducks, geese, trumpeter swans, and other birds. His waterfowl investigations, including work on the North Slope and investigation of a large oil spill in lower Cook Inlet in 1970, generated awareness and protective measures by public agencies.[47] Not least of the accomplishments of King and other waterfowl biologists, their work on the Yukon Flats helped defeat the Rampart Dam project that would have destroyed one of North America's topmost waterfowl breeding areas.

Most of King's work consisted of waterfowl surveys, but his early warden years produced some memorable moments in law enforcement. On a spring day in 1957, he and agent John Klingbiel investigated an allegation of illegal goose shooting at Kotzebue. Refused entry to the suspect's house, they returned bearing a warrant. The suspect departed in a jeep, waving at them. Pursuing the jeep, they found a stash of white-fronted geese in a snowbank. They carried the geese to the marshal's house next door to that of the suspect, who tried to bar their entry until the marshal emerged, ordering him away. At the trial the prosecutor, allergic to feathers, had to stand in the back of the courtroom and shout questions at the agent holding the evidence. The court convicted and fined the suspect, a non-Native guide.[48]

Typically, though, King flew over waterways and nesting sites the length and breadth of Alaska—the Southeast islands, the ponds of the interior and the Yukon Delta, the river courses, the Aleutians and the Bering Sea, the Arctic tundra—to band or census ducks, geese, and swans. Managers needed the numbers to control hunting and conserve the various species. Survey agents got to know people, Native and white, in nearly all the cities and villages; some dated from the Gold Rush and others came from Oklahoma for oil. When male agents declined to ride in the plane flown by the first female survey pilot, King volunteered to be her assistant. She proved a fully competent flier.[49]

While manager of the Clarence Rhode refuge, King proposed the reservation of Cape Newenham to protect nesting seabirds. This resulted in action by Interior Secretary Stewart Udall in 1969, and the tract became part of the Togiak National Wildlife Refuge in 1980. King and agent Jim Bartonek formed a Pacific Seabird Group that contributed to the expansion of the Alaska Maritime National Wildlife Refuge. In 1975 King and agent Calvin Lensink went to Washington to brief Interior Department officials and members of Congress on lands appropriate for wildlife refuges. Lands settlement bills envisioned

U.S. Fish and Wildlife Service agent Jim King and Nunamiut Eskimos examine a wolf pelt, Anaktuvuk Pass, mid-1950s. By J. Malcolm Greany. Alaska Game Commission, 18th Annual Report, July 1, 1956 Thru June 30, 1957. *A waterfowl expert, King remained active in environmental concerns for half a century.*

vast acreage under federal jurisdiction, enabling the two agents to draft liberal boundaries for the refuges. Their proposals for waterfowl habitat at Innoko, Kanuti, Koyukuk, Nowitna, Tetlin, Yukon Flats, and other lands largely determined their 1980 designation as national wildlife refuges.[50]

In the private sphere, King helped organize the Trumpeter Swan Society (1968), the Pacific Seabird Group, and the Steller Society (renamed Juneau Group of Audubon Society); served on the boards of Alaska Conservation Society and Territorial Sportsmen; and presided over the state chapter of the Wildlife Society. On the state and Juneau parks advisory boards he played a leading role in preservation of the Mendenhall Wetlands and 2,000 acres of Juneau beach properties. He and his wife, Mary Lou, led efforts to establish the 2,800-acre Point Bridget State Park (1988) and the 13-acre Ernest Gruening State Historical Park (1989). The Kings helped create bike and forest trails and other recreational facilities in the Juneau vicinity. In the 1990s King initiated an effort to establish a Juneau Icecap International Park. He received many conservation citations and, in 1989, an honorary doctorate at the University of Alaska–Southeast.[51]

Dufresne, Rhode, Brooks, and King exemplify the many territorial era officials—wardens, researchers, managers, and others—who carried the effort to safeguard Alaska's wildlife populations during the long period between the heyday of influential private elites and the rise of national environmental public opinion in the 1960s. Paralleling the Bureau of Biological Survey–Fish and Wildlife Service directors who in some cases had been their agency superiors, they promoted the evolution of environmental management values in Alaska. All supported species protection, although Dufresne and Rhode expressed a traditional view of predators. They saw their main objective as ensuring a stable supply of game, fur, and fish for residents and, to a lesser extent, for nonresident sportsmen.

Schooled in more modern concepts of wildlife management, Brooks and King perceived their goal as something closer to ecological sustainability. Rhode, Brooks, and King all actuated this value through protective land designations. All four of these leaders articulated the necessity of a strong and responsible government role in wildlife management backed by sound research. As men-on-the-scene they also believed in grassroots participation in policy. In the absence of environmental groups in pre-statehood Alaska, most participation involved settlers, sport hunters and fishers, trappers, and guides. The success of Game Commission and fisheries agents in bridging the gaps between government and settlers gradually reinforced utilitarian conservationist values in Alaska, a step toward later and broader ecological concepts.

12

Grizzly Bears in Politics

No more powerful emblem of the Alaskan frontier existed than the grizzly bear. It drew forth intense feelings of fear and admiration in its detractors and sympathizers. To those who wished to meet one or, to the vastly greater number who preferred to imagine doing so, the bear stood as a manifestation of Nature's raw power; of the mystery, vigor, honesty, and freedom of wilderness; of beauty, excitement, and danger. Some sought to transfer the power to themselves through elemental (if unequal, given the capacity of modern firearms) combat against the bear. Some settled for purchase of a hide. Others, empowered through contemplation of Nature, endeavored to preserve the bear and its habitat. Those immersed in the settlement dream sought not excitement, danger, or beauty but stability, security, comfort, and material gain. They perceived the bear as a pest, a challenge, a threat, even an insult. For more than half a century before statehood the competing elements—hunters, preservationists, wildlife managers, settlers, developers—fought for the hearts and minds of the American public; in essence, for the soul and future of Alaska. During most of this period, their quarrel revolved in part around the grizzly bear.

Brown and grizzly bears, now considered varieties of the same species, are found throughout mainland Alaska and some adjacent islands and occurred as far south as Mexico in the early 20th Century. Adults vary in facial features, in size from about 400 to 1,500 pounds or more, and in fur color from pale yellow to nearly black. The 1902 Alaska game law classified them as big game. They are also predators: of salmon, moose, caribou, deer, and, sometimes, livestock. They occasionally attack humans, almost always as a result of some provocation. Among the most magnificent of the world's land carnivores, the bears occupied a unique position in pre-statehood Alaskan wildlife management. Their special character and ambiguous status between "big game" and "predator," or menace, guaranteed them endless trouble in Alaska, as it had in the States. Controversy over their status persisted throughout the territorial period and gave rise to sanctuaries for their protection. The debates articulated and implemented models for the values of unlimited exploitation, utilitarian conservation, species and ecosystem preservation, and nonconsumptive use.

BROWN BEAR HUNTING

Eskimos, Athabaskan Indians, and other Alaska Natives traditionally killed brown bears for meat, skins, and fat. The fat served as food and as fuel for stone lamps. Hunters employed long spears to brace against the ground and impale a charging bear or to drive into the neck of a bear standing upright. They also attacked bears in hibernation or at night on fishing creeks or bear trails. An estimated total pre-contact population of 71,000, many of whom hunted brown bears, may have been a significant determinant of the size of brown bear populations as well as their fear of humans.[1]

Alaska Natives also hunted bears for the Russians as early as the start of the 19th Century. Between 1803 and 1822, Russian fur-trading vessels carried away 2,650 bearskins, many or most presumably of brown bears.[2] In the 1842–1860 period another 2,280 bearskins left Alaska.[3] Commercial harvest apparently slackened in the early years of American rule. Ivan Petroff related in his 1880 census report that

> their skins are not very valuable, and, owing to this fact and to the fierce disposition of the animals, they are not commonly hunted. All natives of Alaska respect them, and it is the universal custom of hunters to address a few complimentary remarks to the intended victims before attempting to kill them. Perhaps the skins of fully one-half of the brown bears of Alaska are retained by the natives for bedding and to hang before the entrances of houses in the place of doors. The smaller skins are tanned and cut up into strips and lines, and the natives of the interior utilize them for manufacturing sledge fastenings and the net work bottoms of snow shoes, because this leather does not stretch when exposed to moisture, as moose and deer skins do.[4]

Brown bear at Karluk Lake, Kodiak National Wildlife Refuge, 1958. By Earl Fleming. FWS 4863, Alaska Resources Library and Information Services. As a symbol of wilderness, the bear evoked powerful but conflicting reactions from its admirers and detractors.

Beginning in the late 1880s, brown bears on Kodiak Island and the Alaska Peninsula underwent intense hunting for their skins, fashionable in Europe. Observing the Iliamna-Katmai region, federal biologist Wilfred Osgood described brown bears as scarce in 1902, whereas "not more than fourteen years ago it was not uncommon to see eight to fifteen bears scattered about on one mountainside." A prime bearskin brought $75 from Russian nobility in 1904, and skins adorned military hats in Russia, Germany, Austria, and England. The Gold Rush era kept the bears under fire well after the turn of the century, by which time their numbers in some areas had been greatly reduced.[5]

English sportsman Charles R.E. Radclyffe, who hunted the Kenai Peninsula in 1903, noted that the law forbade the sale of heads and skins of game animals. Nevertheless, he said,

> [T]he natives bring in regularly a supply of brown bear skins to all the local stores, and if not already sold to the shopkeepers, they offer these skins to any one who visits the local settlement. . . . [A]t three of the largest stores on the coast of Alaska . . . I saw a total of 120 brown bear skins sold by the natives to the shopkeepers, and afterwards shipped out of the country openly, and with the full cognizance of the authorities. One only needs to pay a visit to the sale-rooms of Messrs. Lampson in London, where hundreds of Alaskan brown bear skins are always on offer, to see how loosely this portion of the game law is enforced.[6]

A woman who lived on the Alaska Peninsula for three years ending about 1910 related that "my husband shot during the three years over one hundred of the big brown bears for the hides."[7] Yet Harold McCracken, who traveled around the western end of the Alaska Peninsula in the spring and summer of 1922, stated, "I saw 190 brown bears. The fact that we saw 28 bears in one day, and as high as 12 in sight at the same time, is in itself good evidence of the numbers to be found."[8] Almost certainly bears stood a better chance of survival in remote than more accessible locations.

Adding to the impact of commerce in skins, sport hunters began to seek brown bear heads and hides shortly before the end of the 19th Century. British gentleman-hunter Claude Cane, in the summer of 1902, felt disappointed when for the second time he lost an opportunity to shoot a mother and her two cubs on the Alaska Peninsula. Bears in the vicinity had become wary of humans. Cane had already downed two adult bears elsewhere on the coast of the peninsula and another on the Kenai. His friend Frances Paget bagged five brown bears that summer.[9]

Charles Sheldon, as a Boone and Crockett hunter-naturalist, walked an indistinct line between conqueror of fearsome big game and scientific observer, collector, and preserver of that game. He shot females and cubs but felt ambivalence about it. In his first Alaskan brown bear hunt on Montague Island in May 1905, he unsuccessfully pursued a mother and cub on two occasions. Eventually, he caught up with a pair on a steep mountainside just below the snowline. Creeping up to them,

> I saw the cub pushing its head into the body of its mother. The mother, stretched at length in a slight depression among the spruces, was distinctly

> visible, and I saw that her left forefoot was raised. The cub was nursing. It seemed excited with hunger and moved its head about in a wild frenzy, all the time bawling in a low, strange tone. . . . [T]he bear half rose, her head turned in my direction. I quickly fired at her foreshoulder. With a woof and a jump she came to her feet and I fired again. In savage fury, she slapped at the point where the bullet had struck, rushed a few feet in the direction away from me, then a few up and a few down, all the time woofing in pain or fright. . . . I fired three more times, and at the fifth shot she dropped. . . . The cub soon emerged from the bushes and started running to follow its mother. I shot it before it had gone three feet."[10]

As he lit his pipe to relax, Sheldon mused,

> I was burning with the glow produced by that rare glimpse of animal life—the very essence of wild nature. I could not resist a strong feeling that I had intruded on sacred moments in that old bear's life, moments forbidden to the members of the human race by some deep law of nature. Faithfully she had fulfilled her duties. Her last hours had found her still performing them, having hidden so well, on such difficult ground, in a spot high and secluded—taking every precaution to give food to her young. It seemed to me that I had a right to kill her, but not thus to detect her at the time she was giving her breast.

Looking back on the experience, Sheldon reflected that "one thing stands out more vividly than all the rest—that sight of the mother bear nursing her moaning cub. . . . Wounded once, she had taken every care of her offspring. . . . But, in spite of all, fate had overtaken her."[11]

During the hunt of several weeks' duration, Sheldon killed at least five bears and continued to look for more. One of the five fell into a canyon where it could not be retrieved. A wounded male escaped. In recounting the hunt Sheldon wrote more as a ritual sport hunter than as a collector for science. Yet his discourse differed considerably from that of popular sport magazines. After a bear accidentally ran into him and knocked him down, he commented that he "could have written a fine story about a vicious, charging bear." In that case and most others, though, bears ran away from the perceived source of danger. He concluded that "every experience I have had with them . . . leads me to doubt most of the stories of their aggressiveness in times past." Later in life he told an outdoor sporting writer that over a period of 35 years he had killed more than 500 big game animals including 70 to 80 brown or grizzly bears.[12]

Other well-educated hunters seemed oblivious to their contributions to the depletion of wildlife species. George Mixter, his brother, and a friend, all influential men from the East, conducted a spring hunt for brown bears on the north side of the Alaska Peninsula in 1908. They killed eighteen bears shortly after the animals had emerged from hibernation. They captured three orphaned cubs to be taken to the National Zoological Park. Immediately after his narration of the hunt in *National Geographic* and without apology, Mixter quoted Wilfred Osgood: "The brown bears of Alaska will undoubtedly become very rare or extinct at no distant date. . . . Already they have become scarce on Kodiak Island, where formerly very abundant, and on the Alaska Peninsula, though still fairly numerous, they are being killed at a rate probably greatly in excess of their increase."[13]

Some including Sheldon collected their kills for museums or other scientific purposes. Most seemed to want trophies for their dens and for status among their peers. Russell Annabel aptly described the phenomenon, rating the grizzly bear, which he distinguished from the brown bear, as

> tops among American sportsmen. . . . The animal's legendary courage, craftiness, and willingness on occasion to charge hell-bent into gunfire makes its pelt more than a souvenir of a hunting trip; it is a trophy certifying you have accomplished just about the ultimate in American big game shooting. The old-time Indians felt the same way about the grizzly when they rated a necklace of grizzly claws or teeth as the badge of a hunter who had been places and done things. Then, as now, it was the spice of danger, the possibility of getting batted down and chewed up, plus the primary difficulty of finding a grizzly and maneuvering yourself into position for a shot at it, that made hunting the animals an outstanding he-man behavior.[14]

POLITICAL CONFLICT OVER BEARS

As a result of Boone and Crockett's work, two provisions of the 1902 Alaska game law protected the grizzly bear: no sales of hides beyond fifteen days after close of the season and an annual per-person limit of four adult bears. These measures provoked a strong reaction from Alaskans opposed to federal restrictions. They enlisted Vermont senator William P. Dillingham, convincing him that bears would put livestock ranchers out of business and that the 1902 game law should be abolished. Settlers named a town after Dillingham, but Boone and Crockett fought off the attack on the game law.

A revised 1908 game law authorized the territorial governor to hire game wardens and control the licensing of nonresident hunters and export trophies. It reduced the annual limit of brown bears to three per hunter and required permits for hide exports but bowed to Alaskan critics by abolishing the season on brown bears north of 62 degrees. Hunters could still sell brown bear skins in or outside Alaska on a very limited scale. The 1902 and 1908 laws may have saved the species from extinction in parts of its range. Boone and Crockett went on advocating sanctuaries for the bears.[15]

Resentment of the 1902 and 1908 game laws persisted. Asserting the potential of Kodiak Island and the Kenai Peninsula as "great cattle ranges" if the bears could be cleared away, F.E. Kleinschmidt complained in a 1913 *Outdoor Life* article, "Men who formulated laws for us called us the riff-raff of the Western Federation of Miners; of low intelligence, unable to govern ourselves or to make our own laws suited to our own needs. . . . One of the great monuments of stupidity erected to this, our great Northern Territory, is The Alaska Game Law." Kleinschmidt charged that outsiders protected the brown bear so they could hunt it themselves.[16] Beyond the normal frontiersman's resistance to outside interference, his remarks reflected the class difference between local citizens and outside conservationists.

Warden Charles Madsen, asked by territorial governor J.F.A. Strong to advise on the status of wildlife on the Alaska Peninsula, assessed the brown bear in anthropocentric terms:

> Its flesh is useless as food; its pelt is of no great value; and it destroys anything and everything that comes within its reach. It even seems to enjoy an opportunity of getting into a trapper's or prospector's cache or place of residence, and tearing to pieces his supplies. . . . They help materially in destroying caribou, and make the raising of domestic stock in the peninsula an almost impossibility. . . . Were it not for the bear this peninsula would be a quite ideal range for both reindeer and domestic stock.

When among domesticated animals, said Madsen, the bear's typical behavior is "killing and maiming without discretion or other intent than demonstrating its power as a mighty slaughterer." Madsen recommended that "the protection now being given the brown bear be abolished."[17]

Alfred H. Brooks, pioneer geologist and name source for the Brooks Range, stated the settler philosophy regarding brown bears in broad terms:

> If the farmer, sheep-herder, and cattleman make progress at the cost of driving out the moose, the caribou, the big bear, and the wolf, it is but an evidence of the progress of civilization. A fundamental principle of advancement of civilization is that the land must be put to its best possible use for the benefit of mankind. Our people have never taken kindly to the European system of game preserves which benefit the few at the expense of the many. All this does not mean that we shall not make every effort to preserve wildlife so long as it does not conflict with the legitimate demands of the settlers.
>
> There have been some wise restrictions put on the killing of game and fur-bearing animals, but some actions taken have been regarded by Alaskans as of more benefit to the non-resident hunter and the occasional visiting naturalist than to the residents of the Territory. For example, some of the game laws indicate a desire to preserve for the use of the large brown bear

> areas which might be used for cattle or sheep. So far, these laws have worked few hardships, as the land is but little settled. As soon as the settlers demand it, such laws will inevitably disappear before advancing civilization, and the bear will be relegated to haunts not available for better purposes.[18]

Governor Strong spoke for the cattle and sheep ranchers in his 1915 and 1916 annual reports to the secretary of the interior: "[T]he Brown Bear is a serious menace to the live-stock industry on Kodiak Island. . . . If these conditions are continued, it will be necessary to abandon the live-stock industry altogether on Kodiak Island and other places where this pestiferous brute is protected by law."[19] A year later, probably having read Madsen's report, he heated up the rhetoric: "[The brown bear] is rapacious and predacious, and he is esteemed to be worthy of a congressional iron cross, presumably because of his fierce and warlike disposition. This animal should not be given protection. . . . It is safe to say that an Alaskan Legislature will not protect the brown bear."[20]

In 1919 Governor Thomas C. Riggs Jr. echoed his predecessor. Taunting his buffalo-loving opposition, he alluded to big game hunters who took trophies and wasted meat, venturing, "It seems to me that the brown and grizzly bears are being protected for the sole benefit of the nonresident sportsmen. They have no place in the economic development of the territory any more than the herds of wild buffalo would have in the wheat fields of Minnesota and the Dakotas." A year later he rated brown bear protection by the federal government as "probably the most serious difference of all" in federal-territorial relations concerning wildlife. He added, "I advocate not only the removal of all restrictions covering them, but a bounty for their destruction. I also believe that protection to brown bears can be found to be unconstitutional." He offered no explanation of the alleged constitutional violation.[21]

Alaskans condemned the brown bear not only as a danger to livestock and human life but also as a predator of valuable game. Governor Walter Clark noted in 1912 that on the Kenai Peninsula "the moose are not menaced by overhunting, but their calves are killed in large numbers by the brown bear." Governors Strong and Riggs also mentioned bear predation of game but cited no details.[22] The difficulty of observing and measuring such predation, and expressions of sympathy for the bears, forestalled bounties and other territorial government efforts to remove brown bears.

In his 1921 summary, Bureau of Biological Survey (BBS) representative Alfred Bailey commented, "Alaskans kill bear at every opportunity regardless of law, and I venture to assert that it would be impossible to find an Alaskan jury which would convict a man for killing a brown bear during the closed season." He recommended that protection of brown bears be lifted to retard the momentum of an attempt by the territorial legislature to gain control over Alaskan wildlife.[23]

The grizzly bear functioned as a scapegoat for Alaskan frustrations. Governor Riggs gathered and publicized accounts of bear attacks on humans, citing several in his 1920 game report. He then discovered a vulnerable spot in the position of the bears' New York and Washington friends. Former BBS director C. Hart Merriam, a "splitter" mammalogist, had published a study identifying up to 86 species of grizzly and brown bears, most of them found in Alaska. It treated grizzlies and browns as separate species. BBS chief Edward W. Nelson had publicly endorsed the classification.[24] Aware that the 1908 game law mentioned only "brown bears," Riggs threatened to lift restrictions on the export of grizzly bear hides. Nelson, Charles Sheldon, and George Bird Grinnell strove to refute the bear attack stories, arguing that in each case the bear had been provoked. Riggs's move put them in a weak position to combat market hunting, a threat that could have eliminated bear populations in some locales.[25] Boone and Crockett mobilized its allied groups and put a stop to Riggs's attack. Riggs responded by threatening court action to test the 1908 law. Madison Grant, who had defended the bears for twenty years, and Grinnell met with Riggs in Washington and persuaded him to withhold the lawsuit. They calmed the waters between Riggs and William T. Hornaday, who had publicly insulted one another during the debates and both threatened libel suits. Soon thereafter the 1920 elections brought Republicans into office and ended the contest over brown bear definition.[26]

Defense of the Brown Bears

Feeble enforcement of the 1908 Alaska game law induced Nelson and the Eastern nature and sporting groups to work for a new law. Hornaday cooperated in this effort, as did Dan A. Sutherland, a candidate for Charles Sulzer's congressional delegate seat. "A vote for Sutherland is a vote for Hornaday and the Alaskan Brown Bears," suggested the Juneau *Daily Alaska Empire*. But Sutherland won.[27]

Largely as a result of Nelson and Sheldon's diplomacy, the furor over the bears and the meat hunting issue quieted enough in the early 1920s to enable smooth passage of the 1925 Game Law. But more trouble lay in wait for the bears. The new Alaska Game Commission received numerous complaints about bears, mostly from residents objecting to their protection or demanding a bounty on them. The loudest protest came from the Kodiak Island cattlemen. The commission responded. Its most politically useful argument consisted of an incident involving a brown bear encountered by Forest Service surveyor Jack Thayer on Admiralty Island in 1928. Thayer and his companion Fred Herring surprised the bear at close range in thick cover. Herring climbed a tree and Thayer fired at the bear, which proceeded to terminate Thayer's career. Herring did not see whether the bear charged before being fired upon. Whatever the case, Thayer had used a light rifle and steel-jacketed ammunition, inadequate for stopping a brown bear.[28] Effective in mid-1930 the commission adopted a regulation permitting citizens "to kill a bear at any time when such animal is considered a menace to person, livestock or property" or appears within one mile of any human residence. The regulation exempted most coastal brown bear habitat.[29]

Outside environmentalists reacted in dismay. Hornaday weighed in with acid commentary:

> The present flurry of demand for the "extinction" of the big brown bears of Kadiak Island and other points north . . . is like the breaking out of heat rash on children. It is to be cured by a salve of equal parts of Truth and Reason. . . . There is no such thing as the "edge of civilization," and the wild beasts of New York and Chicago annually kill and maim about 50 times more innocent people than do all the wild beasts in Alaska.[30]

Letters poured in to the Game Commission, many from nature enthusiasts in the States. Executive director H.W. Terhune dismissed those from outside as "written for purely sentimental reasons." The Hoonah Alaska Native Brotherhood chapter sent a petition declaring that "both the black and brown bears are a menace to human life and safety and there is no particular reason for protecting them." Thomas Gardner of Petersburg wrote, "I have been on the frontier for sixty years and have yet to see the bear that would bother you if you left him alone. The cannerymen say the bear destroy a lot of salmon, but don't say anything about the salmon they take and cannot can. . . . All the bears in Alaska wouldn't eat the salmon wasted that way."[31]

John Pegues, a reporter who had attended every meeting of the Game Commission, held that the new regulation would not be a threat to the grizzly bear population. Introducing another argument unlikely to be well received by the preservationists, he noted that "hundreds of hunters come here annually because of [the bear's] presence. They spend many thousands of dollars in outfitting, hiring guides, on transportation, hotel bills and otherwise. Men have become interested in Alaskan industries directly as the result of hunting trips. The people of Alaska . . . have no desire to exterminate their biggest attraction to the sportsmen." "In fact," he added, "the Alaska Game Commission has since its creation adopted a policy of encouraging big-game hunters to come north."[32]

Brown bears faced guns pointed at them by sport hunters, by settlers who feared them, by ranchers guarding cattle and sheep, by salmon fishers who perceived them as competition, and by loggers who entered their forests. In the Southeast, especially on Admiralty and Chichagof islands, plans for clearcut logging menaced the bears' protective habitat. John M. Holzworth, who passed three summers and falls in the late 1920s studying and filming brown bears in the Southeast, wrote *The Wild Grizzlies of Alaska* in their defense. He attacked the claim of Alaska's officials characterizing Jack Thayer's death as unprovoked. He had personally encountered brown bears on more than 250 occasions, he said, frequently at close range. They had charged twice but not touched him. His guide Al Hasselborg had lived among the bears for 30 years and been charged twelve times, all by bears he had wounded. "The bear's criminal offense, apparently," Holzworth concluded, "is in defending himself. . . . Decimate the bears in Alaska and a great part of the appeal of adventure and the wilderness, the charm of romance which surrounds its islands and mountains, will be gone." He accused the Game Commission of assisting a land grab by grazing interests and called for retraction of the offending regulation and the setting aside of Admiralty and Chichagof islands as bear sanctuaries. For the consideration of prospective hunters he suggested:

> Good photography requires far more skill and ingenuity than hunting with the modern high-power rifle. . . . I also hope that such success as I have had in taking motion pictures, particularly of the grizzly bear, may help to stimulate the use of the motion picture camera rather than the rifle. It affords a much better thrill, and one is soon weaned away from the rifle, with beneficial results both to the hunter and to what remains of the fast dwindling big game animals of the wilderness.[33]

Indeed, photographers began to supplement sport hunters in quest of the most interesting wild creature in Alaska, adding to the employment of guides and outfitters and helping to moderate local attitudes toward the brown bears.

Holzworth chaired the Alaskan Bear Committee organized by the American Society of Mammalogists and the New York Zoological Society. He received the endorsements of Madison Grant, C. Hart Merriam, and Edward W. Nelson and enlisted a large number of conservation groups, magazines, and newspapers. One prominent nature writer, Stewart Edward White, authored numerous articles demanding protection for the bears. In the April 12, 1930, *Saturday Evening Post* he declared, "There is no doubt in the world that if the regulation is permitted to remain in effect, our unique brown bear of Alaska is doomed to as complete extinction as the California grizzly." He called for retraction of the 1930 regulation, defended the bear involved in Thayer's death, and ridiculed the notion that the bears constituted a threat to the salmon industry.[34]

In the 1935–1936 Alaska Game Commission report, director Frank Dufresne mentioned the continuing tendency of coastal fishers and old-timers in the interior to shoot brown bears on sight and the

> frequent but oftentimes exaggerated reports of persons being attacked without apparent provocation. While there are no authentic cases of death

> or severe mutilation from this source during the past year, it is significant to note that several of these so-called "charging brownies" were found to be carrying pieces of old bullets—mute testimony to a former painful but non-fatal encounter with man. This condition, which often produces a crazed and dangerous animal, is largely unwarranted and directly attributable to careless sniping by thoughtless persons.[35]

Apart from hunting regulations, brown bear advocates hoped to establish Admiralty and Chichagof islands as bear sanctuaries. But the Forest Service coveted the voluminous stands of timber on the islands. Accordingly, the agency supported the National Park Service in protecting bear habitat elsewhere. This understanding facilitated the 1931 expansion of Katmai National Monument and the 1939 additions to Glacier Bay National Monument.[36]

On the question of logging on Admiralty and Chichagof islands, Arthur Newton Pack seconded White's views in *Nature Magazine*: "Alaskans of the promoter type, and some government officials, like to talk in terms of 'Economic Development.' They envision employment in lumbering and paper manufacture and the industrialization of Alaska for all Alaskans, all a very fine-sounding theory." Pointing out the failure of pulp industries in British Columbia hundreds of miles closer to markets, Pack asked, "Should Alaska run the risk of destroying the unreplaceable asset of its wildlife and trading this birthright for a mess of pottage? . . . Alaska will do better by preserving the forests on [Admiralty Island] as a public recreation area and wildlife refuge than cutting it."[37] Pack's argument would be heard for decades to come, eventually winning the day.

Shifts in Americans' attitudes had begun to transform the grizzly bear from feared predator to valued symbol of wilderness and integral element of ecosystems. Ecological science and animal rights concepts brought the BBS policy of predator control under critical scrutiny. Nature writers such as White and Holzworth reacted to reports that the Forest Service had tried to arrange for Crown Zellerbach Corporation to log off most of Admiralty Island at low timber rates, for pulp. Senator Frederick C. Walcott, chair of the newly formed Committee on Conservation of Wild Life Resources, visited Alaska to investigate brown bear killing and held hearings in Washington, DC, in 1932. First of the major federal agencies to reflect the attitude changes toward wildlife, the National Park Service in 1931 adopted habitat and species protection as an explicit component of its mission. Joseph S. Dixon, a Park Service biologist and former student of leading ecologist Joseph Grinnell, conducted surveys of the Glacier Bay environs. To institute the brown bear as the premier wildlife species of Glacier Bay National Monument (Chapter 8), he recommended widening the boundaries to take in surrounding forests and the grasslands near Gustavus.[38]

Responding to bear advocates, in 1925 the Alaska Game Commission had designated much of the forest bordering Glacier Bay National Monument as a bear sanctuary. In 1927 Game Commission director Terhune approached the Forest Service to suggest adding the bear habitat to the monument. Eventually, the Forest Service reached an agreement with the National Park Service: it would transfer jurisdiction over the habitat from the Tongass National Forest to the monument in exchange for Park Service cooperation in heading off the drive to make Admiralty and Chichagof islands national parks. To avoid a clash over mining, Park Service leaders decided to seek a presidential proclamation expanding the monument rather than a law creating a national park. President Roosevelt signed the document on April 18, 1939. While making no specific reference to the brown bear whose welfare had been its central purpose, the proclamation made Glacier Bay National Monument larger than any other in the national park system and incorporated virtually all bordering lands necessary for the bears' protection.[39] But it did not end the effort to designate Admiralty Island a bear sanctuary.

Brown Bears and Livestock

Livestock raising, primarily on Kodiak Island, endured as the outstanding reason or excuse for opposition to the brown bear. The industry had a long and troubled history. Russians first introduced cattle in 1794 and maintained small herds on Kodiak and other islands. American ranchers began operating in the late 19th Century. The Department of Agriculture set up an experimental station and cattle herd at Kodiak in 1906 to facilitate a ranching industry in the region. It moved the herd to Seattle for two years following the Katmai eruption and transferred everything to the Matanuska Valley in 1931. Private individuals owned a total of 349 cattle on Kodiak in 1939, 974 in 1956, and 1,350 in 1965.

American settlers also imported sheep. They introduced a flock of 300 to Kodiak Island in 1883; none remained in 1898. Of 9,000 imported in 1902, only 80 survived in 1904.[40] Like beef ranching on Kodiak, sheep ranching never did well, and the brown bear received a large share of the blame. Governors' reports on game conditions repeatedly complained about the threat of brown bears to ranching. Warden Charles Madsen noted in 1916 that "brown bears killed during the fall of 1915 every one of the sheep kept at the U.S. Agricultural Experimental Station at Kodiak."[41] Investigating such complaints, warden Homer Jewell judged in 1930 that losses of large numbers of sheep on Kodiak Island attributed to bears had actually been caused by loose dogs or by starvation and cold.[42]

Beginning in 1927 the Interior Department's General Land Office, attempting to promote economic development, had issued leases for cattle ranching on Kodiak Island. Within a year leaseholders launched a campaign for removal of the brown bears. Complaints of cattle kills by bears in the 1920s precipitated a 1930–1931 investigation, finding that most cattle deaths resulted from starving and from accidents such as falls and entrapment in bogs. Bears often ate the cattle upon finding them dead. Wardens Clarence Rhode and Jack O'Connor drew similar conclusions in 1937.

Meanwhile, a 1933 survey by warden Hosea Sarber had indicated large numbers of brown bears being killed on Kodiak and Afognak islands. Sarber investigated in 1938–1939 and found a maximum of 9 bear-killed cattle, 3 of them questionable, among a total of 74 lost cattle blamed on bears. The rest had died of starvation and accidents. Kodiak Island, he advised, did not suit livestock, and cows had to eat seaweed to survive. He observed that "cattlemen will often go to any extremes to kill or injure the bear. They have extermination first on their minds and state that every bear on the island should be killed. They strongly advocate the bounty system and feel that the Kodiak bear should be destroyed, the government, of course, to pay the bounty."[43] Attempting to target problem bears, Game Commission agents shot eleven on Kodiak Island in 1939.[44]

Alaska Game Commission policy could hardly satisfy all claimants simultaneously—ranchers who wished to eliminate the bears, guides and sport hunters who wanted access to them, salmon fishermen who viewed them as competition, settlers who feared them, and conservationists who insisted on preserving them. The territorial legislature seized upon the issue, accusing the Game Commission of mismanagement and calling for Alaskan jurisdiction over natural resources. Congressional delegate Anthony Dimond introduced a bill to effect the change, but it died.[45] Control over natural resources remained in federal hands until statehood, generating recurring displays of resentment among Alaskans, who pointed to the fact that other territories had been given control. Federal officials, in part beholden to exploitative industries such as salmon canners, also felt reluctant to grant power over a sixth of the nation's land to a very small, largely transient group of people who often behaved irresponsibly in their treatment of the resources.

In 1939, legislation transferred the Bureau of Biological Survey from the Department of Agriculture to the Department of the Interior, effective in 1940, and renamed it the Fish and Wildlife Service. Immediately upon assuming jurisdiction over mainland Alaskan wildlife in 1939, Interior investigated the situation on Kodiak Island. Two inspectors from the San Francisco office visited Kodiak Island in 1939–1940. Ranchers told them that in their five locations they had lost a total of 202 cattle since 1928. Several ranchers had allegedly been driven out of business. Bears in the ranching area appeared to be few but active, and the ranchers claimed an increase of bears since 1935. In their appraisal the inspectors stated that the supply of vegetation and mostly mild

Cow killed by brown bear, Pagashak, Kodiak Island, August 1952. In Russell R. Hoffman, Refuge Narrative Report: Kodiak Wildlife Refuge, May to August 1952, *Kodiak: Fish and Wildlife Service, 1952. Bears killed some cattle, but ranchers exaggerated the numbers and treated the bear as predator or vermin.*

winters could permit a substantial increase in the numbers of cattle on the island. Moving the ranches to the mainland would not work because of harsh winters and bear or wolf predation there. As for Kodiak Island, the inspectors commented, "If the bears are not to be controlled, it will not be possible to raise cattle at a profit."[46]

Fish and Wildlife Service director Ira Gabrielson's recommendation for a Kodiak National Wildlife Refuge succeeded in 1941. The executive order marked off most of the southwestern two-thirds of the island for bears but excepted a vital one-mile coastal strip for commercial fishing and homesteading.[47] This strip, frequented by bears, bred endless tension. A land trade in 1958 added the strip to the refuge in exchange for giving up the Shearwater and Kupreanof peninsulas to be leased for cattle ranching. After the deal, the refuge took in 1.6 million acres of Kodiak and Uganik islands.[48]

Stepped-up conflict over the Kodiak bears followed the 1951 organization of the Kodiak Stock Growers Association, whose leaders badgered the Alaska

Chamber of Commerce and the legislature for resolutions requesting withdrawal of protection for the bears. Guides, sportsmen, and conservationists resisted and persuaded the Alaska Game Commission not to end the protection.[49] Wildlife Management Institute director Ira Gabrielson declared, "If it comes to a choice between killing off the bears and trying to develop the optimistically estimated herd of 3,800 range cattle, it is my belief that this country ought to set aside the entire island to preserve the splendid Kodiak bears." He questioned whether people who would kill off the Kodiak bear for the sake of minute gains for the cattle industry possessed the qualifications for statehood.[50] The Bureau of Land Management, holding jurisdiction over ranch leases, permitted cattle ranching in a few more bear-intensive areas during the 1950s. It set minimal leasing fees—60 cents per animal per year—and required no fencing to keep bears out or cattle in. Responsibility for leasing shifted to the state in 1966 after it selected the ranch areas as part of its land quota.[51]

The Kodiak Island bear-cattle issue went on unresolved. In its final report the Game Commission noted 23 head of cattle killed by a bear in 1959. "Such losses," it stated, "seriously slow down the building up of cattle numbers on the Kodiak ranches."[52] At a Kodiak airport in the fall of 1963 a light plane appeared, a gun on its top. Investigation revealed its owner as cattle rancher Joe Zentner, who had used the plane to kill about 100 bears during the previous decade. The pilot, Dave Henley, presided over the Kodiak Stock Growers Association. His gunning partner during the spring, Kodiak representative Gilbert Jarvela, had done the shooting from the back seat. The operation had been covertly organized and paid for by the Alaska Department of Fish and Game (ADF&G).

When the scandal broke, bear hunting guides and conservation and sporting groups protested. Jim Rearden investigated for *Outdoor Life* and pieced the story together. Cattlemen had been claiming losses to bears and complained to the governor and game officials. One rancher cited a loss of 61 cattle in 1963 and Zentner claimed 30, although he could find only 10. ADF&G initiated the airborne control program in 1962, killing 15 bears; at least 35 died in 1963. Thirteen of these had been gunned down by a semiautomatic M-1 Garand rifle affixed to the top of the plane. Whereas the law permitted killing in defense of property, gunners dispatched some of the bears at least ten miles from the nearest ranch.

Ranchers, who leased the land from the federal government for twenty-year periods, had eliminated approximately 200 bears on Kodiak Island over the previous ten years, about half by the use of aircraft. Nine ranches sat so close to bear country as to experience recurring problems. The economics, Rearden reasoned, did not make good sense. An average cow sold for $250–$400. Sport hunters, on the other hand, contributed over $2,000 to the Alaskan econo-

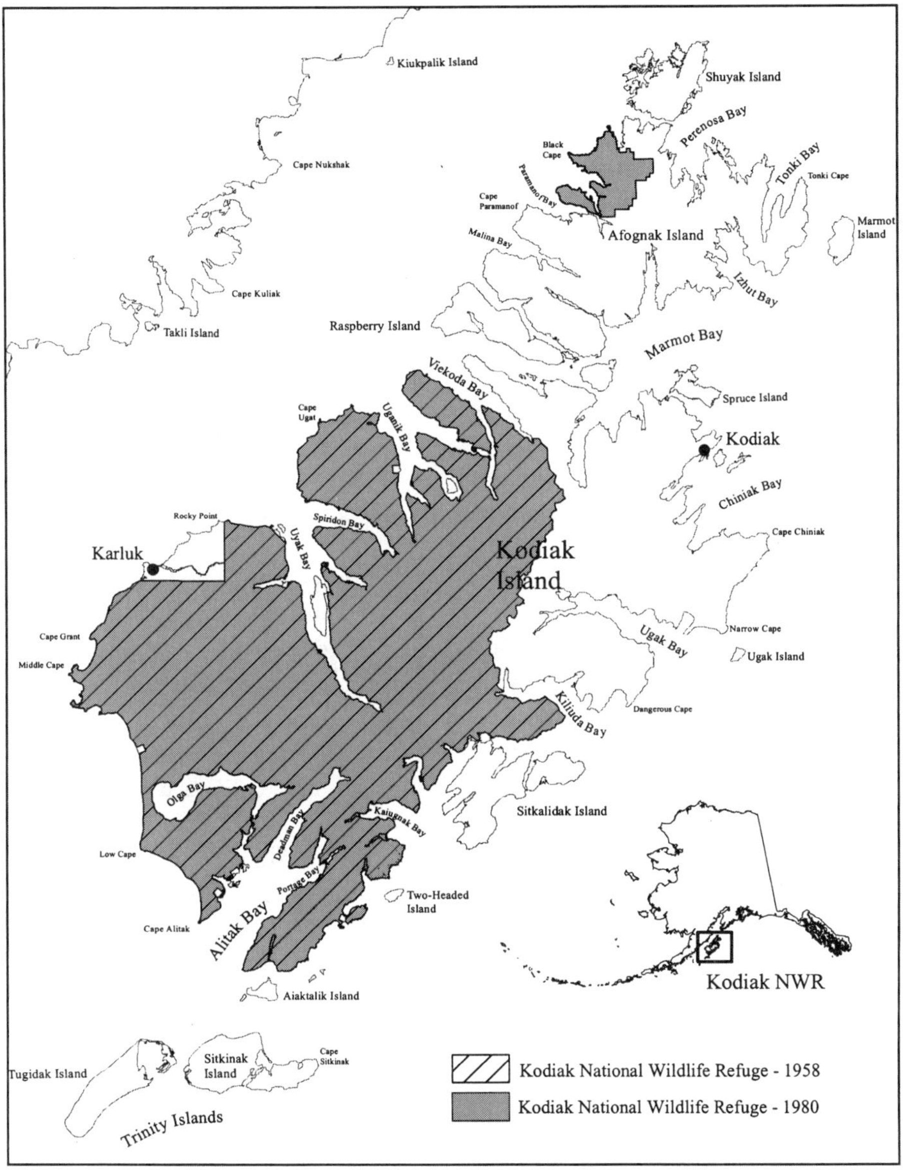

Kodiak National Wildlife Refuge, 1958 and 1980. Courtesy Jason Geck

my for each bear killed and shot more than 100 annually on Kodiak-Afognak islands.

Embarrassed ADF&G officials halted the aerial gunning immediately, but neither this nor the economics of the matter deterred the ranchers. "With our expanding population, people are looking for a place to live, such as Kodiak

Island," one reasoned. "The Indians didn't stop them in the West, the mountains didn't stop them. They pushed on because they were pioneers. The same thing will happen around here, and the bears will have to give. It's only a matter of time."[53]

A 1964–1965 ADF&G survey indicated that 1,350 adult cattle grazed on Kodiak Island on eight ranches covering 180,000 acres. Over a fourteen-month period bears killed at least 33 and injured 6 more. One bear that killed 5 cattle traveled twenty miles through deep snow in a region of steep hills. Most predation occurred in June, a time of food shortage. Adult males appeared to be the most frequent cattle killers.[54] Focusing on specific animals thought to be killing cattle, ADF&G continued to control the Kodiak bears. Between 1964 and 1969, agents killed 43 more bears. Thereafter, they left control to the ranchers, authorized to use deadly force only after exhausting all other methods.[55]

SPORT HUNTING OF BROWN BEARS AFTER 1925

Sport hunting of Alaskan brown bears never approached the point of threatening regional extinction. It may have supplemented other killing or disruption in depleting local populations and, for better or worse, it may have kept the bears in fear of humans. To achieve sustainability, the Alaska Game Law of 1925 ended market hunting of bears by prohibiting all sales of bear hides within or outside the territory. The new Game Commission kept the annual per-person bag limit at three in 1925, during specified seasons and subject to trophy hide export fees. The commission reduced the limit to two in 1927 and to one in 1942. Fifteen years later it prohibited killing females accompanied by cubs. When the State of Alaska assumed responsibility for wildlife management in 1960, it employed similar regulations.[56]

Harvest figures from the prewar era are imprecise. On Kodiak Island, the most popular destination for brown bear sport hunters, the annual kill averaged about 25 between 1930 and 1940. A larger but unknown number fell to salmon fishers, cattle ranchers, and to Koniag Eskimos for subsistence purposes. Hunting dropped off during the war and then rebounded rapidly. It peaked at 225 bears in 1953, inducing tightened regulations. By the late 1950s, both legal and illegal kills fell off because of fewer local military personnel and of stream guards protecting the bears from salmon fishers. A flourishing guiding business earned the town of Kodiak more than $100,000 annually. Koniags harvested about 10 to 12 bears each year for food.[57]

Sport hunting may have done genetic damage to bear populations on Kodiak Island and elsewhere. Warden Jack O'Connor noted in 1937 that "Kodiak reports mostly all large brown bears have been killed off and a plentiful supply of smaller bears." High kill rates in the 1950s and perhaps later also reduced av-

Hunter and brown bear trophy, Kodiak Island, 1957. By Will Troyer. Alaska Resources Library and Information Services. Throughout the 20th Century, sport hunters from around the world came to hunt the great bears.

Table 12.1. Estimated Harvests of Brown or Grizzly Bears in Alaska, 1945–1966

Year	*Harvest*	*Year*	*Harvest*	*Year*	*Harvest*	*Year*	*Harvest*
1945	543	1951	1,080	1957	830	1963	568
1946	789	1952	952	1958	600	1964	627
1947	996	1953	830	1959	550	1965	771
1948	1,107	1954	800	1960	505	1966	856
1949	854	1955	615	1961	473		
1950	886	1956	890	1962	547		

Source: Alan M. Courtright, *Game Harvests in Alaska* (Juneau: Alaska Dept. of Fish and Game, June 1968), 31.

erage bear size because hunters wanted the biggest bears they could find. Once attaining a possible 1,600 pounds, large Kodiak bears seldom weighed 1,200 pounds in the mid-1970s. At that time biologists estimated a total of 3,300 bears on the island, 2,000 in the refuge. Game officials set the sustainable level for Kodiak bear kills at 63 to 127 in the early 1970s.[58]

Reported statewide annual kills of brown or grizzly bears averaged approximately 757 between 1945 and 1966 (Table 12.1). The figures showed a significant reduction in the toll between the late 1940s and early 1960s. This may have reflected a change of sentiment along the lines suggested by Holzworth or that of former Game Commission chairman and bear admirer Will Chase: "The primitive instinct and inclination of youth to hunt down and kill for sport diminishes until it is fairly absorbed in the knowledge of truth that creeps into the life of every man that is privileged to go out into the great open places and virgin forests and commune with nature."[59] Data from 1961–1984, however, indicated an average annual kill of 772, 56 percent taken by nonresident hunters. Stable populations existed in the protected ranges of Admiralty, Chichagof, and Kodiak islands and in other national parks and wildlife refuges. But the brown bear population as a whole faced the prospect of decline from a range of human activities including oil and gas activity, logging and other habitat destruction, agriculture, and miscellaneous conflicts related to human settlement.[60]

RESERVES FOR BROWN BEARS

Madison Grant and John Holzworth's dream of an island-wide Southeast bear sanctuary did not materialize during the territorial period; however, Glacier Bay National Monument protected bears and the Forest Service designated 81 square miles of bear management areas in the Pack Creek and Thayer Mountain locales of Admiralty Island in 1935. Interior Secretary Harold Ickes favored designation of Admiralty as a national park for preservation of bears. However, Alaska's delegate Anthony Dimond objected to the idea, as did National Park Service officials. The U.S. Geological Survey resisted closing off mineral exploration, Hoonah Tlingits wanted tribal control, and loggers, hunters, trappers, and fur farmers sought entry rights. Budgetary limitations also influenced a late 1941 decision by Interior officials to drop the proposal for monument or park status.[61] In part because of the sanctuary lands, no imminent danger threatened the bears. Frank Dufresne and Ralph Young conducted counts of bears on Admiralty, Baranof, and Chichagof in the 1930s, finding healthy populations. No cattle existed on the three islands, and sport hunting left no significant impact.[62]

By the mid-1940s grizzlies enjoyed some protection on Afognak Island (1892), Unimak Island (1913), Mt. McKinley National Park (1917), Katmai National Monument (1918), Glacier Bay National Monument (1925, 1939), the two reserves on Admiralty Island (1935), the Kodiak National Wildlife Refuge (1941), and the Kenai National Moose Range (1941). The Alaska Game Commission had also protected bears on Kruzof and Partofshikof islands in the Southeast, at Eyak Lake near Cordova, and in Keystone Canyon near Valdez.[63] Sport hunting could occur by permit on some of these reserves, as in nearly all other parts of Alaska.

After World War II, logging reappeared as the foremost hazard for grizzly bears in Alaska. Decades of efforts by the Forest Service to stimulate a timber industry in the Southeast paid off in 1947 through the Tongass Timber Sales Act, designed in part to defer competing Native claims. Chief forester and later governor B.F. Heintzleman crucially assisted the passage of the law.[64] He had consistently opposed park or monument status for Admiralty Island and other repositories of wood, arguing that "the harvesting of timber from the island will not materially affect the bear."[65]

Pulp companies received uniquely generous long-term contracts. Ketchikan Pulp Company opened its mill in 1954, and the Alaska Pulp Company commenced operations at Sitka in 1959. The contracts committed huge tracts of Tongass National Forest land to logging, much of it prime brown bear habitat. *Field and Stream* editors Frank Dufresne, Corey Ford, and others called for measures to safeguard the Southeast bears. On a 1956 trip to inspect the effects of the lumber and pulp industry, Ford and Dufresne witnessed, among other impacts, the devastation of a clearcut at Whitewater Bay. They delivered a powerfully negative judgment:

> The menace is the pulp mill, destroyer of essential timbered watersheds, polluter of clean waters so necessary to the life cycle of the salmon, enemy of all wildlife including the brown bear, ruthless despoiler of a nation's recreational heritage. The progress of the pulp industry in Alaska—a progress that appears to be the pet pride of the Territory's present governor—does not represent a vague threat lurking somewhere in the future. Its shadow hangs over Admiralty Island at this very moment.[66]

Dufresne wrote his popular book *No Room for Bears* (1965) to support bear preservation on Admiralty.[67] But the Forest Service had only begun to build up the timber industry in Alaska. Logging in the Southeast precipitated one of the longest-running environmental conflicts in the American experience, lasting throughout the century and beyond. The quest for a bear sanctuary at Admiralty Island continued until the island became a national monument in 1978 and a designated wilderness area in 1980.

The Alaska National Interest Lands Conservation Act of 1980 increased the size of most existing national parks and wildlife refuges, added many more, and classified 56 million acres as wilderness in which no hunting would be allowed. Kodiak National Wildlife Refuge took in part of northwestern Afognak Island. But Native land selections created hundreds of thousands of acres of land inholdings within the boundaries of Kodiak and other refuges and parks, threatening their natural integrity. These inholdings, added to mining and other claims, necessitated a lengthy and expensive effort to purchase them back.

CHANGING PERCEPTIONS OF THE BEAR

Alaska's tug-of-war over brown bear policy evoked local and national reactions ranging across the spectrum of environmental values. Some economic boosters would gladly have seen the beasts extirpated; most tolerated the bear as long as it did not bother humans in any way; others called for species or ecosystem preservation through bear reserves; a few argued that the bear deserved to live as much as or more than some humans. Perhaps because of the confusion of images of the bear as predator, pest, game trophy, wilderness monarch, and winsome furry creature, many private organizations shied away from the debate. Scientific data made a difference, but probably less than sentiment did. Critics called government and corporate interests to account on Kodiak Island and, to a lesser extent, on Admiralty Island. All participants save those favoring extinction got some of what they wanted.

Over time, policy and values shifted toward the preservationist end of the spectrum. Educated members of the Boone and Crockett Club and related groups, while retaining elements of sport hunting as a manhood ritual, could see inherent value in such creatures as the grizzly bear. They also knew that, without safeguards, bear populations could be cut down by commercial or mass sport hunting or by the numerous encroachments of civilization. Thus they encouraged management for sustainable use of the bears and, to some degree, nonconsumptive use. Hornaday, Holzworth, and Stewart Edward White openly insisted on a measure of rights for the bears.

Wildlife managers, in large part brought into being by interest groups led by Boone and Crockett, responded to conservationist appeals. Not beholden to commercial market hunters, they endorsed laws to curb such use of the bears. Notwithstanding their ties to agricultural interests, Bureau of Biological Survey officers did not view brown bears as such serious predators of cattle and sheep as to warrant systematic removal. Rather, wildlife managers felt closest to hunters and trappers, who wanted a reliable store of game and fur. Unlike the wolf, the grizzly bear escaped being targeted as a significant predator of moose and caribou. And the bear itself rated as big game. The managers accordingly applied utilitarian conservation values to the bear, to the end of sustainability. Knowing that, in the case of the grizzly bear, species sustainability necessitated ecosystem protection, they instituted bear sanctuaries at Katmai, Glacier Bay, Kodiak Island, and elsewhere.

After statehood, valuation of the grizzly bear continued to evolve. Wildlife managers still catered to resident and nonresident sport hunters who treasured the ritual of slaying a large and savage beast. Settlers and even hikers could legally kill bears they perceived as a threat. In the 1990s, conservative legislators passed a measure to suppress bears, by shooting them from aircraft if necessary, to enlarge stocks of moose and caribou.[68] Meanwhile, hunting and conquest of wild animals faded as a national pastime, in part because of nature shows and advancing ecological science. Environmentalists grew more numerous and effective in translating their values into public policy. Both federal and state governments designated or enlarged bear sanctuaries. The McNeil River and Katmai parks attained world status as bear viewing sites. Television nature shows elevated bears to iconic status as exponents of the wild. Ecotourism institutionalized nonconsumptive uses—aesthetic, recreational, spiritual—as the brown bear's prime value.

Grizzly bears had won important rounds in the struggle for legitimacy. Yet swelling human population and development left open the question of whether in the long run this magnificent wilderness mammal could survive in more than a few isolated refuges.

13

Frontier Justice: Predator Control

LAST AMONG THE TERRITORIES TO HOLD VIABLE POPULATIONS OF LARGE PREDATORY mammals, Alaska became a battleground over predator control. As a nearly intact ecosystem it also offered a chance to examine natural predator-prey relationships. Beginning in the 1930s the studies and disputes helped reverse traditional attitudes toward predators on the national level and, ultimately, in the far North as well. They helped move policy toward more enlightened utilitarianism and preservationist nonconsumptive values.

Alaska's 1925 Game Law constituted "an Act to Establish an Alaska Game Commission to Protect Game Animals, Land Fur-bearing Animals, and Birds in Alaska, and for other Purposes."[1] It "protected" the species considered most immediately useful to people: the game as food supply and object of sport hunting and the furbearers as a source of cash income. Six species held prominence among the inland wild game mammals: moose, caribou, Dall sheep, mountain goat, Sitka deer, and brown bear, the last acquiring a tenuous status between game animal and predator. Black bear joined the "big game" list in 1938. Among land furbearers, beaver and marten enjoyed the most insistent protection. Game and furbearers needed safeguarding against abuse and over-exploitation by humans, as well as from predators. "Predators" meant animals, excepting the superpredator, who appropriated "game" and "furbearers" for themselves, thereby contesting humans for the resource. Predators needed to be "controlled," a word interpreted by different people to mean everything from limited cropping to extermination. The law permitted the use of poison against wolves, coyotes, and wolverines, regarded as the most troublesome predators.

Predation existed from time immemorial, but it did not spur humans to action until it visibly impinged on their interests and until they felt capable of doing something about it. Such conditions might have applied to the valuable fur seals in the late 19th Century. Capt. A.W. Lavender, Treasury agent on St. George Island, depicted attacks by killer whales on fur seals in the 1880s. His journal entry for September 15, 1881, related, "A school of apparently 10 or 12 killers ran into the [swimming fur seals] around the near rookery to-day and soon made havoc among the pups. It was estimated from the manner in which the seal were thrown up out of the water that 20 or 30 were eaten by their greatest enemies." Similar notations appeared through the decade. Writing to Henry W. Elliott, Lavender recommended that "this species of whale must be destroyed or the seal rookeries will be something of the past in a short time. . . . The next Congress should make an appropriation sufficient to furnish two whale boats and crews with all the modern implements for the killing of whales, and to . . . destroy this whale whenever an opportunity is afforded."[2] Elliott endorsed the idea, although he may have differed as to who rated as the seals' greatest enemy. Nevertheless, the government abstained from any systematic effort to suppress the whales.

As a government policy, predator control sprang primarily from Progressive Era conservation, which emphasized efficient management of natural resources to benefit the public. Long before the science of ecology demonstrated the beneficial roles of predators, scientists and the public considered them a threat to resource supplies analogous to thieves or murderers in the human social sphere. Progressive conservationists therefore expected the federal government to take the lead in suppressing predators. As agencies of the Department of Agriculture, the Division of Economic Ornithology (1886–1905) and its successor Bureau of Biological Survey (BBS) (1905–1940) oriented their concerns largely to the demands of farmers and ranchers. Accordingly, agency chief C. Hart Merriam initiated a program of prairie dog poisoning in 1901 to clear the way for cattle grazing in the West. In 1906 the BBS began functioning as an information center for state bounty systems, and a year later it supervised the killing of 1,800 wolves and 23,000 coyotes on national forest lands. By 1915 BBS fielded a well-organized and well-funded contingent of federal predator control officers.[3]

For several decades the BBS war against predators reflected the will of the people, most natural scientists, and even many nature writers. Antagonism toward "bad" or "immoral" species stemmed not only from competition for game and zeal for efficiency but also from the revulsion of humanitarians and others against cruelty and violence wrought by predators. It seemed obvious that getting rid of them would improve both wildlife abundance and justice. Among his lengthy list of villainous species, the respected William T. Hornaday regarded the wolf as a "black-hearted murderer and criminal" and the mountain lion an "intolerable pest" that "must be hunted down and destroyed regardless of cost." Theodore Roosevelt termed the wolf "the beast of waste and desolation." Few appreciated John Muir's reverence for all creatures or his 1910 observation that plagues of jackrabbits in California had been caused by the elimination of hawks, coyotes, and other predators.[4] Institutionalized in BBS policy, the anti-predator campaign devastated several species in the States before it lost the sanction of science and public opinion.

INITIATION OF ALASKA WOLF CONTROL

Wolves headed the predator list in Alaska. Bearing the burdens of old European fairy tales, a recent experience of persecution by livestock interests in the West, and the fear, resentment, and, perhaps, envy of the human mammal, wolves ran into trouble before the turn of the 20th Century. Commercial game hunters regarded the wolf as a threat to their business during the Gold Rush era. Trappers slew large numbers, using poison illegally to acquire fox furs. An unknown, perhaps substantial number of wolves died from diseases brought in by miners' dogs.[5] In his 1912 report to the secretary of the interior, Governor J.F.A. Strong complained, "In certain portions of southeastern Alaska deer have become very scarce as a result of the depredation of wolves." Calling for a bounty, he made no mention of the slaughter and waste of deer by meat and skin hunters.[6] Two years later fisheries official E. Lester Jones reported deer "rapidly disappearing on many of the islands. I observed a number of instances where the wolves had killed deer, and in others I saw specimens of deer that were thin because of the ceaseless chasing."[7] The territorial legislature placed a ten-dollar bounty on the wolf in 1915, although wardens had reported no decrease in game over the previous several years.[8] In 1922 Governor Scott Bone declared, "Wolves and wolverines are ruthless destroyers of game and fur animals. Predatory and destructive by instinct, they are a menace to game life. The Territory has shown liberality in providing a bounty on wolves and this should be supplemented by the Federal Government in aid of the necessary extermination."[9]

This "liberality," accompanied by requests for federal funds, reappeared throughout the territorial period. Bald and golden eagles acquired bountied status in 1917, hair seals in 1927, coyotes (which entered Alaska in numbers around 1912–1915 and spread rapidly in the 1920s) in 1929, the Dolly Varden in 1931, and wolverines in 1953.[10] Letters streamed in to the Game Commission calling for bounties on these animals, black and brown bears, hawks, falcons, owls, and ravens. A 1928 letter asked, "What are you going to do about coyotes? They have cleaned up everything here in this section, rabbits, grouse, local ducks, foxes and now ptarmigan and muskrats." A 1935 letter from Cache lamented, "About all there is around here now is owls, chicken hawks, ravens and some eagles. There should be a bounty on them." Except for bears, Alaskan writers expressed virtually no sympathy for predators. Trappers favored the bounties but objected to poison because it killed small furbearers in addition to targeted predators.[11] Bounties won popular approval not only as predator control but also as a source of income for hard-pressed local residents, particularly during the Depression.

Agent Alfred M. Bailey recommended to the BBS in 1921 that the wolf bounty be increased from $10 to $25. He requested that BBS hire trained predatory animal destroyers "to protect deer from wolves in the Southeast" while acknowledging that excess hunting had wasted the deer.[12] Catering to the powerful stock-raising interests, BBS had practiced wolf control in the States since 1907. It felt little compulsion to do so in Alaska prior to the 1940s, in part because of the heavy kill of wolves by poison during and after the Gold Rush era. Rising concern within Alaska, however, resulted in a $10,000 appropriation by the 1927 territorial legislature for the hiring of a "predatory animal hunter," to be under the joint control of the governor and the Alaska Game Commission. Underwritten by territorial and later federal funding, R.K. Stewart, followed by Harlan P. Gubser, Frank Glaser, and others, operated in various regions of Alaska from 1927 through the late 1950s. Their work consisted primarily of instructing trappers in wolf and coyote trapping and poisoning techniques. The commission assigned additional personnel to the Southeast in the 1940s. It sought to protect traplines, reindeer herds, and deer and other game populations.[13]

Stewart reported in 1929 that wolves seriously menaced reindeer at St. Michael and big game in McKinley Park. Wolverines, he said, engaged in trapline robbery and property destruction. He offered an honest interpretation of his job: "All nature strives to keep uniform balance. . . . Man's killing of the various so-called game animals tends to keep the balance tipped against them permanently. The only possible thing to do, therefore, other than enforcing game and fur laws, is to control the predatory animals." BBS biologist Olaus Murie, who researched caribou in the 1920s, saw it differently: "The caribou's greatest menace is not the wolf, not the hunter, but man's economic developments, principally the raising of reindeer." He suggested setting limits on reindeer grazing areas and avoidance of mixing the herds, which might alter the genetic purity of the caribou.[14]

DEFENSE OF PREDATORS

Predator control raised biological and ethical questions about the proper role of humans in relating to Nature. On either plane, viable policy called for a sound understanding of predator-prey ecology. But emotion and perceived short-term gain, not science, dictated policies toward predators well past the mid-20th Century. The beginnings of a sympathetic view of the wolf accompanied its scarcity and the passing of the frontier. Ernest Thompson Seton featured a wolf as the protagonist in his popular story "The King of Currumpaw: A Wolf Story" in 1894. Seton and some others based their nature writing on a degree of scientific knowledge. Nevertheless, large predatory mammals had almost no organized defense. The new Forest Service hired its first wolf killers in 1905, and BBS began field efforts culminating in its permanent predator program in 1915. The receipt of money from private groups and states encouraged BBS to elevate its predator control program to a top priority.[15]

By the mid-1920s the wolf and mountain lion had been actually or practically eliminated in nearly all their habitat in the contiguous United States. Relief for predators awaited the advancement of ecological science to dispel fears and deflate excessive claims of harm to prey species and economic loss to ranchers and sheepherders. Accumulating knowledge led to publication of the first ecology book in 1913. Aldo Leopold, teaching at the University of Wisconsin, coauthored the first text on ecologically based wildlife management in 1933. The BBS and its successor Fish and Wildlife Service, tied to their anti-predator clientele but staffed by some officers dubious of predator control programs, remained conflicted from within and without well past midcentury. The National Park Service, hosting swelling flocks of visitors looking for closeness to Nature, assumed the lead among national agencies by halting predator control in its parks in 1935.

Scientists' objections to predator killing had begun to surface by the 1920s. Joseph Grinnell and other members of the American Society of Mammalogists confronted the BBS at the society's 1923 meeting, accusing it of "modern poison warfare." The society persisted as the main institutional adversary of the bureau's policy for about three decades. The bureau responded by shifting its goal from extermination of predators toward more restrained forms of control. Some BBS leaders modified their attitudes, but field operations, driven by funding and ties to farming and ranching, carried on until their demise in the early 1970s. Most critics argued for an ecological view of predators, citing their useful functions in the balance of nature. A few such as Olaus Murie maintained that predators had a moral right to exist.[16]

Murie wrote a tactful memo in 1929 to his chief, BBS director Paul Redington, conveying some of the concerns of the agency's critics. He asserted the existence of a dynamic, although not well understood, balance of nature. In a desirable balance, "[O]ur native animal life may be represented in a reasonable way in our woods and fields." Regarding predators, "The public is more and more pleading for a place in our Nature scheme for our predatory animals. Unfortunately, a number of the sportsmen are not willing to sacrifice some of the 'game.'. . . Many people, as you know, are advocating a certain balance between predatory species and the game, merely that the predatory animals may have some small place in our fauna." Projecting a decline of sport hunting, Murie commented that "'manliness' is no longer acquired by the pursuit of game; it is too absurdly easy. 'Sterling qualities' must assuredly be gained in some other manner."[17] Wildlife appreciation would be the trend of the future, he predicted.

Murie gently suggested that the BBS change its priorities. In contrast to its excellent research work in some endeavors, he argued, the predatory animal division indulged in

> constant effort to produce hatred . . . to kill offending creatures in a spirit of hatred, calling them "murderers," "killers," "vermin," in order to justify our actions. . . . Glaring posters, portraying bloody, disagreeable scenes, urging some one to kill, are working against the efforts of our other selves, who are advocating conservation, appreciation of wild life. Stirring up any part of our population to kill in a spirit of hatred has no part in a government program.

Murie recommended concentrating on research rather than being "a policeman, a sort of handy man." Other agencies needing wildlife data, he noted, had begun to look elsewhere.[18] Murie's prescient views would find wide acceptance 30 or 40 years later.

The BBS, Murie's employer for more than a quarter-century, did not feel ready to adopt his views and declined to publish his studies. But the ecological perspective slowly gained ground. Aldo Leopold, once an enthusiastic killer of predators, co-founded the Wilderness Society in 1935. By the time of his death in 1948 his thinking had evolved to the position that humankind should act as a member of the natural community and had no right to arbitrarily kill other species. Animal rights philosophy, however, possessed weak prospects in a world of vested material interests. Ecological science began to take hold in the 1930s and 1940s, partly as a result of Leopold's work. But rather than casting humans as citizens of the natural community, it moved toward management and control of complex ecosystems.[19]

Studies in Alaska furthered the science of predator-prey relationships. In 1941 Fish and Wildlife Service wildlife biologist Lawrence J. Palmer produced a report identifying fire, not wolves, as the prime cause of diminishing caribou herds in the interior. Fires tended to destroy lichens totally, and full recovery took decades. Overgrazing had an effect similar to fire.[20] Palmer's study drew little attention. A 1952 survey by biologists A. Starker Leopold and F. Fraser Darling corroborated Murie and Palmer's findings. "We seriously doubt that wolves have played any major role in the decrease of caribou which started far back when wolves were very scarce," they said. Caribou attrition in the central region resulted from fires that destroyed the slow-growing lichens: "One fire easily could outdo the work of decades in protecting a local caribou population from man and wolves." In the west coastal region they found reindeer overgrazing to be the main cause of the caribou's downward trend as well as that of the reindeer itself. They also concluded that wolves did not significantly affect moose or deer populations. They did not flatly reject predator control, acknowledging that it might be a necessary means of restoring specific game populations. But they cautioned that excessive predator removal could create game overpopulation, exhausting the food supply and leading to parasitism, lowered fertility, starvation, and damage to the range.[21]

WOLVES IN McKINLEY PARK

Disagreement over the status of the wolf found its first national public expression in a lengthy quarrel centering on Mt. McKinley National Park. Wildlife protection, particularly for the Dall sheep herd, had been a prime rationale for the park; other national parks had been established for scenery or tourism. Notwithstanding the continuation of commercial meat hunting in McKinley Park until 1921, the sheep herd numbered in the thousands. Few wolves existed in the region, possibly because of the widespread use of poisons. But in the spring of 1929 and winter of 1932, heavy snows cut the sheep herd to 1,500. The National Park Service, although leaning toward an ecological view of predators as recommended by the American Society of Mammalogists and other scientists, felt increasing pressure to control wolves and coyotes in the park. Alaska's governor George Parks, the legislature, congressional delegate Anthony Dimond, and the *Alaska Sportsman* and its allied outdoor sporting community all insisted on predator control. So did the Alaska Game Commission, most BBS officials, and the Camp Fire Club. A 1936 *Fairbanks Daily News-Miner* editorial demanded, "If Alaska is to preserve her game and fur animals she—with the aid of the federal government—must wake up and carry relentless warfare into the ranks of the enemy—not tomorrow but today—not at some convenient season but in this hour of emergency." Like other Alaskan critics of the Park Service, the editors believed coyote and wolf predation in the park threatened game outside as well.[22]

Highly vocal elements demanded wolf control but, as in other resource disputes in the territory, some silently held more moderate opinions. Hjalmar "Slim" Carlson, a Swedish immigrant who trapped alone on the fringes of McKinley Park for several decades beginning in 1924, viewed wolves sympathetically. Once he caught a beautiful black wolf by two toes in a trap. He tried to let it go but it seized his leg in its jaws, holding but not biting. He talked to the wolf, and it wagged its tail and made a whining sound. But he dared not approach it again and, reluctantly, decided he had to kill it. He did not favor bounties and refused to blame the wolves when the caribou herds receded in the 1930s. In his judgment, the caribou had migrated elsewhere.[23]

McKinley Park officials occupied uncomfortable ground between National Park headquarters and Alaskan citizens. They monitored sheep and wolf populations in the park. They regarded wolf predation claims as exaggerated but shot a few wolves in an attempt to quiet the critics. A 1935 order, however, directed them to stop killing wolves. Superintendent Harry Liek wrote the Alaska Game Commission in 1936 relating the results of four surveys he had personally conducted. He had found the remains of sheep killed by wolves, but no evidence of an unusual number of wolves. Three sheep had been killed by coyotes, which Liek believed to be on the increase and a danger to the sheep. "The coyote," in his estimation, "is an exotic animal, and we are endeavoring to eliminate coyotes."[24]

Support for the Park Service came from the American Society of Mammalogists, Ecological Society of America, New York Zoological Society, Boone and Crockett Club, Audubon societies, and prominent biologists including Olaus Murie. Responding to a Camp Fire Club critic in 1938, Assistant Park Service Director Arthur Demaray proposed that "if sheep, wolves and caribou have lived together for many thousands of years without one exterminating the other, then, other things being equal, there seems no reason why they cannot now." In the future, he predicted, people would want to "see and hear a timber wolf in its natural state." Nevertheless, to fend off the political assault, officials killed 37 wolves in the park between 1930 and 1938.[25]

Battered by pugnacious opposition for nearly a decade, in 1939 the Park Service hired biologist Adolph Murie to study predation in the park. Adolph had assisted his brother Olaus in researching caribou in 1922–1923 and had completed a master's degree and a PhD in wildlife ecology at the University of Michigan. During 1937–1939 he investigated coyote-elk predation in Yellowstone National Park. Applying more modern scientific methods than had Olaus, who carried out a similar study at Yellowstone a decade earlier, he nevertheless reached the same conclusion—that coyotes had no detrimental effect on the elk population. From April through October 1939 and April 1940 through July 1941, Adolph examined wildlife in McKinley Park. Based on this experience—a landmark study in predator-prey ecology—he judged, "It appears that wolves prey mainly on the weak classes of sheep, that is, the diseased, the young in their first year. Such predation would seem to benefit the species over a long period of time and indicates a normal predator-prey relationship in Mt. McKinley Park." Few coyotes lived in the park, grizzlies ate mostly vegetation and carrion, and golden eagles, accused of taking young sheep, fed primarily on ground squirrels, he noted.[26]

Murie's book *The Wolves of Mt. McKinley* came out in 1944. It heartened naturalists, scientists who believed in ecosystem integrity, and National Park Service leaders. But critics of wolves in the park interpreted it as propaganda on behalf of the Park Service. Meanwhile, apparent shortages of game intensified demands for wolf control. Governor Ernest Gruening led a chorus picturing McKinley Park as a breeding ground for wolves that spread out to attack game elsewhere. They characterized wolf protection in the park as an egregious example of federal mismanagement of Alaska. The Park Service responded by sending Murie back to survey the sheep in August-September 1945. Murie found only 500. He recommended that 10 to 15 wolves be killed to help the sheep recover, and the Park Service agreed.[27]

The alarmingly low sheep tally in 1945 and the buildup of sentiment for wolf control prompted a congressional hearing in 1946. At the urging of the Camp Fire Club, the House Committee on Public Lands debated a bill to require the secretary of the interior to act against predators in McKinley Park. Marshall McLean, chairman of the Camp Fire Club, reminded the committee that

> it was the purpose and intent of those men who initiated this project to have the area set aside as a national park, to provide there a sanctuary and refuge for the home and breeding grounds of the game, in particular for the white mountain sheep and caribou, from which they could spread to the surrounding territories. . . . [T[his purpose has failed because of the predators which have moved into the area, and because of the refusal of the National Park Service to recognize this area as a refuge and sanctuary for these game animals.[28]

Belmore Browne also spoke for the club. He pointed out that the enabling bill identified the park as a "game refuge" and opined that wolves did not qualify as game. To save the sheep, he argued, "a most terrific effort has to be made right away." He recommended that professional wolf killers be employed.[29] H. Bradford Washburn of the New England Museum of Natural History and James R. Clark of the American Museum of Natural History in New York both testified in firm support of the bill. Appended letters from the Boone and Crockett Club, former National Park Service director Horace M. Albright, and Alaska Game Commission game management supervisor Jack O'Connor concurred. O'Connor stated that "personally, I can see no place in the scheme of things for wolves in the future of game in Alaska."[30]

Notwithstanding the reduction of the sheep herd to 500, Murie had stated in his 1945 report that "in a national park, the objective is to preserve a piece of primitive nature where natural relationships may prevail." Browne, who subscribed to the game refuge concept, energetically attacked Murie's approach to park management: "[T]he only persons in America who could take an interest in Murie's ideal would be a handful of biologists. It was on account of the Park Administrators being misled by these theories that the park has been depleted of its game." To Murie's hypothesis that predation benefited sheep by removing the weak, Browne replied that "the killing of the young . . . is, in reality, the race murder of the sheep of tomorrow—the slaughter of the species." Browne speculated that fear instilled by being chased aggravated sheep losses. He rejected Murie's positing of a beneficial balance of nature: "The only way that equilibrium will be obtained in the Mt. McKinley National Park is by the practical elimination of the wolf."[31]

Further congressional hearings planned for 1947 did not take place, but a national debate on wolf policy evolved. Park Service officials organized a counteroffensive, writing articles and encouraging wolf sympathizers to back their position. Nearly every prominent conservation group objected to legislation requiring wolf control in the park. *Living Wilderness* articulated the ecological view, while *Field and Stream* and *Outdoor Life* featured primarily anti-wolf articles. Further debate within the Boone and Crockett Club caused withdrawal of its anti-wolf resolution and adoption of a neutral stance.

In August 1948 an inspection team visited McKinley Park. It included park superintendent Frank Been, full-time park biologist Adolph Murie, Camp Fire Club representative Belmore Browne, American Museum of Natural History director and Boone and Crockett member Harold Anthony, and Anthony's friend Ralph Friedman. At the end of a ten-day survey the team signed a compromise statement approving wolf control pending recovery of the sheep herd. The Park Service reinstated control measures. Murie counted 1,200 sheep in 1951 and 1,500 in 1953. Sheep recovery and an aggressive federal wolf control program elsewhere in Alaska allowed the McKinley Park issue to fade away. Since 1930, at least 76 wolves had been killed in the park.[32]

Realizing that wolves could become a tourist attraction that would dampen criticism without harming the ecology, the Park Service permitted Herb and Lois Crisler to film a wolf family in the park in 1952. To support the filming the service halted wolf control and never renewed it. Lois Crisler's book *Arctic* Wild came out in 1956, portraying wolves sympathetically and in detail. The Disney film *White Wilderness* appeared in 1958, containing wolf footage by the

Crislers. The film and book made decisive contributions to the changing image of the wolf.[33]

Adolph Murie's studies in Wyoming and Alaska advanced the science of ecology by providing some of the first quantitative data on relations between large predators and their prey. The emerging field of ecology put conservation groups and the National Park Service on firmer ground. Evidence that predators performed useful functions enabled their admirers to avoid reliance on unproven concepts of the "balance of nature" or attempts to persuade others to preserve predators because of their beauty or spiritual values. The Park Service renewed its commitment to protection of all species in McKinley Park, Katmai National Monument, and other park units.[34]

ESCALATION OF WOLF CONTROL

Scientific assessments did little to diminish Alaskans' devotion to predator control. Increased human population and hunting following World War II, and an apparent revival of wolf numbers, generated demands for an intensified predator control program. Four ungulate species received primary attention: moose, caribou, Dall sheep, and reindeer. Coyote numbers had plunged since 1940;[35] therefore, officials placed the dominant emphasis on wolf control. In the prevailing view, wolves needed to be thinned out to the point where they would no longer be a detriment to the meat supply. Virtually no conspicuous private individual or group in Alaska regarded wolves as valuable in their own right or as an integral part of an ecological balance. The negative image of the wolf had a firm hold in the legislature and the Alaska Game Commission. Describing his work in caribou country, predator control agent Frank Glaser declared that "wolves had overrun the country" and that a great herd of caribou "was being slaughtered. . . . I was waging war on the wolves, a war that began 38 years ago when I went to Alaska. For 17 of those years I was a government wolf hunter, and I figure I've personally accounted for over 500 of the killers."[36] Frank Dufresne termed the wolf "the villain in Alaska's pageant of life."[37] Clarence Rhode's official pamphlet on Alaskan wildlife stated that "wolves prey on the valuable big-game animals, except bears, and have contributed to the great decline of the caribou herds."[38]

Outdoor sporting interests generated strong momentum for action against wolves. Russell Annabel cited numerous instances of alleged wolf atrocities in his 1948 book, *Hunting and Fishing in Alaska*. In the Chickaloon-Knik district, "Everyone traveling through the mountain passes has reported finding the wolf-torn remains of sheep piled in the valley heads where the animals come in winter for browse. . . . The district has been reduced by wolves to a fifth-rate hunting ground." Of moose in the Matanuska-Susitna range, "[E]ach

Eskimos displaying reindeer killed by wolves, mid-1950s. By Maurice W. Kelly. Alaska Game Commission, 19th Annual Report, July 1, 1957 Thru June 30, 1958. *Claims of heavy losses of reindeer added impetus to wolf control.*

returning guide, trapper, or hunter has reported finding anywhere from five to twenty carcasses indisputably killed by wolves." On the north side of the Alaska Peninsula, "[T]rappers told me the heavy-antlered caribou are being 'piled up in windrows' by wolves." Caribou migrations in Broad Pass near Mt. McKinley "were wiped out by wolves. Dotting the tundra flats and the willow thickets are the whitening bones and antlers of the grand animals that fell victim to the blood-lust of the packs." As for the western mainland, "At Nome, officials of the Reindeer Service reported that virtually all the caribou along the rim of Bering Strait and the Arctic Sea have been killed by wolves and that the predators are now in a fair way to exterminate the reindeer." Supervisor Sidney Rood told Annabel that during his eleven years of service, "[W]olves destroyed more than 1,000,000 reindeer, each of which had a wholesale value of $22." Waterfowl also suffered according to Annabel: "At Unalakleet, on Norton Sound, gunners for years have complained that wolves were killing countless ducks, geese, and swan in the vast nesting grounds." Annabel painted the game situation "as grim and sickening a composite picture of destruction, with nothing being done to prevent it, as a sportsman could imagine in a nightmare."[39]

Not every commentator shared such an alarmist view of the situation. Returning from an inspection trip in 1946, Ira Gabrielson reported to the Fish and Wildlife Service that "everywhere I went people were talking about the decrease of the reindeer herds" and "wolves were widely blamed." Seeking out those he thought better informed, Gabrielson noted that "they and others generally believed that poor herding and the reckless killing of the reindeer for dog food by the Eskimos were both more important factors than wolf predation in their reduction. Frank Glaser, the Service trapper, is very strong in this belief. . . . Some of the Eskimos and a few of the Indian Service employees expressed the same point of view, one or two quite enthusiastically." Gabrielson termed wolf predation "a convenient alibi for carelessness and mismanagement" of the reindeer.[40]

Annabel also fixed coyotes in his crosshairs. Clarence Rhode advised him that coyotes, not wolves, bore the main responsibility for the atrophy of Dall sheep herds. Annabel considered the coyote an even more formidable threat to nesting waterfowl. A chairman of Ducks Unlimited in Alaska told him in military terms that "the coyotes are spreading westward toward the mouths of the Yukon and the Kuskokwim. If they once get a foothold there, some of the finest duck-shooting grounds of America will be affected. In time they'll cut off a good share of the western migration at its source, and then they'll work north and raid the nesting areas of the ducks and geese that swing across Canada into the big Mississippi flyway."[41]

Annabel demanded corrective action:

> [T]he wolf menace to Alaska's game exists throughout the territory and is past exaggeration. All woodsmen with whom I have discussed the matter believe that unless immediate and drastic steps are taken to control the predators, the sheep, moose, and caribou populations will soon be reduced to the point where Alaska's great hunting grounds will be mediocre and their rich promise to the next generation of American hunters gone.

He shamed sport hunters for their "almost unbelievable apathy" and territorial and Washington legislators for failing in their duty. Pointing to an estimate valuing Alaska's game at $300 million, he belittled the 1947 congressional budget item for predator control as grossly inadequate to "hire pilots and maintain airplanes for patrolling and aerial wolf hunting, and for hiring and training wardens and year-round wolfers."[42]

Responding to such appeals in 1948 and again in 1949, Congress made two $104,000 appropriations for Alaska. In September 1948 a Branch of Predator and Rodent Control set to work under the Fish and Wildlife Service in Alaska. By 1950 the branch fielded nine agents.[43] A survey identified the areas of greatest apparent need: reindeer ranges on the Seward Peninsula, the Alaska Peninsula and Nelchina caribou herds, mountain sheep ranges in the interior, and Sitka deer habitat in the Southeast. Some of these ungulate populations had sunk to low levels. Relying on aircraft travel, agents spread poisoned seal blubber in open areas crossed by wolf or coyote trails. Alaska Game Commission

Seal blubber cubes used in wolf control, ca. 1956. By J. Malcolm Greany. Alaska Game Commission, 18th Annual Report, July 1, 1956 Thru June 30, 1957. *Each cube, dipped in seal oil and fish sauce to attract wolves, contained a pellet of strychnine.*

agent Hosea Sarber had discovered in 1943 that small furbearers like mink and martens disliked the blubber, whereas wolves and coyotes loved it. This afforded the control effort a measure of selectivity.[44]

Territorial Sportsmen, Inc., of Juneau participated actively and financially in wolf control in hopes of increasing the deer population in the Southeast. Maurice Kelly, a club member and director of the Predator Control Branch, wrote the group in 1951, "It does appear that the wolf pack on the Taku was wiped out as well as the three wolves ranging in the Dyea Valley. . . . I feel it was a very successful operation and one which I feel was possible only through the cooperation of your organization."[45] Territorial funds supplemented federal funding beginning in 1953, appropriated through the endorsement of "most sportsmen's clubs, farm organizations, women's clubs, civic organizations and many individuals."[46]

Predator control agents and private wolf hunters employed three methods against wolves during the 1948–1960 period: strychnine-laced carcasses and blubber cubes, "getters" that fired cyanide into the victims' mouths, and

Wolves recovered from poison bait stations, ca. 1957. By J. Malcolm Greany. Alaska Game Commission, 18th Annual Report, July 1, 1956 Thru June 30, 1957. *A storm of complaints from hunters and settlers about loss of game set off an intensive wolf control effort in the late 1940s and 1950s.*

buckshot fired from light aircraft. Each method accounted for an approximately equal number of wolves and coyotes taken by agents.[47] Strychnine had the side-effect of poisoning foxes and other furbearers, although agents normally placed it on frozen lakes while bears hibernated. "Getters" used in the summer and early fall sometimes killed black bears, and an occasional wolf would run as much as a mile before dying. In 1951–1952, wolf and coyote control accidentally killed at least 70 furbearers in addition to 374 wolves and 57 coyotes (Table 13.1).[48]

Shooting from aircraft normally involved a pilot, who flew over the wolf or the pack, and a gunner, who fired a 12-gauge shotgun out a door or side window. This procedure, done in late winter and early spring, could be dangerous to both wolves and fliers. Private bounty hunters obtained aerial shooting permits beginning in the late 1940s, and several died in accidents.[49] One pair experienced two accidents in a single day. As they chased a wolf over a hilltop, a ski struck the creature, disabling the landing gear. After repairing it in Fairbanks

TABLE 13.1. Furbearers Purposely and Accidentally Killed in Predator Control, 1951–1952

	Trap	*Getter*	*Poison*	*Snare*	*Shooting*
TARGETED					
Wolf	—	44	80	—	250
Coyote	—	32	5	1	19
ACCIDENTAL					
Fox	1	30	21	—	—
Wolverine	—	3	4	—	—
Black bear	—	8	3	—	—
Lynx	—	1	—	—	—

Source: Alaska Game Commission, *13th Annual Report to the Secretary of the Interior, July 1, 1951 to June 30, 1952* (Juneau, 1952), 15–17.
Note: Includes 223 wolves shot and 36 poisoned in Operation Umiat and one wolverine collected for the Cooperative Wildlife Unit.

they returned to the North Slope and, while pursuing a wolf, crash-landed the plane. Uninjured but without food or sleeping bags, they snowshoed 60 miles to Chandler Lake.[50] The Predator Control Branch obtained its first aircraft in 1949 and lost at least one plane during a wolf control operation.[51] While firing at a wolf on the North Slope, director Maurice Kelly shot the tip off a propeller. Pilot Bob Burkholder landed; they sawed off the opposite tip for balance and resumed the hunt.[52]

Aerial wolf control reached its apex in a quasi-military event on the North Slope titled Operation Umiat. Pilots, wardens, traders, and military personnel in the Arctic had formed a consensus that a large population of wolves threatened to eradicate a shrinking caribou herd. Clarence Rhode explained that "my dream is to do enough wolf work in the Brooks to see if we can build that herd to the point where it will move back into the Yukon-Kuskokwim-Tanana areas where they [caribou] have been absent for so long."[53] During several weeks beginning in March 1952 all seven Fish and Wildlife predator control agents in Alaska participated in Umiat, flying two Piper Super Cubs and a Piper J-5. Flying mainly out of the airfield at Umiat, the agents destroyed a total of 259 adult wolves and pups, keeping 102 for their skins or for research.[54] Agent Frank Glaser described the process:

> In the ski-equipped planes we searched for wolves at an altitude of about 400 feet. When we found a wolf or a pack of wolves (generally from five to ten animals) we circled a mile or so away, dropped to within 40 or 50 feet of the ground, and flew directly toward them. The wolves usually ran straight away in single file. We'd fly on their left, and the gunner, using a shotgun loaded with buckshot, shot the wolves out the right side of the plane, often at ranges of 20 or 30 feet.

A few wolves learned to weave back and forth in defense, and some darted left under the plane out of the gunner's sight. The operation nearly claimed the life of Glaser, who had killed a wolf on a mountain near the Killik River. Pilot Joe Miner landed the plane in a precarious spot, and Glaser got out to skin the wolf. The skis slipped and the plane took off before Glaser could get to his seat; Miner pulled him into the climbing aircraft.[55]

In a sequel to Operation Umiat, private bounty hunters using caches of gasoline left by the military flew the area throughout the 1950s. They boosted the North Slope wolf toll to at least 1,500.[56] Considering that almost no research had been done on the Arctic caribou herds and plenty existed for consumption by Eskimos, some critics regarded Operation Umiat as a bureaucratic excess and an excuse for killing large numbers of wolves rather than an exercise of needed predator control.[57]

Jay Hammond, who flew one of the planes at Umiat, summed up the Game Commission's justification for wolf control:

> To those of us who live in Alaska our game means food, money and recreation. Big business! Last year hunters, trappers and sport fishermen spent in the vicinity of $13,000,000 here in the Territory. This, by the way, is more than is derived from Alaska's fabled mining industry. . . . In an effort to maintain adequate game herds in the face of a snowballing population, it is obviously necessary to reduce the numbers of animals killed by factors other than hunting. One of the few positive steps we can take toward this goal is to reduce the number of animals cut down by wolves. I wish there were enough game to go around for everyone—the wolf included. The big fat truth is, however, there isn't![58]

A gunning team set a record of eighteen wolves in a single day in the Steese-Fortymile district in 1957.[59] In that same year the new Alaska Department of Fish and Game initiated a limited wolf control and research project as part of the Fish and Wildlife Service program. Near Wrangell and Ketchikan, agents set out poison stations to reduce predation of Sitka deer.[60]

Between 1927 and 1958 the territory paid bounties on approximately 25,000 wolves and 20,000 coyotes at a cost of about $1.5 million (Table 13.2). Predator control officers added a minimum 2,000 wolves and 1,000 coyotes (Table 13.3).[61] Although game officials believed wolves increased in most regions during the 1950s,[62] the controls appeared to be drawing them down by the end of the decade. Efforts to reduce wolf populations gained force from recurring complaints of their killing reindeer and from their apparent slaughter of over 200 moose (about 75 percent of the local population) during a period of hard snow crust in the Koyukuk River Valley in the spring of 1957.[63] Officials claimed success in restoring herds of caribou to the point where hunting could resume. Control of the Nelchina wolves may have been overdone: a population

TABLE 13.2. Alaska Bounty Expenditures, 1927–1958

Wolves and coyotes	$1,530,743
Bald eagles	164,561
Hair seals	1,174,084
Dolly Vardens	96,344
Wolverines	31,875
Total	$2,997,607

Source: Donald E. McKnight, *The History of Predator Control in Alaska* (Juneau: Alaska Dept. of Fish and Game, February 1973), 4.

Table 13.3. Species Bountied and Taken in Predator Control Programs, 1927–1958

Species	*Bountied*	*Predator Control*
Wolves	(25,000)	(2,000)
Coyotes	(20,000)	(1,000)
Hair Seals	358,023+	36,000
Sea Lions	—	90
Belukhas	—	128
Grizzly bears	—	16+
Foxes	—	n.d.
Bald eagles	129,273	—

Sources: Donald E. McKnight, *The History of Predator Control in Alaska* (Juneau: Alaska Dept. of Fish and Game, February 1973), 2–5; Alaska Game Commission, *Annual Report of the Executive Officer*, 1927–1946; Alaska Game Commission, *Report of Wolf and Coyote Bounty Payments*, 1940, 12+; *Annual Report of the Alaska Game Commission, July 1, 1956–June 30, 1957*, 33; Alaska Dept. of Fish and Game, *Annual Report for 1958*, 95–103; Alaska Dept. of Fisheries, *Annual Report for 1955*, 100–101; *1956*, 50–51; Willard A. Troyer and Richard J. Hensel, "The Brown Bear of Kodiak Island" (Typescript, Alaska Resources Library and Information Service, 1969), 193–196; Amos Berg, "Alaska's Bald Eagles," *Alaska Fish and Game Trails* (January-February 1971): 11.

of about 200 shrank to only a dozen by 1953, and by 1956 the caribou herd swelled to 36,000, nearly triple the normal size. In the spring of 1957 the Game Commission protected Nelchina wolves and coyotes and initiated a long-term predator-prey study.[64]

Anecdotal reports from residents, guides, and agents, followed by brief surveys, identified bears as predators of moose on the Kenai Peninsula. Wolves had been exterminated there by 1915, and black bears had increased as a result of protection from 1935 to 1945. A more thorough study in 1949 produced stronger evidence that black bears frequently killed moose calves. Brown bears did also and sometimes took down adult moose. More than three decades later, a study in east-central Alaska showed that grizzly bears had killed more than three times as many moose calves as wolves had.[65] Only after statehood did bears receive general recognition as part of the picture of wild ungulate population dynamics.

The Predator Control Branch invested considerable energy in speeches to community groups and other public relations efforts.[66] In its final reports the branch proudly cited community backing for its predator control program, then employing 22 persons. It predicted, "Under statehood it is not anticipated that there will be any great change in the operations or organization of the Branch of Predator and Rodent Control."[67] But ecologically oriented biologists in the Alaska Department of Fish and Game, eager to assume jurisdiction over Alaskan wildlife, opposed most predator control as unwarranted interference in Nature's balancing mechanisms. When they took over in 1960 the branch nearly expired. Its emphasis shifted to foxes and rats in the Aleutians, feral dogs in the towns, and a small-scale wolf control effort in the reindeer range of the Yukon-Kuskokwim Delta.[68]

PREDATION OF SALMON

As Alaska's most economically valuable natural resource, salmon warranted conservation. But it would not be easy to control the behavior of fishermen aggressively seeking to maximize their catches. They blamed one another and wild creatures for salmon declines. Deputy U.S. commissioner of fisheries E. Lester Jones related the findings of his 1914 inspection trip:

> Those engaged in the great fishing industry say the blame for the diminished number of salmon is due largely to natural enemies, which includes bears, wolves, eagles, gulls, terns, mergansers, hair seals, trout, and sculpins. These enemies undoubtedly destroy enormous numbers of salmon and their eggs. But this condition has gone on for years, and would continue without serious detriment to the supply if it were not for the added drain resulting from heavy fishing. . . . [M]an has as much to do with the waning supply of salmon now apparent in some sections. Of course, this great resource was made for man's use, and . . . the fish are there to be taken, but *properly* and *with discretion*, so that the future supply will not be jeopardized.[69]

Jones "saw hundreds and hundreds of humpbacks, silvers, and chums that had been thrown out of the water" by brown bears. Most lay untouched except for paw marks and missing cheeks, a part favored by the bears. Wolves, said Jones, "play a part similar to the bears in the destruction of salmon, but to a less extent." He rated gulls and terns as the most destructive birds. He watched a huge flock of gulls pick the eyes out of humpbacks ascending a shallow stream. About 5,000 fish flopped helplessly when Jones flushed the gulls. He described eagles as a "contributing cause" of loss of salmon, and terns and mergansers as significant consumers of eggs and young fish. Hair seals destroyed salmon and fishing gear; and sculpins, Dolly Vardens, steelhead, and rainbow trout ate large numbers of eggs. Jones recommended removal of protection of gulls and bears and a bounty on wolves.[70]

An array of fish, birds, and mammals consumed salmon eggs during the spawning runs or, later, ate the salmon fry. Lack of scientific evidence resulted in a hit-or-miss system of predator control. The Dolly Varden, a char found in the coastal salt and freshwaters of the Northwest, embarrassed territorial and federal officials alike. Under the assumption that it laid waste to young salmon and eggs, fisheries agents systematically trapped, killed, and discarded it. Federal hatcheries used it for fish food, and dams or racks prevented its ascension of spawning streams. Seines or gillnets captured it below the dams or in upstream lakes, and dynamite preceded release of fry in the lakes. Its numbers dropped off sharply in West Coast streams from Oregon to Alaska. Then fisheries biologist William Morton discovered that two species of Dolly Varden existed: one anadromous, or sea-run, and the other lake-dwelling. The sea-run char that had been targeted ate virtually no salmon or eggs; the lake dweller turned out to be the predator. A more mundane consideration ended the bounty, however. Payment called for turning in the tails, but checkers had difficulty identifying species. In one group of 500 examined, 355 proved to be salmon, 94 rainbow trout, and only 51 Dolly Vardens.[71] Between 1931 and 1941 when it freed the Dolly Varden from bountied status, the territory paid out $96,344 in bounties.[72]

Bears caught salmon as they ascended rivers and creeks to spawn. Inevitably, some commercial fishers perceived the bears as competition and cited them as a reason, or used them as an excuse, for salmon scarcity. A study done at Karluk Lake in the mid-1940s suggested that Kodiak brown bears took commercially significant numbers of sockeye salmon. Follow-up research over the next eight years convinced biologists that the brown bear did not pose a threat to fish supplies.[73]

Sea lions, hair seals, and belukhas (white whales) also qualified as predators because they ate salmon, halibut, black cod, and herring. Sea lions ranked close to wolves in the negative reactions they inspired. Commercial fishers accused them of taking excessive amounts of salmon at sea, stripping fish off trolling and deep-sea lines, raiding traps or nets, and damaging gear. Salmon trap watchers kept guns onboard to shoot sea lions whenever possible. Captain Casper Hollingstad of Petersburg, longlining for halibut in 1946, filed a typical report: "Sea lions took lots of fish from us. Seemed like there was 2 or 3 around most of the time. We shot and killed one at close range. We could often feel them on the line, and one came up with a large halibut in his mouth. We lost a good many fish to them this trip but don't know how many." Sea lions reputedly learned to strip the lines underwater, swim out of shooting range, and eat the catch.[74]

Interior Department researcher Ralph H. Imler and Alaska Game Commission agent Hosea Sarber carried out a 1945–1946 investigation of sea lion predation in response to the widespread complaints. They found that, while fishers exaggerated their losses, sea lions at times extracted 5 percent or more of halibut and sablefish catches. Of salmon trollers, "[V]ery few . . . lost more than six or eight salmon per year to sea lions." Sea lions could be damaging around nets and traps, but elsewhere, stomach analyses showed only about 14 percent

Silver salmon damaged by harbor seals while in gillnet, Stikine River, 1946. By R.H. Imler. RG22 Box 71, National Archives at College Park. Nearly 2 percent of the gillnetted salmon examined by fisheries biologist Imler showed such wounds.

salmon and halibut by volume. Overall, the researchers judged, sea lions needed to be controlled where found in large numbers near important fisheries. Rifle fire could not effectively suppress them because of the time required and the difficulty of hitting them from moving boats. But "any rookery of 200 or more sea lions located in areas of extensive commercial fishing could be reduced to fifty percent . . . with a great saving of food fish, and without jeopardizing the sea lion population."[75] Subsequent research found evidence of greater predation of halibut by sea lions—approximately $270,000 loss in the Gulf of Alaska in 1958. But stomach analyses again revealed no significant amount of commercial fish, and uncertainties remained.

To combine predator control and commerce the Bureau of Commercial Fisheries arranged for a vessel to experimentally harvest sea lions from five rookeries between Kodiak Island and Unimak Pass in 1959. From the 616 sea lions killed, over 200 tons of meat went to mink farms.[76] But commercial use of sea lions did not prove economically viable, and the 1972 Marine Mammal Protection Act banned most sea lion killing.

Harbor seals closely rivaled sea lions as nuisances to commercial fisheries. They specialized in raiding the nets and eating or biting the salmon caught in

Government seal hunter and harbor seals he killed, mid-1950s. Alaska Department of Fish and Game, 1957 Annual Report No. 9, Juneau, 1958, p. 52. The Territorial Department of Fisheries conducted a vigorous campaign to suppress seals under the assumption that they significantly predated salmon.

them. Ralph Imler visited the two main problem sites, the Copper and Stikine rivers, in 1946. He estimated that about 2 percent of the spring red salmon run in the Copper, and a similar percentage of the fall silver salmon run at the Stikine, had been damaged by harbor seals. The annual monetary loss at the Copper tallied about $30,000. Rifle shooting to collect bounties effectively controlled harbor seals in the 1940s. In "pass shooting," hunters waited onshore in the spring at a point where seals swam by to or from their feeding grounds. Commonly, men cruised along the shore in a powerboat until they came to a haulout site, pulled ashore, and shot as many seals as possible before they swam away. A few hunters approached the faces of glaciers where seals bore their pups on icebergs. Many seals could be shot but could easily sink or disappear in the moving ice. Men, two to a boat, also approached haulout sites at high speed and fired buckshot at mothers and pups.[77]

Bounty hunters and Alaska territorial fisheries employees systematically shot harbor seals in the 1950s. Beginning in 1951 the Department of Fisheries hired marksmen to shoot seals along the Stikine River. In one year a department hunter in Wrangell killed 998 before being stopped by a trigger finger infection contracted from a seal.[78]

Near the Copper River, another major salmon gillnetting locale, the department used depth bombs at haulout sites. A description of this method appeared in the department's report for 1951, the first year of its harbor seal control program:

> The two skiffs were to run abreast at high speed in order to reach the rookery before the herd was able to disperse. As soon as the seal went into the water the dynamite charges, lit from a blow torch, were dropped overboard one after the other. The hunt would usually terminate one-half hour from the time of contact and the seals not killed migrated from the immediate area.
>
> In the initial effort at Aukley Spit 50 seals were killed. Later in the day a small herd of 25 seals was located and killed at Edwards River. On October 18 another hunt was conducted at Aukley Spit and an additional 175 seal were killed. The most successful hunt was at the Big Softuk Bar where 250 seal were killed bringing the total estimated kill to 500.

Agents constructed bombs of 30 to 50 or more sticks of dynamite tied together. Canneries and fishing organizations, particularly the Cordova Seal Committee, donated a portion of the territory's costs.[79] Between 1951 and 1958, agents dispatched an estimated 37,600 harbor seals and 90 sea lions in the Copper, Stikine, and Taku river sectors. Both shooting and bombing methods proved effective, noticeably reducing the damage to salmon caught in gillnets. Control measures had to be taken just before the fishing season and near the fisheries to work efficiently. Before the following season, seals moved in from elsewhere and replaced much of the lost population. In addition to those taken by agents, in the 31 years following 1927, a total of 358,023 hair seals of all species had been bountied at a cost of $1.175 million.[80] The organized seal control program ended in 1959,[81] and bounties continued through 1967.

In the wake of complaints of salmon predation by belukhas, the territory initiated a research program in 1954 at Bristol Bay. During 1954–1956, agents killed 128 belukhas for study. They gave the bodies to Eskimos, who traditionally used them for food. Researchers concluded that the local concentration of 1,000–1,500 whales consumed 70,000–130,000 young red salmon each June and larger salmon later. Nevertheless, they calculated that the whales ate only 1.0 to 2.7 percent of the young salmon run, and "there would probably be no detectable increase in salmon entering the commercial catch or reaching the spawning grounds if predation by belukhas on adult fish were eliminated completely." In the late 1950s experiments began on means of frightening away belukhas by playing killer whale recordings. Studies proceeded on salmon predation by belukhas, seals, sea lions, lake fish, gulls, and other birds.[82] Researchers examined 20 more belukhas at the Kvichak River in 1958–1959 and a final 7 in 1965.[83]

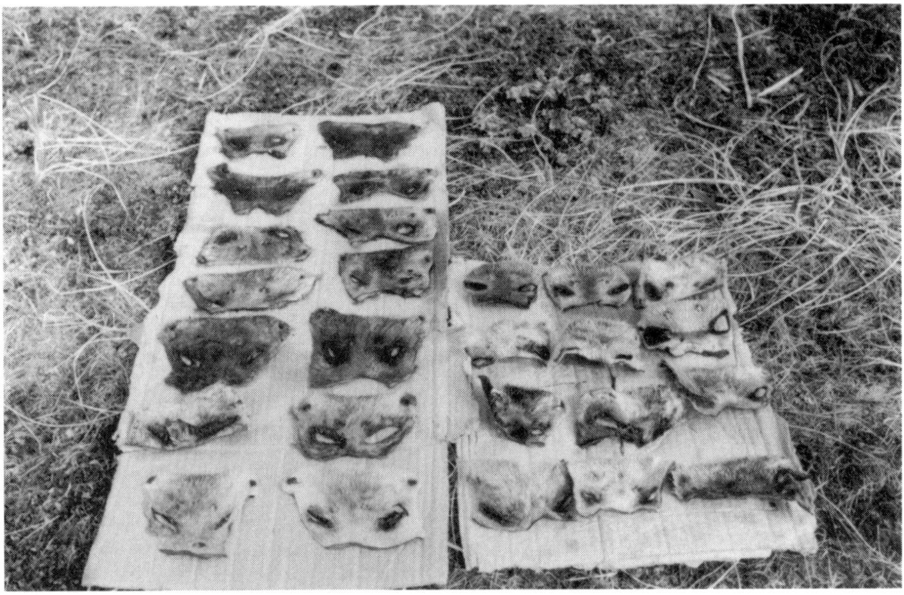

Seal faces collected for bounty, Chukchi Sea, May 1967. By Ken Ross. Over 40 years beginning in 1927, Alaska paid bounties on upwards of 1 million seals, partly as a welfare program.

FOX PREDATION OF SEABIRDS

Foxes, while not subject to bounties, presented problems for other wildlife and for sheep ranching. Fur traders put Arctic foxes (primarily the blue phase) and red foxes (the more valuable cross and silver phases) on islands from Attu to the British Columbia border. Prior to the commercial fur era, Arctic foxes existed only on the Commander and Pribilof islands and north of the Alaska Peninsula. Russians introduced them to Attu in 1750 and, in the late 1700s and early 1800s, throughout the Aleutians and eastward. Introductions occurred systematically by government order after 1819. Americans began stocking Arctic foxes about 1880, eventually placing them on islands all along the south and southeast coasts. Red foxes, native only as far west as the Fox Islands in the eastern Aleutians, were let go by Russians and Americans on islands in the Aleutians, the south, and the southeast. Between 1750 and 1920, fox farming efforts stocked a recorded 455 islands: 86 in the Aleutians, 63 on the south coast of the Alaska Peninsula, 51 in the Kodiak Island region, 73 in the Gulf of Alaska, and 182 in the Southeast.[84]

The 1911 Fur Seal Treaty restricting the harvest of fur seals and sea otters stimulated the fox fur industry. Despite the Aleutians' status as a wildlife refuge, entrepreneurs received licenses for fox farming on the islands. When the value of foxes rose in the 1920s, fox farms reached a pinnacle of 391. Top Arctic fox pelts sold for $460 and silver foxes for up to $2,800 in London. During the Depression the market crashed; the industry nearly expired in the mid-1930s. Island trapping essentially ceased in the late 1940s.[85]

Wild birds, mostly seabird colonies, afforded a natural food supply for the free-running farm foxes. Natural balances soon deteriorated. Aleuts protested in 1812 the loss of seabirds whose skins they made into clothing; they turned to fish skins as a substitute. Russian navigator Vasilev, wintering at Atka in 1811–1812, mentioned that "the Aleuts complain that the foxes drive away the birds, which formerly were numerous and served as a source of feathers for clothing. Nowadays, to get birds they must travel to other islands." Living in extreme poverty, the Aleuts had no footgear and few clothes. Foxes, said Vasilev, had been brought to Atka about twenty years previously and multiplied; a female could produce ten to twelve young annually.[86]

Modern observers noted the work of red foxes placed on Big Koniuji Island in 1916: in less than three months a group of thirteen foxes killed about 100 horned puffins and 800 crested auklets. Foxes sharply reduced or eradicated surface-nesting birds except on inaccessible cliffs. Ground-burrowing species including tufted puffins, Cassin's auklets, Leach's and storm-petrels, ancient murrelets, and rhinoceros auklets virtually disappeared. Other species including rock and willow ptarmigan, common eiders, winter wrens, glaucous-winged gulls, and Aleutian terns steeply declined or vanished. Aleutian Canada geese, once widespread and found in the thousands on Agattu in 1910, survived only on three small islands. Later investigations showed that the loss of bird guano caused the vegetation of most of the Aleutian Islands to change from grasslands to tundra dominated by shrubs and forbs. Mammals introduced as fox food supplemented the effects of fox predation. Arctic ground squirrels, voles, lemmings, house mice, and deer mice ate eggs and young birds, as did Norway rats from supply ships. European rabbits, Arctic hares, and hoary marmots, in addition to the smaller rodents, sometimes overgrazed vegetation, creating erosion and damaging underground bird nests.[87] Feral cattle survived on seven islands where some had existed since the 1890s. They caused erosion, reduced protective vegetation needed for bird nesting, and trampled both surface and subsurface bird nests.[88]

As the reservoirs of nesting birds evaporated and the fur market lapsed, many fox populations died out. Insufficient natural food and unfavorable climate worked against them in the Southeast. Various other phenomena may have caused fox disappearance: interbreeding; predation by brown bears, wolves, and otters; and natural disasters—a 90-foot tsunami cleared foxes off several small islands in 1946. Trappers using poison inadvertently exterminated foxes on

Blue fox at den next to seabirds it killed, Gareloi Island, Aleutians. By Victor B. Scheffer. RG22 WB Box 59, National Archives at College Park. Russian and American fur traders introduced foxes to hundreds of islands, endangering populations of breeding birds.

Shuyak and Dark islands, but in 1970 cattlemen freed Arctic foxes on Sanak Island, whence they spread to nearby islands.

U.S. officials had first expressed concern for the fox impact on birds in 1930. The 1936–1938 Murie-Scheffer expedition reiterated the need for protection of seabird colonies.[89] Examining 1,800 fox scats from 22 islands, they found that birds, predominantly seabirds, accounted for 57.8 percent of the diet of blue foxes. The canines easily caught nesting birds and would also wait for the birds to dive near the shoreline and then jump in and seize them when they surfaced. On small islands and in the case of smaller nesting colonies, the foxes nearly eliminated the birds.[90]

The new Fish and Wildlife Service, under the Department of the Interior, placed more emphasis on ecosystem restoration and land protection than it had under the Department of Agriculture. Aleuts protested a 1944 decision by the Interior Department to prohibit further placement of foxes on Carlyle Island, which had yielded $6,000 in furs in 1940.[91] But fox farming and trapping lost their economic appeal in the 1940s.

Aleutian Islands refuge manager Robert Jones began a fox removal effort in 1949 on Amchitka Island. Fish and Wildlife agents broadcast poisoned bait over the island from a DC-3 aircraft, and no foxes (or feral dogs and cats left by the military) remained in 1960. The agency cleared Agattu between 1963 and 1969; beginning in 1986 it redid an unsuccessful 1963 attempt at Kiska. By 1992 the agency had freed 21 islands of foxes. It planned to complete 19 of the remaining 46 mostly Aleutian islands containing Arctic foxes.[92]

Several difficulties accompanied the removal program. Rats, which thrived on several islands, appeared not to be affected by the control effort. They also preyed on bird eggs and young and may have eradicated song sparrows and winter wrens on Amchitka Island.[93] Removal of foxes increased rat populations. Both ravens and foxes disappeared on Amchitka.[94]

A 1972 presidential order barred the use of poisons in predator control except by special permission for rehabilitation of endangered species. Agents employed this exception only for the Aleutian Canada goose, whose breeding populations they reestablished on Agattu, Alaid, and Nizki following fox removal. After 1986, regulations prohibited all poisoning, and the Fish and Wildlife Service had to rely primarily on trapping and shooting, methods effective only on small islands. Agents restored two islands by the introduction of sterilized red foxes, which killed off the Arctic foxes and then died out.[95] They removed feral cattle from three islands in 1985 but could find no effective method for getting rid of rodents.[96] Many fox removal efforts succeeded, but bird species nesting in burrows recovered very slowly. Surface-nesting birds tended to rebound dramatically.[97]

OTHER EXOTICS IN THE ALEUTIANS

Fox introduction to Alaskan islands illustrated the economic orientation and ecological ignorance of the conservation era. It must have seemed logical that producing valuable crops on near-barren islands represented an improvement, a "conservation" achievement. And ideas for improvement ranged well beyond fox farming. In 1910 the Bureau of Fisheries sent biologist Walter L. Hahn to St. Paul Island to investigate prospects of introducing reindeer, sheep, poultry, muskrats, mink, river otters, crayfish, mussels, water lilies, and other potentially useful animals and plants. Hahn's death by drowning brought the plan to an end.[98]

A few years later scientists from the Bureau of Fisheries observed that swine, chickens, and cats had been brought to the Pribilofs. The cats had a negligible effect on the unwelcome community of house mice. Rats, however, had not gained a foothold. Attempts to establish muskrats and ground squirrels failed either in transit or after release. The scientists recommended against bringing

Red foxes and predated lamb, Unalaska or Umnak Island, ca. 1958. By Lee Ellis. Alaska Game Commission, 20th Annual Report, July 1, 1958 Thru December 31, 1959. *Foxes interfered with sheep raising in western Alaska and the Aleutians.*

in mink and river otters lest they eat the birds, or ptarmigans lest they be killed off by the native Arctic foxes.[99]

Subsequent importations to the Aleutians included more Arctic foxes until the 1930s, sheep (on Umnak and Unalaska), reindeer (on Atka, Umnak, and St. Paul), and caribou (on Adak). Foxes greatly reduced the native ptarmigans on Amchitka but less so on mountainous Adak. Blackflies found their way to Adak and eventually to Shemya and Amchitka, bearing the potential to harm birds through the blood parasites they carried. Placement of rainbow trout on Adak and Shemya and of Sitka spruces on several islands probably entailed fewer possibilities of ecosystem disruption.[100] Increased ecological awareness eventually phased out most exotic transplants by government agencies.

Securing permits from the Bureau of Land Management, sheep ranchers multiplied their flocks on Umnak and Unalaska islands from 1,300 to 6,000 in the late 1950s and planned for expansion to 20,000. They lobbied for fox control; the Game Commission initiated a program in 1957. Ranchers claimed the loss of 400 lambs prior to the 1958–1959 control efforts and very few afterward.[101] The fox control program continued under federal jurisdiction after statehood.

PREDATION BY EAGLES

Unlike most other territorial predator control efforts, the eagle bounty sullied Alaska's image in the States. An American national symbol, the bald eagle lived mostly along the coasts. It courted trouble by feeding on salmon and, allegedly, by stealing pups from fox farms. On Umnak and Unalaska islands, upon installing their sheep herds, ranchers demanded eagle control.[102] Alaskans commonly believed eagles took significant numbers of game mammals as well. Governor Strong reported in 1915 that "the natural enemy of the mountain sheep is the eagle, very numerous on the Kenai Peninsula, which destroys the lambs." In his 1918 report on game, Governor Thomas Riggs attributed the decrease of deer in the Southeast in part to "the greatly increasing depredation from wolves and eagles. The Territory provides a bounty of $15 on each wolf and 50 cents on each eagle. . . . It is my opinion that if the bounty on wolves were placed at $50 and on eagles at $5, in a very few seasons these menaces would be removed." Riggs noted in 1920 that "from the upper Chitina come reports of a great many [mountain goat] kids having been killed by eagles, and one man reports having found the skulls of five kids in one aerie." Riggs called attention to stateside conservationists who had proposed federal legislation to override the territorial eagle bounty. He rated the issue as one of three main points of territorial-federal dispute over game, next to restrictions on the sale of game and protection of grizzly bears. He warned that if the eagle protection law succeeded, "there will be a veritable crusade not only against eagles, but also against all laws of so-called conservation." Riggs again called for higher bounties, to be paid by the federal government.[103]

Some observers regarded the eagle bounty as less vital a measure. Bureau of Biological Survey representative Alfred Bailey noted in 1921 the comment of Fairbanks area warden Protzman that in the vicinity of the Wood, Johnson, and Tanana rivers "there are many eagles, bald eagles also, in the sheep hills, and it is stated that a pair of eagles will account for at least 50 lambs in a single year. . . . In my estimation, the eagle bounty should be fifteen dollars, the same as on wolves." Less convinced of the eagle menace, Bailey thought the fox ranchers "have no evidence that these birds bother the foxes." His recommendation to the bureau:

> Remove the bounty on eagles, using such money as is in that fund for increasing the bounty on wolves. Hundreds of dollars have been paid out on eagles which have been living entirely on herring and dead fish. I believe, however, that it might be of advantage to have a zone system, allowing boun-

ties for birds killed away from the sea coast, for such birds must necessarily live entirely on game birds and animals. The majority of these birds would undoubtedly prove to be the Golden.[104]

T. Gilbert Pearson, president of the National Association of Audubon Societies, visited Alaska in the summer of 1927 to assess the evidence of predation by eagles. Traveling 2,000 miles in the interior, he saw about six pairs of golden and one pair of bald eagles. Twice he witnessed a golden eagle swoop toward a Dall sheep lamb accompanied by its mother. Officials at Mt. McKinley Park said they had no proof of significant sheep predation by eagles. In the Southeast where most bald eagles lived along the coast, Pearson watched them catch fish. He heard scattered claims of eagles taking young deer, furbearers from traps, or foxes from fox farms. Very few people had personally observed such events, however. A sheep ranch manager told Pearson he had seen eagles take dead lambs or wait for dying lambs but not carry off live ones. Pearson found a small number of people to be violently anti-eagle, an even smaller group defending the birds, and a large majority neutral, passively accepting the bounty, or uninterested. People variously attributed the motives behind the bounty to conservation of fish and wildlife, seeking votes of fox farmers, and diverting attention from the predations of commercial salmon fishers.[105]

The bounty, raised to one dollar in 1923, markedly affected the eagle population. Former Alaska Game Commission executive director Ernest P. Walker noted in 1927 that "the Eagle bounty system has considerably reduced the eagles in southeastern Alaska in the ten years that it has been in effect, and to a lesser degree it has reduced Eagles along the southern coastline as far west as the Kadiak region." Comparing his impressions in the pre-bounty period to conditions in 1936, ornithologist George Willett stated that "[t]he eagles had decreased to such an extent that the destruction by them must be very small. This was admitted by many Alaskans with whom I talked. . . . Unfortunately, the question has stopped being one of conservation and has become economic, in that many Indians and some whites . . . have come to consider the eagle bounty as part of their income."[106]

Alaska's treatment of the eagle and the brown bear hatched a great measure of distrust among outsiders, who held the upper hand in deciding the fate of resources in Alaska. In a 1935 issue of *American Rifleman*, sport shooter Lucius Burch waxed eloquent over his Alaska experiences:

> Eagle-shooting, of all the forms of rifle shooting, is a type of sport that is most attractive to the finished rifleman. . . . Unfortunately, there are few spots left where the eagle abounds in quantities sufficient to furnish consistent shooting. . . . [It is the] purest of all the rifle sports; a sport wherein the thorough shooter may have the fun of the game and incidentally pay his way as he goes.[107]

Bald eagle shot for bounty, held by Jim Dolan, Valdez, ca. 1940. Core coll. 01-3891, Alaska State Library. Hunters killed more than 100,000 eagles, ostensibly to protect salmon stocks.

On his most successful day Burch gathered 31 pairs of eagle feet for one-dollar bounties. Frank Dufresne and other game officers, he said, assured him of the bounty's validity "despite the howl of the sentimentalists back in the States." In a lengthy discourse on the relative merits of rifles, bullets, scope sights, and other equipment, Burch decided that, in the case of his Winchester 54, "the killing properties are also excellent; in fact it is too good a killer, as eagles hit solidly are torn up to such an extent that they have a tendency to hang in the trees." His 30-06, he said, "is too much gun for eagles. The great amount of shooting done each day is sure to cause flinching by all but the stoutest." He added that "the eagle is at all times a large and tough customer . . . and he takes some killing."[108]

Reacting to the article, Aldo Leopold wrote president Karl Frederick of the National Rifle Association: "We gun enthusiasts are constantly complaining of restrictive legislation on firearms. Is it likely that the public is going to accord us any more respect and consideration than we earn by our actions and attitudes? . . . I would infinitely rather that [the author] shoot the vases off my mantlepiece than the eagles out of my Alaska."[109]

For years to come, Alaska retained its eagle bounty. A bounty hunter declared, "Alaskans have many definite reasons for their dislike of the great, soaring bald eagle of the craggy mountain fastnesses. They go in for the elimination of this destroyer in no uncertain terms."[110] Hunters climbed nest trees for chicks whose feet brought a dollar a pair.[111] Legislator and later governor William Egan won the nickname "Eagle Bill" for his sponsorship of a measure doubling the bounty on eagles.

Adolph Murie's research exonerated the golden eagle, and separate studies by his brother Olaus and by warden Hosea Sarber determined that bald eagles nearly always fed on spawned-out salmon, not edible by humans. In 1940 a federal law banned molesting of eagles outside Alaska, which suspended its bounty in 1941, repealed the bounty in 1945, and reinstituted it and raised it to two dollars in 1949. An Alaska Game Commission regulation in 1952 permitted killing of eagles only when in the act of taking fish, wildlife, or domestic birds or mammals. The territorial legislature repealed the bounty after federal legislation outlawed the killing of Alaskan eagles in 1952. Over a period of 28 years between 1915 and 1952, Alaska had paid bounties for 129,273 (almost entirely bald) eagles.[112]

EVOLUTION OF PREDATOR POLICY

Predator control policy in pre-statehood Alaska evolved as did ecological awareness: slowly, but ultimately responsive to accumulating scientific information. Bureau of Biological Survey–Fish and Wildlife Service ties to agricultural interests supplemented pre-scientific attitudes in Alaska to perpetuate the suppression of wolves and other creatures. Similarly, Game Commission ties to hunters and trappers inclined it to kill wolves to ensure a game and fur supply. Few officials viewed predators as necessary elements of ecosystems. Field experiences of game agents tended to be anecdotal and often reflected settlers' biases toward predators. Attitudes varied according to the species and its prey, the being the most resented. Some government officials and many settlers excepted the wolf from the generally held notion that species should not be exterminated; almost all thought it should at least be reduced numerically. The fight over wolves in McKinley Park turned the issue into a national debate in which the Park Service, enjoying widespread support, essentially held its ground in defining the wolf as a positive element. Studies by Adolph Murie, Lawrence J. Palmer, and Leopold and Darling constructed a base for a shift to an ecological view of the wolf, which informed policy in the early statehood period.

In the 1960s, attitudes changed toward most predator species. The wolf quickly gained a state and national constituency through popular literature and television nature shows. It became the centerpiece of Alaskan debates ending the bounty system by 1972. When the Alaska Department of Fish and Game renewed wolf control programs in the mid-1970s to raise moose and caribou numbers, it met intensifying opposition. But the need for more research, the persistence of Alaskans' image of the wolf as predator competing for their meat supplies, and the dramatic rise of sympathetic and nonconsumptive uses of the wolf blocked any consensus on its environmental value for the remainder of the century. Protectors and prosecutors of the wolf engaged in ongoing conflict.

Coyotes, almost as frequently killed as wolves in control efforts, won minimal sympathy in Alaska. Perhaps, considering their recent arrival, people classified them as exotics as did Harry Liek. It would have been difficult to argue that they formed an ancient and integral part of natural balances in the North. Their reputation as a common nuisance in the States did not engender fears that they might be exterminated. And perhaps their smaller size and less noble bearing compared to the wolf gave them less potential to win the public's admiration.

Bald eagles proved infinitely easier to rescue from predator status, in part as a consequence of their status as the national bird. Unlike the wolf they bore no significant legacy of threatening economic interests in the States. Studies by Olaus Murie and Hosea Sarber confirmed common-sense suspicions that eagles did not harm Alaska economically. Stateside opinion, expressed through citizen groups, precipitated a shift in national government policy. Essentially no agitation for eagle control endured in Alaska after 1952. While the eagle may not have been thought of as an element of a healthy ecosystem, opinion at least accepted the validity of its preservation as a species.

Sea lion and hair seal control elicited no noteworthy response from the stateside public. It continued in the form of seal bounties until the late 1960s. Federal and state research rationally assessed the belukha and exonerated it. The complexity and unfamiliarity of marine ecosystems acted as impediments to an ecological perspective on these mammals.

Foxes had no significant public following after the fur market declined in the 1930s. Eradication of introduced foxes denoted ecosystem sustainability: the restoration of seabird colonies on subarctic islands. Research as well as casual observation exposed the substantial damage done by foxes. Olaus Murie and other federal officials knew what needed to be done. Remoteness of the islands and the near-total absence of economic stakes permitted them to act without much interference, but not without mistakes. Yet difficulties of exterminating rodents, and modern restrictions on chemical use, deterred final victories for sustainability of the island ecosystems.

Predator control in Alaska represented a similar, belated version of earlier practices in the States. Numerous wild creatures inevitably threatened settlers' economic interests. Large mammals such as wolves and bears elicited fears for personal safety, rarely warranted by the facts. Any challenge to the economic or personal well-being of American pioneers triggered a violently aggressive response. Whereas predators did not vote, politicians responded readily to the emotional demands of hunters, trappers, and settlers. Bounties proved popular regardless of whether they had any meaningful connection to predator-prey relationships. Advancing ecological science could not easily make headway against sentiments based on fear or economic advantage and among people who held little respect for science. Widespread understanding of predators relied on scientific proof but awaited social and economic changes in which the pioneer experience gave way to modern education and to a leisure-oriented society that valued nonconsumptive uses of wildlife.

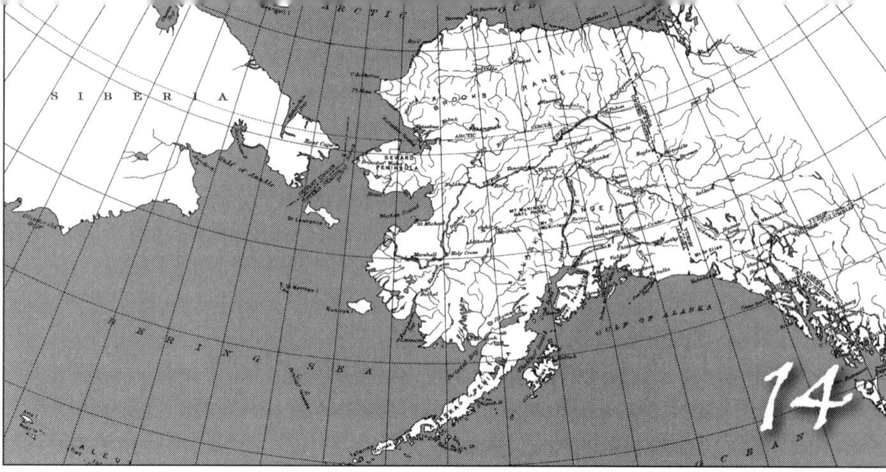

14

Game and Fur Mammals

Conflict over Alaskan land mammals, like that over sea mammals, catalyzed changes in thinking about natural resources. Treatment of "game" and predator species informed the national debate on wildlife management. Efforts to protect mammals motivated the creation or expansion of Mt. McKinley, Katmai, and Glacier Bay national parks. These lands in turn served as models for ecological concepts in natural resource policy. Utilitarian values predominated in Alaska, but wildlife management evolved slowly in the direction of ecosystem preservation.

Mammals, in various ways, ranked high in pre-statehood Alaskan affairs. For aboriginal Natives they provided spiritual sustenance as well as food, clothing, and other implements. Settlers also sought them for food. Russians, Natives, and Euro-Americans engaged in fur trade that at times amounted to a high portion of Alaska's income. Around the beginning of the 20th Century, Native and white entrepreneurs killed for hides and horns, and commercial meat hunters supplied miners, railroad workers, and settlers. Sport hunters arrived to take advantage of some of the world's finest remaining shooting grounds, and

TABLE 14.1. Estimated Harvests of Big Game Species in Alaska, 1945–1963

Year	*Deer*	*Moose*	*Caribou*	*Sheep*	*Goat*	*Black Bear*	*Polar Bear*	*Walrus*
1945	7,204	1,547	4,897	300	229	1,127	76	n.d.
1946	9,077	2,028	1,852	553	320	1,219	117	n.d.
1947	11,280	3,215	5,522	685	493	1,634	110	n.d.
1948	10,922	3,369	6,337	572	660	1,709	102	n.d.
1949	7,476	3,319	6,946	488	580	1,970	105	n.d.
1950	4,520	3,000	4,150	200	580	1,970	69	n.d.
1951	4,600	3,900	5,000	400	600	1,870	60	(1,337)
1952	4,200	3,700	5,600	500	650	1,870	39	(1,337)
1953	3,300	2,880	3,900	420	450	1,500	50	(1,337)
1954	5,100	3,500	16,000	510	430	1,410	100	n.d.
1955	4,600	3,800	17,000	532	500	1,300	128	n.d.
1956	5,900	4,280	17,000	540	420	1,250	135	n.d.
1957	7,800	5,300	19,000	700	470	1,280	206	n.d.
1958	8,000	4,000	16,000	600	250	1,300	128	n.d.
1959	11,000	4,000	13,500	500	125	1,500	225	1,453
1960	12,000	5,500	22,500	1,000	250	1,100	163	2,300
1961	15,000	12,000	30,000	1,000	600	1,100	156	1,486
1962	12,000	9,000	20,000	666	600	1,200	196	1,353
1963	12,000	8,861	21,000	977	600	1,200	167	1,725

Source: Alan M. Courtright, *Alaska Big Game Harvests Data* (Juneau: Alaska Dept. of Fish and Game, November 1964); Courtright, *Game Harvest in Alaska* (Juneau: Alaska Dept. of Fish and Game, June 1968).
Note: Grizzly/brown bear figures in Table 12.1. Walrus figures do not include those struck and lost.

outfitting and guiding them boosted the local economy. But Alaska's remoteness and the seeming abundance of wildlife invited excesses. Settlers and Native and non-Native trappers and hunters poisoned and gunned local populations of some species out of existence. Alarmed at the losses, conservationists in the States took action resulting in the game laws of 1902, 1908, and 1925. Prior to the emergence of ecological science, conservationists joined in the suppression of wolves as a means of conserving game. Different groups valued different mammal species for different purposes, and controversy often surrounded attempts at enforcement of wildlife laws.

A turbulent 35 years passed between the implementation of the Game Law of 1925 and the assumption of wildlife management by the new state in 1960. For a combination of reasons all Alaskan land mammal species including predators survived the period, some restored in numbers. Relatively light hunting activity during the Depression and World War II affected mammal populations, as did fire and weather. Between 1945 and the early 1960s, harvests of most big game species rose moderately (Table 14.1). Observers agreed that the outlawing of commercial meat hunting by the 1925 law and the enforcement of hunting and trapping regulations by the Alaska Game Commission helped conserve several species. Caribou, moose, and deer populations rose in part as a result of wolf control. The Alaska Game Commission accomplished most of what it set out to do.

UNGULATE POPULATIONS

Ungulates, often thought of as "prey species" and generally referred to as "game," supplied necessities of life for both Alaska Natives and terrestrial carnivores. In the near-absence of agriculture, Euro-Americans also relied on them for meat and skins, and some wanted their conspicuous horns and antlers. Human population grew and technology evolved, raising the rate of consumption of ungulate stocks. Disagreements over hunting rules, predator control, and access to game persisted throughout the 20th Century. Most of the debates focused on caribou, reindeer, Sitka black-tailed deer, Dall sheep, and moose.

Caribou

Game management officials made recurring efforts to understand the caribou, a migratory deer inhabiting Arctic and subarctic Alaska and Canada and including a few relict populations in the late 19th Century in several northern tier states. Alaskan herds waxed, waned, and wandered, for reasons not well understood by biologists. A staple resource for predators, Natives, miners, and settlers, caribou stirred anxiety and recrimination when they declined locally. One of the earliest disputes involved the herds of northwest Alaska. During the last quarter of the 19th Century and well into the next, few caribou appeared along the Arctic coast and in the Kobuk and Koyukuk river valleys. Sheldon Jackson and others found Eskimos in a condition of starvation and population loss and blamed the absence of caribou on meat hunting for the whaling industry. Caribou researcher Ronald Skoog determined that the herds had dwindled prior to the high demand for meat and the introduction of numerous guns among the Arctic coast Eskimos. Similarly, Skoog rejected the notion that caribou had been pushed out by reindeer, first introduced to northwest Alaska in 1892.[1] Scarcity of caribou along the northern and western coasts may at least have been exacerbated by excessive killing by Native hunters during the whaling era. Whaling crews each consumed an estimated 10,000 pounds of caribou annually while operating near Herschel Island.[2] In 1878 Eskimos bearing rifles exterminated the herd on Nunivak Island.[3]

Gold seekers, and commercial meat hunters catering to them, further reduced the caribou herds. Bureau of Biological Survey agent Wilfred Osgood, who surveyed the Alaska Peninsula at the turn of the century, addressed hunting's impact on caribou:

> Nearly the year round they are brought in regularly to all the mining camps along the peninsula, being hunted not only for their flesh, but also for their skins, which are in great demand. The mail steamer which runs along the south side of the peninsula takes on a supply of caribou meat on nearly every trip. The animals are usually killed in the Port Moller region, and the carcasses taken to the village of Unga, where the steamer makes regular stops. On the October run, when I was a passenger, caribou chops, roasts, and stews were a feature of the bill of fare. . . . In September, 1902, a trading post was established at Unangashik . . . for the express purpose of trading for caribou skins. . . . [A]pproximately 500 caribou were killed by the natives of Unangashik between October 1, 1902, and May 1, 1903, and the skins disposed of to the trader. . . . The trader pays about $1 in trade for a skin, which is worth to him $2 to $5. The skin of the body is widely used for clothing and bedding material. The short-haired skin of the legs is especially desired for making the tops of the skin boots which are very extensively used by natives and whites alike.

Osgood warned that "if the wholesale traffic in meat and hides . . . is not checked, the animals are surely doomed to speedy extinction."[4]

As of the early 20th Century no caribou survived in the Kenai and Seward peninsulas, the Kuskokwim and Kilbuck mountains, or the Nulato Hills. But at least one large herd existed in the 1920s.[5] Olaus Murie, the game biologist who attempted the first counts, estimated the Yukon-Tanana population at between 500,000 and 1 million.[6] By the late 1940s this enormous assemblage had completely disappeared, but the Kobuk-Noatak herd not seen since the 19th Century now numbered about 100,000. The Yukon-Tanana caribou may have migrated northwestward in 1943.[7]

At the time of statehood biologists estimated the Arctic caribou total at 230,000, and the Nelchina herd south of the Alaska Range had swelled to 50,000. Smaller aggregations of caribou existed in most other regions. Roads, railroads, and airfields made them increasingly available to hunters. Grant's caribou on the Alaska Peninsula had been greatly diminished in number and possibly diluted by interbreeding with reindeer. Assuming the herd had been under siege by wolves, the Game Commission cited its survival as one of the beneficial results of predator control.[8]

Ecologists A. Starker Leopold and Frank Fraser Darling, based largely on their 1952 survey, offered a broader perspective on the causes of caribou population trends. In their view, wolf predation played little or no part. They attributed the decline of the Alaska Peninsula herd to overgrazing of the range by reindeer. They cited fires as the primary cause of caribou losses. Fire destroyed the lichens on which caribou depended as a winter food source. Lichens grew at the rate of one-sixteenth of an inch per year, taking decades to reach even part of their full sixteen-inch height. Gold Rush era and settlement activity had accelerated the frequency of fires compared with the number set earlier by lightning and Natives. An estimated 80 percent of the white spruce forest, where lichens grew in abundance, had been burned in the first half of the 20th Century. A climatic warming trend over the same period aggravated the fire problem, and forest clearing and reindeer grazing further cut back the lichens. Hunting, accelerated by the availability of guns and access by roads, also shrank caribou populations. These combined pressures eradicated some herds, separated most remaining groups and, in general, concentrated the species in the Arctic tundra regions resistant to fire. The researchers saw no prospect of reversing the trend. They recommended fire suppression as a management tool for maintaining caribou populations.[9]

Skoog concluded in the 1960s that, aside from human activity,

> Alaska's caribou population has fluctuated widely during the past 100 years or more. . . . Individual herds have expanded and declined in size; few have remained stable for very long. As the herds increased, their movements have become increasingly complex, more erratic in timing, and more extensive in scope, with the opposite occurring as the herds declined. Major emigrations from one region to another have taken place when peak numbers were reached; other emigrations have occurred when animals from adjacent regions have intermingled during the winter.[10]

Uncertainty about the causes of caribou population shifts infused decades of controversy over predator control.

Moose

Moose protection emerged as one of the Alaska Game Commission's qualified success stories. For flying wardens, the size of moose made them difficult to hide and relatively easy to count in winter. Kenai moose increased as a result of the extermination of wolves and from tightened law enforcement, but lost feed and population as the number of forest fires tapered off. In the wake of fire in a spruce forest, birches, willows, and aspen—crucial winter feed for moose—proliferated. Eventually, in the absence of additional fires, these trees would be succeeded by spruce and moose would decline.

Moose populations gradually increased in the interior for three reasons, according to Leopold and Darling. Since the turn of the century the warming trend had eased their movement northward, even to the Arctic coast, by stimulating the growth of willows. Second, fires usually generated moose browse. Third, on a lesser scale, the clearing of spruce forests for roads, settlements, and other purposes caused more deciduous tree growth. All of these factors, they argued, favored moose and hurt caribou.[11] Other wildlife managers contended that Leopold and Darling gave insufficient credit to the enforcement of bag limits and the prohibition on shooting cow moose as reasons for recovery.[12] Whatever the causes, and despite concerns about wolf predation and excessive hunting by burgeoning numbers of military personnel and civilians, a healthy and widespread moose population greeted the new state. Excepting temporary circumstances in a few locales, moose remained numerous throughout the rest of the century.

Dall Sheep

Mountain sheep, often considered the most desirable game for human consumption, experienced overexploitation by both Natives and non-Natives. Their visibility and herding behavior made them relatively easy to count and, given political will, to protect. Their localized nature allowed Native and Euro-American hunters to reduce or eradicate some of the herds. To supply miners, railroad workers, and other recent immigrants, commercial hunters decimated sheep herds on the Kenai Peninsula (Chapter 16) and in parts of the Alaska Range. Poachers killed them through the 1920s, even in Mt. McKinley Park. Governor Gruening explained the McKinley herd's slow decline in the 1930s and 1940s as "due to predatory animals, and some type of disease may be a contributing factor." Leopold and Darling considered weather, hard winters in particular, the main determinant.[13] To some extent, sheep died from snowslides and predation by wolves, coyotes, and wolverines. Regardless of whether the park sheep benefited from predator control efforts, they gradually rebounded in the 1950s and generally maintained their numbers thereafter.

Mountain Goats

Unlike sheep, mountain goats did not hold wide appeal as a food supply. Neither did they gather in large bands in their steep and rocky mountain habitats along the coast from the Kenai Peninsula southward. Their dispersal made them difficult to count but also difficult to hunt. Except for local areas, particularly along the Southeast coast, they never became seriously threatened. Predation by wolves, coyotes, and wolverines claimed a few goats, and many died in snowslides. In the early 1950s sport hunters killed about 500 annually and Natives about 100, from an estimated statewide population of 11,150 to 13,550.[14] Agents transplanted goats (Table 14.4) to Baranof Island in 1923 and to Kodiak Island in 1952–1953, places where they had not been known to exist. In the statehood period, formation of national and state parks, wildlife refuges, and wilderness areas afforded protection to mountain goats as it did for sheep and other species.

Sitka Black-Tailed Deer

Sitka deer, a variety of mule deer located in the Southeast rainforest, suffered nearly uncontrolled carnage between the 1880s and the 1920s. Prohibition of hide export, and law enforcement generally, relieved pressure on them. Population levels rose and fell according to available food. Heavy winter snows forced them to the beaches where many starved in times of overpopulation. Mild winters allowed more to survive, and wolf control increased the number available to humans. They numbered an estimated 123,000 in 1958–1959 and may have been too numerous in some ranges.[15] Over the second half of the century, logging depleted old-growth forests to the detriment of the deer. Bag limits and protective land designations helped keep the deer populations viable.

UNGULATE TRANSLOCATIONS

For several reasons, government officials and private entrepreneurs or experimenters attempted to introduce wildlife species into various corners of Alaska. Goals included food supply, sport hunting opportunity, commercial profit, and restoration of populations eradicated by humans. Two of the efforts, stocking of foxes (Chapter 13) and importing of reindeer, probably had the greatest environmental impact.

The Reindeer Experiment

Reindeer introduction, an economic, social, and incidentally ecological experiment, got its start when Sheldon Jackson first visited the Arctic in 1890. Jackson, a prominent and charismatic Presbyterian missionary then serving as general agent of education for Alaska, traveled to the northwest coast to set up schools at Cape Prince of Wales, Point Hope, and Barrow. He learned that Eskimo settlements had been depopulated, in some cases entirely, since the coming of whalers and traders. He attributed the losses principally to the commercial killing of whales and walruses and to the extermination of caribou herds by Eskimos using guns. Adopting an idea suggested by U.S. Fish Commission biologist Charles H. Townsend in an 1885 report, Jackson proposed that the government import reindeer from Siberia and establish an agricultural school to teach the Eskimos reindeer husbandry: "To reclaim and make valuable vast areas of land otherwise worthless; to introduce large, permanent and wealth-producing industries where none previously existed; to take a barbarian people on the verge of starvation and lift them up to a comfortable self-support and civilization, is certainly a work of national importance." Jackson pointed out that in Lapland and Siberia, people depended on reindeer as a source of

Rev. Sheldon Jackson, ca. 1880. Portrait file PCA 01-3279, Alaska State Library. An assertive and charismatic figure, Jackson publicized Alaska and drew attention to the needs of the Native population.

meat, milk, clothing, and other useful implements. Moreover, he argued, reindeer could draw sleds much more efficiently than dog teams could.[16]

Realizing no action from Congress on his request for funds to import reindeer, Jackson raised $2,146 from private sources. He went to the Siberian coast in 1891 on the revenue cutter *Bear*, made available by the Treasury secretary. To assess the feasibility of reindeer purchase and transport, he bought sixteen from Native herders. Upon return he released the reindeer on Amaknak and Unalaska islands. All the deer had survived the trip and, a year later, the total increased by two.

Anticipating congressional backing, Jackson made five 1892 trips to Siberia on the *Bear*, bringing back 175 reindeer and assembling a herd at Teller near Port Clarence on the Seward Peninsula. He also brought along four Siberian herdsmen and assigned a few young Alaskan Eskimos to learn herding. In his report to Congress Jackson expanded on his earlier appeals for rehabilitation of the Eskimos. Pointing out that whalers regularly wintered on the Arctic coast, he suggested a "reindeer express" to carry the mail to ice-free ports: "It would enable the owners of the whaling fleet to avail themselves of the latest commercial news and keep a more perfect control over their business." He added that reindeer skins could be made into commercial products such as gloves, military trousers, book bindings, and carriage robes to replace those once derived from buffalo herds.[17]

Jackson's project received funding from Congress after 1892, and he continued to ship reindeer. The additions and the natural increase swelled the Teller herd. Finding the Siberian herders too cruel and otherwise unreliable, Jackson brought in seven Lapps and their families from Norway to train the Eskimos. To improve management efficiency he placed mission stations in charge of herds. Eskimo apprentices received food, clothing, housing, and education and could earn up to 37 deer to start their own herds after five years' training.

Reindeer loaded aboard revenue cutter Bear, *Siberia, 1891.* Bear *1891 Cruise Album 95-034-58, University of Alaska Fairbanks, Alaska and Polar Regions Archives. Sheldon Jackson envisioned a large-scale reindeer industry to sustain Eskimos and develop Alaska's economy.*

Jackson enlarged his vision in the mid-1890s. Partly to replace the dying sea otter industry, he advocated stocking reindeer along the entire Aleutian chain. To meet the food and transportation needs of miners, "[R]eindeer should be widely distributed throughout all northern Alaska."[18] He pictured "400,000 square miles of territory" on which "9,200,000 head of reindeer will support a population of 287,500, living like the Lapps of Lapland." Besides helping Eskimos, reindeer would assist the "opening up of . . . northern and central Alaska to white settlers and civilization." A "vast commercial industry" of reindeer products would benefit all, and to spread herding skills, a "migration" of families from Lapland should be encouraged.[19]

Reindeer entered the 1897–1898 drama (Chapter 3) in which a fleet of whaling ships became trapped in the ice off Point Barrow. News of the event prompted an emergency cabinet meeting chaired by President McKinley. Jackson, invited to attend, suggested the revenue cutter *Bear* be sent to Cape Prince of Wales. A nearby reindeer herd could be driven overland as a food supply for the crew members. The cabinet agreed, and the *Bear* left Port Townsend, Washington, on November 29. Ice forced it into Cape Vancouver, 800 miles short of its goal.[20] Lts. David H. Jarvis and Ellsworth Bertholf and vessel surgeon Dr. Samuel J. Call made the overland trip by dogsled. On the way they borrowed 448 reindeer, including 292 from a herd managed by missionary W.T. Lopp

Eskimo mail carrier, ca. 1905–1910. Lomen coll. 72-71-3557, University of Alaska Fairbanks, Alaska and Polar Regions Archives. Reindeer served as transportation, but dogsleds proved more effective. The reindeer industry held the potential to massively alter the ecosystem of northern Alaska, but it peaked in the 1930s.

and 133 owned by Eskimo herder Charlie Antissarlook. Written agreements promised repayment in reindeer in 1898 or as soon thereafter as possible. More would be added to compensate for expected natural increase. Call, Jarvis, Antissarlook, and seven other Eskimos drove the herd 750 miles north through the Arctic winter, reaching Barrow on March 29. Thanks to Charles Brower's relief effort, the whalers slaughtered only 180 of the animals for food. About 382 reindeer had survived the trip, and new fawns left a total of 439 by fall 1898.[21]

Antissarlook, the first Eskimo herd owner, had been lent 100 reindeer in 1895 by Sheldon Jackson. They increased, but Jackson recalled the loan in 1897, well before the contract deadline, to start another missionary herd. After the drive to Point Barrow in 1898, the surviving reindeer went to missions in Barrow and Point Hope. Left without their herd, the Antissarlook family experienced food scarcity. They received replacement animals in 1899.[22] Such incidents reinforced an impression that Jackson placed the interests of missions ahead of the welfare of Eskimos.

Reports of starvation among miners in the upper Yukon in 1897–1898 induced Congress to appropriate $200,000 to transport reindeer from Lapland. Jackson traveled to Norway to convey the request to his agent William Kjellman, in the process of recruiting more Lapps for the reindeer service. They purchased 539 reindeer and shipped them to the East Coast, to Seattle by train, to Haines by boat, and overland to Circle. Only 114 survived the arduous journey ending on February 28, 1899.[23]

Between 1891 and 1902, when the czar halted reindeer exports, 1,280 had been shipped from Siberia to Alaska. By 1905 natural increase had boosted the total to 12,828. Eskimos owned 38 percent of the herds, the federal government 30 percent, missions 21 percent, and Lapps 11 percent.[24] Critics of the program felt non-Native private parties should not own reindeer herds, and many objected to Jackson's mixing religious instruction and herd maintenance. They suspected his top priority lay in supporting the missions. A 1905 investigation resulted in Jackson's resignation.

Reindeer proliferated and herders found more uses for them. The animals supplied meat, mail service, and freight hauling in the turn-of-the-century Nome gold rush. Beginning in 1911 the Bureau of Education assisted Natives in sales of meat and antlers in Seattle. As a result of the change in government policy, Eskimos owned 66 percent of the 70,000 reindeer by 1916. Over the objections of officials who questioned its legality, the Lomen family of Nome commenced buying reindeer in 1914 from missions and other private owners. They amassed a large herd and sold more than 14,000 carcasses annually to stateside buyers in 1929 and 1930. Both Lomen and Eskimo herds multiplied rapidly, but neither realized much success in securing outside markets. When miners left the Nome goldfields in the 1910s, away went an important source of income for Eskimo herders. The 1918–1919 influenza epidemic dealt the Eskimos another blow by devastating western and northwestern Alaskan villages, claiming the lives of several leading herders and superintendent Walter Shields, who had advocated Native ownership of reindeer.[25]

Participants and commentators carried on a vigorous debate over who should own reindeer herds and whether their purpose should be a means of subsistence for Eskimos or an economic resource for the development of Alaska. The Department of Agriculture attempted to achieve both goals. In 1920 its Bureau of Biological Survey (BBS) set up a reindeer experiment station at Unalakleet on Norton Sound. Dr. Seymour Hadwen, chief veterinarian, estimated in 1922 that Alaska had enough grazing land for 3 to 4 million reindeer but that care must be taken to avoid overgrazing or undergrazing. He believed that "it is evident that the development of the reindeer requires white supervision, with proper markets." BBS and the Lomens jointly carried out breeding experiments for several years at Nunivak Island and Fairbanks.[26] In 1920, 98 caribou had been placed on Nunivak Island. Breeding by 10 caribou bulls conducted in 1925 apparently created hybrids larger than average reindeer.[27] But the experiments revealed no significant economic potential in crossbreeding.

Enthusiasm and optimism accompanied the growth of reindeer herds. One of Jackson's successors declared in the early 1920s that

> within less than a generation the reindeer industry has advanced through one entire stage of civilization, the Eskimo inhabiting the vast grazing lands from Point Barrow to the Aleutian Islands. It has raised them from the primitive to the pastoral stage, from nomadic hunters to civilized men, having in their herds of reindeer assured support for themselves and opportunity to acquire wealth.
>
> It was the earliest and perhaps only government action providing, by the introduction of a new industry, practical vocational training adapted to community needs, and resulting in training a primitive race into independence and responsible citizenship.[28]

Over the ensuing decades, experience would make this assessment appear more like an extravagant hope.

Bureau of Education officials and other critics continued to oppose private ownership of reindeer herds, the Lomen operation being by far the largest. Other problems beset the reindeer industry: weak markets, swelling herds, overgrazing, poor management, mixing of herds, confusion over ownership, and charges of theft.[29] Eskimos preferred to be near the ocean and found the work of tending herds boring in comparison to hunting. When Eskimo associations assumed ownership of herds, hired herders felt less responsibility toward herd maintenance. To take advantage of more far-flung, less depleted grazing ranges, the Reindeer Service advised a change from "close herding," a method that called for constant watch on small herds, to "open herding" of large, free-ranging herds of mixed ownership. Open herding eased the way for predators to seize reindeer and for caribou to entice them to run away. Uncertainty over ownership and responsibility for reindeer in open herds worked to the disadvantage of individual Eskimo owners and generated tension between Natives and non-Natives.[30]

Reindeer provided meat and skins for local and regional use, but this fell far short of the hopes of reindeer visionaries. They planned to sell meat in the States as well as in Alaska. Such a trade, however, would necessitate refrigeration facilities from regional stations to outlets in San Francisco and the East Coast. It needed docks near shipping stations, but no docks existed on the Bering Sea. Infrequent and seasonal boat schedules in the North added to the costs and instability of potential markets. And some states, possibly influenced by the beef industry, banned the sale of reindeer meat on grounds that it constituted wild game. Not least, the vast majority of Americans preferred beef.[31]

TABLE 14.2. Ownership, Size, and Locations of Reindeer Herds, 1949

Ownership	*Location*	*Number of Reindeer*
Native association	Wainwright	270
	St. Lawrence Island	450
U.S. government	Kotzebue	3,500
	St. Michael	150
	Hooper Bay	400
	Nunivak Island	4,500
	Atka Island	1,700
	Umnak Island	1,400
	Pribilof Islands	700
Individual	Barrow (3 herds)	3,000
	Kotzebue (2 herds)	3,000
	Shungnak	400
	Selawik	1,500
	Noatak	1,100
	Wainwright	450
	Golovin	1,500
	Igloo (Seward Pen.)	750
	Candle	650
	Alitak (Kodiak I.)	2,500
Total		27,920

Source: Margaret Lantis, "The Reindeer Industry in Alaska," *Arctic* 3 (April 1950): 38.

A 1933 Interior Department report, one of several investigations in the 1930s, found that Eskimos lacked the facilities to operate a long-range marketing system, that they preferred hunting to herding, that the reindeer population had reached 600,000 to 800,000, that range damage had occurred, and that some herds had wandered out of reach into remote areas. It cited persistent claims that the Lomens had unfairly taken possession of Eskimo reindeer.[32] A court decision had affirmed the Lomens' right to own herds, but it did not stop the criticism. By 1934 the Lomens determined that their commercial venture would not work in the absence of outside markets. Three years later, Congress passed a bill transferring the Reindeer Service to the Interior Department's Office of Indian Affairs. The act authorized the government to purchase all private herds and marketing facilities, a transaction completed in 1940.[33]

World War II interrupted any possibility of immediate revival of the failing reindeer industry. But the Reindeer Service reinstated close herding, discouraged herd ownership by associations, and tried to develop market niches for hides, such as gloves, jackets, and boots. Government agencies continued research on parasites and range conditions and conducted vigorous predator control. But only a fraction of the reindeer survived the war years. Compared to 51 herds in 1932, 22 existed in 1949 totaling 27,920 reindeer (Table 14.2).[34]

TABLE 14.3. Reindeer in Alaska, 1892–1977

Year	*Number*	*Year*	*Number*	*Year*	*Number*	*Year*	*Number*
1892	171	1917	98,582	1942	169,000	1967	33,150
1897	1,466	1922	259,000	1947	n.d.	1972	27,399
1902	5,148	1927	n.d.	1952	26,700	1977	24,100
1907	15,839	1932	641,000	1957	39,800		
1912	38,476	1937	544,000	1962	40,000		

Source: Richard O. Stern, Edward L. Arobio, Larry L. Naylor, and Wayne C. Thomas, *Eskimos, Reindeer, and Land.* University of Alaska Agricultural Experimental Station Bull. 59 (Fairbanks, December 1980), 103.

A highly optimistic projection by the Bureau of Land Management in 1952 foresaw a dramatic restoration of the reindeer industry. Grazing on 200,000 square miles of tundra, up to four million reindeer would supply meat and hides for the nation.[35] On the ground, reindeer herding increased somewhat in the 1950s but did not succeed in becoming more than a regional industry. Many of the same problems—lack of commitment to the arduous and isolated task of herding, lack of adequate winter range, and opportunities elsewhere—retarded the growth of the industry. From a high of 641,000 in 1932, the reindeer total stood at 40,000 in 1962 and 24,100 in 1977 (Table 14.3).[36]

Shortly after statehood, resource economist Arthur D. Little analyzed the prospects for a viable commercial reindeer industry. In a summary issued in 1963 he identified several obstacles: (1) lack of interest in herding, (2) poor winter range, (3) lack of a range management plan, (4) poor animal husbandry, (5) the existence of caribou herds on potential reindeer range, (6) poor nutrition of existing reindeer, (7) the narrow market for reindeer meat, and (8) herder reliance on government grants. Little remarked, "We are not so presumptuous as to believe that we can suggest a program that will resolve all these difficulties. Persons have been working on these problems in Alaska for over sixty years, and the Government for at least thirty years without finding a solution." Little recommended restricting operations to the few highly motivated herders and training them in animal husbandry and marketing.[37] Except for the sale of antlers, nothing more than local use emerged. Reindeer introduction ended in commercial failure, but, in Ernest Gruening's judgment, by saving thousands of Eskimo lives it turned out to be "the most important single contribution made to the natives . . . in the first half-century of U.S. rule."[38]

Some environmental impact flowed from the reindeer experiment. BBS chief Edward Nelson, concerned that multiplying reindeer might threaten the existence of the caribou by appropriating their grazing lands or by interbreeding, had assigned Olaus Murie to survey the caribou in Alaska. Research demonstrated that overgrazing in the form of eating and trampling caused significant deterioration of the range. BBS range scientist Lawrence J. Palmer estimated from his 1920–1935 survey that recovery of lichens, the preferred food for reindeer and caribou, required 20 to 40 years if left undisturbed. He found the 1944 reindeer population on Nunivak Island to be 30,000, far above the sustainable level of 8,000.[39] Experimenters had placed reindeer on Nunivak and several other islands where no predators existed. On St. Matthew Island, devoid of wolves and caribou, the Coast Guard released 29 reindeer in 1944. They intended the animals as food for a U.S. Army weather station and a Coast Guard loran station that operated during the war. After the herd reached 6,000 in 1963, 99 percent died of starvation and cold the following winter, and none remained by 1985. A similar population on St. Paul Island crashed upon attaining a density of 49 per square mile. Palmer had recommended a maximum of 10 to 16 per square mile.[40]

Other environmental impacts included the loss of predators and possible dilution of the caribou gene pool by escaped reindeer. To protect their stock, herders shot or trapped wolves, grizzly bears, coyotes, wolverines, and foxes. Federal predator control agents shot wolves from planes and, in some cases, dropped poisoned bait.[41] Had the BBS expectation of three to four million reindeer (much less Jackson's projection of nine million) eventuated, environmental disruption would have been widespread. Hundreds of square miles would have become pastureland, displacing caribou and altering their gene pool. Predator control would have greatly reduced carnivores and disrupted the ecosystem. Human population buildup, roads, and other facilities would have vastly degraded wilderness quality in Alaska.

The Reindeer Trek

An attempt to introduce reindeer into Canada begot an epic five-year struggle against the elements. Impressed by the seeming success of the Alaska experiment, Canada's Department of the Interior investigated prospects for starting a reindeer industry in the Northwest Territories. The recent introduction of the rifle had heightened killing of wildlife by both Eskimos and whites. Increasingly reliant on goods from trading posts, the Eskimos nevertheless had only the Arctic fox as a source of income. Foxes, in turn, could easily fluctuate in population and market value. A Royal Commission on the Reindeer and Musk-ox instituted in 1919 sought to conserve wildlife and find a stable means of sustenance for the Eskimos. In 1926 the Dominion government decided to acquire reindeer from Alaska. It sent Erling Porsild and his brother Robert north in May to do feasibility surveys, purchase the animals, and oversee the transfer.

The Porsilds evaluated grazing conditions in the Mackenzie River Delta and dog-teamed thousands of miles through Alaska to examine reindeer herds. Primarily through the Lomen company they bought 3,515 reindeer and assembled them at Kotzebue Sound to be driven overland 1,600 miles through the Arctic by a crew of Eskimos and Lapps.[42] To lead the expedition the Lomens called out of retirement a former employee and native of Lapland, Andrew Bahr. Bahr interpreted the project as a mission of mercy for the Canadian Eskimos. More than 60 years old and despite life-threatening illness during the trek, he endured throughout. Once, in the winter of 1931–1932, he spent five months backtracking to find lost reindeer, but by the time he returned to the main herd, as many more reindeer had been lost as he found.[43]

Departing in November 1929, the trek ran into a host of daunting obstacles: deep winter snows in the Brooks Range, plagues of mosquitoes in summer, harsh living conditions causing crews to quit, bands of reindeer trying to return home or otherwise wandering off, and attacks by wolves that "continually harassed the herd, at times taking a great toll and compelling the herders to remain on watch day and night." Calving and rutting season, dark nights, blizzards, and open rivers restricted travel to about four months per year. The herd reached the eastern Mackenzie Delta in February 1935 and put reindeer in the corrals at Kittigazuit on March 6. Only a minority of the original reindeer remained, but births had left the total at 2,370.[44] For reasons similar to those encountered in Alaska, however, reindeer herding did not spread in Canada.

Muskoxen

The muskox, a partial success story in the territorial period, originally resided on the Arctic tundra from northwest Alaska to Greenland as well as Siberia. Explorers, traders, and whalers found it relatively easy to subdue because of its habit of forming and holding a defensive arc. They valued the animal for food and for its exceedingly fine wool coat. Muskox hides from Canada served as warming robes on cutters when buffalo skins grew scarce. Hunters killed adults so the calves could be captured and sold to European zoos. Traders gave cheap guns to Eskimos in return for furs, causing more muskoxen to be killed for sale. As game grew less plentiful this practice made the Eskimos more dependent on the traders.[45] A Stefansson expedition to Melville Island slaughtered 400 muskoxen, and by 1930 only about 500 remained in mainland Canada. In 1927 Parliament created the Thelon Game Sanctuary in Northwest Territories for the muskoxen.[46]

In Alaska, muskoxen appear to have been uncommon or rare at the time Euro-Americans arrived. Inuit hunters (Chapter 9) had apparently eliminated nearly all the scattered herds. Virtually none of the animals survived to the second half of the 19th Century. Barrow trader Charles Brower found muskox skulls at various sites on the North Slope and knew an old Eskimo who had killed the beasts with bow and arrow. Another of his Eskimo acquaintances told of a hard winter about 1858 when few seals appeared and people starved. His father took the family overland about nine miles southeast of Wainwright to Oo-Ming-Muc ("Muskox"), a tributary of the Kuk River. They discovered a band of muskoxen and killed, by one account, all thirteen.[47]

In the eastern Brooks Range far from the coast, muskoxen probably hung on for several more decades. Irving McKinley Reed, a former member of the Alaska Game Commission, related that

> the last two musk ox herds in Alaska had both been wiped out in the general area of the Chandalar River. One slaughter occurred in 1892 or 1893 when a band of Chandalar Kutchin and other Indians destroyed a herd of these animals on the height of land between the Christian and Sheenjek Rivers; the other took place in 1897 or 1898 when two French-Canadian trappers killed an entire herd of 18 muskoxen somewhere to the east of their cabin on Chandalar Lake (on North Fork of Chandalar River).

Whaling captain Hartson Bodfish, who wintered at Herschel and Baillie islands between 1890 and 1900, recalled, "While we wintered in the Arctic [Natives] killed all the musk oxen in an area of 150 miles."[48] These may all have come from Canada, however.

Hunter-naturalist Andrew J. Stone made a point of inquiring about muskoxen during his travels in northern Alaska and northwestern Canada between 1897 and 1899. He noted that "specimens of Musk-Ox are reported to have been recently brought, by Camden Bay" from the Romanzof Mountains of northeastern Alaska. He interviewed Eskimos, Indians, whalers, traders, and others along the Arctic coast and in the upper Yukon drainage. But he could find no knowledge or evidence of surviving muskoxen in Alaska or even closer than 300 miles east of the Mackenzie River.[49]

Some muskoxen may have lasted beyond the turn of the century. Hunter-explorer L.L. Bales wrote in 1908 that, based on information from Natives familiar with the region, the few remaining muskoxen lived in "that section north of the Endicott range of mountains, beginning at a point about 200 miles east of Point Barrow near the Colville River, and extending eastward to the boundary line. They do not range on the low, flat tundra near the Arctic sea coast, but are found on the moss-covered ridges and in the hilly country one hundred miles or more inland."[50] Researchers found no physical evidence of muskoxen living in Alaska after the mid-19th Century.

Vilhjalmur Stefansson and Nome entrepreneur Jafet Lindeberg proposed to Governor Riggs in 1918 that muskoxen be imported from Greenland. Riggs responded positively, seeing an opportunity for economic development in the form of a wool and meat industry:

Muskoxen, College, early 1930s. Keys coll. 88-174-17, University of Alaska Fairbanks, Alaska and Polar Regions Archives. Extirpated from Alaska in the 19th Century, muskoxen were successfully reintroduced.

> Here is an animal which seems to be designed by nature to make a productive country out of barrens now serving no purpose. In the musk-ox are combined all the qualities most to be desired by a pioneer people of a desolate region. The northern portion of Alaska can never serve a better purpose than in becoming the grazing land of vast herds of reindeer and muskoxen, and when so utilized will become one of the great sources of meat supply for the United States.[51]

Edward Nelson and Charles Sheldon endorsed the idea of transplanting the animals, but it attained no action. In 1929 President Herbert Hoover designated Nunivak Island a reserve for reindeer breeding experiments. Bureau of Biological Survey officials used it for reestablishment of the muskox. A congressional appropriation enabled them to bring 34 from Greenland in 1930 and keep them at the reindeer experimental station at the University of Alaska. The Alaska Game Commission moved the remaining total of 31 to Nunivak Island in 1935 and 1936. By 1965 the band had grown to 500.[52] Anticipating overpopulation at Nunivak, wildlife managers established several groups on the mainland between 1967 and 1970 (Table 14.4), and one group crossed on the ice. In 1975, following a 1972 agreement, 40 of the muskoxen went to Wrangel Island and the eastern Siberia mainland where they had been eradicated. Beginning in 1974, sport hunting by permit kept the Nunivak population at a sustainable level and gave Eskimos an opportunity to earn income by guiding or transporting hunters.[53]

Muskoxen survived the Arctic winters in large part by the insulating quality of their wool, or *qiviut.* One of the finest, warmest, and most valuable hairs known, it gave rise to the idea of cottage industries producing fabrics from domesticated muskox herds. In Canada and Alaska the income could supplement the largely subsistence economies of Arctic and subarctic villages. As a result of urging by Stefansson, the Institute of Northern Agricultural Research brought 3 muskoxen from the Thelon sanctuary in Canada to Vermont in 1954. Satisfied that the animals could be successfully domesticated, the institute arranged for 33 to be captured on Nunivak Island in 1964 and 1965 to comprise a herd at the University of Alaska in Fairbanks. In 1975–1977 the institute placed the herd in the Eskimo village of Unalakleet.[54] Small-scale commercial weaving proceeded at several locations.

Other Translocations

Bureau of Biological Survey agents conducted transplants of several species of game as early as 1917 (Table 14.4). In most cases they intended to introduce a species to a new area where it could be hunted rather than restore it to a location where it had become scarce. Agents successfully moved caribou to Adak Island in 1958–1959 and reintroduced them to the Kenai Peninsula in 1965. They released moose on the Copper River Delta between 1949 and 1957, at Berners Bay in 1958 and 1960, at the Chickamin River in 1963–1964, at Kodiak Island in 1966–1967, and at Kalgin Island in the late 1950s. The Chickamin and Kodiak efforts did not succeed. Dall sheep were taken to Kodiak Island without success in 1964–1965 and 1967 and mountain goats to Baranof Island in 1923, Kodiak Island in 1952–1953, and Chichagof Island in 1952–1954. They did not survive at Chichagof. Agents successfully moved Sitka deer to the islands and mainland of Prince William Sound between 1917 and 1923, to Kodiak Island in 1924 and 1934, to Yakutat Bay in 1934, and to Afognak Island, among other locations. Eight Roosevelt elk from Washington, placed on Afognak Island in 1929, prospered. Other attempts to relocate elk came to naught. Legal hunting on Afognak in most years between 1949 and 1963 yielded an average of 73 elk per season.[55]

In the 1920s, when hunting pressure had cut back the moose population, interior Alaskans petitioned the Bureau of Biological Survey for game transplants. They suggested elk, white-tailed deer, and antelope. The bureau appeased them in 1928 by transporting plains bison from the National Bison Range at Moiese, Montana. They set nineteen free near Delta Junction.[56] One of the bulls injured its leg in transit. Frank Dufresne, who had charge of the relocation operation, returned with his wife, Klondy Nelson, to check on the bull's status. Separated from Frank, Klondy came face-to-face with the ema-

TABLE 14.4. Successful Transplants of Wild Terrestrial Mammals in Alaska, 1916–1970

Species	*Number*	*Date*	*Destination*
Sitka deer	24	1916–23	Prince William Sound
Sitka deer	16	1924, 1930	Long Island, Kodiak Archipelago
Sitka deer	9	1934	Kodiak Island
Sitka deer	4	1951–54	Sullivan Island, Lynn Canal
Mountain goat	18	1923	Baranof Island
Mountain goat	18	1952–53	Kodiak Island
Roosevelt elk	8	1929	Afognak Island
Plains bison	19	1928, 1930	Big Delta
Plains bison	17	1950	Copper River
Plains bison	35	1962	Chitina
Plains bison	38	1965, 1968	Farewell
Muskox	21	1935–36	Nunivak Island
Muskox	23	1967–68	Nelson Island
Muskox	63	1969–70	Camden Bay & Kavik River
Muskox	72	1970	Seward Peninsula & Cape Thompson
Moose	15+	1949–58	Copper River Delta
Moose	—	1958, 1960	Berners Bay
Moose	—	1957–59	Kalgin Island, Cook Inlet
Caribou	24	1958–59	Adak Island
Caribou	44	1965–66	Kenai Peninsula
Arctic & red fox	—	1750–1950s	455 islands
Beaver	24	1925	Kodiak Island
Marten	—	1934	Prince of Wales & Baranof Islands
Muskrat	60	1925	Kodiak-Afognak islands
Varying hare	576	1934, 1952	Kodiak-Afognak islands
Red squirrel	145	1930–31	Baranof & Chichagof is.; other Southeast sites
Red squirrel	77	1948, 1952	Kodiak-Afognak islands

Sources: Alaska Game Commission, *9th Annual Report to the Secretary of the Interior, July 1, 1947–June 30, 1948*, 21–22; W.A. Elkins and Urban C. Nelson, "Wildlife Introductions and Transplants in Alaska" (Presented at Fifth Alaska Science Conf., Anchorage, September 7–10, 1954), 3–16; Oliver E. Burris and Donald E. McKnight, *Game Transplants in Alaska* (Juneau: Alaska Dept. of Fish and Game, December 1973), 6–29; Albert W. Franzmann, *Review of Alaskan Translocations*, Appen. 1 (Juneau: Alaska Dept. of Fish and Game, 1986).

Note: Does not include small-scale introductions not sanctioned by government. "Successful" denotes a viable remaining population.

ciated and angry animal, which immediately began to chase her. As the bull bore down on his wife, Dufresne shot it.[57] The bison proliferated and became the source of herds at Copper River in 1950, Chitina in 1962, and Fairwell in 1965. Hunters filled permits for bison in the early 1950s and most years afterward. Severe winters and limited food supply kept a lid on population growth. Beginning in the 1950s and again in the 1970s, bison in the Delta herd ate and trampled crops on farms that had sprung up in their range. To mitigate the problem, game officials attempted to steer the bison away from farms and toward alternate food sources.[58]

Wood buffaloes, a separate subspecies, once inhabited Alaska in large numbers. Of many bones found, the most recent carbon-dated at 140 to 200 years.

Mountain goat released at Hidden Basin, Kodiak Island, 1952. In Russell R. Hoffman, Refuge Narrative Report: Kodiak National Wildlife Refuge, January to April 1952, *Kodiak: Fish and Wildlife Service, 1952. Game officials tried to introduce several species into new localities. Goats survived on Baranof and Kodiak islands.*

Elders in the upper Yukon River Valley described in detail buffalo hunts by their ancestors. Athabaskans prized the meat and skins and used the hair for thread or left it on the hide for warmth. Oral history consistently indicated that buffaloes had been numerous in the early 1800s and that a few had been seen or killed in the 1900s. In 1917 some buffaloes appeared near Eagle and became tangled in moose snares. They had likely come from remnant herds in Canada whose total population had been cut to a minute fraction of the original. Wildlife managers made no move to reinstate the wood bison in Alaska during the 20th Century.[59] Within the context of modern ecology and politics, such a move would be a lengthy process requiring research, interagency cooperation, and consultation of interest groups.

Many transplants happened before ecological perspectives had taken hold within the game management community, and they typically stemmed from demands by hunters or others seeking personal advantages. Single individuals or private groups released organisms without authorization from government,

Unloading first buffalo, College, ca. 1928. Keys coll. 88-174-11, University of Alaska Fairbanks, Alaska and Polar Regions Archives. Alaska Game Commission officials established plains buffaloes in Alaska. Wood buffaloes, a separate subspecies, had been native to the territory.

including raccoons on several islands in Southeast Alaska. The 1925 Alaska Game Law forbade such actions without a permit, although the Game Commission itself actively engaged in transplants it considered beneficial. So did the Fish and Wildlife Service and the Alaska Department of Fish and Game. Guidelines in the 1950s emphasized introduction of species to former habitat or across physical barriers to similar range and avoidance of injury to native species.[60]

The disastrous consequences of fox introduction to seabird nesting islands (Chapter 13) suggested that serious ecological questions needed to be answered before executing transplants. One of the few to question the practice as it related to game mammals, Olaus Murie, urged caution. Reacting to a proposal to release elk in interior Alaska, he pointed out that elk would eat lichens and might compete for food and reduce populations of caribou, mountain sheep, and moose. Exotic species, said Murie, tended to proliferate beyond the habitat's carrying capacity and then die out.[61] Beyond biological considerations, introductions of exotic species involved questions of maintenance of wilderness integrity.

TERRESTRIAL FURBEARERS

Land furbearers in Alaska occupied for the most part a more modest position among political controversies than did ungulates, sea otters, and fur seals. Alaska Natives caught some for clothing and food. In the 18th Century or earlier, European demand for furs projected the trading routes across Siberia into Alaska and perhaps Arctic Canada. Eskimos relayed goods such as seal oil, baleen, tobacco, and copper or iron implements to more easterly Eskimos and interior Indians. In return, the skins of fox, marten, wolf, wolverine, beaver, and river otter moved westward.[62]

The Russian Period

To supplement the profits from sea otters and fur seals, Russian fur traders directed attention toward land mammals. They forced Aleuts and Koniag Eskimos to trap foxes and river otters. Employing what coercion they deemed expedient, they acquired furs from the Tanaina Indians in the Cook Inlet vicinity and from other coastal Natives. The Tanainas, in turn, conveyed Russian trade goods to the Gwitch'in and other Athabaskan Indians in exchange for furs. Motivated in part by a desire to shut off the Eskimo-controlled flow of furs across Bering Strait, Russians erected forts in 1818 on the Nushagak River at Bristol Bay, in 1833 at St. Michael on the lower Yukon, and in 1839 at Nulato at the juncture of the Koyukuk and Yukon rivers. Construction of a trading post at Fort Yukon by the Hudson's Bay Company in 1847 posed a threat to Russian fur profits as well as their control of Alaska. Indians could acquire more guns, ammunition, sugar, tobacco, tea, and other desired trade goods in exchange for furs at Fort Yukon than from the Russians.[63] Moreover, the Russian hold on the interior proved tenuous. By one account, in a dispute among Native groups over control of fur territory, Koyukon Indians attacked the Nulato fort in 1851 and killed nearly all its inhabitants, including the manager.[64]

During the 1860s the Russians sent the more valuable land furs—river otter, beaver, lynx, and red, silver, black, and blue fox—to Siberian trading centers for sale in Russia where buyers prized the silver and black foxes above the sea otter. Some beavers went to Shanghai and some to the United States, which also took white foxes. Aleut workers sewed mink, muskrat, and marten skins into parkas to be sold at Sitka. Bearskins, about 120 annually, went to St. Petersburg. Russians kept the few wolf and wolverine skins for use at St. Michael, their trading post on Norton Sound.[65] In all, they exported a large quantity of land mammal furs from Alaska (Table 14.5), but the total made up a small portion of profits.

Except locally and temporarily, and possibly excepting the beaver, trapping apparently did not endanger any species of land furbearer prior to the 20th

TABLE 14.5. Selected Land Mammal Furs Shipped From Russian America and Alaska, 1745–1890

	1745–97	*1798–1821*	*1822–41*	*1842–62*	*1862–67*	*1868–70*	*1871–80*	*1881–90*	*Total*
River otter	5,039	17,768	29,442	170,473	21,816	6,367	27,730	27,730	306,365
Black fox	16,563	15,112	18,783	15,341	5,860	1,847	20,100	15,910	109,515
Cross fox	20,369	24,535	39,312	29,650	13,675	14,398	37,308	53,151	232,398
Red fox	20,665	35,456	60,579	66,860	16,920	16,461	47,298	62,718	326,957
Blue fox	62,961	50,934	41,000	20,130	11,314	16,263	23,615	21,314	247,531
Beaver	428	56,001	162,034	157,484	37,409	17,041	41,217	60,940	532,554
Marten	—	17,921	15,666	13,682	918	24,311	81,609	127,601	281,708

Source: Samuel Applegate, *Report on Population and Resources of Alaska, Eleventh Census: 1890* (Washington: GPO, 1893), 213–215.
Note: Does not include furs of less valued species, those lost in shipwrecks, those traded across Bering Strait by Natives, those smuggled into British Columbia, and those acquired by Northwest coast whalers and traders.

Century. Russians considered the marten inferior to its Eurasian relative, the sable, so rather than ship it out, the Russian-American Company made the skins available to its higher-placed employees. Russians valued the river otter for trim on army officer uniforms as a substitute for the more prestigious sea otter. Beaver rose to the height of fashion in the mid-19th Century and then faded. Russians sold castoreum (beaver musk) in Asia for medicinal purposes. Some Indians and Eskimos considered the beaver's flesh a delicacy and fashioned chisels and other tools from its teeth. Severe winters in the late 19th Century killed off many beavers. Alaska Natives used muskrat, mink, and wolverine for clothing trim; traders accepted few of these. Wolves comprised little of the fur trade, and traders bought lynx skins for carriage robes and clothing trim. Darker color phases of the red fox held higher value, the jet-black and silver far more prized than the cross and standard red varieties. Of the Arctic fox variations, traders much preferred the blue to the white. Alaska Natives, Asians, Europeans, and Americans all made fox fur into clothing.[66]

Post-1867 Trapping

In the American period, control of the Alaska fur trade by the Treasury Department passed to the Commerce Department's Bureau of Fisheries in 1903 and to the Agriculture Department's Bureau of Biological Survey in 1920. Restriction of trapping rights between 1868 and 1899 to Alaska Natives, relatively conservative in their treatment of furbearer populations, limited the harvest. But many non-Natives came to prospect or trade during the Gold Rush era and supplemented their incomes through trapping.[67] Increasingly common forest fires lowered the numbers of foxes, lynx, ermine, and martens available to both Natives and non-Natives.[68]

The Alaska Commercial Company and smaller independent traders took command of the fur business in the interior. Individual trappers could go directly to them, bypassing the Indian chiefs who had controlled the trading under British and Russian arrangements. Family-managed trapping territories thus evolved and spread to white trappers in the 20th Century. An influx of trade goods increased Natives' material wants and dependence on outside industrial society. Prospectors took up trapping for extra income or as a way of remaining in the bush after giving up the full-time search for gold. They and Natives therefore competed in the fur trade, but trapping continued to be an important income source for Natives in the 20th Century.

Historian William Schneider described the trapping seasonal cycle of many Natives and non-Natives prior to midcentury:

> Leaving the village in the fall before freeze-up with the winter's "grub stake," families headed up a tributary stream until they reached the main cabin.

Trappers and their catch of furs. Core coll. 01-20-34, Alaska State Library. From left: ermine, mink, marten, lynx, wolf, river otter, and wolverine. Land furbearers, trapped throughout the Russian and American eras, did not suffer any species extinctions.

> Before snowfall, wood had to be cut, and the winter supply of meat gotten. Soon after freeze-up the traps and snares would be set and from then until Christmas the trapper was moving, checking his trapline, then back to the cabin to skin and stretch fur. Some families traveled by dog team to the village at Christmas time to visit with friends, celebrate the holiday, and trade furs to the trader in exchange for store goods.
>
> After the holiday the families returned to the trapline routine until spring when the orientation shifted from the major fur animals to beaver and muskrat. Most families stayed out on their trapline until spring breakup, then returned to the village by boat. After a short visit in the village the family had to go to fish camp where they remained until they had sufficient fish dried for their own needs and for dog feed. Then it was fall and time to resupply for trapping.[69]

To get started, a lone trapper had to spend the summer transporting supplies into the interior, usually by poling a boat upriver. Then he would build a main cabin and several smaller ones along the trapline. Trapping commenced in mid-October. If the trapper had no dog team, he would check the traps twice a week on snowshoes, covering up to fifteen miles a day. Naturalist Lee R. Dice figured that in 1912 a hardworking trapper typically sold his seasonal fur catch for less than $500, barely enough for subsistence.[70]

Besides the loneliness, cold, and other discomforts, a single trapper constantly risked accidents. In the Southeast around the turn of the century, a man stepped into a bear trap he had set. Despite crushed shinbones he managed to open the trap and free himself. He dragged himself to the shore, got into his boat, and rowed several miles to his cabin. A day or two later another man found him. The leg needed to be amputated and they had no prospect of reaching a doctor, 100 miles away, in time. They sterilized a hunting knife and an old saw, cut off the leg, and the trapper survived.[71]

As the 20th Century progressed, technological advances changed the trapping industry. Metal snares replaced the work-intensive deadfall; motorboats and eventually airplanes increased outreach. So did snowmobiles, succeeding dogsleds, which had replaced travel on snowshoes. A variety of related implements, such as chain saws and nylon fishing nets, boosted trapping efficiency. At the same time, trappers grew more dependent on outside sources for their supplies, and the desire for schooling and other services dampened families' willingness to stay in remote locations.[72]

Aircraft enabled trappers to operate great distances from home, and in the late 1930s whites from Fairbanks began to fly to better territory. In doing so, they encroached on Native traplines. To protect their rights and their prime source of income, the Chandalar Gwich'in Indians requested a reservation under the 1934 Indian Reorganization Act. Secretary of the Interior Harold Ickes, who had witnessed the success of the Metlakatla reservation and the degradation of other Alaska Native towns, favored reservations as bases for economic viability for Native Americans. In 1943 he approved a 1.8-million-acre Chandalar reservation.[73] The remote location, lack of known valuable mineral resources, and near-absence of white settlers enabled Native ownership of such a large block of land.

Fox Farming

Fox farming, an alternate means of acquiring furs, began when Russians introduced blue-phase Arctic foxes to various Aleutian islands. The rapidly reproducing creatures ran free and fed on native fauna, primarily seabirds (Chapter 13). They constituted a semicaptive population for trapping whenever convenient. Americans followed suit in the 1880s and learned to attract foxes to feeding pens for regular meals of fish and sea mammal meat. Having eliminated the wild birds, the foxes adapted to the pens. An attached trap house allowed the operators to sort out the foxes for breeding purposes or to be slaughtered for the market. On the mainland, fur farmers kept the animals permanently in pens to prevent escape. They also raised mink and martens on a minor scale.

American fox farmers obtained permits from the Treasury Department or, later, the Commerce, Agriculture, or Interior departments. The Forest Service leased islands under its jurisdiction, mainly in the Southeast. Until the 1940s or later the agencies viewed their objective as generating industry on otherwise useless islands. They lacked scientific data or concern for the ecological effects of fox introductions. Farmers stocked two species: Arctic (nearly always in the blue rather than the white color) and red (preferably in the silver or black rather than the red or cross varieties). Black and silver fox pelts reached high peaks of value at various times in the late 19th Century through the 1920s.

Well-publicized top prices for fox furs attracted numerous hopeful entrepreneurs to Alaska. The furs they produced tended to saturate the market and bring down prices, making it difficult for them to realize a profit. Success depended on a substantial capital investment for the license, breeding pairs, buildings, food, and other supplies. It called for knowledge of fox behavior and diligent attention to the details of operation. One also needed the patience to live in a distant location and wait several years before making any monetary gain. Island-raised blue foxes in particular presented a host of problems. Feeding them required money and work. Males often killed pups, and eagles occasionally did. Adults fought one another and sometimes killed and ate others. Breeding for quality could not be well controlled. On the rainy islands in the Southeast, fur became matted and less desirable. Pups died of pneumonia, and dampness aided internal and external parasites. Given the number of obstacles, few fox farmers made any money in Alaska. Licenses hit a high of 356 in 1929 and entered a continual slide accelerated by the Depression and World War II. By 1960 virtually no fox farms remained.[74]

Like commercial fisheries and other enterprises controlled by white people, fox farming worked a hardship on Alaska Natives. In the Southeast, the Forest Service had leased 140 islands to fox farmers by 1923. In apparent violation of the 1884 Alaska Organic Act, the service issued leases without determining use of islands by Indians. In 1925 the Alaska Native Brotherhood, dedicated to improvement of the social and economic well-being of Natives, issued a complaint that fox farmers had "driven the Indians of southeastern Alaska from their homes on many islands. The home of at least one Indian widow with six children has been destroyed and her garden products actually used by the beneficiaries of the Forest Department officials in Alaska. Another Indian, a very old man, was forced out of his island and his home and smokehouse actually made to serve as fox pens."[75] The Indians received little sympathy from the Forest Service and fought for decades more before winning recognition of their land claims.

Outside economic forces dictated the fortunes of fox farmers, trappers, and furbearer populations. Whereas a shift in fashion accelerated trapping of a species of furbearer, it could soon change course and remove the pressure. High prices induced periodic influxes of trappers (post–World War I, the mid- to late 1920s, the late 1930s, post–World War II), and then competition and falling prices would lower the number of trappers.[76] Fur prices plummeted in 1949, remained low through the 1950s, and revived in the 1960s and 1970s.

Snowmobiles appeared in interior villages in the 1960s and replaced dog teams by the end of the 1970s. They permitted trappers to cover far wider areas while living in the villages, but they necessitated increased cash income. Sales of trapping licenses peaked in the 1980s and fell off steadily. Protests by animal rights groups influenced fashion trends. Effective in the mid-1990s the European Union banned importation of pelts from a list of furbearer species originating in nations that permitted leg-hold traps or otherwise failed to adopt internationally recognized humane standards. Banned Alaskan species included beaver, ermine, coyote, fisher, lynx, marten, otter, and wolf.[77]

Law Enforcement

Conservation measures, and the wide distribution and secretive nature of many species of terrestrial furbearers, protected all from extinction. Furbearer harvest (Table 14.6) could be controlled more readily than most hunting, in part because fur sales, unlike poached meat, left a paper trail. Methods of killing normally went unrecorded. The beaver, a prized animal easily located by its dams and houses, experienced the greatest abuse. Early white trappers caught beavers with dynamite, poison, netting, and shooting and by destroying dams and houses. Scarcity of beavers prompted a series of trapping bans. A 1927 regulation stipulated that all beaver and marten skins must be inspected and "sealed"—accompanied by signed statements that they had been legally caught.[78] Some trappers avoided regulations by smuggling beaver and marten pelts into Canada.[79]

Flying wardens performed effectively in monitoring the take of beavers. According to writer Russell Annabel, Clarence Rhode told of a fearsome rogue trapper named 30-30 John who boasted that no warden dared interfere in his rascally operations. One day an exhausted, bedraggled man appeared at a warden station. The puzzled agent in charge investigated his case. Several weeks earlier a warden, while flying over a beaver pond, had spotted a man illegally setting nets. Finding no place to land, he scrawled on a piece of paper, "Turn yourself in to the nearest Fish and Wildlife Station," then flew back over the pond and dropped it out the window. He expected no response.

TABLE 14.6. Reported Fur Exports From Alaska, 1912–1964

	1912–1920	*1921–1930*	*1931–1940*	*1941–1950*	*1951–1960*	*1961–1964*
Land otter	13,779	25,399	29,767	24,583	29,050	9,982
Arctic fox	–	116,299	153,059	52,617	11,875	5,534
Other fox	116,051	187,716	170,879	75,530	10,122	3,449
Beaver	1,571	96,839	219,072	164,479	173,937	74,046
Marten	34,769	29,957	60,971	77,095	48,035	23,172
Lynx	76,040	51,606	14,820	7,776	15,430	9,200
Wolf	1,191	3,178	5,427	3,326	7,923	2,351
Coyote	–	1,772	8,827	3,170	2,979	369
Wolverine	3,341	4,839	2,931	1,489	2,982	1,133
Mink	266,925	346,575	455,712	440,778	242,256	83,484
Muskrat	934,486	2,579,317	2,919,799	2,096,306	1,208,852	260,822
Weasel	75,451	110,202	132,765	72,272	34,807	5,541

Source: Alan M. Courtright, *Alaska Big Game Harvest Data* (Juneau: Alaska Dept. of Fish and Game, November 1964).
Note: Many or most foxes came from fox farms. Many wolf and wolverine pelts remained for use in Alaska.

The man had come to turn himself in. "Well, here I am," he said. "I couldn't git here no sooner, on account of I had to build a raft, an' the damned raft hit a rock an' busted up, an' my outfit went down the river. I had to walk in, livin' on squirrels an' stuff, an' the mosquitoes like to et me alive. Your airplanes are too much for me; I know when I'm licked," lamented 30-30 John.[80]

Martens grew scarce because they could be caught easily and because their pelts sold for high prices. Officials decreed closed seasons in the 1910s, the 1920s, and the 1940s.[81] Mink, solitary and widely distributed creatures, never atrophied as a species. Neither did lynx or foxes, whose numbers paralleled the cycles of rabbits and ptarmigan. Coyote numbers climbed in the 1920s and fell off in the 1940s, possibly because of the increase in wolves. Wolves dwindled in the late 19th and early 20th centuries from poisoning and again in the 1950s following the federal poisoning and aerial shooting campaign. Wolverines, secretive and wily, could not be easily counted, nor could they be greatly imperiled before the snowmobile era without a widespread suppression effort. Their durable fur served for parka ruffs but not fur coats in the fashion world. A brief period of predator control may have made inroads in their population. But their low density and nocturnal nature protected them except in open country.

Black bears existed throughout forested areas except for some islands in the Southeast. They have not been commonly taken for food, in part because dining on salmon gives their flesh an unpleasant taste. They have been less feared or sought after for furs or trophies than grizzly bears, and the commercial value of their pelts dropped precipitously in the 1920s and 1930s. They encountered no serious risk of depletion during the territorial period.

Wolverine in leg-hold trap, Anchorage vicinity, 1949. By Fred Humes. FWS 6674, Alaska Resources Library and Information Services. Trappers pursued this uncommon and secretive wilderness creature both for its fur and as a predator. Note patch of skin chewed off.

Grizzly or brown bears, less amenable to civilization, lived in wilder regions of forest, mountains, and tundra. Support in the States helped them survive the era of hide marketing and won them some protection in reserves and wildlife refuges. Their numbers increased after the 1925 Game Law prohibited the sale of their skins, and educational efforts by the Alaska Game Commission reduced the number killed by commercial fishers who regarded them as competition for salmon. But cattle interests, loggers, settlers, and others often treated them as a menace to human safety and enterprise. Conflicts recurred for decades after statehood.

VALUING WILDLIFE

From the onset of control by the United States to the time of statehood, management of Alaskan land mammals rested predominantly on utilitarian conservation values. Government attempted, often feebly, to assure an ongoing supply of each species to the extent that it provided desirable meat and fur. Division of jurisdiction among the Treasury, Commerce, and Agriculture departments hampered management efficiency before 1924. But the frontier mentality of salmon fishers, miners, settlers, and some Natives posed the greatest barrier. They operated on an assumption of unlimited natural resources or, if limits existed, on the principle that they should grab the resource before someone else did. Early whites in Alaska felt free to kill wildlife wherever and whenever they pleased, and Natives often slaughtered without any sense of conservation. Government, mainly through the Bureau of Biological Survey, strove to shift wildlife utility values from frontier exploitation to sustainable utilitarianism. While some officials appreciated wildlife for aesthetic or spiritual reasons, their public statements focused on sustainable consumptive use.

Alaskan wildlife represented much more than an amenity; it lay at the core of Alaska's economy and identity. The territory, more than any of the 48 states, held relatively intact wildlife populations. But World War II and its aftermath accelerated the assault on wildlife through rising human population, more versatile transportation means, and other modern implements. If wildlife and wilderness were to be retained, greater recognition of their economic and social value would be necessary. John Buckley, research director at the University of Alaska, attempted a quantification of economic values of wildlife in the early 1950s (Table 14.7). He concluded that wildlife yielded nearly three times as much economic value as mining, agriculture, and forestry combined.[82]

Resource analysts projected a 30 percent increase in Alaskan wildlife economic value by 1961, including a disproportionate rise in recreation. National Park Service planner Lowell Sumner expected a rapid increase of wilderness-oriented tourists and believed tourism could become the major industry. Alaskans, he thought, needed to adjust their attitudes toward wildlife accordingly:

> Surely, greater ultimate prosperity and happiness will come to Alaska's people through deliberately accepting and adjusting their way of life to their unique resources of climate, scenery, wildlife, and wild spaces. This is most likely to happen if they take pride in and consciously hold on to the best features of the frontier way of life for its own special values, rather than thinking of it as something to get rid of as rapidly as possible.
>
> To be successful the future economy will have to use, without using *up*, all of Alaska's renewable resources, from seal skins to scenery, under a program which will perpetuate these resources indefinitely and retain more of the income at home. It is within the framework of this picture of the future—in which the frontier remains a living background—that leading persons in Alaska believe the infant tourist industry may outstrip all others in its potentiality.[83]

Sumner's assumptions about tourism increase proved valid. But a year after his article appeared, Alaska entered an oil era that would last well over half

TABLE 14.7. Values of Wildlife and Other Natural Resources in Alaska, 1952

Resource	*Dollar Value*	*Employment*
WILDLIFE		
Commercial value		
Commercial fish	$ 39,260,240	31,623
Subsistence	3,250,000	24,000
Raw land fur	1,942,291	10,500
Raw fur seal	2,702,959	a
Raw ivory	8,000	a
Reindeer	115,000	250
Fur farms	40,000	19
Subtotal	47,318,490	
Recreational value	12,394,000	43,421
Scientific value	50,000	?
Aesthetic value	1,600,000	?
Gross wildlife value	61,362,490	50,000 b
Management expenditures	–2,474,256	
Net wildlife value	58,888,234	
MINING	18,000,000	1,925
AGRICULTURE	2,763,166	525
FORESTRY	255,000	100

Source: John L. Buckley, *Wildlife in the Economy of Alaska. Biological Papers of the University of Alaska No. 1* (Fairbanks, February 1955), 33.

a= under Subsistence and Raw land fur

b= people may be in more than one category; figures are not additive

a century and generate multiple impacts on Alaskan culture, wildlife, and wilderness.

Partially excepting the grizzly bear, which enjoyed somewhat of a public following, the pre-statehood game laws did not protect species for nonconsumptive purposes. Yet a range of intangible values, while difficult to quantify, remained important to many people in Alaska as well as in the States. Sumner argued that if the time spent in wildlife recreation were converted into dollars, it might double the value of wildlife. In the absence of proper measuring sticks, he advised, it would be unwise to diminish wildlife resources. "Many, possibly most, permanent residents," he thought, "would not care to make Alaska their home if the fighting trout and yearly salmon runs were gone except in old pictures, if the trails of bear and moose had faded from the river banks, if the bands of wandering caribou were only a legend handed down from a vanished frontier."[84]

Elements of ecosystem preservation as a valued goal appeared before statehood, as in parks and refuges and in Leopold and Darling's work on caribou, moose, and wolves. Advocating the Arctic Refuge, Sumner pointed out that several wilderness species including caribou, muskoxen, grizzly bears, and wolverines needed large expanses of land not degraded by development: "Looking ahead 50 years, it is becoming clear that the only opportunity for maintaining a pure wilderness area large enough for the indefinite preservation of the caribou and other space-requiring animals, lies in northeast Arctic Alaska."[85]

Most ungulate transplants, carried out before statehood, violated principles of ecosystem sustainability. Reindeer in particular held the potential for vast ecological damage. The new ecological approach to research did not make its presence felt in the field much before the late 1950s. Biological science adequate for understanding population and ecosystem dynamics, especially for such mobile species as caribou, would take many additional years of work beyond statehood.

15

Journey of the Salmon

AMONG ALASKAN WILDLIFE CONTROVERSIES, ONLY THE SALMON GENERATED AS much heat as the fur seal did. Its mysterious life at sea confounded attempts to manage the salmon, yet its value led men to fight ceaselessly over it. Conflict over the salmon altered Native culture, strained relations between the territorial and federal governments, and even contributed to tensions that exploded into World War II.

Salmon ranked first among economically valuable resources in Alaska nearly every year from the 1880s until oil took the lead in 1969. As elsewhere, people viewed fish in utilitarian terms, as a resource to be eaten by humans or perhaps by other animals. Salmon underwent some of Alaska's most blatant episodes of misuse in the pre-statehood period, suffering damage to or destruction of numerous populations. Both federal government overseers and Alaskans who wanted local control of the fisheries invoked conservation to justify their positions. But the high monetary value of the salmon, the remote settings of the fisheries, and the lack of information on salmon ecology combined to undermine rational control of the harvest.

Salmon in the eastern Pacific spawned in rivers from Kotzebue Sound to the Monterey Peninsula.[1] Five species swam in Alaskan waters. Pinks or humpbacks, the most numerous, averaged 4 pounds and emerged from streams north of Washington. Sockeyes or reds, cumulatively the most commercially valuable because of their numbers, reddish flesh, and oil content, ranged from Washington to the Bering Sea. They averaged 6 or 7 pounds, lived four to eight years, and preferred rivers connected to lakes. Chums or dogs, the least valuable, came from rivers between California and the Arctic. They weighed 8 to 15 pounds and lived three to five years. Cohos or silvers ranged from central California to Kotzebue Sound. They averaged 7 pounds and lived only about two years. Kings or chinooks, the largest and individually most valuable, averaged 20 pounds and could reach 100 pounds or more. They originated in rivers from California to the Arctic and lived three to five years. Commercial fishers caught all species as they returned to the rivers and streams where they had been hatched. Canners might use all species, but sport fishers favored kings, cohos, and pinks. Kings and cohos supplied the bulk of the cured, frozen, and fresh salmon market.[2]

Aboriginal Alaskans depended heavily on salmon, catching them by hand, in traps, or with spears or sinew nets and drying them for year-round consumption. They built dams across streams but are said to have let fish continue upstream after catching enough. Russians opened a saltery the year after they built their first permanent settlement on Kodiak Island in 1784. Dried or salted salmon fed Native sea otter hunters, Russians, and their servants. An attempt to export salmon to California and the Sandwich (Hawaiian) Islands failed economically. After 1867 the Alaska Commercial Company bought salmon for sea otter hunters. Limited sales to the West Coast began in the early 1870s. Canneries, to preserve salmon flesh in cans as opposed to packing in salt, first appeared at Sitka and Klawock in 1878. This signaled the commencement of a highly intensified and politically contentious period in the exploitation of salmon in the eastern North Pacific.[3]

CANNERY OPERATIONS

Success in a salmon cannery called for a supply of fish of desirable quality and sufficient quantity to keep production lines going day and night as long as the salmon run lasted. Four methods of fishing accounted for the vast bulk of cannery salmon in pre-statehood Alaska: (1) beach seines (nets tied by one end to the beach, the other end paid out offshore in a loop and pulled back by hand or winch); (2) traps (on piles driven into the bay floor or floating and anchored offshore) into which salmon funneled as they migrated along the shore; (3) gillnets (supported by floats and either tied at one end to the shore of a lake

Fish trap, Thlinket Packing Company, Funter Bay, 1907. Core coll. 01-2385, Alaska State Library. Traps efficiently captured salmon migrating along shorelines, harming some salmon runs, deepening the industry's recession, and intensifying the political controversy over fishing.

or estuary and extending offshore or free-floating in the ocean; fish swam into the net and became entangled, often by the gills); and (4) purse seines (pulled by boats in a circle, to be closed at the ends and bottom). Methods depended on local conditions, but all could be very effective: in the early years at Karluk River on Kodiak Island a 40-fathom beach seine could yield 100,000 salmon in a single haul. One trap in Southeast Alaska captured over a million in a season. Purse seiners made lucrative hauls by intercepting offshore schools before they could enter rivers.[4]

Trolling, or fishing with lines and hooks from moving boats, provided salmon for the salted, cured, frozen, and fresh fish markets. Trolling for chinooks and cohos took place mainly in Southeast Alaska, although most of the fish returned to rivers in British Columbia, Washington, and Oregon. The practice originated at the turn of the century in small boats powered by oars, a method called hand trolling. By the 1920s it had evolved into a mechanized operation. A motorboat crewed by one to three people dragged steel lines and multiple baited hooks or lures, to be retrieved by power winches. Catches by all methods topped out in the late 1930s and dropped by more than half before statehood. Dams, pollution, irrigation diversions, and overfishing in the home rivers hastened the downward trend.[5]

Brailing a salmon trap. Core coll. 01-3330, Alaska State Library. Alaska salmon replaced those of the ravaged rivers of California and the Northwest.

As soon as feasible after capture of the cannery salmon, independently or company-owned boats transported them to the factory. Workers removed the heads, entrails, and tails and packed the bodies in cans for sealing and cooking. English officer Claude Cane, visiting the Kasilof cannery in 1902, observed that of the five Alaska salmon species, canners normally used only two: "The rejected fish are not let loose to swim away, but every fish in the trap is killed and carried off to the cannery, where the selection is made, those for which they have no use being simply thrown over the side of the staging into the river to lay there and rot."[6] Before the turn of the century, canners in central and western Alaska often treated chums and humpbacks as commercially worthless. Discarded humpbacks could be seen piled knee-deep on Kodiak beaches. By 1901 they sold for 50 cents per dozen cans, half the price of sockeyes. Government purchases in World War I to feed troops elevated the less desired fish to general acceptance.[7]

Packing companies sent vessels to Alaska to prepare for the fishing season. The ships delivered supplies, small boats, cannery workers, and fishers; waited out the fishing and canning; and loaded the crews and canned salmon for return. Companies chose old sailing vessels because of low cost and no need for tight scheduling. This gave the great oceangoing ships their last role in American commerce, keeping some in service into the 1930s. Sailor Harold Gill related his experiences in the square-rigger *Berlin* on a six-month round-

Naket Packing Company's Waterfall Cannery near Craig, Prince of Wales Island. Core coll. 01-2217, Alaska State Library. About 159 salmon canneries operated in Alaska during their peak in 1929. They furnished low-cost, high-protein food, especially welcome during the Great Depression.

trip voyage between Astoria and the Nushagak River in 1912. The ship arrived in time to witness the Katmai eruption in June: "burning jewels of fire . . . great glowing rubies dripping fire for an instant and then snuffed out." Loud booms and earthquakes shook the buildings 100 miles from the volcano, and a change of wind brought "showers of ashes, as fine as flour."[8]

Summer storms drowned several men off the mouth of the Nushagak River and kept crews busy repairing damage. After loading, the *Berlin* departed in late August. On a rare warm and sunny day as the vessel passed Amak Island east of Unimak Pass, Gill and his friends climbed to the fore topgallant yardarm:

> It was glorious to sit there on the sharply braced yard, leaning against the backstays, with our legs lying out on the swelling cheeks of the to'gan'sl. The sky was blue above us and the sea was blue beneath, and all around us wheeled the screaming white seagulls. At the foot of the weather-beaten cliffs the swells broke in foamy surges, and we could dimly hear their roar. Close to the lee-beam was a large outlying rock where some walrus had crawled up to take a sun bath. Looking down we could see the sailors walking deck.

Normally, though, fog and cold predominated: "Nothing on earth can you imagine more lonely than those Aleutian Islands, with their sheer brown lava cliffs towering above the sea and capped with snow." Returning home, Gill

Alaska Packers Association ship Santa Clara. *Greely coll. PCA-66-846, Alaska State Library. Launched in Bath, Maine, in 1876, the 1,474-ton vessel sailed from the East Coast to the Orient and California until 1896, carried salmon until 1922, and served in movies until 1939. The Alaska salmon trade gave the square-riggers their last major economic use.*

allowed that "there is not a man but would give a hundred Alaskas for one Oregon."[9]

Between 1872 and 1903 Alaska fisheries came under the jurisdiction of the Treasury Department's Commission of Fish and Fisheries, best known as the Fish Commission. An era of aggressive profit seeking got under way as the canneries multiplied in the 1880s. Competition waxed fierce: companies sometimes sabotaged others' catches to reduce their profits. Greed ran free: fishers dammed or blocked off streams and caught every salmon. Regulation treaded lightly: weak laws went unenforced.[10] Complaints by government inspectors roused Congress to action in 1889. It outlawed damming and blocking streams or placing weirs in them and appropriated money for salmon-related research. It authorized the Fish Commission to enforce the law, but lack of funding limited the commission to a staff of two enforcement agents. As a result, fishers continued their underhanded tactics. One cannery supervisor ordered his men to illegally net the spawning grounds of a nearby river; they pulled out 225,000 salmon. Men openly violated the ban on fishing in the Afognak reserve.[11]

Dam on salmon stream, Helm Bay, ca. 1898. In Jefferson B. Moser, The Salmon and Salmon Fisheries of Alaska, *Washington, DC: GPO, 1899, plate 10. Early commercial fishers blocked streams to maximize their catch, damaging salmon populations in the process.*

In his official report on the Fish Commission's 1889 survey, ichthyologist Tarleton H. Bean had predicted that, in the absence of effective federal regulation,

> we shall have repeated in Alaska Rivers the story of the Sacramento and the Columbia; and the destruction in Alaska will be more rapid because of the small size of the rivers and the ease with which salmon can be prevented from ascending them. For a few years there will be wanton waste of that marvelous abundance, which the fishermen—concerned only for immediate profit and utterly improvident of the future—declare to be inexhaustible. This season of prosperity will be followed by a rapid decline in the value and productivity of these fisheries, and a point will eventually be reached where the salmon-canning industry will no longer be profitable.[12]

Bean's prophecy rested on common experience in the nation's treatment of natural resources. In part it came true, although it took longer than Bean probably expected.

Marine scientist William H. Dall repeated the warnings of Bean and others that "unless more effectively supervised the [salmon] will meet with the same fate as the fisheries of California and the Columbia River." Noting the northward progression of the fisheries, he worried that "the natives of the upper Yukon will go hungry."[13] George Bird Grinnell, who observed the canning industry during the 1899 Harriman Expedition, commented, "The salmon of Alaska, numerous as they have been and still are, are being destroyed at so wholesale a rate that before long the canning industry must cease to be profitable, and the capital put into the canneries must cease to yield any return." The practice of salting the bellies of some species and throwing away the remaining 80 to 90 percent reminded him of his experiences in the West: "This practice may fairly be compared with the old time method of killing buffalo for their tongues alone, and the more recent one of killing elk and deer for their hides or heads or hams." A 1909 law banned discarding salmon backs.[14]

Laws enacted between 1896 and 1903 mandated weekly closed periods for traps and prohibited all commercial fishing above tidewater in streams less than 500 feet wide and setting nets more than one-third of the way across tidewater streams or within 100 yards of another net. The 1896 act authorized the hiring of three inspectors. In practice, until 1912 two agents shared responsibility for policing the far-flung fishing sites. Territorial governor John G. Brady branded the fishing regulations "a farce." Hearing that lack of funds forced federal inspectors to rely on the canneries for transportation, he quipped, "As well send a man to the front without arms and ammunition."[15]

Congress transferred Alaska fish management from the Department of the Treasury to the Bureau of Fisheries, Department of Commerce and Labor, in 1903. This move strengthened regulatory sympathy for the packing companies because of the agency's close ties to business interests. An inspection of 34 fish traps in the Southeast in 1908 showed 29 in violation of the weekly closed period. A second check a week later disclosed 24 still in violation. Courts levied fines in 54 convictions that year, and some supervisors lost their jobs.[16] Dependent on the companies for transportation and sometimes for food, the inspecting agents found it next to impossible to enforce the law. The boats they employed in 1912 lacked the necessary speed to catch violators. Stream guards, introduced in 1918, could be subject to bribery. Should violators be caught, prosecution would be uncertain given the cost, difficulty of showing proof, and lack of will within elements of the judicial system.[17]

SALMON AND ALASKA NATIVES

The salmon business in some respects detrimentally affected Alaska Natives, as did other forms of commercialization of Alaskan resources. Treated as wards of the government, Natives could not stake natural resource claims under U.S. laws. Tlingits and Aleuts honored family rights to fishing grounds and hoped these rights would be respected. At first, canneries in Southeast Alaska recognized Tlingit claims; some bought construction sites from the Natives or paid them royalties based on the number of fish taken. When competition intensified, canneries ceased the practice.[18] In a reversal of the usual cultural clash, the Southeastern Indians tried to defend what they regarded as private rights against the European concept of fish as common property and available to everyone.[19]

By prohibiting dams and weirs, the 1889 law overrode Native claims to stream ownership and measurably increased the difficulty of their catching fish to supply canneries. Minimum distances between traps and nets mandated by the 1896 amendments further disadvantaged Natives and benefited trap owners. Natives lacked the capital, technical skills, and heavy equipment necessary to build stationary pile traps or the more versatile floating traps that came into use in 1907. Natives able to purchase or lease boats could engage in purse seining that began shortly after the turn of the century.[20]

Governor Lyman Knapp, attempting to curb the canneries' behavior, drafted a document for use by the Tlingits. One, circulated in Juneau in 1891, read,

> This is to notify all persons interested, that . . . Suk-ta-han and his father Kitch-noch claim exclusive right of possession of river at Sitkok bay for fishing purposes. . . . Any white persons desiring to negotiate for privileges there must either satisfy ALL CLAIMANTS or have the matter of controversy settled by getting the parties claiming the rights together before me or some magistrate and have a hearing and determination of the questions at issue.

The *Juneau Mining Record* ridiculed the "valuable document" of the "noble siwash" as "worthy of preservation in a museum for rare curiosities" and accused the "heap big governor" of attempting to "create a small sized siwash land office as well as a sort of court for the adjudication of siwash difficulties." Governor James Sheakley, who held office from 1893 to 1897, did not sustain Knapp's efforts.[21]

Chief Johnson of the Taku wrote to a Treasury Department official, "This is the country of my people, who must have salmon to live. Five cannery companies catch salmon last summer in Takou River, and will take all the salmon from my people. . . . The book you gave me when I last saw you . . . you marked the page where the law say no man can catch fish with net in the river. . . . The canneries do not keep that law, they fish in river and fish all the time."[22] Lt. Cmdr. Jefferson Moser, a Naval officer who investigated the salmon fishery for the Fish Commission, explained in 1898 that

> a native, whose ancestors have lived on a certain stream for generations, and whose rights are respected by other natives, supplies a certain cannery with his catch, as possibly he has been doing for years. A rival cannery tells the

> native he must sell his catch to it, and that otherwise the men will fish the native's stream. The result is overfishing, bad feeling, complaints, blows, and threats of bloodshed. So far as can be learned, there are now no legal rights or title to any fishing grounds in Alaska except what force or strategy furnish.[23]

Some cannery operators, Moser stated, paid chiefs a fee for the use of streams, whereas others reneged on payments. Tlingits resented the appropriation of their resources by others to make a profit and could not understand why the whites, whose culture they admitted to be superior, would not respect traditional Native rights. They pointed out the irony of Natives being forbidden to stake mineral claims. Moser, sympathetic toward their plight, felt that little would be done to correct the situation. Natives had lost the contest over fishing territories.[24] A legal opinion issued by the Interior Department in 1942 upheld the validity of aboriginal Native fishing rights, but officials refused to act.[25]

Appropriation of salmon streams by whites may have jeopardized Natives' cash income rather than food supply per se. Fisheries agent George R. Tingle reasoned that even if whites fished a river to commercial exhaustion, enough salmon would return to the numerous tributaries to feed the Natives. When questioned, he said Tlingits objected to loss of the right to sell fish to the canneries and no longer wanted to catch and dry fish for food. They showed little concern for their food supply, Tingle added, when they slaughtered large numbers of deer merely to sell the hides.[26] Laws banning commercial fishing in streams benefited Natives who fished for subsistence. In the Yukon and Kuskokwim rivers the government heavily restricted commercial fishing beginning in the 1920s. This helped guarantee a reliable supply of salmon for Native consumption.[27]

Canning companies sometimes directly assisted the Natives. On Kodiak Island in 1922, Alaska Packers Association set up housing and commercial fishing facilities for the Aleuts at Karluk River. In 1944 the Aleuts won reserve status for 35,000 acres embracing the river, one of the most productive salmon waters in Alaska, thereby securing an economic base. The reserve boundaries extended 3,000 feet offshore.[28] Canning companies challenged the Aleuts' exclusive right to fish in reservation waters and won in a close 1949 Supreme Court decision. For their part, Metlakatla Indians on Annette Island in the Southeast started a community-owned cannery in 1890 and established a reserve in 1891, both ultimately upheld by the courts.[29]

In the 1940s and 1950s the Bureau of Indian Affairs provided loans to Natives for purchase of boats and canneries. It advocated recognition of Native rights to traditional fishing territories. By contrast, the Fish and Wildlife Service, in control of Alaska salmon fisheries from 1940 to 1960, resisted Native land

Athabaskan fish wheel, Tanana, 1918. By Charles H. Townsend. Fish and Wildlife Service coll. PCA 186-23, Alaska State Library. Commercial salmon fisheries could jeopardize Native food supplies, and most Alaskans believed the federal government favored the outside-owned canneries.

claims. A lawsuit settled in 1959 acknowledged the validity of Tlingit and Haida land claims in the Southeast, for which they received $7.5 million in compensation in 1965. Comprehensive settlement of Native claims came in the Alaska Native Claims Settlement Act of 1971 and the Alaska National Interest Lands Conservation Act of 1980.[30]

As soon as Alaska became a state, it abolished all commercial fish traps. The federal government took the position that Natives had the right to build traps on territory belonging to them. A 1962 Supreme Court decision upheld only the traps in the Annette Island Fishery Reserve authorized by executive order in 1916.[31]

Salmon fisheries benefited Alaska Natives by offering an opportunity to earn cash (Table 15.1). Indians worked at American-owned salteries in the Southeast in the 1870s. As soon as the first canneries opened in the region, Indians sold them salmon and provided cannery labor thereafter.[32] At Karluk some Aleuts fished commercially and used equipment provided by canneries. Nonetheless, they felt ambivalent about wage work. Moser observed that "the complaint is made everywhere that Indian labor—that is, the labor of men—is uncertain. After making sufficient wages to supply their personal wants and getting a few dollars ahead, the desire for hunting and fishing seizes them and they are apt to leave when they are most wanted."[33]

TABLE 15.1 Statistical Profile of Alaska Salmon Canning Industry, 1878–1897

Canneries (1897)	29
Salmon canned (cases of 48 1-lb cans, 1878–1897)	
Southeast	1,739,832
Kodiak/Chignik	3,286,505
Prince William Sound	494,567
Bering Sea	1,496,513
Cook Inlet	490,941
Total	7,508,358
Annual average	375,418
1887–1897 average	691,743
Workers (1897)	
White fishermen	1,148
Chinese cannery workers	2,268
Native fishermen	759
Boat/hatchery workers	326
White cannery workers	312
Native cannery workers	439
Total	5,252
Workers by Region (1897)	
Southeast	1,829
Cook Inlet	173
Prince William Sound/Copper River	364
Kodiak/Chignik	1,577
Bering Sea	1,309

Source: Jefferson F. Moser, *The Salmon and Salmon Fisheries of Alaska: Report of the Operations of the United States Fish Commission Steamer* Albatross *for the Year Ending June 30, 1898* (Washington: GPO, 1899), 49–50.

To the extent that Alaska Natives worked in the salmon industry, conversion to a cash economy hastened the dissolution of their subsistence culture. Rather than drying enough salmon for a winter food supply or for barter, they sold the fish to canneries. Unless they carefully managed their money, a practice not part of their tradition, they risked hardship.[34] They craved Western goods, not least the ingredients for brewing liquor, which sold briskly. At the same time, many took pride in their aboriginal culture. Lack of industrially efficient behavior by the Indians and rapid growth of canning operations resulted in the importation of Chinese workers. A turn-of-the-century visitor noted, "In the skillful manipulation of the cans and machines within doors, neither [the Indian] nor the white man can approach the automatic dexterity of the Chinese, who, being paid by the piece, take no account of a day's working hours, and keep the machinery moving as long as there are fish in the cannery."[35] Exclusionary laws forced the departure of most Chinese from Alaska by 1906, and workers of Japanese, Filipino, and Mexican origin replaced them in some canneries.[36]

During World War I most Tlingit men worked seasonally on fishing boats, and women and children labored in the canneries. A 1935 survey in northern Southeast Alaska showed that of a total of 2,444 Tlingit residents, 862 worked on seine boats and 795 in canneries. By the 1940s many operated their own boats. Tlingits resented the competition from cannery-owned fish traps and imported labor. They continued to practice subsistence hunting and fishing, typically in the vicinity of the canneries, where they lived seasonally.[37]

HATCHERIES

Concern for sustainability of the salmon fishery implied a need for more constricted fishing zones or periods, limits on the amount or type of gear employed, or means of increasing the numbers of salmon. Upon its inception in 1871, the U.S. Commission on Fish and Fisheries adopted fish propagation technology as its main conservation mechanism. Livingston Stone, director of hatcheries in California and Oregon, accompanied a Fish Commission team surveying Alaska for possible hatchery sites. He recommended upon returning that Afognak Island be made a "Salmon National Park." He presented his idea to the American Fisheries Society and in George Bird Grinnell's *Forest and Stream*. The Afognak Forest and Fish Culture Reserve came into being on December 24, 1892.

Hatcheries might be owned by cannery companies, other private concerns, or the federal government. Companies, hoping to head off government restriction, built and briefly operated a hatchery at Karluk River in 1891. Four others went into operation, one at Karluk and three in the Southeast, during the late 1890s.[38] At his own expense, trader John C. Callbreath ran a hatchery operation on Etolin Island in Southeast Alaska from 1892 through 1907. He used methods as natural as feasible, penning the salmon in the stream. He did not succeed in getting return runs of fish, possibly because of overfishing near his stream. His request for protection went unanswered, and the reasons his experiment failed could not be determined.

Prompted by warnings of fish scarcity and recommendations that hatcheries be government operated, Congress acted in 1900 to require packing companies to maintain hatcheries. Some compliance ensued, but costs and inexperience yielded avoidance and poor results. Congress repealed the requirement in 1906.[39]

Fish culture experts who dominated the Fish Commission and its successor Bureau of Fisheries emphasized fish propagation rather than regulation as the way to maintain stocks. Canners also preferred weak regulations and wanted to gain title to their cannery and trap sites. The Fish Commission resisted private ownership of sites and hoped to lease them and set catch quotas for each. It offered government hatcheries and no catch quotas as a compromise that canners accepted.[40] In 1905 Congress authorized Alaska's first federal hatchery, opening that year at Yes Bay in the Southeast. A second went into operation at Litnik Lake on Afognak Island in 1908.

In Alaska a typical salmon hatchery collected fish returning to spawning rivers and removed eggs and milt. Inside the hatchery, fertilized eggs incubated in protected enclosures. Hatchlings remained in pens in flowing water until old enough to release. Pinks and chums went back to the ocean as fry, and sockeyes, cohos, and kings lived in the pens or in lakes for about a year to be released at smolt size. Growing to maturity in the ocean, salmon returned to the hatchery stream but did not belong to the hatchery owners.[41]

Canneries continued to operate a few hatcheries in the 20th Century, receiving tax rebates supposedly equal to their costs of producing fingerlings. However, inspectors pointed to release of fry as one of the weaknesses in the hatchery approach to conservation. Dumping them directly into lakes, some frequented by Dolly Varden char, exposed fry to undue levels of predation. Hatchery operators often lacked technical training and made numerous mistakes. Cannery officials and both government and private hatchery operators claimed success for the operations. Between 1906 and 1920 the government spent far more on hatcheries than on fishery regulation and salmon research combined. Yet no solid evidence of hatchery effectiveness existed, and salmon runs continued to shrink.[42]

The two federal hatcheries remained until 1933 when a new Fisheries commissioner, Frank T. Bell, visited and ordered them closed. Bell viewed them as unwarranted and generous subsidies for the fishing industry. A last remaining private hatchery, near Boca de Quadra Bay in the Southeast, shut down in 1936.[43] Rather than enhancing salmon stocks, hatcheries in the first four decades may have functioned as an excuse for the government to avoid unpleasant regulation and for the packers to ignore conservation measures.

Before the 1950s, hatcheries achieved modest results at best. Between 1919 and 1927 the Territory of Alaska operated four hatcheries, but uncertainty regarding their benefits ended the program. During the 1940s the Bureau of Fisheries ran an experimental pink salmon hatchery at Little Port Walter on Baranof Island. It failed to produce useful data on the effects of hatchery salmon on natural pink salmon runs. Beginning in 1950 the new Territorial Department of Fisheries tried to establish chinook salmon runs on Alaskan streams by planting eggs from Washington. The experiment failed completely, but the department successfully initiated sockeye salmon runs. The department ran a research station to study sockeyes and cohos at Kitoi Bay on Afognak Island from 1954 to 1964. Research results were lost. A hatchery at Deer Mountain near Ketchikan, begun in 1955, again tried to create chinook runs without significant results. It had mixed success in generating coho runs in lakes and streams.[44] Pre-statehood experiments supplied vital knowledge of salmon ecology but could not compensate for the losses of salmon.

LAW ENFORCEMENT AFTER WORLD WAR I

Application of effective fishing methods by competing parties threatened to erode salmon runs and generated conflict and temptation to fish illegally. Almost any government attempt to regulate gear drew fire from one or more of the interested groups. Ongoing complaints and projections of a salmon industry collapse created a widely shared consensus on the need for protective action. Sales dropped from the high of World War I, and companies shut down numerous canneries. The companies maintained a strong presence in Bureau of Fisheries deliberations, and the agency lacked the power to regulate fishing beyond the low-tide line.

Disaster along the Yukon River forced action by the federal government. A very low harvest of salmon in 1919 followed the introduction of commercial fishing in 1918. Many Yup'ik Eskimos and Athabaskan Indians died of starvation. All parties including the canning companies agreed on the need for conservation to be overseen by the federal government. But they disagreed on the meaning of "conservation" as it applied to fisheries. In congressional hearings Dan Sutherland, representing Alaska's small fishermen, interpreted "conservation" to mean open and equitable access for all citizens to natural resources and government regulation to ensure access. In effect, Sutherland's conservation would call for abolition of permits, reserves, private ownership of sites, and fish traps, all of which disadvantaged small fishers. By contrast, Secretary of Commerce Herbert Hoover and the canning companies with which he empathized defined "conservation" in terms of efficiency. The companies wanted to own the trap sites and be subject to weak regulation. The most economically and technically efficient means of stopping the falloff of salmon runs implied traps and permits and thus favored the companies. The technology of fisheries led to a split between "equity" conservation and "efficiency" conservation, and the latter won out in the 1920s.

To conserve fisheries the bureau revived the 1892 Afognak Island precedent of salmon reserves to safeguard important spawning rivers. According to this plan the government would set aside a series of reserves in which leases for exclusive harvest could be granted. The plan would advance conservation of fish but would benefit the large companies who could afford the leases.[45]

In 1922 President Warren Harding designated fishing reserves (by permit only) on Bristol Bay, Kodiak Island, Cook Inlet, and the Alaska Peninsula and Aleutians. The battle between Alaska fishers and the canning companies continued. Criticism of the reserves led to a compromise in the 1924 White Act. It empowered the national government, specifically the secretary of commerce, to bring Alaska fisheries under more complete control. It ended exclusive fishing rights, thereby abolishing the reserves. It set regulations on nearly all aspects of fishing and specified that 50 percent of the fish entering each stream must be allowed upstream. It extended Bureau of Fisheries jurisdiction to the three-mile limit. Canning company lobbyists tried in vain to kill the 50 percent escapement provision but managed to stop Sutherland's amendment to abolish fish traps. Alaskans had objected to fish reserves, favored by the large canning companies, and they won stiffer restrictions on fish traps.[46] Enforcement capacity improved from eight boats and 50 stream guards in 1923 to ten boats and 103 guards after passage of the act.[47]

Regulations pursuant to the White Act aimed to achieve sustainable harvesting of salmon. By its nature, the fierce competition among fishers and canneries during the short spring and summer seasons led to excesses and would eventually exhaust the salmon runs if not curbed. Rules stipulated, among other provisions: (1) no wasting of salmon, (2) processing of salmon within 48 hours of death, (3) no driving of salmon from protected to unprotected areas, (3) no fishing during a specified period in each week, and (5) limits on the type, size, and placement of fishing gear; for example, traps in different regions had to be 0.5 to 1.5 miles apart. Restrictions varied for each district, based on different salmon species and environmental conditions.[48]

After a post–World War I recession, the industry again grew rapidly. Debate ensued as to whether the increase in harvest could be credited to conservation measures or to advancing technology and exploitation of new locations in Alaska. Writer-conservationist Stewart Edward White, depicting fisheries in the late 1920s, subscribed to the latter thesis:

> I have seen every regulation on the list flagrantly and repeatedly violated. Seine boats fish the mouths of streams whenever they get a chance. This is obviated to a certain extent by the recent installation of stream watchers. But sometimes one man must look after several widely scattered streams, and a lively seine-boat skipper is quick to seize the absence. And, though most watchmen are honest, there are some willing to wink the other eye, either through friendship or because they sympathize with the poor devil who has had a lean season, or, quite simply, because they are bribed. . . . No one who has not seen it can realize the intensity of the scramble for fish in the brief season. . . . [T]hose bringing in the salmon are quite aware of the fact that any salmon are more than welcome.

White considered the weekend no-fishing period to be discriminatory against the relatively visible seine boats and in favor of trap operators, who often left the gate open unless a patrol boat happened along.[49]

Salmon counting weir, stream watcher's cabin, and Fish and Wildlife Service patrol plane, Red River Lake outlet, Kodiak Island, 1950. By Frank L. Beals. FWS 970, Alaska Resources Library and Information Services. Aircraft measurably enhanced fisheries law enforcement.

Enforcement, however inadequate, tightened in the mid-1920s. Using ten Bureau of Fisheries vessels and chartering eleven others, agents reduced the incidence of trap robbery. Most violations involved fishing in closed waters, fishing out of season, or improper use of gear. Officers seized, for example, four traps for illegal fishing in the Southeast in 1925; the court ordered two sold, fined a watchman $100, and sent him to jail for 30 days. The Coast Guard seized two Canadian vessels for fishing in U.S. waters; the court released them after levying $100 fines.[50]

Aircraft, first employed in 1929, multiplied the range of agents' surveillance and gave them an additional measure of surprise. By 1935 the bureau fielded faster boats and a total of 170 stream guards. One trap owner paid a $750 fine for operating a trap during the weekly closed period; another paid $500 for using traps postseason. Two beach seiners paid $50 fines and forfeited the salmon they had caught in Petersburg Creek.[51]

Salmon scarcity in the 1940s and 1950s heightened fishing competition and the frequency of law violations. Alaska Game Commission agents and pilots assisted the Bureau of Commercial Fisheries in law enforcement. Of 50 cases before U.S. Commissioner courts in 1945, 44 resulted in convictions. Normally, violators paid $100 fines and gave up their catches. In 1955 the commissioner courts pronounced 218 of 244 defendants guilty in 125 cases. Compared with 1945, fines increased for larger operators, but the small man usually paid $50 or $100 or won acquittal.[52]

TERRITORIAL-FEDERAL ANIMOSITY

Management of the salmon fisheries stirred virulent resentment among Alaskans during the entire territorial period. Alaskans believed the canning industry, concentrated largely in San Francisco, Seattle, and Astoria, had been instrumental in shaping the 1912 Alaska Territorial Act that created the territory but denied the legislature managerial control over fish and wildlife. The legislature retained the power to impose limited licensing and property taxes on fisheries, providing the bulk of the territory's revenue for decades. The fishing industry lobbied Congress unsuccessfully for bills removing the territory's right to tax but succeeded in forestalling the territory's repeated attempts to gain management powers.[53]

Local feelings toward stateside fishermen and the federal government ran high. After passage of the 1924 White Act, fishermen complained that their boats and gear could be seized upon suspicion of their location, whereas most fish traps could not. For many years residents in some districts had difficulty being hired to fish for or work in the canneries, even if they joined an outside-based union.[54] Between 1927 and 1938 the Seattle-based Alaska Fishermen's Union maintained a contract clause obligating some canneries to pay a four-cent penalty (one-third of the value) for each fish purchased from an Alaska resident. Another contract set a ratio of thirteen nonresidents for each Alaska resident fisherman allowed to sell to the canneries.[55]

Researchers Homer F. Gregory and Kathleen Barnes of the Institute of Pacific Relations examined claims that canning companies exercised monopolistic control. They pointed out that large companies could better afford the modern vessels increasingly employed to transport workers and fish over long distances; could more effectively bargain with unions, influence policy, and market their products; and possessed the breadth and stability to survive downturns in prices or salmon runs. Moreover, the conservation regulations incidentally favored them by spreading fish traps over a wider range, giving larger operators a relative advantage.[56]

Alaska Packers Association, a San Francisco–based group formed in 1893, put up as much as 80 percent of the salmon pack for most of the 1890s. By declining percentages it headed the Alaska industry until World War I.[57] By the

1930s, however, no company dominated. In 1937, near the all-time peak of production, 113 canneries operated in Alaska, owned by 75 companies. Most companies had 1 or 2 canning factories. In the Pacific Northwest as a whole, the largest company ran 11 factories and the 9 largest had a total of 52. Of 453 traps in Alaska, the 5 largest companies controlled 171 and the 9 largest companies 214. Traps in Alaska caught 46.4 percent of the salmon, seines (mostly owned by small concerns) 27.7 percent, gillnets 24.3 percent, trollers (for fresh or cured salmon) 1.4 percent, and fish wheels (used by Natives only) 0.3 percent. Alaska Packers Association put up 11.5 percent of the canned salmon in 1937 and the leader, Pacific American Fisheries, Inc., somewhat more. Gregory and Barnes concluded that competition among the companies and the variety and mobility of gear prevented formation of a monopoly.[58] Working together, however, the companies exercised a powerful effect on regulatory policy.

Salmon Traps

Probably nothing more clearly focused local resentment of federal control than salmon traps. Alaska Natives had devised various means of trapping salmon, and the Russians built traps for the salted salmon trade. Americans followed suit, improving on the designs to supply large numbers of salmon to the canneries. The two most common forms, stationary and floating, ultimately caught more fish than any other type of gear. Fishers placed these devices in streams and estuaries until the 1889 law banned the practice, and they continued to do so until law enforcement tightened up. By 1901, 57 stationary traps existed: 6 in Bristol Bay, 21 near Chignik on the Alaska Peninsula, 1 at Kodiak, 20 in Cook Inlet, and 9 in Southeast Alaska. Floating traps appeared in 1907 and proved cheaper to operate than stationary traps, which had to be pulled up after every season to reduce navigation hazards. Floating traps could be towed into a harbor for the winter.

A strike by fishers in 1912 caused the canners to increase their reliance on fish traps. Traps enabled companies to reduce labor costs, gain greater control over the fishing and transportation process, and obtain fresher fish to can. The number of traps peaked at 799 in 1927. Required minimum distances between traps cut the numbers steadily. Traps caught more salmon in times of plenty, but purse seines got more in times of scarcity.[59]

Fish traps sat strategically in the pathways of salmon returning to their spawning rivers. Fish swam into a pen from which they could not escape. Traps could be brailed (emptied) at leisure and the fish delivered to a cannery in relatively unspoiled condition. Occupiers of a trap site held an exclusive right to that site by tradition and might sell the lease for a large sum. Those who fished by other means strongly resented the fish traps, accusing the owners of putting them out of business by overexploiting the fish supply. Industry representatives interpreted the dispute as largely a labor issue in that fish traps required few workers. Government fisheries officials defended the traps as a legal and efficient means of harvesting fish.[60]

Between 1915 and 1958 more than 40 percent of the salmon catch came from fish traps, 75 to 90 percent outside-owned. In a 1948 nonbinding referendum Alaskans voted by more than seven to one to abolish fish traps. Federal officials contended they could not legally discriminate in favor of local residents and that, compared to other methods, fish traps wasted less salmon.[61] In any case, the secretaries of Commerce and Interior lacked the authority to abolish traps until 1949. Thereafter, federal reluctance to abolish salmon traps further convinced Alaskans that Washington overrode their wishes for the benefit of powerful outside interests. Critics cited the salmon decline as the outstanding proof of federal mismanagement of natural resources and called for territorial control of resources, or for statehood, as a remedy.

Salmon Decline and Statehood

A long and deep depression in salmon harvests began in the late 1930s (Table 15.2), intensifying mutual recriminations and resentment of federal management. At maximum in 1929 the canneries numbered 160, in the 1930s and 1940s about 110–115, and by 1960 about 50. The number of traps stayed at about 400 from the mid-1930s to the mid-1950s. But gillnet boats increased from 3,000 to 7,500 and seine boats from 700 to 1,500 during the period. Average annual catches declined about 50 percent for traps, 80 percent for purse seiners, and 90 percent for gillnetters. Between the peak harvest year of 1936 and 1959, the total catch fell from 8.5 million to 1.6 million cases, prompting President Dwight Eisenhower to declare Alaska fisheries a disaster area in 1953 and 1954.[62] The emergency resulted in increased federal enforcement and research funds, scarce prior to the mid-1950s. Higher salmon prices, however, tempted more people to fish and inspired more illegal fishing.[63]

The Interior Department's Fish and Wildlife Service had assumed jurisdiction over Alaskan inshore fisheries in 1940. As a wildlife management agency the service saw its main responsibility as maintaining a sustainable supply of salmon and not involving itself in questions of who should get the fish. In effect, this policy favored the large companies who possessed financial and technical advantages in access to salmon. It reinforced Alaskans' impressions that the federal government favored the outside companies. Within the context of tightening competition for fewer salmon, federal-territorial relations worsened in the 1940s and 1950s.

TABLE 15.2. Commercial Salmon Catches in Alaska (thousands of fish), 1878–1982

Year	*Total*	*Year*	*Total*	*Year*	*Total*	*Year*	*Total*	*Year*	*Total*
1878	56	1899	14,358	1920	64,066	1941	103,608	1962	62,801
1879	69	1900	21,546	1921	38,568	1942	80,844	1963	47,471
1880	68	1901	27,165	1922	72,273	1943	86,717	1964	65,717
1881	91	1902	31,794	1923	77,789	1944	70,128	1965	56,331
1882	177	1903	30,095	1924	82,181	1945	74,867	1966	64,033
1883	295	1904	28,631	1925	64,163	1946	72,454	1967	20,881
1884	429	1905	27,257	1926	96,785	1947	69,859	1968	62,292
1885	640	1906	31,312	1927	47,517	1948	58,160	1969	41,902
1886	1,273	1907	34,643	1928	87,737	1949	78,171	1970	68,445
1887	2,060	1908	42,296	1929	71,107	1950	44,816	1971	47,489
1888	4,183	1909	34,938	1930	80,076	1951	49,503	1972	31,950
1889	6,605	1910	33,365	1931	69,629	1952	48,032	1973	22,305
1890	6,625	1911	44,307	1932	72,196	1953	37,041	1974	21,873
1891	7,694	1912	63,169	1933	79,624	1954	44,296	1975	26,217
1892	5,117	1913	59,308	1934	113,433	1955	39,624	1976	44,416
1893	7,266	1914	54,975	1935	71,501	1956	50,591	1977	50,805
1894	8,506	1915	63,655	1936	126,439	1957	34,370	1978	82,281
1895	7,586	1916	69,742	1937	108,687	1958	41,000	1979	88,754
1896	11,536	1917	91,565	1938	100,710	1959	25,127	1980	110,004
1897	13,025	1918	102,041	1939	78,341	1960	42,484	1981	113,325
1898	12,898	1919	57,367	1940	84,800	1961	45,026	1982	111,572

Source: Doug Eggers and Michael R. Dean, *Alaska Commercial Salmon Catches, 1878–1986.* Alaska Dept. of Fish and Game, Div. of Commercial Fisheries. Regional Information Report No. 5J87-01 (Juneau, August 1987), 1–2.

The service held annual hearings in Seattle and Alaskan fishing ports to discuss status of the stocks, report on research results, and hear comments before drafting regulations for the following year. But the meetings did not result in a mutual effort to conserve fish stocks. Despite annual decreases in salmon catches, the canning companies and labor unions united to demand weaker regulations. Fish and Wildlife director Ira Gabrielson confronted industry representatives at a 1941 hearing, castigating them for their greed: "One is therefore to conclude that the governing motive is the desire to take as many fish as possible now without any regard to the future supply. No industry, no matter how potentially profitable it may be, can long endure if the partners engage in indiscriminate looting." After each Seattle meeting the industry lobby went to Washington to seek more receptive ears. During the war they argued for relaxed regulations to feed the troops, and after the war they contended that restrictions prevented rebuilding the fishing fleet. Meanwhile, in most years the salmon harvest continued to go down.[64]

In 1949 the Alaska legislature created a Department of Fisheries in preparation for eventual statehood. Members of its governing board included three fishermen, a canning industry representative, and a member of the public at large, to be nominated by the governor and confirmed by the legislature. The department assisted the Bureau of Commercial Fisheries by fielding additional stream guards, improving spawning beds, and conducting research. The dominant responsibility for salmon management, however, remained with the federal government until after statehood.[65] Secretary of the Interior Fred Seaton abolished fish traps effective in 1959, the last year of federal control.[66]

During and after his 1939–1953 tenure as territorial governor, Ernest Gruening kept up a steady criticism of federal jurisdiction over fisheries. The steep reduction in harvest reinforced his argument that territorial or state control would be better for conservation. In 1954 he wrote that

> forty-two years ago, the Territory of Alaska, deprived as no other territory had been, of the control and management of its fisheries, through the intrigue and political manipulations of the same forces that have helped destroy the resources, began to plead for that right of self-government. . . . But an absentee industry, wealthy and politically potent, little concerned with the morrow of Alaska's resources, has been able to thwart this logical aspiration and long-overdue change, abetted by a bureaucracy equally unwilling to yield an iota of its perquisites.

Gruening charged that in addition to jeopardizing a vital natural resource, the canning industry used its clout to oppose statehood because it would mean Alaskan control over the fisheries.[67]

Salmon symbolized the frustrations of Alaskan boosters, who strove to replicate the American experience of taming the frontier and converting its natural resources into prosperous and self-governing communities. In the view of the business community, newspaper editors, and politicians, this normal and proper goal required that local citizens control the resources. That meant the settlers, not the Native Americans. Yet very little capital existed in Alaska. The salmon industry, like large-scale gold and copper extraction, necessitated investment from outside owners who did not fancy living in remote and primitive conditions. Managers and stockholders in faraway Seattle, New York, San Francisco, and other cities built and owned most of the canneries and the large vessels employed. Companies imported nearly all their supplies and many workers and needed very little from Alaskans. The territory functioned as an economic colony of the United States, its settler population sustained largely by federal expenditures.

Outsider control of natural resources and, to a high degree, of the governance system grated on the boosters. Rather than acknowledge the problem of remoteness, they blamed the canning companies' political power for retarding the growth of their communities. They viewed federal conservation measures in the same light and labeled most such moves "federal mismanagement." Opposition to the federal government, to environmental protection, and to recognition of Native claims became ingrained in the settlers' political culture. Boosters looked for salvation in statehood. Then, they believed, control over natural resources and over their political affairs would at long last enable them to achieve their destiny.[68]

JAPANESE-AMERICAN COMPETITION

An ongoing quarrel between the United States and Japan affected world affairs as well as Alaska salmon. A seafaring nation consuming a high quantity of fish, Japan turned its attention to North Pacific salmon. Victory in the Russo-Japanese War of 1904–1905 gave it access to sites on the Siberian coast for cannery locations. Forced out by the Soviets after 1918, the Japanese designed cannery ships, enabling them to operate offshore.[69] The vessels first appeared in the Bering Sea in 1930 and processed king crabs, a fishery not yet exploited by the Americans. Diplomatic talks produced an informal understanding that Japan would not fish there for salmon and the United States would not encourage a domestic crab fishery. Under the influence of its fishing industry, the Japanese Diet funded a 1936–1939 "study" of the North Pacific salmon fishery. A mother (cannery) ship and six fishing boats appeared in the Bering Sea in 1936 and canned both crabs and salmon. At a meeting of fishery representatives in February 1937, a Japanese delegate proposed a joint venture to operate floating canneries in Bristol Bay. American representatives rejected the plan.[70]

Tensions rose when a Japanese fishing fleet visited Bristol Bay in June 1937. A State Department inquiry evoked Japanese assurances that the fleet had no license to fish salmon there and was "presumably engaged in crab fishing." American fishery companies chartered a plane and photographed the vessels catching salmon. In its response to Japan, the State Department argued that "as a sound principle of justice" no nation should destroy a resource being conserved by another nation and that the United States had "the right or obligation to protect the salmon fisheries." It did not claim legal jurisdiction over the fish as it had attempted to do in the case of fur seals. The Japanese government promised to discontinue the study after 1937.[71]

Japanese military advances in China and multiple indications of deteriorating U.S.-Japan relations transformed the salmon incident into a dramatic confrontation. A *New York Daily News* writer declared in August 1938:

> Aside from commercial aspects, the plain implication of Japan's position is a new definition of her sphere of influence in the Pacific, constituting a direct challenge to our sovereignty over waters hitherto considered exclusively within United States jurisdiction. It amounts also to a continuation of the aggressive policy of territorial expansion applied to Manchukuo and China, only this time by sea instead of land.

The writer charged that the Japanese operated more than 1,000 vessels along the eastern Pacific Coast, crewed by naval reservists rather than ordinary fishermen: "They not only chart the waters off our shores and the channels leading into our bays, inlets, and harbors, between Nome and San Diego; they possess accurate knowledge of our naval bases, our coast defenses, even our gasoline and oil stores."[72]

Rumors of a return of the Japanese fleet in spring 1938 prompted a Coast Guard investigation that found nothing. But the rumors inflamed fishermen and others suspicious of Japan. Newspaper and magazine articles, radio programs, and even movies magnified anti-Japanese sentiment and heightened demands on the government to take action. Bills introduced in Congress declared the salmon to be U.S. property and called for widening national jurisdiction to waters over continental shelves.[73] Almost certainly, the angry mood contributed to American military defense buildup in the Pacific.

World War II interrupted Japanese fishing in subarctic waters. During the postwar occupation, General Douglas MacArthur placed severe restrictions on Japanese fisheries, excluding them from the Bering Sea and Aleutian Islands. The constraints remained in force until 1952 as a means of pressuring Japan to agree to boundaries favorable to the United States.[74] Japan, Canada, and the United States signed a treaty in 1951, ratified in 1953, forming the North Pacific Fisheries Convention. Under its provisions Japan would refrain from catching salmon originating in North American rivers. Lacking certainty of where the fish went at sea, parties agreed that Japan could fish west of 175 degrees West Longitude, a line bisecting the central Aleutians. Meanwhile, research would be done to determine boundaries between eastern and western Pacific salmon so the jurisdictional line could be adjusted accordingly.

Japan stepped up its high seas fishing in 1954, and for the next three years sockeye salmon catches in Bristol Bay fell well below normal while Japan made record catches. As many as 20 percent of fish caught in Bristol Bay bore scars from small-mesh driftnets used by the Japanese. American researchers concluded that a majority of fish caught almost as far as 170 degrees East Longitude, near the tip of the Aleutians, came from North America. American and Canadian fishers, restricted to inshore fishing as a conservation measure, asked the Japanese to move their operations westward. At a 1957 meeting of the Fisheries Convention, the Japanese refused.[75]

Differing interpretations of research results prevented resolution of the fishing boundary question for two decades. Effective in 1977 the United States and others adopted a 200-mile offshore zone for national jurisdiction over fishing rights. Japan and the United States then negotiated a treaty recognizing the new exclusion boundaries. In effect, the agreement moved Japanese fishing to 175 degrees East Longitude and 200 miles away from American-owned islands. In the Bering Sea foreign vessels could fish without permission only in a zone in the center.[76] Even then, high seas fishing by Japan, Taiwan, and Korea intercepted salmon from Alaskan waters.

Americans arrested vessels illegally fishing within the 200-mile limit. Pressured by environmentalists, the U.S. government prevailed upon Japan to stop the use of driftnets that stretched for several miles and captured a wide variety of fish, birds, and mammals. Japan halted the practice in 1991, and subsequent agreements limited the length of driftnets and prohibited all salmon fishing by gillnets on the high seas. In 1992 a North Pacific Anadromous Fisheries Commission, now including Russia, replaced the tripartite 1952 International North Pacific Fisheries Commission.[77]

RESEARCH ON SALMON

Effective conservation and government regulation suffered acutely from a lack of accurate information. Evidence appeared to justify the widespread opinion that overfishing did long-term damage, but proof did not come easily. Without sound research data, congressional committees could not readily be induced to vote for restrictions. Moreover, Alaska's isolation and the territorial government's weak position and emotional stance precluded high visibility or sympathy in Congress or in stateside public opinion. Vocal Alaskans displayed much more interest in improving their own take of salmon than in conserving the stocks.[78]

Federal research on Alaskan salmon began in 1899 when the U.S. Fish Commission vessel *Albatross* identified species and their locations in the Southeast. A year later, the ship surveyed Bristol Bay. The Bureau of Fisheries opened an office in Seattle in 1914 and conducted summer studies of salmon life cycles in Alaska. On a small scale the bureau carried on research into the 1950s. The federal government transferred its research program to Southeast Alaska in 1956 and built the Auke Bay Laboratory near Juneau in 1960. The laboratory maintained stations at King Salmon, Brooks Lake, Karluk Lake, Kasitna Bay, Olsen Bay, Traitors Cove, and Little Port Walter. It concentrated mainly on pink, sockeye, and chum salmon. After the state gained control of inshore fisheries in 1960, the laboratory continued as a federal facility investigating the biology of high seas salmon and other organisms.[79]

Shrinking harvests in the 1940s led the salmon industry to establish a Fisheries Research Institute. Located at the University of Washington, it began fieldwork in 1946. Increasingly through the 1950s, funding from the federal government supplemented that from private sources. The institute carried out thorough, long-term studies of salmon life cycles and focused on escapement as a key to biologically based salmon management.[80] In the decades after statehood, fisheries scientists steadily improved their ability to predict and enhance salmon runs.

Accumulating knowledge of salmon life revealed a host of complexities. Stream water quality and quantity, forest cover, ocean currents and temperatures, weather patterns, hatchery production, escapement, fishing intensity, and other factors affected salmon abundance. Research on escapement showed each salmon run to be a distinct genetic unit, and thousands of such units existed in Alaska, intermingling in the ocean where most fishing took place. Earlier fishing practices had seriously damaged many genetic units. Under the White Act, regulators thought it sufficient to allow fishing for half the season and close it for the other half to achieve 50 percent escapement. Because different units ran upstream at different times, overescapement occurred for some units and underescapement for others.[81] Underescapement could impair a unit by numerical loss, but overescapement could disrupt eggs and lower the survival rate, also weakening the unit. Perhaps for this reason, Tlingits sometimes faced starvation before the era of canneries.[82]

Further reflection on the controversial fish traps yielded a broader perspective. Historian Robert DeArmond observed that in addition to keeping the fish fresher than those caught by other means,

> the salmon trap was an efficient machine for harvesting a natural resource [and] in good part responsible for the low cost of canned salmon when compared to other sources of protein. During the years of the Great Depression, canned pink and chum salmon, No. 1 tall cans, commonly sold at a dollar a dozen wholesale, and in some years as low as 90 cents a dozen, and thousands of poor people depended on it for their protein.

"It is interesting to note," added DeArmond, "that while all Alaskan fishermen—seiners, gillnetters, trollers—united in their efforts to abolish the traps, each now puts an approximately equal effort into fighting the others for a share of the total catch."[83]

Efficiency of the fishery did not concern the individual commercial fisher, who approached the business competitively. Between 1936 and statehood the average catch per operator continually fell, but high fish values balanced low harvests and kept fishermen afloat. Ever-more gear chasing ever-fewer fish meant a more rapid decrease of fish stocks and steadily lowered efficiency in the fishery as a whole.[84] Advocates of statehood had chosen "federal mismanagement" of fisheries as their most potent rallying cry. At statehood Alaska acquired its own opportunity to tackle the increasingly complicated and politically loaded problem of who should have access to which fish under what conditions.

When the state assumed control of inshore fisheries on January 1, 1960, the salmon harvest had reached a low point. Yet the reviled traps had disappeared and advancing research laid an ever-stronger foundation for management. It soon became apparent, however, that competitive fishing by small companies and individual boat owners did not work well either. It multiplied the difficulties of regulation, wasted resources, and put excess pressure on fish stocks. Alaska changed its constitution effective in 1974 to restrict commercial salmon fishing by issuing permits for exclusive fishing rights at specific times and locations. This approach built conservation into the process rather than leaving it an external force pleading for regulation.[85]

Low salmon harvests moved the state to reinstitute public and private hatcheries in the 1970s. Accumulated experience in fish culture brought about success in propagation. Hatchery-nurtured salmon, mostly pinks and chums, eventually comprised 25 percent of the overall catch.[86] But the ecological impact, if any, of large-scale hatchery salmon production had yet to be determined.

Research in the late 20th Century demonstrated a clear connection between Alaska salmon population levels and a cyclical weather pattern called the Pacific Decadal Oscillation (PDO). The PDO appeared to be connected to, but not necessarily caused by, the El Niño phenomenon. PDO periods tend to last two to three decades and are characterized by high or low sea surface temperature, sea level pressure, and precipitation. During "positive" PDO phases, higher winter precipitation along the Gulf of Alaska coast causes high spring runoff, favoring survival of salmon fingerlings. Warmer near-shore waters enhance the growth of plankton, food for the young salmon. Farther south, from British Columbia to California, this climate phase appeared to lower rather than increase salmon production. Positive PDO periods existed from 1925 to 1947 and after 1977, generally corresponding to high salmon catches (Table 15.2).[87] Applying six other indexes of climate, researchers confirmed the change dates of 1925, 1947, and 1977. A century of data suggested that salmon populations probably have fluctuated for centuries, before the era of modern fishing.[88] Ocean changes, therefore, rather than overfishing or mismanagement per se, may have been the primary cause of the salmon decline beginning in the 1940s. To what degree, if any, overfishing may have worsened the downward trend is not known.

By the 1980s Alaska salmon harvests rose in some years to record levels. But the industry encountered new challenges. World price competition drove down profits. Pen-raised salmon from Chile, Norway, Scotland, and Canada seized an increasing share of the market. Alaskans realized they might be forced to abandon their expensive chases at sea and follow suit.[89] Meanwhile, logging in the Southeast threatened to reduce salmon runs by degrading freshwater habitat, and the possibility of oil tanker spills loomed. Pen-raised salmon might spread disease to wild populations or interbreed and genetically dilute them. Perhaps not least, global warming posed uncertainties for salmon habitat, both freshwater and marine. A study of sockeye salmon indicated that an ocean temperature rise of a few degrees could greatly contract the range of sockeyes and perhaps other species.[90]

Conservation proved difficult to apply to Alaska salmon. Unlike charismatic mammals, salmon stood little chance of acquiring a public following. Isolation from public scrutiny, a politically powerful fishing industry, the widespread taste for salmon flesh, and the competitive nature of the industry invited excess in Alaskan commercial salmon fishing in the pre-statehood period. Federal enforcement agents attempted to curb aggressively exploitative behavior and achieve goals and objectives of sustainable harvest of salmon while being accused of favoring outside fishing interests. Although conservation goals usually required generous measures of ecosystem sustainability, science understood too little of salmon ecology in the years before statehood. Treaties and conventions introduced broader elements of stewardship, necessary for a fish traveling from international waters to inland destinations. A combination of tightening regulation, accumulating knowledge, and the uncertainty of annual fish hauls moved federal and state policy toward sustainable management of the salmon. Notwithstanding the achievements in salmon management, however, climatic warming might do more damage to salmon ecology and the salmon industry than all other negative factors combined.

16

Gold and Oil on the Kenai

A PROMINENT PLACE IN ALASKA'S ENVIRONMENTAL AND POLITICAL ANNALS BELONGS to the Kenai Peninsula, a 9,000-square-mile region of surpassing beauty. Few other locales in the North experienced such contention over land use or such rapacious treatment of wildlife. At statehood the contest continued, leaving a partially protected ecosystem facing worrisome prospects for survival.

Bordered on the south and east by glacier-trimmed peaks, the center and west of the Kenai features lakes, muskeg, and low wooded hills. Dominant tree species are black and white spruce and, in burned-over areas, aspen, birch, cottonwood, and willows. Moose, black and brown bears, caribou, Dall sheep, mountain goats, wolves, coyotes, wolverines, lynx, beavers, red foxes, and smaller mammals are sustained by the varied topography. About ten species of game fish are found in the lakes and streams.[1] Whales, porpoises, sea lions, seals, and sea otters can be sighted offshore. Nearly half the land mass is reserved in the Kenai National Wildlife Refuge and Kenai Fjords National Park.

Endowed by fish and wildlife, agricultural potential, and timber and mineral wealth and accessible to the ocean, the Kenai Peninsula bred conflict over

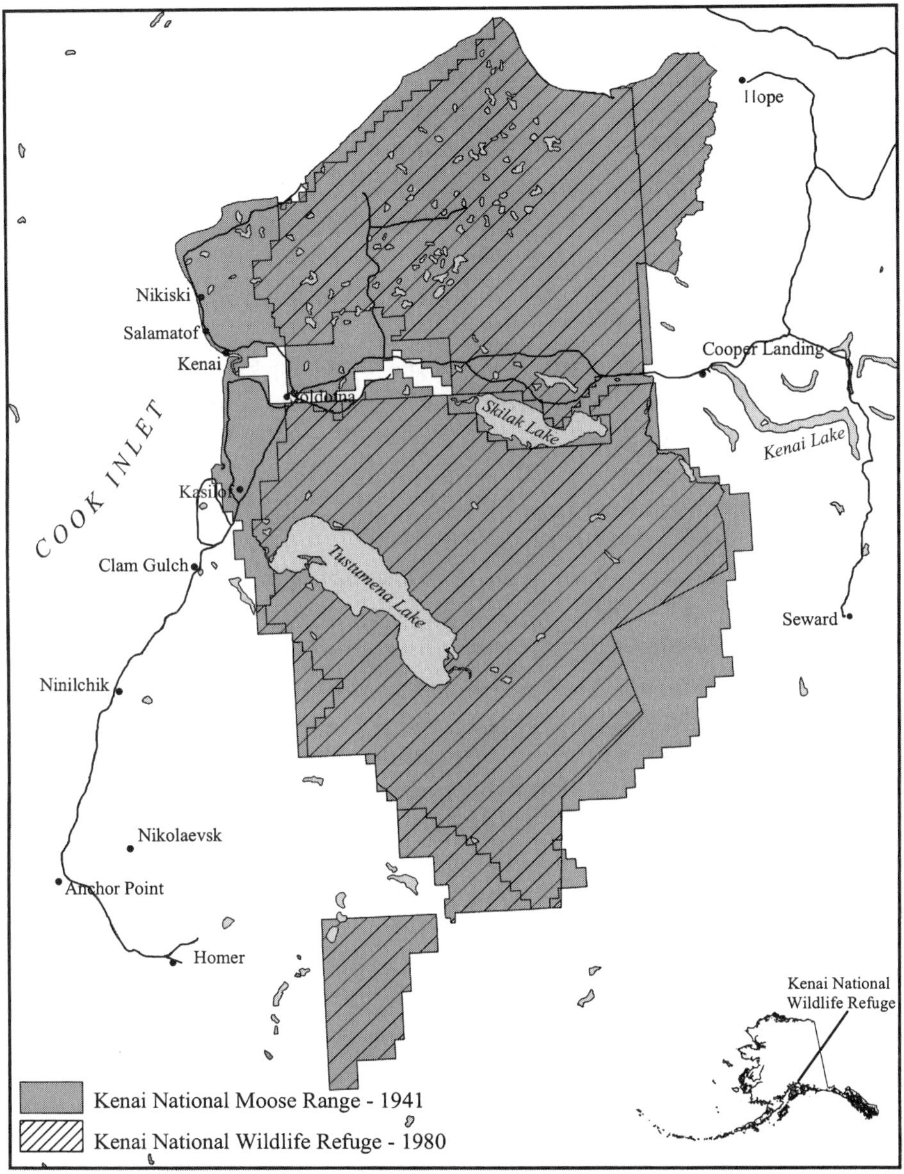

Kenai National Moose Range/Wildlife Refuge, 1941 and 1980. Courtesy Jason Geck

natural resources. Captain James Cook bade his men to survey the shores of his namesake inlet in 1778.[2] Russians hunted sea otters along its coasts and erected one of their first settlements, Fort Alexandrovsk at the southwest tip of the peninsula, in 1786. Others followed at the Kasilof and Kenai rivers in 1787 and 1791 and at Resurrection Bay and Hinchinbrook Island in 1793. Russians acquired land animal skins from Tanaina Indians on the peninsula. After 1867 the Alaska Commercial Company operated several fur trading stations on and near the peninsula.[3] Trapping ranked as an important industry during the territorial period. Salmon canneries operated at Homer, Seward, Seldovia, and other locations. Settlers engaged in commercial gardening and dairying, and tourist ships visited the port of Seward.[4] Compared with other parts of Alaska the Kenai possessed a more diverse economy and ecosystem.

CONFLICT OVER MINERALS

Minerals decisively affected events on the peninsula. Chugach Eskimos and Athabaskan Indians mined and fashioned implements from copper. Smelting iron from ore mined in the Kenai Mountains, Alexander Baranof's men built Alaska's first sailing vessel, the *Phoenix,* at Resurrection Bay in 1794. Russians conducted their only significant coal mining venture at English Bay where an open pit mine operated between 1855 and 1860. They burned the coal in their steamships and in shipyards at Sitka. They lost money in 1857 on their sole attempt to sell coal in California.[5] Americans briefly operated mines at Kachemak Bay beginning in 1889. Like the Russians, they could not find a viable coal market in San Francisco. Coal mining took place at several Kenai Peninsula locations during the territorial period; the coal fired steamships and heated canneries and homes.[6]

Gold added color to the Kenai story. Russians explored the peninsula, finding gold on the Kenai River in 1834 but not exploiting it. American prospectors discovered economically valuable deposits under beaches at Turnagain Arm about 1890 and at Bear and Palmer creeks in 1894. A resultant gold rush in 1896 immediately spawned boomtowns named Hope and Sunrise, whose heyday ended abruptly when word of the Klondike strike spread in 1897. Confidence man and criminal gang leader Jefferson Randolph "Soapy" Smith came to assess the prospects of the Kenai rush but decided not to stay. He went to Skagway in 1897 to win infamy as one of Alaska's most notorious criminals.

Prospecting activity in Cook Inlet gave rise to a supply route across the mountains from Resurrection Bay, where the town of Seward sprang up. Andy Simons, Alaska's most famous and first licensed guide, got his start freighting mail by dogsled over Moose Pass to the goldfields.[7] The Klondike Gold Rush magnified national interest in Alaska and spurred efforts to build a railroad into the interior. In their optimistic projections, economic boosters envisioned large-scale gold and other metal production, and exploitation of the Matanuska Valley coal deposits for locomotive fuel and agricultural and industrial development. Congress passed an enabling act in 1898, and investors built a railway from Seward 47 miles north to Moose Pass in 1903–1906.[8]

The Ballinger-Pinchot Affair

Alaska coal and railroad politics touched off one of North America's most celebrated conservation fights. The Morgan-Guggenheim Syndicate (or Alaska Syndicate), owner of Kennecott Copper as well as a controlling interest in Alaska's main steamship line and some of its fisheries, also owned a mine up the Copper River at Kennicott. Needing coal for its projected Copper River and Northwestern Railroad from Cordova to Chitina and for a planned extension into the Tanana Valley, it hoped to secure coal in Alaska. Coalfields of serviceable quality existed near the Bering River, but the syndicate had no direct legal access to them. A 1904 coal leasing law permitted individuals to file claims on 160-acre plots or to combine claims for joint ownership of up to 640 acres. The law forbade conspiracy to combine claims in advance of their "location," the first stage in processing a claim on federal land, but permitted it after "entry," a later stage.[9]

Theodore Roosevelt disliked both waste and monopoly control of natural resources. He sought coordinated and rational resource use through planning and management by the federal government to achieve sustained-yield production for the advancement of the nation. Resource giveaways and theft, the fruits of compliant laws and weak enforcement, did not fit into his notion of efficient scientific management. Congress responded to the appeals of interest groups seeking access to public lands and only partially and reluctantly accommodated the president. Although he considered conservation policy his most meaningful domestic achievement, Roosevelt had to conduct most of it through executive action.[10] To bring coal leasing into line with market values and prevent it from becoming monopolized, he withdrew nearly all Alaska coal lands from commercial activity in 1906.

One prospector, Seattle businessman Clarence Cunningham, set out to investigate the Bering River coalfields in 1902. He eventually staked out 33 contiguous 160-acre claims on behalf of a group of Seattle-area acquaintances. Whereas observers believed that nearly all of the approximately 900 Alaska coal claims had been filed by stand-ins for companies in contradiction to law, the Cunningham group had no such record. A General Land Office agent investigating the group's claims approved their elevation to entry status. While finalizing the claims in 1907, the group met Morgan-Guggenheim representatives and worked out an agreement to split profits and guarantee the syndicate an unlimited coal supply for 25 years. Morgan-Guggenheim would thereby gain dominant control over the Bering coalfields. A member of the Cunningham group, former Washington governor Miles Moore, went to see Land Office chief Richard Ballinger, who ordered the claims advanced to "clearlisting," a near-final stage of government approval.[11]

Ballinger, a former Seattle mayor known for integrity and devotion to public service, had been selected to reform the scandal-ridden General Land Office. This he proceeded to do before resigning to resume his law practice in March 1908.[12] Louis Glavis, a zealous young official in charge of the Seattle branch of the Land Office, suspected that his chief had improperly favored the Cunningham group. He obtained a copy of Cunningham's journal indicating that the latter's group had agreed prior to the crucial date of location to combine and sell their claims. The journal demonstrated violation of the law but no collusion with the syndicate. Recently resigned and unaware of the journal discovery, Ballinger met Cunningham group members and assisted them in processing the claims.[13]

When William Howard Taft assumed the presidency in 1909, he appointed Ballinger secretary of the interior. Prominent men interested in forwarding the Cunningham claims visited Ballinger and requested action. Disdainful of that form of influence and uncertain of the validity of the claims, Ballinger passed the men off to his assistants. Glavis met one of the assistants, told his story of the journal, and asked for an investigation of the claimants. Ballinger ordered the investigation suspended pending an attorney general's opinion. As soon as Glavis and another agent had drafted a letter of evidence for the attorney general as directed, the Interior Department decided to rely instead on the opinion of its own legal department. Its ensuing opinion upheld the coal claimants. Glavis then took it upon himself to send the evidence to the attorney general, who overruled the Interior Department's decision. Convinced of undue favoritism in Interior, Glavis went to former secretary of the interior James Garfield and his fellow conservationist and chief forester Gifford Pinchot. Adding other conservation issues, Pinchot wrote a letter of complaint to Taft. After investigating the matter, Taft upheld Ballinger.[14]

Pinchot had also arranged for Glavis to personally present his case to President Taft. The meeting took place in late summer 1909. Taft took the position that Ballinger had not known the details of the Alaska coal claims in question; therefore Glavis had been inappropriately aggressive in questioning Ballinger's actions. Ballinger received Taft's approval to dismiss Glavis, and, shortly thereafter, Glavis lost his job. Now more certain than ever of wrongdoing and a cover-up, Glavis wrote a lengthy and hard-hitting article for the muckraking magazine *Collier's Weekly*. He insisted that Ballinger had indeed been aware of the details of the Cunningham leases because he had been fully informed by Glavis and another officer. Moreover, by representing the leaseholders after leaving office, Ballinger appeared to be violating a conflict-of-interest law that prohibited such action for two years. Glavis detailed a list of instances in which Ballinger or others in the Interior Department acted as if determined to validate the coal leases. Believing the department would soon transfer 100,000 acres of valuable coal lands to private parties who in at least some cases had made fraudulent claims, Glavis asserted that he had no choice but to bring the case before the public.[15]

On his last day in office, Roosevelt had ordered an addition to the Chugach National Forest that took in four of the Cunningham claim sites, incidentally creating a basis for Forest Service involvement. Chief Forester Pinchot, the principal architect of Roosevelt's utilitarian conservation policy, hoped to keep that policy alive under the new Taft administration. His bureaucratic rival Ballinger had now been appointed secretary of the interior. Ballinger and Taft, while anti-monopoly Progressives, espoused a form of conservation emphasizing market-value sale of resources to private interests rather than ownership and leasing by the federal government. The new policy, the loss of Roosevelt's direct involvement, and the upsurge of special interest activity threatened Pinchot's conservation principles. In the Alaska coal claims case he found a means of reviving his plan: coupling an attack on his opponents in government to an appeal to the public's anti-monopoly sentiments. He proceeded to nurture the impression that Ballinger personified the influence of the Morgan-Guggenheim Syndicate in government.[16]

Pinchot launched a public attack on Ballinger's policies, and the press picked up Glavis's story of the Alaska coal claims. Ballinger, believing in the integrity of his position and backed by Taft, proved no match for the combative Pinchot. Taft lost faith in Pinchot and fired him, adding fuel to the flames.[17] A congressional investigation of extraordinary length—45 sessions—ensued between January and March 1910. Glavis attorney Louis Brandeis proved that the Taft document exonerating Ballinger had been backdated, a severe embarrassment to Taft. In a partisan vote the committee upheld Ballinger, but Glavis and Pinchot had won in the eyes of the public.[18] Soon after the sick and weary Ballinger resigned in 1911, the Land Office cancelled the Cunningham claims. The coal deposits turned out to be far less valuable than imagined by participants on either side of the debate.

The Alaska scandal left lasting marks on American politics. Magazines and newspapers painted it as a triumph of the public interest in affirming Rooseveltian conservation and rejecting Taft's approach. Roosevelt hoped to revive his policy and his presidency through the Bull Moose Party. He had intended the party name to symbolize his brand of conservation in Alaska, suggesting that Taft favored monopoly capitalists. His campaign split the Republicans and ensured the victory of Woodrow Wilson. Louis Brandeis won fame that carried him to the Supreme Court.[19]

In Alaska, most magazine editors and business leaders assessed Pinchot's brand of conservation as a barrier to economic progress. They believed Ballinger was sincerely interested in the welfare of Alaska, and Clarence Cunningham

Construction train of Alaska Central Railroad, north of Seward, June 1905. Alaska files 11704, University of Washington Archives. The railroad project failed, but its publicly funded successor opened interior Alaska to land travel. Hunting to feed railroad crews put pressure on Kenai Peninsula wildlife stocks.

epitomized the individual entrepreneur frustrated by federal regulations. Some Alaskans adopted Pinchot's argument, portraying J.P. Morgan and the Guggenheims as a threat to Alaskan autonomy and individual enterprise.[20] They linked Taft to the syndicate, suggesting that his proposal for governance of Alaska by an appointed commission amounted to giving the syndicate access to Alaska coal. Taft relented in 1911 and signed a bill creating the Alaska territorial government in 1912.[21]

Alaska Railroads

Notwithstanding the post-1902 gold rush to Fairbanks and some successful agricultural activity in the Matanuska Valley, the planned Seward-Fairbanks railway went bankrupt after being extended to the 72-mile point on Turnagain Arm in 1910. Several factors contributed to the railway's demise: mismanagement, tight investment money, Roosevelt's coal withdrawal, and resistance by the Morgan-Guggenheim Syndicate to a route that might rival their Copper River line.

Believers in Alaskan development redoubled their efforts for a government-financed route to the interior. Taft, a sympathizer, asked Congress in 1912 to authorize an Alaska railroad, something the federal government had not done for other territories or states. A commission sent to the territory carried out a hasty survey and recommended in January 1913 that two routes be constructed to the interior: (1) extension of the Copper River route from Chitina to Fairbanks and a spur to the Bering coalfields, and (2) continuation of the Seward line across the Alaska Range to the Innoko-Iditarod gold mining district and a spur extending to the Matanuska coalfields. President Woodrow Wilson took office in March and shared the enthusiasm for a government-owned-and-operated railroad to catalyze Alaskan economic growth. Pushing aside skeptical questions about economical viability, both houses of Congress voted overwhelmingly in 1914 to give Wilson power to build a railroad from a port site to the interior and to use equipment from the Panama Canal project. Alaska delegate James Wickersham had struck a responsive chord in his call to "do something for Alaska" and in his argument that government involvement would end the syndicate's monopoly plans. Some Alaska boosters promulgated the thesis that Matanuska coal would benefit the Pacific naval fleet, a claim rendered dubious by the shift to oil, among other conditions.[22]

Alaskan boosters wanted both of the railroads and full access to the coal lands. Coal-fueled railroads would open up the interior to mining of gold, copper, and other metals, the presumed key to Alaska's economic progress. The coal would also heat homes and other enterprises, and the railroads would connect to agricultural lands. Boosters interpreted the federal reservation of coal lands as an unconscionable denial of their rights. They received part of what they wished for in October 1914 when Congress made available for leasing nearly all Alaska coal lands. To prevent monopolization, the law limited leases to 2,560 acres. Coal deposits could be exploited but not owned by private parties, and modest per-acre and per-ton fees would be due the federal government, provisions the boosters considered unfair.[23]

A study team fielded by Wilson recommended a single railroad route, from Seward to Fairbanks. They probably sensed the political unwisdom of choosing the Copper River option that would link the administration to the syndicate. Moreover, the westerly route could make connections to Matanuska coal and agriculture, and Ship Creek (later Anchorage) afforded a good main construction site. Wilson rendered his decision in April 1915 for a Seward to Fairbanks route. He rejected or ignored Portage Bay as a port site. It would have shortened the railroad by 64 miles, and a spur eventually ran to it.

Soon after completion of the railroad President Warren Harding rode the train from Seward, making speeches along the way. He drove the golden spike at North Nenana on July 15, 1923. Like Taft and Wilson, he believed in an active federal role in Alaska development and in resistance to monopoly control. Harding articulated these themes in his last major speech at Seattle on the return trip from Alaska. Dead of a heart attack in San Francisco on August 2, he did not live to see the flowering of the Teapot Dome scandal or its echo on the Kenai Peninsula three decades later.[24]

Notwithstanding the booster rhetoric of Wickersham and others, the Alaska Railroad failed to either pay for itself or create a rush of economic activity in the interior. It cost $56 million to build, far more than the $35 million estimated. By 1930 it had lost $8 million in operation. Senate investigators readily identified the shortcomings. Salmon fishing, the main industry, occurred along the coast and did not need the railroad. Neither did the fur industry nor, for the most part, gold mining. Not enough agricultural production existed to make use of the railroad; indeed, food from the States came in by railroad and undercut local prices, reducing the number of commercial farms. Settler population did not significantly increase along the route.[25] Only World War II and the oil era would bring about economic development in the interior.

GAME MAMMALS

Besieged by fortune seekers, limited in size, and in geographical terms relatively separate from the interior mainland, the Kenai Peninsula incurred heavy ecological damage. Forest fires proliferated, converting spruce stands to deciduous forest. Agricultural scientist Hugh Bennett's 1916 report stated that "most of the forest fires are started by homesteaders, timbermen, railroad constructors, prospectors, and hunters, generally through carelessness and without thought of the seriousness of the destruction done."[26] Fires generated side effects of increased moose browse and removal of the lichens preferred by caribou. Commercial hunters slaughtered both moose and caribou for their antlers. Meanwhile, the mammals' natural predator, the wolf, neared eradication by trappers setting out poison. Biologist Wilfred Osgood recorded in 1900 that "wolves are considered common in the Cook Inlet region. Mr. [George] Coon, of Hope told me that during the winter of 1899 he secured fourteen with poison. Among these were six in the black phase."[27] By 1915 trappers had exhausted populations of small furbearers on the peninsula and exterminated the wolves. Few commentators appeared concerned about the wolf, regarded as a competitor for fur and game.

Mammals on the Kenai, once depleted, took long to recover. The human population had relatively easy access to them, and the restricted and ruggedly mountainous connection to the interior inhibited migration. Caribou, described in an 1890 report as abundant, began to disappear soon after the turn of the century. Andrew Stone reported in 1900 that they "are already scarce on

English hunter Col. Claude Cane and trophies, Kenai Peninsula, 1902. In Claude Cane, Summer and Fall in Western Alaska, *London: Horace Cox, 1903, frontispiece. A relatively accessible source of big game, the Kenai attracted some of the earliest sport hunters.*

the Kenai Peninsula, and will doubtless soon be exterminated, the region being greatly frequented by visiting sportsmen, while native hunters kill moose and caribou for their heads, disposing of them at good prices for shipment to San Francisco."[28] Claude Cane noticed the scarcity of caribou in 1902 and mentioned hearing of several mass killings, one by a sport hunter who gunned down all thirteen of a band of caribou he encountered.[29] Regulations based on the 1902 game law banned the hunting of caribou after 1904.[30] Forest fires removed lichens, almost certainly hastening the demise of the Kenai caribou. A last officially confirmed sighting, of a lone bull south of Skilak Lake, entered the records in 1910.[31] No caribou and virtually no wolves existed on the peninsula for more than half a century.

Meat hunting also changed natural balances on the Kenai. Sport hunter E. Marshall Scull described the pattern of moose exploitation:

> Driven out of the southwestern end of the Peninsula by hunters issuing from Homer and Seldovia to supply the canneries there; forced to retreat from Kenai and Hope on the west and north, the moose had withdrawn near to the mountains. . . . Many hundreds were killed yearly by the Indians, the guides and the professional meat hunters, and the continued persecution had herded the remainder together into a comparatively small piece of country [near Skilak and Tustumena lakes].[32]

Special Game Warden L.F. Shaw related in 1915 that Hope and Sunrise at the north end of the peninsula

> depended for a meat supply almost wholly on the moose and mountain sheep, and there was a wanton and wasteful killing of these valuable food animals. Indeed, some of the old-timers made it their boast that they killed a moose merely for what they considered the choice part—the tongue—leaving the carcass to go to waste. The beginning of construction on the Alaska Central Railway in 1903, and continuing on until 1906, on which hundreds of men were employed during the greater part of the time, raised havoc with the moose and mountain sheep. Hunters were engaged at all times to keep the various camps along the line of work supplied with moose and sheep meat, it being cheaper than domestic meats shipped from the States.[33]

Entrepreneurs also shipped meat to the mining towns of Valdez and Cordova.[34] The 1908 Alaska game law curbed some of the practice, as did a 1912 regulation prohibiting the sale of moosemeat outside the Kenai Peninsula and a 1916 regulation banning sale on the peninsula.[35]

Illegal killing and sales persisted during the 1915–1923 construction of the Alaska Railroad. Mountain goats on the Kenai suffered relatively little because of their steep terrain and the fact that people did not prefer their meat. Sheep, estimated at 2,000 in 1916, had been severely diminished, particularly in the northern sector closest to the railroad. Officials thought moose numbered about 5,000. Sport hunters rated them the world's largest, but relatively few hunters journeyed to Alaska prior to World War II.[36]

Market hunting posed a threat to moose in the late 1910s and early 1920s. A twenty-year Kenai resident charged that, after the deletion of the warden post at Kenai,

> our Anchorage warden is a clerk in a haberdashery, and he has not been off the railroad since he was appointed. Our restaurants are serving moose and other wild game meat, both in and out of season. One can find moosemeat at almost all times at the road houses, tie camps, and restaurants in and around Anchorage, Seward, and Seldovia. It is the hind quarters of moose which have been brought in by the market hunters, by natives and whites, and sold for whatever they will bring. In most instances the fore quarters have been left in the woods.
>
> Kenai has a population of some 300 people, whites and natives, and that many more dogs. They all live on moosemeat. The government teacher there told me that the people there kill about 450 moose every year of which 90 percent are cows.

Bulls had remained inland on higher ground, whereas cows moved to lower elevations to bear and raise their calves. The resident estimated that hunting along the Alaska Railroad had driven moose 25 miles back, restricting their

Moose at Kenai River, 1920s. Romig coll. 90-043-835, University of Alaska Fairbanks, Alaska and Polar Regions Archives. Fires and the absence of wolves caused the moose to multiply.

range. Moreover, rabbits had caused starvation among moose calves by eating low-growing vegetation during a hard winter. The resident called for funding to cut birch trees to feed moose in winter and to better enforce the game laws.[37] Such complaints aided passage of the 1925 Game Law, which effectively proscribed commercial meat hunting and alleviated pressure on ungulates on the Kenai. However, it worked a disproportionate hardship on Natives, who did most of the hunting.

Moose continued to be seen as the peninsula's most important wildlife species. Given the advantages of abundant feed and the absence of wolves, the moose increased until the mid-1920s.[38] During rutting season they gathered in large herds, and a sport hunter could look over several hundred bulls within a few days to choose a trophy.[39] The moose herd receded slowly in the 1930s and sharply in the early 1940s. Leading causes appeared to be predation by black bears and scarcity of browse as the forests recovered from the fires of the Gold Rush era. A 290,000-acre fire in 1947 helped moose recover.[40]

Concern over excessive taking of Kenai mammals gave rise to proposals for a wildlife preserve. William Langille, the first Alaska director for the Forest Service, so recommended in 1903. The Alaska Game Commission and the Bureau of Biological Survey made similar requests in 1931 and 1932. Governor George Parks and others disparaged the idea as an impediment to mining and homesteading. Fish and Wildlife Service chief Ira Gabrielson secured a presidential

Henry Lucas, Frank Dufresne, and Lawrence J. Palmer near Killey and Funny rivers, Kenai Peninsula, 1938. FWS 6994, Alaska Resources Library and Information Services. Palmer, an expert on vegetation, conducted research on caribou, reindeer, moose, and muskoxen.

executive order in 1941 creating a Kenai National Moose Range. Gabrielson later resisted efforts to settle European refugees on the Kenai Moose Range or to use it as a military bombing range. The executive order declared the Kenai Moose Range "for the purpose of protecting the natural breeding and feeding range of the giant Kenai moose on the Kenai Peninsula, Alaska, which in this area presents a unique wildlife feature and an unusual opportunity for the study in its natural environment of the practical management of a big game species."[41] Characteristic of pre-ecological thinking, it made no mention of wolves to help balance the moose population or of caribou to complete the ecosystem. Such concerns awaited the statehood period. A different Kenai question occupied the attention of conservationists in the 1950s: wildlife versus oil.

THE OIL ERA

Kenai oil made its presence known to visitors on the lands bordering Cook Inlet, where Russians noticed oil seeps by 1853. Oil prospectors staked claims on the west shore in the 1890s and drilled two wells, pumping small quantities of oil in 1902.[42] At Katalla near Cordova southeast of the Kenai, according to legend, Tom White fell into an oil seep while bear hunting in 1896. He set fire to it and watched it burn for a week, then tried to interest companies in drilling. A British consortium investigated and made Alaska's first commercially viable strike in 1902. Chilkat Oil Company and others drilled 36 holes, and Chilkat built a small refinery in 1911. The field produced modestly until the refinery burned in 1934, terminating the venture.[43]

Taft withdrew Alaska oil lands from public access in 1910. After the reopening in 1920, prospectors showed minimal interest in the Kenai until about 1950. Then, little more than a decade after the executive order creating it, the Kenai National Moose Range figured in two of the most profound changes in Alaskan history: the creation of the 49th U.S. state and the domination of Alaska by the oil industry. David Postman, an investigative reporter for the *Anchorage Daily News*, traced the Kenai oil story from Washington to Anchorage, where a group of local businessmen succeeded in helping an oil company gain a commanding position in Alaskan oil production. In the process, group members enriched themselves and moved Alaska toward statehood.

The Kenai Oil Strike

Oil politics soared to new heights during the Eisenhower years; oil companies heavily financed Ike's 1952 and 1956 campaigns. His western political operator and 1952 fund-raiser, Charles Stone Jones, presided over Richfield Oil Company. W. Alton "Pete" Jones (unrelated), chief of Cities Service Company, which owned 30 percent of Richfield, succeeded him in 1956. Both Joneses belonged to the group of businessmen who persuaded Eisenhower to run for president as a Republican. Soon after the 1952 election, Pete Jones led three oilmen in building a farm for the Eisenhowers at Gettysburg, supplying horses and cattle, paying its operating expenses, and renovating a nearby building as a home for the president's son John and his family. Eisenhower counted the Joneses as friends and treated the oil companies as allies throughout his two terms.[44] His first Interior secretary, Douglas McKay, demonstrated inordinate devotion to oil company preferences and successfully promoted a law granting ownership of offshore oil to the states, a measure that made the oil more available to the companies.[45]

In August 1953 Secretary McKay unexpectedly banned all oil exploration and leasing in wildlife refuges pending a study of their effects on wildlife, a conservation concern he had not previously evidenced. Of several companies exploring in the Kenai Moose Range, all except one abandoned it.[46] Richfield remained and, in late 1954, filed lease applications for 71,000 acres on the range. Locke Jacobs, leasing agent for fourteen Anchorage businessmen, noticed that some of Richfield's leases had been topfiled (claimed by a later party) on those held by his group. Representing the businessmen, Wilbur Wester, manager of the Westward Hotel, visited Richfield headquarters in Los Angeles in January 1955. He proposed that in exchange for the leases Richfield agree to drill a well "somewhere in Alaska" during the next two years. The parties worked out a deal by which Richfield would purchase the leases, drill a well, and pay the group a 5 percent royalty if oil should be produced from the lands. At the same time, Jacobs filed for 52,000 more acres next to the Richfield leases. Later in 1955 Richfield paid the group for all the leases and guaranteed them 5 percent of royalties.[47]

The Anchorage businessmen comprised an elite segment of the Elks Club informally known to some as the "Spit and Argue Club." Two of the most prominent men in Alaska belonged to the group: Robert Atwood, editor and publisher of the *Anchorage Daily Times,* and Elmer Rasmuson, president of the National Bank of Alaska and a brother-in-law whose father had lent Atwood the money to purchase his newspaper. Atwood and Rasmuson recognized oil development as a way to achieve statehood, and they stood to gain financially on the oil deal. As described by Alaska oilman Jack Roderick, "What Atwood, Wester, and other members of the leasing group were trying to accomplish was to gradually convert Anchorage, Alaska into Tulsa, Oklahoma."[48]

Bureau of Land Management officials in Anchorage held the power to dispense leases for oil drilling. Two of them, Chester McNally and Virgil Seiser, issued leases to members of the Spit and Argue Club for lands just outside the boundary of the moose range. According to Postman, McNally and Seiser denied access to persons not connected to Richfield Oil Company. The Interior Department launched an internal investigation in the wake of allegations of bribery of McNally and blatant favoritism by Seiser. Fearing another Teapot Dome scandal involving leases in Louisiana as well as Alaska, Interior officials quietly transferred McNally and Seiser and declared that no corruption existed. Officials destroyed the records of the investigation.[49]

Alaska's territorial delegate to Congress and later senator E.L. "Bob" Bartlett firmly and consistently defended the oil companies, particularly Richfield. He and Spit and Argue Club representative Wilbur Wester marshaled Alaskan support for the submerged lands oil leasing bill. Bartlett pushed for lifting of the wildlife refuge oil drilling ban and for other measures favoring Richfield and its Anchorage allies.[50] The House Committee on Merchant Marine and Fisheries held hearings in 1956 and considered legislation to require congressional consent for all drilling in wildlife refuges. It reported no bills.[51] Bartlett and former governor and nonvoting Senate delegate Ernest Gruening had presented forceful testimony in favor of drilling in the moose range. Committee chairman Herbert Bonner (D-NC) stated that he had no objection to Richfield's going ahead at Swanson River. Fish and Wildlife Service director John Farley and the U.S. Geological Survey also gave Richfield their approval.[52]

Under fire from critics charging excessive subservience to the oil companies, Secretary McKay had resigned in May 1956. Fred Seaton, a former newsman and personal friend to Atwood of the *Anchorage Daily Times* and C.W. Snedden of the *Fairbanks Daily News-Miner*, succeeded McKay. At Snedden's suggestion Seaton chose Alaskan lawyer Ted Stevens as his congressional lobbyist. Within three months after taking office, Seaton approved 72,000 acres of noncompetitive lease applications by Richfield and the Anchorage businessmen for land in the northern part of the Kenai Moose Range. Richfield proceeded to drill and on July 19, 1957, at Swanson River, made the first commercially significant oil strike in Alaska.

A boom atmosphere followed on the heels of the Richfield discovery. Seaton banned further leasing and drilling pending drafting of regulations to apply to all wildlife refuges. A heated debate ensued, focusing on the Kenai National Moose Range. Fish and Wildlife Service regional director Clarence Rhode quietly disapproved of drilling on the refuge, while higher officials endorsed it. The National Wildlife Federation stood against further drilling, as did Ira Gabrielson's Wildlife Management Institute. One conservation organization, the Isaac Walton League, favored oil in the moose range. In a 1957 position paper it reversed its stance of a year earlier. The paper described the roads built through wild areas as a positive influence: "Driving over the oil-well road, one cannot help being impressed by the many beautiful lakes and recreation areas which the new road had made accessible to the ordinary sportsman—the man who cannot afford to charter a plane for his fishing or hunting trips." The moose seemed to "enjoy browsing on the newly felled trees." Switching to a soon-to-become-familiar political theme, the paper added, "Oil from Alaska could be the savior of Western civilization if the Soviet influence on the other side of the world continues to grow." Burton Atwood, national secretary of the league and brother of Robert Atwood, authored the paper.[53]

Shortly after Burton Atwood's visit in August–September 1957, the Anchorage Chamber of Commerce issued a statement on the drilling issue. It argued that oil wells and roads would likely occupy a total of about 699 acres, or "the permanent use of a land area equal to that now allocated for slightly more than one moose (a pregnant cow, perhaps). There are now 4,000 moose in the 2,000,000 acre range which allows 500 acres for each moose." The removal of large trees would spur new growth and "relieve the Fish and Wildlife Service of the present practice of sending crews of men onto the forest to cut down trees to provide moose forage. The oil companies would, free of government cost, maintain and improve the moose range." The statement strongly emphasized the strategic value of a nearby source of fuel for military bases in Alaska. The oil would boost the national economy and "strengthen the position of the United States at a time when the major sources of oil for the Western World are in

Moose in browse cut, Kenai National Moose Range, 1955. Courtesy Alaska Resources Library and Information Services. When post-burn deciduous trees matured, moose starved and refuge managers cut trees for feed.

jeopardy in the Middle East." Appendixes to the chamber's statement included Atwood's paper and a letter from the Anchorage Sportsmen's Association, self-described as "the largest group of sportsmen in the Territory of Alaska," approving of oil drilling in the moose range.[54]

Protection of the natural integrity of the moose range may have been the first priority of Gabrielson, Rhode, and others, but it stood little chance in the atmosphere of the late 1950s. In 1941, when even utilitarian conservation met opposition from Alaskan economic developers, the moose range had to be justified as a moose supply and hunting ground. The Fish and Wildlife Service managed it largely to maximize moose. The absence of wolves and lack of knowledge of bear-moose predation kept predator control out of the Kenai. As forest fires came and went, the quality of moose browse rose and fell. In times when the trees grew too high, the service cut down deciduous species so moose could feed on the tops. Oil advocates cited this practice, and the notion of moose supply as the main purpose of the refuge, to present their own cutting as a benefit. Even a semiurbanized area might not reduce the moose total. Whereas wildlife advocates opposed roads through the woods to lakes as destruction of wilderness integrity, oil companies depicted them as improved access for the average person. Adding national security and national economic benefit to their arguments, oil advocates held a winning hand.

The Interior Department conducted a November 1957 hearing on proposed regulations permitting restricted drilling on the Kenai Moose Range. A.W. "Bud" Boddy registered the support of the Alaska Sportsmen's Council for the plan. All oil company representatives rejected any limits. Ernest Gruening went further, calling for abolition of the range and the Chugach National Forest as well.[55] Gruening wanted to establish himself as the Father of Alaska Statehood. Despite his progressive record as a Democrat and editor of *The Nation*, Gruening turned to the oil companies as allies for the statehood effort and as a source of funding for his future Senate campaign. Moreover, his close friend and a Republican, Robert Atwood, strongly backed Gruening's political ambitions, and vice versa. Describing himself as a "conservationist," Gruening loudly advocated drilling in the moose range.[56] He attacked the Interior Department and conservation organizations as obstacles to statehood and quoted Burton Atwood's paper as evidence that the moose would not be harmed.[57]

Federal officials in late 1957 pondered the question of whether to open the moose range to oil development and, if so, whether leases should be granted on a competitive or on a first-come, first-served basis. Richfield and the Spit and Argue Club had lease applications pending on 100,000 acres; they already held 72,000 acres of approved leases where they had found oil. A rival group of Anchorage businessmen, headed by developer Walter Hickel and First National Bank of Anchorage president Dan Cuddy, challenged first-come leasing, which would give further advantages to Richfield and its allies. Unable to work out a deal, the two groups agreed to prevent an exposé from appearing in the newspapers.[58] Ted Stevens warned Seaton that rumors of favoritism in the leases approved in 1956 could create a scandal. Bob Bishop, an aide to the worried and cautious Seaton, recalled, "We were watching the tracks of the noose, not the moose." Seaton issued orders in January 1958 to prohibit all oil drilling in wildlife refuges except those in Alaska and left the decision of where to drill up to the Fish and Wildlife Service. Overriding the reluctance of its Alaskan officials, the service recommended that half the moose range be opened. Congress raised the annual Alaska leasing fee from 25 to 50 cents per acre to make it comparable to the Lower 48 but took no action on noncompetitive leasing.[59]

Oil companies began to subscribe to statehood for Alaska in the mid-1950s, anticipating greater influence in the new state than in the federal government. Their Alaskan sympathizers worked against higher state royalties for oil extraction, even though the money could help make the new state economically viable. The companies may have hoped to purchase public lands, a prospect that never materialized. W.C. Arnold, veteran lobbyist for the Seattle-based salmon canneries and previously the most active adversary of statehood, softened his position. He had purchased oil leases for himself after privately meeting with members of the Spit and Argue Club. He joined in their demands for opening of the moose range. The statehood bill passed in June 1958, and oil politics may have furthered the statehood effort.[60]

Federal regulations required competitive bids for leases on government land where oil had been found. Nevertheless, the Interior Department commenced noncompetitive leasing in its Anchorage Bureau of Land Management office in August 1958. It honored the 100,000 acres of Richfield–Spit and Argue lease applications filed in 1954 during the leasing ban and accepted them in priority to those of other applicants waiting first in line at the office. Several of the losing applicants took their case to the federal courts. They lost at the District Court level, won at the Appeals level, and lost in the Supreme Court, which ruled that the interior secretary had a right to ignore his own orders.[61] The Richfield group had won an essential monopoly on the most valuable known oilfield in Alaska.

The Kenai During Statehood

Robert Atwood continued employing his newspaper to stoutly promote industrialization and the oil industry in particular. He and others had contested the right of the interior secretary to close any of the Kenai Moose Range to drilling. They lost in the Court of Appeals in 1956 and chose not to appeal to the Supreme Court. Atwood and the thirteen other Spit and Argue Club members ultimately received about $3 million each from the Kenai leases. Gruening won election to the Senate in 1958 and carried on the demand for nullification of the moose range, succeeding in having it reduced by 270,000 acres in 1964. Oil, gas, logging, and other commercial operations proceeded in the northern half of the remainder.[62] In 1965 the legislature passed a resolution calling for discontinuation of the moose range as a game reserve, arguing that it should be used for agriculture. It made no mention of oil.[63] Through the Alaska National Interest Lands Conservation Act, in 1980 the moose range became the 2-million-acre Kenai National Wildlife Refuge, nearly 70 percent designated the Andrew Simons Wilderness Unit. A new Kenai Fjords National Park encompassed 567,000 acres of the central east coast of the peninsula.[64]

Alaskans also sent to the Senate Bob Bartlett, succeeded after his death in 1968 by Ted Stevens, a consistent and powerful opponent of environmental protection. All three senators maintained ties to the oil companies. Richfield (later Arco) went on to make the historic 1967 find at Prudhoe Bay that changed Alaska more than any other event.

Arco discovery well, Swanson River field, Kenai National Moose Range, late 1950s. B87.43.2, Anchorage Museum of History and Art. This well triggered an oil boom that helped bring statehood and economic development to Alaska. It and more than 100 others, plus 1,500 miles of roads and trails, disrupted the ecology of the refuge.

Kenai wildlife realized some gains in spite of the oil extraction in the moose range. Between 1915 and 1960 only a single proven sighting of a wolf occurred on the Kenai. As wolves rebounded from the intensive control efforts of the 1950s, they began to reclaim their territory. The presence of an individual wolf inspired protective measures by the state in 1962. A pair appeared in 1967, and then a large pack arrived in 1968, multiplied, and reestablished the species on the Kenai.[65]

Successful transplant efforts in the 1960s and 1980s returned small caribou herds to the peninsula. But the once-pristine Moose Range had been altered. Fish and Wildlife Service refuges director J.C. Saylor II described it in an internal memo:

> From the air, the area of oil development looks like a site of a major military conflict with cat trails running everywhere, frequent large gravel pits, untreated spoil banks, and sludge pits. . . . Every 80 acres of land has a road on

Kenai National Moose Range supervisor David L. Spencer checking trumpeter swan nest, May 1957. By H.J. Johnson. Alaska Game Commission, 18th Annual Report, July 1, 1956 Thru June 30, 1957. *Protection of nests in Alaska aided recovery of the endangered swan species.*

> it and in most instances it is surrounded by roads on all four sides. Pipelines and power lines radiate to all points of the compass. School buses, kids, cats and dogs abound as in any stateside community. The new oil workers have all turned into moose hunters and the moose population has dropped from 4,736 in 1959 to 2,719 in 1961. It is all one hell of a mess.[66]

About 1,500 miles of bulldozed trails could be seen by 1968, and a gas pipeline crossed the range on its way to Anchorage. By 1980, 115 oil and gas wells had been drilled on the Kenai and in adjacent Cook Inlet.[67] Contamination of the earth and groundwater by toxic chemicals constituted a problem for decades after statehood. Trees cut down for seismic lines incubated beetles and may have aggravated an insect explosion, killing thousands of acres of trees. A 1985 Fish and Wildlife Service assessment stated that "populations of bald eagles, trumpeter swans, mountain goats, Dall sheep, caribou, marten, wolves, lynx, brown bear and beaver have been or are now depressed due to human activities."[68] Dave Spencer, Kenai Moose Range supervisor during the 1950s, summarized the results of oil on the Kenai: "I know there have been a lot of benefits from the oil. But no benefits have accrued to the moose, or the Wildlife Refuge."[69]

Another wildlife success story emerged from the Kenai episode. It involved the trumpeter swan, the largest bird native to North America and a nearly extinct species. Most trumpeters migrated to Alaska to build their nests and raise their young. Some nested on Kenai ponds, and wildlife managers worried about the effects of oil activity. Oil drilling regulations prohibited disturbance of nesting ponds.[70] Within three decades, thanks to the efforts of environmentalists and the Fish and Wildlife Service, the trumpeter population rebounded dramatically.

In terms of wildlife goals and management objectives, the Kenai experience exemplified the shift from untrammeled exploitation to selected species (moose) protection by government experts for sustainable use by humans. Distance from Washington and aggressive frontier behavior forestalled decisive action to sustain Kenai mammals and habitat until the 1925 Game Law and the inception of the moose range in 1941. The naming of the moose range moved the goal closer to ecosystem preservation, although government officials presented it as a moose preserve (open to hunting) and avoided mention of the desirability of reintroducing wolves and caribou. Appreciation of the ecological role of the wolf finally became policy under the new state in 1962. Reappearance of wolves and reintroduction of caribou did much to restore the peninsula's natural character.

Maintenance of the moose range in the face of demands for oil drilling proved more difficult by orders of magnitude than had its creation. As in the case of Bering River coal politics, elements of the federal government fought a seesaw battle for prevalence. In the Progressive Era government could claim enough public support to curb the powerful coal interests. The 1950s, by contrast, featured oil companies, a compliant Eisenhower administration, and a conservative public mood. Moreover, Alaskan business interests had acquired the ability to mold the decision-making process. Both government and corporate responsibility for environmental protection bowed to oil profits. The rush for economic spoils swept aside the meager store of science indicating industrial effects on wildlife. Conservation groups participated modestly, helping to save some of the ecological integrity of the Kenai Moose Range.

From statehood into the 21st Century, a host of disruptive influences beset the wildlife refuge and other natural areas of the Kenai Peninsula: oil and gas operations, swelling tourism, and a perpetually rising resident human population. Their multifarious negative impacts on the wild character of the Kenai energized an ongoing debate over the relative values of wilderness and development in Alaska.

17

Bob Marshall, Olaus and Margaret Murie, and the Arctic Refuge

As Alaska statehood approached, ecological science and evolving public sentiment made possible a more direct appeal for ecosystem preservation. A confluence of events focused attention on a remote corner of the territory to become the Arctic National Wildlife Range. Relatively unspoiled and rich in wildlife, the land had not yet demonstrated industrial potential. Just as important, the campaign to save the land depended heavily on the talents of three uniquely qualified conservationists: Bob Marshall and Olaus and Margaret Murie.

Ongoing losses of wildlife and wildlands gradually tipped the balance of American public values from aggressive exploitation toward preservation of some elements of Nature. Motives varied; some wanted to conserve water, soil, and timber, as in the Adirondacks; some to protect favored species of wildlife, as in the brown bear reserves; others to secure recreation sites, as in most national parks. A few in the 1930s, led by Aldo Leopold, began to acquire an ecological perspective on wildlands, seeing them as integrated complexes of life valuable both in themselves and for the well-being of human communities. Leopold and his colleagues launched a wilderness movement to safeguard large tracts of wildlands. Several of the leaders had strong ties to Alaska, although, compared to the Boone and Crockett founders, they lacked high standing in Washington. Marshall and the Muries knew northern Alaska and envisioned preservation on a regional scale. Their efforts eventually paid off in protective legislation for much of the North, including the Arctic National Wildlife Range.

BOB MARSHALL, WILDERNESS ADVOCATE

John Muir's view of Nature came alive in large measure during the 1930s through another prominent figure in Alaska's environmental history. Robert Marshall (1901–1939) never met Muir, nor did he emerge from Boone and Crockett, Audubon, or other established conservation groups. His love for Nature flowed from reading, hiking, mountain climbing, and exploring rather than from hunting, fishing, or observing wildlife. Like most early environmental leaders Marshall grew up in privilege, his father, Louis, a prominent civil rights attorney in New York City. A conservationist who knew Theodore Roosevelt, Louis helped establish and fought to defend the state's Adirondack Park.

While the family vacationed in the Adirondacks, Bob spent his leisure hours in the woods. At age eleven, confined to bed by pneumonia, he encountered *Pioneer Boys of the Great Northwest*, an adventure tale about the Lewis and Clark Expedition. It so absorbed him that he read it as often as three times a year for the next ten years. His sorties into the woods grew more frequent; he eventually climbed the 46 highest mountains in the Adirondacks. He climbed 28 Alaskan peaks (mostly first ascents), went on more than 200 hikes of over 30 miles a day, and once hiked 70 miles without sleep.

By age fifteen Marshall had resolved upon a career in forestry. Degrees from New York State School of Forestry and from Harvard, and a PhD in plant physiology from Johns Hopkins, followed. He joined the Forest Service and, at his request, received an assignment to the Northern Rocky Mountain Forest Experimental Station in Missoula, Montana, during 1925–1928. There he took full advantage of the opportunity to explore the mountains. Seeking ever-wilder areas to roam, he headed for Alaska. In summer 1929 he adventured and studied tree growth (in that order of preference) in the Brooks Range, enjoying it so much that he returned for a year in 1930–1931 to live in the upper Koyukuk town of Wiseman. *Arctic Village*, his portrayal of the social lives of the sourdough miners and Natives, won literary acclaim. He wrote more than 100 books and articles about Alaska, forestry, and wilderness preservation.[1]

Several aspects of Marshall's upbringing appear to have set the pattern for his life work and philosophy. His father instilled a sense of social responsibility that showed in Bob's earnest efforts to improve society. The family's interest in art gave the boy an aesthetic orientation reflected in his appreciation of natural beauty. Louis read to his children the works of James Fenimore Cooper and other romantic writers who conveyed a message of the superiority of Nature over civilization in building character. Bob enthusiastically participated in athletics. He adopted as a role model Verplanck Colvin, a scientifically oriented explorer of the Adirondacks who loved studying Nature and reveled in the hardships of outdoor life. Bob Marshall evolved a pattern of activity that put him in the wilds as much as possible and combined activity, aesthetics, and benefit to society in his reverent views of Nature.[2]

The more he saw of wilderness, the more convinced Marshall became that it must be cherished. Large tracts of wild continued to disappear, not least through the Forest Service's utilitarian conservationist emphasis on logging. Gifford Pinchot, the first Forest Service director, perceived "conservation" as requiring sustained-yield management of forests on a scientific basis for the benefit of the people as a whole—the greatest good for the greatest number—as distinct from uncontrolled exploitation. Also a Progressive, Marshall nevertheless saw that utilitarian "conservation" would put an end to wilderness. He found a solution in a theory enabling wilderness to rival other amenities by demonstrating its usefulness to modern humans. Wilderness, he asserted, is a source of health, physical independence from civilization, satisfaction of longing for exploration, independent thought, rest and relaxation, and beauty. Such values are important for democracy, he argued; people need escape from the strictures of civilization, which, at its worst, transmutes the quest for adventure into war.

"In the wilderness," wrote Marshall, "with its entire freedom from the manifestations of human will, that perfect objectivity which is essential for pure esthetic rapture can probably be achieved more readily than among any other forms of beauty." By definition, wilderness could not be readily accessible to the masses, Marshall acknowledged. To avoid charges of elitism he presented the utilitarian-sounding argument that "fundamentally, the question is one of balancing the total happiness which will be obtained if the few underdeveloped areas are perpetuated against that which will prevail if they are destroyed."[3] He believed that "quality as well as quantity must enter into any evaluation of recreation, because one really deep experience may be worth an infinite number of ordinary experiences." He considered it appropriate to set aside areas to be visited by few people, considering that unrestricted access would demolish their unique values for everyone.[4]

Beyond the abuse of forests by government, Marshall expressed alarm over the status of those in private ownership. Private forests comprised the bulk of 83 million acres in "ruin," increasing by nearly a million acres annually, and of 200 million acres in a state of "deterioration." He concluded that the nation's forests and their related values of recreation and soil and water conservation could be guaranteed only through public ownership. Accordingly, he advocated public acquisition of 562 million of the 670 million existing acres of forest.[5] Forests, he thought, constituted a national resource and should be treated as such: "The time has come when we must discard the unsocial view that our woods are the lumbermen's and substitute the broader ideal that every acre of woodland in the country is rightly a part of the people's forests."[6] In Alaska Marshall's views informed a raging debate over the Tongass National Forest enduring through the second half of the century.

Applying his extraordinary zeal to government policy, Marshall set out to move government agencies to safeguard wildlands. As early as 1928 he publicly advocated protective regulations. Regardless of whether he influenced the decision, the Department of Agriculture adopted rules in 1929 for specifying primitive areas. A swelling national interest in outdoor recreation made possible by automobiles and roads suggested that the Forest Service needed to accommodate it. The service undertook a comprehensive forest policy review in 1932, just as Marshall finished his PhD program. The survey coordinator, a friend of Marshall's, invited him to participate in writing the sections on recreation. Marshall seized the opportunity and incorporated his idea that 45 million of the 506 million acres of national forest lands should be earmarked for recreation. Between 1933 and 1939, 5.4 million acres received protective status, much of it probably as a result of Marshall's persistent efforts.[7]

Marshall emerged as the government's best-known wilderness proponent. In his position as forestry director in the Interior Department's Office of Indian Affairs between 1933 and 1937, he succeeded in getting 4.8 million acres on Indian reservations designated as roadless or wild. He thought Indians, affected by whites in many negative ways, needed connections to their wildlands for economic reasons and to prevent the loss of cultural traditions. He pointed to the fact that before the Allotment Act of 1887, Indians had owned 138 million acres of reservations. The act, intended by proponents to help Indians become economically independent through ownership of individual plots, instead resulted in land grabs by white men. By 1933 Indians owned 48 million acres of the poorest lands, not sufficient to support their populations. Environmentally unsustainable grazing and logging took place, degrading the lands and further impoverishing the Indians. Marshall advocated governmental purchase of land to be given to Indians, who would otherwise remain in a state of dependency at continuing cost to the government.[8]

In 1937 Marshall returned to the Agriculture Department to assume the directorship of the Recreation and Lands Division. Continuing to push for forest preservation, he proposed a set of revised rules known as the "U" regulations by which the secretary of agriculture could minimize damage to wildlands. Specifically, no logging would be permitted on tracts classified as wilderness (over 100,000 acres) or as wild areas (of smaller size). Shortly before Marshall's death in November 1939 the department adopted the regulations, eventually applying them to about 14 million acres of national forest lands. The process presaged the 1964 Wilderness Act.[9]

Alaska stirred exhilarating feelings within Bob Marshall. In the Brooks Range he fulfilled his dreams of tramping through unspoiled rugged wilds. On what he recalled as "in many ways the greatest one day I have spent," in March 1931 he and sourdough friend Ernie Johnson snowshoed to the pass between the Clear and Hammond rivers:

> I do not know what may be the supreme exultation of which a person is capable, but for me it came that moment I crossed the skyline and gazed over in to the winter-buried mystery of the Arctic, where great, barren peaks rose into the deep blue of the northern sky, where valleys, devoid even of willows, led far off into unknown canyons. Below me lay a chasm so many hundreds of feet deep it seemed no sunlight could ever penetrate its depths. From its upper reaches, bathed in sunshine, a white pinnacle rose into the air for almost a mile at a slope of not less than sixty degrees.[10]

Returning from a climbing expedition accompanied by Nutirwik (also known as Harry Snowden) he wrote, "[N]o man by high-powered instruments and machines can get the thrill which we got with our pocket compass and our field glasses as we made the first rough map of an unknown empire."[11] He named dozens of mountains, creeks, and other places, but none for himself. Of the names he proposed, some of which he made up and some preexisting, the Board of Geographic Names adopted 167. Many names he chose may have replaced those given long ago by Eskimos and Indians. Marshall Lake on Mt. Doonerak became his namesake,[12] as did later the Bob Marshall Wilderness in the North Cascades.

Reflecting on 20th-Century explorations, Marshall judged that they did not add to human happiness as a whole: "In fact, the net result of these activities is to make mankind a little poorer because in each case a slightly diminished possibility for the joy of exploration is left in the world after the exploration is finished." His predominantly egalitarian views contradicted his justification for exploration, "a perfectly laudable pastime in spite of its selfishness because the competition is open, and one person is entitled to enjoy it as much as another."[13] Nor did he confront another irony of his position: his conquest, mapping, and publicizing of wild places accelerated the utilitarian process of cataloging, exploiting, managing, and thereby eroding the mystery and integrity of wilderness areas he so loved. But the mapping would have taken place anyway, and he far more than compensated for the discrepancy in his philosophy by his phenomenal success in wildland preservation.

Nutirwik and Bob Marshall, upper north fork of the Koyukuk, 1939. Bancroft Library, University of California at Berkeley. Marshall's Native and white friends in Wiseman, and the beauty of the land, inspired his leadership in land preservation.

Marshall returned to the Arctic in the summers of 1938 and 1939. Life in Wiseman confirmed his belief that the simple life offered a surer path to happiness than did modern civilization. Just as wilderness represented the last stand for outdoor adventure, Alaska offered the last chance to avoid the resource management mistakes made in the States. Its wild areas would become ever more valuable as recreation replaced minerals, fur, and fishing in Alaska's economy. "Alaska is unique among all recreational areas belonging to the United States because Alaska is yet largely wilderness," Marshall pleaded. "In the name of balanced use of America's resources, let's keep northern Alaska a wilderness." He proposed that everything north of the Yukon, including Native villages and excepting Nome, be set aside as a park.[14]

Perceiving wilderness in anthropocentric rather than biological terms, Marshall valued it for its benefits to humans. The opportunity to experience primitiveness, or connection to unspoiled land, constituted its paramount appeal. A frontier park in northern Alaska, he reasoned, would retain for local inhabitants the values of independence and self-reliance, recognition of the individual, and adventure he had observed on the upper Koyukuk. Visitors to the proposed park could seek adventure without disrupting the lifestyles of residents.[15] Marshall believed or hoped these values, fast disappearing under the crush of civilization, could survive in northern Alaska.

Marshall participated in another, atypical, debate involving Alaska's wilderness. While the pre–World War II turmoil in Europe worsened, FDR asked the Interior Department to identify places where refugees might be resettled. Interior's report suggested Alaska could play a large role and that the United States should help develop Alaska's resources. Marshall's response captured the essence of the debate over Alaskan development, both past and future:

> World history for the last hundred years has been the story of the rapid development of untapped resources which represent the accumulated natural processes of eons, yet the opening of new frontiers has seldom brought more than transient prosperity for the vast majority of those engaged in it. The only reason we have as high a standard of living as we do today is that the more primitive people of past ages saw nothing immoral about leaving resources undeveloped. . . . Although lauding the fact that Alaska is perhaps the last country in the world where a hermit can build a cabin and never see a tax collector, the report fails to recognize that this is due to the scanty population which gives land almost no value, except around a few municipal centers, farming areas and mineralized zones. Furthermore, increasing the population would almost certainly lessen the contribution that wild life now makes to the subsistence of many Alaskans. It would also take away from people the unique possibilities of individuality found in scantily populated countries where men are few and each one is distinctive.

Viable growth, he argued, would be strictly limited by the combination of distance from markets and foreign competition.[16]

Proposals for settlement of European, mostly Jewish, refugees from Hitler's Germany had first surfaced in early 1938. They met resistance from most potential host nations, including the United States. In fall 1938 a Denver group put forward a plan to place refugees and unemployed persons in Alaska; it reappeared in essence in the Interior Department's Slattery Plan of 1939. Alaskan newspapers voiced overwhelming disapproval, despite their repeated previous claims that Alaska possessed abundant resources needing exploitation. Boosters had vigorously objected to Marshall's idea of prohibiting industry north of the Yukon. Marshall, himself Jewish, spoke against the settlement plan. He argued that Alaska could not accommodate large influxes of people, in contradistinction to the 48 states where resources and factories went underutilized. Resistance from Alaskans helped doom the settlement bill in Congress.[17]

Marshall felt an urgent need for a small and dedicated private group to spearhead an effort to maintain wilderness by applying outside pressure on government:

> It will be only a few years until the last escape from society will be barricaded. If that day arrives there will be countless souls born to live in strangulation, countless human beings who will be crushed under the artificial edifice raised by man. There is just one hope of repulsing the tyrannical ambition of civilization to conquer every niche on the whole earth. That hope is the organization of spirited people who will fight for the freedom of the wilderness.[18]

In 1935 Marshall and a few like-minded colleagues organized the Wilderness Society. Marshall financed it and provided its direction until a heart attack struck him down on November 11, 1939, at age 38. The society matured into a prominent actor in shaping the future of Alaska's wildlands, above all through the Wilderness Act of 1964 and the Alaska National Interest Lands Conservation Act of 1980. Part of Marshall's dream of an Arctic park came true in the naming of the Arctic National Wildlife Range in 1960 and Gates of the Arctic and Kobuk Valley national parks and the Noatak National Preserve in 1980. Not least, Marshall publicized Alaska's wilderness assets and the necessity for their conservation, a central theme in debates over Alaskan priorities ever since his death.

Marshall echoed John Muir as a self-styled advocate of wilderness. Like Muir he cast his appeals more in the form of aesthetical, sociological, psychological, and spiritual values than in terms of ecological science. Unlike Muir, he envisioned a wilderness preserve including humans living at low levels of technology and consumption. This rather fanciful prescription for the Alaskan Arctic underwent an endless series of tests in the ensuing decades, centering on questions of land ownership and subsistence rights.

Also, unlike Muir, Marshall displayed little interest in wildlife, nor did he emphasize species preservation or nonhuman rights. Yet his family background and experience tied him to the relatively holistic concepts that inspired the Adirondack preserve, only a step or two away from modern ecosystem sustainability.

Marshall deeply treasured and promulgated nonconsumptive use of Nature. His government positions empowered him to act on his values, setting precedents in wildland management. He argued that government should not only be responsible for but should be the direct steward of the nation's great forests. In founding the Wilderness Society he added a significant element of public participation, albeit somewhat elitist along the lines of Boone and Crockett. The society, in turn, employed and further popularized Marshall's ideas in its central roles in the establishment of the Arctic Refuge and the 1964 Wilderness Act. National support for wilderness ultimately shaped Alaska land status outcomes, as Marshall hoped it would, and fortified notions of ecological sustainability and wilderness values within the Alaskan public.

MR. WILDERNESS: OLAUS MURIE

"The out-of-doors is our true home, and being there gives us solitude and leisure to speak to ourselves and not to others. When we speak to ourselves, we are apt to be more honest."[19] A lifetime of immersion in Nature earned Olaus Johan Murie (1889–1963), a Wilderness Society colleague of Bob Marshall's, the ability and right to speak such words. Another landmark environmental figure, Murie displayed wilderness skills rivaling the most experienced Alaskan outdoorsmen. Yet his philosophy and accomplishments measurably furthered preservationist values.

Murie grew up on a Moorhead, Minnesota, farm and worked hard from age eight because his father died. In his spare time he and his brother Martin built a canoe and traveled the rivers observing wildlife. Ernest Thompson Seton's books kept him busy reading. After study of biology at Fargo College and graduation from Pacific University (Forest Grove, Oregon) in 1912, he served two years as a game warden in Oregon. Then he researched wildlife in Hudson Bay (1914–1915) and Labrador (1917) as a field naturalist and curator of mammals for the Carnegie Museum of Natural History. He over-wintered in 1914–1915 and honed his skills of survival in the North. During World War I he served in the Balloon Corps but did not go to Europe. Bureau of Biological Survey (BBS) chief Edward W. Nelson noticed his Canadian work and thought he might be the right person to survey caribou in Alaska. By 1920 Murie found himself traveling the Arctic and subarctic by dogsled, making the first counts of the northern caribou herds. Other work focused on birds and grizzly bears.

Remaining in Alaska until the fall of 1926, Murie returned south to earn a master's degree at the University of Michigan. At Jackson Hole, Wyoming, he conducted research on elk, coyotes, and other creatures. In 1936–1937 he returned to Alaska to direct the first thorough study of fauna in the Aleutians, where Murie Islets in the Shumagin Islands bear his name.[20]

Nelson, a sober and demanding taskmaster, expected much of Murie. He accompanied the young biologist to Alaska in 1920 and assigned him multiple tasks: collector of bird and mammal specimens, fur warden, and caribou researcher. Enforcement of fur laws, newly assigned to the BBS, did not go well for Murie. His first seizure of illegal furs alienated most of the Fairbanks community. Reflecting the Agriculture Department's orientation, the bureau planned to capture caribou for an experiment to improve reindeer by crossbreeding. A strenuous effort at Mt. McKinley Park in 1922 by Olaus and his brother Adolph ("Ade") ended in failure. They caught three bulls, a cow, and a calf, but one bull died in a wire fence entanglement, a second died for unknown reasons, and the third escaped.[21]

However, Murie excelled as a field scientist and collector. Applying his dog-teaming experience from Hudson Bay and Labrador, he traveled extensively around northern Alaska. Often alone and through the winter months he carried out surveys of caribou. Usually he packed no stove or tent and slept in a rabbit-fur bag. Early trips took him around Fairbanks, Eagle, and Mt. McKinley National Park. From October 1922 through April 1923 he and Adolph ventured into the Brooks Range to Wiseman and the headwaters of the Alatna River. On his fall 1924 honeymoon trip, he and Mardy (Margaret) visited Wiseman and ascended the Koyukuk River. Earlier in 1924 he had dog-sledded 700 miles to the Yukon Delta to study waterfowl. In 1925 he went to the Alaska Peninsula to observe and collect land and sea birds and mammals.[22] He visited Amak Island and recommended that it be set aside as a bird sanctuary. President Herbert Hoover signed an executive order adding it, the Sea Lion Rocks, and other small islands to the Aleutian Islands Reserve.[23]

Murie contributed to the evolution of ecology as a biological science and core of an ecological ethic, and he disapproved of the BBS policy on predator control. A 1923 letter to Nelson expressed his doubts: "I have a theory that a certain amount of preying on caribou is beneficial to the herd, that the best animals survive and the vigor of the herd is maintained. Man's killing does not work in this natural way, as the best animals are shot and inferior animals are left to breed." The theory almost certainly influenced Adolph, with whom Olaus constantly shared perspectives on wildlife.[24] In addition to the research of his colleague Lawrence J. Palmer and that of Adolph on coyotes and wolves, Olaus had observed the case of 700 caribou dying on Unimak Island after overgrazing their range. No wolves had been present. His account of this case did not get published, nor did his later work criticizing federal coyote control policy. Resultant frustration contributed to his resignation from the Fish and Wildlife Service in 1945 to become staff director of the Wilderness Society, a position he occupied until 1962. He correctly predicted that ecological research would help create a shift in public opinion toward predators,[25] and he worked to change the government's policies.

Gifted with an intense, childlike curiosity, Olaus Murie forever observed—questioning what animals were thinking, why they behaved as they did, why the world functioned as it did. In this mind-set he envisioned a form of salvation for humankind: "A poetic appreciation of life, combined with a knowledge of nature, creates humility, which in turn becomes the greatness in man."[26] Murie could hardly be described as a cheechako, or a naive "outsider," yet he displayed a charitable, preservationist attitude toward unpopular animals: "I think we should go beyond proving the rights of animals to live in utilitarian terms. Why don't we just admit we like having them around? Don't we realize that something exciting and satisfying will be gone from the world if we no longer hear coyotes howling?" Asked whether he feared meeting grizzlies unarmed, he replied, "Not much—a little, sometimes. But I never let them know it. I respect them and I meet them on equal terms. They are natural and good. I try to understand them. They have never hurt me."[27] An acquaintance observed that Murie "exemplified the gentleness and natural wisdom that some sensitive people seem to derive from close association with the earth and its creatures . . . a highly civilized being who had acquired an aura of nobleness from the wilds that he loved." Wilderness Society director Howard Zahniser, who also died just before he could celebrate the fruits of his labor on the Wilderness Act, described Murie as "the one person who best personified wilderness in our culture."[28]

As did John Muir, Murie criticized materialism and its impact on Nature:

> I would say that the dollar sign is out of place when it undertakes to ride roughshod over the sensibilities of people who have dedicated a piece of country for the inspiration of its wilderness. . . . It has been pointed out repeatedly that the most dangerous influence we have in our society is not the criminal. We can deal with him more or less. We need to fear much more the half truths, the rationalizations, and the business ethics that are just below par but so universal that we shrug them off with a humorous remark.[29]

"Probably because of our exuberance in coming to a new continent," he thought, "we have acted like children getting into a pantry well-stocked with goodies. We are still exploiting our resources wildly."[30]

He regarded wilderness as "the material of poetry, art and science. Nature gives spiritual values none of us can live without. How can we measure the elation of being in high country in free surroundings?"[31] Destruction of wilderness represented more than the disappearance of wildlife; it also meant the loss of vital heritage: "It is a fragile thing, this natural wilderness, consisting of the material for poetry and art and vigorous clean living. It is easily degraded or destroyed by heedless men. It is not for a single agency, or a single organization, to make ruthlessly a decision which affects the future. Surely it is wisdom to guard the original material on which our culture is founded—and save some of it."[32] This did not mean all people should have access to all of Nature. Echoing Bob Marshall, he believed some wild areas should be reserved "for those who crave a true wilderness experience, for those who can stand weather, who have the stamina to deal with the vicissitudes of camp life, and still enjoy the experience. We surely need this element in American civilization. It should not be lowered to a common denominator to accommodate mass numbers."[33] The Arctic National Wildlife Range fit perfectly his ideal of a wilderness to be left in its natural state.

One of the original governing council members of the Wilderness Society, Murie presided from 1950 to 1957 and served on the council until his death. He wrote scientific and popular works on elk, coyotes, and caribou and on wildlife management, appreciation, and preservation.[34] The activity of the Wilderness Society grew rapidly in the 1950s; through it Murie left a telling impact on the future of Alaska lands. Tirelessly lecturing, testifying, and writing in the cause of wilderness preservation, he won a national and an international reputation.

Olaus Murie earned repute as a writer, artist, lecturer, and conservation leader, as well as a top field biologist. His wife, Margaret (1902–2003), shared his writing and conservation work. Born in Seattle and brought up in Fairbanks from age nine, she majored in English at Reed and Simmons colleges and became the first woman graduate of the University of Alaska in 1924.[35] Her famous book *Two in the Far North* told of dogsled travels with Olaus, including a winter honeymoon trip in the Brooks Range, and of their love for Nature in Alaska. Mardy accompanied Olaus on field expeditions, even after the birth of their son Martin.

Like Muir and Marshall, the Muries discovered in the North a vital connection between its isolation from civilization and a high spiritual quality of life:

> [Mardy and I] often spoke of it even then, as we traveled among scattered villages, trading posts, missions, camps, associating with the men and women of several races—swarthy white men who hardly dared to speak in the presence of a woman for fear of what words might slip out, well-read prospectors who could discuss the classics and philosophy with wisdom, Indian youths (beyond the influence of liquor peddlers) whom we admired for their forth-right-ness and obvious integrity, Eskimos who contributed the brightness of laughter and optimism. I am speaking now of the time previous to the present industrial boom in Alaska.[36]

The Muries found "cold beauty and infinite warmth; physical hardships, as well as times of plenty and fun. We believe it is a life not to be ashamed of, a life of rugged endeavor and high spiritual reward, not to be lightly discarded in the modern reach for ease and gadgets. Surely somewhere in the north we should find it possible to dedicate an area or two to this kind of life."[37]

In May 1926 BBS chief Nelson assigned Olaus to band waterfowl up the Old Crow River on the Yukon side, and Mardy went along. Friends advised against taking the eleven-month-old baby and described the Old Crow as "the worst mosquito place in Alaska," warning that "even the Indians stay out of there in the summer." The party set out up the Porcupine River. Upon ascending the Old Crow to Black Fox Creek they broke a propeller shaft. Undaunted, Olaus and boatman Jess Rust resolved to complete the journey. They transferred the gear, Mardy, and the baby to a barge and poled and lined it for more than 150 miles to the river's headwaters in the Davidson Mountains, stopping to band birds all along the way. Recovering their boat on the way back, they poled it through a dangerous stretch of rapids, descended the Porcupine, and returned to Fairbanks.[38]

Mardy participated in Wilderness Society work as a partner to Olaus. She promoted the efforts to set aside the Arctic National Wildlife Range, a goal she and Olaus had shared since 1924. Following Olaus's death she grew more active, devoting most of her time to wilderness and wildlife preservation through the Wilderness Society and Sierra Club, working from her home at Jackson Hole. She stayed connected to Alaska, visiting in 1975 as a guest of the National Park Service and meeting people around the state to urge a strong Alaska Lands Act. The University of Alaska awarded her an honorary doctorate in 1976. During later visits she worked for the defense of the Arctic National Wildlife Refuge from oil development.

In 1977 Mardy published *Island Between*, a work based on notes taken of Eskimo life at St. Lawrence Island by Alaskan scientist Otto Geist, whom the Muries had known since the 1920s. Four years later she put together *The Alaska Bird Sketches of Olaus Murie*.[39] Her ongoing activity in environmental protection gave her national standing. Presidents Lyndon Johnson and Jimmy Carter invited her to the signing ceremonies for the 1964 Wilderness Act and the 1980 Alaska Lands Act, respectively. President Bill Clinton phoned on her 93rd birthday to promise a veto of any congressional bill to open the Arctic Refuge to oil.[40] The Grand Old Lady of the wilderness movement, Mardy Murie endured as the nation's living icon of wildland advocacy.

Olaus Murie possessed a rare outlay of credentials relevant to Alaskan environmentalism: biologist, frontier explorer, scientific researcher, government official, writer, philosopher, artist, and political activist. He bridged several gaps in the evolving environmentalism of his time. Simultaneously he held the respect of hunters, settlers, government officials, and the publics of both Alaska and the States. He incorporated the hands-on knowledge of a Frank Dufresne and the aesthetic sensitivity of his colleague Bob Marshall. Well ahead of his time, he understood the value of predators and acquired an ecocentric view of the Earth. He articulated and gave force to nonconsumptive use values of the wolf and coyote and, in essence, affirmed the right of species to exist. He worked for ecosystem sustainability, as in his plea for the Arctic National Wildlife Range. He valued and practiced science as a building block for environmentally responsible natural resource management. By no means least, he and Mardy successfully modeled public participation, through the Wilderness Society, in resource management. Their close ties to Alaska, and effective educational work in the Lower 48, registered in Alaska land designations and, eventually, environmentalism in the Alaskan public.

More than any other person, Olaus Murie made possible the Arctic National Wildlife Range. He arranged for the society's 1963 annual meeting to be held in Alaska to focus attention on its wilderness issues and once again made a visit to the Arctic. Three months later he died, not living to see the adoption of the 1964 Wilderness Act to which he had given years of effort.

THE ARCTIC REFUGE

Few lands hold a more exalted ranking in the Alaskan environmental panoply than the Arctic National Wildlife Range (ANWR). Encompassing the northeast corner of the state, it is one of the most remote regions of the United States. It cannot be reached by road; it is almost entirely unpopulated by humans. It contains at least two ecosystems divided by the Brooks Range: the tundra-covered Arctic and the heavily wooded lands to the south. Aborigines first appeared on the South Slope about 11,000 years ago and more recently on the North Slope. Two distinct cultures exist: the Tagmiugmiut Eskimos, who hunt sea mammals and caribou along the Arctic coast, and the Kutchin (or Gwitch'in) Athabaskan Indians, hunters of caribou who live on the South Slope. Both cultures traded along the Arctic coast, connecting the Canadian and Siberian Natives in the 17th to 19th centuries.[41]

Euro-American Explorers

In 1826 British explorer Sir John Franklin initiated the wave of Europeans to visit the coast. He traveled westward from the Mackenzie River Delta in the first of his Arctic expeditions that ultimately led to disaster in his quest for the Northwest Passage. Franklin named Camden Bay for a lord of the Admiralty and another bay for Admiralty hydrographer Captain (later Admiral) Sir Francis Beaufort.[42] The Arctic Ocean above Alaska ultimately took on the name Beaufort Sea.

Later in the 19th Century came more Hudson's Bay Company explorers, searchers for Franklin, and whalers. Advancing civilization left its mark on Arctic ecology. During the commercial whaling era, lasting from 1854 to about 1916 along the north Arctic coast, traders introduced guns to Eskimos. To supply the whaling crews, hunters pursued caribou, mountain sheep, and other mammals far inland, to the point of scarcity. Ernest de K. Leffingwell, a U.S. Geological Survey officer posted to Flaxman Island between 1906 and 1914, reported, "The native hunters have long been furnished guns and ammunition in abundance by the whale ships wintering at Herschel Island. . . . [E]very native in the country has a modern repeating rifle and one or two thousand cartridges every year. As they have no better knowledge of conservation than white men, they soon drove the caribou out of the country." Thereafter, Leffingwell noted, Eskimos sewed most of their clothing from reindeer hides imported from Siberia: "As the caribou decreased in numbers, the natives began to hunt the mountain sheep more energetically. Dall's sheep formerly were abundant everywhere in the mountains, but they have already been cleaned out from the lower part of the larger rivers." Eskimos regarded polar bears as pests and shot them as they attempted to make dens on the high banks ashore. Bear populations dwindled.[43] Whalers and other visitors to the Arctic killed polar bears for their fur or for sport.

Roald Amundsen crossed the divide in the Davidson Mountains by dogsled in 1905–1906 during the first navigation of the Northwest Passage. His ship froze in for the winter, and whale men in over-wintering vessels wanted to send and receive mail and request supplies. Not least, Amundsen planned to telegraph word of his achievement to the outside world. Without money to finance the 1,000-mile round trip to Fort Yukon and Eagle, he accompanied Captain Billy Mogg, who would lead the expedition. Mogg commanded the whaling vessel *Bonanza*, driven ashore by ice while wintering east of Herschel Island. He planned to return to San Francisco and sail another vessel north for spring whaling.[44] A seasoned Arctic whaler, Mogg had wintered at Herschel Island almost every year since 1890. In 1892 he made a round trip by dogsled to the Yukon Valley, the first known traversal of the mountains by a non-Native.[45]

The mail expedition left Herschel Island in late October. Indian guides Jimmy and his wife, Kappa, known for their reliability and competence, served as guides and drove two dog teams. Mogg rode on Amundsen's sled or traveled on snowshoes; Amundsen used Norwegian skis. Mogg pointed out a place where deserting whalers had camped in midwinter on their way to the goldfields. When ordered to surrender they fired on the pursuing officers who returned fire, killing two of them. Two more surrendered, and the rest fled toward Fort Yukon. Five got there, but several perished on the way.

Mogg and Amundsen's party reached Fort Yukon on November 20. They hired another Indian guide, Charlie, to accompany them on the 200-mile trip to Eagle. Upon arrival Amundsen wired the historic news to the king of Norway over the newly installed Alaska telegraph system. On February 3, 1906, Amundsen left Eagle, rejoined the Indians at Fort Yukon, and returned north to his ship and crew, arriving on March 12.[46] The following summer he sailed the *Gjoa* along the Arctic coast on the way to Nome. On that coastal plain, in oil seeps discovered by Eskimos and explorers, lay the seeds of future strife in the Arctic.

An Arctic Ecosystem

Cold, wild, and vast, the Arctic Refuge is a land of awesome beauty and vibrant life. In the words of Averill Thayer, refuge manager from 1969 to 1981, "No other refuge or park encompasses such a continuum of undisturbed, biologically self-sufficient arctic and subarctic habitats—from the interior boreal forest and the central Brooks Range to the coastal plain bordering the Arctic Ocean. No other area affords habitat protection for so many healthy populations of national interest species." He described the caribou herd migration as

Captain Roald Amundsen (left front) and crew of Gjoa, Nome, September 1, 1906, one day after arriving from completion of the Northwest Passage. Bancroft Library, University of California Berkeley. On his 1,000-mile overland trip from Herschel Island in midwinter, Amundsen traversed parts of the future Arctic Refuge.

"the most spectacular wildlife phenomenon on Canadian and American soil."[47] Other mammals in the refuge include moose, Dall sheep, muskoxen, polar and grizzly bears, wolves, wolverines, lynx, porcupines, and Arctic foxes and hares. Offshore are ringed, bearded, and largha seals; occasionally walruses; and gray, belukha, and bowhead whales. Golden eagles, peregrine and gyrfalcons, rough-legged hawks, snowy owls, geese, ducks, loons, and swans are among the 57 species of breeding birds in the area; at least 135 bird species have been seen. Twenty-four species of fish—four freshwater, nine anadromous, and eleven marine—exist in the refuge.[48] This wildlife is a vital source of food for the North Slope Eskimo village of Kaktovik and for Athabaskan villages near the caribou migration routes.

Central to the wildlife complex is the Porcupine caribou herd, named for the Porcupine River in its migration route. Often compared to Africa's Serengeti plain, the coastal tundra of the refuge is the scene of caribou calving in mid-

Bull caribou in forest, Arctic National Wildlife Range, October 1970. By Bob Henning. FWS 6281, Alaska Resources Library and Information Services. The great Porcupine caribou herd, the refuge's central wildlife feature, migrated to the coastal plain for spring calving.

May. This culminating stage of the long spring migration provides abundant food and relief from predators and insects. In late summer the caribou return to the foothills to resume their annual trek of up to 2,700 miles between the coastal plain and their wintering grounds near the Chandalar River to the south or the Ogilvie Mountains in the Yukon.[49] To natural and human predators their biannual journey is part of the pattern of survival. For the reflective observer privileged to behold, it could be a profound aesthetic and philosophical experience. Photographer Wilbur Mills portrayed a herd of advancing caribou at Camden Bay as

> a tight seething mass so dense I could not see the ground beneath it. I heard the approaching thunder of their hooves pounding the tundra. It was more than a sound . . . caribou were coming toward me along an unbroken front perhaps a quarter of a mile wide. Their clicking hooves clattered in the air like a thousand castanets. The air was saturated with the energy of sound. The herd enveloped me. Cows and calves, and bulls with long, velvet-coated antlers reaching high above their heads, rushed by a few yards away as if I were not there.[50]

Wolf at Old Woman Creek, Arctic National Wildlife Range, 1966. By Averill Thayer. FWS 4646, Alaska Resources Library and Information Services. To refuge advocates, the wolf symbolized wilderness; to many Alaskans, a threat to their game supply.

Lois Crisler described the fall migration in the western Brooks Range as

> a spectacle like none other left on earth now. It had power over the spirit. The power lay not only in what you saw—this slender column driving onward into wilderness. It also lay in what you knew. Arctic night and hunger coming. In-gathering far away somewhere of individuals into this traveling column, driven by the great seasons. Knowledge of danger and darkness and fear, built into their tissues by the centuries. Life and the cold Arctic before you for a moment in one silent sweep of land and moving animals.[51]

Ecologist John Milton hiked 300 miles across the Brooks Range in 1967. At the junction of Green Willow Creek and the Aichilik River he found wolf tracks superimposed on those of caribou and mused, "I hope man has the vision to keep his civilization from at least a few such wildernesses as this—wilderness on the old, vast scale—so that wolf and caribou can continue to live as they always have; and for their sake, not ours. . . . And if this wilderness can also be an incidental reservoir for restoring man's spirit, then fine. But that is not the purpose of this place. Its purpose it to *be*. Man's role should be . . . let it be."[52]

Establishment of a Refuge

Such an ecosystem as described by Mills, Crisler, and Milton embodied part of Bob Marshall's dream of a grand national park north of the Yukon. Similarly oriented National Park Service recreation officer George L. Collins and biologist Lowell Sumner investigated the region as part of a general recreational survey of Alaska directed by Collins. Sumner visited the northeast corner in 1951 and wrote Wilderness Society director Olaus Murie suggesting that it be preserved.[53] Collins went to see John Reed, a Naval Arctic research official who had explored oil prospects on the North Slope. Reed advised that any park be located "east of Pet 4," the Naval Petroleum Reserve occupying the central North Slope. Collins and Sumner then flew around the northeast corner in 1952, assisted by the Naval Arctic Research Laboratory at Barrow. "The scenery was magnificent. It was simply stupendous, beyond description," recalled Collins. The two men began to draft boundaries for a proposed national park. They returned in 1953 accompanied by Starker Leopold and Frank Fraser Darling.[54] They wrote to Murie requesting that he lead a campaign for a wildlife refuge. Collins then wrote to Alaska governor B.F. Heintzleman assuring him that the Park Service did not want to make the area a national park or monument, which would close the area to mining and other development.[55] He and Sumner contacted Joe Flakne of the Arctic Institute of North America. Flakne in turn advised Murie, "If you fellows want to save some wilderness in Alaska, you had better begin to do something now."[56]

In a 1953 *Sierra Club Bulletin* article Sumner and Collins highlighted the scientific value of the refuge. Nearly all other areas had been altered, they said. Northeast Alaska presented an opportunity to study the ecology of an essentially undisturbed ecosystem and acquire knowledge applicable to land and wildlife management elsewhere. The refuge should be "planned and dedicated now for perpetual preservation as a scientific field laboratory and also for the education, enjoyment, and inspiration of all outdoor-minded people."[57] As government officials, Sumner and Collins could not freely organize a citizen support effort. In 1954 they formally proposed to the Interior Department the creation of an Arctic reserve, to extend into Canada and be jointly managed.

Olaus Murie and Sigurd F. Olson had flown over the Brooks Range in the fall of 1951. Accompanied by a U.S. Geological Survey official, Murie flew to the Arctic again in 1953. The Wilderness Society had committed itself to the Arctic refuge project, as would the Sierra Club. Others prominently involved included the Conservation Foundation, Isaac Walton League, and Wildlife Management Institute. Funded by the Conservation Foundation and the New York Zoological Society, Murie planned a trip to the region in 1954. His illness forced a postponement until 1956. He and Mardy then undertook an expedi-

Mardy and Olaus Murie, Sheenjek River Valley, 1956. Courtesy Murie Center. The Muries' ties to Alaska and return visit to the Sheenjek brought the proposed Arctic Refuge to the nation's attention.

tion to the Sheenjek River Valley.[58] It reminded them of their travels in the 1920s, but the trip had a political purpose: to publicize the idea of a wildlife refuge. It proved an effective plan. Reporters and other well-chosen people including Justice William O. Douglas and his wife, Mercedes, visited the campsite, and a short film full of life and beauty emerged to counter the image of the Arctic as an icy wasteland.[59] Upon leaving the Arctic the Muries made a series of low-key presentations to Alaskan groups. Sensing the importance of local sentiment, they cautioned the national environmental organizations not to exert pressure prematurely. They returned in 1957, meeting all potentially sympathetic groups and thousands of individuals around the territory. Their respectful approach and solid Alaska credentials stood them in good stead. In the vital Fairbanks area they won the endorsements of the Tanana Valley Sportsmen's Association, Fairbanks Garden Club, Fairbanks Chamber of Commerce, and *Fairbanks Daily News-Miner*.

Arctic reserve advocates knew that Alaskans would more readily accept a wildlife refuge than a national park. And a park meant roads and tourist facilities that would destroy wilderness preservation values. By 1957 the Interior Department publicly backed the creation of an Arctic refuge, and in 1958 it filed a formal request to Congress. Alaska's state and congressional politicians, however, tried to stop the refuge. So did the Anchorage Chamber of Commerce and the Territorial Department of Mines, which termed it "an effort to create a 9,000,000-acre playground at the expense of possible industrial development." The new Alaska state legislature adopted a resolution against the proposal in 1959.[60]

National Parks Magazine ran a series of articles in 1958 touting the refuge proposal. Olaus Murie recounted the exhilarating experience he and Mardy had shared in the Sheenjek country two years earlier. He related vignettes of scenic beauty and wildlife encounters and expressed "a fervent hope that others, a few at a time, can enjoy the spiritual uplift of such a place. We human beings must muster the wisdom to leave a few places on earth strictly alone, to leave them for such esthetic adventures for the next generation." Mindful of the importance of Alaskans' approval, he paid tribute to garden clubs, outdoor sporting organizations, "certain groups of forward-looking teachers at the University of Alaska, and many individuals."[61]

Secretary of the Interior Fred Seaton, who moderately favored preservation of wildlands, contributed an article to the series. Having been shown the proposed refuge by Clarence Rhode, he firmly endorsed it. Adjacent to the 9-million-acre refuge, he noted, the Canadians might set aside 5 million acres of their territory. Straddling the fence on industrial development, Seaton asserted that "no substantial mining or mineral values exist in the Wildlife Range" but added that mineral leasing might be permitted under guidelines protecting the land and wildlife. The refuge would be open to wilderness recreation, scientific study, and hunting and trapping. His recent modification of the 1943 order withdrawing the North Slope would permit oil and mining access to 20 million acres west of the refuge. Thus, Seaton concluded, "it is likely that this American region near the top of the world will contribute as never before to the growth of the Alaskan economy and the recreational enjoyment of United States citizens."[62]

Seaton possessed the legal power either to permit mining and oil and gas drilling under existing laws or to prohibit them entirely. But he wanted to keep the door open for oil and gas while banning mining that would more severely disrupt the surface. This third alternative required congressional approval, and bills to accomplish it appeared in Congress. In addition, he preferred the legislative route to avoid having Alaskans blame the Republicans for an executive withdrawal and to divide the Democrats in Alaska. The designation itself would please environmentalists and reduce criticism of the Eisenhower administration for being too close to the oil industry.[63]

Before a sympathetic House Committee on Fisheries and Wildlife Conservation in spring 1959, representatives of the Interior Department, Wildlife

Management Institute, Wilderness Society, National Wildlife Federation, Citizens Committee on Natural Resources, and Isaac Walton League testified in favor of the refuge bill. Alaska representative Ralph Rivers stated that, in light of the widespread approval in Alaska, he would withdraw his objections if a highway funding problem could be resolved. The distribution formula linked funds to the amount of unreserved lands in a state; therefore, reservation of the Arctic could reduce Alaska's share.[64]

Testifying on June 30 before a Senate subcommittee chaired by Senator Bob Bartlett, refuge advocates received a polite reception. Speaking for himself, Senator Gruening, and many Alaskans, Bartlett said, "[W]e favor a conservation policy but we are increasingly, over the years, alarmed by the fact that the federal government . . . when it desires to make a withdrawal in Alaska, makes it of such a huge size." Appended letters from Gruening, the Alaska Miners Association, Governor William Egan, and Alaska commissioner of fish and game Clarence Anderson registered opposition to the refuge. Anderson wanted to prevent federal control of fish and game: "The only real threat to the wildlife and wilderness of the Alaskan Arctic stems from a handful of wilderness extremists and federal officials." The Juneau Chamber of Commerce objected to the refuge, but the National Audubon Society added its endorsement. Gruening's letter cited five reasons for opposition: (1) the size of the refuge, (2) the possibility of losing highway funds, (3) interference with state selection of lands guaranteed by the Alaska Statehood Act, (4) loss of state control over fish and wildlife, and (5) lack of need to protect such a remote area.[65]

The Sierra Club's biennial 1959 wilderness conference focused in part on the refuge issue. Robert A. Rausch of the Arctic Health Research Center pointed out that little true wilderness remained in Alaska and only a tiny percentage of it had been protected. Excepting the Arctic Wildlife Range, he said, "Nature conservation has enjoyed few advocates in Alaska, as compared with the many spokesmen for those who anticipate monetary gain from exploitation of natural resources." He predicted that the state's economy would increasingly depend on tourism and therefore on protection of natural assets.[66] Notwithstanding the impacts of oil development, Rausch's argument carried on into the 21st Century, slowly gaining force.

In the fall of 1959 hearings took place in Alaska. A.W. "Bud" Boddy of the Alaska Sportsmen's Council, Dixie Baade, Celia Hunter, and Virginia "Ginny" Hill Wood, among others, spoke for the refuge. Hunter testified that "Alaska is considered to be a mining state—mining is our tradition and the first justification for exploration and settlement," and "the whole tone for our state administration is set by the mining interests." She called for recognition of the "decline in the importance of mining, and the increasing emphasis on tourism." Wood, who had first publicly endorsed the refuge proposal in 1954, articulated the environmentalist position that made up part of nearly every Alaska land dispute for the next several decades:

> The rising cry for more wilderness areas, national parks, and recreation sites is more than the pleas of a few starry eyed nature lovers or bird watchers—it is a changing trend in values for a Nation that is finding material goods and higher standards of living not the whole answer to the quest for the good life. . . . Alaska's wilderness and wildlife will become its most valuable asset economically as wild country disappears elsewhere—if we conserve it now. And we don't have to invest vast sums to develop this asset, just maintain the status quo. . . . Always before in history there have been new frontiers to push onto: first the New Hemisphere, then the West, and finally the North, to which those who found life too crowded, exploited and regulated could go.
>
> Now we have come to the end of the line.
>
> We Alaskans must reconcile our pioneer philosophy of conquer, cut, shoot, plow, mine, and move on, to the realization that the wild country that lies now in Alaska is all that is left under the flag.

Otherwise, she warned, wild Alaska would "become a myth found only in books, movies, and small boys' imaginations as the Wild West is now."[67]

In early 1960 legislation to create an Arctic National Wildlife Range passed the House. In the Senate, Ernest Gruening and Bob Bartlett, assisted by Rep. Rivers, blocked it. They fought any move that might restrict mining or other forms of economic activity. Hearings had demonstrated local approval for the refuge; of Alaskans testifying, 73 favored and 53 opposed it. Bartlett stopped the bill in committee in August. Representatives from Alaskan conservation groups went to see him but failed to change his mind.[68]

Clinton "Pink" Gutermuth of the Wildlife Management Institute visited Seaton and demanded action. Sigurd Olson, Seaton's most trusted contact in the environmental community, investigated the refuge site and conferred with Canadian officials at Seaton's behest in the summer of 1960. He recommended action. On December 6 Seaton signed an order to create a 9-million-acre Arctic National Wildlife Range plus the 1.5-million-acre Kuskokwim and 450,000-acre Izembek national wildlife ranges.[69] The Izembek and Kuskokwim ranges, championed by the National Wildlife Federation, had been proposed at the time of the Arctic refuge. Essentially flat and known primarily for migratory waterfowl nesting, they received much less publicity and attention from environmental groups than the Arctic refuge did.[70] Gruening labeled Seaton's move "a total usurpation and disregard for the rights of the state of Alaska."[71] Efforts by the Alaska delegation to persuade Seaton's successor Stewart Udall to rescind the order went nowhere.

Secretary Seaton's order ended surface mining but enabled oil and gas drilling contingent upon agreement between the Bureau of Land Management and the Fish and Wildlife Service, subject to approval by the interior secretary.[72] Oil

Ginny Hill Wood (left) and Celia Hunter, Fairbanks, ca. 1985. Courtesy Northern Alaska Environmental Center. Active in the Arctic Wildlife Range campaign, they helped organize the Alaskan environmental community.

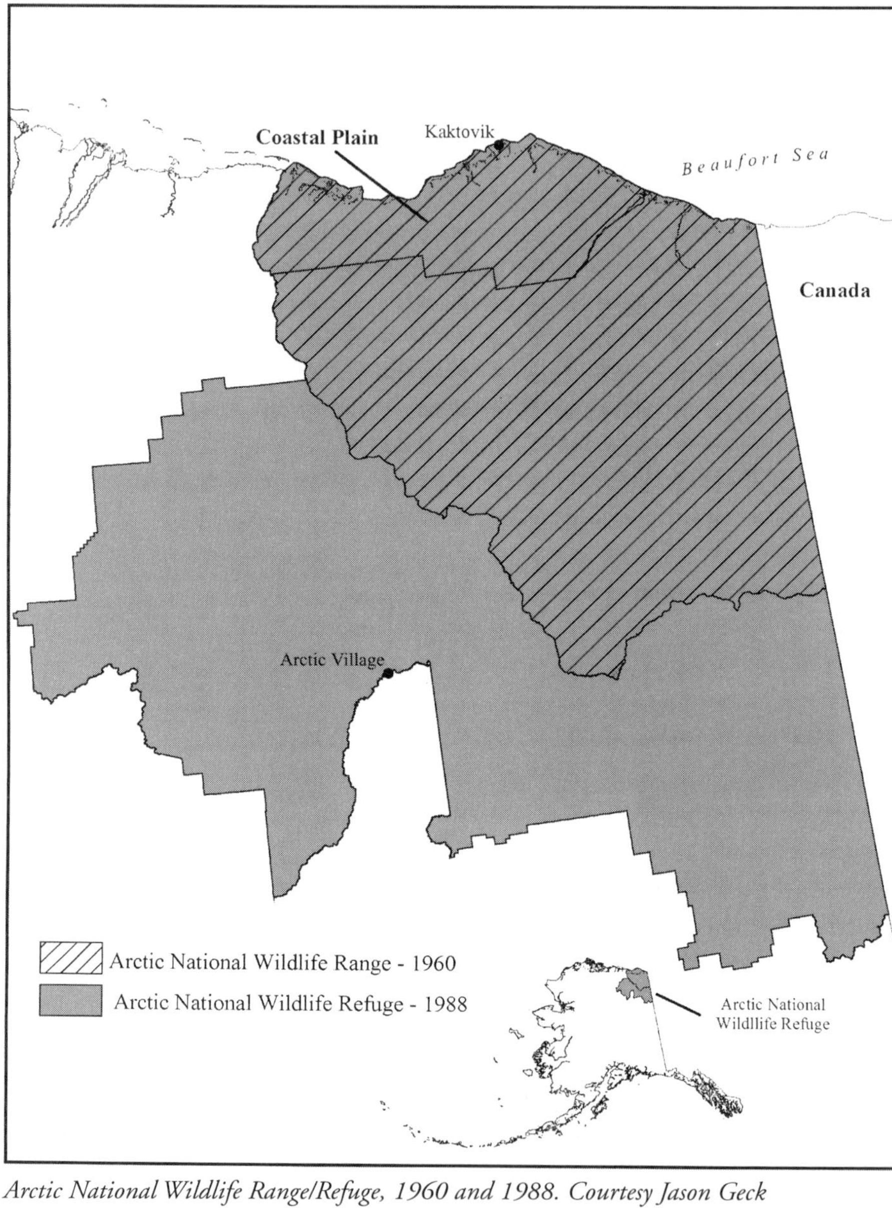

Arctic National Wildlife Range/Refuge, 1960 and 1988. Courtesy Jason Geck

barrels and other litter and scars marked the sites of early oil exploration and an Air Force DEW (Distant Early Warning) station at Barter Island. But the vast bulk of the refuge ecosystem lay undisturbed.

The Arctic National Wildlife Range stood out among environmental events of its time. One of the first federal land designations in post-statehood Alaska, it set precedents in being the first land designation issue to be settled largely in Alaska by Alaskans, and the first in the nation to be so openly dedicated to ecosystem preservation. Wilderness specialist Roger Kaye identified the dominant values sought by the proponents as "wildlife, ecological, scientific, recreational, heritage, and bequest values."[73] While the rules permitted hunting, trapping, and fishing by both Natives and non-Natives, the designation nevertheless imparted a signal victory and inspiration to national environmentalists that carried forth into the Wilderness Act of 1964 and the Alaska Lands acts of 1971 and 1980. It also catalyzed modern environmentalism in Alaska. Celia Hunter and Ginny Wood helped found and lead the Alaska Conservation Society (1960–1981), the state's first such organization and pioneer of one of the nation's most successful environmental communities.

Whither the Arctic Refuge?

In terms of environmental values, the Arctic National Wildlife Range represented a triumph for ecosystem sustainability, a goal consciously pursued by Sumner, Collins, Olaus and Margaret Murie, and other advocates of the refuge. Close behind, the designation embodied nonconsumptive use values; many of those favoring it placed a high spiritual value on a land they knew they would probably never see. Bob Marshall's zealous writing, government activism, and leadership within the Wilderness Society had set the stage for benign treatment of northern Alaska. The Muries' quiet but firm wisdom, carefully presented, did much to bring the vision to fruition. Public participation, both in the States and in Alaska, came to the fore and tellingly affected the outcome in favor of ecosystem preservation. It demonstrated genuine strength of preservation values in a region better known for aggressive resource exploitation. Timing of the issue, just ahead of the oil companies' entry into the Arctic, enabled refuge advocates to overcome resistance from mining interests and Alaskan senators.

Yet the refuge's proclamation left its environmental future in doubt. Most significant, the secretary of the interior could permit oil and gas drilling. Sport hunters or fishers, as well as subsistence users, could seek prey there. Hikers, river runners, bird watchers, photographers, and other sightseers might escalate their visits as economic boosters hoped. Scientists also wanted a presence on the land. At a 1961 symposium in Fairbanks, university biologist William Pruitt portrayed the refuge as a uniquely unspoiled ecosystem crucial for ecological studies, a "control area against which we can evaluate the efficiency of our land practices elsewhere in the Alaskan Arctic." Anthropologist John M. Campbell pointed out the likelihood that early human migrants from Asia had lived in the region: "[N]owhere in the Americas is there a piece of ground that holds more promise for the eventual establishment of a complete Western Hemisphere time-scale than the Arctic Slope," especially the narrow coastal strip bordering the refuge. He cautioned that scientific expeditions could also damage the land: "Let us not spoil the thing that we have set out to save." Olaus Murie, emphasizing the spiritual and psychological values of wilderness integrity, counseled that "we will be wise to go a little bit slower, to leave a few places on our continent undeveloped, with the fewest possible cabins and other structures built by government." He added that "on our trips to the Wildlife Range we saw clearly that it was not a place for mass recreation." Bureau of Sport Fisheries and Wildlife official Urban C. Nelson enumerated the groups hoping to make use of the refuge and advised, "It is not purely wilderness area. It is not a game sanctuary. It is a composite of the interests that are involved."[74]

Alaska entered its modern oil era after the 1957 discovery on the Kenai Peninsula. A decade later came the strike at Prudhoe Bay and recurring attempts to open the nearby Arctic Refuge to oil exploration. Once among the least-known parts of the nation, the region again drew national attention. Drilling for oil necessitated clarification of land ownership, precipitating the Alaska Native Claims Settlement Act of 1971 and the Alaska National Interest Lands Conservation Act (ANILCA) of 1980. A newly invigorated environmental movement won guarantees of wildland protection in ANILCA. The act doubled the size of the renamed Arctic National Wildlife Refuge and classified nearly half of it as wilderness, in which only recreation and subsistence activities would be allowed. In 1983 the state relinquished a temporary selection of 972,000 acres that became part of the refuge. Congress added 325,000 acres in 1988, bringing the total to almost 19.3 million.[75] Rivers and wildlife attracted visitors to the point where they had to be scheduled to avoid environmental and recreational degradation. On the Canadian side, in 1984 the government set aside the 3-million-acre Northern Yukon National Park (renamed Ivvavik) bordering the refuge on the east. As of 1995, 1-million-acre Vuntut National Park bordered Ivvavik on the south and the Arctic Refuge on the east.

Among the many compromises between protection and development in ANILCA, an assessment of oil potential would be made within the Arctic Refuge and drilling could proceed by permission of Congress.[76] Oil companies wanted access, and Alaskans looked forward to more oil royalties. And global warming, in part a product of fossil fuel burning, threatened to further destabilize the Arctic ecosystem.[77] Environmentalists and their opponents both adopted the refuge as a cause célèbre, and the struggle intensified as it continued into the 21st Century. The Arctic Refuge became the nation's preeminent battleground in the debate over exploitation versus preservation, consumption versus sustainability, material production versus wilderness.

18

Evolution of Conservation Values

FROM THE SEA OTTER TO THE ARCTIC NATIONAL WILDLIFE RANGE, ALASKA SERVED as a testing ground for natural resource policy. Cumulatively, the contests registered an evolution of environmental values from all-out exploitation to utilitarian conservation and examples of preservation. They also shaped conservation values both in Alaska and on a national scale. The nation's environmental agenda moved closer to appreciation of Nature and a more holistic approach in relating to it.

Alaska stands out among American states and territories as by far the most recent to go through the frontier experience. It retained territory status for about 70 years beyond the "closing" of the frontier in the States, and settlers could homestead on federal land in Alaska for nearly 20 years after statehood. Remoteness, hardships, a low people-to-land ratio, and the myth of abundant natural resources tempted settlers and adventurers to energetically exploit the territory and obstruct conservation measures, especially those imposed from faraway Washington. Even the preservationist John Muir saw no danger of resource exhaustion. Conservation practices by Natives, to the extent that they existed, exerted almost no influence on the dominant Euro-American culture. Pre-statehood Alaska, especially in earlier years, exhibited an array of primitive environmental values.

VALUES IN ALASKA LAND AND WILDLIFE MANAGEMENT

Environmental values, or prescriptions governing the relations of humans to the natural environment, can be seen as ranging along scales of maturity or advancement. With respect to land and wildlife policy, four aspects are crucial: primary goals, management objectives, information-gathering methods, and decision-making power. By their nature and effects, these value-laden elements determine what happens in practice. They express and create environmental values.

Primary Goals

Primary goals are the fundamental purposes or outcomes we seek. What essentially do we want the human-nonhuman relationship to be? Options span a scale from (a) the absence of any environmental protection to (b) selective species protection to (c) ecosystem sustainability to (d) a holistic ideal of sustainable worldwide existence of humans and nonhumans. This scale parallels the spectrum ranging from uncontrolled exploitation to utilitarian conservation to preservation.

During the first half of the 1741–1867 Russian period, fur seekers pursued a goal of maximal and unrestricted acquisition of pelts, no matter what the impact on wildlife populations, ecosystems, or Native cultures. As of 1806 the Russian government made some headway in moving the goal forward to protection of selected species. After 1867 the basic goal of U.S. policy gradually changed from tolerance of unlimited exploitation to more farsighted purposes. In the whaling period and for most of their initial four decades of control, Americans vigorously engaged in poorly regulated and unsustainable taking of wildlife. No safeguards existed for the whales until after pelagic whaling had all but ceased in Alaska, and much the same applied to the sea otter, sea lion, and walrus. The federal government sought to conserve the fur seal as a valuable commercial resource. Prodded by nature societies and outdoor sporting clubs like Boone and Crockett and the Camp Fire Club, the government attempted to protect selected species through sea mammal treaties and the game laws of 1902–1925. Similarly, the Alaska Game Commission tried to conserve specific mammals and birds as a meat and fur supply for Alaskans. For the most part, large predators did not rank among the favored. Although hampered by the fishing industry's influence in Congress, federal fisheries agents attempted to conserve salmon runs. On the whole, management of Alaskan wildlife made a successful transition to utilitarian conservation. Nearly all species recovered from the depredations of the whaling and Gold Rush eras, in part as a result of government efforts.

Land reserves in Alaska directly or indirectly advanced ecosystem sustainability. Utilitarian conservation of wildlife, scientific curiosities, and tourist attractions may have been the main motives, but the reserves incorporated elements of the preservation ethic. Rooseveltian conservation policies inhibited immediate exploitation of timber, coal, and oil. The Tongass and Chugach national forests incidentally and temporarily shielded extensive terrain from fragmentation and degradation. Land designations in the form of national parks and monuments explicitly recognized elements of ecosystem sustainability. Thanks in large part to the work of Bob Marshall and Olaus and Margaret Murie, the setting aside of the Arctic National Wildlife Range represented an open commitment to ecosystem preservation. But not until the Wilderness Act of 1964 and the Alaska Lands Act of 1980 did national policy endorse the preservation principle on a grand scale.

Aboriginal Alaskans saw themselves as integral elements of a natural system, but few Alaska Natives incorporated traditional conservation practices into their 20th-Century lifestyles. Had they done so, they would have received little recognition prior to the emergence of modern environmentalism in the 1960s and 1970s. Muir, Marshall, and the Muries envisioned elements of a holistic relationship of humans to the nonhuman environment, well ahead of their time. But none of them systematically explicated their views of the proper role of humans. They wrote more for popular audiences than for academic publications. Moreover, they had urgent political work to do and might have weakened their influence by insisting, for example, that humans had no right to arbitrarily destroy ecosystems and their inhabitants. They generated more momentum toward their goals through less direct appeals and arguments for species or ecosystem sustainability.

Management Objectives

Resource management objectives are the shorter-term purposes of wildlife and land managers. They range from (a) unregulated, random exploitation to (b) sustainable consumptive use by humans (utilitarian conservation) to (c) nonconsumptive (scientific, recreational, aesthetic, spiritual) use by humans to (d) nonhuman (individual, species, or ecosystem) rights. Like the primary goals, they advance from (a) to (d) along the scale from exploitation to preservation.

Closely tied to the overarching goals, management objectives evolved similarly. Russia's government shifted the aim of fur-seeking activity from uncontrolled exploitation to utilitarianism or sustainable use of species. American administration featured weak efforts to realize sustainability, slowly improving in effectiveness over the near-century leading up to statehood. The reindeer experiment represented a rare, if doomed, attempt to incorporate the well-being of Natives into sustainable use objectives. Had it succeeded according to its broadest conception, however, it would have massively undermined ecosystem sustainability. Bob Marshall's Arctic park proposal envisioned Alaska Natives and whites living at subsistence levels, a concept partly realized in the post-statehood period through subsistence land use policies.

Nature groups preferred utilitarian objectives to unregulated exploitation, and outdoor sporting groups, trappers, and guides backed regulation as necessary for a continuing game and fur supply. The Bureau of Biological Survey and the Alaska Game Commission concentrated on sustainable use of desirable (primarily ungulate and valuable furbearer) species, an objective that seemed to warrant predator control. As an official management objective, utilitarian sustainable use occupied a dominant position throughout the 20th Century.

Some policy went to the next step and sought nonconsumptive uses, most notably the aesthetic and spiritual valuation of the grizzly bear, Mt. McKinley Park, Katmai, Glacier Bay, and the Arctic Refuge. Scientific and recreational benefits also helped justify the parklands. Arguments based on spiritual values, however, did not generate strong responses from government and the public, at least not in Alaska. Yet their impact is difficult to measure. Muir, Marshall, and Olaus and Margaret Murie appeared to gain stature as they promulgated such views.

Much higher barriers confronted the notion that wild creatures should not be mere "resources" for use by humans but that they are worthy in and of themselves. This idea came naturally to pre-contact Alaska Natives. But to Euro-Americans it had intolerable implications. It implied that nonhumans held rights that would comprehensively restrict human behavior toward them. The idea would also challenge the comforting belief that humans are morally superior, the rightful owners of Earth. Despite these formidable obstacles, arguments in favor of nonhuman rights made some headway. Elliott and Hornaday won admiration in the press and public for their attacks on the injustice of the unnecessary killing of fur seals. Presumably their audiences valued the scals' right to exist as a species. Many must have believed humans had no right to kill individual seals, especially for such trivial reasons as fashion. Even if they rejected the abstract principle of moral or legal rights for nonhumans, people's visceral reaction to the clubbing of wide-eyed, innocent creatures implied a belief in a form of individual animal rights. But legal rights for wild as distinct from domestic animals had no standing in the society. And ecosystem rights as such lay even farther in the future.

Grant, Hornaday, Holzworth, White, and others successfully defended the grizzly bears' right to exist. But wildlife advocates usually found it easier to employ utilitarian arguments. Valuing wildlife species as useful to humans, whether for skins or spiritual benefits, appealed to most people's self-indulgence and achieved much the same result as would legal rights for species. Predators, however, presented a different problem in that they appeared to force a choice between species. Believing that wolves, for example, threatened the well-being or even the existence of desired species such as Dall sheep, most people wanted to control or exterminate the wolves. Yet true belief in species rights required that the wolf be defended. During Alaska's territorial period, only a few naturalists and scientists dared to do so. When they did, their arguments usually rested not on species rights but on the need to complete ecosystems or to ensure the strength and health of prey populations.

Information-Gathering Methods

Information-gathering methods are the cognitive and affective processes that tell managers what is happening and what needs to be done. They range from (a) pre-scientific biases to (b) judgment based on field experience to (c) ecological science to (d) a holistic approach combining natural and social science, intuition, and aesthetic and spiritual perspectives. Generally, these too are correlates of the exploitation-preservation scale.

Human behavior is always linked, however consciously or rationally, to the apprehension of reality or "truth." Means of truth-seeking both reflect and mold environmental values. In the absence of scientific information, people exploited resources according to tradition or narrow self-interest. Tradition in the form of some Native practices consciously or indirectly supported sustainable use. In the case of Athabaskan Indians at least, field observation attained the level of descriptive, if not ecological, science. Europeans and Euro-Americans lacked strong traditions that fostered conservation. Their self-centered behavior, based largely on fear and greed, quickly exhausted resources and impaired ecosystems. Before wildlife management as a science got under way in the mid-20th Century, governments had to rely on the common sense and integrity of field agents using primitive tools of observation and measurement. Fair-minded observers could often see a resource disappearing and realize that its absence might entail serious costs. Far short of creating an understanding of natural processes, field surveys nevertheless contributed building blocks for gradually improving science and for utilitarian conservation.

Russians valued science as a basis for resource management and employed the judgments of informed observers in conservation of the fur seal and sea otter. Under American rule, science usually took a back seat to greed in the case of economically valuable resources (e.g., whales, walruses, sea otters, salmon, gold, oil, and many land mammals) and when the issue involved predators. International controversy brought science to the rescue of fur seals in the 1911 Fur Seal Treaty. Policy makers misapplied science in the introduction of some species, such as foxes on bird-nesting islands. They ventured into realms beyond their capacity to evaluate in their attempts to pastoralize northern Alaska and Eskimo culture through the importation of reindeer. During the early decades of the 20th Century the intuitive judgments of wardens and other agents, relying largely on anecdotal evidence, helped determine management policy. As in the case of predator control and bounties, they often reflected personal biases or served the immediate interests of settlers, hunters, or politicians.

Through the 1920s to the 1950s the Bureau of Biological Survey and the Fish and Wildlife Service increasingly hired university-trained agents, but most of them promoted the bureau's high-priority agenda of predator control. Science in the form of species population surveys assisted the Alaska Game Commission in wildlife management, but it came too late and too little to reform predator control policy before statehood. Newly emerging ecological science helped the National Park Service retain its goal of ecosystem sustainability in Mt. McKinley Park and other units. Ecological science laid a foundation for improved salmon management. It took years or even decades to alter the practices of field managers, especially in such an emotionally loaded matter as wolf control. Moreover, the mechanistic orientation of ecological science hampered its ability to understand the complexity of ecosystems, the more so when taking human actions into account. A more complete understanding of the place of humans in the environment called for integrated application of natural sciences, social sciences, and humanities.

More holistic perspectives characterized the behavior of some pre-contact Alaska Natives, especially Athabaskans. Holism informed the writings of a few Euro-Americans including Muir, Marshall, and Adolph, Olaus, and Margaret Murie. All of these people incorporated intuition, aesthetics, and spiritual or psychological values in their philosophies, and Marshall applied elements of economics and sociology as well. To an extent, holism won tangible expression in the preservation of large tracts of land and in the eventual alteration of predator control policy. A more systematic integration of natural and social sciences emerged in cooperative Alaska wildlife management programs in the late 20th Century.

Decision-Making Power

Decision-making power is the matter of who decides what will be done. It is basic to all politics and social justice. Within the context of natural resource policy the options range from (a) anarchical scramble for resources to (b) government collusion with favored interest groups to (c) management by nonpolitical government resource experts to (d) shared stewardship through government and corporate accountability, public participation, and representation for nonhumans. These options also parallel and express the exploitation-preservation value spectrum.

Participation in decision making is important for at least two reasons. First, it determines which humans benefit from a resource, sometimes making the difference between life and death. Tight Russian control of access to birds, fish, and mammals helped keep Aleut and Koniag subjects in a state of subjugation intended to further Russia's aims in North America. The relative freedom enjoyed by Americans, excepting the Aleuts, resulted in a lawless assault on wildlife that served short-term individual economic purposes. As public access to government and information widened and commercially valuable resources showed signs of depletion, government intervened. Enhanced government control spread the benefits to more people over a longer time span.

Press and public involvement are usually necessary to avoid the appropriation of publicly owned resources for the benefit of narrow interests, as demonstrated in the fights over the fur seals and the Alaska coal lands. Nature and sporting groups, sometimes backed by elements of the national press, protected Mt. McKinley, Katmai, and Glacier Bay from damage by miners and other resource extractors. Alaska newspapers and citizen groups, on the other hand, typically worked to make public resources available to exploitative interests. Alaska Natives, almost entirely excluded from natural resource decision making and without an influential mass media voice, received less than their fair share of benefits under the law until after statehood.

Power to make management decisions is also a key determinant in the fate of the resource. Open availability of resources leads to rapid depletion, and excessive collusion between government and consumptive interest groups can do the same. Control by government experts, in the North American context, normally means long-term conservation of valued resources. But this can cause excessive damage to elements not favored, such as predators, or otherwise disrupt ecosystems. Public involvement, if enlightened, can curb some of the environmental abuses by both government officials and corporations.

Russia's authoritarian government never aspired to involve its general public in decision making, although it sought to control the fur trade for national economic benefit. Following a period of little or no regulation it appointed managers of the fur trade and discouraged uncoordinated profit seeking by individuals. Through the Russian-American Company, as much an arm of government as an interest group, it instituted utilitarian conservation rules. This approach worked best for fur seals because nearly all harvest occurred on land controlled by Russia. Sea otters, spending much of their time in far-flung international waters and pursued by men from several nations, needed more protection than the Russian government could provide. Much the same applied to whales.

The U.S. government found it considerably more difficult to manage the behavior of its fractious and aggressively acquisitive citizens and struggled for decades to incorporate management of wildlife by experts. It failed to protect the sea otters and right whales until they had all but disappeared. Favoritism toward interest groups, notably the Alaska Commercial Company, inevitably emerged during the post–Civil War era of capitalism. But the ensuing Progressive Era set the stage for a political-environmental contest that brought the fur seals and sea otters firmly under government control. The press and attentive public also received a share in the decision making on fur seal management, although the Aleuts had little say in the matter until after statehood.

For better or worse, nature and hunting groups in the States and hunters and trappers in Alaska enjoyed strong influence in wildlife management. In an age of inordinate corporate power, such elite bodies as the Boone and Crockett Club had the best chance of persuading the national government to adopt conservation measures. Fortunately for resource sustainability, the elite nature and hunting groups worked primarily for conservation rather than consumptive exploitation. They advocated management by government experts as an improvement over random exploitation and favoritism toward consumptive interests such as market hunters. The Alaska Game Commission incorporated public representation into its structure but disproportionately served the interests of white hunters, trappers, and guides.

Through such land reservations as the Tongass and Chugach national forests, Theodore Roosevelt managed to curb random and monopolistic exploitation of forests and coal. But in the case of gold mining and Kenai oil drilling in the 1950s, government seldom got beyond minimal oversight of rapacious treatment of the environment. In the case of Kenai oil, it displayed favoritism toward particular private interests.

Land designations, however, and to a lesser extent wildlife disputes, often involved the general public as meaningful participants in policy. Numerous groups had a voice in the formation of the McKinley and Glacier Bay parklands and the Arctic National Wildlife Range. Katmai's designation flowed from extraordinary political access on the part of the National Geographic Society, but the society sought a benevolent public purpose.

Advances in education, travel, and communications technology increased public awareness and participation after World War II. By the 1970s, national legislation encouraged citizen involvement in many aspects of resource management through hearings, appeals, and lawsuits. Alaska Native user groups engaged in cooperative management of specific wildlife species, including whales, polar bears, and geese. Environmental management in Alaska evolved toward shared stewardship.

Environmental goals, management objectives, research methods, and participation in policy evolved toward more enlightened treatment of Alaskan lands and wildlife over the two centuries before statehood (Table 18.1 attempts to quantify the environmental values manifested by the leaders and issues covered in this volume). Alaskan issues have contributed disproportionately to a national value shift. The territory's remoteness encouraged excesses but also deterred human population growth and industrial development until more mature environmental values had evolved.

ALASKA'S IMPACT ON THE NATION

Pre-statehood Alaska disproportionately affected the evolution of American environmentalism, for several reasons. Most ecosystems in the States had been thoroughly disrupted by the eve of the 20th Century; Alaska's had not. Federal ownership (Native claims aside) of nearly all the land, and a dearth of settlers, lent government officials and interested members of the public an opportunity to determine the disposal of a large and relatively unspoiled realm. Ensuing debates illuminated many aspects of environmental concern including resource management goals (as in land designations), objectives (as in game bag limits), research methods (as in McKinley Park wolf control), techniques (as in salmon production and predator control), and participants (as in coal and oil policy).

Alaska's isolation and reputation for drama and grandeur, highly colored by the Gold Rush experience, attracted talented adventurers, hunters, scientists, and government officials. Many attained prominent positions in government and other realms of public affairs, advancing policy and public opinion up the scale of environmental responsibility. John Muir generated a wave of enthusiasm for the northern land and incorporated preservationist messages in his writing. His public stature enhanced his standing as an environmental thinker and activist, molding him into a prominent figure in the environmental movement. The Sierra Club he co-founded and led eventually became one of the most prominent environmental players nationwide and in Alaska. Henry W. Elliott, despite or because of his egotism and eccentricity, turned fur seal management into the first national and international debate on wildlife policy. Wealthy sport hunters such as Madison Grant and Charles Sheldon, initially devoted to conquest of wild beasts, went on to lead efforts to conserve them. For the many entranced by its wildlife and dismayed by what had happened in the States, Alaska tendered the possibility of large-scale species or ecosystem preservation.

TABLE 18.1. Environmental Values Expressed by Alaskan Issues and Leaders, 1741–1960

	Sea Otters	*Fur Seals*	*Whales/Walrus*	*John Muir*	*Boone and Crockett Club*	*Mt. McKinley Park*	*Glacier Bay National Park*	*Katmai National Park*	*Alaska Natives*	*Bureau of Biological Survey*	*Alaska Wildlife Managers*	*Grizzly Bears*	*Predator Control*	*Game Mammals*	*Salmon*	*Kenai Peninsula*	*Arctic Refuge*	*Bob Marshall*	*Muries*
Primary goal																			
A No protection	5	2	5	0	0	-	-	-	?	0	0	3	2	2	3	3	-	0	0
B Selected species	3	5	2	0	5	5	2	3	?	5	5	4	5	5	5	2	0	0	0
C Eco-sustainability	1	1	0	4	3	4	4	4	?	2	2	3	2	2	2	1	4	4	5
D Holistic ideal	0	0	0	4	0	0	0	0	4	0	0	0	0	0	0	0	1	2	2
Management objective																			
A Unregulated	5	3	5	0	0	-	-	-	?	0	0	3	2	2	3	3	-	0	0
B Sustainable use	0	5	2	2	5	2	1	1	2	5	5	4	5	5	5	4	2	3	5
C Nonconsumptive use	1	1	0	5	2	5	5	5	4	1	2	3	2	1	0	0	5	5	5
D Nonhuman rights	0	1	0	4	1	0	0	0	3	0	0	1	0	0	0	0	0	0	2
Information-gathering method																			
A Pre-science	5	5	5	?	0	-	-	-	5	0	0	4	5	3	3	3	-	0	0
B Field experience	3	5	2	3	5	4	4	4	5	5	5	4	5	5	5	4	3	5	5
C Ecological science	1	2	0	2	1	3	1	2	0	1	1	1	2	1	2	1	0	2	2
D Holistic	0	0	0	3	0	0	0	0	2	0	0	0	0	0	0	0	1	3	3
Decision-making power																			
A No control	5	2	5	0	0	-	-	-	0	0	0	2	2	2	2	2	-	0	0
B Favored groups	2	3	1	0	3	1	2	1	?	2	2	1	3	2	2	2	1	1	0
C Government experts	2	4	2	3	5	5	5	4	?	5	5	4	5	5	5	4	4	5	5
D Shared stewardship	0	1	1	2	0	1	1	0	?	0	1	1	0	1	0	0	0	?	1

Note: Emphasis on value is graded from 0 to 5, the highest. Weights are author estimates.

The territory also interested the public because it presented a stage on which pioneer fantasies could still be played out. A surviving facsimile of the Wild West, Alaska seemed to offer a chance, vicariously or viscerally, to return to the past. Coming under American control as the frontier began to disappear in the West, it fell into place as an extension of the frontier, perpetuating the notion of continual American expansion. This idea encouraged Americans to believe that Alaska could be openly exploited and to go there and seek their fortunes at the expense of the environment.

Alaska entered the nation's environmental agenda not long before the Progressive Era, a backlash stemming in part from the destruction of natural resources by powerful economic interests. Resistance to acquisition of Alaska coal lands by the Morgan-Guggenheim Syndicate produced a classic muckraking morality play casting conservationists as heroes. Several prominent New York Progressive leaders, including George Bird Grinnell, Madison Grant, and

Theodore Roosevelt, gave high priority to protection of resources in Alaska. Through the Boone and Crockett Club, New York Zoological Society, and related organizations, they functioned within a network of elites that made numerous and continuing contributions to safeguarding species and natural areas nationwide. Over time, their focus of concern moved from game species toward ecosystem sustainability and preservation.

Early cruise ship tours and the Harriman Expedition of 1899 illustrated Alaska' attraction for the socially prominent, and the *New York Times*, probably the nation's foremost newspaper, displayed an ongoing interest in Alaskan and natural resource issues. Grinnell, Grant, Charles Sheldon, William T. Hornaday, Charles H. Townsend, and, to some extent, Theodore Roosevelt operated out of New York. Bob Marshall, a firmly Progressive New Yorker, may have been responsible for protecting more wildland acreage than any other person save a few U.S. presidents. His achievements and legacy within the Wilderness Society strengthened the nation's commitment to ecosystem sustainability. The New York and Washington elites, motivated in part by their fascination about Alaska, had an extraordinary impact on national policy toward its wildlife and wildlands.

The Progressive Era found expression in utilitarian conservation of wildlife. Theodore Roosevelt's ideal of efficient government management of natural resources permeated agency perspectives. Adopting an aggressively managerial attitude, the Bureau of Biological Survey (BBS) vigorously strove for protection of game species and for reserves. But the managerial bent included an obsessive desire to control predators that lasted far longer than could be justified by evidence. BBS agent Olaus Murie and his brother Adolph in the National Park Service, informed by their Alaska experiences, resisted the policy. Their writings, and the McKinley Park wolf controversy, hastened the decline of predator control nationwide.

Land disposal decisions in the territorial period, notably reservation of the popular Glacier Bay and to a lesser extent Katmai and Mt. McKinley, strengthened national commitment to principles of ecosystem preservation by their example. Robert F. Griggs and William S. Cooper enlisted numerous groups in the States in the campaigns for Katmai and Glacier Bay national monuments. Designation of McKinley Park for mountain sheep, and such lands as the Kodiak brown bear and Kenai moose ranges facilitated by Ira Gabrielson, accomplished some of the same for species sustainability. The Arctic National Wildlife Range enhanced national interest in the nonconsumptive values of wilderness and lent force to the emerging environmental movement. Olaus Murie's work in the Wilderness Society ultimately went far in shaping national wildland policy. He and his surviving wife, Margaret, grew into permanent symbols of Alaskan wilderness and the wisdom of cherishing it.

Lack of population density and resources of interest to mining and logging corporations made possible almost all of the major Alaska land preservation decisions. Yet regardless of the motives behind their selection, the national public valued their spectacular quality, which reinforced the prestige of the National Park and Fish and Wildlife services and the nation's complex of wild parklands.

ENVIRONMENTALISM IN ALASKA

Evolution of environmental values among the Alaskan public lagged well behind that in the States. In the near-absence of opinion polls, uncertainty must exist regarding the balance of sentiments. Anecdotal evidence and the consistent behavior of the business community and territorial legislature suggest that all-out appropriation of resources reigned as the dominant goal. To the extent that Native conservation practices existed, Euro-Americans ignored them. Governors and legislators perpetually badgered the federal government for control of natural resources, not granted the territory in the 1912 act. They accepted the federal government's utilitarian objective of sustainability of economically useful species such as salmon but resisted almost any moves toward nonconsumptive use goals (for such as the grizzly bear) and ecosystem sustainability through federal reserves. They did not encounter public participation by local environmental groups; virtually none existed in Alaska before statehood. They did not respond to scientific evidence questioning the viability of the bounty system and predator control in general. In sum, most pre-statehood Alaskans disdained almost every manifestation of advanced environmental thinking. The impetus for nearly all gains in environmental awareness and policy came from outside, or from federal agents and scholars in Alaska.

After statehood, stout resistance to environmental values persisted in the legislature and other elements of Alaskan society. Many business leaders, state politicians, and the congressional delegation perpetuated the frontier myths of unlimited natural resources and the need to reduce federal control. They brushed aside the fact that most of Alaska belonged to the nation, not to Alaskans for their consumptive use. On into the 21st Century they favored open exploitation of resources, tolerated some utilitarian conservation, and opposed nearly all forms of preservation. Environmental protection and environmentalists represented, to them, barriers to economic development. They persisted in imagining that the land held enough resources to permit them in ever-swelling numbers to fashion comfortable middle-class lifestyles in perpetuity. They ignored or denied the fact that the state's economy rested on one or two nonrenewable natural resources and on subsidies, both controlled from the outside. Essentially residents of a welfare state, they preferred to fancy themselves as rugged individualists. They refused to make preparations for a time when resources or subsidies might disappear. In essence, they rejected economic and environmental sustainability.

But seeds of change, planted earlier, sprouted. Some federal officials of the territorial period joined the Alaska Department of Fish and Game or remained in federal agencies overseeing Alaskan sea mammals, migratory birds, or federal lands. Their ecologically oriented training affected wildlife and land management policy. Research broadened, and emphasis on bounties and predator control lessened. Rising income levels and improved access by air, sea, and highway brought multiplying numbers of visitors to Alaska. Tourism promoters including the state encouraged the "last frontier" image of a romantic, free, relatively unspoiled holdover from the past. The image glamorized consumptive exploitation and ignored conservation, at least until the advent of ecotourism later in the 20th Century. The new state drew increased attention from national media and environmental groups, creating pressure for greater environmental protection. The 1980 Alaska Lands Act demonstrated and reinforced national commitment to values of wilderness and ecosystem preservation, shared by a strong minority of Alaskans.

Initiated by the Alaska Conservation Society, an effective environmental community sprang up in Alaska, composed of long-time residents, outsiders who moved to the state, and branch offices of national environmental organizations. This coalition has significantly shaped state and national legislation, monitored compliance of companies and government agencies, and mounted numerous lawsuits in the service of environmental protection. The state legislature passed a fair amount of environmentally protective legislation until it turned strongly conservative in the mid-1990s. Post-statehood Alaskan resource disputes such as Tongass logging and the *Exxon Valdez* oil spill caught the interest of the American public and set precedents in national policy. As the repository of the nation's greatest store of wildlands, the state assumed a rising position on the nation's environmental agenda. By degrees, the management of both federal and state natural resources in Alaska moved haltingly in the direction of advanced environmental values. Alaskan environmental controversies continued to be a causal force in the evolution of American environmental values.

Maturation of the environmental movement in the last quarter of the 20th Century did not signal the adoption of the most advanced principles by a majority of the national public or even by most environmentalists. It did embody a shift in opinion, public discourse, and management policy toward more advanced, preservationist values. Ecosystem sustainability is replacing the focus on favored species, and nonconsumptive uses are superseding the notion that the purpose of wild creatures is to be killed, skinned, and eaten by humans.

Scholarly inquiry has proliferated, and numerous citizen groups regularly participate in policy making. Holistic perspectives have become part of the debate. Public opinion polls, legislation, media coverage, and other indicators leave no serious doubt that attitudes toward the environment have progressed both in the Lower 48 and in Alaska.

Nor can it necessarily be assumed that adoption of the most advanced (some would say extreme) environmental principles must be preferable to all competing values. Determination of what is best for a society or for Earth under given circumstances is a monumental undertaking, calling at minimum for generous applications of science and philosophy, tempered by discipline and compassion. Yet accumulating knowledge has moved thoughtful Alaskans, and the American body politic as a whole, several steps in the direction of environmentalism.

Notes

CHAPTER 1: SEA OTTERS AND SCIENTISTS

1. R. Fisher, *Bering's Voyages*, 126–129; R. Fisher "Finding America," 4–12; Goldenberg, *Gvozdev*, 26, 64–66. Gvozdev had command in place of the navigator Gens (ill and left in port) and assistant navigator Fedorov (onboard but lacking the authority or strength to command) (Goldenberg, 54–57).
2. Fedorova, *Russian Population*, 40–51, 98–99.
3. R. Fisher, *Bering's Voyages*, 148–150.
4. L. Black, *Russians in Alaska,* 43–48; McCracken, *Hunters of the Stormy Sea,* 22–26.
5. Orth, *Dictionary of Alaska Place Names*, 917.
6. L. Black, *Russians in Alaska*, 67–68; Stejneger, *Georg Wilhelm Steller*, 350–354.
7. Stejneger, "How the Sea-Cow Became Exterminated," 1049.
8. Ibid. It is believed that in modern times the sea cow lived only in the Kommandorski (Commander) Islands, of which Bering Island is the largest, and that the spectacled cormorant nested only on Bering Island. The Kommandorski Islands remained part of Russia following the land transfer in 1867.
9. D. Spencer, "Aleutian Islands National Wildlife Refuge," 16.

10. Scheffer, *Adventures of a Zoologist*, 68.
11. Bancroft, *History of Alaska*, 38–41, 69, 78–79; Golder, *Bering's Voyages*, 1–5; Stejneger, *Georg Wilhelm Steller*, 4, 14, 29–32, 46–52, 368–370, 408–422, 481–486.
12. Golder, *Bering's Voyages*, 233.
13. Steller, *Journal of a Voyage*, 143–144, 146. When first encountered, the otters spent much of their time on land, ranging more than half a mile from shore.
14. Berkh, *Chronological History*, 1, 11–12; Makarova, *Russians on the Pacific*, 2, 97–98, 114.
15. Berkh, *Chronological History*, 11–13; L. Black, *Atkha*, 77–79; Makarova, *Russians on the Pacific*, 98–99, 101–102, 107, 115.
16. Liapunova, "Relations With the Natives," 114–116; Berkh, *Chronological History*, 13, 17; L. Black, *Atkha*, 80–81.
17. McCracken, *Hunters of the Stormy Sea*, 38–39, 56–57, 190.
18. Ibid.
19. Dayvidov, *Two Voyages*, 194, 218.
20. Liapunova, "Relations With the Natives," 108–109; Berkh, *Chronological History*, 4–6, 25.
21. Liapunova, "Relations With the Natives," 105–106, 108, 111; Berkh, *Chronological History*, 31–43; Gibson, "Russian Dependence," 80.
22. Liapunova, "Relations With the Natives," 127; L. Black, *Russians in Alaska*, 110–111, 225–230.
23. R. Fisher, "Finding America," 18–19.
24. L. Black, *Russians in Alaska*, 106–111, 126–127, 209.
25. Liapunova, "Relations With the Natives," 124; L. Black, *Atkha*, 89, 92–93; Gibson, "Russian Dependence," 80–81; Gideon, *Around the World Voyage*, 62–70.
26. L. Black, *Russians in Alaska*, 128–130. Lantis, *Ethnohistory in Southwestern Alaska*, 179, sets the figure at 80 percent.
27. Dayvidov, *Two Voyages*, 191–197.
28. Makarova, *Russians on the Pacific*, 162–164.
29. Gibson, "Russian Dependence," 81–84, 88; Fedorova, *Russian Population*, 131–134; Du Four, "Russian Withdrawal," 60–64.
30. Ogden, "Russian Sea-Otter and Seal Hunting," 217–237.
31. Ibid., 229–230, 234–239.
32. Fedorova, *Russian Population*, 135, 143–144, 198; Okun, *Russian-American Company*, 122–152.
33. Berkh, *Chronological History*, 89–91; Bertrand, "Geographical Exploration," 256–258.
34. Applegate, *Report on Population, 1890*, 201.
35. Gibson, *Otter Skins*, 56–58, 178, 181, 277.
36. Gibson, *Imperial Russia*, 155–157, 167–168.
37. Fedorova, *Russian Population*, 187, 190; Gibson, "Russian Dependence," 81–82; Gruening, *State of Alaska*, 20.
38. Gibson, "Russian Dependence," 81–82; Fedorova, *Russian Population*, 139, 187, 190.

39. Gibson, "Russian Dependence," 98–102; Liapunova, "Relations With the Natives," 134.
40. Gideon, *Around the World Voyage*, 79.
41. Liapunova, "Relations With the Natives," 136–142.
42. Fedorova, *Russian Population*, 155.
43. Gibson, *Otter Skins*, 234–236, 272, 275–277.
44. Lensink, "History and Status of Sea Otters," 12–15; Golovin, *End of Russian America*, 78–79.
45. Berkh, *Chronological History*, 93; Lensink, "History and Status of Sea Otters," 15.
46. Elliott, "Ten Years' Acquaintance," 809.
47. Elliott, "The Sea-Otter Fishery," 489–491.
48. Hussey, *Embattled Katmai*, 194–202; Healy, *Report of the* Corwin, *1884*, 19.
49. Applegate, *Report on Population, 1890*, 203–204.
50. Lensink, "History and Status of Sea Otters," 14–18.
51. Hooper, *Report on the Sea-Otter Banks*, 3–5.
52. Hinckley, "Alaska and the Emergence," 85–87.
53. Gibson, "Russian Dependence," 88–89; Bockstoce, *Whales, Ice, and Men*, 191.
54. Hamlin, "Condition of Seal Life," 453.
55. Applegate, *Report on Population, 1890*, 214.
56. Tansill, *Canadian-American Relations*, 282, 359.
57. Lensink, "History and Status of Sea Otters," 17–18; Kenyon, *The Sea Otter*, 136; 36 Stat. 326, April 21, 1910; *Convention for the Preservation and Protection of Fur Seals in the North Pacific*, TS 563, July 7, 1911; President William Howard Taft, Executive Order 1733, March 3, 1913.
58. McCracken, *Hunters of the Stormy Sea*, 292–294.
59. Eyerdam, "Sea Otters in the Aleutian Islands," 71.
60. D. Spencer, "Aleutian National Wildlife Refuge," 12, 45–51.
61. Alaska Game Commission, *5th Annual Report, 1929*, 4.
62. Merritt, "History, 1741–1967," 124–128.
63. Kohlhoff, *When the Wind Was a River*, 85, 136, 165–168.
64. Merritt, "History, 1741–1967," 128–130.
65. D. Spencer, "Aleutian National Wildlife Refuge," 59–60.
66. Emanuel, "Robert 'Sea Otter' Jones," 41–44.
67. Calkins and Schneider, "Sea Otter," 3.
68. Kenyon and Spencer, *Otter Population and Transplant Studies,* 13–18; Laycock, "Moving Day for Sea Otters," 62, 70–72; Burris and McKnight, *Game Transplantation*, 35–37.
69. U.S. Dept. of Agriculture, *Alaskan Wildlife Refuges*.
70. S. Evans, *Historical View*, 89.
71. Calkins and Schneider, "Sea Otter," 4–5.
72. *Alaska Economic Report*, "Sea Otter Harvest," 7.
73. *Exxon Valdez* Oil Spill Trustees, Exxon Valdez *Oil Spill Restoration, Vol. 1*, 20.
74. Calkins and Schneider, "Sea Otter," 4.
75. Kaiser, "Sea Otter Declines," 390–391; T. Williams et al., "Killer Appetites," 3380–3381.
76. Palmisano, "Sea Otter Predation," abstract, 110–139.

CHAPTER 2: FUR SEAL'S FRIEND: HENRY W. ELLIOTT

1. F. Martin, *Sea Bears*, 31–32, 45–50. In all probability, at least two other vessels visited the Pribilofs earlier and took cargoes of skins. See L. Black, *Russians in Alaska*, 75n22.
2. A. Roppel, *Management of Northern Fur Seals*, 1. Toward the end of the 20th Century, breeding colonies also existed at Bogoslav Island west of Unalaska and on Sea Lion Rock west of Dall Island in the Southeast.
3. Litke, *Voyage Around the World*, 110–113.
4. Veniaminov, *Notes on the Islands*, 342.
5. Busch, *War Against the Seals*, 4, 6, 10–11, 17–18, 36.
6. Gibson, *Otter Skins*, 252–253, 262–264.
7. Stevenson, "Skins of Fur-Seals," 24502–24503.
8. Okun, *Russian-American Company*, 60–62. For a slightly different version of the story of wastage of skins, see Gibson, *Imperial Russia*, 37.
9. Busch, *War Against the Seals*, 99–100; Applegate, *Report on Population, 1890*, 204–205, 208; Veniaminov, *Notes on the Islands*, 344–345; Scheffer, Fiscus, and Todd, *History of Scientific Study*, 3–4.
10. L. Black, *Russians in Alaska*, 262, 267, 275, 280–281.
11. Okun, *Russian-American Company*, 226, 244–261. David Miller, *Alaska Treaty*, also relates causes and events leading to the sale of Alaska.
12. F. Martin, *Sea Bears*, 78, 80, 89; Scheffer, Fiscus, and Todd, *History of Scientific Study*, 5. Martin, p. 78, sets the 1869 kill at 365,000 or more.
13. Scheffer, Fiscus, and Todd, *History of Scientific Study*, 5–7.
14. Murray, *Vagabond Fleet*, 41.
15. Busch, *War Against the Seals*, 110–112, 115.
16. D. Jones, *Century of Servitude*, 5, 7, 10, 15, 20, 22–24, 28–29.
17. Ibid., 27–29.
18. Murray, *Vagabond Fleet*, 41, 45–46.
19. F. Martin, *Sea Bears*, 93–94; Wright, *Lewis and Dryden's Marine History*, 425–426.
20. Murray, *Vagabond Fleet*, 19, 24, 28, 156.
21. Ibid., 21–22.
22. Busch, *War Against the Seals*, 136.
23. Healy, *Cruise of the* Corwin, *1884*, 33–34.
24. Elliott, "Report on the Condition of the Fur-Seal Rookeries," 510–511.
25. Jordan and Clark, *Seal and Salmon Fisheries, Vol. 1*, 229.
26. Elliott, *Seal-Islands of Alaska*, 157, 170; Elliott, *Our Arctic Province*, 232–253.
27. Busch, *War Against the Seals*, 119–121; Gay, "Henry W. Elliott," 214.
28. A. Roppel, *Management of Northern Fur Seals*, 16–17.
29. Morris, "Keeper of the Seal," 2–4.
30. Fitzhugh and Seilig, "Smithsonian's Alaska Connection," 194–198; ibid., 11–12.
31. James, *First Scientific Exploration*, 1–18.
32. Sherwood, *Exploration of Alaska*, 36–54.

33. Morris, "Keeper of the Seal," 12–13, 17.
34. Ibid., 34–37, 65–67; Shalkop, "Henry W. Elliott: Fighter," 8–12.
35. Gruening, *State of Alaska*, 68–70. In the November 1877 *Harper's*, p. 802, Elliott asserted that Alaska "bids fair . . . never to be a treasure trove for the miner or the agriculturalist."
36. Gruening, *State of Alaska*, 90–92, 516n33; Busch, *War Against the Seals*, 123–124.
37. Murray, *Vagabond Fleet*, 57.
38. Tansill, *Canadian-American Relations*, 270, 277, 293, 299, 314–315.
39. C. Campbell, "Anglo-American Crisis," 394–395, 403–414; ibid., 322–324.
40. Tansill, *Canadian-American Relations*, 322–329.
41. Ibid., 336–337, 340, 345–347; F. Martin, *Sea Bears*, 121–127.
42. Stevenson, "Skins of Fur-Seals," 24502–24503. U.S. government reports gathered from vessel owners listed far lower kill totals, e.g., an 1894 high of 61,838 (Scheffer, Fiscus, and Todd, *History of Scientific Study*, 8).
43. T. Bailey, "North Pacific Sealing Convention," 2–3, 2n6, 2n8.
44. Townsend, "Condition of Seal Life," 471.
45. Ibid., 470–471. Spears, better described as harpoons, could be 20 feet long (Robert DeArmond, letter to author, April 12, 2002).
46. DeArmond, "Sailing for Furs," 15–16, 23–24.
47. Austin, *Japanese Fur Sealing*, 16–18.
48. Ibid., 18.
49. DeArmond, "Sailing for Furs," 25.
50. Austin, *Japanese Fur Sealing*, 18–20.
51. Murray, *Vagabond Fleet*, 32, 201–204, 207.
52. T. Bailey, "North Pacific Sealing Convention," 3–5.
53. K. Dorsey, *Dawn of Conservation Diplomacy*, 120, 125–126.
54. Jordan and Clark, "Appendix," 701–702, 705, 711–714.
55. K. Dorsey, *Dawn of Conservation Diplomacy*, 126–129.
56. Tansill, *Canadian-American Relations*, 347–348, 353, 364–365, 369.
57. Busch, *War Against the Seals*, 154–157; Jordan, *Matka and Kotik*.
58. Morris, "Keeper of the Seal," 1, 52, 77, 88, 102, 106–107, 126.
59. Dorsey, *Dawn of Conservation Diplomacy*, 135–141.
60. Booth, "Henry W. Elliott," 22, 25; Geiger, "Saga of the Alaskan Fur Seals," 11–12; F. Martin, *Sea Bears*, 145; Hornaday, *Thirty Years War*, 174–181; 36 Stat. 326, April 21, 1910.
61. Dorsey, *Dawn of Conservation Diplomacy*, 148–152.
62. TS 563, July 7, 1911; T. Bailey, "North Pacific Sealing Convention," 4n11, 5–14.
63. Dorsey, *Dawn of Conservation Diplomacy*, 159–162.
64. *New York Times*, "No More Slaughtering of Seals For Five Years." September 1, 1912, Part 5, 10.
65. Morris, "Keeper of the Seal," 134.
66. D. Jones, *Century of Servitude*, 21, 39–40, 44–47.
67. Scheffer, Fiscus, and Todd, *History of Scientific Study*, 19–20, 26–27.

68. Riley, *Fur Seal Industry*, 9.
69. Bean and Rowland, *Evolution of International Wildlife Law*, 472n14.
70. Robert DeArmond, letter to author, April 12, 2000.
71. Austin, *Japanese Fur Sealing*, 21–22.
72. Bean and Rowland, *Evolution of International Wildlife Law*, 473.
73. Thorne, "Nature Ramblings," 124.
74. East, "Uncle Sam's Prize Fur Factory," 189, 193.
75. Kohlhoff, *When the Wind Was a River*, 8–10, 89–96, 114–115, 147.
76. D. Jones, *Century of Servitude*, 176–177; Busch, *War Against the Seals*, 239–240.
77. Kenyon, Scheffer, and Chapman, *Population Study of Alaskan Fur-Seal Herd*, 41, 44–48.
78. Scheffer, Fiscus, and Todd, *History of Scientific Study*, 27, 42–43; *Convention on North Pacific Fur Seals*, 314 UNTS 105.
79. A. Roppel, *Management of Northern Fur Seals*, 1, 6–9, 19–20; Busch, *War Against the Seals*, 226–227.
80. Murray, *Vagabond Fleet*, 237.
81. Steve Zimmerman, pers. com., July 3, 2002.
82. Angliss, De Master, and Lopez, *Alaska Marine Mammal Stock Assessments, 2001*, 19–22.
83. Sarah Kershaw, "Decline of Hardy Alaskan Fur Seals Baffles Experts," *New York Times*, February 22, 2005: F4.
84. Morris, "Keeper of the Seal," 1, 136, 139, 145; Shalkop, "Henry Wood Elliott," 9–15; Busch, *War Against the Seals*, chaps. 4, 5.
85. F. Martin, *Sea Bears*, 148, 158.
86. Cart, "Struggle for Wildlife Protection," 31–32.
87. Scheffer, *Adventures of a Zoologist*, 92–93.

CHAPTER 3: WAKE OF THE WHALERS

1. Kushner, *Conflict on the Northwest Coast*, 82; Ray, *Eskimos of Bering Strait*, 198. According to Bodfish, *Chasing the Bowhead*, 89, the *Superior* and *Ocmulgee* entered the Arctic Ocean in the fog about the same time, and no one knew which got there first.
2. S. Evans, *Historical View*, 129; H. Collins, Clark, and Walker, *Aleutian Islands*, 29.
3. Petroff, "Report on the Population," 392–393.
4. Durham, "Historical Perspective," 5.
5. Bockstoce, "Eskimo Whaling," 4.
6. Petroff, "Report on the Population," 368.
7. Ibid.; Dayvidov, *Two Voyages*, 225.
8. Bancroft, *History of Alaska*, 193.
9. S. Evans, *Historical View*, 131–132; Petroff, "Report on the Population," 351–352.
10. R. Webb, *On the Northwest*, 40–47, 54, 68.

11. Ibid., 69–72.
12. Scammon, "Northern Whaling," 548–549.
13. Scidmore, "Alaska Fish and Game," 841.
14. Best, "Estimates of Landed Catch," 416.
15. Bockstoce, *Whales, Ice and Men*, 73–74.
16. Clark, "Whale Fishery," 74; ibid., 95.
17. Francis, *History of World Whaling*, 149–151.
18. Best, "Estimates of Landed Catch," 406–407, 410–411.
19. Carroll, "Utilization of the Bowhead Whale," 1–4.
20. Bockstoce, *Whales, Ice and Men*, 94–95.
21. VanStone, "Commercial Whaling," 3–5.
22. S. Evans, *Historical View*, 140–46; ibid., 2–6.
23. Bockstoce, "History of Commercial Whaling," 22.
24. Best, "Estimates of Landed Catch," 416.
25. Bockstoce, "History of Commercial Whaling," 22–24.
26. Bodfish, *Chasing the Bowhead*, 112.
27. Bockstoce, *Whales, Ice and Men*, 260, 327; Vanstone, "Commercial Whaling," 1, 10.
28. Schmitt, DeJong, and Winter, *Thomas Welcome Roys*, 43–44, 47.
29. Clark, "Whale Fishery," 77–78.
30. Gilbert, "Confederate Raider Shenandoah," 188–207.
31. Hawes, *Whaling*, 261–269.
32. Clark, "Whale Fishery," 84–85; Bockstoce, *Whales, Ice and Men*, 151–159.
33. Hegarty, *Returns of Whaling Vessels*, 23–43.
34. Hawes, *Whaling*, 270–273.
35. Tilton, *Cap'n George Fred*, 164–224; Hussey, *Embattled Katmai*, 290–293; J. Cook, *Pursuing the Whale*, 124–125.
36. Joe King, "When Disaster Overtook the Whaling Fleet," 190–193, 196.
37. Bockstoce, "History of Commercial Whaling," 22, 24; VanStone, "Commercial Whaling," 9–10.
38. Marquette and Bockstoce, "Historical Shore-Based Catch of Bowhead Whales," 14, 16.
39. Morgan, "Modern Shore-Based Whaling," 37–41.
40. Reeves et al., "Whaling Results at Akutan," 446–447.
41. Evermann, *Alaska Fisheries and Fur Industries in 1913*, 130–131.
42. Governor of Alaska, *Report of Governor to Secretary of Interior*, 1920, 56.
43. Morgan, "Modern Shore-Based Whaling," 43; Governor of Alaska, *Report of Governor to Secretary of Interior*, 1914, 25–26.
44. R. Webb, *On the Northwest*, 236, 240–241, 244, 250–255.
45. Tonnessen and Johnsen, *History of Modern Whaling*, 115, 124–127, 169, 649.
46. R. Webb, *On the Northwest*, 241–242; Durham, "Historical Perspective," 6.
47. R. Webb, *On the Northwest*, 247.
48. Tonnessen and Johnsen, *History of Modern Whaling*, 453, 457, 461–462, 469–470, 500, 530–532.
49. Ibid., 123, 125, 658, 665–671.

50. Scarff, "Historic Distribution of the Right Whale," 51; Shelden et al., "Historical and Current Habitat Use by North Pacific Right Whales," 130, 133.
51. McClung, *Hunted Mammals of the Sea*, 37–40.
52. Angliss, De Master, and Lopez, *Alaska Marine Mammal Stock Assessments, 2001*, 131–136.
53. Ibid., 139–154.
54. Ibid., 160–167, 170–172.
55. Berkh, *Chronological History*, 99.
56. Bancroft, *History of Alaska*, 193.
57. Gibson, *Imperial Russia*, 36.
58. Perry, *World of the Walrus*, 124.
59. Litke, *Voyage Around the World*, 77–78.
60. Perry, *World of the Walrus*, 123–124.
61. Clark, "Pacific Walrus Fishery," 314–318.
62. Snell, "The Walrus and His Hunters," 16–17.
63. Stevenson, "Oils From Seals," 23615–23616.
64. Chance, *Eskimo of North Alaska*, 13–16; Huntington, *Wildlife Management*, 36–38.
65. Bockstoce, *Whales, Ice and Men*, 137–141, 201; Boeri, *People of the Ice Whale*, 56–59.
66. Brower, *Fifty Years Below Zero*, 77–79.
67. Bockstoce, *Whales, Ice, and Men*, 137–141, 201; Boeri, *People of the Ice Whale*, 56–59.
68. Mudar and Speaker, "Natural Catastrophes in Arctic Populations," 75–80, 99–102.
69. Hinckley, *Americanization of Alaska*, 82–83.
70. Healy, *Report of the* Corwin, *1884*, 17–18.
71. D. Mitchell, *Sold American*, 137–138.
72. Hinckley, "Alaska and the Emergence," 92–93.
73. Burch, *Traditional Eskimo Hunters*, 26.
74. S. Jackson, *Report on Introduction of Reindeer, 1893*, 5–7, 11–12. Anthropologist Dorothy Jean Ray (*The Eskimos of Bering Strait*, 200) argues that for the Bering Strait villages most reliant on walruses, including King Island, an adequate population of the animals remained despite the commercial slaughter.
75. McClung, *Hunted Mammals of the Sea*, 131–132.
76. Bockstoce, *Whales, Ice and Men*, 141; 35 Stat. 102, May 11, 1908.
77. Madsen, *Arctic Trader*, 188, 197–202.
78. Ibid., 188, 197–201.
79. Tonnessen and Johnsen, *History of Modern Whaling*, 122.
80. Madsen, *Arctic Trader*, 205–212.
81. Scull, *Hunting in the Arctic*, 10, 36, 110, 126, 133, 137–138, 141, 143, 160, 292.
82. Bernard, "Walrus Protection in Alaska," 100–101; Fay, *Pacific Walrus Investigations*, 4.
83. Chance, *Eskimo of North Alaska*, 15–17.

84. J. Brooks, "Contribution to History of the Walrus," 79, 86–92.
85. Fay, *Ecology of the Pacific Walrus*, 241–242; Baker, "Walrus," 30.
86. Burns, *Walrus in Alaska*, 1, 36; Sease and Chapman, "Pacific Walrus," 22–23.
87. Courtright, *Game Harvests in Alaska,* 34; Strickland, "Eskimo vs. the Walrus," 51–52, 57.
88. Angliss, De Master, and Lopez, *Alaska Marine Mammal Stock Assessments, 2001*, 193–196.
89. J. Allen, *History of North American Pinnipeds*, 261–274; Elliott, *Seal-Islands of Alaska*, 146–150.
90. A. Roppel, *Management of Northern Fur Seals*, 5.
91. Busch, *War Against the Seals*, 200–204.
92. D. Spencer, "Aleutian Islands National Wildlife Refuge," 27.
93. Dall, "On the Preservation of the Marine Mammals," 687.
94. Kenyon, "History of the Steller Sea Lion," 70–72.
95. Scheffer, *Adventures of A Zoologist*, 58–59.
96. Kenyon, "History of the Steller Sea Lion," 68, 73–75.
97. Dassow, "Utilization of Sea Lions," 6–9.
98. Calkins, "Steller Sea Lion," 4–5; 86 Stat. 1027, October 21, 1972.
99. Lowry, "Alaska's Seals and Sea Lions," 15–16.
100. Angliss, De Master, and Lopez, *Alaska Marine Mammal Stock Assessments, 2001*, 1, 2, 7, 11.
101. Hoover, "Harbor Seal," 138.
102. Dayvidov, *Two Voyages*, 221–222.
103. Catton, *Land Reborn*, 22–23, 110–111, 191–203.
104. Alaska Dept. of Fish and Game, *Annual Report for 1958*, 92, 95, 103.
105. Lowry, "Alaska's Seals and Sea Lions," 16–17.
106. Angliss, De Master, and Lopez, *Alaska Marine Mammal Stock Assessments, 2001*, 26–29, 34, 37, 41–44.
107. T. Williams et al., "Killer Appetites," 3380–3381.

CHAPTER 4: JOHN MUIR AND THE LAND

1. Wolfe, *John of the Mountains*, 317.
2. Fox, *John Muir and His Legacy*, 28–36, 48–50, 86–88; Muir, *Story of My Boyhood*, 2–3, 43–44, 62–75, 231–234; Cohen, *History of Sierra Club*, 1–6; *Dictionary of American Biography, Vol. VII*, 1934, 314–316; *National Cyclopedia of American Biography, Vol. IX*, 1907, 449–450; Sterling, *Biography of American and Canadian Naturalists and Environmentalists*, 563–566.
3. Oelschlaeger, *Idea of Wilderness*, 175–182, 178 (quotation), 186–193.
4. Kimes, *John Muir: A Reading Bibliography*, 165. The trips took place in 1879, 1880, 1881, 1890, 1896, 1897, and 1899.
5. Merrell, "A Wild, Discouraging Mess," 32.
6. Buske, "John Muir: Go To Alaska," 32; Muir, *Travels in Alaska*, 51–55.
7. Muir, *Stickeen*, 46–67, 73. Michael P. Cohen, *The Pathless Way*, 348–350, interprets Stickeen's fearful crossing of the bridge as symbolic of Muir's emotional self,

giving Muir a deeper understanding of his own fears, a greater tolerance for others, and a feeling of responsibility that made him reluctant to lead others into dangerous places in the wild seeking adventure rather than spiritual fulfillment.

8. Dannenbaum, "John Muir in Alaska," 18–19.
9. Muir, *Travels in Alaska*, 13–14.
10. Muir, "The Alaska Trip," 513–526.
11. Muir, *Letters From Alaska*, 66.
12. Norris, *Gawking at the Midnight Sun*, 16; Hinckley, "Inside Passage," 68, 73–74.
13. Buske, "The Wilderness, the Frontier," vii.
14. Kollin, *Nature's State*, 29–37.
15. Muir, *Travels in Alaska*, 25–26.
16. Ibid., 186.
17. Muir, *Cruise of the Corwin*, 162.
18. Muir, *Story of My Boyhood*, 69, 181; Mighetto, *Muir Among the Animals*, 192.
19. Cohen, *Pathless Way*, 166, 170–180.
20. Ibid., 174–180, 187.
21. Wolfe, *John of the Mountains*, 314–315.
22. Dannenbaum, "John Muir in Alaska," 16–18.
23. Muir, *Travels in Alaska*, 34–35.
24. Fleck, *Henry Thoreau and John Muir*, 52, 56–69.
25. Cohen, *Pathless Way*, 185–186; Muir, *Travels in Alaska*, 158, 169–170.
26. Young, *Alaska Days*, 140–141.
27. Catton, *Inhabited Wilderness*, 8–9, 26–27, 62, 68–69.
28. Tompkins, *Alaska: Promyshlennik and Sourdough*, 194; Buske, "John Muir and the Alaska Gold Rush," 40–42, 45.
29. Young, *Alaska Days*, 208–211; Buske, "John Muir and the Alaska Gold Rush," 45–49.
30. Buske, "John Muir: Go to Alaska," 37.
31. Nash, *Wilderness and the American Mind*, 283–285.
32. Morse, "Nature of Gold," 85–86.
33. Tompkins, *Alaska: Promyshlennik and Sourdough*, 227–235.
34. Heller, *Sourdough Sagas*, 183–184.
35. Walden, *Dog-Puncher on the Yukon*, 44–49.
36. Ibid.
37. Ibid.
38. Webb, *Yukon Frontiers*, 63.
39. Ibid., 75–76.
40. Morse, "Nature of Gold," 288–290, 312–317.
41. Ibid., 112–119, 132–137, 141.
42. Gruening, *State of Alaska*, 298.
43. Spence, *Northern Gold Fleet*, 2, 4, 92–93.
44. Baxter, Labaree, and Hildebrand, *On and Off Alaskan Trails*, 52–56.
45. Spence, *Northern Gold Fleet*, 9, 97–98.
46. Morse, "Nature of Gold," 147–160.

47. Hinckley, "Alaska and the Emergence," 106–107.
48. Komarek, "Principles of Fire Ecology," 14–15.
49. Morse, "Nature of Gold," 114, 243–245.
50. Lutz, *Aboriginal Man and White Man*, 4, 6, 11, 26 (quotation), 41–42.
51. Pyne, *Fire in America,* 499–502.
52. Lutz, *Ecological Effects of Forest Fires*. 13–14, 17–18.
53. Ibid., 14–16.
54. Oakes, *Birch Creek*, 3–4.
55. Davis, *Energy/Alaska*, 42–45.
56. J. Dorsey, "Coal Bunkers," 3–4.
57. Davis, *Energy/Alaska*, 44–45.
58. S. Evans, *Historical View*, 507–511, 520, 526–533; Buchanan, "History of Timber Industry," 46–48.
59. Rakestraw, *History of Forest Service in Alaska*, 127–128.
60. Powers, "Public Involvement," 89–105.
61. McNicholas, *Alaska's Agriculture and Forestry*, 190–191.
62. Lutz, *Ecological Effects of Forest Fires*, 19, 80–82, 87, 91–95.
63. U.S. EPA, *Climate Change and Alaska*, 2–4.
64. Naske and Triplehorn, "The Federal Government and Alaska's Coal," 17–21.
65. Kinney, "Copper and the Settlement of South-Central Alaska," 309–317.
66. Stanton, *Alaska Recreation Survey*, 72–75.
67. O. Miller, *Frontier in Alaska and the Matanuska Colony*, 192, 222.
68. Ibid., 207–210, 223–225.
69. Morse, "Nature of Gold," 204–205.
70. Young, *Alaska Days*, 204; Vickery, "Bob Marshall," 81–84.
71. Turner, *Sierra Club*, 44–45.
72. Cohen, *History of Sierra Club*, 1, 5–6; Fox, *John Muir and His Legacy*, 86–88; Bade, *Life and Letters of John Muir*, 394–395.
73. Cohen, *Pathless Way*, 203, 286–294, 298.
74. Wolfe, *Son of the Wilderness*, 270–275.
75. Nash, *Wilderness and the American Mind*, 130, 134–136. Later in life (*Breaking New Ground*, 179), Pinchot acknowledged that "overgrazing does destroy the forest. . . . John Muir called [sheep] hoofed locusts, and he was right."
76. Cohen, *Pathless Way*, 206, 278–280, 300, 308.
77. Nash, *Wilderness and the American Mind*, 139; Bade, *Life and Letters of John Muir*, 409–414.
78. Goetzmann and Sloan, *Looking Far North: The Harriman Expedition,* presents a fascinating account. See 207–212 for list of participants and 214–217 for list of publications.
79. Burroughs, *George Bird Grinnell*, xii–xvi.
80. Cohen, *History of Sierra Club*, 21–22; Cohen, *Pathless Way*, 324.
81. Turner, *Sierra Club*, 63.
82. Orth, *Dictionary of Alaska Place Names*, 663.

CHAPTER 5: THE BOONE AND CROCKETT CLUB

1. Burroughs, *George Bird Grinnell*, xix–xxv.
2. Trefethen, *Crusade for Wildlife*, 325–327; J. Mitchell, "A Man Called Bird," 85–89; Reiger, *Passing of The Great West*, 6–9, 22–31, 108–110.
3. Reiger, *American Sportsmen*, 30–31; J. Mitchell, "A Man Called Bird," 88–89; A. Fisher, "In Memoriam: George Bird Grinnell," 7–8.
4. Dunlap, *Saving America's Wildlife*, 6–15. A full articulation of the gentleman-hunter notion, first promulgated in the United States in the 1830s, is found in Peter J. Schmitt, *Back to Nature: The Arcadian Myth in Urban America*. Schmitt points to access to surrounding areas by trains from the cities as a crucial element in the spreading of sportsmen's clubs.
5. R. Evans, *George Bird Grinnell*, 5–10.
6. Reiger, *American Sportsmen*, 34, 61–62, 80–81, 104–106, 133.
7. J. Mitchell, "A Man Called Bird," 90–91.
8. Reiger, *American Sportsmen*, 118–121, 142–151. Thomas R. Dunlap ("Sport Hunting and Conservation, 1880–1920," 54–58) interprets the Boone and Crockett name as symbolic of manly pioneer virtues. He sees sport hunting as a ritual, appealing at the turn of the century primarily to men of Anglo-Saxon origin, affirming ties to the pre-industrial and pre-urban past.
9. Reiger, "George Bird Grinnell," 219–224, 243.
10. Ise, *United States Forest Policy*, 114–118; Pinchot, *Breaking New Ground*, 85; 26 Stat. 1095, March 3, 1891. The American Academy for the Advancement of Science, American Forestry Association, and irrigation interests helped influence Noble and Harrison (Hays, *Conservation and the Gospel of Efficiency*, 36). Spiro, "Patrician Racist," p. 150, presents the case that Noble's friend and fellow Boone and Crockett member William Hallett Phillips inserted the reserve provision into the bill.
11. Trefethen, *Crusade for Wildlife*, 65–66; Trefethen, *An American Crusade*, 123; Grinnell, *Brief History of Boone and Crockett*, 8, 23–25; President Benjamin Harrison, Proclamation Nos. 343, 343A, December 24, 1892.
12. Cart, "Struggle for Wildlife Protection," 111–112. The Pribilof Islands, declared a preserve by Congress in 1869, are sometimes said to be the first federal wildlife refuge.
13. *National Cyclopedia of American Biography, Vol. XXX*, 1943, 278–279; *Who Was Who in America, Vol. I*, 489; *New York Times*, April 12, 1938, 23; J. Mitchell, "A Man Called Bird," 94–95.
14. A. Fisher, "In Memoriam: George Bird Grinnell," 11.
15. Trefethen, *Crusade for Wildlife*, 327.
16. *New York Times*, April 12, 1938, 23.
17. Spiro, "Patrician Racist," 86–88.
18. Ibid., 6–9, 16, 19–22.
19. Ibid., 22–24, 45–47.
20. Ibid., 28, 32, 152, 155–160, 225–226.
21. Ibid., 239–243.

22. Grant, "Condition of Wild Life in Alaska," 522–523.
23. Ibid., 523.
24. Spiro, "Patrician Racist," 123–136; Grinnell, *Brief History of Boone and Crockett*, 37–39; Cameron, *Bureau of Biological Survey*, 111–112; 32 Stat. 327, June 7, 1902; 35 Stat. 102, May 11, 1908.
25. Spiro, "Patrician Racist," 142–146, 188–192, 739–747.
26. Ibid., 950; *National Cyclopedia of American Biography, Vol. XXIX*, 1941, 319–320; Trefethen, *Crusade for Wildlife*, 81–82, 277–278, 288; Bridges, *Gathering of Animals*, 5–10, 285–289; *Dictionary of American Biography, Vol. XI, Part 2*, 1958, 256; Stone, "An Explorer-Naturalist," 448; *New York Times*, May 31, 1937, 15.
27. Spiro, "Patrician Racist," vii–ix, 116–122. Spiro provides a full treatment of Grant's work regarding race, as well as the most complete available coverage of his conservation work.
28. Bridges, *Gathering of Animals*, 1–13; New York Zoological Society, News Release, May 30, 1937.
29. Alexander, *Museum in America*, 189–192; Sterling, *Biological Dictionary of American and Canadian Naturalists and Environmentalists*, 378–379.
30. Bridges, *Gathering of Animals*, 20–22, 257–261, 276–279, 483–484; *National Cyclopedia of American Biography, Vol. IV*, 1897, 192; *Who Was Who in America, Vol. I*, 588; Blair, "William Temple Hornaday," 47–49; *New York Times*, March 7, 1937, II: 9; *New York Herald Tribune*, March 7, 1937.
31. Alexander, *Museum in America*, 196.
32. Hornaday, "A National Game Preserve in Alaska," 188–189.
33. Hornaday, *Our Vanishing Wild Life*, 269–270.
34. Hornaday, *Wild Life Conservation*, 162–165.
35. Hornaday, *Our Vanishing Wild Life*, 203.
36. Mighetto, *Wild Animals and American Environmental Ethics*, 69, 78–82, 84.
37. Tracy, *American Naturalists*, 138.
38. *New York Herald Tribune*, March 8, 1937; *Who Was Who in America, Vol. I*, 588.
39. Bridges, *Gathering of Animals*, 172–173.
40. *New York Times*, March 7, 1937, II: 9.
41. Bridges, *Gathering of Animals*, 444, 468–469.
42. *New York Times*, January 29, 1942, 13; *National Cyclopedia of American Biography, Vol. XXXII*, 1941, 37.
43. Bridges, *Gathering of Animals*, 202–206.
44. Townsend, "Pribilof Seal Herd," 569.
45. Spiro, "Patrician Racist," 237–238.
46. Trefethen, *Crusade for Wildlife*, 130, 151, 245–246, 299.
47. *Who Was Who in America, Vol. I*, 1113; Carmony and Brown, *Wilderness of the Southwest*, xiii–xviii, xxii.
48. Carmony and Brown, *Wilderness in the Southwest*, xx, xxii; Sterling, *Biological Dictionary of American and Canadian Naturalists and Environmentalists*, 727–728.
49. Carmony and Brown, *Wilderness in the Southwest*, xxiii–xxvii, xxix.

50. Trefethen, *Crusade for Wildlife*, 242–247.
51. W. Sheldon, "Biographical Notes."
52. Carmony and Brown, *Wilderness of the Southwest*, xxxii–xxxv, xl–xli.
53. Trefethen, *An American Crusade*, 191; Trefethen, *Crusade for Wildlife*, 151 (quotation).
54. Brown, *History of Denali–Mount McKinley*, 76–77.
55. Trefethen, *Crusade for Wildlife*, 217–222, 226–228; Sherwood, *Big Game in Alaska*, 34–37.
56. C. Sheldon, *Wilderness of Denali*, ix–xvii (introduction by Merriam).
57. Trefethen, *Crusade for Wildlife*, 180.

CHAPTER 6: CHARLES SHELDON AND MT. McKINLEY NATIONAL PARK

1. C. Sheldon, *Wilderness of Denali*, 8–9.
2. Orth, *Dictionary of Alaska Place Names*, 610.
3. Moore, *Mt. McKinley: The Pioneer Climbs*, 1, 4–5, 9. Other names for the mountain: Doleyka, Traleyka, and Bulshaia Gora (Russian for "Great Mountain").
4. Ibid., 9–10, 14, 17.
5. Brown, *History of Denali–Mount McKinley*, 13–15, 18.
6. Ibid., 19–23.
7. Moore, *Mt. McKinley: The Pioneer Climbs*, 31, 39, 42–44, 52–54, 78, 81, 84, 159–161.
8. Carmony and Brown, *Wilderness of the Southwest*, xxviii, xli; Cook, Frederick A., *To the Top of the Continent* (New York: Doubleday, Page, 1908).
9. Moore, *Mt. Mckinley: The Pioneer Climbs*, 96–98, 108–110, 115–118, 146, 150.
10. G. Pearson, *History of Mount McKinley*, 16, 23–24.
11. Brown, *History of Denali–Mount McKinley*, 84–91.
12. G. Pearson, *History of Mount McKinley*, 24–25, 60–61; Grant, "Establishment of Mount McKinley Park," 439–441. Belmore Browne (*Analysis by Belmore Browne for the Committee on Conservation of the Report of Dr. Adolph Murie's "The Wolves of Mt. McKinley,"* 16) asserted that he first convinced Franklin Lane of the need for a park in 1912 and helped Riggs draw the original boundaries.
13. Trefethen, *Crusade for Wildlife*, 186, 189–191; Bates, *Mountain Man*, xv–xvii, 178; Kennedy, "Belmore Browne and Alaska," 96–100, 103–104.
14. G. Pearson, *History of Mount McKinley*, 27–62; Grant, "Establishment of Mount McKinley Park," 442–444; Bates, *Mountain Man*, 178–179.
15. "Belmore Browne," reprint from *AHFAM Newsletter*.
16. House Subcom. on Public Lands, *Mount McKinley National Park*, 1, 12–13, 20–26.
17. Capps, "A Game Country Without Rival," 81–82.
18. U.S. Dept. of the Interior, National Park Service, *Proceedings*, 195, 197.
19. 39 Stat. 938, February 21, 1917.
20. Brown, *History of Denali–Mount McKinley*, 92–95, 135–136, 162–164.

21. Ise, *Our National Park Policy*, 226–229; Brown, *History of Denali–Mount McKinley*, 186; G. Pearson, *History of Mount McKinley*, 28–30.
22. Catton, *Inhabited Wilderness*, 88; Brown, *History of Denali–Mount McKinley*, 71–72, 127–129.
23. *Brown, History of Denali–Mount McKinley*, 160–162, 196–200.
24. Ibid., 110–113, 206, 235.
25. Capps, "Mount McKinley," 12.
26. Brown, *History of Denali–Mount McKinley*, 101, 141–142, 159, 191.
27. Ibid., 171–172.
28. Stanton, *Alaska Recreational Survey*, 98–99.
29. Brown, *History of Denali–Mount McKinley*, 198, 201, 204, 214–215, 223–224, 237; 94 Stat. 2371, December 2, 1980, Sec. 202(3)(a).
30. P. and C. Martin, "Charlie Ott," 51–54; *Fairbanks Daily News-Miner*, "Four to Receive Honorary Degrees at UAF," February 11, 1989, 7.
31. A. Murie, *Mammals of Mt. McKinley*, 20, 56; A. Murie, *Birds of Mt. McKinley*, 95–96.
32. Orth, *Dictionary of Alaska Place Names*, 162, 863.

CHAPTER 7: ROBERT F. GRIGGS AND KATMAI NATIONAL MONUMENT

1. Griggs, *Valley of Ten Thousand Smokes*, 17.
2. Alaska Travel, *Exploring Katmai*, 50–51.
3. G. Martin, "Recent Eruption of Katmai," 148, 152.
4. Schaaf, "Witness," 4–5.
5. Griggs, *Valley of Ten Thousand Smokes*, 25–27, 31–33; Alaska Travel, *Exploring Katmai*, 54.
6. Bodeau, *Katmai National Park*, 74–75.
7. L. Black, *Russians in Alaska*, 108, 130; Hussey, *Embattled Katmai*, 176–180, 186, 212–213, 273–274 (quotation).
8. Bodeau, *Katmai National Park,* 76–79.
9. Krech, *Victorian Earl in the Arctic*, 86–87, 86 (quotation); Hussey, *Embattled Katmai*, 275–277.
10. Spurr, "A Reconnaissance," 91–92.
11. Hussey, *Embattled Katmai*, 294, 335, 370.
12. Cahalane, "Katmai—America's Largest Nature Reserve," 172–174.
13. Hussey, *Embattled Katmai*, 370–371, 377–378.
14. G. Martin, "Recent Eruption of Katmai," 131–141, 152.
15. Ibid., 145–148, 166–167, 170, 174, 179–181.
16. Evermann, *Alaska Fisheries and Fur Industries in 1913*, 32–33, 161–165.
17. Hussey, *Embattled Katmai*, 370–371, 377–378, 382; Griggs, *We Two Together*, 1, 16, 25–26, 47, 161–162, 168.
18. Alaska Travel, *Exploring Katmai*, 69.
19. Griggs, *Valley of Ten Thousand Smokes,* 81–82, 155, 161–164.

20. Griggs, "Beginnings of Revegetation," 320–324, 329–330, 335–342.
21. Griggs, "Recovery of Vegetation," 6, 24.
22. Ibid., 3, 6, 31–33, 37–44, 47–49, 54–56.
23. Griggs, "Colonization of Katmai Ash," 92–94, 110–112.
24. Hussey, *Embattled Katmai*, 380, 389.
25. Griggs, *Valley of Ten Thousand Smokes*, 153–154.
26. Hussey, *Embattled Katmai*, 398–401, 409–412.
27. Griggs, "Eruption of Katmai," 498–499.
28. Kauffmann, *Katmai National Monument*, 2.
29. Hussey, *Embattled Katmai*, 409–415, 455; President Woodrow Wilson, Proclamation No. 1487, September 24, 1918.
30. Griggs, *Valley of Ten Thousand Smokes*, 231.
31. Norris, *Isolated Paradise*, 41–42.
32. Hubbard, *Cradle of the Storms*, 168, 186; Willoughby, "Volcanoes Packed in Ice," 18–19, 96.
33. Hubbard, *Cradle of the Storms*, 186, 194–197.
34. Ibid., 230–231.
35. Norris, *Isolated Paradise*, 38–41; Hussey, *Embattled Katmai*, 419–420 (quotation).
36. Hussey, *Embattled Katmai*, 421–422, 428; Norris, *Isolated Paradise*, 45–50; President Herbert Hoover, Proclamation No. 1950, April 24, 1931.
37. Norris, *Isolated Paradise*, 42–44.
38. Ibid., 51–52, 55–64, 72–73, 77, 80.
39. Ibid., 68.
40. Bodeau, *Katmai National Park*, 108–109.
41. Ibid., 109; Cahalane, "Katmai—A Wilderness to Be Guarded," 10–11; 68 Stat. 53, April 15, 1954.
42. Norris, *Isolated Paradise*, 76; Cahalane, "Katmai—A Wilderness to Be Guarded," 11.
43. Norris, *Isolated Paradise*, 90–91.
44. Birkedal, "Ancient Hunters," 229–231; Luntey, "Katmai National Monument," 8.
45. Kavanaugh, "Removal of Fish Ladder"; Alaska Dept. of Fish and Game, "Detailed Rationale," 1–6.
46. Luntey, "Katmai National Monument," 8–13.
47. *Science News Letter*, "Wrong Volcano Blamed," 246.
48. Cahalane, *Biological Survey of Katmai*, 68–72.
49. Kauffmann, *Katmai National Monument*, 36.
50. Bodeau, *Katmai National Park*, 109–111; Norris, *Isolated Paradise*, 79–80, 90–94, 107–115, 118.
51. Johnson, Lyndon B., Proclamation No. 3890, January 20, 1969; Alaska Travel, *Exploring Katmai*, 77–78.
52. Simmerman, *Alaska's Parklands*, 173–175.
53. Orth, *Dictionary of Alaska Place Names*, 392.
54. Cahalane, *Biological Survey of Katmai*, 84.
55. Alaska Travel, *Exploring Katmai*, 114, 157.

CHAPTER 8: JOHN MUIR, WILLIAM S. COOPER, AND GLACIER BAY NATIONAL MONUMENT

1. Bohn, *Glacier Bay*, 38, 40–48.
2. Muir, "The Alaska Trip," 524–525.
3. Muir, "The Discovery of Glacier Bay," 239.
4. Catton, *Land Reborn*, 37–39. Orth, *Dictionary of Alaska Place Names*, 369, identifies U.S. Navy Captain L.A. Beardslee as having named Glacier Bay. S. Hall Young (*Hall Young of Alaska*, 204) stated that he suggested naming the glacier for Muir to Navy officers at Sitka immediately after the 1880 visit to the glacier, and Captain Beardslee forwarded it to Washington for approval.
5. Kurtz, *Glacier Bay: Historic Resources Study*, 3; La Perouse, *Voyage, Vol. I*, 367, 371, 378–391, 394–399.
6. La Perouse, *Voyage, Vol. I*, 77–134; *Alaska Magazine*, "Alaskan Adventures of Perouse," 109, 117, 124–137.
7. Makarova, *Russians on the Pacific*, 152.
8. Kurtz, *Glacier Bay: Historic Resources Study*, 6.
9. Bohn, *Glacier Bay*, 33.
10. Ibid., 30–31.
11. Kurtz, *Glacier Bay: Historic Resources Study*, 37–38.
12. Ibid., 25–26.
13. Catton, *Land Reborn*, 39–44.
14. Lawrence, "Memorial to William Skinner Cooper"; Clepper, *Leaders in American Conservation*, 79–80.
15. Catton, *Land Reborn*, 45–49; Cooper, "Recent Ecological History, 1: Interglacial Forests," 93–94; "3: Permanent Quadrats," 355–356, 364–365, 365 (quotation).
16. Cooper, "Contribution to the History of Glacier Bay"; Bohn, *Glacier Bay*, 82, 94 (quotation).
17. B. Black, "History of Glacier Bay," 29–30, 73; Kauffmann, *Glacier Bay: A History*, 6–7.
18. Kauffmann, *Glacier Bay: A History*, 1.
19. Catton, *Land Reborn*, 51–54; President Calvin Coolidge, Executive Order No. 3983, April 1, 1924.
20. *Daily Alaska Empire*, April 28, 1924.
21. Kauffmann, *Glacier Bay: A History*, 6–7.
22. Catton, *Land Reborn*, 56–58; President Calvin Coolidge, Proclamation No. 1733, February 26, 1925.
23. Kurtz, *Glacier Bay: Historic Resources Study*, 48–49, 51–54, 57–58.
24. Catton, *Land Reborn*, 92–96.
25. Bohn, *Glacier Bay*, 87; B. Black, "History of Glacier Bay," 46–70; Rossman, "Geology and Ore Deposits," 37; Cooper, letter to U.S. Rep. Seiberling, July 23, 1976.
26. Bohn, *Glacier Bay*, 99.
27. Ibid., 89; Rossman, "Geology and Ore Deposits," 37.

28. Catton, *Land Reborn*, 173–174, 188–189; 30 Stat. 1342, September 28, 1976.
29. Rakestraw, *History of Forest Service in Alaska*, 113–114; Kauffmann, *Glacier Bay: A History*, 11–34; President Franklin D. Roosevelt, Proclamation No. 2330, April 18, 1939.
30. Bohn, *Glacier Bay*, 101.
31. Kauffmann, *Glacier Bay: A History*, 39–41, 44–52.
32. B. Black, "History of Glacier Bay," 71–78.
33. President Dwight D. Eisenhower, Executive Order No. 3089, March 31, 1955.
34. B. Black, "History of Glacier Bay," 77–78, 77 (quotation); Bohn, *Glacier Bay*, 104.
35. Catton, *Land Reborn*, 29–30, 102, 109, 114, 119.
36. Ibid., 103–106, 109–110, 114, 127–128, 131, 191–202.
37. Ibid., 107–108, 111–114, 122, 198, 202–204.
38. Catton, *Inhabited Wilderness*, 78–85; *Tlingit and Haida Indians of Alaska v. United States*, 177 F. Supp. 452 (Court of Claims, 1959); 85 Stat. 688, December 18, 1971; 94 Stat. 2371, December 2, 1980; 86 Stat. 1027, October 21, 1972.
39. Catton, *Land Reborn*, chaps. 12–15.
40. Ibid., 164, 168–170.
41. Norris, "Lone Voice in the Wilderness," 73–74, 76n34.
42. Cooper, "Remarks at Dedication of Lodge."
43. J. Dufresne, *Glacier Bay National Park*, 24–29; Streveler and Paige, *Natural History of Glacier Bay*, 47–48.
44. Lawrence, "Memorial to William S. Cooper."

CHAPTER 9: NATIVES: THE FIRST ENVIRONMENTALISTS?

1. Grinnell, "American Game Protection," 209–211.
2. Liapunova, "Relations With Natives," 108.
3. D. Spencer, "Aleutian Islands National Wildlife Refuge," 12, 16–17.
4. Veniaminov, *Notes on the Islands*, 215.
5. Elliott, "Ten Years' Acquaintance," 812–813.
6. Rogers, *Alaska in Transition*, 276–278; Robert E. Price, interview by author, July 15, 1989.
7. de Laguna, *Under Mount Saint Elias, Part 1*, 361–362; *Part 2*, 823–824.
8. Birkedal, "Ancient Hunters," 233.
9. R. Nelson, *Make Prayers to the Raven*, 210–211.
10. Ibid., 220.
11. Ibid., 221–222.
12. R. Nelson, *Hunters of the Northern Forest*, 155, 311.
13. M. Webb, *Last Frontier*, 302.
14. Stephenson et al., "Wood Bison," 129–133, 143–146.
15. C. Martin, "American Indian," 245, 248.
16. C. Martin, *Keepers of the Game*, 164, 170–185; see also Krech, *Indians, Animals and the Fur Trade*. Most articles in Krech attribute Native game exploitation to economic motives but view Martin's "war on animals" thesis as overdrawn.

17. Eskimoan peoples are culturally, linguistically, and genetically related groups who live in Arctic Canada, Greenland, Siberia, and Alaska and in parts of subarctic Alaska. Canadian and Greenland Eskimos refer to themselves as *Inuit.* The subgroup *Inupiat* are found in Alaska mostly north of the Bering Strait and include *Nunamiut* in the interior. *Yupik,* or *Yup'ik,* live in eastern Siberia and in Alaska generally south of Bering Strait to the Kuskokwim Delta, Kodiak Island (Koniag Alutiiq), and Prince William Sound (Chugach Alutiiq). Aleuts, living in the Aleutians and on the western Alaska Peninsula, are not considered Eskimoan. Subgroups of Athabaskan Indians live in the interior and Tlingit, Haida, and Tsimshian Indians in coastal Southeast Alaska. The term "Eskimo" is commonly, and incorrectly according to some philologists, believed to be an Athabaskan term meaning "eaters of raw meat." On the assumption that the term is pejorative, attempts have been made to substitute "Inuit" for "Eskimo." The proposed change is not in common use in Alaska. Alaskan Eskimos normally refer to themselves as members of their cultural or geographical subgroups; e.g., Inupiat, Yup'ik, Koniag, Chugach, or Alutiiq. Collectively, Native Americans in Alaska identify themselves as Alaska Natives. (See Borneman, *Alaska,* 19–26; http://www.Dictionary.LaborLawTalk.com.)
18. R. Spencer, *North Alaskan Eskimo,* 268–269.
19. Osterman, *Alaska Eskimos,* 37.
20. J. Campbell, "Aboriginal Human Overkill," 184–193, 200.
21. Coady, "History of Moose," 63–67.
22. Lent, "Alaska's Indigenous Muskoxen," 135, 138–142.
23. Fienup-Riordan, *Eskimo Essays,* 45–48, 167–168, 172–174, 183.
24. Lutz, *Aboriginal Man and White Man,* 4, 6 (quotation), 11, 26, 41–42.
25. Johnson, "Upper Tanana Athapaskan Fire Ecology," 15.
26. Hames, "Wildlife Conservation," 173–178, 182, 188–191.
27. Sherwood, *Big Game in Alaska,* 108.
28. Hames, "Wildlife Conservation," 191–193.
29. Muir, *Travels in Alaska,* 285.
30. Perspectives on identity crisis, particularly involving Eskimos, are well summarized by Pender in "Alaska Natives," 25–27. See also Anders, "Critical Analysis of the Alaska Native Land Claims," 9–10; and Harris, "Survival of Respect."
31. C. Martin, "American Indian," 245, 249–251.
32. Hames, "Wildlife Conservation," 193.
33. Huntington, *Wildlife Management,* 4–12, 30–31.
34. Ibid., 9–10, 23, 28–29; Ross, *Environmental Conflict,* 85–87.
35. Ross, *Environmental Conflict,* 33–38, 82, 86, 284–287, 307.
36. Catton, *Inhabited Wilderness,* 173.

CHAPTER 10: BUREAU OF BIOLOGICAL SURVEY CHIEFS

1. Jordan and Clark, *Seal and Salmon Fisheries, Vol. 2,* 441.
2. Loring, "Notes on the Destruction," 141–143.
3. A. Bailey, *Notes on Game Conditions,* 7.

4. Hornaday, *Our Vanishing Wild Life*, 46.
5. Scott, Chatelain, and Elkins, "Status of Dall Sheep and Caribou," 613, 616.
6. State of Alaska, *Report of Governor to Secretary of Interior, 1899*, 10; *1910*, 22.
7. Cane, *Summer and Fall*, 116.
8. Ibid., 85.
9. Ibid., 87.
10. Ibid., 75, 116, 137.
11. Radclyffe, *Big Game Shooting*, 27, 29 (quotation), 73, 76–77.
12. Madsen, *Arctic Trader*, 222–228.
13. Scull, *Hunting in the Arctic*, 10, 291–294.
14. Madsen, *Arctic Trader*, 223–224; ibid., 85, 151–153, 166, 250–253, 272.
15. Loftus, "Tom Gibson," Part 2, 6–7; Part 3, 20–21.
16. Grinnell, *Brief History of Boone and Crockett*, 37–40; Cameron, *Bureau of Biological Survey*, 111–112; 32 Stat. 327, June 7, 1902; 35 Stat 102, May 11, 1908.
17. *Annual Report of Governor on Alaska Game Law, 1914*, 9–14; *1916*, 3; 35 Stat. 102, May 11, 1908.
18. D. Mitchell, *Sold American*, 181–187.
19. *Annual Report of Governor on Alaska Game Law, 1918*, 8–9; *1920*, 11.
20. Bridges, *Gathering of Animals*, 273–275; Sherwood, *Big Game in Alaska*, 44–48.
21. *Annual Report of Governor on Alaska Game Law, 1911*, 4–5; *1918*, 2–3.
22. Gruening, *State of Alaska*, 151, 165, 301, 323, 327–332.
23. Ibid., 145, 147, 151, 306.
24. Barrow, *Passion for Birds*, 57–58.
25. Osgood, "Clinton Hart Merriam," 421–433; Cameron, *Bureau of Biological Survey*, 18–23; Sterling, *Selected Works*, Introduction.
26. Cart, "Struggle for Wildlife Protection," 5, 49, 54–55, 62–63, 115, 121, 129.
27. Ibid., 30–32, 42, 103, 152–153.
28. Ibid., 4, 8–12, 67–68, 97, 103–106, 145–151, 182.
29. Worster, *Nature's Economy*, 195–198.
30. Sterling, *Last of the Naturalists*, 290, 294–306.
31. Ibid., 256–258, 257 (quotation), 309–310; Sterling, "Builders of the U.S. Biological Survey," 181, 187.
32. Sterling, *Last of the Naturalists*, 319–323; *Who's Who in America, Vol. 20*, 1938–1939, 1735; *New York Times*, March 21, 1942, 17; Osgood, "Clinton Hart Merriam," 430–431; Orth, *Dictionary of Alaska Place Names*, 422–424.
33. Osgood, "Clinton Hart Merriam," 432–434; Sterling, "Builders of the U.S. Biological Survey," 181.
34. Trefethen, *Crusade for Wildlife*, 172–173, 245; Cart, "Struggle for Wildlife Protection," 74–75; Sterling, "Builders of the U.S. Biological Survey," 182–183; Sterling, *Biographical Dictionary of American and Canadian Naturalists and Environmentalists*, 608–609; *Who Was Who in America, Vol. III*, 662–663.
35. Trefethen, *Crusade for Wildlife*, 172; Graham, *Man's Dominion*, 217.
36. De Sormo, *John Bird Burnham*, 178, 180–182, 190.
37. Cameron, *Bureau of Biological Survey*, 119.

38. *National Cyclopedia of American Biography, Vol. XXVI*, 1937, 434; *Who Was Who in America, Vol. I*, 890; Goldman, "Edward William Nelson," 136–142; E. Nelson, *The Eskimo About Bering Strait*, 10–11.
39. E. Nelson, *Report Upon Natural History Collections*, 11–14.
40. E. Nelson, *The Eskimo About Bering Strait*, 7.
41. Orth, *Dictionary of Alaska Place Names*, 681.
42. Lantis, "Edward William Nelson," 8–11.
43. *National Cyclopedia of American Biography, Vol. XXVI*, 1937, 434; *Who Was Who in America, Vol. I*, 890; Trefethen, *Crusade for Wildlife*, 129–130, 156; Goldman, "Edward William Nelson," 147–148.
44. E. Nelson, "Economic Importance of Wild Life," 367–368.
45. Carmony and Brown, *Wilderness of the Southwest*, 37.
46. U.S. House Committee on Territories, *Hearings: To Regulate the Killing and Sale of Certain Game Animals, Part 1*, 4–6.
47. Ibid., 14, 19–20, 43.
48. Ibid., *Part 2*, 65, 68.
49. Ibid., 78, 80–81, 80 (quotation), 87, 92.
50. *Annual Report of Governor on Alaska Game Law, 1920*, 2–3.
51. A. Bailey, *Notes on Game Conditions*, 3.
52. Ibid., 10, 12, 17–18.
53. O. Murie, letter to Edward W. Nelson, January 7, 1922.
54. Sherwood, *Big Game in Alaska*, 50, 119–120; Cameron, *Bureau of Biological Survey*, 119–121.
55. U.S. House Committee on Agriculture, *Hearings: Alaska Game Act*, 8–16.
56. 43 Stat. 739, January 13, 1925.
57. Greeley, *Handbook of Alaska*, 187.
58. Sherwood, *Big Game in Alaska*, 119–120.
59. Redington, "United States Bureau of Biological Survey," 295–306.
60. Cart, "'New Deal' for Wildlife," 114–120.
61. Clepper, *Leaders in American Conservation*, 126–127; Halle, "Gabrielson," 140–143; Gabrielson and Lincoln, *Birds of Alaska*, 25.
62. Gabrielson, *Wildlife Conservation*, 11 and flyleaf.
63. Dunlap, *Saving America's Wildlife*, 128.
64. Fox, *John Muir and His Legacy*, 251; Sterling, *Biographical Dictionary of American and Canadian Naturalists and Environmentalists*, 295–296.
65. Halle, "Gabrielson," 140–142.
66. Fox, *John Muir and His Legacy*, 251.

CHAPTER 11: ALASKAN WILDLIFE MANAGERS

1. 43 Stat. 739, January 13, 1925.
2. Alaska Game Commission, *Annual Report, 1958–59*, 1–2; *Popular Mechanics*, "Man's Law on the Yukon," 291–293.
3. D. Mitchell, *Sold American*, 187–192.
4. Territory of Alaska, *Session Laws, 1935*, HJM No. 7, 206–207.

5. Alaska Game Commission, *1942 Annual Report*, 6; *5th Annual Report, 1943–44*, 2.
6. Alaska Game Commission, *Eleventh Report of Executive Officer, 1935–36*, 18.
7. Alaska Game Commission, *14th Annual Report, 1937–38*, 4.
8. Ibid.
9. Alaska Game Commission, *15th Annual Report, 1938–39*, 4–5; White and Rhode, *Report on Alaska-Yukon Boundary Patrol*, 1, 8–9.
10. S.O. White, letter to Jim King, January 27, 1970; S.O. White, "Sam White, Alaskan," Part 3 (February 1965), 47; Part 4 (March 1965), 48; Part 6 (June 1965), 56. The series by White ran in *Alaska Sportsman* from December 1964 to June 1965.
11. Alaska Game Commission, *4th Annual Report, 1942–43*, 2; *14th Annual Report, 1952–53*, 45; *18th Annual Report, 1956–57*, 26.
12. Sherwood, *Big Game in Alaska*, 138–143; Alaska Game Commission, *6th Annual Report, 1944–45*, Introduction.
13. Alaska Game Commission, *5th Annual Report, 1943–44*, 3.
14. Bezeau, "Realities of Strategic Planning," 26–33.
15. Naske, "The Alcan," 14–18; Borneman, *Alaska*, 236–241.
16. James G. King, interview by author, July 5, 1989.
17. Alaska Game Commission, *10th and 11th Annual Report, 1948–50*, 10.
18. Bowkett, *Reaching for a Star*, 52–55.
19. F. Dufresne, *My Way Was North*, 4–35, 66–75.
20. Sherwood, *Big Game in Alaska*, 9–10.
21. F. Dufresne, *My Way Was North*, 164, 261, 273.
22. F. Dufresne, *No Room For Bears*, 232–252.
23. F. Dufresne, "Whose Wilderness?" 23–26, 56–58.
24. Ibid., 9.
25. F. Dufresne, *My Way Was North*, vii.
26. Rearden, "Clarence Rhode," 11–14; J.G. King, "Pre-Statehood Alaska," 172; S.O. White, "Sam White, Alaskan," Part 4, 48.
27. Annabel, "Trouble in Alaska's Game Lands," 34–35, 48.
28. J.G. King, "Pre-Statehood Alaska," 175.
29. Dugan, "Poacher Patrol," 92–94.
30. J.G. King, "Pre-Statehood Alaska," 175.
31. Annabel, *Hunting and Fishing in Alaska*, 3–7.
32. O. Murie, "Wilderness and Aircraft," 1–2.
33. Ibid., 4, 6.
34. East, "Threat to Alaska Bears," 17.
35. Annabel, "Trouble in Alaska's Game Lands," 35.
36. Ibid., 47–48; Catton, *Inhabited Wilderness*, 180–182, 253n50; photo FWS 1217, Alaska Resources Library and Information Services, Anchorage.
37. Rearden, "Clarence Rhode," 13–14.
38. Ibid., 14, 51; James G. King, interview by author, February 14, 1988.
39. D.S. Miller, "Finding Clarence Rhode's Plane," 17; D.S. Miller, *Midnight Wilderness*, 150–155.

40. Rearden, "Commissioner Jim Brooks," 21; Phinizy, "Savers vs. the Spoilers," 27; J. Brooks, *North to Wolf Country*, chaps. 1–6.
41. James W. Brooks, interview by author, June 30, 1988; J. Brooks, *North to Wolf Country*, 106, 111–113.
42. J. Brooks, *North to Wolf Country,* chaps, 10–13; Rearden, "Commissioner Jim Brooks," 21, 56.
43. Rearden, "Commissioner Jim Brooks," 21, 56–61; Atwood and De Armond, *Who's Who*, 11; *Fairbanks Daily News-Miner*, "Four to Receive Honorary Degrees at UAF," February 11, 1989, 7.
44. J. Brooks, *North to Wolf Country*, chaps. 16, 17, 20.
45. Rearden, "Commissioner Jim Brooks," 58, 61; James W. Brooks, interview by author, June 30, 1988; Alaska Dept. of Natural Resources, *Promised Land*, 28.
46. J. Brooks, *North to Wolf Country*, chap. 28.
47. "Resume, James G. King"; Jim King, letter to author, December 14, 1989; Robert B. Weeden, interview by author, August 15, 1989.
48. James G. King, interview by author, July 13, 1989.
49. J.G. King, "My Fifty Years," 271.
50. "Resume, James G. King"; Robert B. Weeden, interview by author, August 15, 1989; King, letters to author, December 14, 1989, and September 3, 1991; U.S. Fish and Wildlife Service Pioneers Oral History Project, interview of Calvin J. Lensink, February 25, 1998, Tape 1, sides 1 and 2.
51. "Resume, James G. King."

CHAPTER 12: GRIZZLY BEARS IN POLITICS

1. Birkedal, "Ancient Hunters," 228, 231–232.
2. Berkh, *Chronological History*, 110–113.
3. Golovin, *End of Russian America*, 80.
4. Petroff, "Report on the Population," 253–254.
5. Rearden, "Brownie," 35; Osgood, *Biological Reconnaissance*, 42.
6. Radclyffe, *Big Game Shooting*, 33.
7. Thomas, *Trails and Tramps*, 75.
8. O. Murie, *Fauna of the Aleutian Islands*, 269.
9. Cane, *Summer and Fall*, 72, 75, 137.
10. C. Sheldon, *Wilderness of the North Pacific*, 105–110.
11. Ibid., 111, 127–128.
12. Ibid., 79–83; Sheldon, untitled interview by sporting writer.
13. Mixter, "Hunting the Great Brown Bear," 313, 329, 332–333.
14. Annabel, *Hunting and Fishing in Alaska*, 42.
15. Grinnell, *Brief History of Boone and Crockett Club*, 37–41; Sherwood, *Big Game in Alaska*, 27–31; 32 Stat. 327, June 7, 1902; 35 Stat. 102, May 11, 1908.
16. Kleinschmidt, "Alaska: Her Game and Game Laws," 95, 98.
17. Madsen, "Report on Game Conditions," 4–5, 8.
18. A. Brooks, *Blazing Alaska's Trails*, 74–75.
19. *Report of Governor to Secretary of Interior, 1915*, 25.

20. Ibid., *1916*, 62.
21. Ibid., *1919*, 62–63; *Annual Report of Governor on Alaska Game Law, 1920*, 4.
22. *Annual Report of Governor on Alaska Game Law, 1912*, 6–7.
23. A. Bailey, *Notes on Game Conditions*, 16.
24. *Annual Report of Governor on Alaska Game Law, 1920*, 7–8; Sherwood, *Big Game in Alaska*, 35–39; Merriam, *Review of Grizzly*, 2–3, 7–9.
25. Sherwood, *Big Game in Alaska*, 35–41; Sherwood, "Specious Speciation," 49–60.
26. Spiro, "Patrician Racist," 729–730.
27. Hornaday, *Thirty Years War*, 221–222.
28. Senate Special Committee on Wildlife Resources, *Brown Bear*, 46.
29. *Report of Governor to Secretary of Interior, 1929*, 60; Sherwood, *Big Game in Alaska*, 53–55.
30. Hornaday, *Thirty Years War*, 222.
31. Alaska Game Commission, *Annual Report of Executive Officer, 1930*, 55–63.
32. Pegues, "Alaska's Brownie," 36, 62.
33. Holzworth, *Wild Grizzlies of Alaska*, x–xii, 318–322, 338, 352.
34. Senate Special Committee on Wildlife Resources, *Brown Bear*, 1, 29; S.E. White, "An Emergency," 5, 213.
35. Alaska Game Commission, *Twelfth Annual Report, 1935–36*, 34.
36. Kauffmann, *Katmai National Monument*, 12.
37. Pack, "Admiralty's Bears," 112.
38. Catton, *Land Reborn*, 69–77, 81.
39. Ibid., 74, 79–83; President Franklin D. Roosevelt, Proclamation No. 2330, April 18, 1939.
40. Troyer and Hensel, "Brown Bear of Kodiak," 187–189.
41. Madsen, "Report on Game Conditions," 4.
42. Alaska Game Commission, *Annual Report of Executive Officer, 1930*, 60–61.
43. Sherwood, *Big Game in Alaska*, 52–53, 57–60; Sarber, *Report of the Kodiak Brown Bear Control Project*, 24, 27, 34–35.
44. Troyer and Hensel, "Brown Bear of Kodiak," 191.
45. Sherwood, *Big Game in Alaska*, 57–58; Territory of Alaska, *Session Laws, 1935*, HJM No. 7, 206–207.
46. Rowland and Kinsley, *Report on Kodiak Island*, 21–22, 28–30.
47. Troyer and Hensel, "Brown Bear of Kodiak," 192–193.
48. Troyer, *Status of Brown Bear*, 1–2.
49. Troyer and Hensel, "Brown Bear of Kodiak," 193.
50. Gabrielson, "Crisis for Alaskan Wildlife," 348–353, 394–395.
51. Troyer and Hensel, "Brown Bear of Kodiak," 189–190, 194–195.
52. *Annual Report of Alaska Game Commission, 1958–59*, 42.
53. Rearden, "Kodiak Bear War," 17–19, 70–74.
54. Eide, "Nature of Brown Bear Predation," 1–4.
55. McKnight, *History of Predator Control*, 7.
56. 43 Stat. 739, January 13, 1925, Sec. 10; Troyer, "Brown Bear Harvest," 460, 467.

57. Troyer, *Status of Brown Bear*, 2–4.
58. Alaska Game Commission, *Twelfth Annual Report of Executive Officer, 1936–37*, 99; Zimmerman, "Land of the Big Brown Bear," 41, 44–45.
59. Chase, *Alaska's Mammoth Brown Bears*, 122.
60. Rearden, "Brownie," 51.
61. S. Evans, *Historical View*, 534; Rakestraw, *History of Forest Service in Alaska*, 114–116.
62. Powers, "Public Involvement," 64–66; Heintzleman, letter to *Journal of Forestry*, 510.
63. U.S. Dept. of Agriculture, *U.S. Government Reservations in Alaska*, 23–24.
64. Buchanan, "History of Timber Industry," 28–40.
65. Heintzleman, "Managing the Brown Bear," 329–332.
66. Ford and Dufresne, "Lost Paradise," 64.
67. Powers, "Public Involvement," 104.
68. *The Spirit,* "Gunning for Predators," 1, 4.

CHAPTER 13: FRONTIER JUSTICE: PREDATOR CONTROL

1. 43 Stat. 739, January 13, 1925.
2. Jordan and Clark, *Seal and Salmon Fisheries, Vol. 3*, 510–511.
3. Worster, *Nature's Economy*, 262–264.
4. Mighetto, *Wild Animals and American Environmental Ethics*, 76, 79–80, 84–85, 95.
5. James G. King, interview by author, July 13, 1989.
6. *Report of Governor to Secretary of Interior, 1912*, 19.
7. E. Jones, *Report of Alaska Investigations in 1914*, 112.
8. *Report of Governor to Secretary of Interior, 1915*, 62–63.
9. *Annual Report of Governor on Alaska Game Law, 1922*, 3.
10. Lensink, "Predator Control," 94.
11. Alaska Game Commission, *Annual Report, 1928*, 19, 32–34; *1929*, 51–62; *1930*, 83–84; *1934*, 69; *1935*, 63–64; *1936*, 31–32, 61. Sherwood (*Big Game in Alaska*, 90) mentions a coyote seen on the Stikine River in 1899.
12. A. Bailey, *Notes on Game Conditions*, 7.
13. Alaska Game Commission, *Annual Report, 1927*, 28; *1928–29*, 20; *1931–32*; *1945*, 7; *1946*, 7; Dufresne, *Quarterly Report*, 1937, 7; 1941; *Annual Report of Alaska Game Commission, 1958–59*, 38–39.
14. Stewart, *Report to Governor*, 13, 16, 18–19, 28; O. Murie, *Alaska-Yukon Caribou*, 7.
15. Dunlap, *Saving America's Wildlife*, 19, 22, 38–39, 45, 48, 58–60, 79–83; Seton's wolf story first appeared in *Scribner's* 16 (November 1894): 618–628; reprinted in *Wild Animals I Have Known* and *Lives of the Hunted* (Scribner's, 1901). See also Adams, *Guide to the Study of Animal Ecology*; Leopold, and Brooks, *Game Management*.
16. Worster, *Nature's Economy*, 274–279, 288–290.
17. O. Murie, "Memorandum for Mr. Redington," 1–3.

18. Ibid., 3–5.
19. Worster, *Nature's Economy*, 279–285, 288–290.
20. L. Palmer, *Caribou Versus Fire,* 6–7, 32–33.
21. Leopold and Darling, *Wildlife in Alaska*, 53–60, 93–95; Leopold and Darling, "Effects of Land Use," 555–558.
22. Rawson, "Alaska's First Wolf Controversy," 3, 35–36, 59–60, 73, 93, 120, 128, 131–135, 139–140, 149 (quotation).
23. Brown, *History of Denali–Mount McKinley*, 122–125.
24. Alaska Game Commission, *Report of Executive Officer, 1935–36*, 62–63.
25. Rawson, "Alaska's First Wolf Controversy," 107, 115–117, 126, 137, 143–144.
26. Dunlap, *Saving America's Wildlife*, 74–76; A. Murie, *Wolves of Mt. McKinley*, 230–231; Trefethen, *Crusade for Wildlife*, 300.
27. Rawson, "Alaska's First Wolf Controversy," 179–189.
28. U.S. Congress, House Comm. on Public Lands, *Hearings: HR 5004 and 5401*, 1–5.
29. Ibid., 11–12.
30. Ibid., 18, 22, 32–33, 37.
31. Browne, *Analysis by Belmore Browne*, 11, 20–21, 29.
32. Rawson, "Alaska's First Wolf Controversy," 207–211, 216–217, 220–221, 225, 342–243.
33. Ibid., 245, 249–251; Crisler, *Arctic Wild.*
34. Dunlap, "Values for Varmints," 160–161.
35. *Annual Report of Alaska Game Commission, 1956–57*, 32.
36. Glaser, "My Lady Judas," 44.
37. Dufresne, *Alaska's Animals and Fishes*, 80.
38. Rhode, *Alaska's Fish and Wildlife*, 33–34.
39. Annabel, *Hunting and Fishing in Alaska*, 147–149.
40. Gabrielson, "Report on 1946 Observation," 7–8.
41. Annabel, *Hunting and Fishing in Alaska*, 149–150.
42. Ibid., 133, 153–154 (quotation).
43. *Annual Report of Alaska Game Commission, 1948–49 and 1949–50*, 16.
44. Green, "Predator Control Problems," 7, 9–11.
45. Grummett, *Territorial Sportsmen*, 23.
46. *Annual Report of Alaska Game Commission, 1952–53*, 16. Sporting groups supporting the predator control program included Ketchikan Wildlife Club; Anchorage, Cordova, and Petersburg chapters of Isaac Walton League; Territorial Sportsmen of Juneau; and Tanana Valley Sportsmen's Association.
47. *Annual Report of Alaska Game Commission, 1956–57*, 32.
48. *Annual Report of Alaska Game Commission, 1951–52,* 15–17; *1954–56*, 47–48; O'Connor, *Quarterly Report*, 6.
49. Alaska Game Commission, *Annual Report, 1947–48,* 11; Calvin R. Lensink, interview by author, July 28, 1989.
50. Fowler, "Wolf Hunt," 18, 40–41.
51. *Annual Report of Alaska Game Commission, 1951–52,* 16.
52. Calvin R. Lensink, interview by author, July 28, 1989.

53. Hammond, "Strafing Arctic Killers," 38.
54. *Annual Report of Alaska Game Commission, 1951–52*, 15; Hammond, "Strafing Arctic Killers," 112. The seven agents: Bob Burkholder, Doyle Cisney, Frank Glaser, Jay Hammond, Buck Harris, Maurice Kelly, and Joe Miner.
55. Rearden, *Alaska's Wolf Man*, 306–308.
56. *Annual Report of Alaska Game Commission, 1957–58*, 34.
57. Calvin R. Lensink, interview by author, July 28, 1989.
58. Hammond, "Strafing Arctic Killers," 120.
59. *Annual Report of Alaska Game Commission, 1956–57*, 30.
60. Alaska Dept. of Fish and Game, *Annual Report for 1957*, 53–54.
61. Alaska Game Commission, *Report of Wolf and Coyote Bounty Payments, 1940*, 12ff; *Annual Report of Alaska Game Commission, 1956–57*, 32.
62. *Annual Report of Alaska Game Commission, 1957–58*, 33.
63. Ibid., *1956–57*, 29.
64. Ibid., *1954–56*, 49; *1956–57*, 29; *1957–58*, 33; Laycock, "Alaska's Wildlife," 81.
65. Chatelain, "Bear-Moose Relationships," 224–226, 231; *Alaska*, "Alaska Sportsman," 58.
66. *Annual Report of Alaska Game Commission, 1953–54*, 15–16; *1958–59*, 42.
67. Ibid., *1957–58*, 35; *1958–59*, 38–39.
68. U.S. Fish and Wildlife Service, *Alaska District, Branch of Predator Control, Annual Report, FY 1960*, 2–3; *1962–64*, 1–8.
69. E. Jones, *Report of Alaska Investigations in 1914*, 48.
70. Ibid., 52, 54, 112.
71. Morton, "The Dolly Varden Is Innocent," 14–15, 62–63; P. Roppel, *Alaska's Salmon Hatcheries*, 68.
72. McKnight, *History of Predator Control*, 4.
73. Troyer, *Status of Brown Bear*, 4–5.
74. Imler and Sarber, *Harbor Seals and Sea Lions in Alaska*, 13–14.
75. Ibid., 13–15, 19.
76. Thorsteinson, Nelson, and Lall, *Experimental Harvest of Sea Lion*, 1–2, 14.
77. Imler and Sarber, *Harbor Seals and Sea Lions in Alaska*, 1, 3–5.
78. Lensink, "Predator Control," 91–94.
79. Alaska Dept. of Fisheries, *Annual Report for 1951*, 44–45. Cooperating groups in 1951 included Copper River Co-op Cannery, Cordova District Fisheries Union, Cordova Fish and Cold Storage, New England Fish Company, Parks-Western Fisheries, and Whiz Halferty Company.
80. Alaska Dept. of Fish and Game, *Annual Report for 1958*, 92–93, 95, 103.
81. McKnight, *History of Predator Control*, 7.
82. Alaska Dept. of Fisheries, *Annual Report for 1954*, 51–53; *1955*, 100–101, 106; *1956*, 52, 58; Alaska Dept. of Fish and Game, *Annual Report for 1957*, 53.
83. McKnight, *History of Predator Control*, 7.
84. E. Bailey, *Introduction of Foxes*, 4–5, 8–12, 17, 22.
85. Ibid., 9–12.
86. L. Black, *Atkha*, 157.

87. E. Bailey, *Introduction of Foxes*, 31–38; Croll et al., "Introduced Predators," 1959–1961.
88. Kenton Wohl, interview by author, July 27, 1989.
89. E. Bailey, *Introduction of Foxes*, 16–17, 29–31.
90. O. Murie, *Fauna of the Aleutian Islands*, 296–297, 302–303.
91. Kohlhoff, *When the Wind Was a River*, 23.
92. E. Bailey, *Introduction of Foxes*, 39–44.
93. Kenyon, "Birds of Amchitka," 307–309.
94. Scheffer, *Adventures of a Zoologist*, 22, 112.
95. E. Bailey, *Introduction of Foxes*, 41–43; U.S. Fish and Wildlife Service, *Alaska Maritime National Wildlife Refuge*, 54.
96. Kenton Wohl, interview by author, July 27, 1989; U.S. Fish and Wildlife Service, *Alaska Maritime National Wildlife Refuge*, 56. Cattle were removed from Caton, Simeonof, and Chernabura islands and remained on private lands of four other islands.
97. Kenton Wohl, interview by author, July 27, 1989.
98. Scheffer, Fiscus, and Todd, *History of Scientific Study*, 20.
99. Osgood, Preble, and Parker, "Fur Seals and Other Life," 128–131.
100. R. Jones and Byrd, "Interrelations Between Seabirds and Introduced Animals," 221–224.
101. *Annual Report of Alaska Game Commission, 1958–59*, 41.
102. R. Jones and Byrd, "Interrelations Between Seabirds and Introduced Animals," 222.
103. *Annual Report of Governor on Alaska Game Law, 1915*, 5; *1918*, 3; *1920*, 4, 13.
104. A. Bailey, *Notes on Game Conditions*, 5, 16, 27.
105. T. Pearson, "Eagles and the Alaskan Bounty," 86–89.
106. U.S. Dept. of the Interior, Fish And Wildlife Service, *Bald Eagle*, 20–21.
107. L. Burch, "Eagle-Shooting in Alaska," 14.
108. Ibid., 14–15.
109. Meine, *Aldo Leopold*, 360–361.
110. Sweazey, "In the Tallest Trees," 18.
111. Perkins, "Bounty Hunter," 11.
112. Burg, "Alaska's Bald Eagles," 11; Sherwood, *Big Game in Alaska*, 92–93; U.S. Dept. of the Interior, Fish and Wildlife Service, *Bald Eagle*, 19–20; 54 Stat. 250, June 8, 1940; 73 Stat. 143, June 25, 1959.

CHAPTER 14: GAME AND FUR MAMMALS

1. Skoog, "Ecology of the Caribou," 245–246, 251.
2. Bockstoce, *Steam Whaling*, 42–43.
3. O. Murie, *Alaska-Yukon Caribou*, 60.
4. Osgood, *Biological Reconnaissance*, 28–29.
5. Klein, "Caribou: Alaska's Wilderness Nomads," 201.
6. O. Murie, *Alaska-Yukon Caribou*, 6. Murie's method, visual observation from the ground, was primitive and his count probably high.

7. Scott, Chatelain, and Elkins, "Status of Dall Sheep and Caribou," 613, 621–623.
8. *Annual Report of Alaska Game Commission, 1952–53*, 16; *1958–59*, 15–17. Skoog, "Historical Resume—Reindeer," asserted that reindeer characteristics (squatness, short legs, and white coloration) probably reflected recessive genes and would not long survive in a wild population. Two decades after reindeer joined the Alaska Peninsula caribou herd, Skoog noted, no sign of their presence remained.
9. Leopold and Darling, "Effects of Land Use," 553–562.
10. Skoog, "Ecology of the Caribou," 304.
11. Leopold and Darling, *Wildlife in Alaska*, 82–90; Leopold and Darling, "Effects of Land Use," 553–556.
12. James G. King, interview by author, July 13, 1989.
13. *Annual Report of Governor to Secretary of Interior, 1946*, 30; Leopold and Darling, *Wildlife in Alaska*, 104.
14. Klein, "Reconnaissance Study of Mountain Goat," ix, 1, 5–6, 100.
15. *Annual Report of Alaska Game Commission, 1958–59*, 20–21; Klein, *Black-Tailed Deer.*
16. S. Jackson, *Introduction of Reindeer, 1890*, 4–9, 13.
17. S. Jackson, *Report on Introduction of Reindeer, 1893*, 6, 9–10, 14–15.
18. Ibid., *1894*, 10–16.
19. Ibid., 16–18.
20. R.L. Stewart, *Sheldon Jackson*, 400–402.
21. Stern et al., *Eskimos, Reindeer and Land*, 26–28; U.S. Revenue Cutter Service, *Report of Cruise of* Bear *and Overland Expedition*, 143–144.
22. Ray, *Ethnohistory in the Arctic*, 126–129.
23. Stern et al., *Eskimos, Reindeer and Land*, 26–28.
24. Lazell, *Alaskan Apostle*, 195.
25. Stern et al., *Eskimos, Reindeer and Land*, 29–44.
26. Hadwen and Palmer, *Reindeer in Alaska*, 3, 69.
27. Greeley, *Handbook of Alaska*, 165.
28. Lantis, "Reindeer Industry," 37n18.
29. Stern et al., *Eskimos, Reindeer and Land*, 47, 49–52.
30. Lantis, "Reindeer Industry," 30–34.
31. Ibid., 34–35.
32. U.S. Dept. of the Interior, *Survey of Alaska Reindeer Service.*
33. Stern et al., *Eskimos, Reindeer and Land*, 59, 62, 66–67, 70–72.
34. Lantis, "Reindeer Industry," 35–38.
35. O. Miller, *Frontier in Alaska and Matanuska Colony*, 192.
36. Stern et al., *Eskimos, Reindeer and Land*, 73–80, 92–93, 101.
37. Little, *Evaluation of Feasibility of Native Industry*, 4–5.
38. Gruening, *State of Alaska*, 359.
39. A. Murie, *A Naturalist in Alaska,* 1–2; L. Palmer and Rouse, *Study of Alaskan Tundra*, 1, 46–48.
40. Klein, *St. Matthew Island*, iii, 2, 30; U.S. Fish and Wildlife Service, *Alaska Maritime National Wildlife Refuge Conservation Plan*, 56.

41. Stern et al., *Eskimos, Reindeer and Land*, 95–96.
42. Porsild, "Reindeer Journey," 1–5, 12.
43. Scotter, "Reindeer Industry," 57–60. Accounts of the trek vary as to numbers of reindeer and other details.
44. Porsild, "Reindeer Journey," 12–15.
45. Drury, "Natural History of Musk Ox," 27–34.
46. Stefansson, *Northward Course of Empire*, 140; Bergman, "Brave Return," 71–72.
47. Hone, *Present Status of Muskox*, 7; Hornaday, "Musk Ox in Alaska," 754; J. Allen, "Probable Recent Occurrence of the Musk-Ox," 720. There is some inconsistency among the reports. That attributed to Brower appears the most accurate except for identifying the site as southeast of Barrow rather than Wainwright.
48. McKennan, *Chandalar Kutchin*, 18; Bodfish, *Chasing the Bowhead*, 186.
49. J. Allen, "Musk-Oxen of Arctic America," 84–86.
50. Bales, "Habits and Habitat," 3.
51. *Annual Report of Governor on Alaska Game Law, 1918*, 6–7.
52. Bergman, "Brave Return," 72; Trefethen, *Crusade for Wildlife*, 223; *Report of Governor to Secretary of Interior, 1919*, 60; Burris and McKnight, *Game Transplants*, 12.
53. Lent, "Musk-Ox," 144, 147; J. Brooks, *North to Wolf Country*, 302–303.
54. Wilkinson, "Oomingmak," 24–25.
55. Burris and McKnight, *Game Transplants*, 6–29; Franzmann, *Review of Alaskan Translocations*; Courtright, *Alaska Big Game Harvest Data*.
56. Alaska Dept. of Fish and Game, *American Bison*, 3–9.
57. K. Nelson, *Daughter of the Gold Rush*, 138.
58. Alaska Dept. of Fish and Game, *American Bison*, 3–5.
59. Alaska Dept. of Fish and Game, *Reintroducing Wood Bison*, 1–5; Stephenson et al., "Wood Bison," 129–137.
60. Elkins and Nelson, "Wildlife Introductions," 2–3, 14.
61. O. Murie, "Wildlife Introductions," 434–436.
62. Schneider, "Trapping Furbearers," 4–5.
63. Ibid., 6–10.
64. L. Black, *Russians in Alaska*, 266.
65. Ibid., 65, 69; Golovin, *End of Russian America*, 80.
66. Applegate, *Report on Population, 1890*, 207–214.
67. M. Webb, *Last Frontier*, 295, 302.
68. Lutz, *Ecological Effects of Forest Fires*, 80–81.
69. Schneider, "Trapping Furbearers," 11–17.
70. Dice, "Interior Alaska in 1911 and 1912," 69.
71. Thomas, *Trails and Tramps*, 58–59.
72. M. Webb, *Last Frontier*, 295–296.
73. D. Mitchell, *Sold American*, 276–277.
74. E. Jones, *Report of Alaska Investigations in 1914*, 116–117; Huston, "Geographical Analysis of Fur Farming Industry," 19, 87–89, 95–100.
75. D. Mitchell, *Sold American*, 227–229.
76. M. Webb, *Last Frontier*, 300–304.

77. Anderson, *Trapping in Alaska and the European Economic Community*, 12, 14, 24–25.
78. *Popular Mechanics*, "Man's Law on the Yukon," 292.
79. Ford and MacBain, "Hot Fur," 29.
80. Annabel, "Trouble in Alaska's Game Lands," 48.
81. M. Webb, *Last Frontier*, 300.
82. Buckley, *Wildlife in the Economy of Alaska*, 32–33.
83. Sumner, "Your Stake in Alaska's Wildlife," 57, 67.
84. Ibid., 60–62, 70.
85. Ibid., 68.

CHAPTER 15: JOURNEY OF THE SALMON

1. P. Roppel, *Alaska's Salmon Hatcheries*, 3.
2. Cooley, *Politics and Conservation*, 4–8.
3. P. Roppel, *Salmon From Kodiak*, 1–4; S. Evans, *Historical View*, 265–266, 271.
4. P. Roppel, *Salmon From Kodiak*, 15, 63, 73; Moser, *Salmon and Salmon Fisheries of Alaska*, 22.
5. Netboy, *The Salmon*, 408–409; Ted Merrell, pers. com., April 20, 2002.
6. Cane, "Salmon Fishery," 107–108.
7. P. Roppel, *Salmon From Kodiak*, 25, 31, 36; *Pacific Fisherman, 1944 Yearbook*, "Pack of Canned Salmon in Alaska, by District and Species—1884 to 1943."
8. Gill, "Six Months in a Salmon Ship," 310.
9. Ibid., 309, 312, 314.
10. Cooley, *Politics and Conservation*, 27.
11. P. Roppel, *Salmon From Kodiak*, 39, 45–46; 25 Stat. 1009, March 2, 1889.
12. Bean, *Report on Salmon and Salmon Rivers*, 5.
13. Hinckley, "Alaska and the Emergence," 97, 99.
14. Grinnell, "Salmon Industry," 343, 350–351; P. Roppel, *Salmon From Kodiak*, 33.
15. Scudder, *Alaska Salmon Trap*, 15; P. Roppel, *Alaska's Salmon Hatcheries*, 6, 26; Gruening, *State of Alaska*, 248–249; 29 Stat. 316, June 9, 1896; Brady quoted in Hinckley, "Alaska and the Emergence," 98–99.
16. Scudder, *Alaska Salmon Trap*, 16.
17. P. Roppel, *Salmon From Kodiak*, 45–46, 52–53.
18. Kurtz, *Glacier Bay: Historic Resources Study*, 45.
19. Royce, "Alaskan Salmon Management," 21.
20. Augerot, "Environmental History of Salmon Management," 220–221.
21. Hinckley, "Alaska and the Emergence," 97–98.
22. Ibid., 98–99.
23. Moser, *Salmon and Salmon Fisheries of Alaska*, 22–23.
24. Ibid., 43–44.
25. S. Evans, *Historical View*, 264–265, 338.
26. Tingle, *Report on the Salmon Fisheries, 1896*, 19.

27. Netboy, *The Salmon*, 417.
28. P. Roppel, *Salmon From Kodiak*, 87–89.
29. D. Mitchell, *Sold American*, 278–279; Moser, *Salmon and Salmon Fisheries of Alaska*, 66.
30. Augerot, "Environmental History of Salmon Management," 222–224; *Tlingit and Haida Indians v. U.S.*, 177 F. Supp. 452 (Court of Claims, 1959); 85 Stat. 688, December 18, 1971; 94 Stat. 2371, December 2, 1980. The Alaska Native Claims Settlement Act of 1971 abolished all reservations in Alaska except Metlakatla and conveyed title of the former Venetie reservation to the local Gwitch'in corporations, which transferred it to the Village of Venetie. See *Alaska v. Native Village of Venetie Tribal Government* (96–177), 101 F. 3rd 1286 reversed, February 25, 1998.
31. Scudder, *Alaska Salmon Trap*, 21–22.
32. D. Mitchell, *Sold American*, 105–108.
33. Moser, *Salmon and Salmon Fisheries of Alaska*, 22, 25, 66.
34. D. Mitchell, *Sold American*, 106–107.
35. Hinckley, *Americanization of Alaska*, 127–128.
36. P. Roppel, *Salmon From Kodiak*, 29.
37. Catton, *Land Reborn*, 24–25, 104–108, 112–113.
38. P. Roppel, *Alaska's Salmon Hatcheries*, 3–6; Pat Roppel, pers. com., April 24, 2002.
39. Hunt, *History of Marine Hatcheries*, 3–5, 16–17.
40. Augerot, "Environmental History of Salmon Management," 105–109.
41. P. Roppel, *Alaska's Salmon Hatcheries*, 3–4, 13–14; Pat Roppel, pers. com., April 24, 2002.
42. Hunt, *History of Marine Hatcheries*, 13–18.
43. P. Roppel, *Alaska's Salmon Hatcheries*, 30.
44. Ibid., 21–23, 265–275.
45. Augerot, "Environmental History of Salmon Management," 111–112; Taylor, "Well-Thinking Men and Women," 361–369, 377, 382–387.
46. Crutchfield and Pontecorvo, *Pacific Salmon Fisheries*, 96–97; Naske and Slotnick, *Alaska: A History*, 98–99; P. Roppel, *Salmon From Kodiak*, 54–56, 72; 43 Stat. 464, June 6, 1924.
47. Gruening, *State of Alaska*. 268.
48. Gregory and Barnes, *North Pacific Fisheries*, 49–51.
49. S.E. White, "Kidding Ourselves Along," 17, 173.
50. Bower, *Alaska Fishery, 1925*, 86–89.
51. Koughan, "Account of Alaska Salmon Industry," 92–93; ibid., *1935*, 8–11.
52. Bower, *Alaska Fishery, 1945*, 5–7; Thompson, *Alaska Fishery, 1955*, 12–14.
53. Whitehead, "The Governor," 364–366; Gruening, *State of Alaska*, 152, 192–198, 233; 37 Stat. 512, August 24, 1912.
54. Gruening, *State of Alaska*, 382–392.
55. S. Evans, *Historical View*, 307, 324.
56. Gregory and Barnes, *North Pacific Fisheries*, 84–85, 99–100.
57. Fitzgerald, "Days of the Seafaring Canners," 10–11.

58. Gregory and Barnes, *North Pacific Fisheries*, 86–87, 97, 102, 105–108.
59. Scudder, *Alaska Salmon Trap*, 1–6, 8–10, 16.
60. Gruening, *State of Alaska*, 170–171, 524n31.
61. Rogers, *Alaska in Transition*, 7–14; Rearden, "Alaska's Commercial Salmon Fisheries," 20; Naske and Slotnick, *Alaska: A History*, 169.
62. Cooley, *Politics and Conservation*, 36, 43, 49–50; Rogers, *Alaska in Transition*, 106.
63. S. Evans, *Historical View*, 336–337.
64. Cooley, *Politics and Conservation*, 155–161, 157 (quotation), 177–181.
65. Gruening, *State of Alaska*, 404.
66. Scudder, *Alaska Salmon Trap*, 23.
67. Gruening, *State of Alaska*, 406–407.
68. Haycox, *Frigid Embrace*, 3–18, 27–35, 48–51.
69. Committee for Protection of North Pacific Fisheries, *Japan's High Seas Salmon Fishery*, 3.
70. Leonard, "Alaskan Salmon Controversy," 40–43.
71. Ibid., 43–46.
72. Pasley, "Salmon Battle," 146–147.
73. Leonard, "Alaskan Salmon Controversy," 46–47, 50–55.
74. Augerot, "Environmental History of Salmon Management," 248, 324.
75. Committee for the Protection of North Pacific Fisheries, *Japan's High Seas Salmon Fishery*, 4–8, 11–12, 15, 19–20.
76. U.S. Senate, Committee on Commerce, *International North Pacific Fisheries Convention*, 10–11.
77. Augerot, "Environmental History of Salmon Management," 9–10, 256–259.
78. Crutchfield and Pontecorvo, *Pacific Salmon Fisheries*, 85, 87–88.
79. Stansby, *Federal Fishery Research*, 1–4, 10–15.
80. Augerot, "Environmental History of Salmon Management," 300–302.
81. Royce, "Alaskan Salmon Management," 18, 20, 23.
82. DeArmond, "Page and Line Comments on 'History of Alaskan Fisheries' by Sheila Evans," 1–3, appended to S. Evans, *Historical View*.
83. Ibid., 6.
84. Crutchfield and Pontecorvo, *Pacific Salmon Fisheries*, 58.
85. Royce, "Alaskan Salmon Management," 25, 27, 29.
86. Augerot, "Environmental History of Salmon Management," 117–119.
87. Mantua et al., "Pacific Interdecadal Climate Oscillation," 1072–1078.
88. Beamish et al., "The Regime Concept," 521–524.
89. D. Barry, "Salmon Industry's Changing Currents," 60–63.
90. N. Williams, "Temperature Rise Could Squeeze Salmon," 1349.

CHAPTER 16: GOLD AND OIL ON THE KENAI

1. Simmerman, *Alaska's Parklands*, 180.
2. Bennett, *Report on Reconnaissance*, 43–45.

3. Fedorova, *Russian Population*, 115–122, 128.
4. M. Barry, *History of Mining*, 159–160.
5. Ibid., 6, 13–15; Fedorova, *Russian Population*, 195.
6. M. Barry, *History of Mining*, 19; Bennett, *Report on Reconnaissance*, 44–45.
7. M. Barry, *History of Mining*, 6, 47–50, 103, 107; Bennett, *Report on Reconnaissance*, 44. The date of the first Russian gold discovery is commonly cited (e.g., Fedorova) as 1850 or 1851.
8. Wilson, *Railroad in the Clouds*, 3, 6–7; Bennett, *Report on Reconnaissance*, 45.
9. Penick, *Progressive Politics*, 78–83. Kennecott Copper Company and the Kennecott mines derived their names from Western Union expedition leader Robert Kennicott; the company changed the spelling for taxation reasons. The town and glacier retained the original spelling. (Sally Gilbert, secy., Friends of Kennicott, letter to author, August 1, 1991.)
10. Penick, *Progressive Politics*, 5–18.
11. Ibid., 79–86.
12. Ibid., 20–21, 24, 26.
13. Ibid., 85–89, 94–101.
14. Richardson, *Politics of Conservation*, 66–69.
15. Glavis, "Whitewashing Ballinger," 15–17, 27.
16. Penick, *Progressive Politics*, 13–14, 27–29, 38–39, 101.
17. Richardson, *Politics of Conservation*, 67–79.
18. Penick, *Progressive Politics*, 144, 157–162, 173.
19. Ibid., 172, 175, 192–196; Haycox, *Alaska: An American Colony*, 228.
20. Slotnick, "Ballinger-Pinchot," 340–344.
21. Tompkins, *Alaska: Promyshlennik and Sourdough*, 268–271.
22. Wilson, *Railroad in the Clouds*, 6–7, 17, 23–26.
23. Gruening, *State of Alaska*, 177–181, 188.
24. Wilson, *Railroad in the Clouds*, 28–30, 85; 38 Stat. 305, March 12, 1914.
25. D. Mitchell, *Sold American*, 171, 178.
26. Bennett, *Report on Reconnaissance*, 42.
27. Osgood, *Natural History of Queen Charlotte Islands*, 67; Peterson and Woolington, "Apparent Extirpation," 337–341.
28. Stone quoted in J. Allen, "Description of a New Caribou," 148; Lutz, *History of Early Occurrence of Moose*, 2. Lutz refuted the popular theories that moose had only recently arrived on the Kenai and that fire as opposed to hunting was the prime cause of the caribou removal.
29. Cane, *Summer and Fall*, 171.
30. U.S. Dept. of Agriculture, *Regulations for Protection of Game in Alaska, 1904*, 3.
31. Peterson and Woolington, "Apparent Extirpation," 339.
32. Scull, *Hunting in the Arctic*, 210.
33. *Annual Report of Governor on Alaska Game Law, 1915*, 4.
34. Shiras, "White Sheep," 494.
35. *Annual Report of Governor on Alaska Game Law, 1912*, 6; *1916*, 3.
36. Ibid., *1915*, 4–5; Bennett, *Report on Reconnaissance*, 118–121.
37. U.S. House Committee on Agriculture, *Hearings: Alaska Game Act*, 12–14.

38. Chatelain, "Bear-Moose Relationships," 225.
39. Eddy, *Hunting on Kenai Peninsula*, 44–45.
40. Chatelain, "Bear-Moose Relationships," 225, 232–233; D. Spencer and Chatelain, "Progress in Management of Moose," 539–540, 550.
41. Naske, "Kenai National Moose Range," 121–132; President Franklin D. Roosevelt, Executive Order Nos. 8978–8979, December 16, 1941.
42. Moffitt, "Petroleum on West Shore," 135–137.
43. Davis, *Energy/Alaska*, 198–201.
44. Postman, "Oil Industry Built Close Ties With President Eisenhower," *Anchorage Daily News*, February 5, 1990, 1, 5.
45. Postman, "City Leaders Struck a Deal for Oil," *Anchorage Daily News*, February 4, 1990, 9.
46. Ibid., 9–10.
47. Roderick, *Crude Dreams*, 73–77. Coincidence of the Wester negotiations and leasing by Jacobs, and the deals between Richfield and the Anchorage group, suggested collusion, which would violate federal law. Postman ("City Leaders," 10–11) concluded that Richfield needed the group's political backing to get preferential access to oil leasing on the Kenai. According to Roderick (76–77), Jacobs denied any such collusion and pointed out that only one member of the business group had agreed to the January leases. In a 1990 interview, Robert Atwood acknowledged that his group of fourteen had acted as leaseholders for Arco but claimed they had no prior ties to the company and only wanted someone to drill a well to advance economic development in Alaska. Of the oil companies they approached, only Arco showed interest. Arco insisted on paying some of the group's leasing expenses, amounting to about half. When Arco eventually struck oil on the group's leased lands, it paid them royalties. Atwood denied ever having heard the name "Spit and Argue Club." (See Neiswonger, "Robert Atwood," 43–45.) Postman (10–11) quoted former Arco geologist Ray Arnett as saying that Arco sought out the leaseholders to supplement its leased lands, and "[w]e were asking them to go in there and lease that land. . . . We kind of gathered those people together." Arnett stated that Jacobs had acted for Richfield: "We got Locke started. I wanted somebody who could follow the lease activity in Alaska. . . . We paid him a certain amount of money and Locke was capable of doing the job."
48. Postman, "City Leaders Struck a Deal," 9–10; Roderick, *Crude Dreams*, 62–65.
49. Postman, "BLM Aided Chosen Few," *Anchorage Daily News*, February 5, 1990, 1, 4–5.
50. Postman, "Territorial Delegate Aided Oil Company, Businessmen," *Anchorage Daily News*, February 6, 1990, 1, 9.
51. Hanley, Hemming, and Morsell, *Natural Resource Protection*, 168.
52. Roderick, *Crude Dreams*, 78.
53. Postman, "New Interior Secretary Accelerated Oil Development on Moose Range," *Anchorage Daily News*, February 7, 1990, 1, 9–10.
54. Anchorage Chamber of Commerce, *Alaska's 1957 Oil Discovery*, 12–13, 15, Exhibits K, M.

55. Poole, "Stand Firm, Mr. Secretary," 4, 71.
56. Postman, "Gruening Took up the Cause of Oil," *Anchorage Daily News*, February 8, 1990, 9.
57. Postman, "New Interior Secretary Accelerated Oil Development," 10.
58. Postman, "A Nasty Schism," *Anchorage Daily News*, February 8, 1990, 8–9.
59. Postman, "Potential Oil Lease Scandal Worried Interior Secretary," *Anchorage Daily News*, February 9, 1990, 12–13.
60. Postman, "Oil Interests United Opponents, Proponents on Statehood Issue," *Anchorage Daily News*, February 10, 1990, 1, 12.
61. Postman, "Challenge to Spit and Argue Club Leases Fails After 6-Year Fight," *Anchorage Daily News*, February 11, 1990, 1, 8–9; Hanley, Hemming, and Morsell, *Natural Resource Protection*, 178–179.
62. Hanley, Hemming, and Morsell, *Natural Resource Protection*, 179; Postman, "Challenge to Spit and Argue Club," 1, 8–9; Postman, "Epilogue: Upshot of an Oil Lease Deal," *Anchorage Daily News*, February 11, 1990, 8; *Alaska Conservation Society News Bulletin*, October 1964, 3.
63. State of Alaska, *Session Laws, 1965*, SJR3.
64. 94 Stat. 2379 Sec. 201(5); 94 Stat. 2391 Sec. 303(4); 94 Stat. 2418 Sec. 702(7), December 2, 1980.
65. Peterson and Woolington, "Apparent Extirpation," 340–341.
66. Postman, "Epilogue," 8.
67. Hanley, Hemming, and Morsell, *Natural Resource Protection*, 179–180.
68. U.S. Dept. of the Interior, Fish and Wildlife Service, *Kenai National Wildlife Refuge*, 10.
69. Postman, "Epilogue," 8.
70. Borneman, *Alaska*, 408, 412.

CHAPTER 17: BOB MARSHALL, OLAUS AND MARGARET MURIE, AND THE ARCTIC REFUGE

1. Fox, *John Muir and His Legacy*, 206–209; R. Marshall, *Arctic Wilderness*, xiv–xv, 1–3; Vickery, "Bob Marshall," 59–60; Vickery, *Wilderness Visionaries*, 130–133, 141; Clepper, *Leaders in American Conservation*, 219–220. See also R. Marshall, *Arctic Village*.
2. Glover, "Romance, Recreation, and Wilderness," 24–31.
3. R. Marshall, "The Problem of the Wilderness," 142–145.
4. R. Marshall, "The Universe of the Wilderness Is Vanishing," 11.
5. R. Marshall, *People's Forests*, 209–210.
6. Ibid., 217.
7. Glover, "Romance, Recreation, and Wilderness," 30–31; Nash, "Strenuous Life," 23–24.
8. Glover, *Wilderness Original*, 209–211; R. Marshall, "Ecology and the Indians," 159–161.

9. Nash, *Wilderness and the American Mind*, 204–206; Allin, *Politics of Wilderness*, 80–85; Nash, "Strenuous Life," 24.
10. R. Marshall, *Alaska Wilderness*, 74; Vickery, *Wilderness Visionaries*, 154.
11. Quoted in Glover, *Wilderness Original*, 137.
12. Nash, "Tourism," 15–17; Orth, *Dictionary of Alaska Place Names*, 624.
13. R. Marshall, "Adventure, Arrogance and the Arctic," 25.
14. R. Marshall, *Arctic Wilderness*, xx; Cameron, Marshall, and Gordon, "Recreational Resources," 127–129, 137–138.
15. Catton, *Inhabited Wilderness*, 134–143.
16. R. Marshall, "Should We Settle Alaska?" 50.
17. Ibid., 49–50; O. Miller, *Frontier in Alaska*, 164–175.
18. R. Marshall, "The Problem of the Wilderness," 148.
19. Murie quoted in Scheffer, "Exploring With Olaus Murie," 15.
20. Weddle, "Wilderness Champion," 228; *Living Wilderness*, "1889–Olaus J. Murie–1963," 6–7; Curry, "Portrait," 16; Glover and Glover, "Natural Magic," 69–71; Orth, *Dictionary of Alaska Place Names*, 666; Margaret Murie, letter to author, June 26, 1990; Sterling, *Biographical Dictionary of American and Canadian Naturalists and Environmentalists*, 566–567.
21. Glover, "Sweet Days of a Naturalist," 132–135.
22. Ibid., 133–138.
23. D. Spencer, "Aleutian Islands National Wildlife Refuge," 50.
24. Quoted in Glover, "Sweet Days of a Naturalist," 135–136.
25. Wild, "Science and Sympathy"; O. Murie, "Wolf," 220–221; Fox, *John Muir and His Legacy*, 267–268. David L. Spencer ("Aleutian Islands National Wildlife Refuge," 59) stated that military activities caused the Unimak dieoff.
26. O. Murie, *Journeys to the Far North*, 245.
27. Quoted in Curry, "Portrait," 18–20.
28. *Living Wilderness*, "1899–Olaus J. Murie–1963," 3.
29. O. Murie, "Beauty and the Dollar Sign," 22.
30. O. Murie, "Wolf," 221.
31. Quoted in Curry, "Portrait," 16.
32. O. Murie, "God Bless America," 9.
33. O. Murie, "Wilderness Philosophy," 64, 67.
34. Murie quoted in Scheffer, "Exploring With Olaus Murie," 10, 15; Clepper, *Leaders in American Conservation*, 233–234.
35. *Alaska*, Obituary of Olaus J. Murie, 45; M. and O. Murie, *Wapiti Wilderness*, 303.
36. O. Murie, "Wild Country," 12.
37. O. Murie, "Beauty and the Dollar Sign," 27.
38. M. Murie, *Two in the Far North*, 229–258.
39. Graham, "Mardy Murie," 122, 127.
40. Breton, *Women Pioneers*, 260–263.
41. U.S. Dept. of the Interior, Fish and Wildlife Service, *Arctic National Wildlife Refuge Conservation Plan*, 127–128; Chance, *The Eskimo of North Alaska*, 10–12.
42. Orth, *Dictionary of Alaska Place Names*, 117, 176.

43. Collins and Sumner, "Northeast Arctic," 20; Leffingwell, *Canning River Region*, 62–63.
44. Amundsen, *My Life as an Explorer*, 52–54; Underwood, *Alaska: An Empire*, 425–427.
45. Kilian, *Voyage of the Schooner Polar Bear*, vi–vii.
46. Amundsen, *The North West Passage*, 180, 215–218, 224, 229–230, 241, 246.
47. Thayer, "The ANWR," 1.
48. U.S. Dept. of the Interior, Fish and Wildlife Service, *Arctic National Wildlife Refuge: Coastal Plain*, chaps. 4–6; Simmerman, *Alaska's Parklands*, 93.
49. D.S. Miller, *Midnight Wilderness*, 12.
50. D. Jackson, "Floor of Creation," 16.
51. Crisler, *Arctic Wild*, 136.
52. Milton, *Nameless Valleys, Shining Mountains*, 105–106.
53. Naske, "Creation of Arctic National Wildlife Range," 101.
54. Collins, *Art and Politics of Park Planning*, 189–194.
55. Naske, "Creation of Arctic National Wildlife Range," 104.
56. M. Murie, "Return to the Sheenjek," 5.
57. Collins and Sumner, "Northeast Arctic," 23, 25–26. The appeal reflected the ideas of Bob Marshall, whom Collins had known personally (Kaye, *Last Great Wilderness*, 15).
58. M. Murie, "Return to the Sheenjek," 5; Nelson, *Northern Landscapes*, 45; Naske, "Creation of Arctic National Wildlife Range," 103, 105. Dr. Brina Kessel of the University of Alaska, as well as Bob Krear and George Schaller, accompanied the Muries.
59. Wood, "From the Woodpile," 11.
60. Naske, "Creation of Arctic National Wildlife Range," 106–109; Kauffmann, *Alaska's Brooks Range*, 102–103; *Alaska State Session Laws, 1959*, HJM 23.
61. O. Murie, "Nature in the Arctic," 29–31.
62. Kauffmann, *Alaska's Brooks Range*, 103; Seaton, "America's Largest Wildlife Area," 117, 119, 122, 144.
63. Findlay, "History and Status of Arctic National Wildlife Range," 16; D. Nelson, *Northern Landscapes*, 48–49.
64. House Subcom. on Fisheries and Wildlife Conservation, *Hearings*, 139, 157, 164, 171–173, 177, 179.
65. Senate Committee on Interstate and Foreign Commerce, Merchant Marine Subcom., *Hearings, Part I*, 57, 62–63, 66–69.
66. Rausch, "Outlook for Conservation," 15–16.
67. Senate Committee on Interstate and Foreign Commerce, Merchant Marine Subcom., *Hearings, Part I*, 335–337, 340, 344.
68. *Alaska Conservation Society News Bulletin*, March 1960, 3; May 1960, 10; August 1960, 1–4; November 1960, 3–4. Rivers explained that he met so much opposition he let the bill pass the House, assuming it would be easier to stop in the Senate (Kaye, *Last Great Wilderness*, 255n6).
69. Ibid., January 1961, 3–4; D. Nelson, *Northern Landscapes*, 52–53; D.S. Miller, *Midnight Wilderness*, 172, 180; President Dwight D. Eisenhower, Proclamation Nos. 1960–03–2213 to 2215, December 6, 1960.

70. James G. King, interview by author, February 14, 1988.
71. Wood, "From the Woodpile," 11.
72. Findlay, "History and Status of Arctic National Wildlife Range," 16–17.
73. Kaye, *Last Great Wilderness,* 213–214, 224.
74. Pruitt, "Animal Ecology," 46; J. Campbell, "An Anthropologist," 55–58; O. Murie, "Wilderness Philosophy," 68; U. Nelson and Spencer, "Bureau of Sport Fisheries and Wildlife's Position," 71.
75. U.S. Dept. of the Interior, Fish and Wildlife Service, *Arctic National Wildlife Refuge: Draft River Management Plan, 1993*, 5.
76. 94 Stat. 2390 Sec. 303(2), 94 Stat. 2449 Sec. 1002, December 2, 1980.
77. Braasch, "Coveted Slope," 27, 40.

Works Employed

Adams, Charles C. *Guide to the Study of Animal Ecology*. New York: Macmillan, 1913.

AHFAM NEWSLETTER. "Belmore Browne." April 1973.

Alaska. "Alaska Sportsman" (August 1986): 58.

———. Obituary of Olaus J. Murie (January 1964): 45.

Alaska Conservation Society News Bulletin. March, May, August, November 1960; January, May 1961.

Alaska Dept. of Fish and Game. *The American Bison in Alaska*. Juneau, March 1980.

———. *Annual Report, 1957, 1958*.

———. "Detailed Rationale for Decision by the Alaska Department of Fish and Game (ADF&G) to Deny Approval for the Removal of the Brooks River Fish Ladder." Typescript, ca. 1986. Katmai Administrative Records N1619 Waterlife: Brooks Falls Fish Ladder. Lake Clark Katmai Studies Center, Anchorage.

———. *Reintroducing Wood Bison to the Upper Yukon Valley, Alaska: A Feasibility Assessment*. June 1994.

Alaska Dept. of Fisheries. *Annual Report, 1951, 1954, 1955, 1956*.

Alaska Dept. of Natural Resources. *Promised Land: A History of Alaska's Selection of Its Congressional Land Grants*. Juneau, 1987.

Alaska Economic Report. "Sea Otter Harvest on the Rise." September 10, 1993, 7.

Alaska Game Commission. *Annual Report of the Alaska Game Commission to the Secretary of Agriculture, 1925–1939.*

———. Annual Report of the Alaska Game Commission to the Secretary of the Interior, 1940–1959.

———. *Annual Report of the Executive Officer to the Alaska Game Commission. 1927–1936, 1945–1948.* Continues in *Annual Report of the Alaska Game Commission to the Secretary of the Interior.*

———. *Report of Wolf and Coyote Bounty Payments, 1940.*

Alaska, Governor of. *Annual Report of the Governor of Alaska on the Alaska Game Law, 1909–1923.* Washington, DC: GPO.

———. *Report of the Governor of Alaska to the Secretary of the Interior, 1899, 1912, 1914, 1915, 1916, 1919, 1920, 1929, 1946.* Washington, DC: GPO.

Alaska Magazine. "The Alaskan Adventures of Jean Francois Galoup de La Perouse" (March 1927): 108–143.

Alaska, State of. *Session Laws and Resolutions, 1959, 1965*. Juneau.

Alaska, Territory of. *Session Laws, Resolutions and Memorials, 1935*. Juneau.

Alaska Travel Publications. *Exploring Katmai National Monument and the Valley of Ten Thousand Smokes*. Anchorage, 1974.

Alexander, Edward P. *The Museum in America: Innovators and Pioneers*. Walnut Creek: Alta Mira, 1997.

Allen, Joel A. "Description of a New Caribou From the Kenai Peninsula, Alaska." *Bulletin of the American Museum of Natural History* 14 (1901): 143–148.

———. *History of North American Pinnipeds*. U.S. Geological Survey Misc. Pub. No. 12. Washington, DC, 1880.

———. "The Musk-Oxen of Arctic America and Greenland." *Bulletin of American Museum of Natural History* 14 (1901): 69–86.

———. "The Probable Recent Occurrence of the Musk-Ox in Northern Alaska." *Science* 36 (1912): 720–722.

Allen, Thomas B. *Guardian of the Wild: The Story of the National Wildlife Federation, 1936–86*. Bloomington: Indiana University Press, 1987.

Allin, Craig W. *The Politics of Wilderness Preservation*. Westport: Greenwood, 1982.

Amundsen, Roald. *My Life As An Explorer*. Garden City: Doubleday, 1928.

———. *The North West Passage*. 2 vols. New York: E.P. Dutton, 1908.

Anchorage Chamber of Commerce. *Alaska's 1957 Oil Discovery and Its Strategic Importance*. Anchorage, October 1957.

Anders, Gary C. "A Critical Analysis of the Alaska Native Land Claims and Native Corporate Development." *Journal of Ethnic Studies* 13 (Spring 1985): 1–12.

Anderson, David B. *Trapping in Alaska and the European Economic Community Ban on Furs Taken With Leghold Traps*. Alaska Dept. of Fish and Game, Div. of Subsistence. Tech. Paper No. 223. Juneau, July 1993.

Andrews, C.L. *The Story of Alaska*. Caldwell, ID: Claxton, 1938.

Angliss, R.P., D.P. De Master, and A.L. Lopez. *Alaska Marine Mammal Stock Assessments, 2001*. U.S. Dept. of Commerce, National Marine Fisheries Service. Alaska Fisheries Science Center. December 2001.

Annabel, Russell. *Hunting and Fishing in Alaska*. New York: Knopf, 1948.

———. "Trouble in Alaska's Game Lands." *Saturday Evening Post*, January 1, 1949, 34–35.

Antonson, Joan M., and William S. Hanable. *Alaska's Heritage*. Anchorage: Alaska Historical Commission, 1985.

Applegate, Samuel. *Report on Population and Resources of Alaska, Eleventh Census: 1890*. Washington, DC: GPO, 1893.

Atwood, Evangeline, and Robert DeArmond. *Who's Who in Alaskan Politics: A Bibliographical Dictionary of Alaskan Political Personalities, 1884–1974*. Portland: Binford and Mort for the Alaska Historical Commission, 1977.

Augerot, Xanthippe. "An Environmental History of the Salmon Management Philosophies of the North Pacific: Japan, Russia, Canada, Alaska, and the Pacific Northwest United States." PhD diss., Oregon State University, 2000.

Austin, Oliver L., Jr., and Ford Wilke. *Japanese Fur Sealing*. U.S. Dept. of the Interior. Special Scientific Report—Wildlife No. 6. Washington, DC, September 1950.

Bade, William Frederick. *The Life and Letters of John Muir, Vol. 2*. Boston: Houghton-Mifflin, 1924.

Bailey, Alfred M. *Notes on Game Conditions in Alaska*. Juneau: Bureau of Biological Survey, January 1, 1921.

Bailey, Edgar P. *Introduction of Foxes to Alaskan Islands: History, Effects on Avifauna, and Eradication*. Homer: U.S. Fish and Wildlife Service, 1993.

Bailey, Thomas A. "The North Pacific Sealing Convention of 1911." *Pacific Historical Review* 4, 1 (1935): 1–14.

Baker, Christopher. "Walrus." *National Parks* 62, 11–12 (November-December 1988): 28–33.

Bales, L.L. "Habits and Habitat of Alaskan Big Game, Part II: Musk Ox." *Outdoor Life* 22 (July 1908): 3–9.

Bancroft, Hubert Howe. *History of Alaska, 1730–1885*. Darien, CT: Hafner, 1886. Rept. by Antiquarian, New York, 1960.

Barrow, Mark V. *A Passion for Birds: American Ornithology After Audubon*. Princeton: Princeton University Press, 1998.

Barry, Doug. "Salmon Industry's Changing Currents." *Alaska Business Monthly* (April 1992): 60–63.

Barry, Mary J. *A History of Mining on the Kenai Peninsula*. Anchorage: Alaska Northwest, 1973.

Bartonek, James C., ed. *Conservation of Marine Birds of America*. U.S. Fish and Wildlife Service. Wildlife Research Report No. 11. Washington, DC, 1979.

Bates, Robert H. *Mountain Man: The Story of Belmore Browne*. Clinton, NJ: Amwell, 1988.

Baxter, Don V., Benjamin Labaree, and William Hildebrand. *On and Off Alaskan Trails*. No listed publisher, 1937.

Beamish, R.J., D.J. Noakes, G.A. McFarlane, L. Klyashtorin, V.V. Ivanof, and V. Kurashof. "The Regime Concept and Natural Trends in the Production of Pacific Salmon." *Canadian Journal of Fisheries and Aquatic Sciences* 56 (1999): 516–526.

Bean, Michael J., and Melanie R. Rowland, eds. *The Evolution of National Wildlife Service.* 3rd ed. Westport: Praeger, 1997.

Bean, Tarleton H. *Report on the Salmon and Salmon Rivers of Alaska.* U.S. House of Reps., 51 Cong., 1 sess., Misc. Doc. No. 211. Washington, DC, 1890.

Bennett, Hugh H. *Report on a Reconnaissance of the Soils, Agriculture and Other Resources of the Kenai Peninsula, Alaska.* U.S. Dept. of Agriculture, Bureau of Soils. Washington, DC, 1918.

Berg, Ames. "Alaska's Bald Eagle." *Alaska Fish and Game Trails* 1971 (January–February): 10–12.

Bergman, Charles. "A Brave Return From the Brink for an Ice Age Relic." *Smithsonian* 16 (February 1986): 68–72.

Berkh, Vasilii Nikolaevich. *A Chronological History of the Discovery of the Aleutian Islands or the Exploits of Russian Merchants.* Transl. Dmitri Krenov; ed. Richard A. Pierce. Kingston: Limestone, 1974.

Bernard, Joseph F. "Walrus Protection in Alaska." *Journal of Mammalogy* 6 (May 1925): 100–102.

Bertrand, Kenneth J. "Geographical Exploration by the United States." In Herman R. Friis, ed., *The Pacific Basin: A History of Its Geographical Exploration,* 256–291. New York: American Geographical Society Special Pub. No. 38, 1967.

Best, Peter B. "Estimates of the Landed Catch of Right (and Other Whalebone) Whales in the American Fishery, 1805–1909." *Fishery Bulletin* 85, 3 (1987): 403–418.

Bezeau, M.V. "The Realities of Strategic Planning: The Decision to Build the Alaska Highway." In Kenneth Coates, ed., *The Alaska Highway: Papers of the 40th Anniversary Symposium,* 25–35. Vancouver: University of British Columbia Press, 1985.

Birkedal, Ted. "Ancient Hunters in the Alaskan Wilderness: Human Predators and Their Role and Effect on Wildlife Populations and Implications for Resource Management." *Proceedings of Seventh Conf. on Research and Resource Management in Parks and on Public Lands,* 228–234, Jacksonville, FL, Nov. 16–20, 1992. Hancock, MI: The George Wright Society, 1993.

Black, Bruce W. "A History of Glacier Bay National Monument, Alaska." Typescript, 1957. Alaska Historical Library, Juneau.

Black, Lydia T. *Atkha: An Ethnohistory of the Western Aleutians.* Ed. R.A. Pierce. Kingston: Limestone, 1984.

———. *Russians in Alaska, 1732–1867.* Fairbanks: University of Alaska Press, 2004.

Blair, W. Reid. "William Temple Hornaday." *New York Zoological Society Bulletin* 42 (March-April 1937): 47–49.

Bockstoce, John R. "Eskimo Whaling." *Alaska* 43 (September 1977): 4–5.

———. "History of Commercial Whaling in Arctic Alaska." *Alaska Geographic* 5, 4 (1978): 16–25.

———. *Steam Whaling in the Western Arctic.* New Bedford: Old Dartmouth Historical Society, 1977.

———. *Whales, Ice and Men: The History of Whaling in the Western Arctic.* Seattle: University of Washington Press, 1986.

———, and Daniel B. Botkin. "Harvest of Pacific Walruses by the Pacific Whaling Industry, 1848–1914." *Arctic and Alpine Research* 14:3 (1982): 183–188.

Bodeau, Jean. *Katmai National Park and Preserve, Alaska*. Anchorage: Alaska Natural History Assn. and Greatland Graphics, 1992.

Bodfish, Hartson H. *Chasing the Bowhead*. Cambridge: Harvard University Press, 1936.

Boeri, David. *People of the Ice Whale*. New York: Dutton, 1983.

Bohn, Dave. *Glacier Bay: The Land and the Silence*. San Francisco: Sierra Club Books, 1967.

Bonehill, Ralph. *Pioneer Boys of the Great Northwest: or, With Lewis and Clark Across the Rockies*. New York: Stitt, 1905.

Booth, Kay F. "Henry W. Elliott." Typescript, 1963. Anchorage Museum of History and Fine Arts Archives.

Borneman, Walter. *Alaska: Saga of a Bold Land*. New York: HarperCollins, 2003.

Bower, Ward T. *Alaska Fishery and Fur Seal Industries in 1925*. U.S. Dept. of Commerce, Bureau of Fisheries. Doc. No. 1008. Washington, DC: GPO, 1926.

———. *Alaska Fishery and Fur Seal Industries in 1935*. U.S. Dept. of Commerce, Bureau of Fisheries. Admin. Report No. 23. Washington, DC: GPO, 1936.

———. *Alaska Fishery and Fur Seal Industries in 1945*. U.S. Dept. of the Interior, Bureau of Commercial Fisheries. Statistical Digest No. 15. Washington, DC: GPO, 1946.

Bowkett, Gerald E. *Reaching for a Star: The Final Campaign for Alaska Statehood*. Fairbanks: Epicenter, 1989.

Braasch, Gary. "The Coveted Slope: Nearby Oil Drilling and Global Warming Threaten the Nation's Most Pristine Wildlife Reserve." *Animals* 132 (January 1, 1999): 22–40.

Breton, Mary Jo. *Women Pioneers for the Environment*. Boston: Northeastern University Press, 1998.

Bridges, William. *Gathering of Animals: An Unconventional History of the New York Zoological Society*. New York: Harper and Row, 1974.

Brooks, Alfred Hulse. *Blazing Alaska's Trails*. Fairbanks: University of Alaska and Arctic Institute of North America, 1953.

Brooks, James W. "A Contribution to the Life History and Ecology of the Pacific Walrus." Master's thesis, University of Alaska, 1954.

———. *North to Wolf Country: My Life Among the Creatures of Alaska*. Kenmore, WA: Epicenter, 2003.

Brower, Charles D. *Fifty Years Below Zero: A Lifetime of Adventure in the Far North*. New York: Grosset & Dunlap, 1942.

Brown, William E. *A History of the Denali–Mount McKinley Region, Alaska, Vol. 1—Historical Narrative*. Santa Fe: National Park Service, 1991.

Browne, Belmore. *Analysis by Belmore Browne for the Committee on Conservation of the Report of Dr. Adolph Murie's "The Wolves of Mt. McKinley."* New York: Camp Fire Club of America, 1946.

Brownell, Robert L., P.B. Best, and John H. Prescott, eds. *Right Whales: Past and Present Status: Proceedings of the Workshop on the Status of Right Whales, New England Aquarium, Boston MA, 15–23 June 1983*. Cambridge, UK: International Whaling Commission, 1986.

Brueggeman, J.J., T. Newby, and R.A. Grotefendt. "Catch Records of the Twenty North Pacific Right Whales From Two Alaska Whaling Stations, 1917–39." *Arctic* 39, 1 (March 1986): 43–46.

Buchanan, Robert K. "The History, Growth, Use and Future Development of the Timber Industry in Southeast Alaska." Master's thesis, University of Washington, 1969.

Buckley, John L. *Wildlife in the Economy of Alaska*. Biological Papers of the University of Alaska No. 1. Fairbanks, February 1955.

Burch, Ernest S., Jr. *The Traditional Eskimo Hunters of Point Hope, Alaska: 1800–1875*. Barrow: North Slope Borough, 1983.

Burch, Lucius E., Jr. "Eagle-Shooting in Alaska." *American Rifleman* 83 (February 1935): 14–15.

Burg, Amos. "Alaska's Bald Eagles." *Alaska Fish and Game Trails* (January-February 1971): 10–12.

Burns, John J., ed. *Marine Mammals Species Accounts*. Juneau: Alaska Dept. of Fish and Game, December 1984.

———. *The Walrus in Alaska: Its Ecology and Management*. Juneau: Alaska Dept. of Fish and Game, 1965.

Burris, Oliver E., and Donald E. McKnight. *Game Transplants in Alaska*. Juneau: Alaska Dept. of Fish and Game, December 1973.

Burroughs, Polly. *George Bird Grinnell: Alaska 1899: Essays From the Harriman Expedition*. Seattle: University of Washington Press, 1995.

Busch, Briton Cooper. *The War Against the Seals: A History of the North American Seal Fishery*. Kingston and Montreal: McGill and Queens Universities, 1985.

Buske, Frank E. "John Muir and the Alaska Gold Rush." In Lawrence Murphy and Dan Collins, eds., *The World of John Muir*, 37–49. Stockton: University of the Pacific Press, 1981.

———. "John Muir: Go to Alaska. Go and See." *Alaska Journal* 9 (Summer 1979): 32–37.

———. "The Wilderness, the Frontier, and the Literature of Alaska to 1914: John Muir, Jack London, and Rex Beach." PhD diss., University of California–Davis, 1976.

Cahalane, Victor H. *A Biological Survey of Katmai National Monument*. Smithsonian Misc. Coll. Vol. 138, No. 5. Washington, DC, 1959.

———. "Katmai—America's Largest Nature Reserve." *Oryx* 3 (May 1956): 172–179.

———. "Katmai—A Wilderness to Be Guarded." *National Parks Magazine* 32, 132 (January-March 1958): 10–15.

Calkins, Donald G. "The Steller Sea Lion (*Eumetopias jubatus*)." In John J. Burns, ed., *Marine Mammals Species Accounts*, 1–6. Juneau: Alaska Dept. of Fish and Game, December 1984.

Calkins, Donald G., and Karl B. Schneider. "The Sea Otter." In John J. Burns, ed., *Marine Mammals Species Accounts*, 1–7. Wildlife Technical Bulletin No. 7. Alaska Dept. of Fish and Game, Juneau, December 1984.

Cameron, Jenks. *The Bureau of Biological Survey: Its History, Activities and Organization*. Baltimore: Johns Hopkins University Press, 1929.

Cameron, John, Robert Marshall, and Paul Gordon. "Recreational Resources and Facilities." In *Regional Planning Part IV: Alaska and Its Resources*, 127–144. Washington, DC: National Resources Committee, 1938.

Campbell, Charles S. "The Anglo-American Crisis in the Bering Sea, 1890–91." *Journal of American History* 48 (December 1961): 393–414.

Campbell, John M. "Aboriginal Human Overkill of Game Populations: Examples From Interior Alaska." In Robert C. Dunnell and Edwin S. Hall, eds., *Archaeological Essays in Honor of Irving B. Rouse*, 177–208. New York: Morton, 1978.

———. "An Anthropologist Looks at the Arctic National Wildlife Range." In *Science in Alaska, 1961: Proceedings of Twelfth Alaskan Science Conf.*, 53–58. College: Alaska Div., AAAS, 1962.

Cane, Claude. "The Salmon Fishery at the End of the Century." In Morgan Sherwood, ed., *The Cook Inlet Collection*, 105–109. Anchorage: Alaska Northwest, 1974.

———. *Summer and Fall in Western Alaska: The Record of a Trip to Cook's Inlet After Big Game.* London: Horace Cox, 1903.

Capps, Stephen R. "A Game Country Without Rival in America: The Proposed Mount McKinley National Park." *National Geographic* 31 (January 1917): 69–84.

———. "Mount McKinley: A New National Park." *Travel* 29 (May 1917): 7–12.

Carmony, Neil B., and David E. Brown, eds. *The Wilderness of the Southwest: Charles Sheldon's Quest for Desert Bighorn Sheep and Adventures With the Havasupai and Seri Indians.* Salt Lake City: University of Utah Press, 1993.

Carnahan, John. "Fox Farming in the Aleutians." In David L. Spencer, Claus-M. Naske, and John Carnahan, eds., *National Wildlife Refuges of Alaska: A Historical Perspective, Part I*, 77–96. Anchorage: Arctic Environmental and Data Center, 1979.

Carroll, Geoffrey. "Utilization of the Bowhead Whale." In *International Whaling Commission's Deletion of Native Exemption for the Subsistence Harvest of Bowhead Whales: Final Environmental Impact Statement, Vol. 2*, Appendix B, 1–7. U.S. Dept. of Commerce, National Marine Fisheries Service. Washington, DC, 1977.

Cart, Theodore Whaley. " 'New Deal' for Wildlife: A Perspective on Federal Conservation Policy, 1933–40." *Pacific Northwest Quarterly* 63, 3 (July 1972): 113–120.

———. "The Struggle for Wildlife Protection in the United States, 1870–1900: Attitudes and Events Leading to the Lacey Act." PhD diss., University of North Carolina, 1971.

Catton, Theodore. *Inhabited Wilderness: Indians, Eskimos, and National Parks in Alaska.* Albuquerque: University of New Mexico Press, 1997.

———. *Land Reborn: A History of Administration and Land Use in Glacier Bay National Park and Preserve.* Anchorage: National Park Service, 1995.

Chance, Norman A. *The Eskimo of North Alaska.* New York: Holt, Rinehart and Winston, 1966.

Chase, Will H. *Alaska's Mammoth Brown Bears.* Kansas City: Burton, 1947.

Chatelain, Edward F. "Bear-Moose Relationships on the Kenai Peninsula." In *Trans. of the Fifteenth North American Wildlife Conf., 1950*, 224–234. Washington, DC: Wildlife Management Institute, 1950.

Chevigny, Hector. *Lord of Alaska.* New York: Viking, 1944.

Clark, A. Howard. "The Pacific Walrus Fishery." In George Brown Goode, ed., *The Fisheries and Fishery Industries of the United States, Sect. 5, Vol. 2, Part 17,* 313–318. Washington, DC: GPO, 1887.

———. "The Whale Fishery." In George Brown Goode, ed., *The Fisheries and Fishery Industries of the United States, Sect. 5, Vol. 2, Part 15,* 3–318. Washington, DC: GPO, 1887.

Clepper, Henry, ed. *Leaders in American Conservation*. New York: Ronald, 1971.

Coady, John W. "History of Moose in Northern Alaska and Adjacent Regions." *Canadian Field-Naturalist* 94, 1 (1980): 61–68.

Coates, Kenneth, ed. *The Alaska Highway: Papers of the 40th Anniversary Symposium.* Vancouver: University of British Columbia Press, 1985.

Cohen, Michael P. *The History of the Sierra Club, 1892–1970.* San Francisco: Sierra Club, 1970.

———. *The Pathless Way: John Muir and the American Wilderness.* Madison: University of Wisconsin Press, 1984.

Collins, George L. *The Art and Politics of Park Planning and Preservation, 1920–1979.* Berkeley: Regional Oral History Office, Bancroft Library, 1980.

Collins, George L., and Lowell Sumner. "Northeast Arctic: The Last Great Wilderness." *Sierra Club Bulletin* 38 (October 1953): 13–26.

Collins, Henry B., Jr., Austin H. Clark, and Egbert H. Walker. *The Aleutian Islands: Their People and Natural History.* Washington, DC: Smithsonian Institution, 1945.

Committee for the Protection of the North Pacific Fisheries. *Japan's High Seas Salmon Fishery: What Are the Plain Facts?* Seattle, January 1958.

Cook, Frederick A. *To the Top of the Continent.* New York: Doubleday, Page, 1908.

Cook, John A. *Pursuing the Whale.* Cambridge: Riverside, 1926.

Cooley, Richard A. *Politics and Conservation: The Decline of the Alaska Salmon.* New York: Harper & Row, 1963.

Cooper, William S. "A Contribution to the History of the Glacier Bay National Monument." Boulder, Colorado. Typescript, March 1956. Alaska State Library Archives, Juneau.

———. Letter to U.S. Rep. John F. Seiberling, July 23, 1976. William S. Cooper coll., University of Minnesota Archives, Minneapolis.

———. "The Recent Ecological History of Glacier Bay, Alaska: 1: The Interglacial Forests of Glacier Bay." *Ecology* 4:2 (April 1923): 93–128.

———. "The Recent Ecological History of Glacier Bay, Alaska: 3: Permanent Quadrats at Glacier Bay: An Initial Report Upon a Long-Term Study." *Ecology* 4:4 (October 1923): 355–365.

———. "Remarks at Dedication of Lodge at Bartlett Cove, Glacier Bay, Alaska." Typescript, June 4, 1966. William S. Cooper coll., University of Minnesota Archives, Minneapolis.

Courtright, Alan M. *Alaska Big Game Harvest Data.* Juneau: Alaska Dept. of Fish and Game, November 1964.

———. *Game Harvests in Alaska.* Juneau: Alaska Dept. of Fish and Game, June 1968.

Crisler, Lois. *Arctic Wild.* New York: Harper & Bros., 1956.

Croll, D.A., J.L. Mason, J.A. Estes, E.M. Danner, and G.V. Byrd. "Introduced Predators Transform Subarctic Islands From Grassland to Tundra." *Science* 307 (March 25, 2005): 1959–1961.

Crutchfield, James A., and Giulio Pontecorvo. *The Pacific Salmon Fisheries: A Study of Irrational Conservation.* Baltimore: Johns Hopkins for Resources for the Future, 1969.

Curry, Peggy Simpson. "Portrait of a Naturalist." *Living Wilderness* 28 (November-December 1963): 15–21.

Dall, William H. *Alaska and Its Resources.* Boston: Lee and Shepard, 1870.

———. "On the Preservation of the Marine Mammals of the Northwest Coast." Smithsonian Institution, *Annual Report, 1901,* 683–688.

Dannenbaum, Jed. "John Muir in Alaska." *Alaska Journal* 2 (Autumn 1972): 14–20.

Dassow, John A. "Utilization of Sea Lions in Alaska." *Commercial Fisheries Review* 18 (January 1955): 5–9.

Davis, Neil. *Energy/Alaska.* Fairbanks: University of Alaska Press, 1984.

Dayvidov, G.I. *Two Voyages to Russian America, 1802–1807.* Ed. Richard A. Pierce. Kingston: Limestone, 1977.

DeArmond, Robert. "Page and Line Comments on 'History of Alaskan Fisheries.'" In Sheila T. Evans, *An Historical View of Selected Natural Resources,* 1–3. Anchorage: Alaska Historical Commission and Alaska Dept. of Education, 1981.

———. "Sailing for Furs." *Alaska Life* 9 (March 1946): 15–17.

De Laguna, Frederica. *Under Mount Saint Elias: The History and Culture of the Yakutat Tlingit, Parts 1 and 2* of 3. Washington, DC: Smithsonian Institution, 1972.

De Sormo, Maitland. *John Bird Burnham—Klondiker, Adirondacker and Eminent Conservationist.* Saranac Lake: Adirondack Yesteryear, 1978.

Dice, Lee R. "Interior Alaska in 1911 and 1912: Observations of a Naturalist." Lee Raymond Dice coll., Box 1, Fol. 4. University of Alaska Fairbanks, Alaska and Polar Regions Archives.

Dictionary of American Biography. New York: Scribner's, 1934, 1958.

Dorsey, Janine Davis. "The Coal Bunkers and the Fairbanks Community: A Social History." Master's thesis, University of Alaska–Fairbanks, 1998.

Dorsey, Kurkpatrick. *The Dawn of Conservation Diplomacy: U.S.-Canadian Wildlife Protection Treaties in the Progressive Era.* Seattle: University of Washington Press, 1998.

Drury, Herbert R. "Natural History, Conservation and Ecology of the Musk Ox." Master's thesis, University of Michigan, 1955.

Du Four, Clarence John. "The Russian Withdrawal From California." In E.O. Essig, Adele Ogden, and John Du Four, *Fort Ross: California Outpost of Russian Alaska,* 60–98. Ed. Richard A. Pierce. Kingston: Limestone, 1991.

Dufresne, Frank. *Alaska's Animals and Fishes.* New York: Barnes, 1946.

———. *My Way Was North: An Alaskan Biography.* New York: Holt, Rinehart and Winston, 1966.

———. *No Room For Bears.* New York: Holt, Rinehart and Winston, 1965.

———. *Quarterly Report.* Juneau: Alaska Game Commission, 1937, 1941.

———. "Whose Wilderness?" *Field and Stream* (January 1961): 23–26.

Dufresne, Jim. *Glacier Bay National Park: A Backcountry Guide to the Glaciers and Beyond.* Seattle: Mountaineers, 1987.

Dugan, C. Budd. "Poacher Patrol." *Flying* (May 1946): 70–71.

Dunlap, Thomas R. *Saving America's Wildlife.* Princeton: Princeton University Press, 1988.

———. "Sport Hunting and Conservation, 1880–1920." *Environmental Review* 12:1 (Spring 1988): 51–68.

———. "Values for Varmints: Predator Control and Environmental Ideas, 1920–1939." *Pacific Historical Review* 53 (May 1984): 141–161.

Dunnell, Robert C., and Edwin S. Hall Jr., eds. *Archaeological Essays in Honor of Irving B. Rouse.* New York: Mouton, 1978.

Durham, Floyd E. "A Historical Perspective on Eskimo Whaling and the Bowhead Controversy." *Orca* 1 (March 1979): 5–6.

East, Ben. "Threat to Alaska Bears." *Outdoor Life* 120 (July 1957): 17.

———. "Uncle Sam's Prize Fur Factory Closes Down." *Natural History* 51 (April 1943): 188–195.

Eddy, J.W. *Hunting on the Kenai Peninsula.* Seattle: Lowman and Hanford, 1924.

Eggers, Doug, and Michael R. Dean. *Alaska Commercial Salmon Catches, 1878–1986.* Alaska Dept. of Fish and Game, Div. of Commercial Fisheries. Regional Information Report No. 5J87-01. Juneau, August 1987.

Eide, Sterling. "The Nature of Brown Bear Predation on Cattle, Kodiak Island, Alaska." Presented at 45th Annual Conf. of Western Assn. of State Game and Fish Commissioners, Anchorage, July 1965.

Elkins, W.A., and Urban C. Nelson. "Wildlife Introductions and Transplants in Alaska." Presented at Fifth Alaska Science Conf., Anchorage, September 7–10, 1954.

Elliott, Henry W. *Our Arctic Province: Alaska and the Seal Islands.* New York: Scribner's, 1887.

———. "Report on the Condition of the Fur-Seal Rookeries of the Pribilof Islands, Alaska." In David Starr Jordan and George A. Clark, eds., *Seal and Salmon Fisheries and General Resources of Alaska, Vol. 3,* 315–538. Washington, DC: GPO, 1898.

———. "The Sea-Otter Fishery." In George Brown Goode, ed., *The Fisheries and Fishery Industries of the United States, Sect. 5, Vol. 2, Part 18,* 483–491. Washington, DC: GPO, 1887.

———. *The Seal-Islands of Alaska.* Washington, DC: GPO, 1881.

———. "Ten Years' Acquaintance With Alaska." *Harper's New Monthly Magazine* 55 (November 1877): 801–816.

Emanuel, Richard P. "Robert 'Sea Otter' Jones." *Alaska Geographic* 22, 2 (1995): 36–51.

Epps, Alan C., and Edward D. Kerr. "Agricultural Lands." In Helen L. McNicholas, ed., *Alaska's Agriculture and Forestry.* Fairbanks: University of Alaska Cooperative Extension Service, 1983.

Essig, E.O., Adele Ogden, and John Du Four. *Fort Ross: California Outpost of Russian Alaska, 1812–1841.* Ed. Richard A. Pierce. Kingston: Limestone, 1991.

Evans, Robley. *George Bird Grinnell.* Boise, ID: Boise State University Western Writers Series No. 122, 1996.

Evans, Sheila T. *An Historical View of Selected Alaskan Natural Resources.* Anchorage: Alaska Historical Commission and Alaska Dept. of Education, 1981.

Evermann, Barton Warren. *Alaska Fisheries and Fur Industries in 1913.* U.S. Dept. of Labor and Commerce, Bureau of Fisheries Doc. No. 797. Washington, DC: GPO, 1914.

Exxon Valdez Oil Spill Trustees. Exxon Valdez *Oil Spill Restoration, Vol. I: Restoration Framework.* Anchorage, 1992.

Eyerdam, Walter J. "Sea Otters in the Aleutian Islands." *Journal of Mammalogy* 14, 1 (1933): 70–71.

Fay, Francis H. *Ecology and Biology of the Pacific Walrus,* Odobenus rosmarus divergens. Illiger, WA: U.S. Fish and Wildlife Service, 1962.

———. *Pacific Walrus Investigations on St. Lawrence Island, Alaska.* Anchorage: Arctic Health Research Center, November 1, 1958.

Fedorova, Svetlana G. *The Russian Population in Alaska and California, Late 18th Century–1867.* Ed. and transl. Richard A. Pierce and Alton S. Donnelly. Kingston: Limestone, 1973.

Fienup-Riordan, Ann. *Eskimo Essays: Yup'ik Lives and How We See Them.* New Brunswick: Rutgers University Press, 1990.

Findlay, John D. "History and Status of the Arctic National Wildlife Range." *University of British Columbia Law Review* 6 (June 1971): 15–20.

Fisher, Albert Kendrick. "In Memorium: George Bird Grinnell." *Auk* 56 (January 1939): 1–12.

Fisher, Raymond H. *Bering's Voyages: Whither and Why.* Seattle: University of Washington Press, 1977.

———. "Finding America." In Stephen W. Haycox and Mary Childers Mangusso, eds., *An Alaska Anthology,* 3–20. Seattle: University of Washington Press, 1996.

Fitzgerald, Roger. "Days of the Seafaring Canners." *The Journal* (February 1982): 10–12.

Fitzhugh, William, and Ruth O. Seilig. "The Smithsonian's Alaska Connection: Nineteenth Century Explorers and Anthropologists." *Alaska Journal* 11 (Winter 1981): 193–208.

Fleck, Richard. *Henry Thoreau and John Muir Among the Indians.* Hamden, CT: Archon, 1985.

Ford, Corey, and Frank Dufresne. "Lost Paradise." *Field and Stream* (September 1956): 63–65.

Ford, Corey, and Alastair MacBain. "Hot Fur." *Collier's* 104 (December 2, 1939): 22.

Fowler, Howard G. "Wolf Hunt." *Flying* 54 (June 1954): 18.

Fox, Stephen. *John Muir and His Legacy: The American Conservation Movement.* Boston: Little, Brown, 1981.

Francis, Daniel J. *A History of World Whaling.* New York: Viking, 1990.

Franzmann, Albert W. *Review of Alaskan Translocations.* Juneau: Alaska Dept. of Fish and Game, 1986.

Friis, Herman R., ed. *The Pacific Basin: A History of Its Geographical Exploration.* New York: American Geographical Society Special Pub. No. 38, 1967.

Gabrielson, Ira N. "Crisis for Alaskan Wildlife." *Audubon* (November-December 1951): 348–351.

———. "Report on 1946 Observation in Alaska." Typescript, 1946. Denver Public Library Archives, CONS 37, Box 3.

———. *Wildlife Conservation,* 2nd ed. New York: Macmillan, 1959.

Gabrielson, Ira N., and Frederick Lincoln. *Birds of Alaska.* Harrisburg, PA: Telegraph, 1959.

Gay, James Thomas. "Henry W. Elliott: Crusading Conservationist." *Alaska Journal* 3 (Autumn 1973): 211–216.

Geiger, Glenn A. "The Saga of the Alaskan Fur Seals." *The Explorer* (Summer 1975): 4–12.

Gerlach, S. Craig, and Maribeth S. Murray, eds. *People and Wildlife in North America: Essays in Honor of R. Dale Guthrie.* Oxford: British Archaeological Reports International Series 944, 2001.

Gibson, James R. *Imperial Russia in Frontier America: The Changing Geography of Supply of Russian America, 1784–1867.* New York: Oxford University Press, 1976.

———. *Otter Skins, Boston Ships, and China Goods: The Maritime Fur Trade of the Northwest Coast, 1785–1841.* Seattle: University of Washington Press, 1992.

———. "Russian Dependence Upon the Natives of Alaska." In S. Frederick Starr, ed., *Russia's American Colony,* 77–104. Durham: Duke University Press, 1987.

Gideon, Hieromonk. *The Around the World Voyage of Hieromonk Gideon, 1803–1808.* Transl. Lydia T. Black; ed. Richard A. Pierce. Kingston: Limestone, 1989.

Gilbert, Benjamin Franklin. "The Confederate Raider Shenandoah." In Morgan Sherwood, ed., *Alaska and Its History,* 188–207. Seattle: University of Washington Press, 1967.

Gill, Harold D. "Six Months in a Salmon Ship." *The Rudder* 29 (May 1913): 309–314.

Glaser, Frank. "My Lady Judas." *Outdoor Life* 113 (May 1954): 44–45.

Glavis, L.R. "The Whitewashing of Ballinger." *Collier's* 44 (November 13, 1909): 15–17.

Glover, James M. "Romance, Recreation, and Wilderness: Influences on the Life and Work of Bob Marshall." *Environmental History Review* 14, 4 (Winter 1990): 22–39.

———. "Sweet Days of a Naturalist: Olaus Murie in Alaska, 1920–26." *Forest and Conservation History* 36 (July 1992): 132–140.

———. *A Wilderness Original: The Life of Bob Marshall.* Seattle: Mountaineers, 1986.

Glover, James M., and Regina Glover. "The Natural Magic of Olaus Murie." *Sierra* 72 (September-October 1987): 69–83.

Goetzmann, William H., and Kay Sloan. *Looking Far North: The Harriman Expedition to Alaska, 1899.* New York: Viking, 1982.

Goldenberg, L.A. *Gvozdev: The Russian Discovery of Alaska in 1732.* Ed. James L. Smith. Anchorage: White Stone, 1990.

Golder, F.A. *Bering's Voyages, Vol. II: Steller's Journal of the Sea Voyage From Kamchatka to America and Return on the Second Expedition 1741–2.* New York: National Geographic Society, 1925.

Goldman, Edward A. "Edward William Nelson, Naturalist." *Auk* 52 (April 1935): 135–148.

Golovin, P.N. *The End of Russian America: Captain P.N. Golovin's Last Report, 1862.* Transl. Basil Dmytryshin and E.A.P. Crownhart-Vaughn. Portland: Oregon Historical Society, 1979.

Goode, George Brown. *The Fisheries and Fishery Industries of the United States, Sect. 5: History and Methods of the Fisheries, Vol. 2.* Washington, DC: GPO, 1887.

Graham, Frank, Jr. *Man's Dominion: The Story of Conservation in America.* New York: M. Evans, 1981.

———. "Mardy Murie and Her Summer of Dreams." *Audubon* (May 1980): 106–127.

Grant, Madison. "Condition of Wild Life in Alaska." In *Twelfth Annual Report of the New York Zoological Society, 1907*, New York. 521–529.

———. "The Establishment of Mt. McKinley National Park." In George Bird Grinnell and Charles Sheldon, eds., *Hunting and Conservation*, 438–445. New Haven: Yale University Press, 1925. Rept. by Arno, 1971.

Greeley, A.W. *Handbook of Alaska: Its Resources, Products, and Attractions in 1924.* New York: Scribner's, 1925.

Green, Dorr D. "Predator Control Problems in Alaska." Presented at Alaska Science Conf., Anchorage, November 9–11, 1950.

Gregory, Homer F., and Kathleen Barnes. *North Pacific Fisheries: With Special Reference to Alaska Salmon.* American Council, Institute of Pacific Relations, Studies of the Pacific No. 3. San Francisco, 1939.

Griggs, Robert F. "The Beginnings of Revegetation in Katmai Valley." In Robert F. Griggs et al., *Scientific Results of the Katmai Expeditions of the National Geographic Society I-X*, 318–342. Columbus: Ohio State University Bulletin 15 (February 1920).

———. "The Colonization of Katmai Ash, a New and Inorganic 'Soil.'" *American Journal of Botany* 20 (February 1933): 92–113.

———. "The Eruption of Katmai." *Nature* 101 (August 22, 1918): 497–499.

———. "The Recovery of Vegetation at Kodiak." In Robert F. Griggs et al., *Scientific Results of the Katmai Expeditions of the National Geographic Society I-X*, 1–57. Ohio State University Bulletin 15 (February 1920).

———. *The Valley of Ten Thousand Smokes.* Washington, DC: National Geographic Society, 1922.

———. *We Two Together.* Pacific Grove, CA: Boxwood, 1961.

Griggs, Robert F., J.W. Shipley, Jasper D. Sayre, Paul R. Hagelbarger, and James S. Hine. "The Recovery of Vegetation at Kodiak." In Robert F. Griggs et al., *Scientific Results of the Katmai Expeditions of the National Geographic Society I-X*, 1–57. Ohio State University Bulletin 15 (February 1920).

———. *Scientific Results of the Katmai Expeditions of the National Geographic Society, I-X.* Columbus: Ohio State Bulletin 15 (February 1920).

Grinnell, George Bird. "American Game Protection: A Sketch." In George Bird Grinnell and Charles Sheldon, eds., *Hunting and Conservation*, 201–257. New Haven: Yale University Press, 1925. New York: Rept. by Ayer, 1970.

———. *Brief History of the Boone and Crockett Club.* New York: Field and Stream, 1911.

———. "The Salmon Industry." In Edward Henry Harriman and C. Hart Merriam, eds., *Alaska, Vol 2: Harriman Alaska Expedition: History, Geography, Resources*, 337–355. New York: Doubleday, 1901.

Grinnell, George Bird, and Charles Sheldon, eds. *Hunting and Conservation*. New Haven: Yale University Press, 1925. New York: Rept. by Ayer, 1970.

Gruening, Ernest. *The State of Alaska*. New York: Random House, 1954.

Grummett, Karleen Alstead, ed. *Territorial Sportsmen, Inc, 1945–88: A Chronological History.* Juneau: n.p., 1988.

Hadwen, Seymour, and Lawrence J. Palmer. *Reindeer in Alaska*. USDA Bull. No. 1089. Washington, DC: GPO, 1922.

Halle, Louis J., Jr. "Gabrielson." *Audubon* (May-June 1946): 140–145.

Hames, Raymond. "Wildlife Conservation in Tribal Societies." In Margery L. Oldfield and Janis B. Alcorn, eds., *Biodiversity: Conservation, Culture, and Ecodevelopment*, 172–199. Boulder: Westview, 1991.

Hamlin, Charles S. "Condition of Seal Life on the Rookeries of the Pribilof Islands, 1893–1895." In David Starr Jordan and George A. Clark, eds., *Seal and Salmon Fisheries and General Resources of Alaska, Vol. 1*, 445–501. Washington, DC: GPO, 1898.

Hammond, Jay S. "Strafing Arctic Killers." *Field and Stream* (February 1955): 37–39.

Hanley, Peter T., James E. Hemming, and John W. Morsell. *Natural Resource Protection and Petroleum Development in Alaska*. Anchorage: U.S. Fish and Wildlife Service, Office of Biological Services, 1981.

Harriman, Edward Henry, and C. Hart Merriam, eds. *Alaska, Vol. 2: Harriman Alaska Expedition: History, Geography, Resources*. New York: Doubleday, 1901.

Harrington, Fred H., and Paul C. Paquet, eds. *Wolves of the World*. Park River, NJ: Noyes, 1982.

Harris, Bruce. "The Survival of Respect: Economic Power and the Persistence of Community." In Theodore Lane, ed., *Developing America's Northern Frontier*, 161–180. Lanham, MD: University Press of America, 1987.

Hawes, Charles Boardman. *Whaling*. New York: Doubleday, Page, 1924.

Hawkins, A.S., ed. *Flyways: Pioneering Waterfowl Management in North America*. Washington, DC: U.S. Fish and Wildlife Service, 1984.

Haycox, Stephen W. *Alaska: An American Colony*. Seattle: University of Washington Press, 2002.

———. *Frigid Embrace: Politics, Economics and Environment in Alaska*. Corvallis: Oregon State University Press, 2002.

Haycox, Stephen W., and Mary Childers Mangusso, eds. *An Alaska Anthology*. Seattle: University of Washington Press, 1996.

Hays, Samuel P. *Conservation and the Gospel of Efficiency: The Progressive Conservation Movement, 1890–1920*. Cambridge: Harvard University Press, 1959.

Healy, Michael A. *Report of the Cruise of the Revenue Marine Steamer* Corwin *in the Arctic Ocean in the Year 1884*. Washington, DC: GPO, 1889.

Hegarty, Reginald B. *Returns of Whaling Vessels Sailing From American Ports, 1876–1928*. New Bedford: Old Dartmouth Historical Society and Whaling Museum, 1959.

Heintzleman, B.F. Letter to Editor. *Journal of Forestry* 37 (June 1939): 510–511.
———. "Managing the Brown Bear." *American Forests* 38 (June 1932): 329–332.
Heller, Herbert. *Sourdough Sagas*. Cleveland: World, 1967.
Hinckley, Ted C. "Alaska and the Emergence of America's Conservation Consciousness." In *The Prairie Scout 2*, 79–111. Abilene: Kansas Corral of the Westerners, 1974.
———. *The Americanization of Alaska, 1867–1897*. Palo Alto: Pacific Books, 1972.
———. "The Inside Passage: A Popular Guided Tour." *Pacific Northwest Quarterly* 56 (January 1965): 67–74.
Hoffman, Russell R. *Refuge Narrative Report: Kodiak Wildlife Refuge, January to April 1952*. Kodiak: Fish and Wildlife Service, 1952.
———. *Refuge Narrative Report: Kodiak Wildlife Refuge, May to August 1952*. Kodiak: Fish and Wildlife Service, 1952.
Holzworth, John M. *The Wild Grizzlies of Alaska*. New York: Putnam's, 1930.
Hone, Elisabeth. *The Present Status of the Muskox in Arctic North America and Greenland*. Cambridge: American Committee for International Wildlife Protection, 1934.
Hooper, C.L. *A Report on the Sea-Otter Banks of Alaska*. Washington, DC: GPO, 1897.
Hoover, A. Anne. "Harbor Seal." In Jack W. Lentfer, ed., *Selected Marine Mammals of Alaska*, 125–157. Washington, DC: Marine Mammal Commission, 1988.
Hornaday, William T. *The Extermination of the American Bison, With a Sketch of Its Discovery and Life History*. Washington, DC: U.S. National Museum, 1887. Rept. by Smithsonian, 2002.
———. "The Musk Ox in Alaska." *New York Zoological Society Bulletin* 45 (May 1911): 754–755.
———. "A National Game Preserve in Alaska." *Recreation Magazine* 16 (May 1902): 188–189.
———. *Our Vanishing Wild Life: Its Extermination and Preservation*. New York: Zoological Society, 1913.
———. *Thirty Years War for Wildlife*. New York: Scribner's, 1931.
———. *Wild Life Conservation in Theory and Practice*. New Haven: Yale University Press, 1914.
Hubbard, Bernard R. *Cradle of the Storms*. New York: Dodd, Mead, 1935.
Hunt, William R. *Arctic Passage*. New York: Scribner's, 1975.
———. *History of the Marine Hatcheries of Alaska*. Alaska Sea Grant Report 76-10. Fairbanks: University of Alaska Press, 1976.
Huntington, Henry P. *Wildlife Management and Subsistence Hunting in Alaska*. Seattle: University of Washington Press, 1992.
Hussey, John A. *Embattled Katmai: A History of the Katmai National Monument*. National Park Service, Office of History and Historical Architecture, Western Science Center. San Francisco, August 1971.
Huston, John Robert. "A Geographic Analysis of the Fur Farming Industry in Alaska." Master's thesis, University of California, 1963.
Imler, Ralph H., and Hosea R. Sarber. *Harbor Seals and Sea Lions in Alaska*. U.S. Dept. of the Interior, Fish and Wildlife Service. Washington, DC: Special Scientific Report No. 28, 1947.

Ise, John. *Our National Park Policy: A Critical History*. Baltimore: Johns Hopkins for Resources for the Future, 1961.

———. *The United States Forest Policy*. New Haven: Yale University Press, 1920.

Jackson, Donald Dale. "The Floor of Creation." *Wilderness* (Fall 1986): 12–20.

Jackson, Sheldon. *Introduction of Reindeer Into Alaska: Preliminary Report of the General Agent of Education for Alaska to the Commissioner of Education, 1890*. Washington, DC: GPO, 1891.

———. *Report on Introduction of Domestic Reindeer Into Alaska, 1893*. U.S. Senate, 53 Cong., 1 Sess. Misc. Doc. No. 22. Washington, DC: GPO, 1893.

———. *Report on Introduction of Domestic Reindeer Into Alaska, 1894*. U.S. Senate, 53 Cong., 2 Sess. Ex. Doc. No. 92. Washington, DC: GPO, 1894.

———. *Report on Introduction of Domestic Reindeer Into Alaska, 1895*. U.S. Senate, 54 Cong., 1 Sess. Doc. No. 111. Washington, DC: GPO, 1895.

James, James A. *The First Scientific Exploration of Russian America and the Purchase of Alaska*. Chicago: Northwestern University Press, 1942.

Johnson, Roy D. "Upper Tanana Athapaskan Fire Ecology." In Alaska Anthropological Assn., *Eighth Annual Conference, March 20–21, 1981, Abstracts*, 15. Anchorage, 1981.

Jones, Dorothy Knee. *A Century of Servitude: Pribilof Aleuts Under U.S. Rule*. Washington, DC: University Press of America, 1980.

Jones, E. Lester. *Report of Alaska Investigations in 1914*. U.S. Dept. of Commerce, Bureau of Fisheries. Washington, DC: GPO, 1915.

Jones, Robert D., Jr., and G. Vernon Byrd. "Interrelations Between Seabirds and Introduced Animals." In James C. Bartonek, ed., *Conservation of Marine Birds of America*, 221–226. U.S. Fish and Wildlife Service. Wildlife Research Report No. 11. Washington, DC, 1979.

Jordan, David Starr. *Matka and Kotik: A Tale of the Mist-Islands*. San Francisco: Whitaker and Ray, 1897.

Jordan, David Starr, and George A. Clark. "Appendix." In David Starr Jordan and George A. Clark, eds., *Seal and Salmon Fisheries and General Resources of Alaska, Vol. 3*, 689–714. U.S. Dept. of the Treasury. Washington, DC: GPO, 1898.

Jordan, David Starr, and George A. Clark, eds. *Seal and Salmon Fisheries and General Resources of Alaska, Vols. 1–4*. U.S. Dept. of the Treasury. Washington, DC: GPO, 1898.

Kaiser, Jocelyn. "Sea Otter Declines Blamed on Hungry Killers." *Science* 282 (October 16, 1998): 390–391.

Kansas Corral of the Westerners. *The Prairie Scout 2*. Abilene, KS, 1974.

Kauffmann, John M. *Alaska's Brooks Range: The Ultimate Mountains*. Seattle: Mountaineers, 1992.

———. *Glacier Bay National Monument: A History of Its Boundaries*. Washington, DC: National Park Service, 1954.

———. *Katmai National Monument, Alaska: A History of Its Establishment and Revision of Its Boundaries*. Washington, DC: National Park Service, 1954.

Kavanaugh, Ross C. "Removal of Fish Ladder at Brooks River Falls, Katmai National Park, Alaska." Typescript, 1986. Katmai Administrative Records N1619, Waterlife: Brooks Falls Fish Ladder. Lake Clark Katmai Studies Center, Anchorage.

Kaye, Roger. *Last Great Wilderness: The Campaign to Establish the Arctic National Wildlife Refuge*. Fairbanks: University of Alaska Press, 2006.

Kennedy, Michael S. "Belmore Browne and Alaska." *Alaska Journal* 3 (Spring 1973): 96–104.

Kenyon, Karl W. "Birds of Amchitka Island, Alaska." *Auk* 78 (July 1961): 305–326.

———. "History of the Steller Sea Lion at the Pribilof Islands, Alaska." *Journal of Mammalogy* 43, 1 (February 1962): 68–75.

———. *The Sea Otter in the North Pacific Ocean: North American Fauna No. 68*. Washington, DC: Bureau of Sport Fisheries and Wildlife, 1969.

Kenyon, Karl W., Victor B. Scheffer, and Douglas G. Chapman. *A Population Study of the Alaska Fur-Seal Herd.* Special Scientific Report—Wildlife No. 12. U.S. Fish and Wildlife Service. Washington, DC, June 1954.

Kenyon, Karl W., and David L. Spencer. *Sea Otter Population and Transplant Studies in Alaska, 1959*. U.S. Fish and Wildlife Service. Special Scientific Report—Wildlife No. 48. Washington, DC, March 1960.

Kilian, Bernhard. *The Voyage of the Schooner Polar Bear: Whaling and Trading in the North Pacific and Alaska, 1913–1914*. Ed. John Bockstoce. New Bedford: Old Dartmouth Historical Society and Alaska Historical Commission, 1983.

Kimes, William F., and Maymie B. Kimes. *John Muir: A Reading Bibliography*. Fresno: Panorama West, 1986.

King, James G. "My Fifty Years Flying With Alaska's Birds." Juneau. Typescript, 2003.

———. "Pre-Statehood Alaska." In A.S. Hawkins, ed., *Flyways: Pioneering Waterfowl Management in North America*, 170–175. Washington, DC: U.S. Fish and Wildlife Service, 1984.

———. "Resume: James G. King." Typescript, 1989.

King, Joe. "When Disaster Overtook the Whaling Fleet." *Alaska-Yukon Magazine* 7 (December 1908): 190–202.

Kinney, John M. "Copper and the Settlement of South-Central Alaska." *Journal of the West* 10 (April 1971): 307–318.

Klein, David R. *The Black-Tailed Deer in Alaska: An Outline of Management Methods.* Petersburg, AK: U.S. Fish and Wildlife Service, 1957.

———. "Caribou: Alaska's Wilderness Nomads." In Harmon Kallman, ed., *Restoring America's Wildlife, 1937–87*, 190–207. Washington, DC: U.S. Fish and Wildlife Service, 1987.

———. "A Reconnaissance Study of the Mountain Goat in Alaska." Master's thesis, University of Alaska, April 1953.

———. *St. Matthew Island Reindeer-Range Study*. U.S. Fish and Wildlife Service. Special Scientific Report—Wildlife No. 43. Washington, DC, February 1959.

Kleinschmidt, F.E. "Alaska: Her Game and Game Laws." *Outdoor Life* 31 (1913): 95–102.

Kohlhoff, Dean. *When the Wind Was a River: Aleut Evacuation in World War II.* Seattle: University of Washington Press, 1995.

Kollin, Susan. *Nature's State: Imagining Alaska as the Last Frontier*. Chapel Hill: University of North Carolina Press, 2001.

Komarek, E.V., Sr. "Principles of Fire Ecology and Fire Management in Relation to the Alaskan Environment." In C.W. Slaughter, Richard J. Barney, and G.M. Hanson, eds., *Fire in the Northern Environment: A Symposium*, 3–22. Portland: Pacific Northwest Forest and Range Station, U.S. Forest Service, 1971.

Koughan, Helen Rita. "An Account of the Alaska Salmon Industry Since 1878, With Reference to Conservation." Master's thesis, University of California, 1931.

Krech, Shepard, III. *Indians, Animals and the Fur Trade: A Critique of Keepers of the Game*. Athens: University of Georgia Press, 1981.

———. *A Victorian Earl in the Arctic: The Travels and Collections of the Fifth Earl of Lonsdale 1888–9*. Seattle: University of Washington Press, 1989.

Kurtz, Rick S. *Glacier Bay National Park and Preserve: Historic Resource Study*. Anchorage: National Park Service, 1995.

Kushner, Howard I. *Conflict on the Northwest Coast: American-Russian Rivalry in the Pacific Northwest, 1790–1867*. Westport: Greenwood, 1975.

Lane, Theodore, ed. *Developing America's Northern Frontier*. Lanham, MD: University Press of America, 1978.

Lantis, Margaret. "Edward William Nelson." *Anthropological Papers of the University of Alaska* 3 (December 1954): 4–16.

———. *Ethnohistory in Southwestern Alaska and the Southern Yukon*. Lexington: University of Kentucky Press, 1970.

———. "The Reindeer Industry in Alaska." *Arctic* 3 (April 1950): 27–41.

La Perouse, Jean Francois de Galaup, Compte de. *Voyage Round the World, Performed in the Years 1785, 1786, 1787, and 1788, by the Beussole and the Astrolabe,* 3rd ed. London: S. Hamilton for G. and J. Robinson and Rogers, 1799.

Lathrop, John E. "Shall the Mineral Wealth of Alaska Enrich the Guggenheim Trust or the United States Treasury?" *McClure's Magazine* 34 (January 1910): 539–554.

Lawrence, Donald B. "Memorial to William Skinner Cooper 1884–1978." Pamphlet. Dept. of Botany, University of Minnesota, 1980. Cooper coll., University of Minnesota Archives, Minneapolis.

Laycock, George. "Alaska's Wildlife: An Abundance to Destroy." *Audubon* (July 1969): 60–66.

———. "Moving Day for Sea Otters." *Audubon* (January-February 1969): 58–78.

Lazell, J. Arthur. *Alaskan Apostle: The Life Story of Sheldon Jackson*. New York: Harper and Row, 1960.

Leffingwell, Ernest de K. *The Canning River Region, Northern Alaska*. U.S. Geological Survey Professional Paper No. 109. Washington, DC: GPO, 1919.

Lensink, Calvin J. "The History and Status of Sea Otters in Alaska." PhD diss., Purdue University, 1962.

———. "Predator Control With the Bounty System." In *Alaska Dept. of Fish and Game Annual Report for 1958*, Juneau, 91–104.

Lent, Peter C. "Alaska's Indigenous Muskoxen: A History." *Rangifer* 18, 3–4 (1998): 133–144.

———. "Musk-Ox." In John L. Schmidt and Douglas L. Gilbert, eds., *Big Game of Western America*, 135–147. Harrisburg, PA: Stackpole, 1978.

Lentfer, Jack W., ed. *Selected Marine Mammals of Alaska*. Washington, DC: Marine Mammal Commission, 1988.

Leonard, L. Larry. "The Alaskan Salmon Controversy Between the United States and Japan." Master's thesis, Columbia University, 1939.

Leopold, A. Starker, and Frank Fraser Darling. "Effects of Land Use on Moose and Caribou in Alaska." In *Proceedings of the Eighteenth North American Wildlife Conf., 1953,* 553–562. Washington, DC: Wildlife Management Institute, 1953.

Leopold, A. Starker, and Frank Fraser Darling. *Wildlife in Alaska: An Ecological Reconnaissance*. New York: Ronald, 1953.

Leopold, Aldo, and Allan Brooks. *Game Management*. New York: Scribner's, 1933.

Liapunova, R.G. "Relations With the Natives of North America." In S. Frederick Starr, ed., *Russia's American Colony*, 105–143. Chapel Hill: Duke University Press, 1987.

Litke, Frederick. *A Voyage Around the World, 1826–1829, Vol. I: To Russian America and America*. Ed. Richard A. Pierce. Kingston: Limestone, 1987.

Little, Arthur D. *An Evaluation of the Feasibility of Native Industry in Northwestern Alaska: Report to Bureau of Indian Affairs, United States Department of the Interior*. Cambridge, MA: Arthur D. Little, 1963.

Living Wilderness. "1889–Olaus Murie–1963" (Summer-Fall 1963): 3–14.

Loftus, Audrey. "Tom Gibson—Meat Hunter." *Alaska Sportsman* 33 (Part 2: June 1967): 6–8; (Part 3: August 1967): 20–21.

Loring, J. Alden. "Notes on the Destruction of Animal Life in Alaska." In *Sixth Annual Report of the New York Zoological Society, 1901,* 141–144. New York: NYZS.

Lowry, Lloyd F. "Alaska's Seals and Sea Lions: Where Are They Going?" *Alaska's Wildlife* 22 (September-October 1990): 14–16.

Luntey, Robert S. "Katmai National Monument." *National Parks* 30 (January-March 1956): 7–15.

Lutz, Harold J. *Aboriginal Man and White Man as Historical Causes of Fires in the Boreal Forest, With Particular Reference to Alaska*. Yale University School of Forestry Bull. No. 65. New Haven, 1959.

———. *Ecological Effects of Forest Fires in the Interior of Alaska*. U.S. Dept. of Agriculture. Tech. Bull. No. 1133. Washington, DC, March 1956.

———. *History of the Early Occurrence of Moose on the Kenai Peninsula and in Other Sectors of Alaska*. Juneau: Alaska Forest Research Center, 1960.

Madsen, Charles. *Arctic Trader*. New York: Dodd, Mead, 1957.

———. "Report on the Game Conditions on the Alaska Peninsula." King Cove, Alaska. Typescript, December 1916. Alaska Resources Library and Information Services, Anchorage.

Makarova, Raisa V. *Russians on the Pacific, 1743–1799.* Transl. and ed. Richard A. Pierce and Alton S. Donnelly. Kingston: Limestone, 1975.

Mantua, Nathan J., Steven R. Hare, Yuan Zhang, John M. Wallace, and Robert C. Francis. "A Pacific Interdecadal Climate Oscillation With Impacts on Salmon Production." *Bulletin of the American Meteorological Society* 78 (June 1997): 1069–1079.

Marquette, Willman M., and John R. Bockstoce. "Historical Shore-Based Catch of Bowhead Whales in the Bering, Chukchi, and Beaufort Seas." *Marine Fisheries Review* 42 (September-October 1980): 5–19.

Marquis Who's Who. Chicago: A.N. Marquis, 1943.

Marsh, George Perkins. *Man and Nature: Physical Geography as Modified by Human Action.* New York: C. Soribune, 1864.

Marshall, George. "Bob Marshall and the Alaska Arctic Wilderness." *Living Wilderness* (August 1970): 29–32.

Marshall, Robert. "Adventure, Arrogance and the Arctic." *Wings* (May 1933): 9–12.

———. *Alaska Wilderness.* Berkeley: University of California Press, 1970. Rept. of *Arctic Wilderness*, 1956.

———. *Arctic Village.* New York: H. Smith and R. Haas, 1933.

———. *Arctic Wilderness.* Berkeley: University of California Press, 1956.

———. "Ecology and the Indians." *Ecology* 18 (January 1937): 159–161.

———. *The People's Forests.* New York: Harrison Smith and Robert Haas, 1933.

———. "The Problem of the Wilderness." *Scientific Monthly* (February 1930): 141–148.

———. "Should We Settle Alaska?" *New Republic* 102 (January 8, 1940): 49–50.

———. "The Universe of the Wilderness Is Vanishing." *Living Wilderness* (Summer 1971): 8–14.

Martin, Calvin. "The American Indian as Miscast Ecologist." *History Teacher* 14 (February 1981): 243–252.

———. *Keepers of the Game.* Berkeley: University of California Press, 1978.

Martin, Frederika. *Sea Bears: The Story of the Fur Seal.* Philadelphia: Chalton, 1960.

Martin, George C. "The Recent Eruption of Katmai Volcano in Alaska." *National Geographic* (February 1913): 131–181.

Martin, Pete, and Claudia Martin. "Charlie Ott: Wizard of McKinley Park." *Alaska Journal* 10 (Summer 1980): 51–54.

McClung, Robert M. *Hunted Mammals of the Sea.* New York: Morrow, 1978.

McCracken, Harold. *Hunters of the Stormy Sea.* Garden City: Doubleday, 1957.

McKennan, Robert. *The Chandalar Kutchin.* Arctic Institute of North America. Technical Paper No. 17. Fairbanks, 1965.

McKnight, Donald E. *The History of Predator Control in Alaska.* Juneau: Alaska Dept. of Fish and Game, February 1973.

McNicholas, Helen L., ed. *Alaska's Agriculture and Forestry.* Fairbanks: University of Alaska Cooperative Extension Service, 1983.

Meine, Kurt. *Aldo Leopold: His Life and Work.* Madison: University of Wisconsin Press, 1989.

Merrell, Bruce. " 'A Wild, Discouraging Mess': John Muir Reports on the Klondike Gold Rush." *Alaska History* 7:2 (Fall 1992): 30–39.

Merriam, C. Hart. *Review of the Grizzly and Big Brown Bears of North America: North American Fauna No. 41.* U.S. Dept. of Agriculture, Bureau of Biological Survey. Washington, DC, 1918.

Merritt, Melvin L. "History, 1741–1967." In Melvin L. Merritt and R. Glen Fuller, *The Environment of Amchitka Island, Alaska*, 115–137. Springfield, VA: Energy Research and Development Administration, 1977.

Merritt, Melvin L., and R. Glen Fuller. *The Environment of Amchitka Island, Alaska.* Energy Research and Development Administration, 1977.

Mighetto, Lisa, ed. *Muir Among the Animals: The Wildlife Writings of John Muir.* San Francisco: Sierra Club Books, 1986.

———. *Wild Animals and American Environmental Ethics.* Tucson: University of Arizona Press, 1991.

Miller, David H. *The Alaska Treaty.* Kingston: Limestone, 1981.

Miller, Debbie S. "Finding Clarence Rhode's Plane." *Alaska* (January 1980): 16–17.

———. *Midnight Wilderness: Journeys in Alaska's Arctic National Wildlife Refuge.* San Francisco: Sierra Club Books, 1990.

Miller, Orlando W. *The Frontier in Alaska and the Matanuska Colony.* New Haven: Yale University Press, 1975.

Milton, John. *Nameless Valleys, Shining Mountains.* New York: Walker, 1969.

Mitchell, Donald Craig. *Sold American: The Story of Alaska Natives and Their Land, 1867–1959: The Army to Statehood.* Hanover, NH: University Press of New England, 1997.

Mitchell, John. "A Man Called Bird." *Audubon* (May 1987): 81–105.

Mixter, George. "Hunting of the Great Brown Bear of Alaska." *National Geographic* (April 1909): 313–333.

Moffitt, Fred H. "Petroleum on the West Shore, 1882–1906." In Morgan Sherwood, ed., *The Cook Inlet Collection,* 133–137. Anchorage: Alaska Northwest, 1974.

Moore, Terris. *Mt. McKinley: The Pioneer Climbs.* Fairbanks: University of Alaska Press, 1967.

Morgan, Lael. "Modern Shore-Based Whaling." *Alaska Geographic* 5, 4 (1978): 34–43.

Morris, Lisa Marie. "Keeper of the Seal: The Art of Henry W. Elliott and the Salvation of the Fur Seals." PhD diss., University of Alaska–Fairbanks, 2001.

Morse, Kathryn T. "The Nature of Gold: An Environmental History of the Alaska/Yukon Gold Rush." PhD diss., University of Washington, 1997.

Morton, William Markham. "The Dolly Varden Is Innocent." *Alaska* (May 1975): 14–15.

Moser, Jefferson F. *The Salmon and Salmon Fisheries of Alaska: Report of the Operations of the United States Fish Commission Steamer Albatross for the Year Ending June 30, 1898.* Washington, DC: GPO, 1899.

Mudar, Karen, and Stuart Speaker. "Natural Catastrophes in Arctic Populations: The 1878–1880 Famine on St. Lawrence Island, Alaska." *Journal of Anthropological Archaeology* 22, 2 (June 2003): 75–104.

Muir, John. "The Alaska Trip." *Century Magazine* 54 (August 1897): 513–526.

———. *The Cruise of the Corwin: Journal of the Arctic Expedition of 1881 in Search of De Long and the Jeanette.* Ed. William F. Bade. Boston: Houghton-Mifflin, 1917.

———. "The Discovery of Glacier Bay." *Century Magazine* 28 (June 1895): 234–247.

———. *Letters From Alaska.* Ed. Robert Engberg and Bruce Merrell. Madison: University of Wisconsin Press, 1993.

———. *Stickeen.* Boston: Houghton-Mifflin, 1909.

———. *The Story of My Boyhood and Youth*. Boston: Houghton-Mifflin, 1913.

———. *Travels in Alaska*. Boston: Houghton-Mifflin, 1915.

Murie, Adolph. *Birds of Mt. McKinley National Park, Alaska*. McKinley Park: Mt. McKinley Natural History Assn., 1963.

———. *Mammals of Mt. McKinley Park, Alaska*. McKinley Park: Mt. McKinley Natural History Assn., 1962.

———. *A Naturalist in Alaska*. New York: Devin-Adair, 1961. New York: Rept. by American Museum of Natural History, 1963.

———. *The Wolves of Mt. McKinley*. Seattle: University of Washington Press, 1985. Originally printed as Fauna Series No. 5. Washington, DC: National Park Service, 1944.

Murie, Margaret. *Island Between*. Fairbanks: University of Alaska Press, 1977.

———. "Return to the Sheenjek." *Living Wilderness* (July-September 1977): 4–12.

———. *Two in the Far North*. New York: Knopf, 1957. 2nd ed., Anchorage: Alaska Northwest, 1978.

Murie, Margaret, and Olaus Murie. *Wapiti Wilderness*. New York: Knopf, 1966.

Murie, Olaus J. *The Alaska Bird Sketches of Olaus Murie*. Anchorage: Alaska Northwest, 1979.

———. *Alaska-Yukon Caribou: North American Fauna No. 54*. U.S. Dept. of Agriculture, Bureau of Biological Survey. Washington, DC, June 1935.

———. "Beauty and the Dollar Sign." *Living Wilderness* (Summer 1953): 15–27.

———. *Fauna of the Aleutian Islands and Alaska Peninsula*. Washington, DC: U.S. Fish and Wildlife Service, 1959.

———. "God Bless America . . . and Let's Save Some of It." *Living Wilderness* (Summer 1953): 1–9.

———. *Journeys to the Far North*. Palo Alto: Wilderness Society and American West, 1973.

———. Letter to Edward W. Nelson, chief, Bureau of Biological Survey, January 7, 1922. Alaska State Library, Historical Section, Juneau, USFWS MS 51, Group 162, Entry 162.

———. "Memorandum for Mr. Redington." Typescript, April 30, 1929. Denver Public Library Archives, CONS 90, Box 3.

———. "Nature in the Arctic." *National Parks Magazine* 32 (January-March 1958): 29–31.

———. "Wild Country Around the World." *Living Wilderness* (Summer 1953): 10–18.

———. "Wilderness and Aircraft." *Living Wilderness* (Autumn 1947): 1–6.

———. "Wilderness Philosophy, Science and the Arctic National Wildlife Range." In *Science in Alaska: Proceedings of Twelfth Alaska Science Conf.*, 58–69. College: Alaska Div., AAAS, 1962.

———. "Wildlife Introductions in Alaska." In *Trans. of Fifth North American Wildlife Conf., 1940*, 432–436. Washington, DC: Wildlife Management Institute, 1940.

———. "Wolf." *Audubon* (September-October 1957): 218–221.

Murphy, Lawrence, and Dan Collins, eds. *The World of John Muir*. Stockton: University of the Pacific Press, 1981.

Murray, Peter. *The Vagabond Fleet: A Chronicle of the North Pacific Sealing Schooner Trade*. Victoria: Sono Nis, 1988.

Nash, Roderick. "The Strenuous Life of Bob Marshall." *Forest History* 10 (October 1966): 18–25.

———. "Tourism, Parks and the Wilderness Idea in the History of Alaska." *Alaska in Perspective* 4, 1 (1981): 1–2.

———. *Wilderness and the American Mind, 3rd ed.* New Haven: Yale University Press, 1982.

Naske, Claus-M. "The Alcan: Its Impact on Alaska." *Northern Engineering* 8 (Spring 1976): 12–18.

———. "Creation of the Arctic National Wildlife Range." In David L. Spencer, Claus-M. Naske, and John Carnahan, eds., *National Wildlife Refuges of Alaska: A Historical Perspective: Part 1*, 97–116. Anchorage: Arctic Environmental Information and Data Center, 1979.

———. "The Kenai National Moose Range." In David L. Spencer, Claus-M. Naske, and John Carnahan, eds., *National Wildlife Refuges in Alaska: A Historical Perspective: Part 1*, 117–138. Anchorage: Arctic Environmental Information and Data Center, 1979.

Naske, Claus-M., and Herman E. Slotnick. *Alaska: A History of the Forty-Ninth State*. Grand Rapids, MI: Eerdman's, 1979.

Naske, Claus-M., and Don M. Triplehorn. "The Federal Government and Alaska's Coal." *Northern Engineer* 12 (Fall 1980): 11–23.

National Cyclopedia of American Biography. New York: James T. White, 1897, 1902, 1937, 1941.

Neiswonger, Michael. "Robert Atwood: 'It Was a Pretty Busy Time . . . The Opportunities Were Everywhere.' " *Anchorage Magazine* (May 1990): 13–17.

Nelson, Daniel. *Northern Landscapes: The Struggle for Wilderness Alaska* Washington, DC: Resources for the Future, 2004.

Nelson, Edward W. "The Economic Importance of Wild Life." *Scientific Monthly* 14 (April 1922): 367–373.

———. *The Eskimo About Bering Strait*. Washington, DC: Smithsonian Institution, 1983.

———. *Report Upon Natural History Collections Made in Alaska Between the Years 1877 and 1881*. Washington, DC: GPO, 1887.

Nelson, Klondy, with Corey Ford. *Daughter of the Gold Rush*. New York: Random House, 1958.

Nelson, Richard K. *Hunters of the Northern Forest: Designs for Survival Among the Alaska Kutchin*. Chicago: University of Chicago Press, 1973.

———. *Make Prayers to the Raven: A Koyukon View of the Northern Forest*. Chicago: University of Chicago Press, 1983.

Nelson, Urban C., and David L. Spencer. "Bureau of Sport Fisheries and Wildlife's Position on the Arctic National Wildlife Range." In *Science in Alaska, 1961: Proceedings of Twelfth Alaska Science Conference,* 69–75. College: Alaska Div., AAAS, 1962.

Netboy, Anthony. *The Salmon: Their Fight for Survival.* Boston: Houghton-Mifflin, 1974.

New York Zoological Society News Release PR-28 CNA (May 30, 1937). Madison Grant coll., NYZS Archives.

Norris, Frank. *Gawking at the Midnight Sun: The Tourist in Early Alaska.* Anchorage: Alaska Historical Commission, June 1985.

———. *Isolated Paradise: An Administrative History of the Katmai and Aniakchak NPS Units, Alaska.* Anchorage: National Park Service, 1996.

———. "A Lone Voice in the Wilderness: The National Park Service in Alaska, 1917–1969." *Environmental History* 1 (October 1996): 66–76.

Oakes, Patricia. *Birch Creek and the Circle Mining District, Alaska: An Historical Overview of an Economic Entity.* Central, AK: Oakeservices, 1983.

O'Connor, Jack. *Quarterly Report, July 1–September 30, 1946.* Juneau: Alaska Game Commission, 1946.

Oelschlaeger, Max. *The Idea of Wilderness: From Prehistory to the Age of Ecology.* New Haven: Yale University Press, 1991.

Ogden, Adele. "Russian Sea-Otter and Seal Hunting on the California Coast." *California Historical Quarterly* 12 (1933): 217–239.

Okun, S.B. *The Russian-American Company.* Ed. B.D. Grekov; transl. Carl Ginsberg. Cambridge: Harvard University Press, 1951.

Oldfield, Margery L., and Janice B. Alcorn, eds. *Biodiversity: Conservation, Culture, and Ecodevelopment.* Boulder: Westview, 1991.

Orth, Donald J. *Dictionary of Alaska Place Names.* U.S. Geological Survey Professional Paper No. 567. Washington, DC, 1967.

Osgood, Wilfred H. *Biological Reconnaissance of the Base of the Alaska Peninsula.* U.S. Dept. of Agriculture, Bureau of Biological Survey. North American Fauna No. 24. Washington, DC, 1904.

———. "Clinton Hart Merriam, 1855–1942." *Journal of Medicine* 24 (November 17, 1943): 421–436.

———. *Natural History of the Queen Charlotte Islands, British Columbia; Natural History of the Cook Inlet Region, Alaska.* U.S. Dept. of Agriculture, Bureau of Biological Survey. North American Fauna No. 21. Washington, DC, 1901.

Osgood, Wilfred H., Edward A. Preble, and George H. Parker. *The Fur Seals and Other Life of the Pribilof Islands in 1914.* From *Bulletin of the Bureau of Fisheries, Vol. 34,* 1914. Doc. No. 820. Washington, DC: GPO, June 19, 1915.

Osterman, H. *The Alaska Eskimos: As Described in the Posthumous Notes of the Late Dr. Knud Rasmussen: Report of the Fifth Thule Expedition, 1921–4.* Copenhagen: Gyldendalske, Boghandel, Nordisk Forlag, 1952.

Pacific Fisherman. Yearbook, 1944. Seattle.

Pack, Arthur Newton. "Admiralty's Bears." *Nature Magazine* (August 1935): 111–112.

Palmer, Lawrence J. *Caribou Versus Fire in Interior Alaska: A Study of Burned-Over Lichen Ranges.* Washington, DC: U.S. Dept. of the Interior, Fish and Wildlife Service, 1941.

Palmer, Lawrence J., and Charles H. Rouse. *Study of the Alaskan Tundra With Reference to Its Reactions to Reindeer and Other Grazing*. U.S. Dept. of the Interior, Fish and Wildlife Service. Research Report 10. Washington, DC: GPO, 1945.

Palmisano, John F. "Sea Otter Predation: Its Role in Intertidal Community Structure at Amchitka and Other Aleutian Islands." PhD diss., University of Washington, 1995.

Pasley, Fred. "The Salmon Battle of U.S. and Japan." *China Weekly Review* 86 (October 1, 1938): 145–147. Rept. from *New York Daily News*, August 21, 1938.

Pearson, Grant H. *A History of Mount McKinley National Park, Alaska*. Washington, DC: U.S. Dept. of the Interior, National Park Service, 1953.

Pearson, T. Gilbert. "Eagles and the Alaskan Bounty." *Bird-Lore* 30 (January-February 1928): 86–90.

Pegues, John E. "Alaska's Brownie." *Field and Stream* (December 1930): 36–37.

Pender, Jane. "Alaska Natives: Time of Crisis." *National Parks and Conservation* 44 (November 1970): 23–27.

Penick, James, Jr. *Progressive Politics and Conservation: The Ballinger-Pinchot Affair*. Chicago and Toronto: University of Chicago and University of Toronto Presses, 1968.

Perkins, Elmer. "Bounty Hunter." *Alaska Sportsman* (May 1938): 10–11.

Perry, Richard. *The World of the Walrus*. New York: Taplinger, 1967.

Peterson, Rolf O., and James D. Woolington. "The Apparent Extirpation and Reappearance of Wolves on the Kenai Peninsula, Alaska." In Fred H. Harrington and Paul C. Paquet, eds., *Wolves of the World*, 334–344. Park River, NJ: Noyes, 1982.

Petroff, Ivan. "Report on the Population, Industries, and Resources of Alaska." In David Starr Jordan, ed., *Seal and Salmon Fisheries and General Resources of Alaska, Vol. 4*, 167–450. Washington, DC: GPO, 1898.

Phillips, James W. *Alaska-Yukon Place Names*. Seattle: University of Washington Press, 1973.

Phinizy, Coles. "The Savers vs. the Spoilers." *Sports Illustrated* (January 16, 1961): 26–29.

Pinchot, Gifford. *Breaking New Ground*. New York: Harcourt, Brace, 1947.

Poole, Daniel. "Stand Firm, Mr. Secretary." *American Forests* 64 (January 1958): 4–5.

Popular Mechanics. "Man's Law on the Yukon." Vol. 50 (August 1928): 291–294.

Porsild, Erling. "The Reindeer and the Canadian Eskimo." *Geographical Journal* 88 (July 1936): 1–16.

Postman, David. Series of nine articles on history of oil on Kenai Peninsula. *Anchorage Daily News*, February 4–11, 1990.

Powers, Richard L. "Public Involvement and Admiralty Island, Alaska: Effects of Interest Groups on Natural Resource Allocations." Master's thesis, University of Alaska, May 1972.

Pruitt, William O., Jr. "Animal Ecology and the Arctic National Wildlife Range." In *Science in Alaska, 1961: Proceedings of the Twelfth Alaska Science Conference*, 44–51. College: Alaska Div., AAAS, 1962.

Pyne, Stephen J. *Fire in America: A Cultural History of Wildland and Rural Fire*. Princeton: Princeton University Press, 1982.

Radclyffe, C.R.E. *Big Game Shooting in Alaska*. London: Rowland, Ward, 1904.

Rakestraw, Lawrence. *A History of the Forest Service in Alaska*. Alaska Historical Commission, Alaska Dept. of Education, and Alaska Region, U.S. Forest Service. Anchorage, 1981.

Rausch, Robert A. "The Outlook for Conservation in Alaska." Presented at Sixth Annual Wilderness Conference, Sierra Club, San Francisco, March 20–21, 1959.

Rawson, Timothy M. "Alaska's First Wolf Controversy: Predator and Prey in Mount McKinley National Park, 1930–1953." Master's thesis, University of Alaska–Fairbanks, 1994.

Ray, Dorothy Jean. *The Eskimos of Bering Strait, 1650–1898*. Seattle: University of Washington Press, 1975.

———. *Ethnohistory in the Arctic: The Bering Strait Eskimo*. Ed. R.A. Pierce. Kingston: Limestone, 1983.

Rearden, Jim. "Alaska's Commercial Salmon Fisheries." *Alaska* (February 1975): 18–21.

———. *Alaska's Wolf Man: The 1915–55 Wilderness Adventures of Frank Glaser*. Missoula: Pictorial Histories, 1998.

———. "Brownie: Alaska's Big Coastal Grizzly." *Alaska* (May 1986): 34–36.

———. "Clarence Rhode." *Alaska* (January 1980): 11–14.

———. "Commissioner Jim Brooks: A Profile." *Alaska* (November 1972): 21–22.

———. "The Kodiak Bear War." *Outdoor Life* (August 1964): 17–19.

Redington, Paul G. "The United States Bureau of Biological Survey." *Scientific Monthly* 37 (October 1933): 289–306.

Reeves, Randall R., Stephen Leatherwood, Stephen A. Karl, and Evelyn R. Yohe. "Whaling Results at Akutan (1912–39) and Port Hobron (1926–37), Alaska." In *Reports of International Whaling Commission 35*, 441–457. Cambridge: International Whaling Commission, 1985.

Reiger, John F. *American Sportsmen and the Origins of Conservation*, rev. ed. Norman: University of Oklahoma Press, 1986.

———. "George Bird Grinnell and the Development of American Conservation, 1870–1901." PhD diss., Northwestern University, 1970.

———. *The Passing of the Great West: Selected Papers of George Bird Grinnell*. New York: Winchester, 1972.

Rhode, Clarence J. *Alaska's Fish and Wildlife*, Circular 17. U.S. Fish and Wildlife Service, Washington, DC, 1953.

Richardson, Elmo. *The Politics of Conservation: Crusades and Controversies, 1897–1913*. Berkeley: University of California Press, 1962.

Riley, Francis. *Fur Seal Industry of the Pribilof Islands, 1786–1985*. Circular 275. U.S. Dept. of the Interior. Washington, DC, October 1967.

Roderick, Jack. *Crude Dreams: A Personal History of Oil and Politics in Alaska*. Fairbanks: Epicenter, 1997.

Rogers, George W. *Alaska in Transition: The Southeast Region*. Baltimore: Johns Hopkins University Press, 1960.

Rogers, George W., and Richard A. Cooley. *Alaska's Population and Economy: Regional Growth, Development, and Future Outlook, Vol. 2: Statehood Handbook*. College:

University of Alaska Institute of Business, Economic, and Governmental Research, 1963.

Roppel, Alton Y. *Management of Northern Fur Seals on the Pribilof Islands, Alaska, 1786–1981*. NOAA, National Marine Fisheries Service. Technical Report NMFS 4. Washington, DC, April 1984.

Roppel, Patricia. *Alaska's Salmon Hatcheries, 1891–1959*. Juneau: Alaska Historical Commission Studies in History No. 20, 1982.

———. *Salmon From Kodiak: A History of the Salmon Fishery of Kodiak Island, Alaska*. Juneau: Alaska Historical Commission Studies in History No. 216, 1986.

Ross, Ken. *Environmental Conflict in Alaska*. Boulder: University Press of Colorado, 2000.

Rossman, Darwin L. "Geology and Ore Deposits in the Reid Inlet Area, Glacier Bay, Alaska." *Geographical Survey Bulletin 1958-B*. Washington, DC, 1959.

Rowland, Edgar I., and A.C. Kinsley. *Report on Kodiak Island, Part 1*. U.S. Dept. of the Interior, Office of Investigations. San Francisco, 1940.

Royce, William F. "Alaskan Salmon Management—An Outstanding Success." *Pacific Fisheries Review* 15 (March 1988): 17–32.

Sarber, Hosea R. *Report of the Kodiak Brown Bear Control Project, Kodiak Island, Alaska, March–July 1939*. Juneau: Alaska Game Commission, 1939.

Scammon, Charles Melville. "Northern Whaling." *Overland Monthly* (June 1871): 548–554.

Scarff, James E. "Historic and Present Distribution of the Right Whale (Eubalaena glacialis) in the Eastern North Pacific South of 50 Degrees North and East of 180 Degrees West." In Robert L. Brownell, Peter B. Best, and John H. Prescott, eds., *Right Whales, Past and Present Status*, 43–63. Cambridge: International Whaling Commission, 1986.

Schaaf, Jeanne. "Witness." Typescript, 2002.

Scheffer, Victor B. *Adventures of a Zoologist*. New York: Scribner's, 1980.

———. "Exploring With Olaus Murie: The Aleutian Expedition." *Living Wilderness* (June 1980): 10–17.

Scheffer, Victor B., Clifford H. Fiscus, and Ethel I. Todd. *History of the Scientific Study and Management of the Alaskan Fur Seal, Californius Ursinus, 1786–1964*. NOAA Technical Report NMFS SRF-780. U.S. Dept. of Commerce, Washington, DC, March 1984.

Schmidt, John L., and Douglas L. Gilbert. *Big Game of Western America: Ecology and Management*. Harrisburg, PA: Stackpole, 1978.

Schmitt, Frederick P., Cornelius De Jong, and Frank H. Winter. *Thomas Welcome Roys: America's Pioneer of Modern Whaling*. Charlottesville: University of Virginia Press, 1980.

Schmitt, Peter J. *Back to Nature: The Arcadian Myth in Urban America*. New York: Oxford, 1969.

Schneider, William. "Trapping Furbearers in Alaska: A Legacy and, Perhaps a Destiny!" *Alaska in Perspective* 3, 1 (1980): 1–23.

Scidmore, Elisa R. "Alaska Fish and Game." *Harper's Weekly*, September 2, 1893, 838–841+.

Science News Letter. "Wrong Volcano Blamed." April 21, 1956, 246.

Scott, Robert F., Edward F. Chatelain, and Winston A. Elkins. "The Status of the Dall Sheep and Caribou in Alaska." In *Trans. of Fifteenth North American Wildlife Conf.*, 612–626. Washington, DC: Wildlife Management Institute, 1950.

Scotter, George W. "Reindeer Journey on the Rim of the Arctic." *Alaska Journal* 2 (Summer 1972): 57–60.

Scudder, H.C. *The Alaska Salmon Trap: The Evolution, Conflicts, and Consequences*. Juneau: Alaska State Historical Library Monograph Series, 1970.

Scull, E. Marshall. *Hunting in the Arctic and Alaska*. Philadelphia: Winston, 1914.

Sease, John L., and Douglas G. Chapman. "Pacific Walrus." In Jack W. Lentfer, ed., *Selected Marine Mammals of Alaska*, 17–38. Washington, DC: Marine Mammal Commission, 1988.

Seaton, Fred A. "America's Largest Wildlife Area." *National Parks Magazine* 32 (July-September 1958): 117–122.

Seton, Ernest Thompson. *Wild Animals I Have Known*. New York: Scribner's, 1898.

Shalkop, Robert L. "Henry Wood Elliott 1846–1930: A Retrospective Exhibition." Pamphlet. Anchorage Historical and Fine Arts Museum, 1982.

———. "Henry Wood Elliott: Fighter for a Cause." *Alaska Journal* 15 (Winter 1983): 4–12.

Shelden, Kim E., Sue R. Moore, Janice M. Waite, Paul R. Wade, and David J. Rugh. "Historical and Current Habitat Use by North Pacific Right Whales *Eubalaena japonica* in the Bering Sea and Gulf of Alaska." *Mammal Review* 35, 2 (2005): 129–155.

Sheldon, Charles. Untitled interview by outdoor sporting writer, from William Sheldon personal collection. Charles Sheldon file, Denali National Park Archives.

———. *The Wilderness of Denali: Explorations of a Hunter-Naturalist in Northern Alaska*. New York: Scribner's, 1930.

———. *The Wilderness of the North Pacific Coast Islands*. New York: Charles Scribner's Sons, 1912.

———. *The Wilderness of the Upper Yukon*. New York: Charles Scribner's Sons, 1911.

Sheldon, William G. "Biographical Notes on Charles Sheldon." Typescript, undated. Charles Sheldon coll., University of Alaska Fairbanks Alaska and Polar Regions Archives.

Sherwood, Morgan. *Alaska and Its History*. Seattle: University of Washington Press, 1967.

———. *Big Game in Alaska: A History of Wildlife and People*. New Haven: Yale University Press, 1981.

———. *Exploration of Alaska, 1865–1900*. New Haven: Yale University Press, 1965.

———. "Specious Speciation in the Political History of the Brown Bear." *Western Political Quarterly* 10 (January 1979): 49–60.

———, ed. *The Cook Inlet Collection*. Anchorage: Alaska Northwest, 1974.

Shiras, George, III. "The White Sheep, Giant Moose and Smaller Game of the Kenai Peninsula, Alaska." *National Geographic* (May 1913): 423–494.

Simmerman, Nancy Lange. *Alaska's Parklands: The Complete Guide*. Seattle: Mountaineers, 1983.

Skoog, Ronald O. "Ecology of the Caribou *Rangifer Tarandus Granti* in Alaska." PhD diss., University of Alaska–Fairbanks, 1968.

———. "Historical Resumé—Reindeer." Unpublished paper. Juneau: Alaska Dept. of Fish and Game, 1964.

Slaughter, C.W., Richard J. Barney, and G.M. Hanson, eds. *Fire in the Northern Environment: A Symposium*. Portland: Pacific Northwest Forest and Range Station, U.S. Forest Service, 1971.

Slotnick, Herman E. "The Ballinger-Pinchot Affair in Alaska." *Journal of the West* 10 (April 1971): 337–347.

Snell, Roy, Jr. "The Walrus and His Hunters." *Alaska-Yukon Magazine* 9 (November 1909): 16–20.

Spence, Clark C. *The Northern Gold Fleet: Twentieth Century Gold Dredging in Alaska*. Urbana: University of Illinois Press, 1996.

Spencer, David L. "Aleutian Islands National Wildlife Refuge." In David L. Spencer, Claus-M. Naske, and John Carnahan, eds., *National Wildlife Refuges of Alaska: A Historical Perspective, Part 1*, 11–75. Anchorage: Arctic Environmental Information and Data Center, 1979.

Spencer, David L., and Edward F. Chatelain. "Progress in the Management of the Moose of South Central Alaska." In *Trans. of Eighteenth North American Wildlife Conf.*, 539–552. Washington, DC: Wildlife Management Institute, 1953.

Spencer, David L., Claus-M. Naske, and John Carnahan, eds. *National Wildlife Refuges of Alaska: A Historical Perspective: Part 1*. Anchorage: Arctic Environmental Information and Data Center, 1979.

Spencer, Robert F. *The North Alaskan Eskimo: A Study in Ecology and Society*. Washington, DC: Smithsonian Institution, 1959.

Spiro, Jonathan Peter. "Patrician Racist: The Evolution of Madison Grant." PhD diss., University of California–Berkeley, 2000.

Spurr, Josiah Edward. "A Reconnaissance in Southwestern Alaska in 1898." In U.S. Dept. of the Interior, *Annual Reports of the Department of the Interior for the Fiscal Year Ended June 30, 1899: Twentieth Annual Report of the United States Geological Survey, Part 7*, 31–264. Washington, DC: GPO, 1900.

Stansby, Maurice E. *Federal Fishery Research in the Pacific Northwest Preceding Formation of Northwest Fisheries Center*. Washington, DC: U.S. Dept. of Commerce, NOAA, National Marine Fisheries Service, November 1979.

Stanton, William J. *Alaska Recreation Survey, Part 1, Vol. 1: Economic Aspects of Recreation in Alaska*. U.S. Dept. of the Interior, National Park Service. Washington, DC, 1953.

Starr, S. Frederick, ed. *Russia's American Colony*. Durham: Duke University Press, 1987.

Stefansson, Vilhjalmur. *The Northward Course of Empire*. New York: Macmillan, 1924.

Stejneger, Leonhard. *Georg Wilhelm Steller: The Pioneer of Alaskan Natural History*. Cambridge: Harvard University Press, 1936.

———. "How the Great Northern Sea-Cow (Rytina) Became Exterminated." *American Naturalist* 21 (December 1887): 1047–1054.

Steller, Georg Wilhelm. *Journal of a Voyage With Bering, 1741–1742*. Ed. O.W. Frost. Stanford: Stanford University Press, 1988.

Stephenson, Robert O., S. Craig Gerlach, R. Dale Guthrie, C. Richard Harington, Robin O. Mills, and Gregory Hare. "Wood Bison in Late Holocene Alaska and Adjacent Canada: Paleontological, Archaeological, and Historical Records." In S. Craig Gerlach and Maribeth S. Murray, eds., *People and Wildlife in North America: Essays in Honor of R. Dale Guthrie*, 125–159. Oxford: British Archaeological Reports International Series 944, 2001.

Sterling, Keir B. "Builders of the U.S. Biological Survey, 1885–1930." *Journal of Forest History* 33 (October 1989): 180–187.

———. *Last of the Naturalists: The Career of C. Hart Merriam,* rev. ed. New York: Arno, 1977.

———. *Selected Works of Clinton Hart Merriam*. New York: Arno, 1974.

———, Richard P. Harmond, George A. Cevasco, and Lorne F. Hammond, eds. *Biological Dictionary of American and Canadian Naturalists and Environmentalists.* Westport: Greenwood, 1997.

Stern, Richard O., Edward L. Arobio, Larry L. Naylor, and Wayne C. Thomas. *Eskimos, Reindeer and Land.* University of Alaska Agricultural Experimental Station. Bull. 59. Fairbanks, December 1980.

Stevenson, Charles H. "Oils From Seals, Walrus, Etc." *Scientific American Supp.,* No. 1474 (April 2, 1904): 23614–23616.

———. "The Skins of Fur-Seals." *Scientific American Supp*., No. 1529 (April 22, 1905): 24502–24504.

Stewart, R.K. *Report to the Governor of Alaska on Cooperative Predatory-Animal Investigation and Control in the Territory*. Juneau: Bureau of Biological Survey, March 1, 1929.

Stewart, Robert Laird. *Sheldon Jackson*. New York: Fleming Revell, 1908.

Stone, Andrew J. "An Explorer-Naturalist in the Arctic." *Scribner's Magazine* 33 (April 1903): 438–449.

Streveler, Gregory P., and Bruce B. Paige. *The Natural History of Glacier Bay National Monument, Alaska*. Glacier Bay: National Park Service, 1971.

Strickland, Dan. "The Eskimo vs. the Walrus vs. the Government." *Natural History* 90 (February 1981): 48–52.

Sumner, Lowell. "Your Stake in Alaska's Wildlife and Wilderness." *Sierra Club Bulletin* 41 (December 1956): 54–71.

Sweazey, Manley. "In the Tallest Trees." *Alaska Sportsman* (May 1938): 18–20.

Tansill, Charles Callan. *Canadian-American Relations, 1875–1911*. New Haven: Yale University Press, 1943.

Taylor, Joseph. "Well-Thinking Men and Women: The Battle for the White Act and the Meaning of Conservation in the 1920s." *Pacific Historical Review* 71, 3 (2002): 357–387.

Thayer, Averill. "The ANWR: Start at the Beginning—Please." *Northern Line* (April 1986): 1.

The Spirit. "Gunning for Predators." Fall 1999: 1, 4.

Thomas, William S. *Trails and Tramps in Alaska and Newfoundland.* New York: Putnam's, 1913.

Thompson, Seton H. *Alaska Fishery and Fur Seal Industries in 1955.* U.S. Dept. of the Interior, Bureau of Commercial Fisheries. Statistical Digest No. 40. Washington, DC: GPO, 1956.

Thorne, Frank. "Nature Ramblings." *Science News Letter* 42 (August 22, 1942): 124.

Thorsteinson, Fredrik V., Richard W. Nelson, and Dexter F. Lall. *Experimental Harvest of the Steller Sea Lion in Alaskan Waters.* U.S. Dept. of the Interior, Fish and Wildlife Service. Special Scientific Report—Fisheries No. 371, Washington, DC, 1971.

Tilton, Captain George Fred. *Cap'n George Fred Himself.* Garden City: Doubleday, Doran, 1928.

Tingle, George R. *Report on the Salmon Fisheries of Alaska, 1896.* Washington, DC: GPO, 1897.

Tompkins, Stuart Ramsay. *Alaska: Promyshlennik and Sourdough.* Norman: University of Oklahoma Press, 1945.

Tonnessen, J.N., and A.O. Johnsen. *The History of Modern Whaling.* Transl. R.I. Christophersen. Berkeley: University of California Press, 1982.

Townsend, Charles H. "Condition of Seal Life on the Rookeries of the Pribilof Islands, 1893–1895." In David Starr Jordan and George A. Clark, eds., *Seal and Salmon Fisheries and General Resources of Alaska, Vol. 4,* 453–547. U.S. Dept. of the Treasury. Washington, DC: GPO, 1898.

———. "The Pribilof Fur Seal Herd and the Prospects for Its Increase." *Science* 34 (October 27, 1910): 568–570.

Tracy, Henry Chester. *American Naturalists.* New York: Dutton, 1930.

Trefethen, James B. *An American Crusade for Wildlife.* New York: Winchester, 1975.

———. *Crusade for Wildlife: Highlights in Conservation Progress.* Harrisburg, PA: Stackpole, 1961.

Troyer, Willard A. "The Brown Bear Harvest in Relation to Management on the Kodiak Islands." In *Proc. of 26th North American Wildlife and Natural Resources Conf.,* 460–468. Washington, DC: Wildlife Management Institute, 1961.

———. *The Status of Brown Bear in Alaska: Kodiak-Afognak Islands.* U.S. Fish and Wildlife Service, 1958.

Troyer, Willard A., and Richard J. Hensel. "The Brown Bear of Kodiak Island." Typescript, 1969. Alaska Resources Library and Information Service, Anchorage.

Turner, Tom. *Sierra Club: 100 Years of Protecting Nature.* New York: Harry N. Adams for Sierra Club, 1991.

Underwood, John J. *Alaska: An Empire in the Making.* New York: Dodd, Mead, 1913.

U.S. Congress, House. Committee on Agriculture. *Hearings: Alaska Game Act.* Washington, DC. 68 Cong., 1 sess., March 29, 1924.

———. Committee on Merchant Marine and Fisheries. Subcommittee on Fisheries and Wildlife Conservation. *Hearings: Miscellaneous Fish and Wildlife Legislation.* Washington, DC. 86 Cong, 1 sess., May 5, June 3, June 30, July 1, and August 4, 1959.

———. Committee on Public Lands. *Hearings on HR 5004 and HR 5401: Bills to Provide for the Protection of the Dall Sheep, Caribou, and Other Wildlife Native to the Mount McKinley National Park Area.* Washington, DC. 79 Cong., 1 sess., July 23, 1946.

———. Committee on Territories. *Hearings on HR 7344: To Regulate the Killing and Sale of Certain Game Animals in Northern Alaska, Part 1,* February 5–6; *Part 2,* February 26. Washington, DC. 68 Cong., 1 sess., 1924.

———. Subcommittee of the Committee on Public Lands. *Hearings: Mount McKinley National Park.* Washington, DC. 64 Cong., 1 sess., May 4, 1916.

U.S. Congress, Senate. Committee on Commerce, Science and Transportation. *International North Pacific Fisheries Convention: Hearings.* Washington, DC. 95 Cong., 1 sess., May 10, 1958.

———. Committee on Interstate and Foreign Commerce. Merchant Marine and Fisheries Subcommittee. *Hearings on S. 1899: Arctic National Wildlife Range—Alaska, Part 1,* Washington, DC, June 30, 1959; *Part 2,* Fairbanks, October 29–31, 1959. 86 Cong., 2 sess., 1960.

———. Special Committee on Wildlife Resources. *Hearings: Brown Bear of Alaska.* Washington, DC. 77 Cong., 2 sess., January 18, 1932.

U.S. Dept. of Agriculture, Bureau of Biological Survey. *Regulations for the Protection of Game in Alaska for the Year of 1904.* Circular No. 42. Washington, DC, 1904.

———. *U.S. Government Reservations in Alaska.* Washington, DC, August 1938.

U.S. Dept. of Commerce, Bureau of Fisheries. *Alaska Fisheries Annual Reports, 1905–1939.* Washington, DC.

U.S. Dept. of Commerce, Census Bureau. *Annual Census Data, 1970–2000.* Washington, DC.

U.S. Dept. of Commerce, National Marine Fisheries Service. *International Whaling Commission's Deletion of Native Exemption for the Subsistence Harvest of Bowhead Whales: Final Environmental Impact Statement, Vol. 2, Appendix B.* Washington, DC, 1977.

———. *Marine Mammal Protection Act of 1972: Report, 1986–87.* Washington, DC.

U.S. Dept. of the Interior, Bureau of Land Management, Alaska Fire Service. *1992 Fire Statistics.* Fairbanks, 1993.

———. Bureau of Sport Fisheries and Wildlife. *Alaskan Wildlife Refuges.* 1964. Washington, DC.

———. Fish and Wildlife Service. *Alaska Maritime National Wildlife Refuge: Comprehensive Conservation Plan, Wilderness Review and Environmental Impact Statement.* Anchorage, 1988.

———. Alaska District. Branch of Predator Control. *Annual Report, FY 1960, 1962, 1964.* Juneau.

———. *Arctic National Wildlife Refuge: Coastal Plain Resource Assessment: Final Report: Baseline Study of the Fish, Wildlife and Their Habitats, Vol. 1.* Anchorage, December 1986.

———. *Arctic National Wildlife Refuge: Comprehensive Conservation Plan, Environmental Impact Statement, Wilderness Review, Wild River Plans.* Anchorage, 1988.

———. *Arctic National Wildlife Refuge: Draft River Management Plan and Environmental Assessment.* Fairbanks, June 1993.

———. *The Bald Eagle and Its Economic Status.* Circular 30. Washington, DC: GPO, 1955.

———. *Kenai National Wildlife Refuge: Final Comprehensive Conservation Plan, Environmental Impact Statement and Wilderness Review.* Anchorage, 1985.

———. *Restoring America's Wildlife, 1937–87.* Washington, DC: U.S. Fish and Wildlife Service, 1987.

———. National Park Service. *Proceedings of the National Parks Conference,* January 2–6, 1917. Washington, DC: GPO, 1917.

———. Office of the Secretary. *Survey of the Alaska Reindeer Service, 1931–33.* Washington, DC, February 15, 1933.

U.S. Dept. of the Treasury. *Seal and Salmon Fisheries and General Resources of Alaska, Vols. I–IV.* Washington, DC: GPO, 1898.

U.S. Environmental Protection Agency. *Climate Change and Alaska. EPA 236F-98-007b,* updated May 2002. Washington, DC.

U.S. Revenue Cutter Service. *Report of the Cruise of the U.S. Revenue Cutter* Bear *and the Overland Expedition for the Relief of the Whalers in the Arctic Ocean, November 27, 1897 to September 13, 1898.* Washington, DC: GPO, 1899.

VanStone, James W. "Commercial Whaling in the Arctic." *Pacific Northwest Quarterly* 49 (January 1958): 1–10.

Veniaminov, Ivan. *Notes on the Islands of the Unalaska District.* Ed. Richard A. Pierce. Kingston: Limestone, 1984.

Vickery, Jim Dale. "Bob Marshall: A Hunger for Wilderness." *Sierra* (November-December 1985): 58–82.

———. *Wilderness Visionaries.* Merrillville, IN: ICS, 1986.

Walden, Arthur Treadwell. *A Dog-Puncher on the Yukon.* Boston: Houghton-Mifflin, 1928.

Webb, Melodie. *The Last Frontier: A History of the Yukon Basin of Canada and Alaska.* Albuquerque: University of New Mexico Press, 1985.

———. *Yukon Frontiers: Historic Resource Study of the Proposed Yukon-Charley National Rivers.* U.S. Dept. of the Interior, National Park Service, Cooperative Park Studies Unit. Occasional Paper No. 8. University of Alaska–Fairbanks, November 1977.

Webb, Robert Lloyd. *On the Northwest: Commercial Whaling in the Pacific Northwest, 1790–1967.* Vancouver: University of British Columbia Press, 1988.

Weddle, Ferris M. "Wilderness Champion: Olaus J. Murie." *Audubon* (July-August 1950): 224–233.

White, Sam O. "Sam White, Alaskan," Parts 3 (February 1965), 4 (March 1965), and 6 (June 1965). *Alaska Sportsman.*

White, Sam O., and Clarence J. Rhode. *Report on Alaska-Yukon Boundary Patrol, March 9–April 7, 1939.* Alaska Game Commission, 1939.

White, Stewart Edward. "An Emergency Is Declared to Exist." *Saturday Evening Post,* April 12, 1930, 5–6.

———. "Kidding Ourselves Along." *Saturday Evening Post,* December 14, 1929, 16–17.

Whitehead, John. "The Governor Who Opposed Statehood: The Legacy of Jay Hammond." In Stephen W. Haycox and Mary Childers Mangusso, eds., *An Alaskan Anthology,* 364–377. Seattle: University of Washington Press, 1996.

Who's Who in America, Vol. 20, 1937–1939. Chicago: A.N. Marquis, 1943.

Who Was Who in America, Vol. I, 1897–1942. Chicago: A.N. Marquis, 1943; *Vol. III.* Chicago: A.N. Marquis, 1960.

Wild, Peter. *Pioneer Conservationists of Western America.* Missoula: Mountain, 1980.

———. "Science and Sympathy: Olaus Murie and the Fight for Wildlife." Rept. in Peter Wild, *Pioneer Conservationists of Western America,* 113–129. Missoula: Mountain, 1980.

Wilkinson, Paul F. "Oomingmak: A Model for Man-Animal Relationships in Prehistory." *Current Anthropology* 13 (February 1972): 23–44.

Williams, Nigel. "Temperature Rise Could Squeeze Salmon." *Science* 280 (May 29, 1998): 1349.

Williams, Terrie M., James A. Estes, Daniel F. Doak, and Adam M. Springer. "Killer Appetites: Assessing the Role of Predators in Ecological Communities." *Ecology* 85, 12 (2004); 3373–3384.

Willoughby, Barrett. "Volcanoes Packed in Ice: An Explorer's Adventures in Alaska." *Saturday Evening Post,* August 23, 1930, 18–19.

Wilson, William H. *Railroad in the Clouds: The Alaska Railroad in the Age of Steam, 1914–1945.* Boulder: Pruett, 1977.

Wolfe, Linnie Marsh, ed. *John of the Mountains: The Unpublished Journals of John Muir.* Boston: Houghton-Mifflin, 1938.

———. *Son of the Wilderness: The Life of John Muir.* Madison: University of Wisconsin Press, 1945.

Wood, Ginny Hill. "From the Woodpile." *Northern Line* (February-March 1988): 11.

Worster, Donald. *Nature's Economy: The Roots of Ecology.* San Francisco: Sierra Club Books, 1977.

Wright, E.W., ed. *Lewis and Dryden's Marine History of the Pacific Northwest, Vol. 1.* Seattle: Superior, 1967.

Young, S. Hall. *Alaska Days With John Muir.* New York: Fleming Revell, 1915.

———. *Hall Young of Alaska.* New York: Fleming Revell, 1927.

Zimmerman, David R. "Land of the Big Brown Bear." *National Wildlife* 13 (June-July 1975): 40–47.

Index

Page numbers in italics indicate illustrations

Abler, 82
Academy of Natural Sciences, 130
Adak Island, 21–23, 309, 334
Adele, 34
Adirondack Park, 401, 407
Admiralty Island, 51; and brown bears, 124, 132, 186, 248, 267–268, 270–271, 278–280; and whaling, 69
Afognak, 155
Afognak Forest and Fish Culture Reserve, 111, 120, 355, 362, 364
Afognak Island, 21, 127; brown bears on, 272, 275, 279–280; and fur trade, 12; game translocations to, 334; and Katmai eruption, 158; reserve on, 111, 120
Agattu Island, 22, 306–308
Aghiapuk River, 246
Agricultural Experimental Station (USDA), 271
Agriculture, *110;* and Alaska Railroad 386; economic value of, 348; and Glacier Bay NM, 183–184, 187; potential for, 109–110, *110*
Aichilik River, 417
Aircraft: law enforcement by, 238, 242–245, 249, *251,* 256, 320, 344, *366;* predator control by, 274, 296–298, 308, 330, 345; sport hunting by, 205, 207, 242–244, 249–250; trapping by, 342
Akun Island, 21
Akutan, 21; and whaling, 69–73
Alaid Island, 308
Alaska Bird Sketches of Olaus Murie (Murie), 412
Alaska and its Resources (Dall), 37
Alaska Board of Fish and Game, 245
Alaska Central Railway, *384, 388*
Alaska Chamber of Commerce, 274
Alaska Commercial Company, 68; and fur trade, 155, 340, 351, 380,

434; and fur seals, 32–35, 39–40
Alaska Conservation Society, 257, 425
Alaska Dept. of Fish and Game, 253, *254;* and game transplants, 337; and Katmai NM, 171; and predator control, 274–276, 298–300, 313; and wildlife management, 237, 255, 439
Alaska Federation of Natives, 207
Alaska Fire Control Service, 105
Alaska Fisherman's Union, 367
Alaska Game Commission, 233, *239;* and brown bears, 267–278, 346; and eagle control, 311–313; and fox control, 309; and fur trade, 22; and Glacier Bay NM, 186; and Katmai NM, 169; and Kenai Moose Range, 389; and musk-oxen, 333; and 1925 Game Law, 237–250, 255, 258, 318, 428, 430, 432, 434; origins of, 233; and outdoor sporting community, 205–206, *247,* 258, 434; and salmon, 366; and sea lion control, 301; translocations by, 333–335, 337; and wolf control, 288–299, 313, 317, 319
Alaska Appeal (San Francisco), 79
Alaska Herald (San Francisco), 79
Alaska Highway, 148, 244
Alaska Indian Service, 22, 294
Alaska Maritime National Wildlife Refuge, 256
Alaska Miners Assn., 421
Alaska National Interest Lands Conservation Act (1980), 412; land designations, 150, 190, 280, 396, 407, 425–426, 429; and Glacier Bay NP, 190; and Mt. McKinley NP, 150; and Native claims, 360; and public opinion, 439; and wildlife refuges, 236, 280
Alaska Native Brotherhood, 343; Hoonah chapter, 268
Alaska Native Claims Settlement Act (1971), 190, 205, 253, 360, 425–426, 488n30
Alaska Organic Act (1884), 343
Alaska Packers Assn., *355,* 359, 367
Alaska Peninsula, 127; caribou on, 125, 293, 318–319; cattle and sheep on, 109, 265; exploration of, 140, 409; and fur trade, 13; Katmai eruption, 154–156; market hunting on, 214, 261–262, 318–319; salmon on, 364–368; sport hunting on, 214, 216–217, 264
Alaska Pioneers, Fairbanks Chap., 149
Alaska Pulp Co., 279
Alaska Railroad, 252; and Alaska Game Comm., 238; economics of, 106, 108, 386; meat hunting for, 218, 321, 388; and Mt. McKinley NP, 139–140, 143–144, 150; origins of, 384–385
Alaska Range: and Alaska Railroad, 385; exploration in, 137; mining in, 139, 142, 177; and Mt. McKinley NP, 140, 142–143
Alaska Sportsman, 288
Alaska Sportsmen's Association, 421
Alaska Sportsmen's Council, 395
Alaska Statehood Act (1958), 53, 421
Alaska Syndicate. *See* Morgan-Guggenheim Syndicate
Alaska Territorial Act (1912), 139, 367
Alaskan Bear Committee, 269
Alatna River, 409
Albatross, 130, 374
Albright, Horace M., 163, 290
Alcohol. *See* Liquor
Aleutian Canada goose, 306, 308
Aleutian Islands, 354; cattle and sheep on, 109, *309;* fox farming on, 305–306; fox control on, 308, *309;* and harbor seals, 89; Murie study in, 408; reindeer on, 324, 327, 328; reserves, 21, 26; and Russian fur trade, 8, 11–13, 16–30, 39, 305; and salmon, 373; and sea lions, 88; translocations to, *307,* 309; and whaling, 60, 66, 69–71, 74, 196
Aleutian Islands Reserve/ Wildlife Refuge, 21–23, 26, 409
Aleuts, 55, 203; conservation by, 195; and fox farming, 306; and fur trade, 8–17, 28, 32–33, 35, 40, 50–53, *54,* 57, 155, 192, 338, 433; and Katmai eruption, 154–155; and salmon, 357–359; and sea lion hunting, 85–86; and walrus hunting, 75; wartime evacuation of, 52; and whaling, 59
Allen, Joel A., 221
Allotment Act of 1887, 403
Amak Island, 354, 409
Amaknak Island, 323
Amalik Bay, 158

Amchitka Island, 6; fox removal, 308; imported species, 309; nuclear tests on, 23–24; sea otters on, *9*, 22–24, 195–196; and World War II, 22–23
American Bison Society, 122, 125, 127
American Committee for International Wildlife Protection, 125
American Creek, *99*
American Fisheries Society, 362
American Forestry, 388
American Forestry Assn., 183, 185
American Game Protective Assn., 122, 141, 224, 232
American Geographical Society, 183
American Museum of Natural History, 122, 125, 291–292
American Nature Assn., 185
American Ornithologists' Union, 122, 217, 220–221, 224
American Pacific Whaling Co., 69–70
American Pete, 154
American Rifleman, 311
American Society of Geologists, 183
American Society of Mammalogists: and Boone and Crockett Club, 122; and brown bears, 269; origins of, 232; and predator control, 124, 234, 286, 288–289
American Society of Taxidermists, 126
Amundsen, Roald, 137, 246, 414, *415*
Anaktuvuk Pass, 207, 251, *257*
Anchorage, 250; and Alaska Railroad, 385, 388; and Kenai oil, 391–395, 397
Anchorage Chamber of Commerce, 393, 420
Anchorage Daily News, 391
Anchorage Daily Times, 392–393
Anchorage Sportsmen's Assn., 394
Anderson, Clarence, 421
Anderson, Pete, 138–139
Andreanof Islands, 24
Andrew Simons Wilderness Unit, 396
Annabel, Russell, 249, 264, 292–294, 344
Annette Island, 359
Annette Island Fishery Reserve, 360,
Antarctica, whaling at, 71–73
Anthony, Harold, 291
Antimony, 147
Antiquities Act (1906), 183
Antissarlook, Charlie, 325
Applegate, Samuel, 20
Arctic Health Research Center, 421
Arctic Institute of North America, 418
Arctic National Wildlife Range/Refuge, *423;* caribou in, 413–417; exploration of, 413–414; geography of, 413, 414; management of, 424–426; and Muries, 410–412, 418, 420, 425–426; opposition to, 420–422; origins of, 400–401, 405–407, 418–422, *423,* 434; and Rhode, 252, 420; significance of, 211, *417,* 425, 429, 430, 437; wildlife species in, 415
Arctic Ocean. *See* Chukchi Sea
Arctic Village (Marshall), 401
Arctic Wild (Crisler), 291
Arnett, Ray, 475n47
Arnold, W.C., 395
Associated Mountaineering Clubs of North America, 183
Astoria, OR, 354, 367
Atka Island, 21–22, 305–306, 367
Atlantic Monthly, 112
Atlantic Richfield Co. (ARCO). *See* Richfield Oil Co.
Atomic Energy Commission, 23
Attu, 11, 21–23, 305
Atwood, Burton, 393, 395
Atwood, Robert, 392–393, 395–396, 475n47
Audubon, John James
Audubon, Lucy Bakewell, 117
Auke Bay Laboratory, 374
Aukley Spit, 304
Austria, 262

Baade, Dixie, 421
Bahr, Andrew, 331
Baidaras, 6
Baidarkas, 154, 156; for hunting, 9–10, *10,* 12, 17, 59
Bailey, Alfred M., 227, 231, 245; and brown bears, 266; and eagles, 310, and wolves, 285
Bailey, Vernon, *223*
Baillie Islands, 332
Baird, Spencer F., 35; collecting for Smithsonian, 39, 220, 225; and origin of U.S. Fish Comm., 220, 225
Baja California, 29, 74, 86
Balluta, Andrew, 197
Baked Mountain, *164*
Bales, L.L., 332
Ballinger, Richard, 381–383
Baranof Island: and brown bears, 279; and salmon, 363; translocations to, 321, 334, *336;* and whaling, 69
Baranov, Alexander, 12–14, 16, 155, 380
Barnes, Kathleen, 367–368
Barrill, Ed, 138

Barrow, 69, 80, 322, 325, 331, 418
Barter Island, 424
Bartlett Cove, 185, 188, 191
Bartlett, Sen. E.L. "Bob": and Arctic Refuge, 421–422; and Glacier Bay, 187; and Katmai NM, 170, 172; and Kenai oil, 392, 396
Bartonek, Jim, 256
Beach, Rex, 98, 185–186
Bean, Tarleton H., 356
Bear Creek (Kenai Pen.), 380
Bear (revenue cutter), *66;* and Eskimo starvation, 80; and reindeer introduction, 323, *324;* and whaler rescue, 68, 324
Beardslee, Capt. L.A., 457n4
Beardslee Islands, 185
Bears, black, 150, 191, 218; on Kenai Pen., *215,* 378, 389; poisoning of, 296, *297;* as predators, 299, 389; sport hunting of, *317*
Bears, brown/grizzly, *261,* 346, 408, 415; and Boone and Crockett Club, 124, 132, 264, 267; and Katmai eruption, 158–161; and Katmai NP, 169–171, 174, 191; on Kenai Pen., 215–216, *216,* 266, 378, 398; and logging, 248, 268, 279–280; market hunting of, 260–262, 264, 345; and Mt. McKinley NP, 139, 150, 290; Native hunting of, 197; predator control of, 272–276, 281, *299,* 330; protection of, 217–218, 223, 234–236, 248, 250, 255, 267, 270–271, 274, 276, 279–281, 346, 349, 431; reserves for, 234, 254, 270–271, 278–279; sport hunting of, *215,* 215–216, *216,* 219, 250, 262, 264, 274, 276–278, *278;* views of, 259, 264–270, 280–281, 313, 409–410, 430–431, 438. *See also* Admiralty Island
Bears, polar: in Arctic Refuge, 414; and Eskimos, 413; and global warming, 108; management of, 206–207, 253, 435; sport hunting of, 81, *81,* 94, 216–217, 250, *317*
Beaufort, Sir Frances, 413
Beavers, 175, 379; depletion of, 214, 398; illegal take of, 213, *240,* 344; protection of, 218, 237–238, 240, 282; trapping of, 16, *18,* 338–340, *345*
Been, Frank, 291
Bell, Frank T., 363
Belvedere, 68
Bennett, Hugh, 386
Benson, Jack, *239*
Bering, Capt. Vitus, 4–8
Bering Island, 5–8, 27–28, 441n8
Bering River coalfields, 381, 385, 399
Bering Sea, 156, 252, 253, 256; commercial fishing in, 53; explorations in, 94, 130; and fur sealing, 27, 40–42; and reindeer, 327; salmon in, 351, 372–374; seals in, 89; walrus hunting in, 75–84; whaling in, 59–60, 63–65, 71–74
Bering Sea Patrol, 42
Bering Sea Tribunal, 42, 44, 49
Bering Strait: caribou predation at, 293; fur trade at, 338; Harriman Expedition at, 113; walrus hunting in, 80–83, 448n74; and Western Union project, 36; whaling in, 67
Berlin, 353–354
Bernard, Joseph, 82
Berners Bay, 334
Bertholf, Lt. Ellsworth, 69, 324–325
Bethel, 256
Big Koniuji Island, 306
Big Softuk Bar, 304
Biorka, 22
Birds: and conservation leaders, 117, 125, 127–128, 220–221, 223–225, 228–229, 233–234, 256–257; market hunting of, 13, 232, *232;* in parks and refuges, 150, 174, 187, 191, 414; predation of, 293–294, 306–309; predator control of, 304, 310–313; protection of, 218, 221, 223–224, 228–229, 233–237, 256–257, 307–308, 414, 422; refuges for, 228–229, 233–234, 422; sport hunting of, 233–236, 244, 250, 293–294, 311–312; waterfowl, 207, 218, 256–257, 293–294, 422
Birds of Alaska (Gabrielson), 234
Bishop, Bob, 395
Blaine, James G. (Sec. of State), 41
Black Fox Creek, 411
Black Hills expedition, 118
Blackstone Bay, *182*
Board of Geographic Names, 404
Bob Marshall Wilderness, 404
Boca de Quadra Bay, 363
Boddy, A.W. "Bud," 395, 421
Bodega Bay, 14
Bodfish, Capt. Hartson, 332
Bogoslof Island, 442n2
Bonanza, 414
Bonanza Creek, 98
Bonanza Mine, 108
Bone, Gov. Scott, 284
Bonner, Rep. Herbert, 392
Boone and Crockett Club, 48, 252, 401, 407; and brown bears, 264,

267, 280; and Bureau of Biological Survey, 212, 229, 234; and Katmai NM, 168; and Mt. McKinley NP, 135, 139–143, 150, 234; and 1925 Game Law, 232–233; origins of, 116–117, 119–120; political activism of, 116–117, 120–127, 130–134, 210, 217, 221, 224, 229, 236, 264, 428, 434, 437; and wolf control, 289–291
Boston, 15
Botanical Society of America, 183
Bounties. *See* Predator control
Bowers, George, 49
Brady Glacier, 93
Brady, Gov. John G., 357
Branch of Predator and Rodent Control, 294–300
Brandeis, Louis, 383
Bristol Bay, 253; and fur trade, 374; and Katmai eruption, 154–155; research in, 374, salmon in, 304, 364, 368, 372–374; walruses in, 83, *85;* whaling in, 60
British Columbia, 31, 155; and salmon, 352, 376; and Western Union project, 36; and whaling, 71, 74
Broad Pass, 137, 293
Brooks, Alfred H., 104–105, 137, 183, 265
Brooks Camp, 173
Brooks, James W. "Jim," 83, 253–255
Brooks Lake, 171, 374
Brooks Range, 156, 413; and Arctic Refuge, 252, 414, 415, 418; Bob Marshall in, 401, 404–405; caribou in, 416–417; Muries in, 411; muskoxen in, 332; name origin, 265; Nunamiut hunting in, 199, 252; predator control in, 297; reindeer trek in, 331
Brooks River, 171, *174*
Brower, Charles: and muskoxen, 331, 470n47; and whaling, 65, 68–69, 325
Brown, William E., 147
Browne, Belmore, 138, *139;* and Mt. McKinley NP, 140–142, 290–291, 454n12; and 1925 Game Law, 230; and predator control, 290–291
Browne Tower, 150
Buckley, John L., 255, 347
Buffalo Shirt Mountain, 198
Buffalo, plains, 331; and conservation, 2, 56, 118, 120, 127, 230, 266, 357; sport hunting of, 335; translocation of, 334, *337*
Buffalo, wood, 198, 335–336
Bull Moose Party, 383
Burch, Lucius, 311–312
Bureau of Biological Survey (BBS), *223, 226;* activities of, 231, 233–236; and Boone and Crockett Club, 122, 140, 212, 236; establishment of refuges, 224, 233–234; and fox farming, 21; and fur trade, 340; and game waste, 218, 318–319; and Glacier Bay NM, 186; jurisdiction of, 52, 212, 222, 237, 272; and Kenai Moose Range, 389; and migratory birds, 212, 233–236; and Mt. McKinley NP, 140, 150; and muskoxen, 333; and 1925 Game Law, 229–233, 237, 258, 430, 437; Olaus Murie in, 408–409; origins of, 210, 220–221; political initiatives by, 221–222; and predator control, 222, 233–234, 236, 266, 270, 281, 283–284, 285–288, 313, 409, 430; and reindeer, 326, 329–330; and scientific explorations, 22, 131–132, 432; and sea otters, 22; and wildlife translocations, 334–336; and wildlife values, 211, 347
Bureau of Education (USDOI), 326, 327
Bureau of Commercial Fisheries, 302, 308, 367, 371
Bureau of Fisheries, 308; and Aleuts, 51; jurisdiction of, 217, 340; and salmon, 357, 362–367, 374
Bureau of Forestry, 219
Bureau of Indian Affairs, 83, 359
Bureau of Land Management: and Arctic Refuge, 422; cattle leasing by, 274; and Kenai oil, 392, 396; and Mt. McKinley NP, 147; and reindeer, 329; and sheep ranching, 309
Bureau of Sport Fisheries and Wildlife, 426. *See also* U.S. Fish and Wildlife Service
Burkholder, Bob, 297, 467n54
Burnham, John B., 141–142, 224, 232
Burroughs, John, *114,* 221
Buske, Frank, 94

C.S. White, 44
Cahalane, Victor, *173*
California, 17, 25, *223;* and Alaska coal, 380; and fur trade, 14, 21, 27–29; Muir in, 92–93, 111–114; and salmon, 351, 357, 376; sea lions in, 86; and whaling, 65, 68, 71–73. *See also* San Francisco
Call, Samuel J., 69, 324–325
Callbreath, John C., 362
Camden Bay, 390, 332, 413, 416, 486

Camp Fire Club of America, 428; and Boone and Crockett Club, 122; and fur seals, 49; and Mt. McKinley NP, 140–141, 224, 288–291; and 1925 Game Law 230, 232; and wolf control, 288–291
Campbell, John M, 191, 425
Canada: and Arctic Refuge, 418, 420, 422, 426; and border dispute, 180–181; Bureau of Biological Survey in, 221; and fur seal treaty, 21, 48–49, 52, 56; and fur trade, 21, 33–34, 40–46, 77, 338, 344; and Gold Rush, 97–98, 104, 110; and law enforcement, 241–242, 249; and muskoxen, 331–334; and reindeer, 330–331; and salmon, 253, 373; and timber industry, 106; and Western Union expedition, 36; whaling by, 69, 71–74; and wood buffaloes, 336; in World War II, 22. *See also* British Columbia
Cane, Col. Claude, 353, 387; sport hunting by, 214–215, 262, *387*
Cannikin, Project, 24
Canton, 31
Canuanar, 68
Cape Belcher, 67
Cape Lisburne, *255*
Cape Newenham, 256
Cape Prince of Wales, 5; and reindeer, 322, 324; and walrus hunting, 77–79; and whaling, *66*
Cape Smyth, 68
Cape Spencer, 155
Cape Vancouver, 68, 225, 324
Capps, Stephen R., 143, 148, 153
Carib, 75
Caribou: in Arctic Refuge, 413–417; and forest fires, 107, 288, 386; and global warming, 107; Grant's, 125, 319; and Katmai NM/NP, 160; on Kenai Pen., 214–216, 319, 334, 378, 386–387, 397–399, 474n28; Kobuk-Noatak herd, 319; market hunting of, 100–101, 214–215, 230, 232, *232,* 318–319, 386–387; and Mt. McKinley NP, 139, 150, 289, 290; Native hunting of, 192, 199, 202, *206,* 214, 318, 322; Nelchina herd, 294, 298–299, 319; population trends, 318–320; protection of, 218, 282, 292–299, 313, 317, 349; and reindeer, 285–286, 327, 329–330; sport hunting of, 215–217, *215, 217, 317,* 387; translocations of, 309, 334, 337; in whaling era, 192, 318, 322, 413; Yukon-Tanana herd, 319
Carlson, Carlos, 169
Carlson, Hjalmar "Slim," 289
Carlyle Island, 307
Carnegie Museum of Natural History, 408
Carroll, Capt. James, 177
Carter, Pres. Jimmy, 175, 412
Castle Rock, 28
Castoreum, 340
Catherine the Great, 11
Catlin, George, 116
Caton Island, 468n96
Cats, 308
Cattle, 109; and brown bears, 265–266, 268, 271–276, 281; feral, 306, 468n96; and Glacier Bay NM, 187; and wolves, 283
Century magazine, 111
Chain saws, 342
Champion, 67
Chandalar Lake, 332
Chandalar Reservation, 342
Chandalar River, 332, 416
Chandler Lake, 297
Charlie, 414
Chase, Will, 278
Chatanika, 101
Chatanika River, 105
Chaudiere, Capt. Narcisse, 60
Chernabura Island, 468n96
Chicago Academy of Science, 36
Chicago Audubon Society, 36
Chichagof Island, 176; and brown bears, 186, 269–271, 279; game translocations to, 344
Chickaloon River, 292
Chickamin River, 238, 334
Chignik, 368
Chile, 376
Chilkat Oil Co., 391
Chilkat Pass, 98
Chilkoot Pass, 98
China: and fur trade, 8, 14–15, 28–31; and ivory trade, 76; and sea lions, 86
Chinese workers, 361
Chirikov, Alexei, 5
Chisholm, Red, 165
Chitina, 334, 381, 385
Chitina River, *102,* 310
Christian River, 332
Chugach National Forest, 395; withdrawal by Roosevelt, 219, 383, 429, 434
Chugach Range, 114
Chukchi Sea, *305,* and polar bear research, 255; walrus hunting in, 80, 82, *82;* whaling in, 59, 63–65
Chukotka Natives, 78–79
Church, Donovan B., 162–163
Circle City, 99–100, 104, 326
Cisney, Doyle, 467n54
Cities Service Co., 391
Citizens Committee on Natural Resources, 421

City of Topeka, 179, *179*
Civil War, 67
Clarence Rhode National Wildlife Range, 252, 256–257
Clark, Gov. Walter, 22, 266
Clark, James R., 290
Clear River, 404
Clergy, Russian Orthodox, and Alaska Natives, 11
Cleveland, Pres. Grover, 41, 112
Clinton, Pres. Bill, 412
Coal, 108, 380; and Alaska Railroad, 108, 384–386; leasing controversy, 381–384, 433–434, 436
Cohen, Michael P., 95
Colby, William, 113–114
Cold War, 187, 244
College, *333, 337*
Collier's Weekly, 382
Collins, George L., 418, 425
Collins, Grenold, 239, 242, 249
Colville River, 332
Columbia River, 357
Colvin, Verplanck, 402
Commander (Kommandorski) Islands: and fur trade, 8, 18, 28–31, 32, 44, 51, 305; and sea cow, 441n8. *See also* Bering Island; Copper Island
Committee on Refuges, 123
Conservation: Alaskan opposition to, 230; and coal leasing, 446–447, 429; origins of, 116–117, 120–122, 220–221; by Russians, 1, 17, 31–32, 428, 430–431, 433; of salmon, 364–365; of sea lions 87–88; values, 428–440; of walruses 84; of whales, 72–74. *See also* Environmental organizations; Values, environmental
Conservation, utilitarian, xvii, 2–3, 26, 133, 429–430, 514–515; by Athabaskans, 204; and Boone and Crockett Club, 119, 133; and forests, 112, 402; and fur seals, 50; and 1925 Game Law, 233, 258; and pinnipeds, 89; and sea otters, 26; and wildlife management, 211, 247, 258, 346, 429–430
Conservation Foundation, 418
Constitutional Convention (Alaska), 245
Controller Bay, 5
Cook, Capt. James, 5, 14, 29, 379
Cook, Frederick A., 137–138
Cook Inlet, 13; and explorations, 125, 136, 379; gold at, 380; oil at, 256, 390, 398; and salmon, 364, 368; whaling at, 71; and wolves, 386
Coolidge, Pres. Calvin, 121, 183
Coon, George, 386
Cooper, James Fenimore, 402
Cooper, William S., *182*; and Glacier Bay, 181–185, 191, 437
Copper, 59, 108, 371, 380
Copper Island, 8, 27–28
Copper River, 98, 105; game translocations to, 335; and railroads, 108, 385; salmon predation by seals and sea lions, 303–304
Copper River Co-op Cannery, 457n79
Copper River and Northwestern Railway, 108, 381, 385
Cordova, 244, 279, 390; market hunting at, 388; and mining, 108, 381
Cordova District Fisheries Union, 457n79
Cordova Fish and Cold Storage, 457n79
Cordova Seal Committee, 304
Cormorant, spectacled, 6, 441n8
Corwin, 18, 34, 79, 94–95, 130
Coulter, Jack, *99*
Council on National Parks, Forests and Wild Life, 183
Cowles, Henry Chandler, 181
Coyotes, 191, 378, 409, 465n11; control of, 238, 241, 251, 283–285, 288–289, 292, 294, 296–299, 314, 330, 409; as predators, 222, 289, 294, 321; protection of, 344, 412; study of, 408, 410; trapping of, *345*
Craig, 244, *354*
Crimean War, 31, 60
Cripple Creek, 101, *103*
Crisler, Lois and Herb, 291, 417
Crown Zellerbach Corp., 270
Cuddy, Dan, 395
Cunningham, Clarence, 381–383
Curtis, Garniss H., 172
Custer, Gen. George Armstrong, 118
Cygnet, 34

Dall, William H., *38*, 131, 222; career of, 36–37; in Lituya Bay, 180; and salmon, 356
Dan Creek, *102*
Dark Island, 307
Darling, F. Fraser: and Arctic Refuge, 418; and wolf predation, 288, 313, 319–320, 348
Darling, J.N. "Ding," 234
Davidson Mountains, 411, 414
Dawson (YT), 104, 110
Dayvidov, G.I., 12
DeArmond, Robert, 375
Death Valley expedition, 222–223, *223*, 227

Deer Mountain, 363
Deer, Sitka black-tailed: commercial hunting of, 213, 217, 231, 359; harvest of, *319;* and logging, 322; population trends, 322; and predator control, 284, 294, 298, 317; protection of, 237, 282, 317; translocations of, 334, *335*
Delarof Island, 24
Delta Junction, 334
Demaray, Arthur, 289
Denali, 136. *See also* Mt. McKinley; Mt. McKinley NP
Denali Highway, 149
Denali National Park and Preserve, 149. *See also* Mt. McKinley; Mt. McKinley NP; Sheldon, Charles
Densmore, Frank, 137
Denver Museum of Natural History, 227
Dept. of the Interior, Canada, 330
Depression. *See* Great Depression
Dezhnev, Semyon, 4–5
Dice, Lee R., 341–342
Dickey, William A., 137
Dillingham, 240, 244, 264
Dillingham, Sen. William R., 264
Dimond, Delegate Anthony, 244, 272, 278, 288
Diomede Islands, 39, 254
Disney, Walt, 56, 291
Distant Early Warning (DEW), 424
Div. of Economic Ornithology and Mammalogy, 220, 222, 283
Dixon, Sen. Joseph M., 49
Dixon, Joseph S., 147, 270
Dogs, feral, 300, 308
Dolan, Jim, *312*
Dolly Varden char: bounty on, 285, *299,* 301; salmon predation by, 300–301, 363
Dora, 158
Douglas, 104, 231
Douglas (Kaguyak), 155
Douglas, Justice William O., and Mercedes, 419
Dry Bay, 185
Ducks Unlimited, 294
Dufresne, Frank, *390,* 412; and Alaska Game Comm., *239, 242, 245–248, 258;* and brown bears, 248, 269, 279–280; and buffaloes, 334–335; and eagles, 312; and wolves, 292
Dundas Bay, 185
Dutch Harbor, 22
Dyea, 97, 295

Eagle, 36, *99,* 409, 414
Eagles, bald, 256, 398; bounty on, 284, *299,* 310–313; as predators, 300, 310, 343; protection of, 313
Eagles, golden, 415; bounty on, 284; predation by, 310–311, 313; and sheep, 290
East, Ben, 52
East Cape, 67
Ecological Society of America, 182–183, 289
Ecology, science of: origins of, 221–222, 286; and predator control, 283, 287, 289–292, 315; and wildlife management, 286–287, 432, 439
Edgartown, MA, 67
Edrie, 180
Edwards River, 304
Egan, Gov. William, 313, 421
Eisenhower, Pres. Dwight D., 187, 369, 391, 399
El Nino, 376
Elbe, 60
Eldridge, George, 137
Elk, 334, 337, 408, 410
Elkins, Steven B., 40
Elks Club, Anchorage, 392
Elliott, Henry W., *37,* 196, 202; environmental activism of, *47,* 90, 115, 435; and fur seals, 35–36, 39, 41–42, 45–50, 55–56, 130, 222, 430; and killer whales, 283; and 1925 Game Law, 230
Emerson, Ralph Waldo, 92, 205
Endangered Species Act (1973), 88
Endicott Mountains, 332
English Bay, 380
Environmental organizations: and Alaska conservation, 2, 74, 153, 281, 425, 439; and Arctic Refuge, 418–419, 421, 425–426; and Katmai NM, 185; and Kenai Moose Range, 393; and logging, 106; and predator control, 289, 291. *See also* Nature groups
Ernest Gruening State Historical Park, 257
Esais, *139*
Eskimos, *194, 195;* defined, 459n17; and fur trade, 77, 338, 340; and polar bears, 413; and reindeer, *293,* 294, 322–331; and walrus hunting, 77–85, *193,* 255; and whaling, 59, 65, *66,* 69, 72
Eskimos, Bernik, 200
Eskimos, Canadian, 69, 330, 331, 459n17
Eskimos, Chugach Alutiiq, 88, 380, 459n17; and Russian fur trade, 13, 17, 192
Eskimos, Inuit, 200, 331, 459n17
Eskimos, Inupiat, *194,* 199, *206,* 253, *257,* 459n17
Eskimos, Koniag (Kodiak) Alutiiq, 459n17; and brown bears, 276; and

Russian fur trade, 9, *10,* 14, 16, 192, 338, 433; whaling by, 59
Eskimos, Nunamiut, 199–200, 207, *257,* 459n17
Eskimos, Siberian, 69, 74, 84, 459n17
Eskimos, Tagmiugmiut, 413
Eskimos, Yup'ik, 200, 364, 459n17; waterfowl hunting, 207, 218
Esquimault, BC, 31, 41
Etolin Island, 362
Europe, 177, 331; and fur trade, 29–31, 88, 188, 261, 338, 340, 344; and whaling, 72
Everglades NP, 123
Excursion Inlet, 185
Explorers Club, 183
The Extermination of the American Bison (Hornaday), 127
Exxon Valdez, 25, 439
Eyak Lake, 279
Eyerdam, Walter, 21

Fairbanks, 138, 326; and Alaska Railroad, 108, 384–385; and Arctic Refuge, 419, 425; and Game Comm., *239,* 242, 244, 255–256; and gold mining, 101–103, 217; meat hunting for, 141, 143, 217, 229–230, 231–232, *232;* Muries in, 408, 411, 419; and trapping, 342, 408; wood consumption by, 106
Fairbanks Chamber of Commerce, 419
Fairbanks Daily News-Miner, 288, 393, 419
Fairbanks Exploration Co., 101–102, *103*
Fairbanks Garden Club, 419
Fairweather coast, 179
Fairwell, 335
Falkland Islands, 29
Farallon Islands, 14, 29
Farley, John, 392
Favorite, 43
Field and Stream, 247, 279, 291
Fienup-Riordan, Ann, 200
Fires. *See* Forests, fires in
Fisher, Albert K., *223*
Fisheries Research Institute, 379
Fishers, 344
Fishing, commercial, 347; and conservation, 364; environmental impacts of, 213; and fur seals, 53, 57; in Glacier Bay NM, 190; and harbor seals, 88–90, 301–302; and Katmai NM, 169; and salmon predation, 300–304; and sea lions, 25, 87–90, 301–302; and sea otters, 25; value of, *348;* and walruses, 85. *See also* Salmon
Fishing, sport, 169, 171, 245, *247*
Fitzhugh, William, 227
Flakne, Joe, 418
Flaxman Island, 413
Fleck, Richard, 96
Folsom, Lucius G., 160, 162
Ford, Corey, *247,* 248, 279
Forest and Stream, 118–119, 123, 221, 224, 362
Forest Reserves Act, 111, 120, 183
Forestry Commission, 112
Forests: fires in, 104–107, 201, 288, 319–320, 386; and global warming, 107–108; and gold mining, 1, 104–107; protection of, 115, 120, 434; timber industry, 106
Fort Alexandrovsk, 379
Fort Ross (Russian Colony), 14
Fort Yukon, 36, 209, 338, 414
Foster, John W. (Sec. of State), 41
Fouke Fur Co., 51, 55
Fox farming: and Alaska Natives, 343; coastal, 21, 305–307, 342–343; and eagles, 310–311, 343; and fur seals, 51; in Glacier Bay NM, 86–87; and sea lions, 87
Fox Islands, 66, 305
Foxes, 379, 415; bird predation by, 51, 306, *307, 309;* control of, 308–310, 314, 330; and forest fires, 106, 340; illegal take of, 240, 284; introduction of, 21, 305, 322, 342, 432; protection of, 240; trapping of, 8, 13, *18,* 22, 27, 199, 308, 330, 338–340, 345, *345. See also* Fox farming
France/French: exploration by, 14–15, 179–180; and sea otter trade, 15, 17; whaling by, 60
Franklin, Sir John, 31, 413
Fraser River, 36
Frederick, Karl, 312
Fredericksen, Stanley, 252
Friedman, Ralph, 291
Frontier myths, 109, 119, 371, 436, 438
Funny River, *390*
Funter Bay, 52, *352*
Fur Seal Act (1910), 21, 26, 51
Fur Seal Advisory Board, 49, 130, 222
Fur Seal Convention (1957), 53
Fur Seal Service, 32
Fur Seal Treaty (1911). *See* North Pacific Sealing Convention
Fur trade, 1, *20, 29;* American, 14–17, 29–44, 49–53, *54,* 56–57, 69, 217, 305–308, 310, 340–344; British, 13–16, 29, 31, 340; French, 15, 17; Russian, 4, 7–17, *18,* 21,

27–33, *40,* 305, 338–340. *See also* Europe; Furbearers; Trapping
Furbearers (terrestrial): and forest fires, 106, 340; jurisdiction over, 217–218, 231, 340; in Mt. McKinley NP, 150; poaching of, 213–214, 284; protection of, 218, 240–242, 282; trade in, *18,* 338–342, *345. See also mammals by species*

Gabrielson, Ira N., *235;* background, 234; beliefs, 234–236; and brown bears, 234, 273–274; conservation work, 234–236, 252; creation of refuges, 211, 273, 389–390, 437; and moose, 389, 393–394; and salmon, 370; and wolf control, 293–294
Galapagos Islands, 29
Gambell, 83–84
Game law of 1902, 214, 224, 265, 317; and Boone and Crockett Club, 121, 125, 127, 264; provisions of, 217–218, 231, 238, 260, 264, 387
Game law of 1908, 224, 265, 267, 317; and Kenai game, 388; and Mt. McKinley NP, 139, 150; provisions of, 218, 229, 231, 238, 264
Game Law of 1925, 236, 399; and Boone and Crockett Club, 121, 131–132, 134; enforcement of, 237–245, 248–252, 389; origins of, 128, 224, *228,* 229–232, 267, 317; provisions of, 233, 237–238, 276, 282, 337, 346. *See also* Alaska Game Commission
Game preservation committee (Boone and Crockett), 124, 130–132; and fur seals, 130; and Mt. McKinley NP, 139, 141; and 1925 Game Law, 229
Gange, 60
Gardner, "Dod," *99*
Gardner, Thomas, 268
Gareloi Island, *307*
Garfield, James (Sec. of Interior), 382
Garland, A.H. (Atty. Gen.), 40
Gas, natural, 398
Gates of the Arctic National Park, 407
Gay, Charlie, *99*
Geist, Otto, 412
General Land Office, 184, 271, 381–382
Geographic Harbor, *168,* 170
George W. Elder, 179
Germany, 72, 262, 406
Gibson, Tom and Elmer, 217
Gideon, Hieromonk, 16
Gilbert, Grove Carl, 181
Gilbert Inlet, 180
Gill, Harold, 353–354
Gilley, Capt. George, 77
Gjoa, 414, *415*
Glacier Bay, 176, 457n4; commercial fishing in, 190; exploration of, 176–182, *182;* Muir at, 93–94, 177; seal hunting in, 188; tourism at, 177, 179
Glacier Bay–Kluane-Tatshenshini-Wrangell/St. Elias World Heritage Site, 191
Glacier Bay National Monument/Park, *184,* 219, 222, 433, 437; and Boone and Crockett Club, 121, 123; and brown bears, 270, 278–279, 281; glaciology in, 177, 181–182; and John Muir, 114; management of, 185–191; minerals in, 185–186; Native claims in, 97, 188–190, 192; and nonconsumptive values, 190, 430, 437; origins of, 114, 176, *182,* 182–183, 316, 434; seal hunting in, 188–190; tourism in, 190–191; wildlife species in, 191. *See also* Glacier Bay; Muir, John
Glacier National Park, 121
Glaser, Frank, *239;* and wolf control, 285, 292, 294, 297–298, 467n54
Glavis, Louis, 382–383
Glazunov, Andrei, 136
Glenn, Capt. Edwin F., 137
Global warming, 25–26, 54, 107–108; and Arctic Refuge, 426; and caribou, 107, 323; and forests, 107; and moose, 320; and pinnipeds, 25, 54, 57, 85, 89–90; and salmon, 376, and whales, 75
Goats, mountain, 96–97, 191; eagle predation of, 310; on Kenai Pen., 388, 398; population trends, 321; protection of, 218, 282; sport hunting of, *219, 317;* translocation of, 334, *335, 336*
Goff, Charles, 35, 41
Gold. *See* Gold Rushes; Mining, gold
Gold Rushes: and Alaska Railroad, 384–386; environmental impacts of, 1, 80, 103–107, 210, 213, 262, 284–289, 318–320, 429; and John Muir, 97–98, 110, 435; at Juneau, 210, 213; on Kenai Pen., 380; Klondike, 97–98, 104–107, 137, 213, 380; market hunting for, 213, 217, 318–319; and reindeer, 323–326; and trapping, 340
Golikov, Ivan, 11–12

Golovnin Bay, 71
Grand Canyon, 113
Grant, Madison, *124;* background, 122–123; beliefs, 123–126, 453n27; and Boone and Crockett Club, 122–127, 130, 132–133, 140; and brown bears, 267, 269, 278, 431; interest in Alaska, 124–125, 436–437; and Mt. McKinley NP, 140
Great Britain: and Crimean War, 31; and fur trade, 11, 15–18, 21, 35, 262, 340; and oil, 391; and sealing dispute, 21, 41–42, 45–46, 49, 56; and whaling, 72. *See also* Hudson's Bay Co.; London
Great Depression, 109; and bounties, 285; and fur trade, 306, 343; and hunting, 317; and ivory carving, 83; and Mt. McKinley NP, 148, 153; and salmon, 375; and whaling, 71
Greeley, William B., 232
Green Willow Creek, 417
Greenland, 331–333
Gregory, Homer F., 367–368
Griggs, Laura, *164*
Griggs, Robert F.: and aircraft hunting, 250; and Glacier Bay NM, 183; and Katmai eruption, 160–163, *164;* and Katmai NM, 168–169, 172, 175, 437
Grinnell, George Bird, *122;* background, 117–118; beliefs, 118, 121, 194; and Boone and Crockett Club, 117–123, 131–132; and brown bears, 267; interest in Alaska, 437; and Mt. McKinley NP, 142; political activism of, 115, 119–123, 142, 221, 224, 236; and salmon, 357, 362
Grinnell, Joseph, 270, 286
Grosvenor Camp, 172
Grosvenor, Gilbert, 163
Gruening, Sen. Ernest, 255; and Arctic Refuge, 421–422; and federal control, 219–220, 321, 371; and Katmai NM, 174; and Kenai oil, 392, 395–396; and predator control, 290; and reindeer, 329; and salmon, 371
Guadalupe Island, 29
Guatemala, 227
Gubser, Harlan P., 285
Guides, hunting/fishing: and brown bears, 274; and conservation, 430; economic value of, 268, 276; influence of, 434; licensing of, 233
Gulf of Alaska: fox farming in, 305; and Katmai eruption, 155; and salmon, 376; sea lions in, 88; whaling in, 58, 60, 73–74
Gulls, 300, 304
Gustavus, 184–187, 270
Gutermuth, Clinton "Pink," 252, 422
Gvosdev, Mikhail, 5

Hadwen, Seymour, 245, 326
Hahn, Walter L., 308
Haines, 326
Haines Chamber of Commerce, 183
Hakala, John, 255
Halibut, 301
Hallock, Charles, 118
Hames, Raymond, 202, 205, 207
Hamlin, Charles, 19–20
Hammond, Jay, 298, 467n54
Hammond River, 404
Harding, Pres. Warren G., 183, 364, 385–386
Hares, Arctic, 175, 415
Harper, Walter, 138, *139*
Harriman, Edward R., 113
Harriman Alaska Expedition, 113, 121, 222, 357, 437; and Glacier Bay NM, 179, 181
Harriman Foundation, 223
Harris, Buck, 467n54
Harrison, Pres. Benjamin, 41–42, 111, 121
Hasselborg, Al, 269
Hawaiian Islands, 17, 351
Hay, John (Sec. of State), 48
Hayden Yellowstone Expeditions, 39, 220
Healy, 108
Healy, Capt. Michael, 18, 79–80
Hearst newspapers, 186
Heintzleman, Gov. B.F., 279, 418
Helm Bay, *356*
Henley, Dave, 274
Henry, Joseph, 35
Herendeen Bay, 216
Herring, Fred, 267
Herron, Lt. Joseph, 137
Herschel Island, *415;* whalers at, 66, 318, 332, 413
Hetch Hetchy Valley, 114
Hesse, William A., 158, *159,* 162
Hibbard Stewart Co., 80
Hickel, Walter, 395
Hidden Basin, *336*
Hinchinbrook Island, 379
Hitchcock, Sen. Gilbert, 50
H.M.S. Discovery, 177
Holbrook, Don, *174*
Hollingstad, Capt. Casper, 301
Holzworth, John M., 268–269, 278, 281, 431
Homer, 380, 387
Hoonah, 188, 279
Hooper, Capt. C.L., 19
Hoover, Pres. Herbert, 169, 175, 333, 409; and salmon fisheries, 364
Hope, 380, 386, 388
Hornaday, William T., *129;* background, 126–127; be-

liefs, 127–129; and brown bears, 268, 281, 431; and fur seals, 46–50, 56, 130, 430; and 1925 Game Law, 230, 232; political activism of, 127–130, 221, 437; and predator control, 284
Horner, Mel A., 159, 162
Hosley, Neil, 255
Hubbard, Fr. Bernard, 165–166, *167*
Hubbard, John V., 181
Hudson Bay, 408
Hudson's Bay Co., 31, 36, 413; and fur trade, 15–16, 77, 209, 212, 338
Hunter, Celia M., 421, *423,* 425
Hunting and Fishing in Alaska (Annabel), 292
Hunting, commercial, 123–125, 127, 147, 213–214, 316–317; of brown bears, 260–262, 264; of eagles, 312–313; on Kenai Pen., 214, 386–388; and Mt. McKinley NP, 139, 141–143, *146,* 288, 321; by Natives, 100–101, 192, 202–203, 213–214, 218, 387–388; opposition to, 119, 123–125, 127–128, 210, 217–218, 237–238, 317; and wolf control, 284. *See also* Otters, sea; Sea lions; Seals, fur; Seals, harbor; Walrus; Whaling
Hunting, sport: by aircraft, 249–250; on Alaska Pen., 214, 216; and Alaska economy, 232, 268, 274; of brown bears, *216,* 276–278, *278,* 280; and conservation legislation, 117, 233, 430, 433; of eagles, 312–318; harvests, *215, 219, 317;* on Kenai Pen., 214–217, 233, 261, 387; of mountain goats, 321; of muskoxen, 333; philosophy of, 118–119, 128, 132–133, 452n4, 452n8; political influence of, 120–122, 206, 245, 258, 434; and predator control, 313; regulation of, 217–218, 237–238, 243–245, 249, 276, 317; in Southeast, 214; and translocations, 322; of walruses, 82, *82,* 84. *See also* Guides
Hunting Trips of the Ranchman (Roosevelt), 120
Hutchinson and Kohl, 32, 155

Ibach, Joe and Muz, 185–186
Ickes, Harold (Sec. of Interior), 186, 278, 342
Icy Cape, 5, 67, 199
Idaho, 177–179
Iliamna, 12, 261
Iliamna Lake, 168, 261
Imler, Ralph, 301–303
Indian River, 214
Indians, Algonquin, 194
Indians, Athabaskan, 413; brown bear hunting by, 260; conservation by, 194–195, 197–198, 204, 207, 431–432; and fur trade, 338; and salmon, *360,* 364; use of copper, 380; use of fire, 201; and wood buffaloes, 336
Indians, Black River Kutchin, 198
Indians, Chandalar Kutchin, 332, 342
Indians, Chipewyan, 198
Indians, Dena'ina, 197
Indians, Gwitch'in (Kutchin), 207, 338, 413, 488n30
Indians, Haida, 15, 196, 360
Indians, Kenaitze, 13, 192
Indians, Koyukon, 197–198, 200, 207, 338
Indians, Makah, 34, 74
Indians, Metlakatla, 359
Indians, Taku, 358
Indians, Tanaina, 16, 146, 338, 380
Indians, Tlingit: conservation by, 196–197, 207; and fishing rights, 357–360; and fur seals, 51; and Glacier Bay NM, 177–180, 188–190, 192; and harbor seals, 88; and Muir, 93–94, 96–97, 177, 203; and Russian fur trade, 10–11, 13–17, 19, 192; in salmon industry, *361,* 362, 375
Indians, Tsimshian, 196
Influenza epidemic of 1918, 326
Inside Passage, 93
Innoko-Iditarod district, 385
Innoko National Wildlife Refuge, 257
Institute of Northern Agricultural Research, 334
Institute of Pacific Relations, 367
International Agreement for the Regulation of Whaling (1949), 73
International North Pacific Anadromous Fisheries Commission, 374
International Whaling Commission, 73–74
International Whaling Convention (1931), 72
Inuit, 459n17
Iron, 380
Isaac Walton League: Anchorage chap., 466n46; and Arctic Refuge, 418, 421; Cordova chap., 466n46; and Glacier Bay NM, 185; and Kenai oil, 383; Petersburg chap., 466n46
Island Between (Murie), 412
Ivishak River, 252
Ivvavik National Park, 426
Izembek National Wildlife Range, 252, 422

Jackson Hole, WY, 408, 412
Jackson, Rev. Sheldon, *333;* and Muir, 92–93, *178;* and reindeer introduction, 80, 318, 322–326, 330
Jackson, William Henry, 39
Jacobs, Locke, 391, 475n47
Japan, 79; and fur seals, 34, 44–46, 49, 51–53, 56; and ivory carving, 76; and sea otters, 21–22; whaling by, 71–74; in World War II, 22
Japan, 67
Jarvela, Rep. Gilbert, 274
Jarvis, Lt. David H., 69, 324–325
Jeanette, 94–95
Jeffries, Noah L., 40
Jewell, Homer, 271
Jimmy and Kappa, 414
Johnson, Chief, 358
Johnson, Ernie, 404
Johnson, Pres. Lyndon B., 174–175, 412
Johnson River, 310
Johnson, Robert Wood, 111–112
Jones, Charles Stone, 391
Jones, E. Lester, 284, 309
Jones, Robert D. "Bob," 23, *24,* 308
Jones, W. Alton "Pete," 391
Jordan, David Starr, 45–50, 130
Joynt, Gil, 23
Juneau, 258, 295; and Alaska Game Comm., 238, 244; gold strike at, 104, 210, 213; and Katmai eruption, 155; and salmon, 358, 374
Juneau Chamber of Commerce, 184, 421
Juneau *Daily Alaska Empire*, 183, 187, 267
Juneau Group, National Audubon Society, 257
Juneau Icecap International Park, 257
Juneau Mining Record, 358
Kachemak Bay, 380
Kadachan, 96
Kaflia Bay, 154–155
Kaguyak, 155
Kaktovik, 415
Kalgin Island, 334
Kamchatka Peninsula, and fur trade, 8, 28; and Russian exploration, 5, 7–8; sport hunting on, 216; and whaling, 63, 73
Kanaga Island, 24
Kantishna, 252; and Mt. McKinley NP, 139, 148, 152; mining in, 139, 147, 150
Kanuti National Wildlife Refuge, 257
Karluk, 360, 362
Karluk Lake, *261,* 301, 374
Karluk River, 352, 359, 362
Karstens, Henry B. "Harry," 132, 138, *139,* 143–144
Kashega, 22
Kasilof, 353
Kasilof River, 379
Kasitna Bay, 374
Katalla, 108, 390
Katmai Bay, 160
Katmai National Monument/Park, *166,* 219; and brown bears, 270, 279, 281; eruptions in, 154–155, *159, 168,* 172; management of, 168–175, 292; and Natives, 171; and nonconsumptive values, 175, 430, 437; origins of, 121, 155, *156, 160, 162,* 163, 175, 176, 433–434; tourism in, 168–175; volcanic study in, 157–166, 171–172; wildlife species in, 158, 160, 174–175
Katmai Pass, 68, 155–157
Katmai River, 160
Katmai Project, 171–172
Katmai village, 68; and exploration, 157; and fur trade, 12, 13, 155–156; and Katmai eruption, 155, *156*
Kayak Island, 5, 7
Kayaks. *See* Baidarkas
Kaye, Roger, 425
Kelly, Maurice W., 295, 297, 457n54
Kenai Fjords National Park, 378, 396
Kenai Mountains, 380
Kenai National Moose Range/Wildlife Refuge, *379;* and brown bears, 279; moose on, *384;* oil drilling on, 391–399; origins of, 234, *235,* 243–244, 390, 437; swans on, 398, *398;* wildlife species in, 378
Kenai Peninsula, 127, *390;* agriculture on, 109; brown bears on, *216,* 265–266, 378, 388; caribou on, 321, 334, 378, 386–387, 397–399, 474n28; Dall sheep on, 321, 378, 389; explorations on, 140; geography of, 378; and Katmai eruption, 158; market hunting on, 321, 326–388; moose on, 299, 320, 378, 386–390, 397, 474n28; mountain goats on, 321, 378; oil on, 386, 391–399, 426, 434; and Russian fur trade, 12, 16; sea otters at, 24, 378; sport hunting on, 123, 214–217, 262, *387,* 388; wolves on, 378, 386, 397–399
Kenai River, 217, 380, *389*
Kennecott Copper Co., 108, 384, 474n9
Kennicott, 381
Kennicott, Robert, 36, 474n9
Kessel, Brina, 255, 478n58
Ketchikan, 106, 244, 298, 363
Ketchikan Pulp Co., 279
Ketchikan Wildlife Club, 466n46

Keystone Canyon, 279
Kiakhta, Siberia, 8, 15, 28
Kilbuck Mountains, 319
Killey River, *390*
Killik River, 298
Killisnoo Island, 69
Kimberley, Capt. Martin, 34
King and Winge, 81
King Island, 80, 83, 448n74
King, James G. "Jim," 249, 255–258
King, Mary Lou, 257
King Salmon, 174, 374
Kiska, 22–23, 308
Kipling, Rudyard, 34, 46
Kit, 81–82
Kitch-Noch, 358
Kitoi Bay, 363
Kittigazuit, NWT, 331
Kjellman, William, 326
Klawock, 351
Klein, David R., 255
Kleinschmidt, F.E., 82, 214, 216–217, 265
Klingbiel, John, 256
Klondike. *See* Gold rushes
Knapp, Gov. Lyman, 358
Kobuk River, 130, 318
Kodiak: agricultural station at, 271; and Katmai eruption, 155–156, 158, *160*, 161; and salmon, 368
Kodiak Island, 127, 302; brown bears on, 261, 264–267, 271–278, 280; cattle and sheep on, 109, 265, 271–276; and eagles, 311; and fox farming, 305; and Katmai eruption, 158; and Russian fur trade, 12–13, 16, 351; and salmon, 351–352, 359, 364, *366;* game translocations to, 321, 334, *336*; and whaling, 60, 68, 74
Kodiak National Wildlife Refuge, *275;* and brown bears, *261,* 279–280, 437; origins of, 234, *235,* 243–244, 272
Kodiak Stock Growers Assn., 273–274
Korea, 374
Korean War, 153
Kotzebue, 244, 250, 256
Kotzebue Sound, 250, 331, 351
Koyukuk National Wildlife Refuge, 257
Koyukuk River, 197; Bob Marshall at, 401, 405, *405;* caribou at, 318; moose kill at, 298; Olaus Murie at, 409
Krear, Bob, 478n58
Kruzof Island, 279
Kuk River, 332
Kukak Bay, *170*
Kupreanof Peninsula, 273
Kurile Islands: and fur seals, 28, 34, 44; and sea otters, 7, 17, 44; and whaling, 71
Kuskokwim Delta, 39, 225–227, 294
Kuskokwim Delta National Wildlife Refuge, 252
Kuskokwim Mountains, 319
Kuskokwim National Wildlife Range, 422
Kuskokwim River, 39, 225, 240, 294, 359
Kvichak River, 304

La Farge, C. Grant, 126
La Perouse, Jean Francis de Galaup, Compte de, 15, 179–180
Labrador, 408
Lacey Act (1900): and Boone and Crockett Club, 121, 125, 223; and Bureau of Biological Survey, 210, 217, 223, 236; and Game Comm., 239; origins of, 56, 221
Lacey, Rep. John F., 125
Ladd Field, 140
Laguna, Frederika de, 196–197
Lake Clark, 197
Lane, Capt. Louis, 81
Lane, Franklin K. (Sec. of Interior), 140, 163, 165, 454n12
Langille, William, 389
Langley, Samuel P., 46, 127
Lapland, 322, 324, 326, 331
Lapps, 323–326, 331
Larsen, Capt., 82
Lavender, Capt. A.W., 34, 283
LaVoy, Merl, 138
League of American Sportsmen, 221
League of Nations, 72
Lee, Jack, 157
Leffingwell, Ernest de K., 413
Legislature, Territorial: and Arctic Refuge, 420; environmental values, 438; and grizzly bears, 266, 272–274, 438; and Katmai NM, 169; and Kenai Moose Range, 396; and natural resource jurisdiction, 219–220, 230, 367, 438; and wildlife management, 210, 238–239, 281; and wolf control, 288, 292
Legislature, State, 281, 438–439
Lemesurier Island, 185
Lensink, Calvin J., 255, 256
Lentfer, Jack, 255
Leopold, A. Starker: and Arctic Refuge, 418; and wolf predation, 288, 313, 319–321, 348
Leopold, Aldo: and aircraft hunting, 250; and eagle bounty, 312–313; and ecology, 205, 286–287; and Mt. McKinley NP, 149; and wilderness movement, 400; and wildlife management, 121, 255, 286
Lewis and Clark Expedition, 401
Liek, Harry, 148, 289, 314
Lindeberg, Jafet, 332

Lindley, Alfred, 148
Liquor, 96, 203; and fur trade, 16, 19–20, 32–33, 35, 212; and salmon industry, 361; and whaling/walrus hunting, 77–79
Litke, Capt. Frederick, 28, 75
Litnik Lake, 363
Little, Arthur D., 329
Little Diomede Island, 80, 83, *194,* 255
Little Port Walter, 363, 374
Lituya Bay, 177–180
Lituya Bay Placer Gold Mining Co., 180
Living Wilderness, 291
Lloyd, Tom, 138
Lobos Islands, 31
Logging, 115; and brown bears, 248, 268, 270, 279–280; economic value of, 347; and land degradation, 403; and salmon, 376
Lolita, 78
Lomen family, 78, 326–328, 330
London, UK, 76; and fur trade, 31, 42, 262, 306
London, Jack, 34, 46, 98
Lopp, W.T., 324
Loring, J. Alden, 125, 213–214
Lowther, Hugh Cecil, 156–157
Lucas, Frederick, 45
Lucas, Henry, *390*
Ludlow expedition, 118
Lutz, Harold, 201
Lutz, Lt. John E., 34
Lynx: and American fur trade, 345, *345;* and forest fires, 106, 340; mauling by, 238; in parks and refuges, 150, 175, 378, 415; protection of, 344; and Russian fur trade, 16, *18,* 338

MacArthur, Gen. Douglas, 373
MacBain, Alistair, *147*
Mackenzie River, 68, 125, 156, 332
Mackenzie River Delta, 59, 65–66, 330–331, 413
Madison Grant Forest and Elk Preserve, 125
Madsen, Charles: big game guiding by, 216; and brown bears, 265–266, 271; commercial walrus hunting by, 80–82
Man and Nature (Marsh), 116
Manchuria, 51
Manifest Destiny, 94
Manter, Capt. Fred, 58
Marine Mammal Protection Act, 24, 53, 83–84, 87, 89, 190, 302
Marmots, 13
Marsh, George Perkins, 112, 116, 205
Marsh, Othniel C., 118
Marshall, Bob, *405;* and Arctic Refuge, 400–401, 405–407, 418, 425, 429; background of, 401–402; contributions of, 211, 437; and forest preserves, 403–404; and forest ownership, 402–403; and Native Americans, 403, 430; and refugee plan, 406; and wilderness movement, 400, 403, 407, 437; wilderness philosophy of, 402, 405–406, 411–412, 429, 430, 432
Marshall Lake, 404
Marshall, Louis, 401–402
Martens: and American fur trade, 338, *339,* 345, *345,* 398; farming of, 343; and forest fires, 106, 340; protection of, 238, *240,* 249, 282, 344; and Russian fur trade, 16, *18,* 338, *339*
Martin, Calvin, 188–199, 205, 458n16
Martin, Frederika, 52, 55
Martin, George C., 158
Mary and Helen, 65
Mary D. Hume, 65
Mas Afuera Island, 29
Mashukin, 22
Mastodon, 125
Matanuska Valley, 292; agriculture in, 109–110, 271; coal in, 108, 380, 385
Matanuska Colony, 109–110, *110*
Mather, Stephen T., 115, 140
Matka and Kotik (Jordan), 46
Maynard, Lt. Washburn, 39
McBain, Dunc, 246
McCracken, Harold, 262
McGonagall, Charley, 138
McGrath, 244
McKay, Douglas (Sec. of Interior), 172, 391–393
McKinley Park Station, 145
McKinley, Pres. William, 112, 137, 324
McLean, Marshall, 290
McMullen, Capt. C.B., 158
McMullen, Pete, *239*
McNally, Chester, 392
McNeil River State Sanctuary, 255, 281
Melovidova, Alexandra, 39
Melville Island, 331
Mendenhall, Thomas, 45
Mendenhall Wetlands, 257
Mercury, 79
Merriam, C. Hart, 215, *223,* 236; background, 220; and Boone and Crockett Club, 130, 133; and brown bears, 223, 267, 269; and fur seals, 45, 49, 130; and Harriman Expedition, 222; and predator control, 283
Merriam, John C., 125
Metlakatla, 342, 488n30
Mexico, 73; Bureau of Biological Survey in, 131, 221, 227; and fur seals, 29; and sea otters, 14
Middle East, 394

Migratory Bird Act (1913), 239; and Boone and Crockett Club, 121, 125, 127–128; and J.B. Burnham, 224; and Game Comm., 239
Migratory Bird Conservation Act (1929), 228, 233
Migratory Bird Hunting Stamp Act (1934), 229, 233, 239
Migratory Bird Treaty (1916), 224, 228
Migratory Bird Treaty Act (1918), 121, 218, 224
Miller, Orlando, 109
Mills, Wilbur, 417
Milotte, Al and Elma, 56
Milton, John, 417
Miner, Joe, 298, 467n54
Mining, 21, 438; and Alaska Natives, 100–101, 209; and Alaska Railroad, 385–386; and Arctic Refuge, 420–424; coal, 108, 380; copper, 108, 371; economic value of, 347, *348;* environmental impacts of, *102, 103,* 103–108, 110, 125, 324, 347; in Glacier Bay NM, 180, 185–186, 188; in Gold Rushes, 97–108, 371; in Katmai NM, 169–170; and Mt. McKinley NP, 140, 142, 144, 150, 153; methods, 101–104
Mining in the Parks Act (1976), 186
Mining Law of 1872, 104
Mink: and American fur trade, 338, 345, *345;* farming, 302, 343; and Russian fur trade, 16, *18*
Missionaries, 93; effects on Natives, 11, 96, 199, 203, 323–325
Mixter, George, 263
Mogg, Capt. William "Billy," *64,* 414
Moiese, MT, 334
Montague Island, 262
Monterey, CA, 21
Monterey Peninsula, 351
Moore, Gov. Miles (WA), 381
Moose, 415; commercial hunting of, 100, 215–217, 231, *232,* 386–388; Eskimo hunting of, 199; and forest fires, 105–106, 320; in Glacier Bay NM, 191; and Katmai NM, 160, 174; on Kenai Pen., 215–219, 386–389, *389,* 393–394, 397, 474n28; and Mt. McKinley NP, 139, 150; population trends, 320; predation of, 266, 288, 292–293, 298–299, 313; protection of, 217–218, 234, 237–238, 248, 282, 292, 318, 320–321, *394;* sport hunting of, 215–218, *219, 317,* 334, 389; translocations of, 334, *335,* 337; wasteful kill of, 214, 240, 244, 386–388
Moose Pass, 380
Moran, Thomas, 39
Morgan-Guggenheim (Alaska) Syndicate, 108, 381–384, 436
Morse, Kathryn, 98
Morton, William, 301
Moser, Lt. Cmdr. Jefferson, 358–360
Mosquito Fork Flat, 105
Mt. Cerberus, 163
Mt. Cooper, 191
Mt. Doonerak, 404
Mt. Griggs, 174
Mt. Hornaday, 130
Mt. Katmai, 157, *159, 162,* 162, 165, *167,* 172
Mt. Mageik, *162*
Mt. McKinley, 293; climbing of, 137–139, *139, 142,* 148; and Mt. McKinley NP, 149–150; naming of, 137, 454n3; and Sheldon, 132, 135–136, 138–139, 143
Mt. McKinley National Park, *145,* 163, 219, 230, 255, 409, 433; and brown bears, 279; Dall sheep in, *144,* 321; eagles in, 311; management of, 143–153, 169, 288–292, 432, 437; origins of, 123, 132, 134, 139–143, 224, 316, 434, 454n12; and predator control, 285, 288–292, 313, 437; tourism at, 148–153; wildlife species in, 150. *See also* Sheldon, Charles
Mt. Merriam, 222
Mt. Muir, 114
Mt. Sheldon, 150
Mt. St. Elias, 5
Mt. Trident, 171
Mountain lion, 284, 286
Muir Glacier, *179;* Muir at, 91, 95–96, 176–177; naming of, 457n4
Muir Inlet, 114, 177
Muir, John, *114, 178,* 203, 221, 227; background, 91–92; beliefs of, 2, 91–97, 110–113, 115, 117, 203, 205, 401, 410, 427, 429–430, 432; environmental activism of, 111–115, 407; and Glacier Bay, 177, 181, 183, 191, 457n4; and Pinchot, 112, 134–135, 415n75; and predator control, 284
Muir Point, 114
Mulchatna River, *240*
Muldrow Glacier, *149*
Muldrow, Robert, 137
Murder Cove, 69
Murie, Adolph "Ade": and caribou survey, 408; and Mt. McKinley NP, 147, 149, *151,* 153, 289–292; and predator control, 289–292, 313, 409, 437;

and reindeer experiment, 400
Murie Islets, 408
Murie, Margaret "Mardy": and Arctic Refuge, 400–401, 419, *419,* 425, 429–430; environmental activism of, 211, 411–412, 429; and wilderness movement, 401, 432, 437
Murie, Olaus J., 245; Aleutians expedition, 22, 317, 409; and Arctic Refuge, 400–401, 418–419, *419,* 426, 429; background, 408; beliefs of, 250, 409–411, 429, 430, 432; and caribou study, 286, 319, 408, 468n6; contributions of, 211, 227–228, 409, 412; and game translocations, 337; and Mt. McKinley NP, 147, 149, 408; and predator control, 285–289, 313–314, 409, 437; and sea otters, 22; warden work, 231, *232,* 408; and wilderness movement, 400–401, 410–412, 437
Murray, Joseph, 213
Museum of Natural History, Northwestern U., 36
Muskoxen, *333,* 415; Eskimo hunting of, 200, 331–332; protection of, 331, 349; reintroduction of, 233, 332–333; uses of, 331–334
Muskrats, 308; protection of, 217, 237; and Russian fur trade, 16, 338, 340; trapping of, *345*

Naden Harbor, 71
Nagel, Charles (Sec. of Commerce and Labor), 49–50
Naket Packing Co., *353*
Naknek, 154, 157, 169
Naknek Civic Club, 170
Naknek Lake, 171
Nanook, 81
The Nation, 395
National Audubon Society, 224, 234; activism of, 12, 221, 224; and Arctic Refuge, 421; and eagles, 311; and Glacier Bay NM, 185; and 1925 Game Law, 224, 232; Juneau Group, 257; origin of, 121, 221; and wolf control, 289
National Bison Range, 334
National Conf. on Outdoor Recreation, 131, 133, 224
National Geographic: and brown bears, 264; and Katmai NM, 158, 163, 165, 175; and Mt. McKinley NP, 143
National Geographic Society: and Cook scandal, 138; and Katmai NM, 157–158, 160, 163, 165, 175, 434
National Marine Fisheries Service, 88, 253
National Park Committee, 121
National Park Service, 115, 347, 418; and Alaska Lands Act, 412; and Glacier Bay NM, 185–191, 270–271, 278; and Katmai NM, 163, 168–175; management philosophy, 97, 119, 146–147, 150–153, 190, 270, 292, 313, 432; and Mt. McKinley NP, 144–153, 288–292; and predator control, 288–292, 313, 437
National Parks Assn., 121, 125; and Glacier Bay NM, 183, 185; and Katmai NM, 170
National Parks Conf., 143
National Parks Magazine, 420
National Research Council, 183, 250
National Rifle Assn., 312
National Wildlife Federation, 234, 393, 421–422
National Zoological Park, 127, 264
Natives, Alaska: cannery employment, 360–362; and conservation, 194–207; environmental abuse by, 104, 196, 198–200, 202–203, 255; fishing rights, 177, 188–190, 357–360, 425; Gold Rush impact on, 100–101; land claims/conflicts, 146, 171, 188–190, 209, 252, 279, 372; Muir's views of, 96–97; population, 208, *213;* salmon fishing by, 351, *361;* and sea otter trade, 1–21, 25; slavery among, 17; trapping rights, 340, 425; whaling/walrus hunting impact on, 77–80, 192; and wildlife management, 24, 188–190, 204–208, 211, 238, 251, 389, 434–435
Natural History, 52
Nature, 163
Nature groups: and conservation, 2, 117, 122, 134, 183, 185, 220–221, 234, 430, 433–434. *See also* Environmental organizations
Naval Arctic Research Laboratory, 418
Nature Magazine, 270
Naval Petroleum Reserve, 418
Neah Bay, 34
Near East, 116
Nelchina River, 294, 298
Nelson, Edith and Hans, 180
Nelson, Edward W., *226, 228,* 236, 245–246; background, 225; beliefs of, 229, 236; and brown bears, 267, 269; and Mt. McKinley NP, 140; and

muskoxen, 333; and 1925 Game Law, 229–233; and Olaus Murie, 245, 408–408; and reindeer, 329; and Sheldon, 131–132
Nelson Island, 69, 200, 227
Nelson, Klondy, 334
Nelson Lagoon, 227
Nelson, Richard K., 197
Nelson, Urban C., 426
Nenana, 108, 145, 252
Nenana River, 143, 145
New Bedford, MA, 60, 68
New England Fish Co., 457n79
New England Museum of Natural History, 290
New York Aquarium, 130
New York City, 113, 117, 371; and Alaska conservation, 2, 133, 437; and walrus ivory, 76
New York Daily News, 372
New York *Evening Post*, 42
New York *Sun*, 137
New York Times, 42, 50, 437
New York Zoological Park (Bronx Zoo), 48, 127, 263
New York Zoological Society: and Arctic Refuge, 418; and Boone and Crockett Club, 121–123, 125–127, 213, 217; and brown bears, 269; and 1925 Game Law, 250; political activism of, 221, 437; and wolf control, 289
Newhalen River, *247*
Nikita, Smoky, 248
Nizina River, *102*
Nizki Island, 308
No Room for Bears (Dufresne), 280
Noatak National Preserve, 409
Noble, John W. (Sec of Interior), 120
Nome, *84,* 156, 332, *251;* Amundsen at, 246, 414, *415;* and caribou, 293; and game laws, 247; and reindeer, 326, and walrus hunting, 82; and whaling, 71
North American Commercial Co., 39–42, 49
North American Wildlife Foundation, 121
North Nenana, 385
North Pacific Anadromous Fisheries Commission, 374
North Pacific Fisheries Convention (1953), 373
North Pacific Sealing Convention (Fur Seal Treaty) (1911), 21, 26, 49, 305, 432
North Slope: moose on, 199; muskoxen on, 199–200, 331; oil on, 419; wildlife species on, 415; wolf control on, 296–298
Northeast Point, 85–86, *87*
Northern Consolidated Airlines, 172
Northern Rocky Mountain Forest Experimental Station, 401
Northern Yukon/Ivvavik NP, 426
Northwest Passage, 413–414
Northwest Territories, 330–331
Norton Sound, 225, 326, 338
Norway: and Northwest Passage, 414; and reindeer, 323, 326; and salmon, 376; and whaling, 69, 71–72
Novarupta, 157, 172, *173*
Nowitna National Wildlife Refuge, 257
Nulato, 36, 338
Nulato Hills, 319
Nunivak Island, 39, 80; caribou on, 318; muskoxen on, 334; reindeer on, 327, 330, 333
Nushagak River, 338, 354
Nutirwik (Harry Snowden), 404, *405*
Ocean Spray, 34
O'Connor, Jack, *239,* 272, 276, 291
Ocmulgee, 58, 446n1
Oelschlaeger, Max, 92
Office of Indian Affairs (USDOI), 328, 403
Ogilvie Mountains, 416
Oil: and Alaska economy, 350; and Arctic Refuge, 420, 424–426; on Kenai Pen., 391–399, 434, 475n47; and wildlife, 25, 75, 347–348
Oil pipeline, 253
Old Crow River, 411
Old Woman Creek, *417*
Olmstead, Frederick Law, 117
Olsen Bay, 374
Olson, Sigurd F., 149, 418, 422
Olympic National Park, 123
Oo-Ming-Muk, 332
Operation Umiat, *297,* 297–298
Orca, 68
Oregon, 24, 301, 352, 355
Organic Act (1884), 210
Orloff, Ivan, 155
Osborn, Henry Fairfield, 126–127, 221
Osgood, Wilfred, 131, 386; and brown bears, 261, 264; and commercial hunting, 318–319
Otaru, Hokkaido, 22
Ott, Charles J. "Charlie," 150, *152*
Otter Island, 34
Otters, river, 174, 307; and fur trade, 16, *18,* 338, *339, 345;* protection of, 344
Otters, sea, *9, 175,* 191, 324, 379; and Bering expedition, 6–8; ecology of, 15, 19, 23–25, 89, 195; hunting of, 9–21, 195–196, 338, 432; protection of, 21–25, 128, 305, 434; translocations, 23–24

Our Arctic Province (Elliott), 39
Our Vanishing Wildlife (Hornaday), 127
Outdoor Life, 265, 274, 291
Outdoor sporting groups. *See* Hunting, sport; Fishing, sport

Pacific American Fisheries, Inc., 368
Pacific Coast Steamship Co., 94, 179
Pacific Decadal Oscillation, 376
Pacific Seabird Group, 256–257
Pack, Arthur Newton, 270
Pack Creek, 278
Pagashak, *273*
Paget, Francis, 214, 262
Palmer, *110*
Palmer Creek, 380
Palmer, Lawrence J., 245, *390;* caribou study, 287–288, 409; and reindeer, 329; research by, 227, wolf study, 313
Palmer, Theodore S., 215, *223,* 223–224
Pardee, Gov. James (CA), 113
Parker, Charles, 187
Parker, Herschel, 138
Parks, Gov. George A., 184, 186, 288, 389
Parks Highway, 149
Parks-Western Fisheries, 467n79
Partofshikof Island, 279
Passenger pigeon, 220
Pavlov Bay, 216
Peabody Museum, 118
Pearson, Grant, 148, 150
Pearson, T. Gilbert, 232, 311
Pease, Capt. Henry, 67
Pederson, C.T., 81
Pegues, John, 268
Permanent Wild Life Protection Fund, 127–128, 230, 232
Perryville, 155
Peter the Great, 4, 7
Petersburg, 244
Petersburg Creek, 366
Petersen, Ray, 172
Petroff, Ivan, 59, 79, 155–157, 260
Phoenix, 380
Photography, 269
Pinchot, Gifford: and Boone and Crockett Club, 123; and coal leasing, 382–383; and forest use, 402, 451n75; and Muir, 112
Pioneer Boys of the Great Northwest (Bonehill), 401
Pioneers of Alaska, Fairbanks Chap., 149
Pittman-Robertson Act (1937), 234
Poe, Edgar Allen, 46
Point Barrow, *81*; and reindeer, 327; and whaling, 65–69, 324
Point Bridget State Park, 257
Point Hope, 68; Eskimo whaling at, 59; mission at, 322; reindeer at, 325; walrus hunting at, 80, 82
Poison: of furbearers, 240, 242, 284, 296, *297,* 306, 344; of predators, 238, 254, 283, 286, 294–298, 308, 317, 330, 345, 386
Polar Bear, 81
Polovina Point, 23
Popov, F.A., 4–5
Population, in Alaska, 213, *214,* 220, 244
Porcupine caribou herd, 415–416, *416*
Porcupine River, 156, 411, 415
Porcupines, 175, 415
Porpoises, 59, 191, 378
Porsild, Erling and Robert, 330
Port Armstrong, 69–71
Port Ellice, CA, 75
Port Hobron, 69, 71, *73*
Portage Bay, 385
Postman, David, 391, 392
Poughkeepsie, NY, 60
Powell, John Wesley, 117
Predator control, 211, 233; and Boone and Crockett Club, 123, 128; by bounties, 88–89, 284–285, 301, 303–304, *305, 312,* 313; and brown bears, 281; of eagles, 310–314; of foxes, 307–310; by Game Comm., 238, 240, 245–247, 251, 258, 283, 285, 292–300, 311–313, 319–320, 328, 330; of harbor seals, 88–89, 253, 302–304; in Mt. McKinley NP, 152, 288–292; opposition to, 234, 259, 285–288, 409, 431; origins, 222, 283–285; research on, 253, 301–304; of sea lions, 253, 301–302; of wolverines, 345
Preservationism: and Boone and Crockett Club, 123; and fur seals, 50; and Hornaday, 128; and Katmai NM, 171, 175; and Muir, 110–113, 115. *See also* Values, environmental
Pribilof Islands, *30, 54,* 452n12; Arctic foxes on, 305; and fur seals, 17, 28–35, 38–42, 44–53, 128, 130, 222; sea lion hunting on, 86; sea otters in, 21, 23; translocations to, 308–309; walrus hunting in, 75; and whaling, 59
Pribylov, Gerassim, 28, 75
Prince of Wales Island, 5, *354*
Prince William Sound, 68; bear hunting at, 132; and copper mines, 108; deer translocations to, 334; and fur trade, 14; harbor seals in, 89; whaling in, 63

Progressive Movement: and conservation, 2–3, 55, 111–112, 117, 211, 399, 434, 436–437; and predator control, 283
Promyshlenniki, 8–13, 16
Protzman, warden, 310
Prudhoe Bay, 396, 426
Pruitt, William, 425
Puale Bay, 155
Public opinion, national: and brown bears, 270, 280; and eagles, 314; and fur seals, 56; and Katmai NM, 163; and land preservation, 438; and Mt. McKinley NP, 153; and Nature, 2, 25–26, 117, 221; and pinnipeds, 89–90, and whales, 89–90; and wolves, 291–292, 313–314

Queen, 179
Queen Charlotte Islands, 33, 71
Qiviut, 334

Raccoons, 337
Radclyffe, Capt. Charles R.E., 215, *216,* 262
Rampart Dam, 256
Rasmuson, Elmer, 392
Rasmussen, Knud, 199
Rat Islands, 24
Rats, 23, 300, 306, 308
Rausch, A. Robert, 255
Rausch, Robert A., 421
Rearden, Jim, 253, 255, 274
Recreation and Lands Div. (USDA), 403
Recreation Magazine, 127
Red River Lake, *366*
Redington, Paul, 287
Reed, Irving McKinley, 332
Reed, John, 418
Reid, Harry Fielding, 181
Reid Inlet, 185
Reiger, John F., 120
Reindeer, 253, 318, *325, 328*; and Bureau of Biological Survey, 233, 285–286, 326, 329–330, 333; breeding experiment, 327, 408; to Canada, 330–331; ecological effects of, 319, 329–330, 349, 430, 432, 469n8; industry problems, 326–330; introduction of, 21, 80, 309, 322–326; and Katmai eruption, 160; population trends, 328, *329;* and predator control, 245, 285, 288, 292–294, 298, 300; and whaling, 68–69
Reindeer Service, 293, 327–328
Republican Party, 267, 383, 420
Resurrection Bay, 12, 379–380
Revenue Marine Patrol: and fur seals, 40–41, 44; and Katmai eruption, 155; and sea otters, 19; and walrus hunting, 77, 79. *See also Bear*
Rezanov, Nicolai, 31
Rhode, Clarence, *239, 251;* and Alaska Game Comm., 242, 248–252, 258, 344; and Arctic Refuge, 420; background, 248; and cattle predation, 272; and Kenai oil, 393–394; and wolf control, 292–294, 297
Rhode, Jack, 252
Richardson Highway, 149
Richfield Oil Co., 391–392, 395–396, *397,* 475n47
Riggs, Gov. Thomas Jr.: and brown bears, 266–267; and conservation, 230, 310; and Katmai NM, 168; and Mt. McKinley NP, 140, 454n12; and muskoxen, 332, and 1925 Game Law, 230
Rivers, Rep. Ralph, 421–422
Romanzof Mountains, 332
Robben Island, 28, 44, 49, 53
Roderick, Jack, 392
Rogers, George, 196
Rood, Sidney, 293
Roosevelt, Pres. Franklin D., 129–130; and Glacier Bay NM, 186, 271; and Katmai NM, 175; and refugee plan, 406; and wildlife refuges, 132, 233–234
Roosevelt, Pres. Theodore, 129, 220, 401; and Alaska coal, 381, 383–384, 434; and Alaska conservation, 2–3, 434, 437; and Boone and Crockett Club, 119–120, 122–123, 132; and conservation, 3, 381, 383; and fur seals, 46, 48; and Muir, 113, 115; and wolf control, 284
Root, Elihu (Sec. of State), 48
Roquefeuil, Camille de, 15
Rose Harbor, 71
Round Island, 83
Royal Canadian Mounted Police, 242
Royal Commission on the Reindeer and Musk-Ox, 330
Royal Navy, 41
Roys, Capt. Thomas Welcome, 58, 63, 66–67
Rungius, Carl, 131
Russell, Jim, 231
Russia: and cattle, 271; and conservation, 1, 17, 31–32, 428, 429–431, 433; coal mining by, 380; exploration by, 4–8, 180; and fur seal treaty, 46, 49, 53, 56; and fur trade, 4, 7–17, 21, 27–33, *40,* 260, 262, 305, 338–340, 433; on Kenai Pen., 379–380; and salmon, 351, 374; settlements by, 5, 379; walrus hunting by, 75, 83; and

Western Union project, 35–36; whaling by, 59–60, 73–74. *See also* Russian-American Co.
Russian-American Company: and conservation, 433; and fur trade, 12–17, 19, 31, 155, 209, 239, 340; and whaling, 59–60. *See also* Russia
Russian Colony (Fort Ross), 14
Russian Finland Whaling Co., 60
Russo-Japanese War, 44, 372
Rust, Jess, 411

Sable, 340
Sag Harbor (NY), 63
St. George Island: killer whales at, 283; and sea lions, 86; and sea otters, 28, 31, 34, 44, 52–53
St. Lawrence Island, 39; Geist study of, 412; starvation on, 74–78, *78;* and walrus hunting, 77–78; and whaling, 59, 67
St. Matthew Island, 39, 84, *114,* 330
St. Michael, 36, 39, 69, 104; and fur trade, 338; Nelson at, 225–227; reindeer at, 285
St. Paul, 5
St. Paul Island: and fur seals, 28, *29,* 31, 34, 44, 52, *54;* reindeer on, 309, 330; sea lion hunting on, 85–86, *87;* translocations to, 308–309
St. Paul village, 68
St. Peter, 5, 8
St. Petersburg, 8, 31, 338
Salcha River, 106
Salisbury, Lord, 41
Salmon: canneries, 106, 185, 188, 210, 254, 304, 351–371, 380, 395–396; and conservation, 364; ecology of, 375–376; economic value of, 350; federal-territorial dispute over, 252, 365, 367–372, 374–375; fishing methods, 351–364, 369, 375–376; in Glacier Bay NP, 185, 191; and Gold Rush, 106; harvests of, 369, *370;* hatcheries, 362–363, 376; in Katmai NM, 158, 160, 171, 175; and Native rights, 192, 357–360; predation of, 253, 268, 272, 276, 300–304, 316, 346; regulations, 239, 355–357, 362, 364–368, 376, 429; research on, 363, 374–376, 432; reserves, 120, 359, 364–365; species, 351; U.S.-Japan dispute, 372–374; waste of, 268, 353. *See also* Fishing, commercial
San Francisco, 414; and coal, 380; and fur trade, 32, 34, 36; and Muir, 94, 97–98; and reindeer, 327; and salmon, 367, 371; and trophy trade, 387; and walrus hunting, 65, 75, 79
San Francisco *Daily Evening Bulletin,* 94, 97
San Miguel Island, 28
Sanak Island, 17, 307
Sand Point, 214
Santa Clara, 355
Sarber, Hosea: and eagle predation of salmon, 313–314; bear-cattle study, 272; law enforcement by, 240, *240;* and predator control, 295; and sea lion predation of salmon, 301
Saturday Evening Post, 269
Save-The-Redwoods League, 125
Savonoski, 154–156
Savoonga, 83–84
Saylor, J.C. II, 397
Scammon, Capt. Charles Melville, 62–63
Scarf, Oscar, 44
Schaller, George, 478n58
Scheffer, Victor B., 22, 307
Schneider, William, 340–341
Schurz, Carl (Sec. of Interior), 117
Scidmore, Eliza R., *178*
Science, 130
Science News Letter, 52
Scotland, 91, 376
Scull, E. Marshall, 230, 387
Sea Bears (Martin), 55
Sea Cow, 6–7, 441n8
Sea Lion, California, 49, 86
Sea Lion Rock, 444n2
Sea Lion Rocks, 409
Sea lions, Steller, *87,* 191, 379; conservation of, 87–88, 217–218; control of, 86–87, *299,* 301–304, 314; decline, 25, 86–89; hunting of, 13, 85–87, 89; study of, 253, 301–302, 304
Sea of Okhotsk, 60
Sea-Wolf, 80
Seal Island (Disney), 56
Seal-Islands of Alaska (Elliott), 39
Seals, fur: decline, 53, 87; ecology, 27, *29;* hunting of, 28, 33–35, 42–44, 51–53; predation of, 283; and Russian fur trade, *18,* 21, 27–31, *40,* 338, 434; in Southern Hemisphere, 29–31; and tourism, 53, 56; U.S. management of, 32–35, 39–40, *40, 48, 54,* 130, 222, 305, 428
Seals, hair, 81, 415; control of, 253, *299,* 302–304, *305,* 314; predation of salmon, 300–301, 303–304; research on, 25, 304
Seals, harbor: decline of, 89; and fashion industry, 88; in

Glacier Bay NM, 188–191; hunting of, 88, 188–190; and salmon predation, 88–89, 303–304
Seals, largha, *195,* 415
Seaton, Fred (Sec. of Interior), 371; and Arctic Refuge, 420, 422; and Kenai oil, 393, 395
Seattle, 52, 55, 81, 271, 326; and coal, 381–382; and Gold Rush, 110; and salmon, 367, 370, 371, 374
Seiser, Virgil, 392
Seldovia, 380, 387–388
Sequoia National Park, 111
Service, Robert, 98
Seton, Ernest Thompson, 221, 252, 285, 408
Seward: and Alaska Railroad, 108, 384–385; and commercial hunting, 388; and Game Comm., 244; and Gold Rush, 380; and Katmai eruption, 155; and salmon, 380; tourism at, 380
Seward Peninsula, 69, 294, 319
Shanghai, 338
Shaw, L.F., 388
Sheakley, Gov. James, 358
Shearwater Peninsula, 273
Sheehan, Jack, 172
Sheekjek River, 105, 198; Muries at, 419, *419;* muskoxen at, 332
Sheep, Dall, 13, 318, 379; in Arctic Refuge, 413; and eagles, 310–311; market hunting of, 214–215, 217, 231–232, *232,* 321, 388; and Mt. McKinley NP, 143, *144,* 147, 150, 153, 288–291, 321, 437; name origin, 37; Native hunting of, 199, 321; and E.W. Nelson, 227; population trends, 321; protection of, 217–218, 237, 282, 288–294, 431; and Sheldon, 131–132, 139; sport hunting of, 214–216, *219, 317;* translocations of, 334, *335,* 337
Sheep ranching: in Aleutians, 21, 109, 309–310; and brown bears, 265, 268, 271, 281; and foxes, 305, *309,* 309–310
Sheffield, 66
Sheldon, Charles, 131, 437; background, 131, 435; beliefs, 132–133; and brown bears, 262–264, 267; and Katmai NM, 168, 175; and Mt. McKinley NP, 135–136, 138–143, 153; and muskoxen, 333; and 1925 Game Law, 136, 229–232
Sheldon National Wildlife Refuge, 132
Shelikof Strait, 68, 154–155, 169
Shelikov, Gregorii, 11–12
Shelikov-Golikov Company, 11–12, 155
Shemya Island, 22, 209
Shenandoah, 67
Sherwood, Morgan, 37
Shields, Walter, 326
Ship Creek, 385
Shumagin Islands, 23, 408
Shungnak, *206,* 251
Shuyak Island, 307
Siberia: and fur trade, 338, 413; muskoxen in, 331, 333; reindeer from, 322–323, *324,* 326
Sierra Club: and Arctic Refuge, 418, 421; and Muir, 111, 113–115, 435; and logging, 106, 115; and Mardy Murie, 412
Sierra Club Bulletin, 418
Signal Service, U.S. Army, 225
Simeonof Island, 23, 468n96
Simons, Andy, 380
Sitka (New Archangel), 36, 177, 457n4; and coal, 380; and fur trade, 15–16, 29, 40, 338; and Game Comm., 244; Muir at, 97; Russian fort at, 12–14, 180; and salmon, 351; smallpox at, 17; and timber industry, 106, 278; and whaling, 63
Sitka National Historical Park, 165
Sitkalidak Island, 69
Sitkok Bay, 358
Skagway, 97, 380
Skilak Lake, 387
Skoog, Ronald O., 255, 318, 320, 469n8
Slattery Plan, 406
Smith, Capt. Tom, 186
Smith, Jack, 108
Smith, Jefferson R. "Soapy," 380
Smith, Lynn, 99
Smithsonian Institution, 126–127; collecting for, 6, 36–39, 128, 130–131, 221, 224–227; and wildlife management, 45, 46, 220
Snedden, C.W., 393
Snowmobiles: and hunting, 84, 205, 207, 250, 345; and trapping, 342, 344
Society of American Foresters, 121
Sourdough Expedition, 138–139
South Shetland Islands, 31
Southeast Alaska: Aleuts moved to, 52; brown bears in, 269–271, 278–279; deer in, 213–214, 284, 310, 322; fox farming in, 305–306, 343; harbor seals in, 89; Muir in, 93–97, 177; predator control in, 294, 310–311; and salmon, 352, 357–363, 368, 374, 376; sea lions

in, 88; sea otters in, 10, 12–16; slave trade in, 17; sport hunting in, 214; Stone expedition in, 125, 140; timber industry in, 106, 279; tourism in, 177, 179, *179,* 181; translocations to, 334, 337; and Western Union project, 36; whaling in, 69–71, 74. *See also* Tongass National Forest
Southern Pacific Railroad, 113
Spain, 14
Spence, Clark, 103
Spencer, David L., 398, *398*
Spencer, Robert F., 199
Spit and Argue Club, 392, 395–396, 475n47
Spurr, Josiah Edward, 100, 137, 157
Steese-Fortymile District, 298
Stefansson, Vilhjalmur, 331–332, 334
Stejneger, Leonhard, 6, 45, 49
Steller, Georg Wilhelm, 6–8, 27
Steller Society, 257
Stevens, Sen. Ted, 393, 395–396
Stevenson, Adlai, *174*
Stevenson, John Fell, *174*
Stewart, R.K., 285
Stickeen, 93, 449n7
Stickeen (Muir), 93
Stikine Pass, 98
Stikine River: and fur trade, 15; gold rush at, 31, 98; salmon at, *302,* 303–304
Stone, Andrew J.: and caribou, 126, 386–387; explorations by, 125, 140; and muskoxen, 332
Stone, Livingston, 362
Stony River, 240
Strawberry Island, 185
Strawberry Point, 187
Strom, Erling, 148
Strong, Gov. J.F.A., 266, 284, 310
Stuck, Archdeacon Hudson, 138, *139*
Suk-Ta-Han, 358
Sulzer, Delegate Charles, 163, 229, 267
Sumner, Lowell: and Arctic Refuge, 418; and Katmai NM, 170–171; and valuing wildlife, 347–349
Sumner, Sen. Charles, 36
Sunrise, 380, 388
Suomi, 60
Superior, 58, 63, 446n1
Susitna River, 137
Sutherland, Delegate Dan, 232, 267, 364–365
Sutherland, W.W., 242
Sutkum Island, 12–13
Swans, trumpeter, *398,* 399
Swanson, Capt. Olaf, 81
Swanson River oilfield, 392–393, *397*
Swineford, Gov. Alfred P., 39

Taft, Pres. William Howard: and Alaska Railroad, 385; and Aleutians Reserve, 21; and coal leasing, 382–384; and fur seals, 49; and Muir, 113; and migratory birds, 224; and oil lands, 391
Taiwan, 53, 374
Taku Glacier, 181
Taku Pass, 98
Taku River, 295, 304, 358
Tanaga Island, 24
Tanana River, 137, 201; and agriculture, 109; and Alaska Railroad, 381; eagles at, 310; and gold mining, 101
Tanana River Railway, *107,* 217
Tanana Valley Sportsmen's Assn., 419, 466n46
Tatum, Robert, 138, *139*
Taylor, Billy, 138–139
Teapot Dome, 368, 392
Tebenkof, Capt. Mikhail, 60
Teklanika River, 143
Teller, 323
Tenada, 137
Terhune, H.W., 268, 271
Territorial Dept. of Fisheries, 252–253; and salmon, *303,* 363, 370; and seal control, *303,* 303–304
Territorial Dept. of Mines, 169, 420
Territorial Sportsmen Inc., 257; Juneau chap., 295, 466n46
Tetlin National Wildlife Refuge, 257
Thayer, Averill, 414
Thayer, Jack, 267–269
Thayer Mountain, 278
Thelon Game Sanctuary, 331, 334
Thlinket Packing Co., *352*
Thoreau, Henry David, 91, 116, 205
Thorne, Frank, 52
Tickey, 68
Tilton, George Fred, 68
Timber industry. *See* Logging
Tingle, George R., 359
Tlingit and Haida Indians v. United States, 189
To the Top of the Continent (Cook), 138
Togiak National Wildlife Refuge, 256
Toklat River, 143
Toloumne Meadows, 111
Tongass National Forest: brown bears in, 186, 270, 279; logging in, 115, 270, 279, 403, 407, 439; Native claims in, 188–190, 192; reserving of, 219, 429, 434
Tongass Timber Sales Act (1947), 279
Tourism, 429; and Alaska Highway, 244; and Arctic Refuge, 419, 425–426; and brown bears, 281; and fur seals, 51, 53, 56; in Glacier Bay NM/NP, 177, 179, 181, 184, 190–191;

in Katmai NM/NP, 163–165, 169, 171–175; on Kenai Pen., 380, 399; in Mt. McKinley NP, 146, 148–153; and national forests, 472; post-statehood, 438; and sea otters, 35; in Southeast, 93–94, 114, *179;* and wildlife, 347
Townsend, Charles H., *131,* 437; background, 130; and Boone and Crockett Club, 130–131; and fur seals, 43, 45, 49, 130; and reindeer, 322
Toyatte, 94
Traitors Cove, 374
Transcontinental Railroad, 65
Trapping, 317, *341;* and conservation, 199, 430; in Katmai NP, 169; on Kenai Pen., 380; life cycle, 340–342; and predator control, 284–285, 308, 313; regulation of, 218, 240–241, 244–245, 249, 340, 434; and Russian fur trade, 8, 13, 16, *18,* 339, *339;* and technological change, 342; trends in, 344. *See also* Fur trade; Furbearers
Travel magazine, 148
Travels in Alaska (Muir), 96
Treadwell Mines, 104
Trefethen, James B., 121, 133
Trumpeter Swan Society, 257
Tugidak Island, 13
Turner, Lucien M., 225
Turnagain Arm, 380, 384
Tustumena Lake, 387
Two in the Far North (Murie), 411
Tyee Co., 69

Udall, Stewart (Sec. of Interior), 256, 424
Uganik Island, 273
Ukak River, 173
Ukamok Island, 12–13
Umiat, 297–298
Umnak Island, 21, 309–310
Unalakleet, 36, 326, 334
Unalaska Island, 34; and fur trade, *10,* 17, 31; reindeer on, 21, 323; sheep on, 21, 309–310
Unangashik, 319
Unga, 319
Unimak Island, 279, 409
Unimak Pass, 89, 302, 354
Union Pacific Railroad, 113–114
United States Whaling Co., 69–71
University of Alaska Fairbanks, 103, 150, 255, 411–412; musk-oxen at, *333,* 333–334; wildlife study at, 99, 291, 293–294, 406
University of Alaska Southeast, 258
University of Washington, 374
U.S. Air Force, 425
U.S. Army: exploration by, 137; and Glacier Bay NM, 185; and Katmai NM, 169; and Mt. McKinley NP, 148, 169; and reindeer, 330
U.S. Coast Guard, 330, 366, 373
U.S. Coast Survey, 36
U.S. Commissioner Courts, 367
U.S. Dept. of Agriculture, 271; Bob Marshall in, 403; origin of Bureau of Biological Survey, 210, 220; and fur trade, 21, 307, 340, 343, 347; and migratory birds, 212; and 1925 Game Law, 232, 237; and predator control, 236, 283; and reindeer, 326, 408; wildlife jurisdiction, 21, 217, 272, 347. *See also* Bureau of Biological Survey
U.S. Dept. of Commerce: and fur trade, 21, 51–53, 340, 343; and salmon, 357, 364–365, 369; wildlife jurisdiction, 21, 217, 219, 347
U.S. Dept. of the Interior, 403; and Arctic Refuge, 419–421; cattle leasing, 271; and coal, 382–383; and fox farming, 343; and Glacier Bay NM, 183; and Kenai oil, 392, 395–396; and Kodiak Refuge, 272–273; and Mt. McKinley NP, 148; and Native fishing rights, 359; and 1925 Game Law, 232, 237; and refugee plan, 406; and reindeer, 328–329; and salmon, 369–371; wildlife jurisdiction, 210, 219, 272; and wildlife refuges, 257. *See also* U.S. Fish and Wildlife Service
U.S. Dept. of Justice, 382
U.S. Dept. of the Treasury: and fur seals, 32–35, 39–41; and fur trade, 340, 347; and reindeer, 323; and salmon, 355–358
U.S. Dept. of War, 23
U.S. Fish and Wildlife Service: and Alaska Game Comm., 249–249, 252, 255–258; and Arctic Refuge, 337, 422; and Boone and Crockett Club, 122; and fur seals, 52–53; jurisdiction, 236–237; and Katmai NM, 171; and Kenai Moose Range, 389, 393–395, 397–398; and Native claims, 359; Olaus Murie in, 409; origins of, 210, 220, *223;* polar bear research, 253, *255;* predator control, 286–288, 293–300, 307–308, 313, 409, 432; reputation of, 438; and salmon, *366,* 369–370; and sea lions,

86; and sea otters, 22–24; translocations, 337; and waterfowl, 207, 256–257
U.S. Fish Commission, 130; and fur seals, 39, 45, 49; origins of, 221, 225; and reindeer, 322; and salmon, 355–358, 362–363, 374
U.S. Forest Service: Bob Marshall in, 401, 403; and brown bears, 267, 270–271, 279–280; and coal, 383; and fox farming, 343; and Glacier Bay NM, 184, 186, 418; and Kenai Moose Range, 389; and predator control, 286; and timber industry, 279
U.S. Geological Survey, 100, 117; and Admiralty Island, 278; and Arctic Refuge, 418; exploration, 36, 137, 157–158, 168, 418; and Glacier Bay NM, 181, 183–184, 186; and Kenai oil, 392; and Mt. McKinley, 137; and Mt. McKinley NP, 143
U.S. House of Representatives, committees: Conservation of Wild Life Resources, 270; Fisheries and Wildlife Conservation, 420–421; Merchant Marine and Fisheries, 392; Public Lands, 142, 290; Territories, 220, 229
U.S. Navy, 23, 177
U.S. Postal Service, 156
Usibelli coal mine, 108
USSR, 372, 393. *See also* Russia

Valdez, *99,* 108, *243,* 279, 388
Valdez-Eagle Trail, 105
Valley of Ten Thousand Smokes, 157, 161–165, 172
Values, environmental, xvii, 3, 425, 435, *436,* 439–440; corporate accountability, 3, 56, 115; ecosystem preservation, 150–153, 175, 191, 211, 236, 348, 437, 439; ecosystem sustainability, 3, 56, 115, 133, 175, 197, 204, 211, 258, 280, 425, 429, 439; government accountability, 3, 56, 115; holism, 115, 175, 407, 429, 432, 440; nonconsumptive resource use, 3, 25–26, 53, 56, 115, 152, 175, 204, 280–281, 292, 314–315, 407, 430, 437, 439; nonhuman rights, 115, 133, 205, 281, 430; public participation, 3, 26, 56, 115, 258, 433–434, 440; science-based management, 3, 56, 133, 211, 236, 258, 431–432; species preservation, xvii, 25–26, 115, 133, 175, 280, 428; sustainable utilitarianism, xvii, 3, 19, 26, 119, 201, 204, 211, 258, 280, 346, 429–430, 438. *See also* Conservation, utilitarian; Environmental organizations
Vancouver, Capt. George, 136, 177, 183
Vancouver Island, 33
Vanschoonoven, George, 137
Vasilev, navigator, 306
Venetie, 488n30
Veniamenov, Ivan, 196
Vermont, 334
Victoria (BC), 33–34, 42, *43*
Vint, Thomas C., 187
von Guttman, Baron, 216

Wainwright, 332
Walcott, Sen. Frederick C., 270
Walden (Thoreau), 116
Walden, Arthur, 99–100
Wales, 253
Walker, Charles, 68
Walker, Ernest P., 311
Walrus, *85,* 415; American market hunting of, 75–85, 89–90, 322, 428, 432; harvest data, *76*; hunting methods, 75–76, 80–84; ivory carving, 76, 83, *84*; protection of, 83, *85,* 239, 255; Russian market hunting of, *18,* 75, 83, *193*; sport hunting of, *82,* 82–84, 216, 250, 255, *317*; study of, 253; subsistence hunting of, 79–80, 84, 255, 448n74
Walrus Act (1941), 83, 239
Walrus Island, 86
Walrus Islands State Sanctuary, 83–84, *85,* 255
Walter A. Earle, 44
Ward's Natural History Establishment, 126, 130
Warner, Clarence, 108
Washburn, H. Bradford, 290
Washington, DC: and Alaska Conservation, 2, 133, 437; and Alaska development, 135, 427; and whaling, 68
Washington, State of, 108, 155; elk translocation from, 334; and salmon, 351–352, 363. *See also* Seattle
Waxell, Sven, 5
Weasels: and forest fires, 106, 340; protection of, 344; trapping of, *345*
Webb, Melodie, 198
Wester, Wilbur, 392, 475n47
Western Federation of Miners, 265
Western Union Telegraph project, 35–36, *38*
Whale, Atlantic right, 60
Whale, belukha, 415; hunting of, 59, *70,* 71; and salmon predation, 253, *299,* 301, 304

Whale, blue: hunting by Aleuts, 196; market hunting of, 63, 70–74, 196
Whale, bowhead, 415; conservation of, 206–207; hunting of, 58–59, 63–65, *70,* 72–74
Whale, finback: hunting by Aleuts, 196; market hunting of, 59, 63, *70,* 70–75
Whale, gray, 415; market hunting of, 59, 63, *70,* 74, 171–172
Whale, humpback, 191; market hunting of, 63, *70,* 70–74
Whale, killer, 191; and belukha research, 305; and fur seals, 54, 89, 283; hunting of, 59; and sea lions, 89; and sea otters, 10, 25, 84
Whale, Minke, 191
Whale, North Pacific right, market hunting of, 58–63, 70, *70, 72,* 72–74, 434
Whale, sei, 63, *70,* 71, *72*
Whale, sperm, market hunting of, 58–59, 63, 70, *70,* 73–74, 434
Whaling, 1, 58–59, *72, 73;* Antarctic, 71–72; Canadian, 71, 74; and conservation, 89, 428; deserters, 414; effects on Natives, 77–80, 192, 199; by Eskimos and Aleuts, 59, 65, *66,* 69, 72, 74–75, 77, 196, 206–207; harvests, *18, 61–62, 70;* and fur trade, 13, 15; hazards, 66–69; market hunting for, 318, 322, 413; methods, 59–66; products, 63, 71; by Russians, 59–60; shore-based, 21, 65, *66,* 69–71
White Act (1924), 239, 365, 367, 375
White Pass and Yukon Railway, 110
White Pass, 98
White, Sam O., *239,* 242, *243,* 280
White, Stewart Edward: and brown bears, 169, 279, 281, 431; and salmon, 365
White, Tom, 391
White Wilderness (Disney), 291
Whitewater Bay, 279
Whiz Halferty Co., 457n79
Wickersham, Delegate James, 137, 140, 385–386
Wien, Noel, *243*
Wien, Ralph, 242
The Wild Grizzlies of Alaska (Holzworth), 269
Wilderness: and Alaska Lands Act, 280; and Arctic Refuge, 400–401, 410, 418, 425–426, 437; and Bob Marshall, 400–407; in Katmai NP, 174; in Kenai Moose Range, 396; movement, 400, 407; and Muries, 410–412; philosophy of, 110–111, 402, 404–406, 410
Wilderness Act (1964), 248; origins of, 402, 404–405, 407, 410, 412, 425; and preservationism, 429
The Wilderness of Denali (Sheldon), 132
The Wilderness of the Upper Yukon (Sheldon), 132
Wilderness Society: and Aldo Leopold, 287; and Arctic Refuge, 418–421, 425; and Bob Marshall, 406–407, 437; and Glacier Bay NM, 185; and Margaret Murie, 411; Olaus Murie in, 409–411, 437; origins of, 406–407; and Wilderness Act, 407, 410, 412
Wildlife, economic value of, 274–275, 347, *348*
Wildlife Conservation Society, 153
Wildlife management, 234, *243, 394;* and Alaska Natives, 188–190, 204–208, 211, 238, 251, 389, 433–435; and ecology, 286, 288, 439; federal-territorial conflict over, 211, 310; and interest groups, 205–206, 234, 258, 281, 434; jurisdiction, 52, 212, 217, 219–220, 236–237, 272, 276, 340, 343, 347; 1925 Game Law, 238–245, 247–252, 389; origins, 119–120, 133, 231
Wildlife Management Institute: and Arctic Refuge, 418, 421, 422; and brown bears, 274; Gabrielson in, 234, 236, 252; and Kenai oil, 393; origins, 121
Wildlife Society, 257
Wildlife translocations, 322–337; to Aleutians, 305–306; ecological effects of, 329–330, 349; for fox food, 306; of reindeer, 322–326, 330–331
Willett, George, 311
William H. Allen, 77
Willow Island, 185
Wilson, Pres. Woodrow, 383; and Alaska Railroad, 139–140, 385; and Katmai NM, 165, and Mt. McKinley NP, 143
Wiseman, 401, 405, 409
Wolverines, 345; control of, 238, 245, 283, 285, *297, 299,* 330; in parks/refuges, 150, 160, 174, 191, 378, 415; predation by, 321; protection of, 207, 349; trapping of, 16, *18, 199,* 338, *341, 345, 346*
Wolves, 99, 191, *417;* appreciation of, 222, 412, 417; bounty on, 242, 254,

284, 298, *299;* control of, 222, 238, 240, 245, 247, 251, 255, 283–285, 288–290, *293, 295, 296,* 310, 313–315, 317, 319–320, 322, 330, 345, 386, 431–432; in Katmai NP, 160, 175; on Kenai Pen., 386, 397–399; in Mt. McKinley NP, 147, 150, 288–282; predation by, *293,* 321, 331; protection of, 255, 344, 397; research on, 299, 313, 349; and salmon, 300; trapping of, 199, 338, *345*
Wolves of Mt. McKinley (Murie), 290
Wonder Lake, 145, 148–149
Wood, 104–106, *107*
Wood, Lt. Charles Erskine Scott, 177
Wood River, 310
Wood, Virginia Hill "Ginny," 421, *423,* 425
Woodchopper Creek, 99
Woolford, Ray, *206,* 251
Work, Hubert (Sec. of Interior), 183–184
World War I: and forests, 106; and game, 229; and salmon, 353, 365; and Tlingit employment, 361; and whaling, 71
World War II, 253; and Alaska Highway, 244; in Aleutians, 22–23; and forests, 106; and fur seals, 52; and game laws, 243–244, 347; and Glacier Bay NM, 185; and Katmai NM, 169; and Mt. McKinley NP, 148, 153; and reindeer, 328, and Tlingits, 188; and trapping, 343; and U.S.-Japan salmon dispute, 373; and whaling, 72
Wrangel Island, 227, 333
Wrangell, 93, 94; and Game Comm., 244; and seal control, 304; and wolf control, 298
Wrangell Mountains, *102*
Wrangell Narrows, 214
Wright, George Frederick, 181
Wright, George M., 147

Yakutat, 127; Russian fort at, 11–14, 180; Tlingits at, 196
Yakutat Bay, 13, 334
Yale University, 118, 123, 131
Yanert, Sgt. William, 137
Yellowstone National Park, 118, 130, 289; and Boone and Crockett Club, 120, 124
Yes Bay, 363
Yosemite NP, 111, 113
Young, Ralph, 279
Young, Rev. S. Hall: and Muir, 93, 97, 111, 177; and Muir Glacier, 457n4
Yukon Delta, 39, 256; Nelson on, 225–227; Olaus Murie on, 409; waterfowl on, 218, 294; wolf control on, 300
Yukon Delta National Wildlife Refuge, 252
Yukon Flats National Wildlife Refuge, 256
Yukon River, 80, 156, 332; explorations, 36, 125, 131–132, 137; and fur trade, 16, 338; and Gold Rush, 100–101, 104, 108, 137, 326; Indians on, 198, 201; salmon in, 357, 359, 364, 415, 419, 425; and whaling, 414; wood buffaloes at, 336
Yukon Territory, 46, 125; bird banding in, 411; exploration in, 140; game law enforcement in, 242; gold-seeking in, 98, 213

Zahniser, Howard, 410
Zapadni rookery, 29
Zentner, Joe, 274